Hall & Mooney Lith. Buffalo.

Capitol School – Detroit

SYSTEM

OF

PUBLIC INSTRUCTION

AND

PRIMARY SCHOOL LAW

OF

MICHIGAN,

WITH EXPLANATORY NOTES, FORMS, REGULATIONS AND INSTRUCTIONS; A DIGEST OF DECISIONS; A DETAILED HISTORY OF PUBLIC INSTRUCTION AND THE LAWS RELATING THERETO; THE HISTORY OF AND LAWS RELATING TO INCORPORATED INSTITUTIONS OF LEARNING, &c. &c.

[DOCUMENT NO. 6.]

PREPARED BY

FRANCIS W. SHEARMAN,

SUPERINTENDENT OF PUBLIC INSTRUCTION.

Lansing, Michigan:
INGALS, HEDGES & CO., PRINTERS TO THE STATE.

1852.

TO SCHOOL OFFICERS.

This Document is transmitted to each County Clerk and County Treasurer, and to each Township Clerk for the use of the Township Library, and an additional copy to the latter, for the use of the Township Board of School Inspectors. One copy is also transmitted to each of the school district officers, viz: the Moderator, Director and Assessor, for their use while in office—to be delivered up to their successors at the expiration of their term.

NOTE.—On page 1 an error occurs in relation to the subdivision of lands. The smallest is forty acres.

CONTENTS.

PART I.

PART II.

PART III.

APPENDIX.

STATE OF MICHIGAN.

Report of the Superintendent of Public Instruction.

To His Excellency, Robert McClelland,
Governor:

Sir—When the illustrious Chief and Exile from Europe, whose eloquence and philosophy and patriotism have so recently astonished the world, planted his footsteps for the first time upon the shores of the United States, impressed with a sense of its commercial greatness, as exhibited in the great metropolis of our country, his lofty genius, looking beyond the triumphs of the physical world, ascribed the glory of America to its educational institutions, and the provisions made in the early days of the Republic, for the support and spread of Primary School education. Looking back, not yet a century, American institutions existed not even in name. The struggles of the Revolution established them as a fact: and it is a circumstance well worthy of remembrance, that our educational system is closely allied to the trials of the revolutionary war, and its means of education, for the support of schools, derived from the consequences of that war—the immense public debt which it created. It is an interesting fact in the history of our country, illustrating the sagacity and foresight of our fathers, that as a means of extinguishing that debt, and as one, the most reliable and sure of all others that could be devised, the one thirty-sixth part of the public domain was set apart forever, as a fund for the advancement of education—thus presenting an inducement to the purchase of the lands, and to the settlement of the country, which has effected its purpose, and scattered over the length and breadth of our land, a race of hardy men who have subdued our forests, cultivated our fields, and laid the basis of physical, social, intellectual and moral prosperity and wealth. It is most gratifying, but not wonderful that such a race should be deeply impressed with the idea, that to perpetuate the blessings of liberty and good government, schools, and the means of education should forever be encouraged. New England has long boasted of her system of schools, and means of education; and it has not been vain boasting. From the land of the Rock of Plymouth, from its statesmen, its orators, its poets, and its people, a powerful influence has been sent out in behalf of education. There the principle of schools, free and open to all—the doctrine of universal education—received its first impulse. The glory of New England in her schools is the achievement of more than a century. Her system had its origin among the causes of the revolution—ours is one of its consequences. The success of both—the triumph of education everywhere in our land—the means afforded for its support—educational institutions provided throughout the several States of the Union—constitute the common glory of the Republic, as they afford the only safeguard for its progress and perpetuity. "Each State," says a distinguished living statesman, "is deeply interested in the welfare of every other, for the representatives of the whole regulate, by their votes, the measures of the Union, which must be happy and prosperous in proportion as its councils are guided by more enlightened views, resulting from the more universal diffusion of Light and Knowledge and Education."

The educational history of our country, has not yet been developed in the manner it should be. One of the principal causes which has prevented it from being done, has been the fact that in most of the States of the Union there has been no separate officer charged with the special supervision of Public Instruction. Information could not be concentrated, nor reduced to system. So long as the interests of education are made secondary in importance, in the scale of public offices, so long will its legitimate benefits be greatly retarded. Every State needs a separate officer of Public Instruction, charged with its general supervision, whose special duty it should be to accumulate all the material which is legitimately embraced in a system of Public Instruction, to present it in embodied form before the representatives of the people, and thus secure from time to time, that just share of attention to which the subject is entitled at the hands of those who are placed in authority to frame our laws and to mould and form our local governments.

The State of Michigan was the first in the Union that established a constitutional officer by the name and designation of "Superintendent of Public Instruction." The system contemplated by the framers of the first constitution and laws, embraced the widest field. It consisted of a head of the department, designated as above with general supervision; a University, in which education was free, governed by a Board of Regents, now elected by the people, with a local Faculty; branches of the University, and a system of Primary Schools, under the management of Township officers, designated Inspectors of Primary Schools, and district officers, known as Moderator, Director and Assessor of the school district. It did not contemplate the creation of other incorporated literary institutions; but as their establishment is based upon influences which must always continue to exist, and be more or less powerful, charters were subsequently granted to these institutions. Having received such charters, they are legitimately embraced in the system of Public Instruction, and in most instances, as they should be in all, made subject to the visitation of the Superintendent, and required to make to him an annual report. The institutions and officers as above enumerated, have constituted the educational working force of Michigan for the first fifteen years of its existence. To these has been added by the Legislature of 1850, a State Normal School, the exclusive purposes of which are defined in the organic law, to be "the instruction of all persons, both male and female, in the art of teaching, and in all the various branches that pertain to a good common school education; also to give instruction in the arts of husbandry and agricultural chemistry—in the fundamental laws of the United States, and in what regards the rights and duties of citizens." This school is under the government of a Board of Education, consisting of three members, and the Superintendent of Public Instruction, who are elected by the people. The requisite main building has been erected, at an expense of over twenty thousand dollars, thirteen thousand of which was subscribed and paid by the citizens of Ypsilanti, where the school is located. This institution will be put into operation in the course of the coming fall or spring, when the principal and requisite teachers will be employed, and its course of studies announced.

By an act of the Legislature approved June 23d, 1851, all State officers from whom reports are required to be made to the Legislature, are to report for the year 1851 to the Governor of the State. Under an act prescribing the duties of Superintendent of Public Instruction, it is provided that he shall annually prepare and transmit to the Governor a report containing:

1. A statement of the condition of the University and its branches; of all incorporated literary institutions and of the primary schools.

2. Estimates and amounts of expenditures of the school money.

3. Plans for the improvement and management of all educational funds, and for the better organization of the educational system, if in his opinion the same be required.

4. The condition of the Normal School.

5. All such other matters relating to his office and the subject of education generally, as he shall deem expedient to communicate.

By the third section of the act referred to, it is also made the duty of the Superintendent to prepare and cause to be printed with the laws relating to primary schools, all necessary forms, regulations and instructions for conducting all proceedings under said laws, and transmit the same with such instructions relative to the organization and government of such schools, and the course of studies proper to be pursued therein, as he may deem advisable, to the several officers intrusted with their management and care. Having in view the accomplishment of the work required in both of the acts alluded to, it has been deemed both a measure of economy and a means of disseminating in the best form all information in relation to our system of Public Instruction, to combine the material of the annual report required by law, and the primary school law, with notes and forms, in one document. The legislature, in the law of June 1851, made provision for an extensive distribution of the annual report, providing that one copy should be furnished to each township library, one to each county clerk and treasurer, ten to each city, one hundred and fifty to the State Library, one to each school district in the State, five hundred for binding, and one hundred for the use of the office. By the provisions of section 3, the school law is to be transmitted to the several officers entrusted with the management and care of the schools. For this purpose an additional number of copies have been printed, and also a sufficient number in addition to supply the demands which are constantly arising for copies of the school law, from time to time, until another edition shall be required, which, with the present prospect of permanency in the law, will not probably be for some years. As this document is intended therefore as a permanent one for reference by school officers, it has been deemed essential and of vital importance to the successful developement of our system to embrace in it not only the school laws with notes and forms, but all such information connected with the system, relating to the University, and all of our institutions of learning, and the progress of education in the State, as would afford a full knowledge of the subject, to our people, and to the citizens of other States, whose interest on the subject is identical with ours, in all that relates to educational achievement.

The document partakes of the character of a compilation. The object has been to put together in permanent form such experience and facts as would lead to a knowledge of what has been attained in the past, and from this, to be better enabled to make progress in the future. It has been the design faithfully to record the acts of those who have taken a part in the educational career and affairs of the State. The past is thus secure, and its history is here unfolded in the acts of our successive Chief Magistrates, Legislators, Board of Regents, successive Superintendents of Public Instruction, Board of Visitors, and friends of education.

It will be perceived by those who take an interest in perusing our past educational history, that the efforts of each successive officer have been attended with manifest improvement. To ascertain what course to pursue to ensure progress and stability in a system of education, which was to survive long after those who had participated in its creation and early progress have passed from the field of action and labor, must of necessity be the work of time and reflection. The charge of such a system can not fail to be felt as one of the most solemn and responsible in worldly affairs, requiring investigation and thought, and a thorough practical knowledge of and acquaintance with whatever relates to education, generally, but of the workings of the system established for its promotion. Theory and experiment merely were believed to be an uncertain basis for practical improvement. The reports which have been made from year to year from the Department of Public Instruction, have not been made permanent documents, and the facts which they successively develop were neither preserved, nor can they be referred to, except among the documents in the Library at the Capitol. The annual reports of the present incumbent to the Legislature have been confined chiefly to the consideration of such subjects as seemed to require legislation to perfect the system, without hazarding schemes for further improvement, till time and experience, gained from a knowledge of the subject and of the past, would be most likely to make suggestions for the future, partake of a wise, beneficial and permanent character. *To fit himself* for the performance of the duties devolving upon him, in a manner worthy the efforts of the people, was believed by the present incumbent to be the first requisite and surest process for improvement in all other respects; and if in doing this, other active and outward labors in the field, in the shape of lectures and personal visitations, have been precluded, it is nevertheless the deduction of his own reason, and the conviction of his own judgment, that the documentary history of our educational affairs was of first importance, and that permanent good, and the utmost utility are best secured in the outset, by studying thoroughly to understand and to perfect our system of Public Instruction; by watching the operations of the laws relating to that system; by adapting them to the wants of the people and the requirements of the age, until such time as it shall work with entire harmony and develop the greatest amount of good. Other duties may be no less useful, and perhaps more agreeable, but the general supervision of the system, (enlarging in its scope and sphere of operations from year to year,) both in general and in detail, so as to render it easy of execution in all its parts, and capable of being readily comprehended and understood by those who execute the laws, especially those relating to our primary schools, is above all other things indispensable to real and permanent improvement. In vain may public attention be aroused and public interest excited in behalf of education, if the system adopted be insufficient to meet the requirements and wants of the people and of the age, or so faulty as to be incapable of executing itself with the least degree of burthen to those whose time and labor have to be for the most part gratuitously devoted to the local management of the schools.

The history of the University of Michigan forms an important portion of the sketch on Public Instruction. An important change had taken place in the organic law, by which its management was changed from a Board of Regents appointed by the Governor and Senate, to a Board elected by the people. The institution has passed through a series of reverses since its organization, and it was deemed important to afford facilities of examination as to the causes, by referring with minuteness to the management of its affairs from year to year. But the main reason for including in this document so full and detailed account of its rise and progress, has been to diffuse among the people, for whose benefit the fund was granted, that knowledge concerning it, of which they have been mostly deprived, and on account of which, there has not been felt that warm sympathy with the institution which has been felt for the Primary Schools. That it has not accomplished all that could be desired, is beyond question; but with future good management, by the exercise of prudence, wisdom, and discretion on the part of the Regents in the appointment of a president, and the re-organization of the department of literature, science and the arts, there is no reason why it should not be filled with students, and fulfill the objects of its high mission with the most abundant and satisfactory success. But two departments, as yet, have been organized—that of literature, science and the arts, and that of medicine. The medical department stands upon a footing of the highest order. Although yet in its infancy, it has taken high rank in the medical world; its course of studies is of the severest order; the discipline exacted, of such a character as to unfold the faculties of thought, investigation, reflection and the power of reasoning, analyzing and comparing, while the general advantages offered to the medical student are not surpassed by those of any other institution in the United States. The determination of the Board of Regents, and of the Medical Faculty, to place this department upon the highest basis of improvement, is worthy of all commendation and praise.

A statement of the expenditures and receipts of the University from its commencement in 1837, to December 31, 1851, will be found in the appendix. The whole amount of disbursements for all purposes up to this period is two hundred and eighty-six thousand, nine hundred and twenty-eight dollars and twenty-two cents. The revised law relating to the University does not provide, as the first law did, for the establishment of a branch for the purpose of Female Education; but in this department, to which the public mind has not yet been sufficiently directed, the wants of the State will doubtless be met by the various institutions which have been established without the aid of the State. The revised constitution provides that the Legislature may appropriate the twenty-two sections of salt spring lands now unappropriated, or the money arising from the sale of the same, where such lands have already been sold, and any land which may hereafter be granted or appropriated for such purpose, for the support and maintenance of an agricultural school; and such school may be made a branch of the University, for instruction in agriculture and the natural sciences connected therewith, and placed under the direction of the Regents.

Those institutions which are denominated INCORPORATED LITERARY INSTITUTIONS, a list of which will be found under that title, in the index, are institutions which receive no pecuniary aid from the State. They are the result of the enterprize and zeal of various denominations and communities, and are of a higher grade than institutions of a similar character, in most of the States.

The origin and progress of the PRIMARY SCHOOLS may be traced from year to year throughout this volume. The first primary school law of the State of Michigan was approved on the 20th day of March, 1837, and provided for supporting the schools by a tax upon the taxable property of the district, in proportion to its valuation, which was to be ascertained by a transcript of the township assessment roll; thus virtually making the basis of a system of FREE SCHOOLS. The early legislation of the State upon the subject of primary schools was subjected to repeated change, from the difficulty of adapting a law to the circumstances of a people in a new country. Of late years there has been a gradual approach to stability and permanency. The law is working well in the main, and any radical change in the system is peculiarly to be deprecated. The debates in the Convention to revise the constitution were considered an important portion of our educational history, and will be found under the proper head. The main feature of the revised constitution, in relation to primary schools, is the clause which requires that the Legislature shall, within five years from its adoption, provide for and establish a system of primary schools, whereby a school shall be kept without charge for tuition, at least three months in each year, in every school district in the State, and all instruction is to be conducted in the English language. A school must be maintained in each school year at least three months, or it is deprived the ensuing year of its proportion of the income of the primary school fund, and of all funds arising from taxes for the support of schools.

Under the law, it is made the duty of the supervisor of each township to assess the taxes voted by every school district in his township, and all other taxes provided for in the law chargeable against such district or township, upon the taxable property of the district or township respectively, and to place the same in the township assessment roll. It was made the duty of the supervisor also, to assess upon the taxable property of his township, one mill on each dollar of valuation thereof in each year, and after deducting from the amount thus raised, twenty-five dollars for the purchase of books for the library, the remainder is to be apportioned to the several districts in the township for the support of schools therein. The Legislature of 1850, in order to carry out the provisions of the constitution for free schools, in pursuance of the recommendation of the Superintendent, increased the amonnt required to be assessed by the supervisor, to two mills. In consequence of imperfect and partial returns heretofore, it has been impossible to determine the amount which has been actually assessed. The duty in some instances has been neglected by supervisors, and while with one mill on the dollar's valuation, it should raise some thirty thousand dollars, the returns for several years show that only some seventeen thousand have been assessed. Provision has been made for more accurate and full returns. The supervisors, for the first time, during the past year assessed upon the taxable property the sum of two mills on each dollar of the valuation, and statements of the amounts thus assessed will be returned to the office of Public Instruction in the month of November next, when a reliable estimate may be made as to what further legislation may be required to carry out the provisions of the constitution. The trouble in older States has been to regulate the detail of a Free School Law. In Michigan the change in the system is unfelt. The transition from the old law to the requirements of the constitution, is accompanied with no confusion, and the system of taxation to accomplish the purpose of Free Schools is as equal and just as it is possible to make it.

The sources of revenue for the support of primary schools are, 1st: the income of the primary school fund, which for the past year has amounted to over fifty-seven thousand dollars. The total sale of school lands for the last year has amounted to $83,449 89, being an increase over last year of nearly sixty-seven per cent. The school fund itself now amounts to over $811,000 00. 2d. A tax of two mills upon each dollar's valuation of the taxable property of the township. 3d. A tax not exceeding one dollar a scholar, voted by the district and collected and returned in the same manner as other township taxes. The existing law provides for a rate bill to make up any deficiency. This law will require change or modification when the present constitutional provisions are fully carried out.

Tabular statements will be found in the appendix, showing the amount raised for various school purposes in Michigan, during the year last past. The whole number of school districts in the State is three thousand three hundred and seven. The whole number of children residing in school districts where a school has been taught for three months, is one hundred and forty-three thousand, two hundred and twenty-two. The apportionment of the income of the primary school fund is based upon this number, instead of the number which are actually in attendance on the schools, the latter being one hundred and fifteen thousand, one hundred and sixty-five. Whether a change in the system of apportionment, based upon actual attendance, would not be the means of greatly increasing the usefulness of our system, and be otherwise beneficial, is a question which should deserve the consideration of the people. The whole amount that has been paid to teachers in the State, during the past year, is one hundred and fifty-four thousand, four hundred and sixty-nine dollars and thirty cents. The whole amount of money raised by the districts was one hundred and thirty thousand, one hundred and ninety-six dollars and thirty-eight cents. There has been raised for the following purposes, viz:

Building School Houses	$57,348 52
Repairing " "	11,265 00
For past indebtedness	9,108 34
For other purposes	4,112 90
On rate bill,	69,035 37

The whole number of volumes in the township libraries, as reported, is ninety-seven thousand, one hundred and fifty-eight. The amount of mill tax reported is seventeen thousand one hundred and forty dollars and fifty-nine cents. The returns of this item are erroneous, or if not, a large number of the Supervisors have neglected to assess the tax. The probability is that the deficiency mainly arises from the neglect of the inspectors to report the amounts to the Superintendent.

An important and laborious part of the work has been the preparation of the notes and forms to the Primary School Law. The notes have been based upon the queries submitted to this office by school officers from time to time, and embrace most of the questions that arise in the districts, so far as it is competent and proper for this department to give its decisions. As there is no law requiring such decisions, they are to be considered advisory, but they are believed to be legally correct, and it is earnestly hoped will be found of use, and be the means of avoiding much trouble and difficulty. Access has been had to the volume of decisions published by the Superintendent of Common Schools of the State of New York, and also to the Massachusetts and Rhode Island and Connecticut decisions. The opinions and views of the school officers of these States have been adopted and published, so far as they were applicable to the laws of Michigan; and full liberty has been taken to incorporate into the work, the opinions and views of the Superintendents of our own State, upon subjects connected with the interests of the schools.

The communications in relation to the UNION SCHOOLS in the appendix, do not embrace an account of all that have been established, and more full information in relation to this important branch of our system will have to be left for the future. This class of schools deserve the particular attention of the people. They are destined to fill up the space now left between the University and the Primary Schools, and while they preserve the character of Primary Schools, they are calculated to afford all the advantages of higher Seminaries of Learning.

In concluding this general summary of the work now accomplished, it affords a satisfactory reflection that the subject of Education has received so large a share of attention from the successive Chief Magistrates of the State, and from successive Legislative bodies; and the rewards for the time and labor expended in gathering up the history of our educational achievments, will be ample and sufficient, if the object for which it was designed shall be successfully accomplished, in the promotion of the cause of Education and the development of our system of Public Instruction. It is a source of high gratification that your Excellency has fully appreciated the importance of the subject, and that in the accomplishment of the purpose designed, the undersigned has received your Excellency's strong encouragement and support.

I have the honor to be, very respectfully,

Your ob't friend and servant,

FRANCIS W. SHEARMAN,

Superintendent of Public Instruction.

Lansing, May 1, 1852.

PART I.

ORIGIN, PROGRESS, AND PRESENT CONDITION
OF
PUBLIC INSTRUCTION IN MICHIGAN.

CONGRESSIONAL AND TERRITORIAL LEGISLATION FROM 1785 TO 1836.

The foundation upon which the educational superstructure of Michigan, and the other States comprised in that section of our country, known as the north-west territory, has been raised, was laid in an ordinance of the Congress of the Confederation, in the year 1785, entitled an ordinance for ascertaining the mode of disposing of the lands in the western territory. By its provisions, lot numbered sixteen, of every township, was reserved for the maintenance of the public schools within such township.

The greatest division of land, according to the uniform method of survey of the public lands, contains the quantity of 23,040 acres. This is called a township, and is six English or American miles square, and is subdivided into thirty-six equal divisions, or square miles by lines crossing each other, called sections. The section contains 640 acres, and is subdivided into four parts, called quarter sections, each of which contains 160 acres. The quarter sections are subdivided into two equal parts, containing 80 acres, each called half quarter sections, or eighths of sections, which is the smallest subdivision. Every sixteenth section of land as here described, was reserved by the ordinance, for the support of schools, amounting to the one thirty-sixth part of the public lands.

"The plan," says the venerable Gov. Woodbridge, late Senator in Congress from Michigan, in a letter to this department, "in its application to the 'Western Country,' had doubtless been predetermined, though of course not authoritatively disclosed before the treaty of peace, and before the cessions from the States. After these events, and when the title of the General Government was no longer disputed, a more definite form was given to it. The application of the one thirty-sixth part of each surveyed township for the support of common schools within such township, first appears in a formal ordinance of the old Congress of May, 1785. All subsequent acts of general legislation, both before and after the adoption of the constitution, affirm the plan, and indicate a scrupulous adherence to the principles of it, as indeed every sentiment of common honesty, as well as sound public policy, required. The United States were deeply in debt, and it was an enquiry of the greatest solicitude among all public men in those days, by what possible means that debt could be paid. After the treaty of peace, and especially after the cessions from the States, the immense public domain, which, without further doubt, was then by common consent, admitted to be subject to the disposition of the United States, was regarded as one certain, and perhaps the most productive, of all the means, applicable to that object, in their power. In these circumstances it was expedient to adopt a system which should hold out strong inducements to purchasers, in order to realize any revenue from its sale. Such policy was also enforced, by the consideration that no adequate protection could be given to the then frontier States, until extended settlements in that western country should have first dislodged from it permanently, the hostile savages. Influenced by such considerations, the old Congress passed its ordinance of 1785, This was in fact, an invitation to all the world to buy; and among other inducements held out, it was therein promised to all who should go out and settle there, that one thirty-sixth part of the whole country should be applied forever, as a fund for the advancement of EDUCATION. It contained a promise to all who should buy there—it amounted to a solemn covenant with each purchaser and settler in every township, that he and his posterity forever, should in all future time, in common with the other settlers in the township, be entitled to the usufruct of that fund, as a means of educating his children. What an inducement was this with the father of a family, to go out and settle there!"

In 1787 the ordinance was passed, establishing rules and regulations for the government of the Territory. The provisions of the prior ordinance were respected; and it was further declared that "RELIGION, MORALITY and KNOWLEDGE, being necessary to good government, and the happiness of mankind, SCHOOLS, and the means of EDUCATION shall forever be encouraged."

The negotiations which led to the first appropriations for University purposes in the Northwest Territory were commenced in the year 1786 by the Ohio company, and concluded the following year by a contract for the purchase of one and a half millions of acres of the public lands. In this contract, in addition to a reservation for schools and religious purposes, was a provision for the grant of two entire townships as an endowment for a University. These two townships were selected together at Athens, in Ohio, and the University located upon them. The year after, John Cleves Symmes, cf New Jersey, and his associates, made application for the purchase of another large tract of land, which comprehended what is now Cincinnati. In this contract provision was also made, besides every section 16 for school and every section 29 for religious purposes, for an appropriation of one entire township for a University. It was a condition of the contract between the government and the purchasers of the tract that within seven years from the completion of the survey, unless Indian irruptions rendered it impracticable, they should lay off the whole contract at their own expense, into townships and fractional parts of townships and divide the same into lots according to the land ordinance of 1785. Lot numbered 16 in each township, or fractional part of a township, was given perpetually for the purposes of EDUCATION. Lot No. 29 in each township was granted perpetually for the purposes of RELIGION. Lots No. 8, 11 and 26, were reserved for the future disposition of Congress. One entire township was granted perpetually for the purpose of an academy or college.

In 1788 the quantity of land first applied for by Judge Symmes, was reduced by a subsequent contract, to one million of acres and the right to a college township thereby lost.

The provisions for seminaries of learning and for the other new States and Territories, are found in an act of Congress of 1804, one entire township being reserved for that purpose. In this act provision is made for such a reservation in that portion of the Western Territory which is now Michigan.

In 1817 the administration of the territorial government being vested in a Governor and Judges, the following law which may be viewed as a curiosity in the history of education, both on account of its peculiarity of language and the means provided for its support, was adopted. It was, however, no unusual thing at that early day, and is not so now, in many of the States, to provide for the establishment of literary institutions, schools and colleges, and for benevolent and religious enterprises and purposes, by the organization of lotteries. The law was adopted and published from the laws of the seven original States mentioned in the last clause, by reason of a provision of the Ordinance of 1787, that the laws which the Governor and Judges made and published, both civil and criminal, were to be so taken, and suited to the circumstances of the Territory, and reported to and sanctioned by Congress, until the people were entitled to the organization of a General Assembly.

AN ACT to establish the Catholepistemiad, or University of Michigania.

Be it enacted by the Governor and the Judges of the Territory of Michigan, That there shall be in the said Territory a Catholepistemiad, or University, denominated the Catholepistemiad or University of Michigania. The Catholepistemiad or University of Michigania shall be composed of thirteen Didaxum, or Professorships; first, a Didaxia, or Professorship of Catholepistemia, or universal science, the Didactor or professor of which shall be President of the Institution; second, a Didaxia or professorship of Anthropoglossica, or literature embracing all the Epistemum or sciences relative to language; third, a Didaxia or professorship of Mathematica, or Mathematics; fourth, a Didaxia or professorship of Physiognostica or Natural History; fifth, a Didaxia or professorship of Physiosophica or Natural Philosophy; sixth, a Didaxia or professorship of Astronomia, or Astronomy; seventh, a Didaxia or professorship of Chymia, or Chemistry; eighth, a Didaxia or professorship Iatuca, or Medical Sciences; ninth, a Didaxia or professorship of œconomia, or economical sciences; tenth, a Didaxia or professorship of Ethica, or Ethical Sciences; eleventh, a Didaxia or professorship of Polemitactica, or Military Sciences; twelfth, a Didaxia or professorship of Diegetica, or Historical Sciences, and thirteenth, a Didaxia or professorship of Ennœica, or Intellectual Sciences, embracing all the Epistemum or sciences relative to the minds of animals, to the human mind, to spiritual existence, to the Deity, and to Religion; the Didactor or professor of which shall be Vice President of the Institution. The Didactors or professors shall be appointed and commissioned by the Governor. There shall be paid from the Treasury of Michigan, in quarterly payments, to the President of the Institution, and to each Didactor or Professor, an annual salary to be from time to time ascertained by law. More than one Didaxia or professorship may be conferred upon the same person. The President and Didactors, or professors, or a majority of them assembled, shall have power to regulate all the concerns of the Institution. to enact laws for that purpose, to sue, to be sued, to acquire, to hold and to aliene property, real, mixed and personal, to make, to use and to alter a seal, to establish colleges, academies, schools, libraries, musæums, athenœums, Botanic gardens, labaratories, and other useful literary and scientific institutions, consonant to the laws of the United States of America, and of Michigan, and to appoint officers, instructors and instructri. in, among and throughout the various counties, cities, towns, townships, and other geographical divisions of Michigan. Their name and style as a corporation, shall be "The Catholepistemiad or University of Michigania." To every subordinate instructor and instruxtrix, appointed by the Catholepistemiad or University, there shall be paid from the treasury of Michigan, in quarterly payments, an annual salary, to be, from time to time, ascertained by law. The existing public taxes are hereby increased fifteen per cent.; and from the proceeds of the present, and of all future public taxes fifteen per cent. are appropriated for the benefit of the Catholepistemiad or University. The Treasurer of Michigan shall keep a separate account of the University fund. The Catholepistemiad or University may prepare and draw four successive lotteries, deducting from the prizes in the same fifteen per cent. for the benefit of the Institution. The proceeds of the preceding sources of revenue, and of all subsequent, shall be applied, in the first instance, to the acquisition of suitable lands and buildings, and books, libraries and apparatus, and afterwards to such purposes as shall be, from time to time, by law directed. The *Honorarium* for a course of lectures, shall not exceed fifteen dollars: for classical instruction, ten dollars a quarter, and for ordinary instruction, six dollars a quarter. If the Judges of the court of any county, or a majority of them, shall certify that the parent or guardian of any person has not adequate means to defray the expense of suitable instruction, and that the same ought to be a public charge, the honorarium shall be paid from the Treasury of Michigan. An annual report of the state, concerns, and transactions of the Institution, shall be laid before the legislative power for the time being. This law or any part of it, may be repealed by the legislative power, for the time being. Made, adopted and published from the laws of seven of the original States, to wit: the States of Connecticut, Massachusetts, New Jersey, New York, Ohio, Pennsylvania and Virginia, as far as necessary and suitable to the circumstances of Michigan. at Detroit, on Tuesday the twenty-sixth day of August, in the year of our Lord one thousand eight hundred and seventeen.

WILLIAM WOODBRIDGE,
Secretary of Michigan, and at present acting Governor thereof.

A. B. WOODWARD,
Presiding Judge of the Supreme Court of the Territory of Michigan.

JOHN GRIFFIN,
One of the Judges of the Territory of Michigan.

I hereby certify the above and foregoing to be a true copy of the original, now of record in the office of the Secretary of State, on pages 52 and 53 of the Executive Records of Michigan.

R. R. GIBSON,
Deputy Secretary of State.

In the same year that this territorial law was enacted and published, three sections of land were granted to the "College of Detroit' by the treaty made at Fort Meigs. For the purposes of a seminary of learning therefore, there were at this time two sources of revenue; that derived from the grant of one township and that derived from the treaty.

In 1818, the first sales of public lands were made in Michigan. The Secretary of the Treasury had not then located the college townships. In 1819 Gov. Woodbridge was sent from the Territory as the first delegate in Congress, and gave his attention to the subject with a view to cause the location. The result of his examination was a conviction that in consequence of the rapid sales then making there did not remain within the district designated by the law of 1804, any one entire township of good lands upon which the location could be made. The session was too far advanced to secure the passage of a law to remedy the evil, and in 1820 Gov. W. resigned his seat in Congress.

In 1821, an act was promulgated and adopted by the Governor and Judges, establishing a UNIVERSITY "for the purpose of educating youth." It was to be placed under the management, direction and government of twenty-one trustees, of whom the Governor of the Territory was always to be one, by virtue of his office. The first trustees named in the act were the Governor, John Biddle, Nicholas Bolvin, Daniel Le Roy, Christian Clemens, William H. Puthuff, John Anderson, John Hunt, Charles Larned, Gabriel Richard, John R. Williams, Solomon Sibley, John Monteith, Henry J. Hunt, John L. Leib, Peter J. Desnoyers, Austin E. Wing, William Woodbridge, Benjamin Stead, Philip Lecuyer and William Brown.

Section five of this act provided that the trustees might from time to time ESTABLISH SUCH COLLEGES, ACADEMIES AND SCHOOLS depending upon the University, as they might think proper; made it the duty of the trustees to visit and inspect such colleges, academies and schools, to examine into the state and system of education and discipline therein, and to make a yearly report; to ordain rules for the government of the institution not inconsistent with the laws of the United States or of the Territory, and to appoint a president and professors and to remove them at pleasure. A president was to be appointed without waiting until the state of the funds would allow the establishment of a college. Persons of every religious denomination were capable of being elected trustees, and no person, president, professor, instructor or pupil was to be refused admittance for his conscientious persuasion in matters of religion.

The corporation had control and management of the township of land granted by the act of 1804, and of the three sections granted to the college of Detroit by the treaty of Fort Meigs in 1817, and also were entitled to all property, rights and credits of the corporation established by the act to establish a "Catholepistemiad," which act was repealed.

At the first meeting of the board of trustees, Gov. Woodbridge disclosed to the board the result of his previous inquiries and was appointed one of a committee to memorialize Congress in relation to the lands. A memorial was drawn up by him, adopted by the trustees, and a copy laid before the Legislative Council which held its first session in the Territory. It was transmitted with their approval to Congress in 1824. This document, which may be found at length in the journal of Congress for that year, embodies the motives which led to a location of the township in detached sections, rather than in an entire township.

The evils resulting from the separate interests, adverse to the general interests of the State and of the institution, which could hardly fail to grow up, by embodying together in one county and neighborhood, so large a number of *lessees* (for at this time no thought was entertained of selling these lands in fee,) had been witnessed by the memorialist in the State of Ohio, and formed a leading consideration for locating the land in separate tracts.

The petition of the trustees was attended to with zeal and fidelity, by the late AUSTIN E. WING, and through his earnest efforts, a second township was appropriated for University purposes, both to be located in detached tracts. An addition was made to our University lands by the terms of the treaty of Fort Wayne. The Catholic residents of the city of Detroit were desirous of obtaining land to aid in the building of a church. This wish was complied with in the execution of the treaty, by General Cass, with the condition that another tract should be granted for the benefit of general education. This treaty was confirmed and the grants sanctioned.

Classical and evening schools were established in the city of Detroit, as early as 1822, by private teachers, and a Lancasterian school was kept as part of the University, but no law was passed to provide for a system of common or primary schools, until 1827, four years after the organization of the legislative council. This act provided that every township containing fifty inhabitants or householders, should provide themselves with a schoolmaster, of good morals, to teach children to read and write, and to instruct them in the English and French language, as well as in arithmetic, orthography and decent behavior, for such terms of time as shall be equivalent to six months for one school in each year; every township containing one hundred families or householders, for an increased length of time; and to provide in addition, a schoolmaster or teacher to instruct children in the English language. Every township containing two hundred families or householders, was to be provided with a grammar schoolmaster of good morals, well instructed in the Latin, French and English languages.

For neglect of any township to procure and support such teacher as was required for the various lengths of time, the township incurred a penalty in proportion, from fifty to one hundred and fifty dollars; and the penalty was to be levied by warrant from the court, upon the inhabitants of the deficient township, and was appropriated for the use of such schools as had complied with the law, and whose circumstances most required such assistance.

The inhabitants were to choose five persons within their township, as inspectors of common schools, who possessed similar powers to these officers at the present time.

The inhabitants voted at the annual meetings to raise such sums of money upon the polls and rateable estates, within the respective townships, for the support and maintenance of a schoolmaster, to teach youth to read, write and cipher, as a majority deemed expedient; to be assessed and collected at the same time and in the same manner with the township and county taxes; the moneys were apportioned by the supervisor and township clerk, according to the number of children between the ages of five and seventeen, as appeared by a census of the district, taken under oath by one or more of the trustees of the school, who were appointed in each of the districts.

The moneys were to be applied exclusively in paying the wages of the teacher or schoolmaster. But the law did not apply to any township which at an annual meeting, declared by a "two-thirds vote that they would not comply with the act."

Section six of this act relates to proceedings after the formation of a school district, and also to the power of the inhabitants to vote tax and the manner of its collection, and is deemed to be of sufficient interest, being the first school law, and adapted to a state of things so different from our present condition as a State, to be inserted at length:

Sec. 6. That whenever any township in this territory shall be divided into school districts, according to the directions of this act, it shall be the duty of one of the inspectors of said township, within twenty days after, to make a notice in writing, describing said district, and appointing a time and place for the first district meeting, and deliver said writing to some one of the freeholders or inhabitants, liable to pay taxes, residing in said district, whose duty it shall be to notify each freeholder or inhabitant residing in said district, qualified as aforesaid, by reading such notice in the hearing of each such freeholder or inhabitant, or leaving a copy thereof at the place of his abode, at least six days before the time of such meeting; and if any such freeholder or inhabitant shall neglect or refuse to give such notice, he shall pay a fine of five dollars, to be recovered in the same manner, and for the same use as is provided in the third section of this act. Such district meeting shall have power, when so convened, by the major part of the persons so met, to adjourn from time to time, as occasion may require, and to fix on a time and place to hold their future annual meeting, which annual meeting they are hereby authorized and required to hold, and to alter and change the time and place of holding such annual meeting, as they or a majority of them, at any legal meeting, may think proper. And at such first meeting, or at any future meeting, the said freeholders and inhabitants, or a majority of them so met, are hereby authorized and empowered to appoint a moderator for the time being, to designate a site for their school house, to vote a tax on the resident inhabitants of such district, as a majority present shall deem sufficient, to purchase a suitable site for their school house, and build, keep in repair, and furnish it with necessary fuel and appendages; also to choose three trustees to manage the concerns of said district, whose duty it shall be to build and keep in repair their school house, and from time to time, as occasion may require, to agree with and employ instructors, and to pay them; also to choose one district clerk, to keep the records and doings of said meeting, whose doings shall be good in law, who shall be qualified by oath or affirmation, as the several township clerks are; likewise one collector, who shall have the same power and authority, and have the same fees for collecting, and be subject to the same rules, regulations and duties, as respects the business of the district. which by law appertaineth to the collectors of townships in this territory; and the said trustees, clerks and collectors shall not be compelled to serve more than one year at any one time; and it shall be the further duty of the trustees of each district, as soon as may be, after the trustees have voted a tax, to make a rate bill or tax list, which shall raise the sum voted, with four cents on a dollar for collector's fees, on all the taxable inhabitants of said district, agreeably to the levy on which the township tax was levied the preceding year, and annex to the said tax list or rate bill, a warrant, which warrant shall be substantially as followeth:

County of } *ss.*

To , Collector of the district, in the town of , in the county aforesaid. Greeting:—In the name of the United States of America, you are hereby required and commanded to collect from each of the inhabitants of said district, the several sums of money written opposite to the names of each of said inhabitants, in the annexed tax list, and within —— days, after receiving this warrant, to pay the amount of the money by you collected, into the hands of the trustees of said district. or some one of them, and take their or his receipt therefor. And if any one or more of said inhabitants shall neglect or refuse to pay the sum, you are hereby further commanded to levy on the goods and chattels of each delinquent, and make sale thereof, according to law. Given under our hands and seals, this day of 182 .

[L. S.]
[L. S.] } Trustees.
[L. S.]

In 1828 Congress authorized the Governor and Council to take charge of the school sections, to protect them from waste and injury, and to provide by law for leasing them. In 1833 the school law of 1828 was repealed and another act passed, which provided for the election of three commissioners of schools and ten inspectors, whose duties were similar to those of inspectors under the present law. They were charged with the protection of section 16, with power to lease and manage it, in whatever manner they deemed best calculated to enhance its value. Any moneys arising from such care and management were to be applied to the support of common schools. The mode of taxation to build a school house, after a majority of the inhabitants approved of the estimate of expense, was similar to later provisions, requiring the directors of districts to obtain a transcript of so much of the last assessment roll of the township as related to his district, and to add to it all the property of persons who had become residents, and of residents who had purchased since the last assessment roll was made.

A humane provision of the law gave discretion to directors, whenever there was within any district, any poor and indigent person, unable to pay for the instruction of his or her children, or where there were poor children without parents, to order such children to be instructed at the school, and the expense of such instruction was defrayed by tax upon the property of the district.

This law gave authority to the several commissioners of adjoining townships to constitute and establish conjointly school districts on the line dividing such townships. It also authorized the appointment of some person, by the governor of the territory, as "Superintendent of common schools," who had authority to take supervision of section 16, and all fractional sections for the use of schools, where trustees or commissioners had not been chosen. The directors of districts were to report to the Superintendent, the whole number of scholars taught in the district for three months, and any additional time, together with the amount of moneys received from the commissioners. It was made the duty of the Superintendent to report annually to the Legislative Council, the number of scholars taught, the condition of the school lands, suits or actions brought, and moneys arising from this and other sources, and whatever else might to him appear necessary, concerning the lands and the condition of the schools.

In 1835, the same year in which the law was passed to form a constitution and state government, an amendment to the act of 1833, made it the duty of the school commissioners to make yearly dividends of all moneys coming into their hands by virtue of their office, for rents or damages done to section 16, and distribute and pay over the amount to the directors, in proportion to the number of scholars taught, according to the provisions of the law of 1833. This amendment repealed the sections of the previous act relating to the Superintendent, and provided for his appointment by the Governor, by and with the advice and consent of the Legislature, with the same powers and duties as before.

During the year [1835,] the people of the Territory adopted a constitution and formed a State government. The ordinance of the convention submitted to Congress the following propositions in relation to educational funds:

First. That section numbered sixteen in every township of the public lands, and where such section has been sold or otherwise disposed of, other lands equivalent thereto, and as contiguous as may be, shall be granted to the State for the use of schools.

Second. That the seventy-two sections of land set apart and reserved for the use and support of a university by an act of Congress approved on the twentieth day of May, eighteen hundred and twenty-six, entitled "an act concerning a seminary of learning in the Territory of Michigan," are hereby granted and conveyed to the State, to be appropriated solely to the use and support of such university, in such manner as the Legislature may prescribe: *And provided also,* That nothing herein contained shall be so construed as to impair or affect in any way the rights of any person or persons claiming any of said seventy-two sections of land, under contract or grant from said university.

These propositions became subsequently a part of the ordinance admitting Michigan into the Union and form the basis upon which rests the educational system of the State. Previous to the admission of Michigan, the other States of the Northwest Territory took the grant of the school section "to *each township respectively* in the State for the use of schools," or "to the State for the use of *the inhabitants of the township* for the use of schools." The difficulties under which these states had labored in making the fund available and effective for educational purposes, were avoided in the ordinance admitting Michigan into the Union as a State, and the foundation was laid for a better order of things, the results of which have been witnessed with abundant satisfaction during the sixteen years of its existence. In no other State of the Union, under all circumstances, has education been so amply and abundantly sustained by a sure and steadily increasing fund. This great advantage has been secured, as facts will demonstrate, from two causes: the taking of the grant to the State to be appropriated to the use of all the schools of the State, and to the constitutional provision subsequently adopted, creating a distinct and separate department of public instruction.

A question involving a claim of great magnitude, however, has been raised as to the subsequent and existing rights of the inhabitants of townships under the ordinance of Congress, in consequence of the alleged departure from its original terms. During the senatorial term of Gov. Woodbridge in the Congress of the United States, he eloquently and ably maintained the right and justice of a further claim on Congress in behalf of the individual inhabitants of townships, and at three different sessions introduced and got successfully through the Senate a bill granting a million and a half of acres of land to the State, sustaining it before that body on the ground of a want of fair equivalent for the rights of taxation which the State had given up in the adoption of the ordinance of admission, still leaving untouched all question of compensation to the inhabitants respectively of the several townships. The question may yet in the view of many, become important to Michigan and other States, which have been admitted under similar provisions. Should it become so or not, it is a subject which deserves to be generally understood, or at all events not lost sight of, as a part of the history of our legislation. The substance of the ground thus assumed is, that the provision of the ordinance of the Congress of 1785, amounts to a solemn covenant with each purchaser and settler that he should be forever entitled to the usufruct of that fund, with the other settlers in the township, as a means of educating their children *within such township;* that every man who buys a lot of land and pays for it, buys with it the *right* to his proportion of the use of section 16 *within his township*, establishing thereby a claim of great magnitude in behalf of the inhabitants of each surveyed township; that the right to taxation is a right which no State may surrender or abrogate; that if the right may be commuted for or surrendered for an *equivalent,* no just equivalent has been rendered, and nothing gained but what was before guaranteed to the inhabitants of the townships; that the equitable and available right—the use—the beneficiary interest in it had passed from Congress; that in the case of Michigan, Congress had resumed that which it had before sold, to the purchasers of its wild lands, as if it were an equivalent for the surrender by the State of the brightest jewel of its sovereignty—the right of taxation—no matter how the State may have been required to dispose of these lands; in short that the resulting rights of the people of the townships were the same, as if it were a case between two individuals, where either the second conveyance by the trustee would be pronounced void, or an adequate indemnity for the right taken, would be decreed. The considerations however, which induced the action of the convention which gave its assent to the ordinance of admission embracing the grant of the school lands to the State, were based upon the light of experience afforded in the educational history of the other States of the North West. The States of Ohio, Indiana and Illinois had reserved the grant to the inhabitants of the township; such inhabitants exercising over the section 16 the duties and powers of a landlord, and disposing of it by vote; such management requiring a multiplicity of officers without any identity of purpose, and without the authority or means to consolidate their action to produce an equal amount of benefit to all the citizens. The history of the educational affairs of these States afforded practical evidence, [even if it was a doubtful assumption that these States possessed the right to take the grant to the State,] that the management and disposition of these sections by the inhabitants of the townships was a source of difficulty, embarrassment and expense, fatal to the success of any educational achievement worthy of the people, or productive to them of the greatest amount of good.

Such considerations afford satisfactory grounds for the action of our own Convention, in submitting different terms to Congress for its assent, and to the people for their sanction. In taking the grant to the State, it avoided a multiplicity of officers otherwise located in different counties; it contributed and is still contributing in an unexampled manner to the education of all the youth of the whole State; it has saved many townships from asking legislative aid, where the school section was unavailable, either from prior locations by actual settlers, as was the case in the counties of Wayne, Macomb and Monroe, or where the section was covered with heavy timber, which prolonged the event of its being cleared for a series of years; and in many instances, saving not only time, labor and expense, but the means of education itself, to the inhabitants of those townships where the section was entirely unavailable from natural causes, and relieving the inhabitants in such cases from the management of equivalent sections, at a distance from their townships.

In taking the grant to the State, there was a higher principle of equity involved in relation to the whole people, than would have obtained, had Congress refused its assent to the terms demanded in the ordinance of the Convention. If the original faith of Congress might be considered as pledged to the townships, previous to the adoption of our constitution, the inhabitants by their votes in adopting that instrument, decided in favor of a consolidation of the fund and its management by the legislature, for the common benefit of all the townships. Nor was such policy rendered less sound by the adoption of a system which avoided the repeated applications to Congress which have arisen in other States, and which left all questions connected with these lands, to be settled by Congress and the State, in its sovereign capacity, rather than by township jurisdictions, subordinate in their will and power, to the higher and more general interests of the whole people.

The step thus early taken by the Old Congress, which so materially aided in increasing the settlement of the western country, and providing it with the permanent means of education, has been followed by Congress in later days, in providing for territorial governments. For the government of Oregon, two sections were set apart for school purposes. The grant of an additional school section to the new territories was recommended by Mr. Robert J. Walker, while Secretary of the Treasury of the United States, and his comprehensive and liberal views of the subject, are worthy of a place upon the record of the future educational history of the United States.

"This grant to each of the new States," says Mr. Walker in his report to Congress, "of one section of the public lands in each township, was designed to secure the benefit of education to all the children of that township. This object has failed to a great extent, because one section in the centre of a township, six miles square, is too distant from many of the sections to furnish a school to which all can resort, and because as a pecuniary provision it is inadequate. The grant of one section for every section in such quarter township would be sufficient, whilst the central location would be adjacent to every other section in such quarter township, bringing the school house within the immediate vicinage of every child within its limits. Congress, to some extent, adopted the recommendation of granting two school sections instead of one, for education in Oregon, but even thus extended, the grant is still inadequate in amount, whilst the location is too remote for a school which all can attend. This subject is again presented to Congress, with the recommendation that it shall be extended to California and New Mexico, and also to the other new states and territories composing the public domain. Even as a subject of revenue, such grants would more than refund their value to the government, as each quarter township is composed of nine sections, of which the central section would be granted for schools, and each of the remaining eight sections would be adjacent to that granted. The eight seetions thus located, and each adjoining a school section would be of greater value than when separated by many miles from such opportunities, and the thirty-two sections of one entire township wolud bring a larger price to the government than thirty-five sections out of thirty-six, when one section only, so remote from the rest, was granted for such a purpose. The public domain would then be settled at an earlier period, and yielding larger products, thus soon augment our exports and imports, with a correspondent increase of revenue from duties.

"The greater diffusion of education would increase the power of mind and knowledge applied to our industrial pursuits, and augment in this way also, the products and wealth of the nation. Each State is deeply interested in the welfare of every other, for the representatives of the whole, regulate by their votes, the Measures of the Union, which must be happy and prosperous in proportion as its councils are guided by more enlightened views, resulting from the more universal diffusion of LIGHT, and KNOWLEDGE and EDUCATION."

These are the sentiments of a great Statesman, speaking of education, and the means of its permanent support and spread, as the main spring of national progress and greatness in its intimate connection not only with the intellectual power, but with the wealth of the country applied to its industrial pursuits. But the "failure in the object of the grant" is attributable in a great degree to other causes than to those assigned by Mr. Walker. These causes have consisted in the manner of taking the grant and in the want of a separate officer of public instruction, with general supervision of the subject of education. Whatever may have been the failure in other States, the arguments of Mr. Walker do not apply in this respect, to our condition of things, but furnish a strong argument in support of the action of our own State in taking the grant to itself, whatever claim may be supposed to arise in favor of the inhabitants of the townships.

Facts demonstrate that there has been no such thing as *failure* in MICHIGAN, in the object of the grant, either as a pecuniary provision or as a means of affording the blessings of general education. On the other hand, comparison may be challenged in this respect, with the educational system and progress of any other State in the Union. Our fund for the support of primary schools, after a lapse of only fifteen years of our existence as a State, amounting to nearly a million of dollars, the interest of which, with a principal rapidly accruing from the sales of the lands granted for the purpose, is annually distributed throughout the whole State, affording aid to all sections, for the purpose of instruction, while the school system itself is meeting the educational wants of all, and successfully carrying forward the objects of the great mission, it is destined to accomplish.

The manner of the grant being fixed by the assent of Congress and the people of Michigan, the next question of historical importance, is the adoption of the Constitutional provisions on the subject of education. It is to be regretted that the proceedings of the first Convention have not been preserved, so as to be accessible to public inspection. There was, however, no debate in relation to the importance of making suitable provision for Public Instruction. A committee was appointed to draft an article, of which Isaac E. Crary, of Calhoun, was chairman. It was reported on the second day of June, 1835, and was adopted substantially as it came from the hands of the committee. As reported to the convention, the article provided for a Secretary of Public Instruction. When the article came up in Convention, Judge Woodbridge remarked that he had read it, and although it was new and not to be found in any other constitution, yet he was inclined to give it his support, if the chairman of the committee would consent to make one alteration, viz: to strike out the word "Secretary," and insert "Superintendent." The chairman remarked that the report was beyond his control, but if there was no objection on the part of any member of the Convention, in order to secure the support of the member from Wayne, he would readily consent to the change. The change was accordingly made.

The article, as reported, provided for a library in each school district. This was amended in Convention, by the casting vote of the President, by striking out the words "school district," and inserting "township." The article being then referred to the committee on phraseology and revision, the words "at least," were inserted, where they appear in the old constitution; and the article thus passed, securing by this slight addition and change, the establishment, by subsequent legislation, of libraries in *every school district.* The following is the constitutional article adopted in 1835:

EDUCATION.

1. The Governor shall nominate, and by and with the advice and consent of the Legislature, in joint vote, shall appoint a Superintendent of Public Instruction, who shall hold his office for two years, and whose duties shall be prescribed by law.

2. The Legislature shall encourage, by all suitable means, the promotion of intellectual, scientifical and agricultural improvement. The proceeds of all lands that have been or hereafter may be granted by the United States to this State for the support of schools, which shall hereafter be sold or disposed of, shall be and remain a perpetual fund; the interest of which, together with the rents of all such unsold lands, shall be inviolably appropriated to the support of schools throughout the State.

3. The Legislature shall provide for a system of common schools by which a school shall be kept up and supported in each school district at least three months in every year; and any school district neglecting to keep up and support such a school may be deprived of its equal proportion of the interest of the public fund

4. As soon as the circumstances of the State will permit, the Legislature shall provide for the establishment of libraries; one at least [in] each township; and the money which shall be paid by persons as an equivalent for exemption from military duty, and the clear proceeds of all fines assessed in the several counties for any breach of the penal laws, shall be exclusively applied for the support of said libraries.

5. The Legislature shall take measures for the protection, improvement or other disposition of such lands as have been or may hereafter be reserved or granted by the United States to this State for the support of a University; and the funds accruing from the rents or sale of such lands, or from any other source for the purpose aforesaid, shall be and remain a permanent fund for the support of said University, with such branches as the public convenience may hereafter demand for the promotion of literature, the arts and sciences, and as may be authorized by the terms of such grant; and it shall be the duty of the Legislature, as soon as may be, to provide effectual means for the improvement and permanent security of the funds of said University.

The SYSTEM OF PUBLIC INSTRUCTION which was intended to be established by the framers of the constitution, the conception of the office, its province, its powers and duties were derived from Prussia. That system consisted of three degrees. Primary instruction, corresponding to our district schools; secondary instruction, communicated in schools called Gymnasia, and the highest instruction communicated in the Universities. The superintendence of this entire system, which was formed in 1819, was entrusted to a Minister of State, called the Minister of Public Instruction, and embraced every thing which belonged to the moral and intellectual advancement of the people.

The system in Michigan was intended to embrace all institutions which had for their object the instruction of youth, comprising the education of the primary school, the intermediate class of schools, however denominated, and the University. The idea of the framers of the constitution was to embrace the whole, and in one sense, a wider and different field of supervision than was embraced in the first law established under it—a wider, in all that pertains to the high and peculiar signification of Public Instruction; and different, in the absence of any connection of the Superintendent with the disposition of the lands, or management of the funds granted for the support of education. The Prussian *principle* upon which the constitutional provisions of Michigan were based, asserted the fact "that every State needs a separate officer of Public Instruction, and that there should be nothing to divert his attention from the general supervision of education." Under that system this officer devotes his whole time to schools and the subject of education. The creation of such an officer was intended in the adoption of our own constitution. Its framers looked to this officer for a general supervision not only of primary schools, but of the university, of colleges, academies, high schools and all schools, established or to be established throughout the State. True, the government of these institutions were to be confided to the management and control of local officers, adapted to the character and wants of each—but over all, as representing the guardian watchfulness and interest of the State, was intended to be the general officer of Public Instruction, accumulating all the material of this congregated effort, and laying it in embodied form before the tribunal of the people and their legislatures; devising and maturing plans for improvement; requiring full information in every particular relating to the annual condition and progress of all these institutions; preparing suitable forms of procedure for the expedition and correct transaction of business; suggesting the wants of the system, and perfecting its details where it was found to be wanting; giving his support to the labors of officers entrusted with the care of schools; impressing the importance of education by public lectures and personal visitations in the various counties and districts; infusing life and zeal, and spreading information among all; showing the rewards of labor; and by the energy of his exertions, in common with others, and from advantage of position in acquiring knowledge, ensuring progression in all that relates to educational, intellectual and moral achievement.

This was the field laid out by the framers of the constitution. It was conceived to be sufficiently responsible and arduous; sufficiently vast and comprehensive, to engage every moment of time and consideration, to employ the entire thought and labor of one man, in devising the means of bringing into perfection a system so enlarged and commanding; embracing full knowledge of education and its progress among the people, in whatsoever form and shape it was working its way; by public grant, or private endowment, by State patronage, or by individual exertion or munificence. The history of our State legislation will demonstrate how this conception has been filled, and what progress has been made in Michigan towards the developement and perfection of a System of Public Instruction.

STATE LEGISLATION.

1836.

EXTRACT FROM GOV. MASON'S FIRST MESSAGE.

Ours is said to be a government founded on intelligence and morality, and no political axiom can be more beautifully true. Here the rights of all are equal, and the people themselves are the primary source of all power. Our institutions have levelled the artificial distinctions existing in the societies of other countries, and have left open to every one, the avenues to distinction and honor. Public opinion directs the course which our government pursues, and so long as the people are enlightened, that direction will never be misgiven. It becomes, then, your imperious duty, to secure to the State, a general diffusion of knowledge. This can in no wise be so certainly effected, as by the perfect organization of a uniform and liberal system of common schools. Your attention is therefore called to the effectuation of a perfect school system, open to all classes, as the surest basis of public happiness and prosperity.

The constitution declares that the legislature shall provide a system of common schools by which a school shall be kept up and supported in each school district at least three months in every year; and it also provides for the appointment of a Superintendent of Public Instruction, whose duty it shall be to direct and superintend said schools. Under the direction of the government, section 16 in each township is reserved for schools, and under the act of Congress, of January 20, 1826, 72 sections of land are reserved for the use and support of the University of Michigan. Forty-nine sections of the University lands have been located, and consist of some of the most valuable tracts on the peninsula of Michigan. I would suggest that the proper authority be requested to make the remaining locations. These locations will, when brought under the control of the State, place the University of Michigan, among the wealthiest institutions of the country, and under a proper direction, render it an ornament and honor to the West.

On the 16th of July, Mr. Whipple, from the committee on education, to whom had been referred a resolution of the House of Representatives, instructing them to report whether any law be necessary to give effect to the constitution, regarding the subject of education, reported that full and complete effect could not be given at this session to an article respecting it—that in legislating upon a subject of such vital importance, the proceedings of the Legislature should be guarded—that no measures should be taken without the greatest consideration; that the Congress of the United States, appreciating the vast importance of a universal diffusion of knowledge, so necessary to the very existence of a republican government, had granted to the State, lands, not only for supporting an extended system of common schools, but for the purpose of founding a University—that the framers of the constitution, impressed with the magnitude of the subject, with wise forecast, had adopted an article intended to protect the fund from being diverted, and made other general provisions, well adapted to attain the great end sought to be accomplished—that the committee did not think it expedient then to recommend the adoption of any system of instruction, but had provided a bill for collecting such information as would enable their successors to act understandingly, and hoped that by an efficient and well digested system to be devised thereafter, the intellectual and moral condition of the people would be improved, their happiness promoted, and their liberties established on a firm foundation. The bill thus introduced, resulted in the act of July 26, 1836, a summary of which is embraced in the first report made under it, by the officer charged with that duty. On the same day, Rev. John D. Pierce was nominated by the Governor for the office of Superintendent of Public Instruction, and unanimously confirmed by both Houses of the Legislature. To this gentleman was confided, by the act referred to, the responsible duty, among other things, of preparing a system for common schools, and a plan for a University and its branches.

1837.

EXTRACT FROM GOV. MASON'S SECOND MESSAGE.

The Superintendent of Public Instruction will report to you a system for the government of the University of Michigan, and for the organization of the primary schools of the State. I cannot, however, dismiss the subject of education without endeavoring to impress upon your minds the truth, that in it, is embraced the most vital interests of our country, and that no object within the province of your legislation, should demand so important a portion of your time and attention. The State fund for the support of common schools, with a prudent husbandry, will equal our utmost wants. The University of Michigan will also possess an endowment, which will enable the State to place that institution upon an elevation of character and standing equal to that of any similar institution in the Union. I would therefore recommend the immediate location of the University, and at the same time, the adoption of a system of primary schools.

In the organization of your primary schools, which are the foundation upon which your whole system of education must be based, the first measure essential to their success and good government is the APPOINTMENT OF GOOD TEACHERS, of the highest character, both moral and intellectual. Liberal salaries should be allowed the instructor, and without this, you may rest assured, you must fail in your object; as individuals in all respects competent to the charge of your schools will be excluded from them by the parsimoniousness of their compensation. Let me also suggest that you adopt A PERMANENT AND UNIFORM STANDARD OF WORKS to be used in the schools, and that in the studies selected, they may, to as great an extent as practicable, embrace the useful and practical information of life. Let your youth be taught the first principles in morals, in science, and in government, commencing their studies in the primary schools, elevating its grades as you approach the distinct seminary, and continue its progress till you arrive at the University. By this system your children will acquire practical knowledge for after life, and have instilled in their minds at an early day, their duties as citizens, and above all, their obligations to the Searching Power of another world.

In contemplating the Past, and dwelling on the Future, we are forcibly reminded that if our government is to outlive the term heretofore allotted to Republics, it is to be accomplished by the diffusion of knowledge amongst the people, and that we must depend upon the power of a liberal and enlightened public "as the palladium of a free government—the ægis of our Federal existence." Let us not suppose that WE are beyond the calamities which have befallen other nations. Guard the education of the rising generation. Teach them in earliest lessons of life, the great principle upon which their government was founded, and keep before their minds those scenes of American glory which have chiefly contributed to immortalize the American name.

SYSTEM OF PUBLIC INSTRUCTION—AS REPORTED BY THE SUPERINTENDENT.

The plan reported defined the rights, powers and duties of school districts—the duties of district officers—of township officers, of school inspectors, and of townships—proposed the establishment of libraries, and plans for school houses—the establishment of academies as branches of the University, and a method of organization for the University, and also defined the duties of Superintendent of Public Instruction.

The officers of the system proposed for school districts, were moderator, vice moderator, director and assessor, and three township school inspectors, with the township clerk as clerk of the board.

The following extract from the report of the Superintendent evinces the high estimation in which that officer viewed the system of FREE SCHOOLS, as connected with education in a government like ours. He says:

"It has been said, and rightly too, that common schools are truly republican. The great object is to furnish good instruction in all the elementary and common branches of knowledge, for all classes of community, as good indeed for the poorest boy of the State, as the rich man can furnish for his children, with all his wealth. The object is universal education—the education of every individual of all classes. The great thing which has rendered the Prussian system, so popular and efficient, which has so strongly attached it to the hearts of the people, and made it an essential element of the social state, is its truly republican character. It is this feature of FREE SCHOOLS which has nurtured and preserved pure republicanism in our own land. In the public schools, all classes are blended together; the rich mingle with the poor, and are educated in company. In their sportive gambols a common sympathy is awakened; all the kindlier sensibilities of the heart are excited, and mutual attachments are formed which cannot fail to exert a soothing and happy influence through life. In these schools the poor are as likely to excel as the rich, for there is no monopoly of talent, of industry, or acquirements. It was the ceaseless application and untiring perseverance of FRANKLIN, and not his wealth, which raised him to the highest eminence. It is this system which brings forward and elevates to places of distinction, a due proportion of that class of citizens which the Romans called new men—men who owe nothing either to birth or fortune—but all to the Free Schools and their own exertions. It is this principle of universal education adopted by the Pilgrims, and cherished by their descendants through succeeding generations, which has given them and their sons pre-eminence. Nothing can be imagined more admirably adapted, in all its bearings, to prostrate all distinctions arising from mere circumstances of birth and fortune. By means of the public schools, the poor boy of to-day, without the protection of father or mother, may be the man of learning and influence of to-morrow; he may accumulate, and die the possessor of thousands; he may reach the highest station in the Republic, and the treasures of his mind may be the richest legacy of the present to coming generations. Whilst the reverse of all this may be true of the young scion of wealth and power, proud and accomplished as he may be in person, and gifted also by nature with the highest order of intellect, and blessed with the fairest prospect of usefulness, the long cherished hopes of doating parents and the brightest youthful visions of rising greatness, may all be disappointed in some thoughtless moment of ungoverned passion, and his sun go down in the gloom of midnight darkness. Let Free Schools be established and maintained in perpetuity and there can be no such thing as a permanent aristocracy in our land; for the monopoly of wealth is powerless when mind is allowed freely to come in contact with mind. It is by erecting a barrier between the rich and the poor, which can be done only by allowing a monopoly to the rich—a monopoly of learning, as well as of wealth—that such an aristocracy can be established. But the operation of a Free School system has a powerful tendency to prevent the erection of this barrier."

Another feature which was presented to the consideration of the Legislature, was the obligation on the part of the State to suffer none to grow up in ignorance. For this purpose, the Superintendent suggested that all persons having the care of children, should be required to send them to school, the constitutional portion of each year. The object to be attained was the welfare of the individual instructed, and the security of the State; and the reason given was, that the State had the right to require the education of all children and youth, and to impose upon all to whom their management and care are committed, the duty of educating them. In carrying out this idea, the Superintendent was of opinion that it might not be consistent with the principles of our constitution, to prohibit private seminaries, but that it was consistent, both with the spirit and the letter of our institutions, to place the public schools upon high and elevated ground, to make them adequate to the wants of the whole community; to place them on such a footing as to furnish the best instruction, not only in the more common, but in all the higher branches of elementary knowledge. "But," says the Superintendent, "the most perfect organization of the entire system in all the varied departments of instruction must fail of securing the desired results without a sufficient number of COMPETENT TEACHERS." To this end, it was suggested, as a subject for consideration, whether it would not be expedient to fix, by law, a minimum price, below which no teacher should be entitled to receive aid from the public fund, and to *provide prospectively that every teacher of the public schools shall have been through a regular course of training*, and received his diploma from the academic board, setting forth his qualifications as a teacher. It was suggested, in relation to the public money, whether any township ought to be entitled to its proportion of the income of the fund, which did not comply with the provisions of the law, and maintain an EFFICIENT SCHOOL BOARD. It was recommended that the active agents of the schools, upon whose activity and energy the success of the system would depend, be few as possible, their duties clearly defined, and their services paid for; that the time of any man was his property, and ought not to be taken by the public without remuneration.

It was recommended that the legislature provide, as soon as circumstances would permit, for DISTRICT LIBRARIES. The clear proceeds of all fines, the equivalent for exemptions from military duty, and a district tax of $10, were suggested as establishing the basis of a fund for the purpose.

ACADEMIES OR BRANCHES.

The original plan, as reported, provided that any county containing a given number of inhabitants, should be entitled to an academy of the highest grade, as a branch of the University, on condition that the board of supervisors should procure an eligible site, and cause suitable buildings to be erected, such as should be deemed sufficient, and approved by the Superintendent of Public Instruction. The board of supervisors were to appoint six "wise and discreet persons," who, together with one appointed by the Superintendent, were to constitute the board of trustees. Of this academic board, the judge of probate and the two associate judges of the county, were to be *ex-officiis* members, and the county clerk, clerk *ex-officio* of the board. The trustees were to superintend its general concerns, appoint professors and teachers, and make a report to a *board of visitors*. This board was to consist of three persons, to be appointed annually, one by the supervisors, and two by the Superintendent. It was to be their duty to visit the academy at its annual examination, to inquire into its condition. examine the proceedings of the board of trustees, and forward their report to the Superintendent.

For the support of these institutions it was proposed that the board of supervisors cause to be raised by the county, a sum equal to that which should be apportioned to it from the income of the University fund. In each academy were to be three departments—one for the education of teachers, one for the higher branches of English education, and one for classical learning. The course of instruction for the teachers' class, to be three years; this department to be open, without charge, to all who wished to fit themselves for the business of teaching, on pledge of teaching at least four years, under a forfeiture, if they did not. Tuition for English department not to exceed ten dollars, and for the classical, twelve. Whenever any county complied with these requirements, they were to be entitled to an appropriation of $500 for the purchase of apparatus and books. In the TEACHER'S DEPARTMENT the following studies were recommended: the English language, writing and drawing, arithmetic, mental and written, and book keeping, geography and general history combined, and history of the United States, geometry, trigonometry, mensuration and surveying, natural philosophy and elements of astronomy, geology and chemistry, constitution of the United States and of the State of Michigan, select portions of the laws and duties of public officers, principles of teaching, rhetoric, algebra, the nature of man as a physical, intellectual and moral being, and his relative duties.

THE UNIVERSITY.

The additional and general interest created by a change of the organic law in 1850, in placing the University under the control of Regents elected by the people, and the consequent questions of policy which have arisen in relation to this institution, renders it not only desirable, but an object of the deepest importance to trace with care the history of legislation in regard to it. For this reason, it is deemed important to give much of it, in detail. The following extract contains the plan of government for this institution suggested by the first Superintendent:

In the organization of the University, it will be proper and necessary to create a Board of Regents to superintend and manage its general concerns. The powers to be vested in this Board, and its duties may and ought to be prescribed by law. The Board of Regents shall consist of the Governor, Lieutenant Governor, the Chief Justice and Associate Justices of the Supreme Court, Chancellor of the State, and the Chancellor of the University, who shall be *ex-officio* members, and twelve others to be appointed by the Legislature. Of these twelve, three shall continue in office four years, three three years, three two years, and the remaining three one year, to be determined by drawing. This arrangement will make it the duty of the Legislature, after the first organization, to appoint three annually. Of this Board, the Secretary of State shall be ex-officio Secretary. The Regents shall have the power, and it shall be their duty, to enact laws for the government of the University, to confer degrees, to appoint a Chancellor, and the prescribed number of professors in the several departments, and the requisite number of tutors, also to determine their respective salaries; to appoint a steward and fix the amount of his salary. The university shall consist of three departments:

1. The department of literature, science and the arts.
2. The department of law.
3. The department of medicine.

In the department of literature, science and the arts, there should ultimately be established the following professorships:

One of Ancient Languages.
" Modern Languages.
" Rhetoric and Oratory.
" Philosophy of History and Logic.
" Philosophy of the Human Mind.
" Moral Philosophy.
" Theology.
" Political Economy.
" Mathematics.
" Natural Philosophy.
" Chemistry.
" Geology and Mineralogy.
" Botany and Zoology.
" Fine arts.
" Civil Engineering and Drawing.

The department of law should consist of the following professorships

One of International Law.
" Common Law and Equity.

One of Constitutional and Statute Law.
" Commercial and Maritime Law.
" Jurisprudence.

In the department of medicine there should be the following professorships:

One of Anatomy.
" Surgery.
" Pathology.
" Practice of Physic.
" Obstetrics.
" Materia Medica.

The immediate government of the several departments must necessarily be intrusted to their respective faculties. The Regents shall have the power to regulate the course of instruction, and prescribe, under the advisement of the professorships, the books and authorities to be used in the several departments. And it shall be the duty of the Board of Regents to report annually to the board of visitors, the condition of the University, the amount of its expenditures, the number of its professors and tutors, the number of students in the several departments, and in the different classes, and text-books used, to be accompanied with an estimate of expenses for the coming year. The board of visitors, to consist of five, shall be appointed annually by the Superintendent of Public Instruction. But the question will arise, and it is an important one and must be met, can an institution on a scale thus magnificent be sustained? It is confidently believed that the day is not distant, when the wants of the State will require such an institution, and when its resources will be amply sufficient to sustain it. With a population already exceeding two hundred thousand souls, and floods of immigration of intelligent, enterprising and educated men pouring in upon us, it cannot be otherwise. To suppose that the wants of the State will not soon require a superstructure of fair proportions, on a foundation thus broad, would be a severe reflection upon the foresight and patriotism of the age. And to suppose that such an institution cannot be sustained, would seem to be a contradiction of the known laws by which human affairs are governed. Let the State move forward as prosperously, for a few years to come, as it has for a few years past, and one-half of the revenue arising from the University fund, will sustain an institution on a scale more magnificent than the one proposed, and sustain it too, with only a mere nominal admittance fee; a consummation most devoutly to be desired. And this fee, say $10 from each student, may be applied to the increase of the library. The institution would then present an anomaly in the history of learning, an university of the first order, open to all, tuition free. It is not to be expected, nor will it be necessary, that all the professorships should be filled at the commencement of its career. One-half the number judiciously appointed and arranged could *ad interim* discharge the duties of the whole; they could do so without difficulty, until the wants of the institution and the state of its funds should warrant the completion of the plan.

But in laying the foundations of a superstructure to be raised in just and equal proportions, and to be continued, as we trust, through all succeeding ages, liberal and ample provisions should be made for the anticipated wants of a high-minded and growing people. Present appearances warrant the belief that the income of the University fund cannot fall short of $50,000 per annum. One-half of this sum will be amply sufficient to give life and vigor to the several academies as branches of the University, and the remaining half will be fully adequate to sustain the parent institution on a scale as grand and magnificent as that proposed.

But there is another question to be considered, and one which requires a more detailed examination than can now be given to it. It is the propriety of engrafting upon an institution destined for public education in the higher branches of literature, science and the arts, the departments of law and medicine. Lord Bacon, one of the great master-spirits of the human race, states the true doctrine on this subject, and gives a conclusive reason for it. He says—"to disincorporate any particular science from general knowledge is one great impediment to its advancement. For there is a supply of light and information, which the particulars and instances of one science do yield and present for the framing and correcting the axioms of another science, in their very truth and notion. For each particular science has a dependence upon universal knowledge, to be augmented and rectified by the superior light thereof." In an address delivered on occasion of the dedication of Dane Law College, as a department of Harvard University, President Quincy made the following lucid remarks:—"In no way, perhaps, can the truth of this doctrine be better illustrated, than by the history of the progress of the English law, from its ancient, barbarous, and perplexed, to its present cultivated and lucid state. So long as it was disincorporated from general knowledge, and pursued exclusively under the guidance of professional men, in the Inns of Courts, or in offices of practitioners, its outline was obscure, its aspect forbidding and mysterious; none dared to pretend to master it, except the regularly initiated; and to some of these, its reason was a closed book, which they had not the strength or patience to open. No sooner. however, was the common law introduced among the branches of University education, than it became liberalized and refined. Its particular light was augmented and rectified by the superior light of universal knowledge. Its foreign jargon was abandoned. Its technicalities were diminished—by the labors of Blackstone the rough scene was changed. After the publication of his work, men of general science began to think and to speak of the English law, as of a subject which could be understood without the exclusive devotion of a whole life to it. Professional men also, their progress thus facilitated, found more leisure themselves to pursue general science. From the hour when the great magician, Blackstone, standing in the halls of Oxford, stretched his scientific wand over the 'illimitable ocean, without bound,' where, to the uninstructed eye, 'cold, hot, moist, dry, in their pregnant causes mixed, seemed to strive for the mastery,' confusion disappeared. In its stead was seen a well proportioned, well cemented fabric, pleasing to the sight, satisfactory to the taste, approved by the judgment, its architectural principles just, its parts orderly and harmonious, in which justice was found consorting with reason, and controversy guided by the spirit of truth, and not by the spirit of victory. Thus, under the joint influences of a thorough legal education and of general science, it may confidently be anticipated, that the destinies of the profession of the law will daily become more and more elevated and refined." What the learned President here affirms in regard to the science of law, and its corresponding art and profession, is equally true, with some slight modifications, of the science of medicine, and its corresponding art and profession. The science has been enlarged and rectified, and the profession elevated and rendered more permanently beneficial to the human family, by its connection with general knowledge. It is not easy to imagine a more appropriate place for the investigation of the sciences of law and of medicine, and the study of the professions thereunto belonging, than at the fountain head of light and intelligence. The advantages resulting to each profession, from this connection with general literature and science, must be strikingly obvious. So much so indeed as to excite wonder, on the slightest reflection, that a disconnection should ever have been tolerated.

But whatever may be the advantages of such a connection, it is not to be expected that the study of theology, as a profession, can ever be made a separate department of the University. There is no connection, and it is devoutly to be hoped there never will be, between church and State under our government. We have therefore no establishment, and consequently no ministry to provide for it. The different denominations, being left free in the exercise of their religion, are at liberty to adopt such measures for the training of the ministry of their respective churches as they may deem most advisable. The control and management of this business of right belongs to them; and it would be usurpation on the part of the State to assume to interfere in its direction. But so far as the great principles of the science of theology are concerned, they necessarily come within the compass of that general knowledge, with which every well educated young man ought to be acquainted. The mighty evidences of the divine existence, resulting from the unnumbered manifestations of contrivance and design throughout the universe of matter and of mind; and the basis, on which christianity has reared its stupendous fabric, and founds its claims to the confidence and affection of the world, would be fruitful topics for the predilections of such a professorship as is proposed to be established. Besides, it will be found to be essential to the prosperity of the University. Without something of the kind it would be abandoned by all religious denominations. We should then have presented to our view the spectacle of an University, on the broadest foundation, and splendidly endowed, but without students; while private institutions, struggling for existence, with comparatively few advantages, would be filled to overflowing. As christianity is the religion of our people, it must be recognized as coming within the circle of general knowledge, though they will suffer no interference in the formation of their religious opinions. It is all important to secure the interest of the great body of the people in the welfare of the University. But the great mass of them will be found attached to the different denominations of christians. Nothing, therefore, should be done to excite jealousy, or create alarm. And it is equally important that no religious test be introduced, but that every individual be left free in the exercise of his religion, and to worship as his conscience shall dictate. No flourishing institution can be found, which does not embrace as much as is here proposed; every attempt on a different plan hitherto made, has proved an entire failure. The University lately established in the city of New York, has a professorship of the character here contemplated; and as the first fruit of it, a splendid production has recently been presented to the public in a volume of lectures, written in the most captivating style, and filled with the clearest logical argumentation, and abounding in the most enlarged and liberal views. Such a professorship, thus filled, would secure to any institution unbounded confidence. And the men who founded that seat of learning are to be numbered among the most talented of our country, enlightened and liberal in their views, and belonging to the different religious persuasions. We find among them an ex-president of the United States, and the Hon. Benjamin F. Butler—the present distinguished attorney-general, who is now one of the council of the University, and who has recently been appointed to a professorship in the department of law. The fact is not to be concealed, that there is a strong prejudice in the minds of many worthy and enlightened men, against state institutions. And it is often said of late, that State institutions do not flourish. This feeling has originated from the attempt of two or three States to exclude everything in the form of religion from their Universities. The moral sense of the community was found to be against the plan, and the institutions could not flourish; for they were abandoned by the great majority of those who patronize the higher seminaries of learning. And the consequence was, difficulties ensued, and private institutions rose up around them and prospered. The truth is, the nature of man is such, that the result might have been anticipated. There is a medium between bigotry on the one hand, and atheism on the other. And the success of the University, its life, energy, character and usefulness, will essentially depend on the adoption of that medium course. In Brown University, the different denominations have ever been conjointly engaged in promoting the cause of letters. Difficulties may be created in anticipation, but they will generally be found on a nearer inspection to be imaginary. Some may complain if they cannot have the entire control, but the great body of the people will be satisfied. In respect to the assertion that state institutions do not, and cannot flourish, it may safely be affirmed that the history of the past proves directly the reverse. The oldest and most venerable institutions in our land are emphatically state institutions; they were planted, came up, increased in stature, and attained to the maturity and vigor of manhood, under the guidance and patronage of the state. There have been no failures, except in the cases named, and obviously for the reason assigned. The same is true of nearly all the celebrated European Universities; they are state institutions, founded, sustained and directed by the state. It is all important that the University of Michigan, in its constitution and order, be such as to secure the confidence of the liberal minded of all denominations, and then it may be expected that they will give it countenance and support.

PRIVATE INSTITUTIONS.

But there is another question, involving important considerations, which is intimately connected with the subject that has just now been discussed, and it is one that justly demands the exercise of the soundest discretion. It is the granting to private associations, acts of incorporation with university powers. Such corporations, if the filling of all vacancies is vested in themselves, contain within their own body, the principle of self-preservation and perpetual existence. Thus far, they are independent of the government, and cannot be reached by any power in the state; because the charter is held to be sacred. It is true, the right of supervision may be retained, and also the right of repeal. The principle adopted in New York is to grant university powers only on condition that the company applying shall have $25,000 in appropriate buildings, and $100,000 in funds, secured in double the amount, for the use of the institution; the state reserving to itself the right of visitation. The object of this rule is to prevent the multiplication of such institutions, without any fair prospect of permanent usefulness; and where the practice of granting such charters has obtained, the propriety of the rule cannot reasonably be questioned. With us, as a state, all is new; and we are at liberty to adopt such principles, and form such rules of action, as on mature reflection the great interests of learning may seem to require. It is respectfully suggested to the consideration of the legislature, whether it will be desirable to incorporate such a number of private associations for the purposes of education, as will have the effect to draw off the attention and interest of any considerable portions of the public from the institution founded by the State.

SUPERINTENDENT OF PUBLIC INSTRUCTION.

The duties of this officer were proposed to be as follows:

1. To submit to the Legislature an annual report *exhibiting the condition of the University and primary school funds;* also of the primary schools and of the University and its branches, and all such matters relating to his office and the public schools as he may think proper to communicate.

2. To prepare suitable forms for making all reports which may be required of the district, township, academic and university boards, and suitable regulations for conducting all proceedings under the law relating to public instruction, and transmit the same with such instructions as he may deem proper for the organization and government of the public schools, with such directions as to the course of

studies as he may judge advisable, to the several officers intrusted with their management and care.

3. To appoint the prescribed number of trustees and visitors in the different academic boards, and the annual board of visitors to the University.

4. To take charge of all University and school lands and all other property reserved to the State for the purposes of education, and dispose of the same according to law.

5. To invest all moneys arising from sale of such lands and property as directed by law.

6. To apportion the income of the University fund among its branches and the parent institution, and also the income of the primary school fund among the several townships and cities of the State, on such principles as shall be sanctioned by the Legislature.

7. To prepare annually a table of the amount to be paid to the University and each of its branches; also the amount in the aggregate to be paid to the different counties of the State from the income of the University and primary school funds respectively, and present the same to the State Treasurer.

8. To notify the treasurers of the several counties of the amounts to be disbursed.

9. *To hear and decide all questions arising under the public school system.*

This was designed to give him the power of putting at rest all controversies arising in the administration of the system of which he has the supervision.

The provision was intended to guard against the difficulties which had arisen under the administration of the school system in New York, and in relation to which, the Superintendent of that State, Mr. Dix, had said—"if the system has any defect, it is that the Superintendent has no power by law to enforce the execution of his own decisions."

The report, of which the above is a synopsis, was laid before the legislature on the 5th day of January, 1837. On the 18th day of February, Mr. Ward, from the committee on education, submitted a report concurring in the views presented by the Superintendent, and also a bill authorizing the Superintendent to sell the lands set apart for educational purposes, both school and University, and to invest the proceeds in the manner pointed out by law, and to give him the care and disposition of all the lands and other property reserved and granted to the State for educational purposes. A law was also passed giving to the Superintendent generally, the powers specified in his plan, with the exception of that which related to the decisions of questions arising under the school laws, and on the 20th day of March of this year, was approved the "act to provide for the organization and support of schools."

This law also carried out in its details the views of the Superintendent, but did not give to Michigan a system of FREE SCHOOLS. It provided for the establishment of school districts, with the offices of moderator, director and assessor, and defined their duties; for the appropriation of a share of the proceeds arising from "fines, breaches of penal laws and exemption from military duty." to every district in which the inhabitants voted a tax for a suitable library case, and a sum not to exceed ten dollars annually, for the purchase of books; it established a board of school inspectors, defined the duties of township clerks relative to schools, and provided for the distribution of the income of the school fund among the school districts, in proportion to the number of scholars in each, between the ages of five and seventeen years, and required a report from the inspectors to the county clerk, annually, of the whole number of districts in the township, the number from which reports were received for the year, the length of time a school had been taught for the year by a qualified teacher, the amount of public money belonging to each district, the number of children *taught* in each, and the number belonging to each between the ages of five and seventeen, the amount of public moneys, the amount raised in the township for schools, and the manner of its appropriation. The method of supporting the schools was by the levy of a tax upon the taxable property of the district, in proportion to its valuation, which was to be obtained by a transcript of the township assessment roll. The districts had authority to levy and assess upon the taxable property of the district, all moneys voted by the district, the necessary sums for appendages and fuel, and for purchasing and leasing a site and building, hiring or purchasing a school house—a fund to be raised for this purpose, specially. It was made the duty of the board of supervisors to add to the sums to be raised in each township a sum equal to that apportioned to the townships from the income of the school fund.

THE UNIVERSITY.

The first law under State legislation, establishing this institution, was approved March 18, 1837. Its name and style was to be "THE

University of Michigan;" its objects defined to be "to provide the inhabitants of the State with the means of acquiring a thorough knowledge of the various branches of literature, science and the arts." Its government was vested in a Board of Regents to consist of twelve members and the Chancellor, which member were to be appointed by the Governor, by and with the advice and consent of the Senate. The Governor, Lieutenant Governor, Judges of the Supreme Court and Chancellor of the State were ex-officio members. It was made the duty of the Regents "to enact laws for the government of the University; to appoint the prescribed number of professors and tutors; to determine the amount of their salaries." The University was to consist of three departments—literature, science and the arts; law, and medicine. The professorships to be established under the law, to be appointed as the wants of the institution might require, were as follows:

In the department of literature, science and the arts, one of ancient language, one of modern languages, one of rhetoric and oratory, one of philosophy, of history, logic and philosophy of the human mind, one of moral philosophy and natural theology, *including the history of all religions*, one of political economy, one of mathematics, one of natural philosophy, one of chemistry and pharmacy, one of geology and mineralogy, one of botany and zoology, one of the fine arts, and one of civil engineering and architecture.

In the department of law, one of natural, international and constitutional law, one of common and statute law, and equity, and one of commercial and maritime law.

In the department of medicine, one of anatomy, one of surgery, one of physiology and pathology, one of practice of physic, one of obstetrics and diseases of women and children, and one of materia medica and medical jurisprudence.

The government of these departments was entrusted to their respective faculties, but the Regents had power to regulate the course of instruction, and prescribe, under the advice of the professors, the books and authorities to be used in the several departments; also to confer degrees and grant diplomas. The fee of admission was never to exceed ten dollars, and the institution was to be "open to all persons, resident in the State, who might wish to avail themselves of its advantages, *without charge of tuition*; and to all others, under such regulations and restrictions as might be prescribed by the Regents. A board of visitors, five in number, were to be appointed by the Superintendent of Public Instruction, whose duty it was "to make a personal examination into the state of the University, in all its departments, and report the result to the Superintendent, suggesting such improvements as they deemed important."

It was made the duty of the Regents to make an exhibit of the affairs of the University; the amounts of expenditure; the number of professors and tutors, and their salaries; the number of students in the several departments and in the different classes; the books of instruction used and such other information *as the Board might require*, with an estimate of expenses for the ensuing year. As soon as the State shonld provide funds for that purpose, the Regents were to proceed to the erection of the necessary buildings for the University on the ground to be designated by the Legislature.

It was made their duty, together with the Superintendent of Public Instruction, to ESTABLISH SUCH BRANCHES in the different parts of the State as should be authorized by the Legislature, and to prescribe needful rules and regulations. The branches were excluded from the right to confer degrees. In connection with every such branch, there was to be an institution for the EDUCATION OF FEMALES in the higher branches of knowledge, whenever suitable buildings should be prepared. In each of the branches there was to be a DEPARTMENT OF AGRICULTURE, with competent instructors in the theory of agriculture, including vegetable physiolgy and agricutural chemistry, and experimental and practical farming and agriculture." Whenever such branch was formed, there was to be in each a department especially appropriated to the EDUCATION OF TEACHERS FOR THE PRIMARY SCHOOLS, and such other departments as the Regents deemed necessary. Whenever the branches were established, or any of them, there was to be apportioned to each, in proportion to the number of scholars therein, for the support of its professors and teachers, such sums as the state of the University fund should allow, and also such sums for the purchase of books and apparatus. The Board were required to procure the best and most appropriate plan for the University building, which, if approved by the Governor and Superintendent of Public Instruction, was to be adopted.

By an act approved March 20, 1837, the University was to be located in or near the village of Ann Arbor, in the State of Michigan, upon such site as the Regents should select, which site was to be conveyed to the Regents, for the use of the State, and for that express purpose, free of cost, and the site was to include not less than forty acres.

At the extra session of this year, Gov. Mason, in behalf of the Regents, transmitted to the House of Representatives a communication, asking for the following amendments, which were passed, and became a law on the 21st of June, viz: an amendment to invest the board with power to elect a chancellor, and prescribe his duties—to make the Governor president of the board, and provision authorizing the Regents to create such professorships in the University as they might deem proper, and to establish branches at discretion.

Authority was given to the Regents to expend so much of the interest arising from the University fund, as may be necessary for the purchase of philosophical and other apparatus, a library, and cabinet of natural history. It had, by the previous law of March 21, 1837, been made the duty of the Superintendent to apply the income of the University fund to the payment of such debts as should accrue from the operation of the law establishing the University.

During the year, as an auxiliary to the cause of education, the "Journal of Education" was established in Detroit, under the auspices of the late Senator Lyon, Dr. Pitcher, and H. R. Schoolcraft; and on motion of Hon. J. M. Howard, the Superintendent was instructed to furnish one copy to each board of inspectors, and one to each director of a school district.

1838.

EXTRACT FROM GOV. MASON'S THIRD MESSAGE.

From the report of the Superintendent, you will receive all the necessary information connected with our schools and University. He will present to you the general condition of the common schools, and will at the same time, suggest to your consideration such amendments to our existing school laws, as may appear to him expedient and desirable. I would, however, recommend, by the appointment of an assistant, the *separation of the financial department from the ordinary duties of the office of Superintendent,* so as to relieve that officer from duties too onerous, *and in themselves inconsistent.*

I have so often referred to the subject of education in my former communications, that important as the subject is, I feel indisposed to dwell on it at any great length, sensible that your feelings and interests are alive to its success, and that your most unremitting exertions will be directed to its advancement throughout the State. Every free government is called on by a principle of self-preservation, to afford every facility for the education of the people. The liberty of a people cannot be forced beyond its intelligence. The South American Republics exhibit but alternate scenes of anarchy and despotism. France, in the day of her bloody struggles for freedom, was overwhelmed and plunged in misery, by the very attempt to make her free. In the United States we witness the advantages of education, in the virtue, intelligence and liberty of the people. History points out the ignorance and degradation of other countries, and we are admonished of the duties before us. If our own country is ever to fall from her high position before the world, the cause will be found in the ignorance of the people—if she is to remain where she now stands, with her glory undimmed, *educate every child in the land.*

Whilst the fund will be sufficiently great for the support of the University, on the broad scale intended by the Legislature, if applied to that object alone, it may fall short of that purpose when directed to the numerous branches which seem to be demanded by the people. I would therefore suggest that portions of the seventy-two sections of the salt spring lands be set apart by the Legislature as an exclusive fund for the support of the branches of the University.

SUPERINTENDENT'S REPORT.

The Superintendent refers to the following acts as comprising what might be termed the "MICHIGAN SCHOOL SYSTEM," viz: the act to provide for the disposition of the University and primary school lands; the act to provide for the organization and government of the University with branches; and the act for the establishment and support of the primary schools.

No change was recommended in the system of primary schools. The previous laws were during this year prepared and arranged into a code. The commissioners were not authorized to make alterations, however, and the school laws, with all other laws, were consolidated in the revised statutes of 1838. A question of great importance was brought before the Legislature, by the Superintendent, relating to the policy of granting

CHARTERS FOR PRIVATE COLLEGES.

This question, in the view of the Superintendent, involved the highest considerations of sound public policy as affecting the State in all time to come.

"When this decision is finally made," says the report, "it will not require the inspiration of a prophet to determine whether the State shall eventually assume the first rank in the Republic of Letters, by founding and rearing up an institution of noble stature and just proportions, worthy alike of the State and of learning, and equally worthy the name of University, or whether the State shall ultimately sink to a low level in the world of knowledge, having institutions under the imposing name of colleges, scattered through the length and breadth of the land, without funds, without cabinets, without apparatus, without libraries, without talents, without character and without the ability of ever maintaining them. If one is granted, others must be, and there is no limit. If one village obtains a charter for a college, all others must have the same favor. In proportion as they increase in number, just in that proportion will be their decrease of power to be useful."

In aid of this view of the question, the opinions of distinguished scholars were obtained, among whom were the names of Dr. Wayland, Edward Everett, President Humphrey, President McIlvaine and others. The question was submitted to these distinguished gentlemen in a letter of the Superintendent requesting "the result of their observations as to the effect produced on the higher branches of literature and science by the multiplication of universities and colleges in the United States. In the creation of the higher institutions a question has arisen, in the commencement of our existence as a State, whether we shall grant to an indefinite number of private associations the right of conferring degrees, or for the present concentrate our energies in one university." To this, President Wayland replied: "that so far as he was qualified to judge, the plan of concentrating your energies in one university, is incomparably preferable to that of granting university charters to an indefinite numher of private institutions. By a great number of small and badly appointed colleges you will increase the nominally educated men, but you will decrease the power of education, because it will be little else but the name." The reply of Mr. Everett was in substance, that supposing the condition of Michigan to be the same as most other infant political communities, he should think that one institution of a high order would be as much as we could expect to found and sustain at the first. "You will not understand me," says Mr. Everett, "as at all underrating the importance of acadamies and schools. I deem them quite as important as colleges. Good common schools are the basis of every wise system of popular education. But it is not useful to grant to *academies and schools* the privilege of conferring degrees.

Harvard college in Massachusetts, was founded in 1636. There was no other college in New England till 1700, when Yale was founded. If the question is between one well endowed and amply provided institution, and several languishing on an inadequate public and private patronage—which, if several are attempted, will be apt to be their condition—it is scarcely necessary to say the decision must be for the former."

President Brown, of Pennsylvania, was of the opinion that much depended on circumstances—the public fund, the character and number of the inhabitants, the *probability of uniting* in the patronage of one—people of different talents, prejudices, literary taste, and especially different moral and religious sentiments. If all these could be concentrated harmoniously, it might be best to confine their energies to one, for a time—that if all religious men were excluded, the institution would become infidel. Serious people would not send their sons to such an institution; that no amount of funds per se created a college, and that any amount of talent would not alone command success—that there must be harmony and co-operation, and he suggested "that the Legislature should, for the present, look to the formation of only one State University, to receive the ample endowments the State is able to afford; that they should, from the commencement, guard against the evils of an undue multiptication of colleges, and in order to do this, that no charter should be granted to any association, only on the condition of having procured such an amount of funds as will secure respectability by supplying able professors, and the proper college accommodations. President McIlvaine considered that with the property devoted to college education in Michigan, the State had a noble opportunity of taking and holding dignified ground on this subject: of building a breakwater against the winds and waves, by which other less independent institutions are in danger of being overwhelmed, and recommended that it be improved by having but *one place* of *degrees* in Michigan.

From these opinions and others similar, the Superintendent expressed the opinion that "the multiplication of institutions under the imposing name of universities and colleges, was to be regarded as an evil of great magnitude, as exceedingly detrimental to the interests of literature, science and the arts," and recommended that the Regents of the University be empowered to grant charters for colleges only on condition that the association applying shall have actually secured for the use of the institution the sum of two hundred thousand dollars; that of this sum, fifty thousand, at least, should be invested in suitable buildings and other accommodations, and the balance secured so that the full amount of the interest arising therefrom should be yearly available for the support of the college, so long as it should continue in operation, *reserving to the State the right of visitation, and requiring an annual report.*

On the 19th of January, of this year, a petition was presented to the House of Representatives, by Hon. J. M. HOWARD, "to incorporate the Trustees of Michigan College." The petition was referred to a committee, of which Mr. HOWARD was chairman, who made a majority report, and also reported a bill to incorporate the institution. The majority of the committee did not agree in opinion with the Superintendent, or see the propriety of restricting the power in question, exclusively to the State institution. The institution proposed to be incorporated, in its inception, had contemplated a school, to be organized on the manual labor plan, and was designed ultimately as a college. Owing to financial embarrassments, the "colony scheme" was abandoned. A subscription of about eighteen thousand dollars had been raised and applied to the purchase of a farm of three hundred and seventy-five acres, near Marshall, in the county of Calhoun. In addition to this the trustees had become the owners of a landed interest on Grand River, with a mill privilege upon it, which was estimated at ten thousand dollars, and friends of the enterprise in New York had conditionally invested for the benefit of the college, five thousand dollars. Buildings were proposed to be commenced, to accommodate one hundred and fifty or two hundred students—a preparatory school opened, and a president of the college appointed, who was seeking further pecuniary aid for the institution. The value of the property owned by the trustees, the committee were assured, was not less than from $60,000 to $100,000. It was announced to be the settled determination of its founders "to establish it on a broad and liberal scale—one which would make it an ornament and honor to the State—an efficient means of diffusing the benefits of general and classical education—to open its doors for the instruction of youth of all classes, sects and conditions, and dispense to the indigent as well as to the wealthy, the charities of an ever-wakeful benevolence—the means of solid and useful learning, and the constant healthful influence of religious precept and example."

The following extracts from the report of the majority of the committee, substantially develope their views of the subject.

The committee cannot appreciate the force of the objection, that by granting the franchises asked for, we encourage others to make like requests. We are of opinion that in this, as well as in other matters coming before the Legislature, it is to be governed by a sound discretion, neither granting nor withholding, without sufficient reason, and keeping constantly in view the general good of community.

They deem it the duty of the legislature, not only to prevent all impediments, but to afford facilities to the progress of general education; to speak in words of encouragement rather than of restraint, to those who volunteer to aid it, and not from an overweening fondness for one particular institution, or one particular system, place all others under the ban of power.

As to the fear expressed, that "to permit the establishment of this or other institutions of the kind, would distract public attention and divert patronage from the State University," the committee did not participate in it, but maintained

That an institution, under the immediate supervision and control of the government, with an endowment of one million of dollars, and all the attendant patronage, cannot be prostrated or impeded in its progress by any voluntary association, founded upon individual munificence. The true secret of the success of every such institution, is found in the enterprise, learning and capacity of those at its head; and where these are wanting, the interests of education, like those of commerce and other branches of business, will assuredly decline."

It is also urged that by confining the power of granting diplomas to the State University, and withholding its exercise from all other institutions, the State ensures to that University, at all times, a number of students corresponding to its high literary claims, and the wealth of its endowment. We are at a loss to discover the propriety of this restrictive and exclusive principle. * * * It is certainly at war with the well known freedom of American Institutions and American character. * * * We claim that the ancient and time honored system of New England, now extending over almost the whole country, is more in accordance with the genius of the American people than any known system of foreign nations. We are not to suppose that the settled feelings, habits and opinions of a people can be safely disregarded by their rulers, nor that they can be made to bend and quadrate to any and every innovation, which those in authority may dignify with the name of improvements. Still less can freemen be compelled to countenance a monopoly of those benefits which they have been taught to regard as the gift of God.* * * In our own community, there exists every variety of religious and political opinion, and so strong are men's attachments to their own particular creeds, that any legislative attempt to change or modify them by the course of instruction or otherwise; any system which seeks to make all coalesce in one set of opinions, or to inculcate indifference to all, or which erects a barrier to even the caprices of men, must necessarily prove odious and unavailing. Whatever may be the theories of philosophers and speculatists, among the mass of mankind, religion is not supposed to exist without creed, and to use the language of another, "he is a rash man, indeed, and little conversant with human nature, and especially has he a very erroneous estimate of the character of the people of this country, who supposes that a feeling of this kind is either to be trifled with or despised; it will assuredly cause itself to be respected.

One obvious effect of the system recommended will be to drive from the State every young man wishing to obtain a degree, but unwilling from whatever cause to prosecute his studies in the University. The majority of the committee deem it unjust to individuals and the State, to confer on the State University a monopoly of college honors. It is the right of every parent and guardian, and one which we may be assured will be insisted on, to educate his child or ward in his own way; and it is furthermore the right of the student himself, that the road to literary honors should be opened to him by his own State, in a manner accordant with his own feelings and principles; and it is the correspondent duty of the State, to cherish and encourage all her sons in the way to distinction and usefulness, in order that she may reap her just share of the glory of their achievements. It is made the duty of the Legislature "to encourage by all suitable means. the promotion of intellectual and scientific improvements." It is conceived that the policy proposed is in conflict with the spirit of this provision, inasmuch as it in a manner disfranchises a large portion of the community. We predict that if it be adopted as the governing rule of the Legislature, it will drive from among us a large number of young men, seeking a liberal education, and the usual honors by which it is and ever ought to be distinguished, will engender hatred, rather than create respect for the State institution, and ultimately leave it deserted by all but its immediate government patrons—a place where the idle and curious may find gratification, but devoid of that active, vital energy, which is ever kept awake by peaceful and salutary competition.

Another, and with many a weighty objection, is the fear that the institution [proposed to be established] will be sectarian.* * * Human nature cannot, however, be changed, and religious partialities will exist as long as man is a religious animal. * * * The constitution declares "that the civil and political rights, privileges and capacities of no individual shall be diminished or enlarged on account of his opinions or belief concerning matters of religion;" and it seems unfair and extra legislative to anticipate, and use as an objection, a state of facts against which the constitution requires us to close our eyes.

The majority report was signed by Hons. J. M. Howard, S. Vickery, Wm. P. Draper, and Jer. R. Smith. A minority report was made, signed by Hons. D. B. Wakefield, John Ball, and Wm. H. Montgomery. The report of the minority was in accordance generally with the views of the Superintendent. They regarded the petition referred to them as asking an infraction of a general system adopted by the State; as a precedent, drawing after it all the weight and authority necessary to give it effect and cogency in argument, in favor of further infractions, which as friends of the system established they were bound to look upon with caution and distrust. The decision upon this question was made by the Legislature in 1839, when a charter was granted, the provisions of which are stated hereafter.

THE UNIVERSITY.

The fund of this institution, at this time, was estimated by the Superintendent at one million of dollars, and the interest arising therefrom, at $70,000; yet he suggests that it will not be sufficient to put the present institution, with such a number of branches as it would be desirable to create, into immediate and successful operation. Buildings were to be erected, a library to be procured, a philosophical and chemical apparatus to be purchased, and a cabinet of natural history to be selected, besides the yearly payment of salaries, when the University should have commenced operations; and for years to come, it was suggested the University would need every dollar of the income of its fund to give it a vigorous and manly existence. To relieve the University fund, therefore, for the time being, it was recommended that the income of the *salt spring lands* be devoted, for a limited number of years, to support the branches. The object and importance of the BRANCHES of the University are set forth in the following extract from this year's report:

It is certainly of much consequence to the public interests that these branches be pushed forward with vigor, and be adequately sustained. They form the all-important connecting link between the primary schools and the University. They are specially intended to fit such young men for the regular classical course of the University, as wish to enter the institution; also to prepare some for the PROFESSION OF TEACHING, that the primary schools may be fully supplied with competent instructors; and to qualify others for those numerous employments of life, which require a more extended education than is usually to be obtained at the district school. Unquestionably, then, they are essential to the successful and harmonious action of the system. Without them, every part of it must suffer, and every department languish. Without teachers, thoroughly educated and bred to the profession, what essential benefit can rationally be expected to result from the general establisment of primary schools?

But where can we find such teachers, without furnishing the necessary means to fit them for the work, and where can we better do it than in the contemplated branches of the University? It is indeed of the first importance to the great interests of education in our own State, that these branches be well appointed and vigorously sustained. For the purpose of supporting the department for the education of teachers, it is suggested whether a small amount might not be appropriated to this object, from the income of the school fund? The proposed branches occupy the middle ground, being connected on the one hand with the primary schools, by the establishment of a department in each, for the education of teachers; and on the other with the University itself. by the establishment in each of them, of a preparatory course, and being thus equally designed for the benefit of both the University and district schools, it seems no more than right and just that they should be supported from the funds of each.

On the 8th day of March, of this year, the Governor transmitted to the Legislature a resolution of the Board of Regents, requesting that the President of the Board might be authorized to ascertain whether a loan of State bonds, to the amount of $150,000 might be obtained for the University, during the term of twenty years, the interest and principal of which, to be secured to the Treasurer of the State, and to be paid out of any moneys belonging to the University, or which might be applicable to such purpose. The application was commended to the favorable consideration of the Legislature, on the ground that it would enable the Regents to open the institution at an early day—that it would provide the necessary library and apparatus required—and that without the loan, the opening of the institutiod must await the tardy process of realizing a fund by the sale of University lands, whilst the lands themselves must be disposed of at an immense sacrifice, if sold under the existing financial embarrassments of the country. The committee of the House reported favorably upon the proposition, and an act was passed authorizing the loan, and the same approved April 6, 1838.

An interesting and useful object of the law in relation to the University, was to secure zoological specimens for that institution. A report was this year made by Dr. Pitcher, on the part of a committee of the Regents, stating that from an estimate made on data furnished by the State Geologist, they had come to the conclusion that in the section of ornithology alone, the State of Michigan would yield from three hundred and fifty to four hundred species, and that a complete collection of Michigan birds would contain, at the lowest estimate, one thousand specimens, one-fourth of that number having been already obtained. An appropriation was urged for this purpose to prepare specimens, provide cases, and to go on with the collection of quadrupeds, fishes and reptiles; to provide the University with a complete collection of the subjects of natural science, and especially such as were indigenous to the State.

No change in legislation was made this year, in relation to the primary schools. A resolution was introduced into the House ot Representatives and passed, requesting the Superintendent to recommend to the several school districts in the State, such elementary books to be used in the schools, as he might think best calculated for that purpose.

Before the sales ot the school lands commenced, they were estimated to amount in all, to 1,148,000 acres. In this estimate was included all lands lying within the boundaries of the State at that time, 704,000 acres being situated within the peninsula portion, and 444,160 on the west of Lake Michigan. Under the act for the disposition of the lands, 34,399 acres had been sold already, at an average price of nearly $12 per acre, amounting to $411,794.33, the interest of which, was $28,825.60. The amount for distribution, adding the amount to be raised by supervisors for that purpose for the year, amounted to $57,651.20.

1839.

EXTRACT FROM GOVERNOR MASON'S MESSAGE.

The Governor announced the sales of primary school lands, in addition to the sales of previous years, to amount to $55,650, and those of the University, to $10,104; renews his recommendation for a separation of the fiscal from the other duties of the Superintendent's office, and says:

I have so often referred to the subject of EDUCATION, in my former communications to the Legislature, and its importance to the permanent prosperity and happiness of the American people is so manifest, that I shall refrain from its repetition. In a government like ours, which emanates from the people, and where the entire administration of its affairs is submitted to their supervision and control, *no other subject can equal in importance* that of Public Instruction. As the friends of civil liberty, it becomes our duty to provide for the education of the rising generation. To the intelligence of those who preceded us, we are indebted for our admirable system of government, and it is only upon the intelligence of those who are to come after us, that we can hope for the preservation and perpetuation of that system. Our own State has been highly favored. The Federal Government has secured us an ample fund for all the purposes of a liberal system of education; and it only remains for us to foster it with a scrupulous regard to the important object for which it is assigned.

Our system of education as adopted has not yet had sufficient time to develope its defects, if any exist. It would not be advisable, perhaps, to attempt any material change, for the present.

SUPERINTENDENT'S REPORT.

The Superintendent, in his report, remarks:

The progress of the school system has been as rapid as could rationally have been anticipated. Scarcely two years and a half have elapsed since the first movement was made. In 1836, thirty-nine townships reported fifty-five districts, having two thousand, three hundred and thirty-seven children, between the ages of five and seventeen. In 1837, one hundred and nine townships reported three hundred and eighty-two districts, having fifteen thousand, four hundred and forty-one between those ages. In 1838, two hundred and forty-five townships reported fifteen hundred and nine districts, with rising THIRTY-FOUR THOUSAND between those ages.

The importance of *statistical knowledge* was urged, as becoming every year more and more apparent, it being by such information as statistics furnish, that the wants of a community can be ascertained, and its progress in improvement determined. Several amendments were proposed in the report to the existing school laws, the enumeration of private schools, and the requiring from them annual reports. Defects were found to exist in regard to the collection of taxes for school districts, there being no provision in relation to the sale of any lands or tenements for the collection of taxes.

The establishment of DISTRICT LIBRARIES was recommended, and, in the opinion of the Superintendent, too much value could hardly be attached to this essential agency of Public Instruction.

The Superintendent urged anew the importance of making more ample provision for BRANCHES, again expressing the opinion "that without the aid of these, the University itself could not be expected to prosper,' and that they were equally important to the success of the primary schools being the sole means of obtaining a full supply of competent teachers. He again recommends the appropriation of the salt spring lands to this object. The AGRICULTURAL DEPARTMENT, yet to be established in one of the branches, was also deemed an object of great interest and importance.

FIRST REPORT OF THE REGENTS.

The Regents report that under the act of March 20, 1837, they had selected a site for the University buildings, and obtained a satisfactory title to forty acres of land. At their first meeting they resolved to establish *branches* as soon as could conveniently be done; one in the first Senatorial district, one in the second, two in the third, one in the fourth, and three in the fifth, making eight branches in all; and $8,000 was appropriated to aid in the payment of teachers to be employed in them, when they were organized. Five of these they organized and put in operation; one at Pontiac, one at Monroe, one at Kalamazoo, one at Detroit, and one at Niles; for all of which principal instructors were appointed.

The number of pupils in all of the several branches, was reported to be 161, ten of whom were qualifying themselves as teachers for common schools, and six for the University. It was estimated that in 1840 thirty students would be ready to enter the Freshman, or Sophomore classes; in 1841, thirty-five; in 1842, forty; and that the total number of students, whom parents designed for a liberal education, was 101. The Regents anticipated great accessions to this number. They remark, as a matter of congratulation to the State at large, that "wherever a branch has been established, it has not only received the decided approbation and support of the inhabitants, in its immediate vicinity, but has continued regularly to increase in the number of students, from term to term." A uniform system of studies had been adopted, subject to such alterations as experience might suggest. The Regents further remark, "that the system of branches, their organization, board of visitors, support of instructors, and, in a word, every thing connected therewith, being a new and untried experiment in our country, they feel the necessity and importance of proceeding with caution and deliberation." The branches established did not include any department for Female education.

The loan authorized under the act of April 6, 1838, had been negotiated; a valuable cabinet of minerals from European and other localities of the old world had been purchased, $4,000 having been appropriated for this purpose, $1,000 of which had been already expended.

The first professor chosen was Dr. Asa Gray, in the department of Botany and Zoology. As Dr. Gray was about to visit Europe, the sum of $5,000 was placed at his disposal, for the purchase of books, as the commencement of a University Library. Arrangements had also been made for obtaining such information as was desirable, in procuring the most modern and approved apparatus for the departments of natural science.

With the approbation of the Governor and Superintendent of Public Instruction, in pursuance of the act of March 18, 1837, the Regents had adopted the plan of the University buildings, determined upon the materials to be used in their construction, and taken such other measures for prosecuting the work as they deemed advisable.

The expenditures on Branches during the past year, amounted to $7,800. The estimate for the expenses of the University for the current year, for salaries to professors, principals and tutors of Branches, was $10,000; for buildings, $35,000. The sum of $9,171 42, was reported by the Superintendent, as subject to be drawn in favor of the board, being the interest of the University fund.

At this session, Mr. Adam reported a bill to create a fund for the branches of the University, which did not, however, become a law; and also a joint resolution, which was approved March 4th, 1839, authorizing and making it the duty of the Superintendent to make out and cause to be published, a catalogue of school books, to be recommended by him to be used in the several classes in the primary schools throughout the State, and a list of books to be recommended as suitable for school district libraries; and making it also his duty to report what provision, in his opinion, could or ought to be made, by law, to ensure a regular and sufficient supply of such books to every school district, on the most economical terms, or what other provision, if any, should be made to insure uniformity, as near as may be, in the books to be used in the primary schools. An act was also approved March 4th, of this year, requiring the president of the board of trustees of every organized academy, or literary or collegiate institution heretofore incorporated, or hereafter to be incorporated, to cause to be made out and forwarded to the office of Superintendent of Public Instruction, between the first and fifteenth days of December, in each year, a report, setting forth the amount and estimated value of real estate owned by such corporation, the amount of other funds and endowments, the yearly income from all sources, the number of students in the different classes, the studies pursued, and the books used, the course of instruction, terms of tuition, and such other matters as may be requested by the Superintendent, or deemed proper by the president or principal of such academies or institutes, to enable the Superintendent to lay before the Legislature a full and fair exhibit of the affairs and condition of such institutions.

Mr. Gibbs offered a resolution, instructing the committee on education to enquire into the expediency of authorizing an appeal in all cases from decisions of school inspectors to the Superintendent.

On the 23d day of March, Mr. Adam reported a bill to incorporate the trustees of Marshall College, and the same became a law, and was approved April 16, 1839. The principle suggested by the Superintendent was carried out, in relation to the right of visitation, and the institution was made subject to the visitation of a board of three persons, to be appointed by the Governor and Legislature. During the same year, an act was passed, incorporating the Marshall Female Seminary. The charter to Spring Arbor Seminary was amended; the act to incorporate St. Philip's College at Detroit, was passed; and also an act to amend the chapter of the Revised Statutes relative to primary schools. The petition of John R. Williams, J. McDonnel, John Biddle, and others, was presented to the Legislature, to constitute the colored citizens of Detroit into a school district by themselves.

During the year, a resolution was introduced to effect a change in the constitutional provisions, relating to the disposition of the moneys arising from exemptions from military duty. It was proposed that the funds thus arising, should not be appropriated to libraries, but the proposition did not meet with success.

In 1839 the first provisions appear for a *rate bill.* The county commissioners, (in lieu of supervisors,) were required to add to the tax roll of each township, such sum as the inhabitants at their annual meeting, directed to be raised for the purpose of purchasing a site, and building a school house, for the year. A meeting of the inhabitants was to be called, to make provisions for the continuance of the school, after the apportionment of the school moneys was exhausted. The expenses of the school thus continued, was to be assessed upon, and paid by parents or guardians of the scholars, in proportion to the time they were sent to school. No tax could be levied without the consent of two-thirds of the voters, at a regular meeting, and no school district was to be deprived of its proper proportion of any school or library fund, by reason of its not having collected a district tax within and for such district, nor incur any penalty. The directors were required, for the first time, to report the number of scholars attending private schools in the district, between the ages of five and seventeen years inclusive; the number residing therein, and the number out of the district, as near as it could be ascertained. Every school district was entitled to demand its proper proportion of library and school money, notwithstanding by reason of accident, negligence, or any other cause, the proper officers may not have exercised their powers fully and regularly; or may not have made their returns regularly in time; provided, there had been a school kept in the district, at least three months in the year.

1840.

Gov. Woodbridge assumed the duties of his office on the first of of January of this year. The Governor in his message, stated the embarrassments which existed, in communicating the "condition of the State," the reports and public offices not having been accessible to his inspection till he assumed the gubernatorial chair. For this reason, the subject of education and its condition, was not presented.

The Report of the Superintendent again presents the importance of a full and thorough course in the University. The Superintendent says, "nothing short of this can satisfy the demands of the public, and the general expectation of its numerous friends.

The branches should fill up the intermediate space between the parent institution and the primary schools. In no circumstances should the appropriate ground of these schools be occupied by the branches. The primary schools are the all important institutions of our country; and hence in carrying out the system, nothing should be tolerated which may have the remotest tendency to endanger their usefulness."

THE REPORT OF THE REGENTS for this year, announces the *discontinuance* of the branch established at Kalamazoo, and the establishment of one at White Pigeon, and one at Tecumseh. Six teachers were now employed as principals of branches, and six tutors, two of whom were females. The average number of pupils under instruction was two hundred and twenty-two. With a view to ensure uniformity in the system of instruction, in the discipline, and books used, the principals of the branches were convened, and a uniform system adopted. One-tenth of the funds arising from tuition was pledged for the establishment of a library in each of these institutions. The Board state that from communications received by them, they learn with regret, that many young men who have sought admission into the branches have been turned away for want of appropriate places of study, and of boarding houses adapted to the wants and and pecuniary abilities of the applicants for admission.

The report of the Regents was accompanied by the code of laws adopted for the government of branches, which may be found at length in document No. I, of the Senate, or No. II, of the House, for this year, as well also as a detailed report of the financial affairs of the University. Dr. Houghton had been also appointed Professor of geology, mineralogy, &c. Four buildings had been erected and completed, designed ultimately for the residence of the Professors; but for the time being, two were appropriated for recitation rooms, for specimens in zoology, mineralogy, botany, &c. The Regents remark that "they have great satisfaction in view of the onward course of education, as well in our common schools as in the branches of the University." They report, however, that they were much embarrassed on account of want of funds.

During this session, on motion of Mr. Turner, a select committee was appointed, consisting of Messrs. Turner, Renwick, Hammond,

Brown and Miller, to enquire into the condition of the University, and to ascertain what steps were necessary, if any, to ensure its full and permanent success. The majority of this committee reported: first, that the system established, contemplated one University: second, that having but one, it might make the standard of education and the course of instruction, the *best:* third, that the plan of having BRANCHES, conducted on a uniform system, training youth expressly for one institution, was unlike, and better, than any thing else in the Union.

The committee say:

If the system is carried out as commenced, the Regents will command the services of the ablest men in the country, to conduct these branches. In other States, preparation for college is left to voluntary, independent academies, no two following the same course of instruction, nor preparing students for any institution in particular. * * * Michigan, by putting the BRANCHES on the same footing of permanence and respectability with its University, and by enforcing uniformity of studies, has the advantage of having the best things taught, and from first to last, taught in the best manner. The multiplication of colleges beyond what is needed, multiplies the expense of education to the State, and in the same proportion, diminishes the value of the institution. The UNIVERSITY of OXFORD had at one time, ten thousand students. If these had been distributed in separate colleges, containing two hundred each, with its separate faculty, libraries, apparatus, building, &c., and if these were to be as perfect in all its parts, the expense would have increased beyond calculation; but no *one* of them could be as perfect as the University.

The working of the system, the committee maintained, was watched with interest by men of learning, for the following reasons: because

1. No STATE INSTITUTION in America has prospered as well as Independent Colleges, with equal, and often with less means; and the reasons why they have not, the committee ascribed to the following causes, viz: that they had not been guided by that *oneness of purpose,* and *singleness of aim,* (essential to their prosperity,) that *others,* whose trustees are a permanent body—men chosen for their supposed fitness for that very office—and who having become acquainted with their duties—*can* and are disposed to pursue, viz: a *steady* course, which inspires confidence and ensures success.

The following extract is from their report:

STATE INSTITUTIONS have fallen into the hands of the several Legislatures—fluctuating bodies, chosen with reference to their supposed qualifications for *other* duties than cherishing literary institutions. Where Legislatures have legislated directly for colleges, their measures have been as fluctuating as the changing materials of which they are composed. When they have acted through a board of trustees, under the show of giving a representation to *all*, they have appointed men of such discordant and dissimilar views, that they never could act in concert; so that whilst supposed to act for, and represent *every body*, they, in fact, have not, and could not act for *any body*.

Again, legislatures wishing to retain the power of the State in their own hands, have not been willing to appoint trustees for a length of time, sufficient for them to become acquainted with their duties; to become interested in the cause, which they were appointed to watch over, and to feel the deep responsibility of the trust. A new board of trustees not knowing well what to do, generally begins by undoing and disorganizing all that has been done before. At first they dig up the seed a few times, to see that it is going to come up, and after it appears above the surface, they must pull it up to see that the roots are sound, and they pull it up again to see if there is sufficient root to support so vigorous branches, then lop off the branches for fear they will exhaust the root, and then pull it up again to see why it looks so sickly and pining, and finally to see if they can discover what made it die. And as these several operations are performed by successive hands, no one can be charged with the guilt of destroying the tree. * * * Thus has State after State, in this American Union, endowed universities, and then by repeated contradictory and over legislation, torn them to pieces with the same facility as they do the statute book, and for the same reason, because they have the right.

Whilst State institutions have not flourished hitherto, from the causes mentioned, the University of Michigan *has one point of exposure* peculiar to itself; its greatest danger arises from its greatest excellence; its system of BRANCHES connected with the University and training students for it. *These are destined to accomplish more good* than the University itself, for all students must pass through them, and great numbers will be educated there who will never go to the higher University, as thousands will be educated in the common schools who will never enter the branches. They form a dependent and connected series, the number of students necessarily diminishing as they rise from the schools to the branches, and from the branches to the University. As soon as these branches are fully appreciated, every village will desire and feel itself entitled to one; and members will come to the Legislature pledged to their constituents to use their efforts to get a branch of the University in the *immediate neighborhood of all*. Such universal importunity will at first cause perplexity and embarrassment to the Regents, and as they cannot support such branches as are *best*, and locate them everywhere, members will come pledged to get a branch, or depose or change the Regents, or break up the University. Whilst there are many who would hope to profit by despoiling the University of its land, and its funds *which are loan-*

ed, it would not be difficult to get up a cry against it. As these dangers are less, and can be more easily guarded than at any future day, they should be met immediately, before it is too late—before the ignorant and interested shall combine against it, and ensure its destruction.

The University is a trust too sacred to be made the foot-ball of party. If it sinks once, life will be extinct before it will rise again. To secure to the University and thereby to the State, the benefit of a Board of Regents having experience and enjoying the confidence of the entire community, and having time and opportunity to carry out the noble plan that has been devised, the committee herewith submit a bill. It proposes to exempt this subject from becoming the prey of politics; to give permanence and thereby efficiency to the Board charged with executing the great work of rearing a University with dependent branches; and to put upon this permanent board of well known individuals the *entire responsibility* of accomplishing this work and that to secure these ends, does not require any Regent to be displaced, any plan to be changed, or any deed to be undone.

This report is of great length, and discusses many subjects of importance. The committee suggest that if any change had been contemplated, they would have recommended a reduction of the Board, but this they did not deem expedient; that if they could undo, they would perhaps substitute less expensive buildings. The amendments which they proposed, were to give the power to the Regents instead of a Governor, to appoint members of their own Board, that the existing Regents be continued, and to provide against the annihilation of the Board from the action of legislatures. It was proposed that the Chancellor and Judges should continue members of the Board; that the Lieutenant Governor should not be a member—*that the presiding officer of the college should be President of the Board*—that as tutors were not permanent officers, the Chancellor of the University may know what particular qualifications are desired; that the several faculties be made the judges of the qualification of candidates for degrees; that the Regents should be cautious in the appoinment of professors, and that the Superintendent of Public Instruction might perplex but never benefit the Regents. The report concludes with the following remarks:

What the legislature should attempt in reference to the University, is in the opinion of the committee, to put the whole subject into the hands of competent men, leaving it with undivided responsibility on their shoulders, and then the legislature not meddle with it again except to protect as guardians, not to destroy as capricious despots. Repeated legislative interference, known by experience to be the ruin of a cause like this, would soon dishearten every Regent who takes an interest or active part in the duties of his office. * * The duties of the Regents in their turn, will be mostly to provide the means and apparatus, and the like, and fill the several faculties with able men, *and throw the undivided responsibility of carrying on the work of education on them.* The further duties of the Regents are only to watch and defend, and not to interfere with the growth of what they have planted. A Board of experienced Regents can manage the funds and machinery of a University better than any Legislature; and the faculty can manage the business of education—the interior of a college, better than any Regents.

The report of the minority of the committee, [Joseph Miller, Jr.,] embraced suggestions in opposition to the views of the majority, from which the following is an extract:

1. That any new modeling of the plan is not called for by experience.

2. The new plan proposes giving the direction of literature to the Regents. Good—but so does the old. It also proposes to give the direction of the funds to the Regents. Bad—as chosen for their science only, they are usually the worst men to manage the concerns of practical business.

3. The new plan proposes making the office of Regent for life, except he may be removed for cause. Bad—for the term is too long. The course of education would fall behind the improvements of the age. Old men do not like the idea of change.

4. The old plan is that the Regents be appointed by the Governor, by and with the advice and consent of the Senate, for three years, &c. If this mode is not wise, (as it exposes the University to the conflicting influences of State and national politics,) and if it would be better, were the period longer, yet a plan to shut out change, and to provide for superannuated control, would be a remedy worse than the disease. Again, if a different mode of appointment, viz: by Regents, might to some seem to be expedient, as the choice would be guided by literary capacity and merit of candidates, yet more might be lost, by the want of practical wisdom and experience.

5. The new plan excludes from certain professions of business life, *self-made men*, on the ground that incompetency must be found in those not educated in Universities. It is not true that our self-made men are behind their compeers because they have not seen the inside of a college; nor is it true, that our collegians are inferior because they have been so educated. But it is true that where indolence attaches, inferiority will exist; and that where zeal, industry and perseverence exist, united with good sense, eminence will be attained.

No further action was had at this session upon this subject, except the passage of a joint resolution, approved March 25, 1840, which required the Regents to report to the next Legislature, at the commencement of their session, if any changes, and what, are necessary to be made in the organic law of the University, in order to secure more effectually the objects of the same.

PRIMARY SCHOOLS.

The idea of abolishing all fees to inspectors was presented by resolution, and referred to committee on education. A petition was also presented, in relation to a common school, established by the Irish adopted citizens in the city of Detroit, under the care of the Pastor of Trinity church, praying the "interposition of the Legislature." The committee of the Senate to whom it was referred, reported by their chairman, D. G. Jones, and the following is extracted from the report, as showing the substance of the petition:

The petitioners are compelled, under the general law, regulating common schools in the city, to pay each one his proportion of all the expenses of *organizing*, maintaining and supporting the common school in the district where he may reside. Does he derive from that school *his proportion* of the benefits and privileges arising from its existence and continuance, for which he is annually subjected to a tax? The petition declares that he does not. But it will be asserted that it is at his option—that he rejects the privileges that are offered under the general plan—that his children, with those of his neighbors, are amply provided for, by the means afforded, and that they are rejected by no one, except by the dictate of his own peculiar prejudices.

Your committee cannot and do not deem this an answer to the proposition stated. They know and feel that upon the subject of the education of our children, our institutions, our liberal sentiments, our past and present history forbid for a moment, the thought of dictation and control. If the petitioners desire that those who are to come after them should have the benefit of pastoral instruction from persons educated with the same views and feelings of themselves, it is their *right*, nay, their sacred *duty*, to seek such instruction; and it is our privilege to see that the taxes paid by them for education should be appropriated to their own use, and subject to their own control. By denying them these privileges, you subject them to a double tax, the first of which is expended upon schools, from which, either from prejudices or religious principles, they cannot derive any benefit; and the last is produced by supporting such institutions as may best accord with their early education and be under the direct charge of those entertaining the same religious views as themselves.

Your committee cannot assent to such a course inasmuch as they believe it to be duty of the Legislature to further by every means in their power the education and well being of the rising generation, and that special care should be taken that no odious distinctions of a sectarian or political character should be permitted to exist, and that the sons of every native and naturalized citizen, of the catholic and protestant, should be placed in every respect upon an equal footing.

So far from discouraging, they feel it their duty to encourage here and elsewhere, the organization of schools among our adopted fellow-citizens; and they believe that the stability of our schools can in no event be more certainly increased than by diffusing learning and knowledge over the whole mass. They further believe, that sound policy demands that every inducement to foreign immigration should be held out to the oppressed of other nations, and that the mass of our people should be thoroughly enlightened and qualified for the important duties of American citizens by the influence of education, and that no barrier to the diffusion of knowledge should ever be erected.

Believing therefore that the school referred to in the petition should be encouraged and sustained; that the taxes the petitioners pay for the support of schools should be expended for the benefit of their children, under their *own control;* and believing also that the petitioners are prevented by the most conscientious and pure motives from embracing the advantages offered in the schools in the city, they recommend that an act be passed providing that from the common school fund distributed in the city, there shall be paid towards the support of the school referred to, an annual sum equal to the amount that the petitioners would be entitled to as component parts of the several districts in which they reside.

No innovation was made, however, upon the system as established, and no further action had upon the subject before the Legislature.

This year an act was passed to amend the revised statutes relative to primary schools.

This law provided that the amount of tax to be raised in any one year to purchase or lease a site and build a school house, should not exceed the sum of one hundred dollars, unless the inspectors certified in writing that a larger sum was needed, and no larger amount could be raised; and provided, that not more than three hundred dollars should be raised in any one year. All expense for fuel was to be paid by a tax upon those who sent to school. It was the duty of the assessor to obtain a transcript of the last assessment roll of the township, and having added to it all the property of persons who had since become residents, all property purchased by non-residents, and all property both personal and real, omitted by the township assessor, to assess and collect the tax upon the taxable property of the district in proportion to its valuation on the township assessment roll.

1841.

EXTRACT FROM GOVERNOR WOODBRIDGE'S MESSAGE.

In any attempt to review "the condition of the State," the attention of the observer is first very properly directed to the consideration of the moral and intellectual character, actual and prospective, of its people. Civil commotions and wars have an end; the evils of misgovernment are temporary in their nature, and may be corrected; the chastisements of heaven, even, through the merciful Providence of God, are, in this world, of short duration. But who can measure the extent, or see the end, or estimate the intensity, of the evils which flow to a people, from ignorance and vice? If any political axiom be better established than another, it is this, that no republic can long exist, unless intelligence and virtue predominate among, and characterize the great body of its people. Gathered principally from the older States of this happy Union, our fellow citizens have, for the most part, participated, more or less, in the benefits of their excellent and long established institutions—their common schools, and all their highly improved literary and religious establishments. We may, therefore, justly claim for them the present possession, in equal degree with our fellow citizens of the older and more favored States, of those high and ennobling attributes of human nature, intelligence and virtue. But in so far as we may justly claim this high distinction, in the same proportion are the motives stronger and the obligation more imperative, to secure to those who shall come after us—to our own children—at least, an equally elevated rank in the scale of intellectual being. But, have we been sufficiently mindful of this great duty? Not experiencing in our own person, perhaps, or but in a slight degree, the immeasurable evils likely to result from a deprivation, in early life, of the benefits of such institutions, have we not accustomed ourselves to think but seldom, and then with too much indifference upon the vital importance of the establishment, multiplication and perfection of similar systems, in our own beautiful, but recently reclaimed, peninsula? The character of our State, the happiness and the destinies of our people, are fast passing into the custody of those who shall come after us; and shall it in future times be said of them, that through the improvidence of their fathers, it was their unspeakable misfortune, to be deprived of those advantages of early mental, moral and religious education, that we ourselves have possessed?

The importance of the early and methodical development and culture of the intellectual faculties of man; the influences which habits formed, and knowledge attained in early life, (through a general and judicious system of education,) cannot fail to exert, not only upon individual happiness. but upon the political institutions of our country, have been too frequently the topics of discussion among the learned, the wise and the eloquent of the land, to render it necessary or proper for me to delay you by further comments upon the subject. I recommend a careful review of all existing statutory enactments, relative to the system of education heretofore adopted in the State, and especially relative to that part of it, which concerns the broad basis of the whole—the common schools.

I know of no section of the Union, in which the subject of education, (comprehending a system of common schools,) has engaged more the attention of the public authorities, or for a longer time, or more successfully, than in Connecticut. And appreciating very highly the benefits to be derived from long-tried experience, I respectfully lay before you some well reasoned reports, made to the Legislature of that State, exhibiting the present condition and the leading features of their system. I am not in favor of a literal and too servile adoption of the legislation of other States; our system should, in general, be *our own*, and be made to accord with whatsoever may be peculiar in our circumstances, or in the condition of society among us. But considering the success which has attended the efforts of our fellow citizens of that State, in the great cause of education, I have supposed that an attentive examination of their greatly perfected plans, might suggest important improvements in our own. That *our* system is susceptible of amelioration in many particulars, I have little doubt; while at the same time, it is proper to remark, that in this, as in all other matters of legislation, no innovation should be made, but with great caution, and the more especially, because its establishment has been so recent, that its merits can scarcely yet have, in all things, been fully tested. For reasons, however, which heretofore I have had the honor to communicate to your immediate predecessors, and which I propose again to advert to, I do not hesitate to recommend, that a more equal and just mode of taxation for the sustainment of common schools, be substituted in lieu of the existing provisions of the law in that respect. And also, that the fiscal arrangements and pecuniary affairs of the system be either separated entirely from the other more intellectual functions of the Superintendent of Public Instruction, or else, that by some other appropriate modification of the law, the existing powers and duties of the Superintendent, relative to pecuniary affairs, may be made more entirely subject to the direct control of the head of the financial department.

The revenues necessary for the erection of school houses, and the sustainment of the system generally, are derivable, first and principally, from a course of taxation provided for by existing laws. The entire plan upon which this course of taxation is founded, seems to me obnoxious to the most serious objections. The legislation of last year, though beneficial, in no wise removed the evil.

Every system of taxation, to be just, should be reasonable, equal and uniform. It is a proposition as notorious as it is lamentable, that the assessments of taxes for school purposes as well as for highways, are neither uniform nor equal, and in some instances have been most highly unreasonable. The Legislature has prescribed no uniform standard by which assessments are made; the same species of property, and of the same estimated value, may be taxed a hundred fold more in one district than in another bordering upon it; and every little neighborhood may be erected into a separate school or road district, with power to tax almost at pleasure. But the power of taxation is one of the highest attributes of sovereignty. It should never be exercised but with much caution—the most mature consideration, and the most scrupulous regard to justice, uniformity and equality. If otherwise exercised, it becomes unjust and oppressive. No tax, I am persuaded, would be paid by the people of Michigan, with more cheerfulness, if it be just, equal and uniform, than a tax for the hallowed purposes of education. But it deeply concerns the honor and good faith of the State, that the practical injustice of our present system should be avoided, and the evils I have alluded to, promptly corrected.

The remaining source of revenue, applicable to the support of our common schools, consists in the annual interest accruing upon the purchase money; for which sales of school lands may have been, or may be effected; and the rest reserved for the use and occupation of such as may be leased.

This resource, upon which so much expectation was founded, seems too likely, for present purposes, in a great measure, to fail us. The overthrow of the general currency of the nation, which has produced so much distress, and the continuing process by which, what little remains available, seems rapidly passing out of the State, have already prostrated all uniform standard of value; and the ruinous diminution in the prices of agricultural products, have rendered all real estate of little present worth. School lands, therefore, are no longer sought after by purchasers; and, hitherto, in times of so great pressure and general distress, the legislature have found it difficult to resist applications for relief, and delay of payment on the part of those who have heretofore purchased these lands.

From this source, therefore, little, comparatively, has been realized, and the sanguine hopes of the friends of education have been thus far disappointed. The same general cause, very materially affects also the present condition, and, for a time, the future capacities of the University.

SUPERINTENDENT'S REPORT.

This document was the last annual report of the first Superintendent, to whom had been entrusted the high responsibility of reporting a system, adapted to the constitutional provisions and the wants of the State; and in presenting the subject of education to the Legislature, he urges anew the importance of adapting the system to the entire wants of the great mass of community. He says:

We must multiply our school houses, educate teachers, procure libraries. and provide indeed all the necessary means of instruction for the whole population, or increase greatly the number of our jails, penitentiaries, and standing armies. * * * We must EDUCATE, or forge bars, bolts and chains. One system or the other we must adopt—there is, and can be no alternative. Besides the experience of all the past—of all ages and nations, demonstrates that is more economical, much less expensive to educate the young, and form them to high moral principle and honorable conduct, than to support paupers, restrain, imprison and punish aged criminals.

If the people of Michigan, instead of bequeathing to their children, the noble inheritance derived from a high minded, intelligent, moral and religious ancestry, wish to see them cast down from that proud elevation on which they have stood, and become ignorant, debased and poverty-stricken, the dupes of a selfish priesthood, or the serfs of an avaricious oligarchy, or the fit instruments of an ambitious military disposition, they have only to dismiss their teachers, burn up their books and school houses, and abrogate all laws for the support of schools, and in a few short years, the work is done. As a State we are but of yesterday; and on the day of our coming into being, we were thrown entirely upon our own resources. We inherited no richly endowed establishments, or time honored institutions; all was to be formed—to be created anew. True, Congress reserved from sale and granted to the State a certain amount of wild land for the support of schools. It is our labor and our capital, expended in the cultivation of the soil, in the general improvement of the country, in the formation of republican institutions, and the support of government, which has given to that land its present value. The circumstances of the times have been exceedingly adverse. We commenced our career when the whole country was in the midst of the wildest scene of speculation, and have seen it sunk in three short years, to the lowest state of depression. Howbeit for the time, much has been done towards promoting the great cause of education within our borders—more indeed than could be expected. But though much has been achieved, much remains to be accomplished; and having *put our hands to the plow*, we cannot go back if we would.

In a pecuniary point of view, it is cheaper to educate the young than to support multitudes of paupers and an increased number of criminals. Few indeed are the men that have ever become paupers or criminals, who in early life were brought within the reach and under the salutary influence of schools, books and teachers.

It follows therefore that the PROPERTY OF THE STATE ought to be held liable for the education of all within its borders, and on this principle every school system should be based. As already intimated much has been done, and it is obvious that the people of the State are determined upon the education of their children. No sooner is a settlement formed than a district is organized and a school commenced. The reports of the past year show that large sums have been voluntarily raised for the erection of SCHOOL HOUSES. True many of them are of logs and might be taken by an unreflecting passer-by, as evidence that little or no interest was felt in the subject of schools; but these buildings, though rude they may be, are as good as the circumstances of a people in their infancy, will allow—good indeed as their own dwellings. * * * They entitle the newly formed settlements to the highest commendation. They betoken a zeal worthy of all praise. * * * The present population are generally well educated—*but how will it be* with those who are immediately to take our places? who are soon to succeed us in all the departments and responsibilities of life? True, a good beginning has been made, but unexpected difficulties have arisen. These must be met and overcome, or we are thrown back in our course, time only can tell how long. Should there be any relaxation of efforts, or suspension in the course of instruction, who can calculate the loss, or assess the amount of damages to those immediately concerned? It depends solely upon us, upon our action at the present time, whether a race of men are to come after us and occupy our places, well qualified for a faithful discharge of the high trusts committed to them, or be ignorant, debased or degraded.

Five years of the system have now elapsed, and it is in the tide of successful experiment. The work of organization is still progressing. No system in the Union, with the exception of that of Massachusetts, is now more complete in its organization, or perfect in its parts. The following table shows the increase of school districts and the number of children reported during this period, between the ages of five and seventeen:

In 1836,	39	townships,	55	districts,	2,337	scholars.
" 1837,	109	"	382	"	15,441	"
" 1838,	245	"	1,020	"	34,000	"
" 1839,	302	"	1,325	"	45,892	"
" 1840,	324	"	1,506	"	49,850	"

BRANCHES.

The Superintendent in this, his last communication, expressed his deep conviction of the importance of this part of our system. The parent institution, he maintained, as heretofore, could not succeed without them. Its main dependence from year to year, must be upon the branches; and it was deemed to be equally important to the primary schools, as a source for educated, well-qualified and competent teachers. It was again recommended that the lands granted to the State, in connection with salt springs, be appropriated for the support of these institutions.

REPORT OF REGENTS.

The following is an extract from the report of the committee of Regents to the Superintendent, consisting of Henry R. Schoolcraft, Dr. Pitcher, and Rev. George Duffield.

In organizing a Board of Regents to carry out the views of the Legislature, in the establishment of a University, it is conceived to have been the primary object of this body to extend its benefits as widely, and at as early a period, throughout the State, as the wants of the community, and the means at their disposal would permit. Their attention was therefore called, at an early day as possible, to the location and establishment of branches of the University, at suitable points, where the branches of a classical and English education, preparatory to the entrance of the students into the parent institution, should be taught. This object has been steadily pursued, not only from its being the appointed means for preparing classes for the final collegiate course, but from the additional consideration that in a new and hastily settled community *it would be one of the best and most practical* means of arousing attention to the value and importance of the plan of education, submitted to the people in the organic act, and of thus preparing the public mind to appreciate and foster it * * The committee on branches, charged with this duty, have encountered an arduous task in the management of the correspondence, the selection of principals, and the pecuniary questions which required decision and adjustment; and the Board owe to it much of the success which has attended that effort. Of the seven branches established, five are under the direction of clergymen, and two of laymen, of various religious denominations. The Board cannot, they believe, be mistaken in the importance they attach to the connection between learning and morals, science and religion, and at any rate, would be unjust to themselves, not to express the belief that success cannot permanently crown the institution committed to their management, after this ligament is severed.

Twenty teachers and professors of all grades have been employed, who have instructed an average number of two hundred and thirty-six scholars. A steady increase of number has taken place in the respective terms for the year. At four of the branches, namely, at Monroe, White Pigeon, Niles and Tecumseh, there have been female departments under appropriate instructors, where only English branches have been taught. The effect of home schools in this department has been propitious, and they constitute a branch of higher instruction, contemplated by the act which has been appreciated by the inhabitants. In view of the whole amount of instruction furnished—its character and distribution, it may be asserted that in no previous year has the institution, through its branches, rendered equally important services to the State.

THE UNIVERSITY.

The Regents report the main building to be in process of completion, and the grounds enclosed. The collections in natural history were about to be arranged by Dr. Houghton. To these mineralogical collections, purchased of Baron Lederer, of Austria, had been added the extensive and valuable collections in geology, mineralogy, botany and zoology made within the geographical area of Michigan, by the State Geologist and his exploratory corps. This collection was due to the forecast of the Legislature, who directed their attention to the subject at one of their earliest sessions after the admission of the State into the Union. Dr. Gray had expended the five thousand dollars placed at his disposal, and three thousand seven hundred and seven volumes had been received, a catalogue of which was transmitted with the report of the Regents, and will be found in House document 9 of this session, or in the same number of the Senate document.

In relation to the fiscal affairs of the University and the policy pursued by the Regents, the committee say:

That they would not fully acquit themselves of their duty to the board or the community, in closing this report, without adverting to the fact that the receipts for lands sold, and the instalments and interest, accruing thereon, have fallen short of the estimates. Acting on the principle, which is believed to be true, that intellectual labor, in all the departments of instruction should be well paid and encouraged in carrying it out, by the actual condition of the permanent funds of the institution, liberal salaries were awarded to the principals of the branches and professors, (so far as appointed,) and have been paid without delay or deduction to the present time. And they cannot but regard this course of policy as one of the causes of the actual efficiency and success which has marked the course of instruction generally at the branches. * * * That the branches, although affording a sound and reputable description of instruction, have been maintained at a comparatively high expense, to the parent institution is not to be denied, *and it is a question*, in view of the prospective and diminishing state of the funds, and the increasing demands of the University at its central point, whether the same system should be indefinitely continued, or a connection established between the amount of salary paid and the numbers taught. Disconnected with the principle of finance, sound principle is taught to forbid any respect to this relation. A teacher's best abilities are as fully required to teach a few as many.

We have arrived at a point in the establishment of the institution, when the organization of a Faculty and the opening of the UNIVERSITY proper is a consideration of moment, and the hope is entertained that this may be brought about before the close of another year. A limited number of professors would temporarily answer all the purposes of the incipient and limited classes, and the duties of Chancellor could be performed ex-officio. * * * To accomplish this, however, with our *present funds* without crippling the branches. or devising some additional means for their support from the surrounding communities, will not be of easy attainment. While the permanent funds of the institution are of undiminished intrinsic value, and confidence is felt in the final ability of the purchasers of University lands, there need be no well grounded apprehension that the present annual receipts from these sources will be eventually diminished. Whether sources thus really ample, and which may be eventually relied on without fallacy, constitute grounds in the present state of the institution to justify the anticipation of their proceeds by a further loan, in order to consummate an object so closely identified with the cause of education, is a question that has suggested itself to the Board.

The total expenditures for the University proper, during the year past, were $41,852 43. The cost of sustaining the branches for the same period, $10,188 33.

The Regents, in obedience to the joint resolution approved March 25, 1840, reported to the Legislature, through A. Ten Eyck, Esq., their Secretary, that having duly considered the subject, their views were that "the first change in the organic law deemed essential, is the *proper restriction of responsibility to the* Board of Regents. At present the responsibility is divided, and the Board would be greatly facilitated in their action, were such amendments made as would throw entire responsibility on them, and require them to report their annual proceedings to the *Legislature.*

"The second change relates to the *trust and management of the funds of the University.* Under the existing law it is impossible for the Board to adopt their measures to their means, to project or execute such plans as the interests of education, the wants of the State and the resources of the University demand. The duties of Superintendent in connection with the University, are unnecessary and onerous."

A report was made by Mr. ADAM, as chairman of the committee of the Senate, in reply to certain queries regarding the branches. The resolution of the Senate directed the committee to enquire and report, what number of branches of the University had been established, and at what places—how many scholars had attended each during the past year—what limitations as to age, sex and acquirements, had been imposed by the Regents, regulating the admission of students—what amount of charges for tuition, &c., had been received by the Regents, at the several branches—what number had been taught gratis—how many teachers had been employed in each branch, and what regulation had been adopted in relation to compensation of teachers.

The committee reported that there were seven branches established, viz: at Detroit, Monroe, Tecumseh, Pontiac. White Pigeon, Niles and Kalamazoo, with female departments at Monroe, Tecumseh, White Pigeon and Niles.

That there were in all these branches during the the first term of the year, 222 scholars; during the second, 233; and during the third, 247.

That in the code of laws for the government of the branches, the committee found no limitation as to the age of the students, at their admission, and that in regard to acquirements, each applicant for admission had to undergo an examination satisfactory to the principal, in reading, writing, spelling and arithmetic. For admission to the female department, there was required a satisfactory examination in "reading, writing, spelling, and the rudiments of geography."

That the tuition fees, as established in the code of laws, were in Detroit and Monroe for the first year, $19 50; second year, $18 00; third, and each succeeding year, $12 00. One-tenth of tuition fees was to be applied to the purchase of books for the branch library.

That the committee had no means of stating positively, the number taught gratis, at any of the branches; but that it might not be irrelevant to state, that one of the laws for the branches, provided for refunding to each student, one year's salary for each year he might be engaged in teaching primary schools, until the whole should be refunded.

That it appeared there had been employed during the year, at the branches at Pontiac and Kalamazoo, each one principal, at a salary of $1,200; at Detroit, Monroe, Tecumseh and Niles, each, one principal and one assistant, the salary of the principals being as follows: at Detroit, $1,500 a year; at Monroe, $1,300; at Tecumseh and Niles, each $1,200. In the branch at White Pigeon there appeared to have been employed, one principal, one tutor, and one assistant tutor; the principal at a salary of $1,200. The assistants and tutors received from $300 to $600 a year. In the female department of the branch at Monroe, two, and at Tecumseh and Niles, one each.

The total salaries for the year amount to $10,300. Receipts of tuition estimated at $2,460. The balance of estimated tuition fees amounted to $2,348 33, to be reimbursed to the Board of Regents. The committee also reported that at the first establishment and organization of the branches, a resolution was adopted by the Board of Regents, appropriating $1,000 for every branch in operation, to be divided and apportioned as follows: $500 to each one and the remaining $500 in proportion to the number of scholars. This rule did not however appear to have been adhered to. The committee not having been so instructed, made no further recommendations or suggestions.

In the House, the committee to whom was referred so much of the Governor's message and report of Superintendent as relates to education, made a lengthy report through their chairman, Mr. William Sprague. They remark, "that they have been led to believe that the imposition of all the fiscal duties connected with the educational fund, and the general care and superintendence of education itself, where one and the same obtain, is one of those defects which were connected with our generally excellent laws on this subject; that they were strengthened in this belief by the fact that both the former Executive officers of this State have brought the subject before the Legislature and recommended a change; and the committee believe such a change necessary because the duties themselves are incompatible with each other and because it was impossible to find the requisite qualifications for their performance united in one man; that let whoever may be called upon to fill the station, while the law remains as it is, it would be found that while the duties for which his habits and taste best fit him, may be well performed, the other duties imposed on him would be immeasurably neglected, and that it was not in the nature of things to be otherwise." Complaint is made in this report of the want of *statistical* knowledge; of the insufficiency of the returns, to show the state of education; that they did not show whether the teachers were male or female, good or poor, well or illy paid; whether the course of studies was wise or unwise; whether the government was tyrannical or parental; whether school houses were conveniently or inconveniently constructed; whether parents were interested in the education of their children and in the success of the schools or not. The committee believed that in no way could the Superintendent so well devote his time as to these subjects and to making the primary schools the object of his chief care. They also were in favor of introducing into the bill proposed on this subject, a provision that so far as concerned the sale of University lands—the investment of the proceeds—the Treasurer be required to act with the advice and consent of the Board of Regents.

The general legislation on this subject remained unchanged. An act was passed approved April 13th, reducing the price of University lands and establishing it at fifteen dollars per acre, and the minimum price at not less than five dollars. An act was passed incorporating the Wesleyan Seminary, and also an act providing for the organization of a district in the city of Detroit for colored children. An act was passed to amend the revised statutes relative to primary schools.

An amendatory act to the law of 1840, was passed in 1841, but without any other alteration of the system of taxation except that the electors of any township, at the annual meeting, might raise such sum of money for the support of common schools in their township as they shall deem expedient, provided that such sum did not exceed one dollar for each child in the township between the ages of five and seventeen years. A provision was enacted requiring the directors to ascertain the number of children between those ages, belonging to families habitually using the French, German or other language than the English, and the children attending the districts schools and the number of such, if any, attending schools where the schools books in any other than the English language are used; also the number of adults, above the age of seventeen, who can read the French, German or other language and cannot read the English, together with such other facts and statistics in regard to schools and the subject of education as the Superintendent might direct.

1842.

EXTRACT FROM GOVERNOR BARRY'S MESSAGE.

The universal education of all classes of our citizens is so necessary, and its propriety so generally conceded, that I need hardly urge upon you its importance. By reference to history we learn, and from observation we know, that, just in proportion as the masses have been enlightened, in the same proportion have their rights as men been protected. The rights of personal liberty and of personal security, were never conceded by lords to their vassals, until the latter, after ages of galling oppression and ignominious servitude, by degrees, obtained a hold on the fountain of knowledge.

The moral and political condition of a people depends, in the main, upon the degree of knowledge and amount of useful information diffused abroad among the mass. Within our own recollection, other republics have risen and fallen, and the scenes of intestine commotion which they have constantly exhibited, and which, sooner or later, have caused their overthrow, resulted from a want of general education, and the consequent destitution of virtue in their inhabitants. The democracy of learning, if I may be permitted to use the expression, is, then, essential to the permanency of a republican government, and we can transmit to the rising generation the happy political freedom which we enjoy, only by granting them the benefits of education. They are committed to our keeping, and without our fostering care, will grow up in ignorance and vice.

The revenue for the support of common schools, not derived from taxation, consists, mainly, in the interest arising from the proceeds of the sale of school lands, and the rents of such portions of them as may have been leased. If a judicious and proper use be made of this revenue, it is probable that, at a period not very remote, if not sufficient to educate all the youth of the State, it will at least contribute much towards that desirable object.

Above all others, the laws on the subject of common schools should be plain, simple, and easy to be understood. They should be as independent of all other enactments, as the nature of the case admits, and, to a proper understanding of them, it should not be necessary to refer to legislation on other subjects. Such, however, is not the present condition of our legislation on this important subject. The enactments are various and are scattered through many volumes, and it is with difficulty that even their meaning can, in all cases, be ascertained. To obviate these objections, I respectfully recommend their entire revision. All the various enactments on the subject, should be condensed into one, and published in such convenient form as will insure a circulation in every neighborhood and district in the State. The lights of experience, and a reference to common school systems of other States, may enable you to make such improvements as, by giving a new impulse to education, will result in general and permanent good. I am, however, induced to believe, that the main provisions of the system, as it now exists upon our statute books, should be retained, as far as you think the best interests of the public will permit. Innovations should not be admitted, but with abundant caution, and after the most careful examination. Servile adherence to ancient precedents and long established customs, should not, however, be permitted to take such entire possession of our minds, as thereby to induce us to reject the benefits resulting from an adoption of the improvements of the age. Among the alterations you may deem advisable to make, perhaps none is more worthy of your consideration, than the subject of taxation necessary for the support of the system. The right to impose taxes, is one of the highest prerogatives of sovereignty, and the delegation of that right should be made with the greatest caution. Complaints have been made, perhaps in some degree well founded, that, in the assessment and collection of taxes, for the erection and repair of school houses, great injustice has been done from the unequal manner in which such taxes have been levied. If, after inquiring into the causes of such complaints, you find they really have foundation in truth, you will doubtless correct the evil, by interposing such legislation as the exigency of the case may require.

The office of Superintendent of Public Instruction, is established by the constitution itself, and cannot be abolished by law were it even deemed advisable. I cannot, however, refrain from calling your attention to the fact that the duties of a fiscal character, by law imposed upon that officer, are in no wise consistent with the duties of a literary character, which it is more particularly his province to perform, and to which end the office itself was constituted.

The annual report of the Regents of the University of Michigan, will, doubtless, be transmitted to you by the Superintendent of Public Instruction. The usefulness of that institution has, hitherto, been restricted to its branches. In them have been taught the elements of knowledge and science usually taught in high schools and academies in the eastern States of this Union. Next to common schools, the branches of the University are destined to be of the greatest importance to the people of the State. In the year 1840, the number of students was two hundred and forty-seven. During that year, seven branches were in operation, and the sum of $10,188 37, was expended in the payment of salaries of teachers. The two preceding years, the sum of $13,150 09, was expended for that purpose in the same number of branches. In making these large and apparently enormous expenditures, the motives of the Regents are above suspicion. They were, beyond all doubt, actuated by no other than motives of public good. It is, however, respectfully submitted to your consideration, whether the interests of education would not be more eminently promoted by some provision of law, having for its object the increase of the number of branches, if available funds for that purpose be at command, and the limitation of the amount to be appropriated to each. It is believed that a sum of from three to five hundred dollars, appropriated by the board, together with such sums as should be received for tuition, superadded to such other encouragement as would, of course, be voluntarily afforded at the places of location, would secure the services of persons well qualified to teach, and every way competent to take charge of the branches. If such be the case, of which there can be little doubt, then, with a much less expenditure in the aggregate, the number of branches might be greatly increased and the benefits of education more extensively diffused. I press the subject upon your attention with great earnestness, because I am of opinion, that the usefulness of the University will be incalculably greater to the people of the State through its branches, than through the mother institution itself. By means of its branches, the blessings of a high grade of education will be brought within the reach of nearly all the rising generation, while the number to be instructed in the University proper, must comparatively speaking, be necessarily few. Keeping always in view, then, the object for which the fund was granted, and in no degree departing from the intentions of the grantors, it is our duty to give such direction to the control of this important institution, as will result in the greatest good to our fellow citizens and best insure the extension of the cause of science.

By a joint resolution relative to the University of Michigan, approved March 25, 1840, it is made the duty of the Board of Regents to report to you such alteration as they deem necessary to be made in the laws of the State relative to the University. The only report, made in compliance with this resolution, may be found in the joint documents of the last session, and to which I respectfully invite your attention. In that report, the Regents recommend such alteration in the law on that subject, as will give to them the entire trust and management of the funds, and in all other respects, the absolute control of the institution, subject and responsible only to the Legislature, to which body they wish to make all reports of their proceedings. I respectfully recommend this proposition to your serious and attentive consideration. The high character of the Regents, and their experience, derived from long exercise of the functions of their office, give additional weight to their recommendation, and will, I am certain ensure that attention from you, which the importance of the subject demands.

It is greatly to be desired, that the true and exact condition of the University fund be made known to the public, in order that its capacity for usefulness may be fully understood. The public have an intense anxiety to be informed of its ability to give assistance to education, as well by means of its branches already in operation, as by others desired in various portions of the State. Such a knowledge of the condition of the fund, is also indispensably necessary to such ulterior legislation as, in your wisdom, may be deemed expedient. I therefore respectfully reccommend, that you give the subject in charge to some appropriate committee, accompanied with the instruction, that, after having made the inquiry and investigation, they report the result of their labors for the use of the public.

REPORT OF SUPERINTENDENT OF PUBLIC INSTRUCTION.

The term of the Rev. John D. Pierce having expired, FRANKLIN SAWYER, jr., was appointed at the last previous session of the Legislature, to succeed him. This report unfolds in an interesting and minute manner, the condition of the primary schools at this time, and gives in fact, the first full and detailed account of the operation of the laws in the practical working of the system. The documents accompanying it, showed the whole number of districts integral and fractional, in the State to be two thousand, three hundred. Of them 1,486 embraced in 330 townships, reported 47,066 scholars, between the ages of five and seventeen, and 8,757 under five and over seventeen, making an aggregate of 55,823. The whole number reported at school, 51,254. The Superintendent was of opinion that of this number, too many reported as attending school, passed most of their hours elsewhere than at school, and suggested, that if by the law, the directors were required to report as carefully, as the teacher is to note the time of attendance of each aud every scholar, the real amount would be known.

The average number of months schools had been kept, were reported in twenty-eight counties, at 4 4-7; most of them being kept up only for the constitutional time of three months. The amount apportioned in 1839, was $18,360 86, being several thousand dollars less than the year previous. The Superintendent admonishes those who rely *chiefly* on the fund as a means of supporting their schools, not to be too sanguine—that the true policy was to rely mainly upon their own available resources to advance the cause of popular education. The number of scholars attending private schools was reported at 2,807, which was thought to be below the real number. The returns are complained of, as being doubtful and contradictory. It was suggested that directors be required to report on oath, as being likely to ensure greater fidelity in matters of detail, and preventing a practice, reprehensible in the extreme, and unjust towards other districts, of reporting more scholars of legal age, than were to be found within the district, for the purpose of augmenting its apportionment of funds. In opposition to the views of the legislative committee of the Senate, of the year previous, the Superintendent says:

It is the undoubted policy of every State in the Union, so to frame its system of public instruction, as not only to educate its own native born children, but to Americanize, both in intellect and feeling, every child of a foreign stock, that in the Providence of God, is brought to our shores, to become a part of its society. No encouragement should be given to parents, constituting portions of our Republic, under such circumstances, to educate their offspring through any other medium than the common language; but on the contrary, all conceivable inducements should be held out for them to keep their children at the public schools, where they may learn to think in that language, and by a frequent intercourse with their fellow citizens, forget, not the land of their nativity, but the necessity of the mother tongue, as a medium of communication between man and man, in a country which they have adopted for life, and whose institutions they wish to leave safely in the hands of their posterity.

It was mentioned as a gratifying fact, that only eighty-eight, out of two thousand attending schools, were reported as using other books than the English. Under the act of 1840, giving authority to require such facts and statistics as the superintendent might direct, Mr. Sawyer addressed interrogatories to every school director, requiring reports in relation to the working of the system—suggestions for its improvement—the general operation of the laws—the difficulties encountered in its administration—the frequency of visitation by inspectors and others—the general character, deportment and qualifications of teachers—the discipline of the schools—the system of rewards and punishments—the punctuality of the scholars—the amount paid to teachers—the methods of teaching—the uniformity of books—the religious instruction, and branches taught in the schools—the kinds of school houses, and their situation and location—the common diseases prevalent—the kind of books in the libraries, forfeitures incurred, and the amount of proceeds from fines or military exemptions, &c., &c. To these queries the Superintendent remarks, some paid attention, others, none; by a few, they were deemed inquisitorial, and in three or four cases, uncivil answers returned. Many of them, however, were prepared with a minuteness of detail, creditable to the head and heart of the officer, the facts sought to be elicited, furnished with promptitude and good will, suggestions, made with a frankness becoming the dispenser and recipient of common school education, and pledges of co-operation so amply given as to compensate for any amount of labor bestowed upon the subject by the department. The substance of all the facts thus accumulated, are condensed under the following heads: parents and teachers, duties of inspectors, male and female teachers, government of the schools, character of instruction, uniformity of school books, school houses, libraries, and the working of the system. The Superintendent recommends however, that the board of inspectors be exempted from transmitting to the county clerks, all the particulars set forth in their reports. His conclusions were, from all these reports, that while the facts showed that in many districts sufficient interest on the part of parents was manifested, they also demonstrated the general indifference felt in others—that although the law requiring visitation by the inspectors had been unfortunately repealed, inspectors in many instances, had continued to visit the schools—that an improvement might be made in our system, by the appointment for each county, of a deputy superintendent, whose duties of supervision should be co-extensive with the schools of his circuit—that to his care might be committed the examination of teachers, the visitation of schools, the collection of statistics, the execution of the laws, and the duty of ascertaining their defects, and suggesting plans for improvement—that in relation to teachers, it appeared that while the ages of male teachers ranged from seventeen to twenty, those of females ranged from fourteen to eighteen—that few of the males made teaching a business—that one obstacle to good teaching was the want of adequate compensation. The average pay of male teachers was shown to be $15 61 per month, and that of females, $1 27 per week—that as to the government of the schools the reports evinced that the old fashioned mode of "beating knowledge into the brain," was yet kept up—that the usual appliances were pinching, cuffing, pulling hair and noses, throwing books and rulers at the heads of unruly urchins, compelling them to stand, until fatigued into submission, and locking up in dark places to scare away the evil genius that possessed them shaming, and other varieties of torture—that the character of instruction in some districts, was unexceptionable; but in too many schools, behind the improvement of the age—that *sectarianism* was not taught, while a certain amount of religious instruction was encouraged—that in relation to uniformity of books, it was the great burthen of complaint, and that the variety was almost endless—that if a general uniformity could be brought about, the responsibility should not be imposed upon any *one* individual—that it might be accomplished under a system of county superintendents, or that the plan adopted in some other State, of leaving the work to the township committees, might perhaps be found useful—that as to school houses, the object of the circular addressed to officers, had not been attained—that the replies were not full, and that no judgment could be formed, of their accommodations, yet there was enough to show that many of the houses were good, substantial, comfortable frame buildings—that the disposition was to make the improvements of the school house keep pace with the dwelling house and barn—that a gratifying indication was shown in the location of the school house upon elevated ground, away from marshes, and the salubrity of their position was inferred from the general health of the scholars, and that the people were attentive to the subject—that as to LIBRARIES, only $170 86 had been raised in the State—that nothing as yet, had been received, either from fines, for breaches of the penal laws, or from the equivalents from military exemption—that whether any fines had been collected, was a matter of conjecture, as the county clerks had made no reports on the subject. In consequence of this, it was suggested that they should be required by law, to state the amount of fines imposed by the courts, the amounts collected, and the clear proceeds of such in the Treasury.

In relation to the working of the system, the Superintendent believed that as a whole it was giving satisfaction—that *the principle* embodied in it—the education of all—elicited general admiration, while its practical operation, seen and felt only *in its details*, developed faults of no ordinary magnitude. The frequent change of the law was deprecated, not because the system could become perfect without many modifications, but because it seemed to be impossible under the existing circumstances, for districts and township officers to keep pace with such alterations.

"A law," says the Superintendent, "is hardly known in many districts before it is repealed or amended, and it not unfrequently happens that while the original law governs the official acts of one portion of a township, amendments to it, or even amendments to the amendments, regulate the conduct of another portion of the same township or county. Strange as it may appear to those not familiar with the reasons, some of the reports just received comply only with the requisitions of the revised statutes; others with the law of 1840; and others with the law of last session. The school laws are not promulgated seasonably and *extensively* enough. The remedy proposed is, not to stint the system, in its proper growth, by warring against further modifications, amendments or repeals, whenever or wherever necessary, but to provide that a *printed copy of every new school act be sent to each district as soon as possible after its approval.* Then may the hand of legislation be applied without hesitation or danger to our school system; uniformity in returns and fidelity in details be exacted to the letter, and districts will then cease to be agitated by dissensions, springing, in nine cases out of ten, from imperfectly understood school laws."

The repealing act of 1840, substituted a new system for that contained in the revised statutes, and subsequent amendments made thereto. The Superintendent says that the most striking defect of the new system, as contended in the reports made to him, consisted in ITS INADEQUATE PROVISION FOR THE SUPPORT OF SCHOOLS. A limited tax for a school house, its repairs and appendages, and for a library, case and books, might be imposed by the qualified voters and assessed upon the *property* of the district, but not a dollar for the support of the teacher. The amendatory act of 1841, provided that the organized townships *might*, if they deemed expedient, raise a sum not to exceed a dollar a scholar, for each child, for the support of the school, but made no adequate provision to secure its vote.

There was a general complaint on account of the ambiguity of the law, the inconsistency of one provision with another, and sometimes apparent contradictions. The difficulties and their remedies, which were presented in the correspondence of the office, were various, and too lengthy for enumeration. Recommendations were made to amend the laws, most of which were subsequently adopted, and one of them was the exemption of indigent parents from all charges for tuition of their children.

The Superintendent also referred to the necessity of some publication as an organ of communication between the numerous districts and his office. Such necessity was daily felt, and it was recommended that a definite amount of the school moneys should be appropriated to secure its establishment and existence. Reference was made to the establishment of such an organ in other States. Among the uses of such a publication, the following were enumerated:

To urge the supremacy of common schools over all others, as upon them depend the very existence of higher seminaries, colleges and universities.

To keep the people of the State familiar with the condition and prospects of primary school education everywhere, and follow up the improvements in school houses, books, apparatus, mode of teaching, &c.

To publish and explain the school laws, answer the numerous questions growing out of them, and enable the officers under them, more readily to perform their many important duties.

To record the vast variety of valuable statistical matter, accumulating from time to time, in the several townships, and condense and arrange it systematically for common use, and especially to have the best portions of the school reports that come in at the end of the year.

During the administration of Mr. Sawyer, he delivered addresses upon the subject of education in various counties, and though crowded houses did not greet him, in all cases, he says that "at these popular gatherings were found individuals of all political parties and representatives of most religious sects, and their zeal for common schools, and pledges of co-operation to advance them beyond their present standard, are ample guarantees that hereafter the great work of educational reform will not rest exclusively upon one individual. Incipient measures were taken at these meetings to establish county associations, for frequent and unreserved interchange of sentiment, touching the various branches of common school education." One thing, he remarks as attracting his painful attention, and that was to see how neglectful, with few qualifying exceptions, the populous, and in every other respect, thriving villages, had been of their common schools; but as exhibiting the relative condition of children in the villages, he alludes to the statistics furnished by the praise-worthy efforts of the Common Council of the city of Detroit, to provide the means of full and general instruction in that city.

Mr. Sawyer says: "the Common Council of Detroit, impressed with the necessity of moving to the rescue of its character from imputations of neglect in matters of public education, appointed a committee with the Mayor as chairman, to examine into the operation of the common school system of that city. The committee went to their work, gathered up all the materials within its reach, and finally reported an array of facts that might well startle from their slumbers the most apathetic. The following extract from the report speaks trumpet-tongued to the citizens of our large villages, and in favor of taxation to support public schools:

"From the examination of returns so far as they have been made, and from careful estimates where the returns are defective or wanting, the committee had confidence in the opinion that there are in the city of Detroit, eighteen hundred and fifty children who ought to be at school at least one half of the year. Your committee have also from personal enquiry ascertained that there are within the corporate limits of the city twenty-seven schools in operation, in which are taught seven hundred and fourteen children and youth, at an aggregate sum of twelve thousand six hundred dollars per annum, averaging nearly eighteen dollars a piece. Yet more than half of our youth are coming up in ignorance, the offspring of which are vice and wretchedness, nothwithstanding this enormous tax voluntarily levied and paid by our fellow citizens."

The recommendation of the committee, based upon such facts, was that the Common Council, with the assent of the freemen, ask for a grant of power to raise a school fund by direct taxation. This was in 1841, and subsequent and successive legislation was had, commensurate with the importance of the subject. A sketch of the establishment, rise, and progress of the schools of the city, prepared by D. BETHUNE DUFFIELD, Esq., a gentleman whose interest in the subject of education has been devoted and unceasing, will be found in a subsequent part of this document. It will be read with interest, not only as a faithful and eloquent exposition of the facts connected with the schools, and for its high moral tone and sentiment, but as a tribute justly due to the public spirit and philanthropic feeling of those whose early and continued efforts laid the foundation of the present system of free schools in that city.

The report of the Superintendent further presents the necessity of a system of free education, based upon taxation of the property of the State. From this portion of the report, as evincing the estimation in which this policy was held, the following extract is taken:

Education is a common right—the exclusive property of no man, of no set of men. The great fountain which supplies one portion of society, should be accessible to all—not monopolized by the few or an engine of power—even the many. Our Pilgrim Fathers understood the value of this right. Here, though faulty in other respects, the puritan character developed its true greatness. In the eloquent language of Bancroft, "every child, as it was born into the world, was lifted from the earth by the genius of the country, and in the statutes of the land, received as its birth right, a pledge of public care for its morals and its mind." The principle of popular education was adopted as fundamental. It was imbedded in their public acts, and sacredly cherished through all the trying vicis itudes of their moral and eventful career. In their code, as it ought ever to be in ours, it was the principle without which liberty could not exist, and with which no people could be slaves. Next to the erection of altars for the worship of God, they took care that school houses should be built. The common schools should be as accessible as the mountain spring that gurgles joyously forth to meet and bless all who approach it.

THE UNIVERSITY.

The Superintendent reports that notwithstanding the embarrassments under which this institution is destined to struggle for some time, every citizen of Michigan must rejoice that the main institution is now fairly in operation, and endorses the views of his predecessor, in relation to the importance of sustaining the branches, as the sole means of a full supply of competent teachers. He says:

This is conceived to be one of the most cogent reasons that can be adduced, in favor of the branch system. *Merely* as preparatory seminaries for an admission to the main University, branches could hardly claim an expensive support out of the public fund; but as the means of giving to the State qualified teachers for the common schools, every consideration unites to have them sustained. Are the branches made to subserve this double purpose? *The art of teaching* is not adequately taught. Until a regular school for teachers shall be established in the State, it is right that one or more of the branches make teaching a part of its instruction. Having capable teachers, our schools will begin to flourish. When the schools flourish the University will flourish. The organic law requires in each branch "a department especially appropriated to the education of teachers of the primary schools." A MODEL SCHOOL connected with this department, would afford all the aid that a young man or woman could want to perfect him or her, in the practice, as well as theory of teaching.

He also says:

A department of agriculture in at least one of the branches, is required by the organic law, with competent instructors in the theory of agriculture, including vegetable physiology, agricultural chemistry and experimental farming, and practical farming and agriculture. If, as the late Judge Buel assures us, in his admirable work on American Husbandry, "the great objects of the farmer should be to obtain the greatest returns for his labor without deteriorating the fertility of the soil, and to restore fertility in the most economical way, where it has been impaired or destroyed by bad husbandry," how indispensable to success is a knowledge of the principles upon which these practical results depend!

The Superintendent also remarks in relation to the report of the Regents, that their views in reference to sectarian influences commend themselves to the feeling, and enlightened judgment of all true christians; and that it was a matter of no ordinary gratification, that sentiments so in unison with the liberal spirit of the age, should exist with such perfect unanimity, throughout all our departments of Public Instruction—that the precincts of the University, as well as the school room of the districts, should be effectually barred through the operation of a wholesome public opinion, from all intrusions of a sectarian or partisan nature.

To the attention of the Legislature was commended the appeal of the Board of Regents for such legislation as would render them the responsible guardians of the University, and more practically masters of their own movements; but whether the power asked for could be consistently granted, was considered to be a question which should not be hastily decided. The separation of the fiscal from the more legitimate duties of the Superintendent was also recommended.

The relation between the progress of the schools and University, and the condition of their respective funds, at this time, is shown by the following statement, the value of the lands being fixed, at their minimum price, as established by law:

University lands—45,440 acres at $15, ...	$681,600 00
Amount sold by trustees of old University, ...	5,000 00
Primary school lands—1,148,160 acres, at $5, ...	5,740,800 00
	$6,427,400 00

The total number of acres sold, up to this time, was 75,463.87—of University lands, 12,585.03—of school lands, 62,878.84. The aggregate amount of sales, $824,609 09. The amount distributed to the districts, $13,239 32.

A reduction of the price of these lands was recommended.

REPORT OF THE REGENTS.

In the fourth annual report the Regents announce that as their attention had been previously directed to the branches, and through them to the means of much higher instruction than could be had in primary schools and private academies, they had seduously bestowed their attention also on the necessary means and preparation for the organization of a Faculty and the opening of the institution. During the past year the main edifice had been completed; the cabinet of natural history and the library transferred to the main building and put under care of a librarian, where they were to be arranged by Dr. Houghton, who had not yet commenced a course of lectures, and who had generously tendered his services to the institution free of charge. Valuable additions had been made to the library, the mineralogical cabinet increased by a donation of Baron Lederer, and by specimens collected by the gentlemen engaged in the geological survey. The collection purchased of Baron L. contained almost every known mineral, with the greater portion of the varieties, and was estimated to equal, if not to excel any collection of foreign minerals in the United States. In addition to this, the entire cabinet of minerals of the University now comprehended a very extensive collection of rock specimens, fossils, American minerals, together with a zoological collection of great value, altogether forming greater facilities and inducements for study in natural history than could be found in any institution in this country.

The necessary expenses incurred in the erection of buildings, in the procuring of a library and cabinet, and the support of seven branches were so great, that the sum of $100,000, obtained on loan, was reported to be so far expended as to embarrass the further operations of the Board, unless there should be a greater amount of interest and instalments paid in by purchasers than it was feared would be realized. The reduction of the price of the lands by the Legislature of 1840–41, it was believed by the Board, would have a contrary effect to that intended, and cause much less money to be received during the coming year, instead of replenishing the means of the Board. It was therefore stated to be foreseen by the Board, *that to continue the branches on the system originally established* would be impracticable without further resources, and that those at command of the Board would not be sufficient to continue them for more than a year or eighteen months at furthest. *The value of the branches* was felt to be great, and the importance of opening the main institution still greater, inasmuch as the interests of education called for it, and all the necessary buildings and preparations had been completed.

The idea was conceived, that possibly now, since the branches had been established and were in successful operation, *a change might be made in the system,* which would subject the Board to less expense, continue to foster the branches, and afford means to justify the opening of the University. A change therefore was resolved upon, and instead of the Board undertaking to support the branches by paying the principals' and teachers' salaries, and receiving the avails of tuition, it was determined that from and after the 19th of August, there should be the sum of $500 only appropriated to each branch, the principal to be allowed to appropriate the proceeds of tuition to his own use, and to be at the expense of employing and paying necessary assistants, as well as of meeting all expenses for repairing buildings. The effect of this change was the cessation of the branches at Pontiac, Monroe and Niles. The remainder continued to flourish and extend their advantages to the places where they were situated. The change, however, enabled the Board to organize a Faculty, and open the main institution. It was not deemed prudent to appoint a full Faculty, and it was not thought to be necessary. A professor of languages and a professor of mathematics it was thought, would perform all the duties required for the present, and thus save the Board the expense of the salaries of a chancellor, and other professors. The expense for the support of a full Faculty, was represented to be so disproportionate to the limited number of students at this time, and the expenditure so great, that jealousies might arise and destroy confidence in the Regents. The Regents also doubted whether, with so much uncertainty as to the future means of the Board, under the existing state of things, and with no power whatever, possessed by the Board, *to collect and manage the revenue of the University*, or to urge the fiscal officers to expedite or coerce the collection of taxes, it would be possible to induce any gentleman, fully qualified for the office of chancellor, or persons selected for their attainments and worth for the different professorships, to accept of appointments, should they be tendered to them. The Board remark that,

The disastrous history of universities and colleges in different States, where the appropriations for their support were dependent on legislative bodies, changing with every year, and no permanent body of trustees or Regents held responsible, and furnished with competent power for the collection and management of the revenue, we fear would have been appealed to, in opposition to all our most sanguine hopes, that such would not be the history of the University. These, and such like considerations, induced the Board to adopt the most cautious and prudent plan, and one which would not be so likely to end in disappointment, and in the rejection of their invitations.

Mr. George P. Williams, and Rev. Joseph Whiting, both having been principals of branches, were appointed to the professorships, the former of mathematics, and the latter of Latin and Greek languages; and the 20th of September, of this year, was ordained for the opening of the collegiate department of the University. A preparatory school was also opened, for the reception of such as might wish to qualify themselves to enter the University. The sum of

$500 was voted to each of the professors, and the use by each of one of the houses built as residences for the professors, and they were allowed to appropriate to their own use the moneys received for tuition in the preparatory school.

The committee of the Board remark, that the affairs of the University had reached a crisis, and one which had been looked forward to by the Board with much anxiety—that it was hoped by them the Legislature of 1840 would have made such changes in the organic law of the University as would have rendered the collection of the funds of the institution more efficient, and given the Board, who had to bear all the responsibility for the well and faithful management of the trust, the powers *absolutely necessary* for the prompt and punctual discharge of their duties—that a communication on this subject, being the unanimous expression of the views of the Board, was submitted at that time to the appropriate officers of government—that they were disappointed in not having action then taken, and that when the Legislature of 1841 required from the Board a prompt report, it was again hoped that the subject would not be lost sight of, but that the Board would have the powers conferred on them, which they deemed so indispensable to the welfare and permanent prosperity of the University. In this too, they were disappointed; and being utterly destitute of all power to look after moneys due to the University, and having but little put into their hands for the last two years, by the payment of interest, the Board had no other means than the proceeds of the loan, negotiated by authority of the Legislature of 1838. It is due to the Board that their views should be here given in their own language. They remark that

The public expected, and the state of things called for, the opening of the University at the earliest possible period. This could not be done without appropriate and necessary buildings. The board lost no time, therefore, in constructing what, in the commencing of the University, might be necessary. These have been finished, in a style which does credit to the State, and at a very reasonable cost, compared with the excellence, durability and classic taste of the workmanship, and the value of the materials. Moreover, it was required that branches should be organized and supported, and the wants and demands of several interesting sections of the State called for it. The board endeavored, in both respects, to meet the wishes of the Legislature and the expectations of the public. They did not anticipate any embarrassment from the want of means necessary for the carrying on of the University, until it was ascertained that the interest due on the sales of land, would not be paid, and the action of the Legislature, reducing the minimum price of lands and delaying the payment of the interest, excited the fears of the Board, that there would not be money enough collected to meet the current expenses, to pay the interest on the loan, and to liquidate it when it became due. The Board are confident, that had the changes in the organic law, which were asked for in 1840 and again in 1841, been authorized, the affairs of the University would have been, not only at this time but prospectively, as prosperous as could be desired. There is much to encourage the Board, and to give the prospect of permanent success, could they but realize the moneys due to the University, and receive the interest regularly accruing from the sales of lands. Should their plans be defeated, to this source only may that defeat be traced. It appears from the statement of the committee of finance, that the resources of the Board for moneys due and receivable during 1842, without reference to the interest due on University lands sold during the year 1841, amount to $58,210.62. This sum would be more than adequate to meet all the necessary expenses of the University and branches, to increase the Faculty, if the number of students should require it, to pay the interest due on the State bonds for the loan of $100,000, to purchase a philosophical apparatus, to commence the botanical garden, to erect a laboratory, to contribute to a sinking fund, as well as to meet such unforeseen and contingent expenses as are incident to the commencement of such an institution. The Board feel a deep solicitude on this subject; for judging from the experience of the two past years, there is but little reason to believe that even the amount necessary to prevent the actual suspension of all appropriations to branches, and the dismission of the Faculty, will be collected during the coming year. Nor can the Board, according to the existing laws, move in the matter, or employ any means, or influence, or agency whatever, for the collection of the funds of the University. It is judged but reasonable, that they who are held responsible to the public, and will be looked to by the Legislature for the faithful discharge of their trust, would be able to know what are their means and resources, and what they may reasonably expect and calculate upon from year to year. It is impossible to give any thing like consistency and permanency to their plans without this. Already have they been necessitated to derange their plans, and to adopt measures which have involved them in unpleasant difficulties with some in their employ, and which have given occasion to others, unacquainted with the facts, to reproach the integrity and rectitude of the Board.

It is understood that payments of money due to the University, are, and will be made in State scrip, a depreciated currency, which, in their judgment, is in violation of the sacred trust reposed in the guardians of education in this State, by the splendid gift of the donors, and which if not arrested and prevented, cannot fail to subject the Board to the most ruinous embarrassments.

The committee of finance have made some suggestions on the subject of relieving the debtors of the University from a portion of the burthen, resulting from the extravagance of former years, as an expedient for increasing the annual receipts. But the Board think that the experiments already made on this subject, afford no ground for such a hope, and that the trust reposed in them and in this State, by the government of the United States, as well as their obligations to the community at large, the interests of science, the welfare of our entire population, and the character of Michigan hereafter, and of unborn generations, require a sacred adherence to existing engagements, which may be done without diminishing the resources of the University, or perpetrating injustice or oppression toward any of its debtors. The Board deprecate Legislative action in this matter, and feel persuaded, that a judicious investigation of the entire relations and responsibilities of the Regents, of the claims of the community for the best disposal of the munificent grant of the United States for the purposes intended, and of the immense importance and necessity for such a trust to be totally disconnected from and unembarrassed by any party political action whatever, will convince every unprejudiced mind, that these funds should be deemed sacred; and while the Board should be held, at all times, fully responsible for the right and best management of them, in carrying out the design of the donor, they should be furnished with the powers essential to the discharge of such duties and responsibilities. The history of all collegiate institutions, in this country, dependent immediately on the State, has shown, that they have never prospered, as long as they have been subjected to the influence of desultory legislation, of the uncertainty from year to year, whether any system adopted by one Legislature might not be changed by the next, and of the want of an efficient board of trustees or Regents, of sufficient permanence, and possessed of adequate powers, for the responsible care and management of their interests, both literary and pecuniary. The establishment of a collegiate institution in a free State, and the conducting of its interests, should ever be upon liberal principles, and irrespective of all sectarian predilections and prejudices. Whatever varieties of sect exist in these United States, the great mass of the population profess an attachment to CHRISTIANITY, and, as a people, avow themselves to be CHRISTIAN. There is common ground occupied by them all, sufficient for co-operation in an institution of learning, and for the presence of a religious influence, devoid of any sectarian forms and peculiarities, so essential, not only as the most efficient police, but also for the development and formation of the most valuable traits of youthful character, and of qualifications for future usefulness. Experiments, made in other States, by catering to the morbid prejudices of sectarians, have only embarrassed the institutions of the State, and matured the growth of numerous and rival colleges, avowedly sectarian. Attempts made to exclude all religious influence whatever from the college, have only rendered them the sectarian engines of an atheistical or infidel party or faction, and so offended and disgusted the majority of the population, agreeing in their respect for a common christianity, that they have withdrawn their support, confidence and patronage, and left them to drag a miserable existence, till they invoked the presence and influence of the christian religion in them. The only security that can be had for the avoidance of sectarianism, and the necessary and desirable influence of christianity, in the conduct of a collegiate institution, intended to be the common property of the State, is to be sought in the character and principles of the men who are placed over it, and held responsible for its administration. There are men to be found in all the different christian sects, of sufficiently expanded views and liberal spirit, and enlightened minds, devoid of the spirit of bigotry, and narrow prejudices of sect and of party, that can be selected and deputed to such a work, whose public spirit and philanthropy, and whose love of country, and attachments to the interests of their State and its entire population, will always furnish the best and only true guaranty against the evils of sectarianism. The Board are happy to state the fact, without meaning in the least to commend themselves, that while they consist of gentlemen from almost, if not all, the principal christian sects in our State, there has nothing occurred, in their individual intercourse, their deliberations or debates, or any of their official acts, which has ever elicited occasion for the expression, or even the existence of jealousy and suspicions, growing out of sectarian prejudices or attachments.

As to the local policy and administration of the University, it was judged best by the Regents to avail themselves of the advantage of experience, and not to draft any very extensive code of laws, such as the University might need, when its course became more extended. A few general laws, capable of application by the Faculty to all the exigencies of the government of the institution, in its incipient condition, were thought to be preferable in every respect, to more detailed and minute legislation, prospectively to meet contingencies which might not be realized, and which experience, ere they would arise, would require to be modified. "Much," say the committee, "in the early age of the institution will depend on the wisdom and fidelity, the prudence and zeal, the vigilance and energy, the industry and discernment of the Faculty." The schedule of studies adopted, may be found on page 388, of Joint Documents of 1852. The report of the Faculty shows that there had been, during the current term, thirty-one students, pursuing studies preparatory to the University course. The amount of previous attainment required as much as was required by the best colleges in the United States. In relation to this subject, the Faculty makes the following remarks:

Assuming that the object of the Board of Regents is to furnish to the youth of our State an opportunity of acquiring a superior education, we have considered mental *discipline* and mental *furniture* as the two great points to be kept in view in the arrangement of studies, the selection of text books and the method of instruction. Although the latter of these two points may never be lost sight of, yet the former seems to require special attention in the early part of the academic course. . In this part, therefore, those branches of study are prescribed, and those methods of instruction pursued, which seem best adapted to form in the student habits of fixing the attention, directing the train of thought, analyzing with nice discrimination, balancing carefully evidence presented to the judgment, and arranging and systematizing the knowledge acquired by the memory. The study of ancient languages and of pure mathematics, therefore, occupy the greater part of the first two years of the course. The recitations and exercises in these branches are conducted in a manner that is designed to throw the student as much as possible upon the resources of his own mind—to rouse his individual energy, and to give those habits of mental activity without which the best apparatus of libraries and scientific collections can do little more than afford the means of idle amusement.

We are of opinion that the text books named in our schedule of studies for the first two years, should, so far as the department of languages is concerned, be regarded as indicating rather the *amount* of such languages to be read in the proposed time, than the *authors* whose works are to be read. For, while there are certain authors of such acknowledged excellence in both the Latin and Greek languages, that no man of liberal education should be unacquainted with their writings, there are others among those ordinarily read in colleges in this country, whose claim to preference is by no means such as to warrant their exclusive use. Nor do we see any sufficient reason for requiring each class to read precisely the same authors, whilst some variety in this respect might promote the taste for classical learning. We, therefore, respectfully suggest to the committee that this matter be left subject to such arrangements, from year to year, as the progressive standard of liberal education in the country shall require.

Natural history has been inserted in the list of studies of the first two years, under the impression that, with the means provided for this purpose, the subject might be commenced early in the course, with advantage. Besides the knowledge that would be acquired, it would serve to vary the objects of attention for the student, and could be made valuable as a means of forming habits of classification and arrangement. We are aware, however, that a knowledge of the principles of chemistry must precede any attempt to give thorough instruction in natural science.

The University lands remaining unsold at this date amounted to 36,000 acres.

The Committee on Education of the House of Representatives, through Mr. Crary, reported during the session of the Legislature of this year, in relation to that part of the Governor's message and report of the Regents under the joint resolution of the Legislature of 1840, which related to changes in the organic law establishing the University. In relation to the care and disposition of the lands granted to the State for the support of the University and of moneys accruing from their sale, the committee reported that by present laws they were to be deposited in the treasury and then loaned by the Superintendent; that the accruing interest was paid into the treasury and passed to the credit of the University fund; that the Regents from year to year had had the avails of the interest and the rents of the land, and that if these were not sufficient to furnish the necessary means for putting the University into operation, it was better that present embarrassments should be submitted to rather than any change be made in the law; that the change proposed would give the Regents power to expend not only the interest and rents, but also the principal of the fund.

The second change proposed by the Regents related to the Superintendent of Public Instruction, and proposed to strike out those sections of the law which connects his duties with those of the Regents, viz: that of appointing a committee of visitors to make an examination into the condition and state of the University, and reporting to him, suggesting such improvements as they might deem proper, &c.; and also proposed that instead of making their annual report to the Superintendent, exhibiting the affairs of the University, it should be made directly to the Legislature. The committee upon this subject remark:

That they see no good reason for the change. The law places the Superintendent at the head of Public Instruction. He is as much the Superintendent of the University and its branches, as of the primary schools. This was the design of the constitution, and if carried out by legislation, will make our system of Public Instruction one of harmony in all its parts. With these views, the committee do not deem it advisable to concur in the recommendation of the Regents.

The report was adopted and the committee discharged from the further consideration of the subject.

Mr. Fessenden, from the educational committee of the House, made a report upon the subject of the primary schools, announcing that the committee had given the subject full consideration, and were *unanimously* of the opinion *that an entire revision and condensation of the enactments relating to primary schools* was imperiously demanded by the wants, if not the wishes, of the people. Of the report of the Superintendent they say that "it contains many valuable hints and suggestions, while it abounds with statements showing how obnoxious the whole system, as it now stands, is to the censure and complaint of all interested in the success of schools."

The committee were anxious to revise the law, and to incorporate in it the system of taxation, but despairing of success in perfecting it at this session, they concluded to propose but few changes in existing enactments, indulging the hope that a succeeding Legislature would carry out their views, and mature a system, the leading features of which should be THE TAXATION OF PRORERTY for their support.

An act was passed this year making the schools of the city of Detroit public and free. It provided for a consolidation of the city, into one district, and placed all the schools under the direction and regulations of a Board of Education. The school inspectors, twelve in number, elected under it, together with the mayor and recorder, were created a body corporate, under the name of the Board of Education of the city of Detroit. It had power and authority to purchase school houses, apply for all moneys appropriated for school and library purposes, to make by-laws and regulations relative to all subjects connected with the schools, or to any thing whatever which might relate to the interest of education in the city. It had authority to levy a tax not exceeding $200, to be collected like other city taxes, for the purposes of a library. The Board was authorized also to levy a tax on the real and personal property of the city, not to exceed a dollar a scholar, for every child in the city between the ages of five and seventeen years.

1843.

EXTRACT FROM GOV. BARRY'S SECOND MESSAGE.

The promotion of science and literature deserves your fostering support. The happiness of all political communities, in an eminent degree, depends upon the intelligence of their inhabitants. Where ignorance prevails, vice and misery predominate. In a free government, if rulers be abandoned and profligate, it is because vice reigns among the people. Universal education is the only sure basis on which republican institutions can permanently exist. If we recur to history, whether of ancient or modern times, the examples we there find confirm this important truth. An ignorant, a degraded and an immoral people would be neither prosperous nor happy under a free constitution. Their ignorance would prevent them from understanding and appreciating their rights, and their degradation and immorality would make them fit tools for demagogues more wicked than themselves. * * * Education should not be restricted to a few, or to a favored class—the mass of the people produce the wealth and constitute the strength of the body politic, and to them should instruction in all useful branches of knowledge be extended. * * *

Among the subjects that are likely to engage your attention during the coming session, that of COMMON SCHOOLS is, perhaps, second in importance to no other. These primary institutions constitute the only sure medium by which the education of all can be secured. The enactments on this subject, above all other subjects, should be certain. definite, and easy to be understood. Such, however, is not their condition, and an entire revision is required. * * Without assuming to dictate in regard to the details necessary to give efficiency to the system you may adopt, I may be permitted to suggest that provision should be made for the establishment of SCHOOL LIBRARIES, as numerous and extensive as the means devoted to that purpose will permit.

The [University] fund is embarrassed by anticipation of its revenue. A loan of $100,000 has been made on its account, for the payment of which and accruing interest, the fund is pledged; and this is calculated greatly to impair the present usefulness of the institution. The money has been expended, and except the buildings at Ann Arbor, and the library and apparatus they contain, little or nothing remains to show the usefulness or beneficial results of its expenditure.

The facilities and inducements for study at the University are not excelled by those of any other similar institution of so recent establishment, and in some of the sciences, particularly that of natural history, greater advantages are afforded than elsewhere can be had in the United States.

The office of Superintendent of Public Instruction is created by the constitution, and if the obvious meaning of that instrument be carried into effect, its incumbent should be required exclusively to devote his attention to the superintendence of public education, while duties, wholly fiscal in their character, should be assigned to other officers, to be designated by law.

REPORT OF SUPERINTENDENT.

The report of this officer, [Franklin Sawyer, Jr.,] embraces the following account of the condition of the school and University funds:

From the time of the first sales, July 5, 1837, to the first of December, 1842, five years and five months, 78,436.76 acres of school land have been sold, at an average price of nine dollars and a few cents per acre, for $711,404 85; and 13,013.53 acres of University lands, at an average of $16 94 and a fraction, for $220,-496 05.

Of school lands, 19,328.09 acres, which sold originally for $240,-004 35, or $12 43 and a fraction per acre, have been *forfeited* for non-fulfillment of contract; also 3,422.10 acres of University lands, which sold originally for $77,293 92, or an average of $22 29 and a fraction.

Of the perfected school lands, 10,202.57 acres have been re-sold, at an average price of $7 52 and a fraction, for $76,769 54; and of the forfeited University lands, 969,38 acres have been re-sold, at an average of $14 35 and a fraction, for $13,914 95.

By virtue of the appraisement, or reduction act of 1842, 26,117.-38 acres of school lands, which originally sold for $287,930 87, or an average per acre of $11 02; and 3,936.91 acres of University lands, which originally sold for $87,504 59, or $22 22 and a fraction per acre, have been reduced in price. Purchasers of the former have already been credited $101,770 47, and of the latter $34,-651 17. The reduction in school lands has averaged about thirty-six per cent., and on University lands, very nearly fifty per cent. of the price contracted to be paid.

At the present minimum, the unsold school lands are worth $5,-000,000, and the unsold University lands, $418,550 28. Added to present amounts, the result stands as follows:

School lands sold,	$474,632 73
" " unsold,	5,000,000 00
University lands sold,	137,167 74
" " unsold,	418,550 28
Total,	$6,030,350 75

School fund,	$5,474,632 73
Interest at 7 per cent.,	383,224 29
University fund,	555,718 02
Interest at 7 per cent.,	38,900 26

The Superintendent remarks, in relation to the above, that these are results on paper—that it was not expected the school fund will realize what it thus exhibits, and yet that it was a singular fact, connected with these *chance* locations, that a very large proportion, as examination had proved, belonged to the choice lands of the State. As the University lands were selected, they were not expected to fall much below the estimate.

The aggregate amount originally contracted to be paid for school lands, had been reduced by forfeitures and relief-legislation, from $711,000 to $474,000; and for University lands from $220,000 to $137,[illegible]0, The interest on the former, which upon the certificates issued would have amounted to nearly $50,000 annually, was sunk to $33,000, and on the latter, from $15,000 to $9,000. The 78,000 acres of school lands, once sold at an average price of $9 an acre, and the 13,000 acres of University lands once sold for nearly $17, had thus dwindled down to $69,000 and $10,500, at average prices of less than $7 and $12 50. The too high prices of other years, sad reverses of fortune, and the consequent failure to fulfil contracts, encouraged by hopes of annual relief, were the causes which, in the opinion of the Superintendent, had placed our educational funds in their present condition.

The attention of the Legislature was called to the report of the Regents, and to the first report of the Board of Visitors appointed by the Superintendent. The policy of their views touching the finances, and the power asked for by them of controlling the fiscal operations of the University, met with his unqualified confirmation. In his opinion the Regents were not merely the immediate guardians of the University, but in the enlightened estimation of many, virtually *the trustees of its funds*. It was argued that they were a corporation, and as such subject to responsibilities that ought by no means to exceed the resources within their own control; that if more immediately connected with the finances of the University, they could act more understandingly, more economically, and consequently with greater satisfaction to themselves and the public.

The first board of visitors appointed, consisted of the following gentlemen: Hon. Samuel W. Dexter, Samuel Denton, M. D., Rev. F. H. Cumming, Hon. Henry Chipman, and John L. Talbot, Esq. The recommendation by this board of the immediate appointment of a chancellor, accorded with the views of the Superintendent, and of this he observes, that "if for the contemplated appointment of a new professor, that of chancellor were to be substituted, the peculiar qualifications required for that station would enable him to take charge, for some time at least, of the department of belles-letters and moral science. This course would fully organize the institution, give it the appearance and dignity of a University, contribute to its standing abroad, concentrate its means of usefulness, and obviate the necessity and expense of a new professorship at this time."

THE PRIMARY SCHOOLS.

Reports were received from twenty-nine counties, embodying reports from 355 townships. The township reports returned 2,312 districts; and of this number, 1,656 reported, leaving 656 from which the school inspectors received no reports. The whole number of children between the ages of five and seventeen, was reported to be 54,790; under five and over seventeen, 10,081; attending district school, 56,173; private schools, 3,196. The number between five and seventeen, belonging to families, using habitually any other than the English, was 1,019; and the number of all ages belonging to such families reported at the district schools, was given at 7,-665. The number attending school, where books not in the English language were used, was 160. The French and German adults who could read their own, but not the English language, were reported to number 260. The amount of money actually raised in the districts was $38,259 61—received from the school inspectors, $13,396 26; for libraries, $101 96.

A table, showing the returns of the previous year with those of the present, was prepared by the Superintendent, the importance of which will be appreciated upon examination, as furnishing material and valuable data to the Legislatures, to the office of Superintendent especially, and to the public generally. The preparation of this table was the means of discovering serious defects in the system, among which was the partial and unequal distribution of the income of the school fund. The table itself, and the conclusions of the Superintendent, are therefore given at length, as follows.

YEARS.	Counties rep'ing.	Population.	Towns report'g.	Whole No. of districts.	No. districts reporting.	Children between 5 and 17.	Between 5 & 17 attending district school.	Under 5 and over 17 attend'g district school.	Between 5 and 17 att'ding private schools.	Between 5 and 17 not att'ding district school.	Children attending no school.
1841.	28	209422	330	2300	1486	47066	42497	8757	2807	4569	1762
1842.	29	210345	355	2312	1656	54790	46092	10081	3196	8698	5502
Difference	1	923	25	12	170	7724	3595	1324	389	4129	3740

The foregoing table presents many important facts, from which inferences no less important may be deduced. But the first thing worthy of notice is an apparent disproportion between the population as given by the national census and that in the table between 5 and 17 years. This may accord with fact; but as returns are not under oath, and powerful inducements exist to swell the number between those ages which determine the amount of public money going to a district, it may do no harm to inquire into its probability in all cases. The population in 2,300 districts is, in round numbers, 210,000. The children between 5 and 17 in 1,650 districts is reported at 54,400. In the 650 districts not reporting, being more than one-third of the number reporting, must number, even after making proper allowances for sparse population, at least one-fourth as many, or 13,500. But put it at one-fifth, or 10,800, and we have, in the 2,300 districts, 64,800 children between 5 and 17, or nearly one-third of the entire population, youthful and adult. Can this be so? A table has been carefully compiled from the national census returns for the purpose of showing, at least, good reasons for doubt. The 29 counties reporting were taken. And, supposing the 2,300 districts to include all in those counties, they contain 54,400 persons between the ages of 5 and 15, and 21,600 between 15 and 20. If we take two-fifths of these last, or 8,600 as the probable number between 15 and 17, we shall arrive at something like the following result:

Children between 5 and 17 in 1,650 districts, as reported,	54,700	
Children between 5 and 17 in 650 districts, as estimated,	10,800	
		65,509
Children between 5 and 17 by the U. S. census,	54,400	
" " 15 and 17, as estimated,	8,600	
		63,000
Difference,		2,500

Now, this result will not appear very strange, when it is stated, as a fact susceptible of proof, that the entire number of children between five and seventeen, residing in a fractional district composed of parts of adjoining townships, have, in more than one instance, been returned to the inspectors of each township, thus doubling, trebling, or quadrupling the aggregates in that district, and in this way laying the foundation of a most unequal and unjust apportionment in the particular district or township. An alteration of the law, requiring every director to return his census under oath, to the district board, long enough, say five days before the annual meeting, to have it read and corrected at such meeting, and the annexation of every fractional district, for all school purposes, to the township having the school house, or in which a majority of the district board reside, will preclude all possibility of the glaring injustice alluded to.

The above table also presents facts to cheer the hearts, and, at the same time, to mortify the pride, but, in each case, to stimulate the zeal of all who seek to exalt the character of the State by means of its common schools. It is cheering to know that even one county has come up to the work since last year; still more cheering to find twenty-five additional towns in the field; and most cheering to hail an accession, in a single twelve month, of 170 districts, organized for vigorous and permanent action. All this is cheering; for every new influence, however silent in its approach, or imperceptible in its operation, becomes, like unseen particles of heat falling upon the cold earth, appreciable in the power of its great results. It is gratifying, moreover, to be able to say, as the above table authorizes us to say, that, in addition to the number reported last year, more than 3,000 children of legal age, and one thousand and three hundred under and over that age, have found their way to school. But there is also something in that table to mortify State pride—something to chill the public heart for a moment at least. Notwithstanding this proud array of counties, towns and districts, standing at the outposts of our school system, like sentinels on duty, we have only to pass watchword, and cross the lines, to find mutiny glorying in its partial success. For what but mutiny among the people shall we call that state of things, which prevents 5,000 children or more from ever looking into a school house? Yet that table exhibits such a state of things. Last year, in the districts reporting, only 4,500 children were kept from the district schools, and only 1,700 from any school; but this year, with an increase of 170 districts, while 8,600 have not entered a district school, 5,500 have been permitted to run wild in the street, or to vegetate, like so many noxious weeds, at home. This is the dark side of the picture; and is held up to view, that in admiring the brighter side, on which are painted the happy and almost speaking countenances of 59,000 children at school, other thousands, with destinies as immortal as their prospects are forbidding, may not be forgotten.

Another subject to which the Superintendent bestowed his attention was the *irregularity* of attendance of scholars at the schools. In his opinion, correctly formed, next to the establishment of schools and employment of teachers, was the great object of securing the *greatest amount of attendance*, compatible with the means attained. Occasional attendance can never meet the intentions of any system. Local statistics were not at hand, to furnish correct information on this point, but the Superintendent inferred a necessary state of things in our own State, from data furnished by other States, that made *daily registers* as indispensable in their schools, as books, blackboards or other things of utility.

The annual report of the Secretary of State of Ohio, represented this year 137,870 children as enrolled in the public schools. Of these, only 51,514, or less than two-fifths, on an average, attended school daily, for the term of three and a half months.

Connecticut, in 1840, had 85,000 children between the ages of four and sixteen. Of these, only 65,000 attended the common schools. To these were added about 6,000 under and over the legal age, making 71,000 in attendance. On careful examination of the register, it was found that of this number, only about 44,505, a little over three-fifths, attended regularly during an average term of eight months.

Massachusetts, acknowledged on all hands to have a better system of Public Instruction, and more good schools than any other State, in 1842 reported 171,000 children of the legal age. And even in that State, the average attendance in summer schools was only 89,000, and in winter schools only 107,000—being an average during eight months of 98,000, or a little more than one half.

New York, whose school children alone doubled our entire population, cannot be cited, because the reports from that State do not embrace the requisite statistics. The city of New York, in 1841, reported 40,000 children, and an average quarterly attendance of 25,000, and 16,000 during the year.

In view of these facts, the Superintendent asks, if it is a concession on the altar of State pride, after making allowances of any and every sort, to say that not more than *one half* of our school-attending children are in the habit of attending regularly, summer and winter?

Another subject of importance to the progress of education, and the present and future wants of the school system, was presented in relation to the distribution of the income of the fund. The Superintendent says:

It certainly was an object of the constitution, in emphatically enjoining upon the Legislature the establishment of three months' school in every district, and in appropriating funds for that purpose, to secure to every child in the State, the best common school education attainable in that time, and with that money. *It never was designed* that such money should be scattered broadcast, over the State, and left to fall indiscriminately upon the deserving and the undeserving. Nor is it just that those who neglect to provide schools, or having provided them, *to secure the greatest amount of attendance*, should have an equal share of the fund with those who do their *whole duty* in the matter. Take two adjoining districts, for instance: In one the children attend school punctually and regularly—in the other the reverse. Each exhibits a census of fifty children, between the legal ages, and each keeps a school open three months. The teacher registers the daily attendance, strikes the weekly average, and at the close, that for the term. In one district the average is fifty—in the other twenty-five; yet by the present ratio of distribution, every child reported in each district, gets fifty cents. In one case, $25 has gone to educate fifty children—in the other, only twenty-five children. Those who, by an effort worthy of all praise, have done what the constitution exacted of them, draw only the amount awarded to the neglectful district. Suppose the district sending scholars only one-half the time, had drawn but $12 50? The other $12 50 wrongfully withheld from the faithful district, would have enabled it, by continued fidelity, to prolong its school six weeks. Apply the principal generally. The 8,000 children who never go near a school house, draw into their respective districts just as much of the $33,000 in proportion to their numbers, as the 46,000 who attend; and of these, the 23,000 irregular scholars draw just as much as the 23,000 regular ones.

Such is the picture drawn of the *injustice* that any considerable degree of non-attendance, or irregular attendance, works to the deserving districts, to say nothing of the injustice of a higher and more intellectual character. Of course, allowance must be made for the embarrassments of a new State—but this necessity is of itself a monitor of our increased responsibilities. Notwithstanding this, there was a brighter side. This year had a decided advantage over those that preceded it. Twenty-two districts had kept up schools over ten months, and forty-eight about nine months; in addition to the public moneys they had raised upwards of $5,000. Of 3,629 children living in the districts between the ages of five and seventeen, 3,437 had attended public schools, and the rest private schools. From a second table prepared this year by the Superintendent, it appears that out of 958 districts, 583 had supported schools only three months, fifteen less than three months, *and ninety-seven had had no schools.*

Up to this year, the condition of our primary schools had only been ascertained by the legal returns. Entertaining the idea that barren statistics but partially facilitated investigation, the Superintendent issued a circular to the school inspectors, similar to that sent to districts the previous year, asking for detailed information. The object was to obtain, by a more familiar process, *as exact a picture* of the operation of the system and the condition and prospect of the schools as could be drawn by officers executing the one, and more or less in contact with the others. The object was accomplished but partially. Many inspectors neglected to furnish the information sought, probably deeming the labor extra official, or the solicitations too unimportant. The replies which were received were full of detail and to the point. Many inspectors not satisfied with mere categorical replies, enlarged upon the subject, with good feeling, clearness and force. The materials thus furnished develope the conflicting no less than the coincident views of the people. The topics discussed were, generally, teachers' wages, school houses, black board exercises, the comparative economy of public and private instruction, moral training and religious culture, uniformity of books, the operation of the system, and the policy of taxation to support schools. The highest monthly wages paid to male teachers in 44 townships was $14 28; the lowest $11 53; the highest monthly wages paid to female teachers, $5 72; the lowest, $4 29. "It may be asked emphatically," says the Superintendent, "what *man* will think of qualifying himself to become permanently a school teacher with such prospects ahead, or what *female*, with visions of usefulness and happiness painted upon her imagination, can be induced to study teaching as an art? Is it true that in Michigan, liberal wages make good schools?"

To test the question, the Superintendent referred to the statistical information derived from answers to his circular. It was ascertained that the highest amount paid for teachers was $19 per month. Of this district, the school inspectors said:

The condition of our schools is probably better than most of the other towns in this county, having had for the most part, teachers very well qualified—instruction and discipline good.

The next highest amount paid was $18 per month and board, to males, and $6 to $7 to females. This district was in a new county, (county of Shiawassee,) sparsely settled, but in spite of the embarrassments incident to their position, the school inspectors said:

Notwithstanding all the obstacles, we have some good schools, and many are beginning to see the difference between a good and a poor school. The children attend regularly and punctually.

Another township, in a more densely settled county, paid its teachers from $10 to $16, and from $4 to $6 to females. The inspectors said:

There is not much improvement, either in the qualification of teachers, kind of instruction, discipline, nor in any other respect.

Another township, nearly at the foot of the table, paid to male teachers $9 per month. The inspectors said:

The failure has been in a want of ability, either to govern or instruct. Services of teachers are not sufficiently estimated.

The inspectors of another district, paying $11 per month, said:

The remark will hardly admit of an exception, that all, who are in fact most interested in schools, are governed by mistaken and short-sighted views of economy—cheapness or low wages, too frequently constituting the principal qualification of teachers employed. * * Persons employed as teachers, with hardly an exception. are persons who engage in teaching as a present expedient, not as a permanent business. They are, as a consequence, but little interested in anything but the receipt of their wages.

These are solitary extracts from a large amount of information, verifying the aphorism, that "as is the teacher, so is the school—and as is the pay, so is the teacher." "It is enough," says the Superintendent, in concluding this subject, "to say, that however gratifying may be the fact of an average increase in the number of schools, and of the length of time they have been kept, the average *reduction of teachers' wages*, indicates a gain of amount, not of the quality given."

PRIVATE SCHOOLS.

Five thousand nine hundred and sixty-seven children were reported at this time as attending private schools. Of these the Superintendent observes:

It is altogether fair to presume that, if the public schools could be forced up to the standard of the private ones, the latter would, as a general thing, cease. Such an event has actually happened in some towns of this Union, and there is no very cogent reason why, under like circumstances, it might not in Michigan. So long as the people neglect their own schools, they have no right to complain, if those, who now sustain private schools, continue to contribute largely to that purpose. In this country, notwithstanding schools may be and are supported by the government, there can be no law compelling parents to educate their children in them. Such a law would violate individual rights. At the same time, it cannot be doubted that the distinction between public and private schools generates other and more odious distinctions; and, where that distinction becomes marked and permanent, that it occasions those grades in society which result in so many evils, both of feeling and conduct. No engine of despotism is so potent as that of knowledge over ignorance; and, on the other hand, there exists no surer indication of freedom among the people, than the universality of education, vigorously sustained. The kingdom of Prussia, so much exalted at the present day, for its enlightened population, is no exception to this remark. The monarch now upon the throne, is as enlightened as he would make his people; but it is well known, that the character of the instruction given to them, is, in its details, nicely adapted to their condition as the subjects of a despot. Even if it were true, as many suppose, that his thousands of teachers are free to educate freemen, yet continued acquiescence in the existing form of government, proves only their attachment to the despot, not to his despotism, and that any attempt by future kings to exercise powers, now merely on parchment, will develope in the people an energy and concentration of resistance that universal education alone can prepare them for. No people on the face of the earth can be so free as those among whom education, rightly conducted and rightly valued, is most equally and generally diffused. It becomes, then, a question of intense moment, how far the people of Michigan, in withholding the proper stimulus from their own schools, and thus giving it to their more successful rivals, are sapping the foundation of that very liberty and equality in which they glory.

Another consideration, in this connection, is the comparative economy of public and private instruction. On this point, one or two facts must be conclusive. Last year, it was ascertained that at least 1,850 children resided within the corporation limits of Detroit; and 27 private schools were then in operation. These schools educated 714 children only, at an average price of $18 each, and an aggregate of $12,600 a year! Between four and five hundred children attended no school. Then, no *public* school in fact existed. Last winter, an act was passed, giving the Common Council power to raise an annual tax of one dollar for every child, between 5 and 17. The amount realized under that act, says the Secretary of the board of Education, is $1,800. This liberal sum, paid by a people whose taxes otherwise amount to one-half of one per cent upon their assessments, with $530 apportioned to the city out of the school fund, educates, at least six months in the year, more than 1,000 children, who, before the establishment of *free* schools, were dependent upon high priced private schools, generally beyond their reach, or upon the precarious means afforded by the poorest kind of district schools, open but a small portion of the year in some wards, and in others not open at all. The six summer schools, under the new system, taught by females, registered nearly 700 children, and the winter schools at the time the board made the report, had registerd about 400, with a prospect of 600. Better still, nearly that number was in regular attendance. Last year, as appears from the returns in this office, only 418 children of the legal ages attended the district schools! Here, then, is the astonishing fact, that, in the city of Detroit, while only 418 children between 5 and 17 years, or only 687 of all ages, attended the district schools under the present *State* system, not less than 1,100, certainly, and 1,300, probably, have been educated in *free* schools. But, more astounding still, while it costs nearly $13,000 to educate 700 children in *private* schools, it has only cost $2,300 for six months, or $4,600 for a year, to educate at least 1,000 in the *public* schools! *Now*, every child in the city can be educated; *then*, only 700! and it costs $8,000 less to educate the *whole* than it did to educate *one-third!*

Taking the 5,867 resident children of the State who had attended private schools, the average tuition out of Detroit and Ann Arbor was estimated at about $6,000. This sum would have supported, at $13 each, about FOUR HUNDRED AND SIXTY primary school teachers for one month, or one hundred and fifty-three for three months. And taking as many districts, with an average of fifty scholars each, it would have educated nearly EIGHT THOUSAND CHILDREN in them, three months. It was the opinion of the Superintendent, supported by facts, that the entire population could be educated in common at far less expense than any portion of them could be in select schools, and that it was time that public opinion should set itself in that direction, which could alone exalt the people's schools to the position usurped and held by intelligent and hence more dangerous rivals.

A draft of the revision of the school laws, embodying what was believed to be the necessary provisions, was submitted to the Legislature. It provided that common schools should be supported by the income of the school fund, a State tax of one mill on the dollar, and such other sums as might be voted in the district meetings; it prescribed the branches that should be taught, the books that should be excluded, defined the mode of distributing the public money; provided for county Superintendents; devolved the duty of examining teachers upon the inspectors, and regulated the reports from fractional districts by directing their annual reports to the township where the school house was situated. Sites were proposed to be selected by the inspectors; their financial duties thrown upon the township treasurer; and made it the duty of the inspectors, in conjunction with county superintendent, to select and purchase books for the libraries. The *possible dissolution* of a district was carefully guarded against, the qualifications of voters prescribed, and also penalties for neglect of duty on the part of officers. The school laws of different States had been consulted in making the draft and such provisions adopted as seemed to be adapted to our circumstances.

The Superintendent concludes his remarks by suggesting that school laws to be popular and permanent should be sent in pamphlet, and with every requisite form in blank, to the officers of districts, and that all amendments from time to time, indispensable to meet unforeseen difficulties, should be made known in the district as soon as may be after their adoption, laws becoming in this way intelligible and easy of execution and a vast amount of litigation and expense avoided.

In reviewing the labors of the first two Superintendents, to whom had been confided not only the duties which pertained to the system of Public Instruction, but the management of the educational funds, it is apparent that the complete accomplishment of all the labor devolving upon them, was accompanied with unceasing diligence and devotion on their part, and their literary labors distracted by duties inconsistent with their performance. It devolved upon the first of these to devise and prepare a system of Public Instruction and put it into operation. This was a great and responsible task, to the performance of which, it may be seen by a review of his labors, he devoted himself with assiduity, care and judgment. That it was, or could be perfect, no one—not even he—ventured to expect. His successor [FRANKLIN SAWYER, JR., a summary of whose last annual report is now just concluded,] entered upon his duties, comprehending the vastness of the educational scheme laid out by the framers of the constitution—the wide and varied scope of the system devised by his predecessor and adopted by the Legislature; conceiving the immense importance of a thorough acquaintance with the nature of that system, its adaptation to our wants and its power to produce the greatest amount of good results, and bestow most widely the greatest amount of benefits; appreciating the necessity of a supervision embracing the whole system, in its general and widest sense, and in the minute details of its practical operations through all its various agencies, and in all its different channels. The work of his hands was all important in its bearings upon the future educational career of Michigan, and conceiving it to be so, it occupies no small space in the present compilation of the origin, progress and condition of our system of Public Instruction. He has been the first among those who have been successively placed at the head of that system, who has been called by Providence from the scene of his earthly labors. He is beyond the reach of worldly praise or blame; but it is conceived to be due to his memory, that his untiring industry and unchanging fidelity to the interests of education in our own State, should be made the subject of faithful record—a source of gratification to those who cherish the recollection of his services in life, and a memorial as well as an example to those who have been and who will continue to be recipients of the benefit derived from the faithful performance of his PUBLIC DUTIES.

The condition of the University at this time was the subject of deep and painful interest. In their last report, the Regents had announced the organization of a Faculty, and the commencement of a collegiate department, with the prospect of as large a share of success as could rightfully have been anticipated during the first year of a new institution. That prospect, the Regents remark, has been fully realized; but they also say,

That for several months after the commencement of the year just expiring, there seemed to settle around the affairs of the University a deep and thickening gloom. The circumstances of the Board were made known to the gentlemen appointed professors, and also to the principals of the branches; and they have cheerfully and promptly expressed a willingness to endure privations and hardships, as long as there might be hopes of ultimate success, in getting the University under way; yet the moneyed concerns of the Board became much more embarrassing and perplexed than they anticipated, insomuch, that for a season it seemed as if the entire and absolute cessation of all instruction in the University proper, and in its several branches, must speedily take place, and the gentlemen employed by the Board, be advised of the necessity of seeking some other sphere for their useful labors.

The circumstances which had brought about this result, it is due to the Regents and the people, should be detailed at length, and they are given in the following extract from the report of the Board:

The amount of available funds in the treasury, at the time of the last report, was but $1,721 91 in State scrip, nominally equal to the amount of outstanding warrants, and proved by subsequent settlement to be less by one-half. The moneys due for interest on lands sold previous to 1841, amounted to $58,210 62, a sum far more than adequate to meet all the necessary and contingent expenses of the University and of its branches, to pay the interest on the loan of $100,000, to purchase philosophical and other apparatus, to commence a botanical garden, to erect a laboratory, and additional buildings, now imperiously needed, and to contribute to a sinking fund. The fear was expressed that, judging from the experience of the two preceding years, there would scarcely be received an amount sufficient to prevent the suspension of the branches, and the dismission of the Faculty. Still, it was hoped, if we could struggle through a few months, the treasury would be so far replenished as to prevent such a result.

The legislature designed to administer relief to the purchasers and settlers of the University lands, postponed the period for the payment of interest due till March, 1842, before which, it was intimated, the Superintendent would not collect, and would be unable to pay, any thing to the relief of the board. It was also thought doubtful, whether, even after that date, there would be sufficient collected and paid over to the board, to meet the interest on the loan, viz: $3 000, falling due in January last, and the farther sum of $3,000, falling due in July last, besides the necessary current expenses.

Under the influence of such prospects and fears, the board earnestly desired that the attention of the Legislature should be given to the subject, and that such changes might be made in the organic law as would secure more efficiency, and are indispensable to the permanently successful discharge of the duties devolving on them, and to the management of the interests of education entrusted to them, especially as the subject had been brought before the Legislature, both of 1840 and 1841, with hope of more definite action. The board are under the necessity of again calling the attention of the Legislature to the subject, and of urging such further legislation as may be necessary to give the requisite powers and efficiency to the Regents that they may meet the expectations which the public entertain from them. It is owing to the zeal and measurable success of the Superintendent of Public Instruction, beyond what was anticipated, that the institution has been enabled to continue, during the past year. Of the $58,210 62, due and receivable, during the past year, there have been but $9,946 45, received by the Treasurer of the State, leaving a balance from the last year yet due, of $48,264 17, which, in addition to the amount of $14,000 00 more, falling due in 1843, will make the total sum due to the University for interest $64,264 17.

Of the sum of $10,146 45, received during the past year by the treasurer of the board, there have been paid six thousand one hundred and fifty dollars, for interest and expenses of transmission, due on the loan of $100,000. Three thousand nine hundred and ninety-two dollars and ninety-six cents for the necessary and contingent expenses of the University and its branches.

The expenses of the board for the ensuing year will be, interest on loan and expenses of transmission, $6,150 00. Expenses of University including Professors' salaries, preparatory department at Ann Arbor, and estimated contingencies of the University, and of its branches, $2,550 00; total, $8,700 00. The expenses of the University proper, at present, for the support of Professors, amount to $1,260 per annum.

The services of Doct. Abraham Sager were secured, in place of Doct. Grey, who had resigned the professorship of botany and zoology, and who, while rendering Doct. Houghton important aid in opening and arranging the mineralogical and zoological cabinet, did not expect to receive any salary until his services were wanted in the actual instruction in the classes. A small chemical and philosophical apparatus, sufficient for immediate demands, had been procured. The report of the Faculty showed ten students in the sophomore, and thirteen in the freshman class. The annual necessary expenses of the students ranged from $80 to $100. The Faculty reported, in regard to the local government of the institution, that they had "kept it in mind, that most of the students were of an age which rendered absolutely necessary some substitute for paternal superintendence—that no college in this country could secure public confidence without carefully watching over the morals of its students, and making strict propriety of conduct, as well as diligent application to study, a condition of membership—that considering the government of the students as a substitute for the regulations of home, they had endeavored to bring it as near to the character of paternal control as the nature of the case would admit, and to attain the end not wholly, nor chiefly, by restraint and dread of penalty, but by the influence of persuasion and kindness."

The Board conclude their report by the following appeal to the Legislature, which, as it embraces valuable imformation for reference, is here inserted in full:

It is sincerely hoped that the attention and wisdom of the Legislature will be given to the subject of the resources of the board, and the powers necessary to the permanent and successful prosecution of the interests of education. Of so large a sum as $64,246 17, now due, it is impossible to conjecture what amount will be paid during the ensuing year. Uncertainty attendant on the collection of the revenue, postponement of the times for the payment of interest, liquidation of claims, and any other measures which might excite a hope of successful delay of payment on the part of debtors, it is obvious cannot fail to prove disastrous to an institution on its annual income. The Board of Regents do not impeach the wisdom or motives which have influenced the legislation for several years, relative to the sale of University lands and the collection of the proceeds thence arising. Having the immediate responsibility for the welfare and success of the University, however, devolved on them, they feel it due to themselves, to the Legislature, and to the community at large, whose interests are to be subserved by the faithful discharge of their duties, when making their annual report, once more, under circumstances embarrassing and perplexing, and while soliciting such Legislation as may be necessary to give efficiency to the Board, to present the following brief historical statement of the Legislative enactments on the subject:

1. An act to provide for the organization and government of the University of Michigan, approved March 18, 1837.

2. An act to locate the University of Michigan, approved March 20, 1837.

3. An act to provide for the disposition of the University and primary school lands, approved March 21, 1837.

4. An act to amend an act entitled an act to provide for the organization and government of the University of Michigan, approved June 21, 1837.

5. An act to amend an act entitled an act to provide for the disposition of the University and school lands, approved June 22, 1837.

6. An act releasing to the United States fourteen sections on the Niles, and sections twenty-five and twenty-six on the Nottawasepie reserves, upon certain conditions, approved March 20, 1838.

7. An act to *extend the time of payment* of the University and school moneys, approved April 6, 1838.

8. An act to authorize a loan of a certain sum of money to the University of Michigan, approved April 6, 1838.

9. An act to provide for the payment of the expenses of the Regents of the University in certain cases, approved February 14, 1839.

10. An act to *extend the time of payment* of the University and school moneys, approved March 4, 1839.

11. An act to provide for the sale of certain lands to settlers thereon, approved March 25, 1840.

12. An act to amend an act to *extend the time of payment* for the University and school lands, approved March 30, 1840.

13. An act to reduce the price of the University and school lands, and for other purposes, approved April 13, 1841.

14. An act to reduce the price of University and school lands, approved April 15, 1842.

15. An act to provide for the sale of certain lands to the persons therein named, approved February 9, 1842.

Besides these acts, two joint resolutions have been adopted by the Legislature relative to the University; one relating to public documents, and the other requires the Board of Regents to report to the Legislature convened in 1841, "what changes were necessary to be made in the organic law relative to said University, in order to secure more effectually the objects of the same."

By the act of March 21, 1837, the Superintendent of Public Instruction was authorized to sell at public auction, so much of the University lands as shall amount to the sum of $500,000, at the minimum price of twenty dollars per acre; one-f urth of the purchase money to be paid down, the remainder in annual instalments of five per cent., to be paid annually. In June of that year, this act was so amended as to require only one-tenth of the purchase money to be paid at the time of sale, and one-tenth annually thereafter, with interest on the amount unpaid, and when, in the opinion of the Superintendent of Public Instruction, one-tenth of the purchase money did not sufficiently secure the interest of the State, he was authorized to require additional security of the purchaser.

The act of March 20, 1838, was never carried into effect, the person named therein as the executor of the law declining, for obvious reasons, to perform the duties required of him.

From the report of the Rev. J. D. Pierce, Superintendent of Public Instruction, it appears that there were University lands sold in 1837, amounting to $150,447 90, at the average price of $22 85½ per acre; subsequently, sales were reported to have been made, amounting, in all, to upwards of $200,000. In April (the sixth) of 1838, the time of payment of the University and school moneys was extended to December next ensuing, upon conditions to be, in the opinion of the Superintendent, not prejudicial to the said funds respectively.

By the act of March 4, 1839, all delinquencies were cured which took place in December, 1838, if the delinquent made payment by the first day of May, 1839. All further payments were extended to the first day of December, 1839, "at which time, on the payment of all interest then due, and enough of the principal to make twenty per cent, with what shall have been overpaid heretofore, the said Superintendent may suspend the further payments one year from that time, at which he may receive the interest, and five per cent of the principal, to be paid by the first day of December, 1840."

Up to this period in the history of the University, its resources had not been diminished. Embarrassments had been experienced, growing out of the delay in the payment of the interest due on the University fund, upon the regular receipt of which, obviously, the success of the University essentially depends. Under the act of March 25, 1840, which provides for the sale of certain lands to the settlers thereon, 4,743.12 acres of *appraised* University lands were sold, at the average price of six dollars and twenty-one cents an acre. In the year 1841, 367.66 acres of University lands were *sold* at an average price of seventeen dollars per acre. During the same year, as appears from the report of F. Sawyer, Jr., Esq., Superintendent of Public Instruction, there were sold 160 acres of *appraised* University lands at eight dollars per acre, and of the forfeited lands, resold, 168.-32 acres, at an average price of $1 52 per acre.

The agent appointed by the Legislature to re-locate sixteen sections of University lands, in lieu of those proposed to be relinquished to the United States by the act of March 20, 1838, found the faithful execution of his trust to be impracticable, because there were no lands unlocated as valuable as those already selected. The average price of lands sold in 1840, was seventeen dollars; that of *appraised* lands, sold the same year, was six dollars and twenty-one cents, and in 1841, eight dollars per acre. Forfeited lands were re-sold in 1841, at $19 52 per acre.

In March, 1840, the time of payment for University and school lands was extended. In 1841, the minimum price of University lands was reduced to fifteen dollars per acre, and in 1842, to twelve dollars per acre.

In review, therefore, the Board of Regents, on whom the actual and ostensible responsibility for the successful establishment of the University, and for the distribution of its branches, rests, respectfully submit to the consideration of the Superintendent of Public Instruction, to the Legislature, and to their fellow citizens, the embarrassments attendant on their efforts, which must shortly prove disastrous and ruinous to the interests of education in the State, unless some permanent and stable measures can be adopted for the management and collection of the revenue of the University. The Board do not wish to shrink from responsibility. They are ardently devoted to the trust which has been devolved upon them, and ambitious to prosecute and discharge it in such a way as to render the munificent appropriation of the United States, for the purpose of an University, most efficient and diffusive, and so as to accomplish the intent of the donors, do credit to their munificence, and to render it a blessing to the State, and the State conspicuous for its advantages and facilities for education. All they desire is the necessary powers to accomplish their trust, and measures to render the revenue of the University regularly and permanently available.

THE BRANCHES.

The committee reported branches in continuance at Detroit, Kalamazoo, White Pigeon, Tecumseh and Ann Arbor, with a total number of scholars of 174. Pecuniary considerations had induced the Board to reduce the appropriations for sustaining them, to $200 to each branch, exclusive of tuition fees. The principals at Tecumseh and White Pigeon resigned, and two others were appointed.

REPORT OF VISITORS.

The provision of law establishing this board, was founded upon the principle that the selection of such a number of gentlemen from among the body of the people, to examine into the state of the University in all its departments, and to suggest such improvements as they might deem important would be likely to secure the views and opinions of competent and able men, (disconnected otherwise with the system,) as to its wants and requirements, and its adaptation to the circumstances of the public. The Superintendent, the Regents and the Faculty, are the *active agents* in the system, in carrying out the laws, and government of the institution—the visitors, sentinels of the people, who not being in any way connected with the administration of affairs, are to be presumed to be unbiased and unprejudiced witnesses of the actual state of things, and better able to judge of their operation and effects. The board, after examination of the plan and buildings, pronounced them worthy of the great objects for which they were designed, and believed that the exigencies of the institution would, before the lapse of many years, demand the completion of the buildings, and more than had been contemplated. They were satisfied with the examination of the students, mode of instruction, and competency of the professors, who consisted at this time, of Rev. Joseph Whiting, George I. Williams, Douglas Houghton, and Abram Sager. They were of opinion that the opening of the University had given a new impetus to the cause of education in the State, and that the number of students would soon create a necessity for multiplying the professorships, and for an extension of the building accommodations, to a degree equal to, if not exceeding the means which the best and most rigid administration of the funds would permit—that while they appreciated the reasons assigned by the Board of Regents, they could not withhold the opinion that the interests of the institution would be greatly promoted by the appointment of a chancellor, and that it ought not to be delayed—tha the duties of the two acting professors would soon become too laborious, and render necessary the appointment of a tutor or additional professor—that a spacious and appropriate place for specimens in geology, botany and natural history, should be provided. These specimens were reported to be as follows:

Zoological specimens, including mammalia, birds, fishes and shells,	5,500
Specimens of plants, about	15,000
" " minerals,	8,000
" " geological,	10,000
Total,	38,500

Five thousand five hundred and fifty of these were classed and arranged, and occupied the entire space of a room 25 feet by 44. The visitors expressed the belief that no institution in the United States could boast of a similar collection, of greater number, value and variety. The scientific arrangement of them was due to Dr. Houghton, and the board expressed their acknowledgement of the great value of his gratuitous and invaluable services. His labors were conducted under the eyes and with the assistance of the students, the effect of which had infused into them a spirit of enquiry, and awakened a lively interest in the study of natural science. The library, which consisted of nearly 4,000 volumes of well selected standard works, formed the basis for further enlargement, and the board recommended an addition of all the classical writers in the original, and a larger portion of American and modern works.

They represent that the Superintendent and Regents had seemed to have appreciated the importance of establishing branches, as the means of a more general diffusion of the benefits of education, and of preparing students for the University, and regretted that it should have been necessary from the want of means, to have made a retrograde movement in regard to them, by discontinuing those at Monroe, Pontiac and Niles, though they concurred in the prudential reasons which induced the step. They recommended as early a resuscitation and extension of the system, as an improvement in the financial condition of the University would admit.

They represent the resources of the University, if they could be realized, as *abundantly sufficient* to meet the expenditures further needed, after paying the interest on the loan, and defraying all the current expenses of the institution and its branches, the balance due the fund, after deducting estimated current expenses, being $48,980 63. But they express regret in learning, that out of such abundant means, barely sufficient had been collected for the current yearly expenses, and even that, only by the great energy and exertion of the Superintendent of Public Instruction, *without which aid, the University and its branches must have been suspended.*

The board were of opinion that so long as the Legislature permitted those indebted to the fund to look to them, as virtually invested with the character of creditor, and with the power of relief, the legislative halls would be crowded with applications to the prejudice of the fund, and they sustain the views of the Regents in their application for the management of the fund, the duties of the Superintendent being substituted in this respect, by the Regents, without other change in the laws.

LEGISLATION.

A report was made to the Senate by Hon. E. A. Warner, chairman of committee of Public Instruction, in which it is stated that the committee believed the great defect of the law to be in not providing for the education of every child in the State, of proper age. The objection to taxation for this purpose was the great pecuniary embarrassment of the State and people. The means of education, however, it was asserted, must be furnished to children of indigent parents. The committee adopted the *township library system*, and proposed a change in the mode of assessing school district taxes by requiring the supervisor of the township to place them upon the township roll, and reported a bill to amend the laws.

The committee on education in the House, also reported that they had carefully examined into the system of primary schools, and compared it with that of other States; that they find much wanting; that direct taxation to a limited extent would have to be resorted to, and also reported a bill. The committee believing that the House bill was more systematic and shorter, decided to incorporate into their bill such portions of the Senate bill as was deemed advisable.

The ALLEGAN ACADEMY was incorporated this year. A joint resolution was passed requiring the Secretary of State to furnish annually one hundred copies of the printed annual report of the Superintendent, for the purpose of being by him distributed into the several States.

On the 6th day of March, the act was passed to organize the LAND OFFICE—the Commissioner of which was hereafter to have charge and supervision of all lands belonging to or which might become the property of the State, or held in trust by the State for any purpose. All the books and papers connected with the subject, in the office of the Superintendent, were to be transferred to the Land Office. Thus the separation of the fiscal duties of the office of Superintendent was accomplished, and the office restored to the proper sphere contemplated in its creation by the framers of the constitution.

Dr. O. C. COMSTOCK was nominated and confirmed as Superintendent of Public Instruction; and the following abstract embraces the substance of the school law which was the result of this year's legislation.

The act of 1840, the act of 1841, the act amendatory thereto, and all acts and parts of acts contravening the law of 1843, were repealed. A new law was passed, providing for the formation of districts, and the holding of district meetings, with power to locate site, purchase, build or lease school house, and to impose a tax not to exceed, in any one year, two hundred dollars, unless the inspectors certified as in the previous law; in which case a sum not to exceed the amount so certified, and in no case more than $300 for one year could be raised. A tax could be voted in addition, to keep the school house in repair, and for necessary appendages; to determine the length of time a school should be kept, when the moneys should be applied, and various other provisions similar in many respects to the general provisions of the other laws. A rate bill was to be made out, containing the names of every person liable for tuition and fuel, for attendance of children. The inhabitants of the district were empowered to make such provision as they deemed proper to raise the school money, necessary for the town, in addition to the moneys apportioned, and any money received from other sources appropriated to maintain the school. The amount so received was to be assessed upon and paid by the parents or guardians of scholars, not exempted from payment for tuition and fuel, in proportion to the number of such scholars, and the length of time for which the parents or guardians have sent to school. The district board made out and delivered to the supervisor a report of all taxes voted by the district during the year preceding the second Monday in October, to be raised on the taxable property of the district, and of all taxes which the board were authorized to impose on such property. It was made the duty of the supervisor to assess the taxes so voted, and all other taxes provided for in the act on the taxable property of the district, and for the year 1843, to assess twenty-five dollars; for 1844, a tax of one-half of a mill upon each dollar of the taxable property of the township, one mill upon each dollar for 1845; and annually thereafter one mill on each dollar of the total valuation of the taxable property of the townships; and of the amount so received $25 was to be applied to the township libraries, and any sum not so applied, was to be apportioned to the several school districts. Not less than this sum was to be assessed in a township in any one year, and when the library contained two hundred volumes, the qualified electors might vote to reduce the amount to any sum not less than ten dollars. The Superintendent was required to make out a full set of forms under the act, and cause a sufficient number to be printed to furnish all the State and school officers with one copy. It was also made his duty to publish a list of such books of instruction as he shall deem best adapted for the use of schools; a list containing not less than one hundred volumes for township libraries, with such rules as he thought proper to recommend. He was further to publish in each annual report hereafter, a list of such text books as in his opinion should be used in the schools, and a list for township libraries. A tax not exceeding $50, in addition to the sum required for libraries, could be voted for the purchase of books for the use of the adult residents of the township, or for their children. District libraries, already established, were not subject to the law relating to township libraries without the assent of the district and townships which adopted the district system—the entire amount of money raised by township tax for this purpose should be applied to the support of schools. The school moneys were to be apportioned in proportion to the number of children between the ages of five and eighteen years. Boards of inspectors and other officers were liable to a penalty for neglect, as well as refusal to deliver their report in time.

1844.

EXTRACT FROM GOVERNOR BARRY'S SECOND MESSAGE.

The amount received into the treasury the last fiscal year, to the credit of the common school interest fund, was $19,418 39, and during the same period, $20,890 09 was distributed for the support of common schools throughout the State.

The amount received to the credit of the University interest fund, was $7,234 32. Of this sum, $6,000 was appropriated to the payment of interest due on the loan made for the University, and the remainder expended by the Regents for the beneficial purposes of the institution. Of this fund, $6,000, and the difference of exchange between Detroit and New York, is annually required to pay interest, and the balance, under existing circumstances, cannot be estimated much above $1,000, which is insufficient to render the University, in any considerable degree, useful, and scarcely sufficient to contiuue it in operation. You will, therefore, see the necessity of adopting measures, at the present session, for its relief.

Of the seventy-two sections of land, which constituted its endowment, about one fourth part has been sold. The minimum price now fixed by law, is twelve dollars an acre; and, as this sum exceeds the present value of the unsold land, it will depend on you to decide whether a reduction may now be made with advantage to the permanent prosperity of the University. Large quantities of other public lands are in market, and may be purchased at rates so low that sales of University lands might not be made, even at a minimum corresponding with their true value. On the other hand, the institution is now in its infancy, and the present use of the funds with which it is endowed, is required to ensure its permanence. The lands cannot be sold at their present estimated value for many years to come, and, in the meantime, the University may cease to exist for want of adequate support. The subject commends itself to your serious consideration.

At the time of the adoption of the organic law of the University, its anticipated revenue was expected to be much greater than it has subsequently proved, and the Legislature, actuated by a laudable desire to promote knowledge and extend science, offered, without charge, the means of a collegiate education to all the youth of Michigan. No fees for tuition were permitted to be charged to any student resident in the State. This was a liberal provision, but, unhappily, subsequent events render it uncertain whether the original design, so munificent and worthy of commendation, can be carried out to the full extent intended by its generous projectors; and for the removal, at least in part, of the pecuniary embarrassments of the institution, I would respectfully call your attention to the propriety of authorizing the board of Regents to charge the students in attendance such reasonable fees for tuition, as, with other accruing means, will secure the services of the necessary professors and teachers, in the various departments. If you should deem it expedient to confer this authority upon the board, I would respectfully suggest that while you fix a maximum which should not exceed the charge for similar purposes in other seminaries of learning, you leave to the Regents a discretion in regard to the subject, and authorize them to make discrimination in the exercise of the power granted.

Five professors have been appointed, of whom two only have entered upon the discharge of their duties. The number of students in the main institution is about fifty. Branches at Tecumseh, White Pigeon, Kalamazoo and Romeo, are continued in operation at an annual expense of two hundred dollars for each.

Since the issue of State scrip, the sum of $32,226 23, in that species of State indebtedness, has been received for sales of school lands, and the further sum of $6,484 36, for the sale of University lands, which, amounting altogether to $38,710 59, remains in the State Treasury. As scrip cannot be re-issued but for claims against the general fund, the above sum should properly be considered as a loan and accruing interest paid thereon, as upon other claims against the State.

REPORT OF SUPERINTENDENT.

The Superintendent announces to the Legislature the publication of the school laws in pamphlet form. The school law being a new one, and considerably extended, embracing many principles and objects, and prescribing to numerous officers multifarious duties, accumulated the correspondence of the office and augmented its labor. The following is an extract from the report:

The undersigned is happy in the conviction, that at no former period, have the high interests of popular education, been so justly and generally appreciated in this State, as at the present time. The disposition of the public mind in favor of the universal diffusion of the blessings of knowledge and virtue, must be peculiarly gratifying to your honorable body. It is, moreover, inspiring to the feelings, and animating to the hopes of the friends of education of the country and of man. In view of the ample and enduring foundation, laid in the magnificent grants by the general government, of the University and school lands, grants, the proceeds of which are inviolably secured by the constitution and laws of the State, to the high and holy objects for which they were intended—and in view of the fact, now admitted by most of the civilized world, that mind is public property, and should be educated at the public expense, all must perceive the facility with which the rising generation, with the innumerable multitudes who shall succeed them on our lovely peninsula may acquire an education, which shall develope and discipline all their intellectual faculties—unfold and refine all their moral sentiments—an education, which shall enable them to enjoy and accomplish all that a beneficent Creator designed in their being. * * * *

Michigan seems ordained to have her full share of population. Her physical advantages, rapidly unfolding, are surpassed by no State in the Union. We trust she will ever shine among the brightest stars in the national constellation. But ends involve means. Without a due regard to education, all our fair prospects will be blasted—our bright star of hope will set in thick darkness. We have now many immortal minds to educate. Their numbers will vastly increase with the revolution of years. To education so fundamental to the prosperity and glory of States and empires, the general and State governments have benignly turned their attention. To educate all the rising generation however, not only requires the liberality and fostering care of governments but the cordial and vigorous co-operation of the whole community. Public opinion, feeling and conduct are powerful and prevailing. Teachers and scholars should be universally encouraged and animated in the glorious career of mental and moral improvement. Their attainments—power of accomplishment and usefulness, are identical with the highest interests and honor of the country. By far the greatest portion of our youth will receive all their scholastic education in our primary institutions of learning. These should afford every practical facility for the acquisition of this great object. *

The Superintendent adds his testimony to the value of the branches, believing "the interests of the University—its branches and the primary schools, to be one and indivisible." The whole number of children between 4 and 18, residing in the districts, was 66,756. The whole number that had attended school, 55,555. Schools had been taught upon an average four months of the year. The amount of money raised in the district was $44,705 90. A list of books was recommended for the schools.

REPORT OF REGENTS.

The Board represent the embarrassments heretofore reported as still existing in relation to the University. The number of students had increased, and another professorship was established. There were at this time but *three* branches in existence. The unavoidable expenditures for the coming year were estimated at $2,922 55. A further cause of pecuniary embarrassment was stated to be the failure of the Michigan State Bank, which found the University fund its depository to the amount of $6,000, and the Bank of Michigan more than $9,000. To liquidate these debts the Board had been obliged to take real estate or mortgages thereon. The deficit of revenue thus arising, would have to be provided for, and the committee of Regents, consisting of J. Kearsley, Lewis Cass and Dr. Pitcher, remark:

That to do this, several expedients had claimed the attention of the Board. Shall the parent institution be closed? The Board answer no. The condition of the University, both as to reputation and numbers, had exceeded the expectations of the most sanguine, and it is confidently believed that it will afford the means of a most thorough education to the sons of our own and other States who may appreciate its advantage. *If once closed,* even for the shortest period, years must elapse before it could regain the confidence and prosperity it now possesses. A reduction of the number of professors was impracticable, but the increase of one necessary. Shall all appropriations to the branches be suspended? The Board would adopt this measure with great reluctance, and only under a conviction of its imperious necessity. The manifest intention however of the original grant of the two townships of land (the basis of the University fund) and the ultimate advantages to be attained, indicate to the Regents that should necessity compel the adoption of one or the other of these measures, the *branches must be the sacrifice.* The Board yet cherish the hope that such Legislative aid may be extended to the institution as will meet the demands upon its treasury. To effect this object, the Regents recommend such alteration in the organic law as shall provide for the assessment of such tuition fees, to be paid by the students individually, as the Board may deem reasonable.

The report of the executive committee announce the appointment of Rev. Edward Thompson as professor of moral and mental philosophy; and of Mr. J. Beach as tutor to relieve the professor of mathematics; and that the appointment of a professor of chemistry and also of natural philosophy should be made at an early day. The Faculty consisted of the following gentlemen: Rev. Joseph Whiting, George J. Williams, Abram Sager and Rev. Edward Thompson.

The report of the Faculty showed the whole number of students to be fifty-three.

The report of the committee on branches showed 174 students in attendance. A branch was organized at Romeo.

The board of visitors, consisting of Rev. George Duffield, Hon. Robert McClelland, Hon. E. M. Cust, Hon. J. Wright Gordon, and Hon. Franklin Sawyer, Jr., announced that they had inspected and examined into the general affairs of the University—that a majority attended the examinations and were satisfied with the progress made by the students, and the diligence, zeal and faithfulness of the professors, and that the present organization of the Faculty, if fostered by the Legislature, would render the institution a blessing and an honor to the State.

The question of the expediency and policy of reducing the price of school and University lands, again presented itself to the Legislature, in connection with the subject of education. Mr. Henry N. Walker, as chairman of the committee on public lands, made a report to the House of Representatives, in which it was urged that,

A forced sale now, before they have acquired their proper value, would be sacrificing for the present advantage, the future prosperity of our schools and University; and it is well worthy of the enquiry of every one, whether the object in view would justify the sacrifice which must be submitted to if we undertake to force a sale of the lands. So far as the University is interested, it would be, in the opinion of your committee, of doubtful policy to offer for sale more than sufficient to relieve the parent institution from embarrassment. It was conceived by those who furnished the means to endow our University, that it would be a long period before the wants of the country would require the institution to be fully organized in all its various departments. All establishments of this kind must depend for their maturity and success upon the advancement made in society. It is not wealth alone which keeps an institution like our University, in a prosperous and flourishing condition. The common schools must first be organized, for they are the ever living springs which furnish the pupils to the University. History and experience teaches us that in the early settlement of a country, there is little time or opportunity for the pioneer to devote to the higher branches of edution. It is not until the wants and necessaries of life are furnished, that time and money can thus be expended. In the present situation and condition of our State, it is extremely doubtful whether our

University could take and maintain a high rank and standing at once, even though it had an income equal to the interest on the sum at which the entire of these lands are held. It would be a premature existence, and we should greatly fear that the fund itself would be diverted to some other purpose, which would place it beyond our reach when required, if not endanger its existence. In answer to the argument attempted to be drawn from the supposed increase of interest equal to the amount of difference between the present minimum price and the one proposed, your committee would say, that they might admit the proposition, and still find sufficient reasons for doubting the policy of reducing the price. It would be far better to hold the lands, and thus secure the increased value to the fund, than to sell them now, though we might derive the amount of interest assumed. In one case we have the increase as a paramount fund for all future time. In the other, it is received as interest, and distributed throughout the State as fast as received. But the position we do not believe tenable. The reduction, if made, takes place on all the unsold lands, and the interest is only received upon such amounts as may be disposed of. If we could sell at once all the lands, and recover the pay therefor, then there might be some more reason for the assumption.

There is one evil complained of, which your committee have not referred to, and it is the one, we regret to say, which seems to have an overpowering influence. We allude to the complaint, that it is a great injury to the townships, because the lands are unsettled, and not liable to taxation It is undoubtedly an evil, but one of small magnitude, when placed beside the welfare of our schools and University. The argument, so far as it is valid, would stop at nothing short of sale, and that at once. A sale is the only remedy; and if we act upon this principle, it must be brought about at a fair price, if we can obtain it; if not, then at such price and on such terms as can be obtained. We should look upon the adoption of such a course as an evil of a thousand times more magnitude than the one complained of. Entertaining these views, your committee cannot consistently, with their sense of duty, recommend a general reduction in the price of the University and school lands.

But while your committee cannot believe it expedient to reduce the price of their lands, we do believe it would be both wise and politic to receive in payment of the unsold lands, to a limited amount, all the outstanding obligations drawing interest. It will be remembered, that to anticipate the sale of the University lands, the Regents procured a loan of the bonds of this State, to the amount of $100,000. The University pays interest on this sum annually, and it absorbs nearly the entire income of the University fund. Now, if we could sell sufficient of the University lands for this class of our State indebtedness, to cancel these bonds, or as the University would have due it an amount of interest equal to that which it owes the State, it would be all the relief the University requires. It is well known that one class of our State warrants on the Treasury are worth only about fifty cents on the dollar. This is their market value. They bear interest at [the] rate of seven per cent. per annum. The reception of these in payment of the University and school lands would be to the purchaser equivalent to a reduction equal to the discount on the warrants, while to the fund itself, and as an offset against the claim of the State, they would count as money at their face. No injury could possibly occur to the State or University by an exchange of the lands for this class of our State indebtedness. The State honestly owe the warrants—it has bound itself to pay them, and the faith of the State is pledged to that effect. Why then should the University and school fund, when an opportunity is presented, (of making a good bargain by the exchange,) be prevented from availing themselves of it? Capitalists from other States have invested money in the purchase of these warrants, and if it is an object for them to pay money for them, it is certainly an object for the University and school funds to part with their lands for them. A large increase of sales might be relied upon if this course should be adopted, and probably to the extent, it would be desirable to sell at present. Your committee would, however, limit the amount to be received for University lands, to $100,000. This sum would cancel the bonds received from the State, and thus leave the entire of the interest moneys now annually due, to be applied to the support of the University. This sum would be as great as could be judiciously expended at this stage of its existence, if proper discretionary powers were placed in the hands of the Regents as to the charges for tuition.

An important item in the history of our educational affairs, was the presentation during this session of a PETITION purporting to be signed by one hundred and fifty citizens of the county of Berrien. It was referred to the commitee on education, who, through their chairman, William N. McLeod, made a report which is here introduced at length, not only as showing its substance, but also as furnishing general legal information in relation to the establishment of the University and schools:

The petitioners vouchsafe the information that, in their belief, "the University is of little or no benefit to the State, or the people generally, and that if its fund was added to the common school fund, it would prove of great and lasting benefit to the State and the whole people." They therefore most earnestly and respectfully petition the Legislature "to adopt measures to bring about such an event as early as possible."

The subjoined reasons have influenced your committee, in instructing me, as their chairman, to return the petition with the recommendation that its prayer be not granted.

First. The object sought to be attained is repugnant to the educational policy which has obtained since the organization of our State.

That a public provision for scientific, as well as elementary education, should be made by governments professedly republican, was a maxim incorporated with the earliest efforts of our State legislation.

Republics modified, if not dependent upon popular sentiments and impulses, require the restraints of enlightened education as a mean of prosperity, and indeed of self preservation.

So obvious was this principle that the framers of our State constitution. incorporated in that instrument an injunction upon the legislative department of government, to "encourage, by all suitable means, the promotion of intellectual, scientifical and agricultural improvement. Not only common education, or that elementary instruction which is limited to that humble knowledge which is necessary in the pursuit of the ordinary avocations of life, but the cultivation and diffusion of scientific knowledge was duly inculcated and judiciously enjoined.

A common school system was established through the State, libraries in every district were maintained by the appropriation of fines and penalties exclusively for their support, the government, in this manner, subserving the welfare of the whole by the commutation money paid for the vices of the few; a University, nobly endowed by the munificence of the central government, was founded and protected by wise and liberal legislation; departments of geology, zoology and topography were maintained by the public purse, and the State lent, at once, the sanction of her name and the protection of her laws to the encouragement of science and the diffusion of intelligence and knowledge.

Second. Your committee have been induced to report adversely to the prayer of the petitioners from the further consideration that it is limited to a very small number of the citizens of a single county, and is wholly unprecedented in the history of the State.

Out of a population of 5,011, only one hundred and fifty have been found to memorialize the Legislature on this subject. The representation in the judgment of your committee, is not sufficiently general to warrant so important a change as would be effected by conceding to the prayer.

Third. The petitioners have furnished no facts, statistics or *assertions* by which your committee can guide their opinion in concluding on so momentous a change. They have deigned only to favor us with their belief, "that the University is of little or no benefit to the State, or the people generally." The *data* on which this opinion is based is confined to the bosoms of the petitioners.

Much therefore, as your committee desire to quadrate their faith by any article which the citizens of Berrien may incorporate in their creed, they are yet unwilling to recommend to the House a course so precipitous and unadvised as that embraced in the prayer of the petitioners.

Fourth. The Legislature of Michigan have no power to grant the petition in matter or in form.

In the constitution of the State, article 10, section 5, it is declared that "the funds accruing for the rents or sale of lands reserved or granted by the United States to this State for the support of a University, *shall be and remain* a PERMANENT FUND, for the support of said University, and such branches as the public convenience may hereafter demand, for the promotion of literature, the arts and sciences, and as may be authorized by the terms of such grant."

The Legislature is further enjoined "to provide effectual means for the improvement and *permanent security* of the funds of said University."

If, therefore, your committee were disposed to concede to the modest wishes of the petitioners, they would hesitate lest, peradventure, some doubt might arise as to the authority of a Legislature to dissolve so solemn an injunction, or to violate so palpable a mandate of the constitution they are sworn to support.

Fifth. If the proposition of the petitioners were submitted, by resolution of the Legislature, to the people of Michigan, or by memorial to the Congress of the United States, there is no authority vested either in the people or in Congress to accede to its terms. By the provisions of an act "concerning a seminary of learning in the territory of Michigan," approved May 20, 1826, the secretary of the treasury of the United States is authorized to set apart and reserve from sale a quantity of land, not exceeding two entire townships, *for the use and support of a University within the territory aforesaid, and for* NO OTHER USE OR PURPOSE WHATSOEVER.

By a further act of Congress, approved June 23, 1836, "supplementary to the act entitled 'an act to establish the northern boundary line of the State of Ohio, and to provide for the admission of the State of Michigan into the Union, on certain conditions,'" it is provided in section second, "that the seventy-two (72) sections of land set apart and reserved for the use and support of a University, are granted and conveyed to the State, *to be appropriated solely to the use and support of such University*, in such manner as the Legislature may prescribe."

The acceptance or rejection of this donation, under the restriction specified in the grant, was submitted propositionally to the Legislature of Michigan, and by them was accepted; thus, by the terms of the act, making it "obligatory upon the United States."

Sixth. The inhabitants of Berrien county have no just cause of complaint, under the present organization of the educational system of the State.

From the "abstract of school returns," accompanying the report of the Superintendent of Public Instruction, it appears that out of 1,278 children between the ages of four and eighteen years, 1,167 have attended school four months on an average, in the year. The amount of money received from the treasurer and inspectors of school districts in the county, is $583 92; amounting to a little more than forty-nine cents for each scholar, for the attendance on school *one-third* of the year, or about *twelve and one-fourth cents* per month.

To estimate the *cheapness and universality* of the educational advantages enjoyed by this county, your committee would institute a comparison between it and the county least favored in both these particulars, to wit: the county of Michilimackinac.

The whole number of children between the ages of four and eighteen years, in this county, is one hundred and four, (104) as stated in the "abstract of school returns," although undoubtedly under-estimated.

Of this number but eighteen have attended school, and that too, on an average of only three months in the year.

The amount of money received from the treasurer and inspectors is thirty-five dollars ($35) as stated in the "abstract," manifesting that the county of Michilimackinac pays an average of two dollars ($2) per quarter of a year for every child attending school, or about *sixty-six cents* per month, which is more than quintuple the price paid by the inhabitants of Berrien county for the same amount of instruction.

In addition to this, the subjects of instruction as compared with the total number of children in the last mentioned county, are more numerous than the like subjects compared with the total number of children in Michilimackinac county, in the ratio of six to one. So that the educational advantages of the former, compared with the like advantages of the latter, are, in reference to the price of instruction, five-fold, and in regard to the subject of instruction, six-fold.

Your committee have set forth thus at large the reasons of their adverse report, not so much with a view to satisfy the petitioners as to afford the House an opportunity, by endorsing their opinions, of vindicating the sacredness of the trust committed to their keeping, and of cherishing the high purposes for which that trust was created.

In one word, your committee are unanimously of the opinion that the object sought by the prayer of the petitioners is unnecessary, unprecedented and unconstitutional; that there is no wisdom in the change desired, and no power in the Legislature or the people to comply with their wishes; and that, under this state of facts, no legislative action is either necessary or practicable.

The committee on education also reported, that the school law was still liable to many objections, yet they were of opinion that it was preferable to submit to temporary difficulties rather than to legislate anew upon a subject in which *a permanent and settled policy* is as much to be consulted as correctness of principle and propriety of detail; that the only change which appeared to be called for under this view, was in the basis of *classification* when parity of age, and not advancement in knowledge, had been unfortunately adopted. To remedy this evil a bill was reported.

On the 12th of March an act was approved providing for the more faithful collection of fines and penalties, which were appropriated by the constitution to the township libraries. Grand Rapids academy was incorporated. An act was approved March 9th, requiring moneys paid into any township, village or city treasury under the provisions of an act approved Febuary 17, 1842, where there was no township, city or village poor recognized, to be appropriated to the purchase of libraries. By an act approved February 28, the University fund was relieved from the payment of interest on an amount of bonds loaned from the State by the passage of a law authorizing the receipt of obligations of the State in payment of University lands, not to exceed $100,000.

On the 11th of March, another act was passed for the relief of this institution, providing that upon the Regents conveying to the State by deed their interest in the lot of ground and building in Detroit known as the female seminary, the Treasurer of the State should credit the Regents with $8,095, as so much money paid by them on the principal of the University State stock, issued under the act of April 6, 1838. The minimum price of the unsold unimproved University lands was fixed at $12 per acre, and the same description of school lands at $5 per acre. The Utica female seminary was incorporated. During this session an act was passed providing for the revision and consolidation of the laws of the State.

1845.

EXTRACT FROM GOVERNOR BARRY'S MESSAGE.

During the last fiscal year, the amount received into the treasury, to the credit of the common school interest fund, being the revenue of the common school fund for that year, was $20,989 41 and during the same period $28,076 06 were distributed in accordance with existing provisions of law for support of schools.

The revenue of the University fund, the last year, was $9,703 52. In accordance with the provisions of "an act authorizing the receipt of obligations of this State in payment of University lands," approved February 28, 1844, and of "an act for the relief of the University of Michigan," approved March 11, 1844; the indebtedness of the University, on account of the money borrowed for its use, is reduced to $60,787 52. This diminution of its debt, will greatly relieve the institution from its previous embarrassments.

I am not aware that any legislative action is expected or required at the present session, essentially altering the system of education, now existing in the State. If any change be deemed necessary, it is believed that it should be restricted to the management of the funds devoted to that purpose. The strictest accountability should be required of all in any way intrusted with the sale of school and University lands, or with the investment of their proceeds. Losses in some instances have already been sustained, and the utmost caution should be observed to prevent their recurrence.

The number of students in the University is about fifty; and the number in its branches, though varying at different periods of the year, exceeds one hundred and fifty. The number of children in the State, between the ages of four and eighteen years, reported to the Superintendent of Public Instruction, is eighty thousand four hundred and seventy-five; and the number taught in common schools, seventy thousand two hundred and twenty-seven. The low standard of the qualification of teachers in these primary institutions, is found to be one of the greatest impediments to the advancement of education. The interest, however, that seems recently awakened, and the increased attention that is every where paid to the subject will, it is believed, correct this evil.

EXTRACTS FROM REPORT OF THE SUPERINTENDENT.

Authority of law will be required to empower a district to raise by taxation upon its property, an amount of money considerably larger than it is now authorized to raise upon any occasion.

Further--No authority now exists to enable a district to tax itself, for the purpose of raising a sum of money, however small, to purchase some philosophical apparatus, and other appliances in the acquisition of learning. A portion of the tax-payers in some districts have expressed a wish that such authority might be granted.

It is gratifying to know that more general attention is now being paid to popular education and to witness the rapid increase of the number of scholars, taught in the primary schools. It will be seen by adverting to the statistics of the past, and present years, that there were reported last year, sixty-six thousand eight hundred and eighteen scholars, between the ages of 4 and 18 years: and that there were taught of these, in the public schools, fifty-five thousand five hundred and fifty-five. And that, in the present year, there were reported eighty thousand four hundred and seventy-five scholars between the ages of 4 and 18 years; and that of these, seventy thousand two hundred and seventy-seven have been taught in the public schools. Besides, there has been, it is believed, a proportionate increase in the number of pupils instructed in the various grades of private schools.

The undersigned is happy to report, that the township libraries are generally considered eminently important and useful. They are rapidly multiplying. The selection of books has been very judicious. For various valuable matter, adapted to readers of all ages, they may be justly esteemed a rich treasure. They are an ample source of general knowledge, and of rational pleasure and amusement. A fondness for books is a very great blessing. One who enjoys it is rarely inclined to spend his leisure hours in the haunts of idleness and folly—dissipation and gambling, with all their kindred vices. Home, retirement and study, have for him superior interests and attractions. Reading affords him topics of profitable thought and conversation. It exerts a salutary influence on his taste, moral sentiments and manners. It enables many to improve the arts—to enlarge the circle of learning and science. Such are happy and honored while they live—and after they have gone to repose, they shall be long and gratefully remembered as the benefactors of mankind, A studious disposition, like all other propensities, is strengthened by indulgence. A capacity for lofty achievement, in any department of valuable science, is augmented by all wisely directed efforts of the mind in the investigation of truth. This is the food of the soul, and the more it is fed upon, the more its abundance and delicacies are seen and enjoyed.

The condition of the University is sufficiently communicated in the reports of the Regents and visitors of that noble institution. The Faculty continue, of course. to sustain their high reputation for learning, instruction and faithfulness.

The proficiency of the students, with their exemplary deportment, command esteem, and inspire a hope of their future usefulness and honor.

The branches exhibit renewed evidence of their great utility and success. Their able and laborious teachers, have a strong hold on the respect and confidence of their patrons and of society.

Many cogent reasons induce the hope that the branches of the University, as circumstances shall permit, may be multiplied and fostered.

REPORT OF REGENTS.

A brighter day appeared to be dawning in the history of the University. The Regents say:

It affords the Board the greatest pleasure, to express the deep and grateful sense of obligation under which they feel themselves placed by the very efficient and opportune aid extended to them by the last Legislature. For the two previous years, it has been their painful task and duty, to set forth the embarrassments already experienced, and yet further anticipated, in sustaining the University and its branches. Happily, all ground of fear and cause of complaint have been removed by the Legislative enactments, during the last session of the Legislature, which have enabled the Board of Regents to reduce their permanent debt, nearly forty thousand dollars, and their floating incidental debt one-half. Nor, is it the least gratifying circumstance, that the arrangements, by which this has been effected, has operated as propitiously to the interests of the State as to the Board, by putting the former in possession of a valuable lot and building adjacent to the railroad depot—which, while it furnishes convenient offices for the various functionaries of the government, affords peculiar advantages from its location, to citizens from the interior of the State who have business to tranact with them.

The *fears* once entertained have given place to *sanguine hope,* and the Board take special satisfaction, in the assurance, thus given by the Legislature, that they feel a deep interest in the success and prosperity of the University, and are determined to render it, what its ample resources are abundantly capable of making it, an ornament, as well as a blessing, to the State.

The number of students in the University has increased during the past year, so much as to bring into requisition the whole of the dormitories in the large and commodious building erected for their use, which now, is insufficient for the accommodation of all. An extension of these edifices for this purpose, and the erection of a chemical library, will very shortly become necessary.

The entire classes, commonly organized in collegiate institutions, are now formed, and making progress in their studies in the University. During the coming year, the first class will be graduated, which from past examinations, may be confidently anticipated, will prove the first fruits and pledge of yet greater numbers of the youth of our State, to be introduced to the different professions, through the instrumentality of the University.

The services of a gentleman having been secured for a season, without expense to the Board, in the professorship of chemistry, so as to meet the reasonable expectations and demands of the class to be graduated, and leave the professorship open for the appointment of a permanent professor when the funds of the institution will justify it, and the number of the students render it necessary.

The report of the committee of finance, with its appended documents, shows the amount by which the permanent debt has been reduced to be $39,212 48. The disbursements of the Board, during the past year, will be seen in the documents of the finance committee hereto appended, to have been less than the receipts, and to have extinguished about one-half of the incidental debt of last year, thus affording hope, that at the expiration of the present year, the Board will be able to meet all its outstanding liabilities, after paying the current expenses.

The Executive Committee of the board, gives an assurance of the fidelity of the professors and the progress of the students. The Rev. Mr. Thompson had resigned, and was succeeded by Rev. Andrew Ten Brook. The preparatory department was discontinued, and a tutor of languages appointed. Silas H. Douglass was also appointed assistant to the professor of Geology and Mineralogy.

The report of the Faculty announced the aggregate number of students to be fifty-two, and suggested to the Regents that their representatives, in the form of a visiting committee, should attend at all examinations.

The committee reported the number of students in attendance at the branches, to be 133. The Academy at Romeo had been made a branch, and the branch at Monroe had been revived under the direction of Mr. Mayhew, but without the aid of an appropriation.

The Board of Visitors appointed by the Superintendent, consisting of the following gentlemen, Rev. Chauncey W. Fitch, Rev. Andrew Ten Brook, C. N. Ormsby, Esq., and Dr. Samuel Denton, had attended the examinations and expressed their satisfaction at the results they had witnessed. They remark that the State has reason to be more than satisfied with the fidelity with which the professors had attended to the duties of their own appointments, and the general interests of the University.

The public buildings were found in excellent order—especially that which was appropriated to the students. The library was well kept and in good preservation. The cabinet of natural history was likewise in a perfect state. The public grounds were under cultivation, preparatory to further improvements. There was a deficiency in philosophical apparatus, which the visitors recommended should be supplied. They remark further, that the measures adopted by the last Legislature, were designed to benefit the interests of education; that they were wisely planned for the purpose, and secured the objects to the full extent that was sought. They conclude by saying, that "greatly to the relief of the Regents and the joy of those who wish well to the rising generation, the legislation of the last winter, without taxing the State, saved the University *from being closed*—enabled it to go on with fair prospects of ultimate success, and to liquidate, in a few months, $30,000 of its debt. The hope may now be reasonably indulged, that the action of the Legislature, for some time to come will be favorable, and that a few more years of that prudent and liberal spirit, which devised and matured the measures of last winter, will accomplish most of those objects which the founders of the institution contemplated, the best interests of education demand, and the Regents have been laboring to effect."

LIBRARIES.

The committee on education, through Hon. Andrew Harvie, their chairman, reported that they had had under consideration, a petition praying an alteration of the primary school laws, so that the assessment, levy and collection of money for the purchase of books for the township libraries might be optional with the qualified electors. They did not think expedient to grant the prayer of the petitioners, because,

1. The school law of 1843, had, in the opinion of the committee, not been in operation a length of time sufficient to test its merits, and the provisions of the law were believed to be well adapted to the wants of the State.

2. While the township libraries are intended for the use of all the inhabitants of the township, there could be no doubt but that the youth who have not reached the age of qualified electors, would, for the most part, avail themselves of and derive the principal benefit from these libraries, and the exclusion of that portion of the inhabitants from any voice in the establishment of these libraries, seemed unjust.

3. The committee were aware of the general truth, that mental indolence, and a reluctance to the acquisition of knowledge, are inherent vices of the human mind; and therefore they were of opinion that all proper means, consistent with the spirit of our institutions, should be devised and adopted, to stimulate the public mind to rational exertion, and to furnish means for the action of that stimulated mental exertion, and this opinion was the more strengthened by the reflection that as public opinion is the only basis of our government, in proportion as public opinion was informed and enlightened, would the government become more stable and respectable.

4. The amount required for the libraries was utterly insignificant, compared with the vast general benefit which would flow from their establishment.

The question of conferring upon incorporated literary institutions the powers of conferring degrees, was again presented to the consideration of the Legislature, and Mr. Harvie made a report in relation thereto.

The committee on education have had under consideration a petition of the Trustees of the Kalamazoo Literary Institute, praying that their charter may be so amended as to give them the power of conferring the honors and degrees, usually conferred by collegiate institutions, on such students as may have completed the ordinary course of studies in that institution, and have instructed me to report, that, in the opinion of your committee, the usefulness and reputation of a seminary of learning, depend on the excellence of the system of instruction adopted and pursued therein, and not on any power possessed by the managers thereof, of conferring empty degrees and diplomas. If a young man has undergone a mental discipline which has aroused his intellect, fortified his virtue, stored his memory with useful knowledge, and induced habits of application and thought, he will enter the world with a certainty of attaining, in due time, to a respectable position among his fellow men, and this without the aid of a parchment certificate, and an idle "A. B." or "A. M." attached to his name. The institution where such a discipline prevails will not depend for patronage and success on its power of conferring literary degrees and honors, but on the recognized excellence of its system. When the trustees of an institution of learning ask for, and urge the necessity of receiving, the power of conferring degrees, "to enable them to adapt the institution to the present time and circumstances, to carry out its original design, and to promote the interests of education generally," a suspicion is engendered that the trustees are laboring under a slight misapprehension of the true objects and aims of, and the internal economy adapted to, such an institution. Your committee are of opinion that this power should be exercised by those institutions alone, which, by the possession and control of ample means, the employment of distinguished and well known professors, and the enjoyment of a wide spread and deserved reputation, will afford a guarantee against the abuse of the power. Experience teaches us that colleges in some of the States have been so reckless and indiscreet in conferring honors on unworthy subjects, that it is not uncommon to encounter an A. B. or an A. M. incapable of construing and translating his own diploma. Though your committee apprehend no such foolish consequences from granting the prayer of this petition, yet, they think that great caution should be used, lest the standard of education be lowered. Former legislatures have been laudably careful in bestowing this power on chartered schools, and the only two instances in which it has been extended, are so guarded and restricted, that the clause is little better than a dead letter in the acts of incorporation. But your committee doubt the policy of conferring these degrees at all. They are inconsistent with the spirit of our institutions, and a vestige of the aristocratical distinctions of monarchical Europe. The hope of attaining them is a motive addressed not to the reason or generous emulation of youth, but merely to their vanity. Intellect, morality and knowledge, confer a patent in their possessor universally recognized and respected—a patent which schools can neither give nor take away. And it is a remarkable fact in our nation's annals, that while a majority of those great and good men, whose names are identified with the national glory, were ardent and untiring devotees at the shrine of knowledge, still they never attained the distinction of an academical degree.

Mr. Carter, from the committee to whom the subject was referred, reported against a bill to incorporate seminaries of learning, on the ground, mainly, that all *general* incorporation laws were unconstitutional.

During the year, an act was passed incorporating Ann Arbor Female Seminary; the Michigan Central College, at Spring Arbor; the charter of the Wesleyan Seminary amended, and the Ypsilanti Seminary incorporated; a further act for the relief of purchasers of University and school lands. Misses Clarks' school, at Ann Arbor, was incorporated.

An act was passed relative to primary schools, providing for the organization of districts; and that whenever any school district should be so large as to contain more than one hundred scholars, between four and eighteen years of age, the district might raise a sum of money from the taxable property, for leasing and purchasing a site and building a school house, not to exceed in any one year, *four dollars* a scholar. It enacted *that in no case* should the school house be connected with any other building; and further provided that a majority of two-thirds of the voters voting at a school district meeting, called for that purpose, should vote for such tax. It gave power to the inspectors, annually to appoint a librarian; and took the charge of the library from the township clerk, as provided by a prior law.

Ira Mayhew, of Monroe, was nominated and confirmed as Superintendent of Public Instruction.

1846.

EXTRACT FROM GOV. FELCH'S FIRST MESSAGE.

The subject of common schools is universally acknowledged to be one of vital interest in every free government. The liberal reservation by the general government of section sixteen in each of the townships of the State, for that purpose, has enabled us to secure a fund that will do much in support of our common schools, and for the diffusion of knowledge among the youth of the State. The report of the Superintendent of Public Instruction, will give the necessary information on the important subjects coming within his supervision. The whole number of scholars that have attended the common schools during the past year, is 75,770. Of these, 69,253 are between the ages of four and eighteen years, 2,289 under four years, and 4,228 over eighteen years. There are also in the State 20,752 persons between the ages of four and eighteen years, who have not attended the common schools; the whole number of children between four and eighteen, being 90,006. The amount of school interest money distributed in the last year, for the support of the schools, was $22,113.

A provision having been made by Congress, May 20, 1826, by which the State was authorized, when the school section in a township was fractional merely, or entirely wanting, to select other lands to supply the deficiency, the State geologist was, by act of March 1, 1845, anthorized and required to ascertain the quantity thus deficient, and to report the same to the Legislature, at the present session. This duty has been performed under the direction of the State Geologist, and the result will be reported to you by the Topographer, to whose charge, since the death of the Geologist, the documents relating to the same were committed. These returns contain maps, and complete descriptions of all the fractional sections of common school lands in the lower peninsula, and of lands which have been located to supply such deficiency. The quantity of land to which the State is entitled, for such deficiency in the lower peninsula, is 20,729.68 acres. This, added to the quantity of entire sections in the several townships, and also of the fractional sections, gives for the whole amount of school lands in the lower peninsula, 759,518.69 acres. The quantity of school lands in the upper peninsula is estimated at 380,481.31 acres. The whole number of acres of school lands in the State, is 1,140,000. The minimum value of these lands, as fixed by law, would be $5,700,000, yielding an annual interest, at seven per cent., of $399,000. A sale of all these lands, at the present minimum price of five dollars per acre, is certainly not at present anticipated, and may not take place for many years; yet the statement exhibits a noble fund, from which the amount actually realized is now very considerable, and must continue greatly to increase.

A wise provision of the school law, in connection with a requirement of the constitution, designed to promote the same object, has laid the foundation for valuable township and district school libraries, and during the past year many such libraries have been established. A more effectual method of fostering a taste for reading, and a thirst for knowledge, and of diffusing intelligence and enlarged views of morals and patriotism, could scarcely be devised. Their influence is at the fire-side, and in silence, yet it is an influence that will do much to elevate the people of Michigan.

Our State University, although it has been in actual operation less than five years, has already given promise of great usefulness, and assumed a rank as a literary institution, of which Michigan may well be proud. There are now connected with the University, seventy students. The ability of its professors, the extensive library and cabinets, and the liberal principles upon which it is conducted, are constantly attracting students to its halls. The fact that no tuition fee is charged to any resident of the State opens its door to all, and makes knowledge literally free.

The University fund, at an early day of its existence, became indebted to the State for loan of $100,000, and the interest of this debt has been liquidated from the interest received annually on the fund. The acts of the Legislature, approved February 28, 1844, and March 11, 1844, authorized the State Treasurer to receive certain property and State warrants belonging to the University fund, and to credit the same on this loan, and also authorized the sale of University lands for internal improvement warrants, which were to be paid into the State treasury, and credited in like manner. The effect of these provisions have been materially to aid in relieving the fund from its embarrassments. The amount received by the State, under these provisions, and credited to the University fund, is $56,774 14, leaving due to the State from that fund, for principle, $43,225 86. The amount received on this fund during the past fiscal year, for interest on account of lands sold, and on loans, was $9,724 74. Deducting from this sum the interest due the State on the loan before mentioned, above the interest allowed on warrants paid in, the available income for the past year is found to be $6,138 39, while in 1843, it was but little over $1,100. The embarrassment of the fund has occasioned a withdrawal of pecuniary aid from most of the branches of the University. Six of these branches have been continued in operation, three of which are supported entirely by the avails of private tuition; to each of the others, the sum of $200 has been allowed during the year. The number of students in these branches, and in the preparatory department of the University, is 396. It is to be hoped that returning prosperity may again enable the Regents to afford them such aid as necessity and good policy shall demand.

REPORT OF SUPERINTENDENT.

The Superintendent embraces in his report the following subjects: the duty of States in relation to education; the condition of the public schools, visitation of schools, libraries, school houses, the condition of the University and its branches; the system of public schools, proposed modifications of the school law, teachers' associations, female influence, and other subjects of interest and practical importance.

His appreciation of the important duty devolved upon the State, in the work of education, is manifested in the following extract from his report:

The education of children in a manner suitable to their station and calling is generally conceived a branch of parental duty of very great importance to the welfare of the State. *Education,* (as here used,) *implies every preparation that is made in youth for after life.* This parental duty is strongly and persuasively inculcated by writers on national law. Says Kent, "a parent who sends his son into the world uneducated, and without skill in any art or science, does a great injury to mankind, as well as to his own family, for he defrauds the community of a useful citizen, and bequeaths to it a nuisance." Paley says, "to send an uneducated child into the world, is a public injury, and little better than to turn a mad dog or a wild beast into the streets." Solon, the great Athenian lawgiver, was so deeply impressed with this obligation, that he even excused the children of Athens from maintaining their parents if they had neglected to train them to some art or profession.

Enlightened and liberal minded individuals of every age and nation have regarded it the duty of State to provide for the education of the children of the poor. Distinguished exertions have been made in several parts of modern Europe, for the introduction of elementary instruction accessible to the young of all classes. This has been the case particularly in Denmark, Prussia, and some parts of Germany and Switzerland. In this branch of political economy, Scotland attained to early and very honorable pre-eminence. More than two centuries ago, the Scottish parliament adopted measures for settling and supporting a common school in each parish at the expense of the landed proprietors. And what has been the result? The Scotch are, as a nation, better instructed, and more moral and religious in their habits, than any other people in Europe. * * * * * *

Great pains have been taken, and munificent provision has been made, in this country, to diffuse the means of knowledge, and to render elementary instruction accessible to all. The first legal provision for sustaining free public schools was in 1647, and Massachusetts has the honor of taking the lead in this country, in this great and wise policy. In the colonies of New Haven and Connecticut, early provision was made for the establishment and maintainance of common schools, which were placed upon a permanent foundation a century before the Revolution. The State of Connecticut has, by its constitution, declared the school fund to be perpetual and inviolate. Ordinary education is so far enforced, (and indeed was long prior to the Revolution,) that if parents will not teach their children the elements of knowledge, by causing them to read the English tongue well, and to know the laws against capital offences, the select men of the town are enjoined to take their children from such parents, and bind them out to proper masters, where they will be educated to some useful employment, and be taught to read and write, and the rules of arithmetic necessary to transact ordinary business. This regulation, said the late chief justice Reeve, has produced very astonishing effects, and to it is to be attributed the knowledge of reading and writing so universal among the people of that State. During the twenty-seven years in which that distinguished lawyer was in extensive practice, he informs us he never found but one person in Connecticut who could not read and write.

The total number of scholars that had attended common schools during the year was 75,770. The number that had not attended school, 20,753. The Superintendent says:

There is one entire county from which no returns have been received. There are, also, in the twenty-nine counties from which reports have been received, eighteen entire towns that have made no report. There are, in addition to these, in the three hundred and ninety.nine towns from which reports have been received, 588 districts from which reports have not been received. This is, indeed, alarming. But what adds to the darkness of the picture, there are in the 2,095 districts from which reports have been received, 4,578 children between the ages of four and eighteen years, who have not attended *any school* during the year, and who cannot read, write and cipher. This is by no means a favorable omen: But are there no schools in those townships and districts from which no reports have been received? In many cases there are. They are not, however, *common schools*. They are not entitled to participate in the avails of the school fund. They are private schools, or what are ordinarily denominated *select schools*.

The average length of time scholars between the ages of four and eighteen years have attended school, was a fraction less than four months. The average wages per month paid male teachers in the State, $11 98. The average monthly wages paid female teachers, exclusive of board, $5 24. The Superintendent remarks:

For such compensation it is not reasonable to expect that a high degree of literary attainment, coupled with professional skill, would be called into service. The wages and qualifications of teachers must be proportional. The payment of high salaries to inferior teachers will not insure good schools. The tendency, however, of paying higher wages will be to direct the attention of a greater number of persons to the profession of teaching. A competition will thus be created, and soon higher literary attainments and greater professional skill will be brought into the service.

Neither will the payment of moderate or low salaries to good teachers necessarily produce poor schools. It will not, however, long secure the services of good teachers. As is the demand, so will be the supply. If a reasonable compensation is offered for the services of good teachers, young ladies and gentlemen of the first order of talent will attain the requisite qualifications, and cheerfully tax their best capabilities in the interesting though arduous duties of this profession. He who can teach a good school can engage with proportionate success in other pursuits. If he is not reasonably compensated for teaching, he will seek a more lucrative employment. It is the opinion of some that a second or third order of intellect is all that is desirable to constitute a successful common school teacher. This is evidently erroneous. It may be all that the present compensation will long retain in the service. But it is not all that its importance claims. As is the teacher, so will be the school. And as are our common schools, so will be our future legislators and statesmen.

The total amount of school money received in the several districts,

as reported, was	$23,293 33
Amount raised by tax,	59,931 62
" received from local funds,	1,649 58
" paid unqualified teachers,	5,880 75
Total,	$90,775 28

The total amount for building and repairing school houses, and for the payment of teachers qualified and unqualified, embracing the public money, was only one dollar a scholar for each child between the ages of four and eighteen years. Four thousand four hundred and ninety-two children had been taught in select schools, at an average of $2 64 per quarter, and 3,013 of these were between the ages of four and eighteen. The Superintendent says:

A simple arithmetical calculation, based upon these data, shows that the expense of teaching a given number of scholars in select schools, is more than three times as much as common schools, embracing the amount paid for building and repairing school houses.

In relation to visitation, the report shows that the inspectors had paid 1,956 visits to the schools, deducting 274 for the city of Detroit. On this subject the Superintendent says:

The several district boards have visited their schools a less number of times than the inspectors; the entire number of visits being less than half the number of schools. Parents are the natural guardians and teachers of their children. The work of education cannot safely be conducted exclusively by delegation. Indeed, were it *safe*, it would seem as though parents who are properly interested in the education of their offspring would esteem it a *privilege* to visit their schools at least once a month. But the district officers have not, on an average, visited them once in eighteen months! Frequent visits to the school by inspectors and parents, encourage both teacher and scholars. The teacher will pursue his labor of love with a lighter heart, and with increased devotion, feeling that he has the countenance and co-operation of the parents of his charge. Children, too, will be inspired to redouble their diligence in climbing the rugged hill of science.

A useful purpose was accomplished by the Superintendent, in directing his efforts to apply to the purposes to which they had been devoted by the constitution and laws, the moneys arising from *fines, penalties and forfeitures.*

He addressed a letter of inquiry to the Attorney General, who replied that the board of supervisors had no power to remit fines imposed by courts of law, and that all money collected or received by the county treasurers, on fines, penalties, or forfeiture of recognizances, must be paid to the school inspectors, and by them invested in a township library, and also that a neglect of the supervisor to assess the half mill tax, rendered him liable for neglect of official duty.

The amount of money apportioned for this year, was $22,113 00.

Under the head of "examination of our system of public schools," the Superintendent says:

Our system of education possesses many admirable features. Any child residing within an organized district is entitled to attend the common school, whether his parents are able to pay his tuition or not. The law also provides for supplying the children of indigent parents with such books as they may need.

Our system of township libraries is an admirable one, and is particularly adapted to the wants of townships with a sparse population.

It is superior to the district system, inasmuch as it enables the township to purchase a greater number of more valuable books, to which, also, each individual of the township is enabled in due time to have access. The principal impediment to the usefulness of these libraries lies in the circumstance that directors are frequently remiss in the discharge of their duties. For the manner in which it is thought this impediment may be removed, see the sequel of this report.

The total number of volumes in all of the township and school district libraries of the State does not yet equal one-third of the number of children between the ages of four and eighteen years.

Statutory provision is also made for the establishment of union schools in cities, villages and densely settled townships. In this manner the advantages of the common school, and the highest order of select schools may be happily combined, without any of the mischievous consequences resulting from an inviduous distinction. It is hoped that villages generally in which there are two or three districts, will avail themselves of the provision of the 37th section of the school law.

Our University system, with branches in different parts of the State, is justly entitled to the commendation which it has so generally received wherever it is known.

Our common schools, the branches of the University, and the parent institution, are intimately connected. If properly conducted, the success of each will exert a healthful influence upon both of the others. Each should hold its own appropriate place in our system of public instruction, and neither should attempt to do the legitimate work of another. Our system will thus be prosperous and efficient. Otherwise, it will suffer in all its departments. For example, if a branch attempts to do the appropriate work of the common school, and opens wide its doors for the reception of scholars in the common English branches, the common schools in the vicinity will manifestly be weakened, and sustain sensible loss. The branch itself will be injured *as such,* and become a semi-common school. It will hence prepare a less number of students for the University than it would otherwise be likely to do. There seems to be a deficiency in the supervision exercised over our schools—particularly our common schools. Our district officers have each their particular work assigned them. The duties of the moderator are not arduous. His office is rather an honorary one than otherwise. The assessor is required to collect rate-bills for teachers' wages, for which he is allowed his regular per centage. The director is charged with more important and responsible duties than either of the other members of the district board. It is his duty to keep a record of the proceedings of the district, with the consent of the moderator or assessor to employ a teacher, to call district meetings under certain circumstances, to take the census, to furnish the teacher with a copy of the same, to make out a rate bill, and annex thereto a warrant for its collection, to provide the necessary appendages for the school house, to give notice of the annual meeting, to draw books from the township library, and act as district librarian, to make an annual report, &c., for all of which he is allowed nothing. This seems, in many instances, to operate injuriously upon the schools, particularly when we take into account the fact that the man who is best qualified to officiate as director, has frequently no personal interest in the school. This service is too arduous to be well performed gratuitously. There are other duties also, that the director should perform, which will be considered in part four of this report.

It is believed our system of school inspectors might be rendered more efficient, and at the same time less expensive. At present, a meeting of the board is necessary to examine teachers, and indeed, to transact any business. It takes time to assemble the board, and is also attended with expense. When met for the examination of teachers, generally the person who is regarded as the literary member of the board, conducts the examination chiefly. The certificate is made out and signed by all the members of the board. If their action proves to be unwise, each member being a minority, the responsibility is thrown upon the other two. Thus, one man labors, three men are paid for it, and nobody is responsible for what they do.

It is respectfully suggested that it would be better to elect one inspector in each town, pay him for what he does, and hold him responsible for it. As the board is now constituted, the Legislature have regarded it necessary to limit the number of meetings in a year at the expense of the township. This limitation is thought by many to operate injuriously to the interests of schools.

Complaint is made of the general incorrectness of the reports of the county clerks. Less time also remained in which to make out the annual report of the Superintendent, than the law allowed for county clerks to make out their reports, while the labor of making it, was, in the opinion of that officer, not less than thirty times as much as that of the clerks.

The Superintendent proposed various modifications of the school law; the two leading features of which were to incorporate into the law the establishment of common schools, *to which every child of the State* should have access—and to secure a more efficient supervision of the schools. He estimated that there were in the State, at a moderate calculation, 15,000 children between the ages of four and eighteen years, whose parents did not reside in any organized districts, and who were cut off from access to the primary schools, and suggested, among others, the following provisions of law:

In case any district neglects to organize, or if organized, neglects or refuses to open a school, according to the provisions of law, until the 10th day of May, in any school year, it shall be the duty of the inspector to open a school in said district, for three months at least, and longer at his discretion; to rent or provide a room, in case the district has not a school house; to take the census, and discharge all the duties required by law of the district board, and apply the public money to which the district is entitled, towards defraying the expense of the school. The residue of the expense, which shall not exceed fifty dollars, any one year, together with the salary of the inspector, while engaged in the discharge of the legitimate duties of the district board, shall be assessed by the supervisor upon the taxable property of the district, to be collected in the same manner, and for the same compensation as other taxes, and to be drawn on the order of the instructor; *Provided*, That no school district shall contain less than fifteen children within the legal ages, unless the territory of the district shall embrace nine sections, or its equivalent; *And provided also*, That no district shall contain less than twenty-five children within the legal ages, unless the territory of the district shall embrace four sections, or its equivalent.

At the next annual township meeting, and annually thereafter, one school inspector shall be elected in each township of the State, who shall discharge all the duties hitherto devolving upon the board of school inspectors.

The school inspectors of every county shall meet at the office of the county clerk the third Monday in April, and elect, by ballot, one of their number as president of the board. They shall also elect a vice president and corresponding secretary. The county clerk shall be *ex-officio* recording secretary of the county board of school inspectors. * * * * *

Directors shall be allowed a day for their services. Their account shall be audited at the annual district meeting, and paid on the presentation of a certificate from the school inspector signifying that they have discharged their duty and made their report according to law.

Inspectors shall be entitled to a compensation of a day, for their services. Their account shall be audited by the township board, and paid on the presentation of a certificate from the Superintendent of Public Instruction, signifying that they have discharged their duty, and made their report according to law. * * * *

The provision of the 78th section of the school law operates injuriously upon the interests of weak districts in many instances; and the propriety of its repeal is respectfully suggested. The statutes define the word "month" to mean a calendar month, which, exclusive of Sundays, is twenty-six days, or four and one-third weeks. In many parts of the State, four weeks are, by common consent, considered a school month. I would suggest the propriety of defining a school month to signify four weeks, and allow the teacher to dismiss school Saturday afternoon, without losing time. This would be merely lending the sanctions of law to a time honored usage. A quarter, or three months, in a common school, would still be one week more than according to common usage it now is in our higher institutions of learning.

The following suggestion was made to the Superintendent by a board of school inspectors, relating to LIBRARIES in fractional dis- districts:

"The law appears to be deficient in regard to fractional districts, there being no way for such districts to obtain their books. It should be the duty of the inspectors to attach fractional districts to whole districts, when necessary, for library purposes." I think the change suggested would render the 31st section of the school law more simple and equitable. One part of a fractional district is frequently situated in a township possessing a library, while the other part is in a township possessing no library. Each part of fractional districts might be attached to an adjacent whole district, in the same town, for library purposes; and the director of the whole district might be authorized to draw from the township library the equitable proportion of books for his own district, and the fraction attached thereto. In case of joint districts, teachers are sometimes rejected by the inspectors of one town in which a district is in part situated, and subsequently certified by the inspectors of the town in which the other part of the district lies. To obviate this difficulty, the teacher should receive his certificate from the inspectors of the township to which the director is required by law to make his annual report.

The following means of increasing the usefulness of the public schools were suggested as among the most important, viz: TEACHERS' ASSOCIATIONS—TEACHERS' INSTITUTES—an educational journal, and female influence—and the organization of a college of teachers. NORMAL schools were considered indispensable to the perfection of the system.

"TEACHERS' INSTITUTES," says Mr. MAYHEW, "are teachers' associations with protracted sessions. Where teachers' institutes have been established, the teachers of a county usually spend almost two weeks in session, fall and spring, with a competent principal and experienced board of instruction, employed by a committee provided for that purpose. The several branches of study ordinarily pursued in our common schools are reviewed; the different methods of instruction and modes of government are discussed, and plans are laid for concert of action. Lectures are generally delivered before these institutes by professional gentlemen and others, who, from their devotion to the great work of popular education, might appropriately be denominated common school missionaries.

Teachers' institutes are of recent origin. They were first established in New York, in 1843. * * * * * Would it not be well to encourage their establishment by legislation? I entertain the opinion, that if the State has $25,000 to appropriate annually to the promotion of common school education, it would be productive of a greater good to apply one or two thousand dollars, or even five thousand dollars, to assist in defraying the necessary expense of maintaining teachers' institutes in the different counties, and the residue to the support of schools, than to apply the whole to the payment of unqualified teachers, or even to those of ordinary attainments."

From the suggestions made by school inspectors, the propriety of placing a copy of the annual reports of the Superintendent into the hands of school inspectors and school directors, was submitted.

REPORT OF THE REGENTS.

The Board congratulated themselves and the friends of literature and science in our State, in view of the continued and increased prosperity of the University, whose interests have been by law confided to their management. They pay the following marked but merited tribute to the memory of Prof. Whiting, whose death had but recently occurred:

In the death of Professor Whiting, the University has sustained a severe loss. He had been with us from the beginning, had been thoroughly acquainted with the history, cares, interests and condition of the University; participated with earnest and zealous effort in the Board's desire to promote the usefulness of the institution; and was particularly qualified for his station, not only by his classical attainments and aptness to teach, but by his urbanity and gentleness of manners, by his knowledge of character and other properties which especially fitted him to act the part of a governor and counsellor of youth.

A fourth professor had been appointed, viz: the Rev. D. D. Whedon, who had accepted the appointment, and was discharging the duties of professor of logic, rhetoric and the philosophy of history. The annual meetings of the Regents was fixed in August: and the report of this year was brought down only to that period, instead of December. The amount of warrants drawn for the past year was reported at $10,162 33, leaving a balance in the treasury of over $1,000.

The board of visitors consisted of the following gentlemen, viz: Henry Smith, Andrew Harvie, John R. Finley, George W. Wisner, and F. J. Littlejohn. They say:

In general the affairs of the institution appear to be well managed, and their immediate guidance in competent, safe and skillful hands. So far as could be judged, the instruction in the various branches is thorough and efficient. The board were highly pleased with the portion of the examinations witnessed, and consider them very creditable to the students themselves, as well as to their instructors. In the conduct of the studies of the senior year, especially, the plan of instruction and examination to a considerable extent by means of essays written by members of the class, has been very successfully adopted, and is worthy of strong commendation.

It is a subject of great satisfaction to be able to say that the University is generally and manifestly in a flourishing condition, the number of students annually increasing, and every department bearing evidence of competency, efficiency and fidelity in its management; yet, the board of visitors cannot close their report without once more calling the attention of the proper authorities to a portion of the very able report of the visitors in the year 1842, as contained in the "joint documents" of the legislature for 1843, page 377, and following. The want of additional buildings for the University is much more strongly felt at this time than in 1842. It is only by great exertion, and by crowding the rooms to excess, that the faculty have been able to provide for the present number of students (about seventy) during the last term, and in the very probable, nay almost certain event of the increase of this number, at the beginning of the coming year, it will be necessary to refuse admittance (at least as residents of the college buildings) to new comers, an event greatly to be deprecated by all well-wishers to the institution.

Another very serious evil resulting from the want of a proper edifice is the great danger of loss or irremediable injury to the very valuable specimens of zoology and botany of Michigan, collected and prepared at very great expense to the State, by the late and lamented State Geologist, Dr. Houghton. There being no room in which to place these valuable preparations in natural history, they remain in a state liable to destruction by vermin, and in which, even natural decay can hardly be averted. It is believed that more than 4,000 zoological specimens, and many thousand specimens of plants remain in this condition, the value of which may very fairly be set down as greater than the probable cost of *a chapel*, which should not only contain the rooms requisite for the reception, safe keeping and exhibition of this collection, and the library and cabinets belonging to the institution, but also contain the necessary recitation and lecture rooms for the University, thus restoring nearly one-half of the present building to the use for which it was intended, namely, dormitories; and rendering it capable of accommodating nearly double the present number of students. A chemical laboratory building, detached from any other, should also be erected; its cost would be very small. The soundest economy would be consulted in the immediate erection of these buildings.

An increase to a moderate extent, of the philosophical and astronomical apparatus is greatly required; of the latter, particularly, there is hardly enough to deserve the name.

The professor of languages recently appointed, had not arrived, and his duties were of necessity discharged, and his place, so far as possible, supplied by the other professors, whose duties, from the smallness of the number of the faculty of the institution, were already onerous and severe. If the resources of the University will justify an addition to the number of professorships, such increase is respectfully suggested—particularly in reference to greater attention to RHETORIC and ORATORY, to MODERN LANGUAGES, and to BELLES LETTRES—branches of education more necessary, perhaps, in this country than in any other country in the world.

The system established in almost every collegiate institution in the United States, of graduating the merit of the senior class, and awarding collegiate honors at commencement, seems to have been abolished in the University of Michigan. The board of visitors cannot close this report, without respectfully suggesting a doubt, as to the good results from abandoning the well tried and time honored mode of exciting emulation amongst the students in an institution like ours. Perhaps the present system has not had a fair trial, but one class having as yet taken their diplomas, without a special graduation; yet it is believed that in the end it will be found wise to restore the old order of things in this respect.

For the purpose of a reference to those who may wish to enquire into the location of the school sections and the subject generally, it may be stated that in the joint documents for this year (1846) a report will be found which comprises the following statements:

The registers of all school lands in Michigan.

The maps of fractional sections.

A tabular statement of the townships, with reference to section sixteen.

A tabular statement of all the available school lands of the lower peninsula.

A condensed and tabular statement of the quantity of land the State is entitled to, in lieu of fractional section sixteen, and for townships deficient.

A statement of the same in detail, and also letters of the Commissioner of the General Land Office, &c., &c.

From this document the following is extracted as containing the result of the labors of the State Geologist and his corps, and their general conclusions:

It will be seen that the whole amount of school lands of the lower peninsula, is *seven hundred and fifty-nine thousand five hundred and eighteen acres, and* 69-100*ths*, and when those of the upper peninsula, which are estimated at fully one half as much, or about *three hundred and eighty thousand, four hundred and eighty-one acres, and* 31-100*ths*, are added, we have for the total school lands of the State, *one million, one hundred and forty thousand acres,* (1,140,000,) which, at the minimum price, as fixed by law, of five dollars per acre, would produce the sum of *five millions and seven hundred thousand dollars,* and that again at the legal interest of *seven per cent.* would yield an *annual income of three hundred and ninety-nine thousand dollars.* Although these lands may not all bring the fixed price of five dollars per acre, yet as nearly all of them are of the first quality for agricultural purposes, or valuable for their timber or mineral resources, their product may be anticipated to approximate very nearly to the sum named, and it must afford high satisfaction to the hardy pioneers who first reared their cabins amidst the uncultivated wilds of the "beautiful Peninsula," and endured all the hardships and privations incident to new settlements, to see their children thus amply provided for in that great essential under a free government—*education;* and the enterprising emigrant from the eastern States, accustomed to look upon the advantages of school house and academy as more than counterbalancing the disadvantages of a stubborn soil and rigorous climate, may turn with confidence to Michigan, satisfied that from her prolific and easily tilled soil, he will receive an abundant return for his labor—that in her richly endowed schools and University, means of education are provided for all.

A resolution of the Senate was passed relative to the geological, mineralogical, zoological and botanical department of the University, in reply to which, Major Kearsley reported that the Regents had not had in their charge and custody, any of the specimens collected for the State, except one full suit in geology and mineralogy—that the mass of these collections had been under the control of the State Geologist;—that in the department of geology every specimen had been enclosed in paper, and labelled, and the hope was expressed, that the representatives of a people determined to perpetuate the blessings of enlightened freedom, would not suffer these depositories of knowledge, valuable in every pursuit and condition of life, to be lost through the ravage of time, or their developments postponed until too late for the instruction and self-interest of those who must soon take their places upon the theatre of self-government.

In reply to a resolution of the Senate, the same gentleman, in behalf of the Regents, made the following statement in relation to the views of the Regents, as to whether the interests of the University would be promoted by a reduction of the price of the lands:

The undersigned, to whom the resolution was transmitted, as chairman of the executive committee of the Board of Regents, having consulted with two others, members of that committee, who alone reside at Detroit, and whose views he could at this time obtain, submits the following facts and results, from the past history relative to the legislation upon the subject of University lands:

The act of congress, approved May 20th, 1826, provides that the secretary of the treasury be authorized to set apart and reserve from sale a quantity of land not exceeding two entire townships, (46,080 acres) for the use and support of an University within the then territory of Michigan, *and for no other use or purpose whatever.* This may be termed the fundamental law upon which the present University is based.

In pursuance to this act of Congress, the secretary of the treasury addressed a letter to General CASS, then Governor of the territory of Michigan, requesting him to designate the selections. Governor Cass convened a meeting of the trustees of the then existing University of Michigan, and submitting to them the letter of the secretary, requested that said trustees would adopt measures for making said selections. A committee was accordingly appointed, to whom this matter was confided. That committee employed a suitable person, who selected and reported a large portion of said two townships. This committee subsequently transmitted to Governor Cass, then temporarily at Washington, a list of these selections, which it is believed were confirmed by the secretary.

Congress so far recognized the control of the trustees of the former University of Michigan over part of these lands as to pass an act, approved March 3, 1835, authorizing a committee of that board to offer at public auction, and to sell certain selections previously made. The trustees declining to sell or carry out the provisions of that act, congress, through the importunity of a certain Ohio land company, who held lands in the vicinity, was induced to repeal this act, to give authority, or rather require said trustees to sell these same lands to William Oliver, agent of said Ohio company, under the allegation that the trustees had made contract with said Oliver for such sale; this act was approved March 22, 1836. A conveyance was executed in compliance with this act, and thus the University fund was divested of that portion of land selected, embracing the mouth of Swan Creek, upon which Toledo, now in Ohio, is built, and where, it is understood, the canal terminates. For this land the trustees received about a section of land in that vicinity, and $5,000 in cash. These lands were not disposed of by the trustees and formed part of the fund of the present University, and the $5,000, with the interest thereon, were transferred by a committee of the board of trustees to the treasurer of the present Board of Regents. The next legislation, it is believed, was the act of Congress, approved June 23, 1836, being supplementary to an act for the admission of Michigan, upon certain conditions, the second proposition whereof is as follows: That the seventy-two sections of land set apart and reserved for the use and support of a University, &c., are hereby granted and conveyed to the State, to be appropriated solely to the use and support of such University in such manner as the Legislature may prescribe: And provided also, that nothing herein contained shall be so construed as to impair or effect in any way the rights of any person or persons claiming any of said seventy-two sections of land, under contract or grant from said University. It may here be proper to remark, that the *constitution* of the State of Michigan had been previously submitted to Congress for their action, (see article X, section 5.) This act provides—the Legislature shall take measures for the protection, improvement, or other disposition of such lands as have been, or may hereafter be reserved or granted by the United States to this State, for the support of a University; and the funds accruing from the rents or sale of such lands, or from any other source for the purpose aforesaid, shall be and remain a permanent fund for the support of said University, with such *branches* as the public convenience may hereafter demand for the promotion of literature, the arts and sciences, as may be authorized by the terms of such grant. And it shall be the duty of the Legislature, as soon as may be, to provide effectual means for the improvement and permanent security of the funds of said University. How far the terms of the constitution relative to *branches* conflict with the provisions of the subsequent act of Congress, limiting the grant "solely to the use and support of a University," is left for others to discuss, deliberate and determine. * * *

By reference to the annual reports of the Superintendent of Public Instruction, embracing the report of the Board of Regents to him, much important information may be obtained, as well as admonition gleaned from past legislation.

The Superintendent, under date of Dec. 27th, 1837, (see House Document No. 5, dated January 9th, 1838,) shows that the *interest* which fell due and was payable in July and August, 1838, amounted to the sum of $10,881 32; the Legislature, however, of 1838, relieved the debtors of this interest fund, and notwithstanding the large amount of sales since that period, there has never been paid as large a sum for interest in any one year since.

It may be said that interest would not have been paid; but the only answer that can be given to this, is, that the Legislature did not allow time to prove the positive of this negation. Six thousand five hundred and eighty-three acres of University land were sold prior to 27th December, 1837, at an average price of $22 85½ per acre. In the year ending December 31st, 1838, 527.72 acres were sold at an average price of $20 29 per acre, showing manifestly that the Legislature of 1838, releasing lands upon which there were settlers and improvements, on favorable conditions, held out the expectation and cherished the hope of others that some more favorable terms would be thereafter provided for them. In both the years 1837 and 1838, it will be observed, that, notwithstanding the minimum price, $20 per acre, subsequently deemed so extravagantly high, all the University land offered at auction, brought an average above that minimum. Notwithstanding the diminished sales for 1838, we find by the report of the Superintendent of Public Instruction that interest amounting to $9,171 42, had been actually paid by purchasers, and the further sum of $2,000 or $3,000 more, was by him expected to be paid as interest for that year.

1839. By the report of the Superintendent for this year, it appears that, although the total amount, being ten per cent. instalments, paid as *principal*, was only $1,607 90, yet the interest paid that year was $6,402 91.

1840. During this year the Superintendent reports only 43.70 acres sold, and $763 61 as interest. To account for this extraordinary diminution as well in sales as in receipt of interest due, it may be well to observe the effect of the acts of March 25th and March 30th, 1840. From the provisions of these acts, purchasers were induced to defer further payment, under the expectation that their interested petitions and applications for relief would be granted; nor were they disappointed in their calculations, as appears by the enactment of 1841, by which University lands were reduced to $15 per acre, and interest reduced in like proportion.

To advert to the several and various provisions of the continued annual legislation on this subject from 1837 to 1844 inclusive, would swell this communication, and render it alike tedious to the writer and the Senate. It may, therefore, suffice to remark, that the continued legislation has most naturally induced and encouraged continued application on the part of individuals interested for relief. In the opinion of the undersigned, this legislation has been not only inexpedient but *unjust*. Inexpedient, because thereby purchasers have been induced to postpone payment agreeably to their contracts with the State, and thus introducing by the example a like disregard to punctuality in the observance of contracts between individuals. Unjust, because the Board of Regents make contracts with professors and principals of branches, relying upon existing provisions of law to furnish the means for fulfilling on their part.

But another act is passed—a new provision introduced—perhaps the payment of interest deferred—and thus, the professor with his family, is turned out, if not to starve, certainly with sufficient cause to complain of gross injustice somewhere. Men qualified for the chair of a professor in the University, who have devoted as well the elastic energies of youth, as the matured development of the judgment and understanding, in the pursuit of science and intellectual attainment, are rarely equal to a successful combat with the vicissitudes of a mercurial life. Possessing the "ingenii benigna vena," they are content with a comparatively small pecuniary reward, even a bare sufficiency to meet the frugal and necessary demands of life. Justice demands that this should be certain, and specially does she expect at the hands of the representatives of honorable and enlightened freemen that this just compensation should not be dependent upon a contingency so vacillating and temporary as annual enactments.

Sed nos immensum spatits confecimus æquor,
Et jam tempus equum fumantia solvere colla.

Yet the undersigned cannot close without remarking, that owing to the Legislative enactment prior to 1844, the Board of Regents, in the early part of that year, were so far as within their means or power of redress, inextricably involved in financial embarrassment. Recourse was had to the only source competent to relieve, the Legislature—representatives worthy of their free and intelligent constituents. That Legislature more than responded to the call of the Regents, in the act for the relief of the University of Michigan, approved March 11th, 1844. This act, while it enabled the Regents to meet their contracts with professors and others, and thus saved the professors from great difficulty, and the Regents from bankruptcy, avoided the train of evils consequent upon the great precedent, the general bankrupt law of Congress. A repetition of either law would be calamitous and uncalled for. The act of February 28th, 1844, provides for the receipt of State Treasury notes and warrants bearing interest in payment of principal on purchases of University lands, and had the two-fold beneficial effect upon the purchaser and the University—of enabling the former to pay, if he so elected, the entire debt due by him, and secured to the latter the payment of the interest thereon. The same act had the further indirect effect to lessen the price of University lands, and yet not detract from the amount of the interest fund. Upon careful enquiry, it may be assumed, beyond contradiction, that the *cash* price of University lands during the year 1845, did not exceed 5-8 of $12—that is $7 50 per acre.

A review of past legislation and its effects, must convince that legislation, whether for bank charters or for other individual and sinister objects, does not promote the general public welfare. Every act relating to a trust so highly beneficial and so sacred as the cause of education, it is hoped will be approached with the greatest circumspection, and will be consummated only after the assiduous deliberation recommended in the accomplishment of another object—

Vos exemplaria—
Nocturna versate manu, versate diurna.

From the best sources of information, of gentlemen whose judgment may be confided in, it is estimated, that internal improvement warrants, bearing interest, will probably, for the current year, not command beyond seventy-five cents in cash, for the dollar; it follows that University lands may be purchased, in cash, for nine dollars per acre. The experience of the past sufficiently demonstrates that reduction in the price of University lands, where these lands are designed only for agricultural purposes, cannot greatly increase the sales, unless indeed the reduction should be such as to bring these lands into competition with those of the United States or of the non-resident land holder. But such a policy, all will agree, would be suicidal, alike to the University and to every benefit anticipated from its present fund. If the Regents of the University be permitted to rely upon the resources now provided by law, and those provisions be complied with by purchasers, which it is confidently thought they will do, if no hope is extended to them of future enactments for their special and individual benefit, the Regents, having, as is hoped, profited by their past errors, will take care to limit their appropriations to their receipts, and thus the necessity of a sale of University lands, beyond the exigencies of ordinary increase of population in this State, and for the purpose of revenue only be obviated. Thus, this munificent fund, while it shall furnish the means for educating the youth of our State, who, at present, may appreciate its benefits and desire to participate them, may be handed over unimpaired to endless generations of the sons of Michigan.

Believing that the Board of Regents, if convened, would accord in sentiment with the foregoing, howmuchsoever they might have regretted that it could not have been placed in abler hands for digestion and arrangement; the undersigned, with those whom he has opportunity to consult, is of the opinion that the reduction of the price of University lands is at this time inexpedient, and would result in the lasting diminution of the fund.

In conclusion, therefore, and having the best interests of that State in view, in which, for weal or woe, he anticipates the residence of his descendants—he closes with the liberty of repeating the admonition:

Parce—stimulis; et fortius utere loris,
————medio tutissimus ibis.

This year, Adrian Seminary was incorporated, also the Clinton Institute; the charter of Michigan Central College, at Spring Arbor, amended; the Owosso Literary Institute incorporated and the Vermontville Academical Association; the law relating to the Board of eductaion of the city of Detroit amended; an act was passed providing that the various specimens pertaining to mineralogy, zoology, botany, and all other specimens pertaining to natural history, be transferred to the Board of Regents, to be held in trust for the use and benefit of the University and its branches; and by a subsequent joint resolution they were authorized to take possession of them, and to cause them to be properly arranged into perfect suits (and fractional suits) and report the number, quality, character and condition thereof to the Legislature, and to exchange specimens (in case there were over ten suits) with any other government, institution or individuals.

The PRIMARY SCHOOL LAW was amended by adding a provision that the district board should not in any case build a brick or stone school house upon any site, without having obtained a title in fee, or a lease of ninety-nine years; and should not build a frame school house for which they had not the title in fee or a lease for fifty years, without reserving the privilege of removing the house, &c. The school laws were revised as they are found in the revised statutes of 1846. They were changed in several important particulars. The revised law allowed every white male inhabitant of the age of twenty-one years residing in the distrist, liable to pay a school district tax, to vote at any district meeting. The previous law gave the right to any person to vote, if he was liable to pay a school tax, without confining it to the district; it provided that whenever a district was without officers, or neglected or refused to hold two successive annual meetings, the district was dissolved. It did make the request of five legal voters necessary to call a special meeting. The code reported provided *for the enumeration of children at the county poor houses*, in taking the census of the district, but the Legislature struck out the provision. The clause authorizing the raising of the fifty cent tax, was not in the reported code, but was re-established by the Legislature.

1847.

EXTRACT FROM THE MESSAGE OF GOV. FELCH.

The total amount of money distributed among the several townships, during the year, for the support of primary schools, is $27,-925 72, being thirty-one cents to every child between the ages of four and eighteen years, and exceeding the amount of last year's distribution, by the sum of $5,812 72. The number of scholars in the State, between the ages last mentioned, is reported at 97,658. The whole number of children that have attended the common schools during the year is 77,807. This number is greater by 7,037 than during the preceding year. The number of volumes in the township libraries in the State, are, according to the returns, 36,998.

The laws on the subject of common schools, it is believed, are such, when faithfully executed, as generally to secure, in a manner highly satisfactory, the great interests of education.

The chief obstacles to the realization of all the benefits of our noble school system, are found in the want of punctual attendance on the part of scholars, and deficiency in the qualifications of teachers. To correct the former, rests principally with parents and guardians. The latter is an evil, deplorable in its consequences, and difficult of correction. Voluntary associations of teachers for mutual instruction, have given an earnest of much improvement in this respect. In several of the States, Normal schools, having for their object the qualification of instructors for the great work of education, have been fostered by private munificence and legislative aid, and have been attended with the most beneficial results. Teaching, itself an art, is properly made a subject of instruction. The mission of the teacher demands high qualifications. As the object of his profession is of the greatest importance, so his employment should be considered most honorable, and his efforts be seconded by every friend of the rising generation. It is difficult to say, what method, if any of a public character, should be adopted to raise the standard of excellence in this important department, but I cannot refrain from recommending it to your consideration as a subject in which the interests of the public are deeply involved.

The number of students in the University of Michigan, is seventy. The Faculty consists of seven professors. By the assiduous labors of all connected with the several departments of instruction, the advantages pertaining to education in the higher departments of literature, the arts and the sciences, have been enjoyed to a degree highly creditable to the State and useful to the community. The rare example of the principle of free schools applied to an institution of the highest order, is here presented. Without charge for tuition, every citizen of the State is entitled to the benefits of a liberal education.

The nett proceeds of the University fund, applicable to the support of the institution, have been, during the year, $7,993 02.

REPORT OF SUPERINTENDENT.

The annual report of the Superintendent announced that within the last year he had made an educational tour through eighteen counties of the State, embracing chiefly the more northern organized counties, and had delivered lectures, attended public meetings, participated in public discussions and co-operated with the friends of education in every possible manner. The result of his convictions, derived from these labors, was that "we might reasonably hope to achieve what had been accomplished in other States, and *more;* and that all we had to do, was to adapt the means to the end and difficulties would disappear, and ere long our brightest hopes be realized."

The formation of the first Teachers' Association was announced under his auspices, being in Lenawee county. Another was formed in the county of Macomb. A Teachers' Institute, the first held in the State, was held in the county of Jackson, under the auspices of the Jackson County Teachers' Association, at which about thirty teachers attended. He recommended, in order to awaken a more general interest among all classes of citizens, and lead them to feel the necessity of improving the primary schools, the formation of county educational societies, the object of which he explained to be, to awaken the community to a sense of the real condition of the schools, and to point them to the means of removing the great and alarming evils that existed, and to the means of improvement in the schools. All the organized counties of the State were visited by him with the exception of four, and these he proposed to visit during the winter. In most instances, the result of these visitations was the organization of county societies. Of these, he says:

In many of the counties auxiliary town societies have been organized in most of the towns, and in some counties, in all of them. Although in a few instances there has been much to discourage, no proper notice of the proposed meetings having been given, and no suitable arrangements having been made; in short, nobody appearing to be interested in the subject, yet in the majority of cases it has been far otherwise. In several instances I have been greatly encouraged, finding many worthy citizens ready to co-operate in this work, and disposed to second any efforts that might be proposed for the improvement of teachers and schools. All we want is to have community awake to the interests of this subject and possess a zeal that is according to knowledge, and the work is half accomplished. It should not be disguised that for want of this interest some of these societies have not held a regular meeting since their organization. This will generally be the case where too much reliance is placed upon foreign aid. Their permanency and usefulness must depend upon the activity, zeal and discretion of the friends of education in the different counties. * * *

Public attention, in many parts of the State, seems to be somewhat awakened in relation to the interests of common schools. Many causes have tended to bring about this desirable state of things. The work of reform, however, has scarcely commenced. These societies should continue to hold frequent meetings, and thus keep the subject before the people. By this means the growing interest will continue to increase, and a better organization of our schools, and a general improvement in all that pertains to them will be the result. It has been specially gratifying to see not only clergymen, but members of all the learned professions, and men in public life, in attendance at a great majority of the educational meetings I have attended. And not only to see them there, but to see them, in many instances, actively at work with their fellow citizens in a cause upon which dedend more, perhaps, than upon all other causes combined, the improvement and permanency of our domestic, social and political institutions.

Among the causes which had contributed to advance the subject of education, the Superintendent mentioned particularly the INFLUENCE OF THE PRESS. The propriety of establishing an educational journal was again suggested. Of this, the Superintendent says:

Should such a periodical be issued monthly, or only quarterly, and be forwarded officially to the school inspectors of every town in the State, or to every director of a school district to be by them preserved among the papers of their office and transmitted to their successors, with instructions to have them bound at the end of the year and placed into the township libraries for general circulation, I have no doubt it would soon be regarded a very profitable investment.

This would open a ready means of communication between the head of the school department and the county, township and district officers, whereas we have now to rely solely upon a laborious correspondence and the issue of circulars. With our school law as it now is, should a journal be published devoted exclusively to the cause of education, as has been proposed by an association of two or three individuals, it must depend solely upon individual subscription for support, like any other periodical. With the apathy on this subject which is everywhere too manifest, we could hardly hope for the continuance of such a journal should its publication be commenced. But even should it be sustained it could not be relied upon as a medium of official communication, unless brought so far under the patronage of the Legislature as to insure its regular receipt by school inspectors.

STATISTICAL INFORMATION.

The report says:

The number of scholars reported within the legal ages, (between 4 and 18,) is 97,658, or 7,652 more than were reported last year. Twenty-one more towns have reported this year than did last, and 177 more districts; the entire number of districts reporting the present year, being 2,272. The whole number of children that have attended primary or common schools during the year is 77,807, or 7,037 more than attended the preceding year. Two thousand, two hundred and sixty-three male teachers, (26 less than last year,) have been employed at an average compensation of $12 71 per month, exclusive of board, being 73 cents more than was paid the preceeding year; 4,336 female teachers, (108 more than last year,) have been employed at an average compensation of $5 36 per month, exclusive of board, the same being twelve cents more than was paid last year. The average number of months schools have been taught by qualified teachers is five, the same as reported last year.

Last year the primary school interest fund apportioned among the several counties and towns of the State was $22,113 00, the same being 28 cents to every child between the ages of 4 and 18 years. The amount apportioned the present year is $27,925 72, or 31 cents to every child within the legal ages, the same being $5,812 72 more than the amount apportioned last year.

The late tabular returns show a large increase alike in the number of township libraries, the number of volumes they contain, and the number of districts that draw regularly therefrom. According to the returns received at this office, last year there were only 203 township libraries of the State. Two hundred and seventy two are reported the present year, showing an increase of 69. The last year's report represents that there were 24,905 volumes in said libraries. According to the report for the current year there are 36,938, showing an increase of nearly 50 per cent. These books are circulated and read in 230 more school districts the current year than they were the preceding one. * * *

The law has for several years made it the duty of the Supervisor to assess a half mill tax upon each dollar of the taxable property of his township for the purchase of a township library, a portion of which tax may, when certain conditions are complied with, be applied to the support of schools. This tax has been raised in only 220 of the 420 towns from which reports have been received, a fraction more than one half of the entire number.

The constitution of the State provides that "the clear proceeds of all fines assessed in the several counties for any breach of the penal laws, shall be exclusively applied to the support of said libraries." In consequence of a misapplication of these fines, the Legislature, in 1844, passed "an act to provide more effectually for the completion and disposition of fines, penalties and forfeitures of recognizances."

Notwithstanding the passage of this act there are 360 townships which have received nothing from this source for libraries, and only 46 that have. Lenawee, Oakland and Washtenaw, are the only counties that report any receipts in more than four towns, and neither of these counties reports receipts in one half of their towns, when these moneys should be distributed equally among them all.

The recommendations made in the report of the previous year were renewed, and especially as to that portion which proposed the election of only one school inspector, in each township, and the system of county and town superintendents. Maternal co-operation was invoked, for the purpose of supplying the immediate wants of destitute children, and co-operating with teachers, encouraging scholars, &c. Common school celebrations were held, and in the opinion of the Superintendent, were the means of much good. It was also deemed, thus far, to be impracticable to do much in this State, in the formation of TEACHERS' ASSOCIATIONS, or the establishment of TEACHERS' INSTITUTES, for general reasons, alluded to in his report, yet, he observes that much had been accomplished by the extensive organization of educational societies, a deeper and more general interest awakened, not only with teachers, but among all classes of citizens.

The main design of teachers' institutes, the Superintendent states, was to impart professional instruction; to consider and discuss the best means of interesting and governing children in our primary schools, and the most approved and successful methods of imparting instruction in the several branches of study ordinarily pursued therein; and he entertained the conviction, that with the interest already begotten, should a series of institutes, five or six in number, be held in different parts of the State, they would be well sustained, numerously attended, and prove highly beneficial in their influence. The organization of a State educational society was urged. The friends of education had met at Chicago and organized the North Western Educational Society, the design of which was to embrace in its operations the States of Ohio, Michigan, Indiana, Illinois, Wisconsin and Iowa, and such other States as might be represented.

The Superintendent announces that during the past year, Union Schools had been organized in several villages, and in some instances, large and commodious school houses had been erected, which constituted the pride and ornament of the village. He speaks of this form of common school organization as admirably adapted to villages and densely settled neighborhoods; that they combined, when properly conducted, all the advantages of the ordinary primary school and the academy for young gentlemen and the seminary for young ladies.

To the statistical tables attached to his report, the Superintendent prepared notes which developed the facts that the returns of school officers, and reports of county clerks, were incorrect in many or all of the most important particulars. Columns were not footed, or erroneously footed, requiring great labor in re-examination; averages were incorrectly given, or not given at all; important portions of the school blanks were not filled; in many instances reports from counties were so erroneous or unintelligible that they had to be returned; directors from fractional districts made reports wrongfully, showing in short that the school returns were in almost all cases so inaccurately made out that it was impossible to arrive at general conclusions with any degree of correctness or justice.

NINTH ANNUAL REPORT OF REGENTS.

During the past year, Rev. J. Holmes Agnew had been appointed professor of the Latin and Greek languages in the place of Rev. Joseph Whiting, deceased, Doctor Silas H. Douglass, professor of chemistry, and C. Fasquelle, of modern languages. The $100,000 debt had been reduced $66,150, and the resources of the interest fund had been adequate to meet the current demands on the treasury of the University.

The Regents in their report, which is short, express the hope that the system relative to the University fund, may be considered as permanently settled, and that future legislation may not again disturb the finances, upon which alone they must rely for the advancement of that literature designed by the original grant of Congress.

BRANCHES.

There were this year reports from four branches, viz: those at White Pigeon, Romeo, Kalamazoo and Tecumseh, in which were 287 scholars, 126 of which were females.

REPORT OF VISITORS.

The report of this board, consisting of the following gentlemen, viz: Rev. James Inglis, Hons. Charles Noble, Wm. T. Howell, Samuel W. Dexter, and Samuel Denton, was as follows:

The board of visitors appointed by you for the current year, present their report with much satisfaction, in view of the whole circumstances and prospects of the University. In particular, the efficiency of the Faculty, and the conduct and progress of the students, are such as to inspire public confidence and courage—high hopes of the future standing of the institution. It is to the credit of the Board of Regents, and matter of congratulation to the friends of learning and education, that in every appointment, professors have been secured so well qualified, and so well disposed to foster its infant interests. The zeal and devotion of its early professors to the promotion of these interests, demand the grateful acknowledgment of the public. Since the last board of visitors reported, two members of the present Faculty have entered upon their important functions. One, the successor of the lamented professor Whiting, and the other, a professor of Logic and Rhetoric; both eminently qualified to carry out the objects of the University.

A variety of circumstances prevented a majority of the board from being present during the whole of the minute and thorough examination which preceded the last commencement. So far as it can be reported upon, it was satisfactory. It is not to be expected that in the circumstances in which students are here collected, the studies of the several classes should be of so advanced a character as those of corresponding classes in older institutions. But in nearly every class, the examination gave evidence of a thoroughness and exactness of teaching, which would bear a comparison with those of any college. It is important to notice, that one of the greatest disadvantages under which these classes seem to labor, is the great variety and inequality of attainments with which students enter. The consequences of this were apperent during the examination in almost every department of study. Doubtless it will, for some time be difficult, if not impracticable, to maintain a high standard of admission to an institution circumstanced as this is, but the importance of a more thorough preparatory course ought to be kept before the public. A more liberal encouragement of public schools and academies of the higher order is demanded, and probably a revival and reinforcement of the branches would prove the most effectual means of promoting this object. A comparison of the qualifications of students at present in the University, would afford unequivocal testimony to the past utility of this part of our University system.

It would be unjust to omit to express the gratification with which the commencement exercises were witnessed. The large attendance of citizens—many of them from distant parts of the State—gave encouraging evidence of a growing interest in the fortunes of the University; and there was probably not an individual of the many who left the scene of this literary exhibition, disappointed or dissatisfied. A gentleman, whose opinion is valuable, remarked that he had rarely heard the exercises surpassed in point of thought or composition at any of the eastern colleges, although in those, the commencement exercises are by selected speakers, while in this case they were by all the members of the graduating class without distinction. This was probably the conviction of all present, whose opportunity enabled them to make the comparison.

The condition of the buildings and grounds calls for no remarks further than the repetition of the well known and urgent need of increased accommodations. The library and museum were found in good order. The latter is being improved by the addition of the remainder of the State collection, when under the superintendence of Prof. Douglass, in accordance with the provisions of an act of last legislative session. The value and interest of the collection will also be increased by an exchange of duplicate specimens, which is being arranged by Dr. Z. Pitcher.

The entire management of this important interest is in the highest degree creditable to all connected with it. The character of the tuition and discipline within—the judicious and frugal administration of its affairs without—the progress and promise of students who have enjoyed its advantages—and the increasing number of its classes—all speak encouragingly of its future prosperity and influence. It is thus commended to the confidence and the fostering care of the State.

LEGISLATION.

The committee on public instruction of the Senate, reported a joint resolution, for adoption by the Legislature, requiring the Board of Regents to cause so much of the journal of their proceedings to be published as the public good might require, to be printed as soon as practicable after each session of the Board, and that at the opening of each session of the Legislature, they should report their full proceedings for the year, including the names of all the Faculty—their salaries and duties—the number of students and their classes, and all such other incidental matters and subjects as might be necessary to enable the Legislature to determine with accuracy the propriety of the course pursued by the said Board, and the people at large properly to appreciate the character and importance of the University.

The reasons which led to this resolution, as thus detailed by the committee, through their chairman, Hon. N. A. Balch:

1. Your committee feel that there is an unwarrantable prejudice existing in the minds of many good and intelligent citizens of this State against the University, which it is in the power of the Regents to utterly dissipate and banish, by properly laying before the public the facilities and advantages that institution affords for a thorough education, and the efforts the Board and the Faculty have made and are making to render it not only popular, but useful.

2. In view of the rising importance and ultimate effect of our University, not solely upon those who may pass their halcyon days within its consecrated walls and be made the recipients of its final honors, not alone upon the sons of the affluent, or those for whom genius selects a high station and marks a bright career, as many suppose, but upon the entire character of the whole people of this State and surrounding country. It seems to your committee that in advancing that progress, and in widening that influence, a labored and learned report of the honorable Board of Regents annually, would be of immense utility.

3. If the University of Michigan ever arises to that proud eminence which those who originated it designed, and which your committee verily believe it will ultimately attain among kindred institutions in our land, it seems to them of vital importance that such a report should be annually made, and carefully preserved in the archives of the University, as the best chronicler of its origin and progress; and no other course, in the opinion of your committee, can preserve for posterity many important facts which it is certain will fall into oblivion and perish, when the memory of those who now watch with anxious care the interests of that institution, shall cease to record them.

4. Your committee are of opinion, that the course recommended by the resolutions offered, would be not only a source of present, but of ulterior benefit to the people at large, and to the University itself. It would disarm jealousy of its sting, and suspicion of its malice. It would place the requisite knowledge within the reach of all, and thereby cause them to know and feel that the rights of the people and the University are secure and inviolate, and that all its affairs are transacted with skill and fidelity; that wisdom presides in its halls, and integrity in its councils.

5. Your committee, while they disclaim all idea of censure, respectfully submit whether the last annual report of the Board of Regents is of that character that will best subserve the rights and interests of the University or such an one as the people might have reasonably expected. Your committee, deeply feeling as they do, that the interests of education in a free government, and to a free people, are paramount to all others, and that those interests will always find favor and support, in the bosoms of philanthropic, patriotic and

christian statesmen, and believing as they do the members of the honorable Board of Regents, to be such, humbly hope the foregoing resolutions will be adopted, and that the beneficial results designed to be obtained by the resources, may, thereby be fully realized.

During this session, Hon. R. P. ELDREDGE, chairman of a select committeee of the Senate upon the subject, made a report in favor of electing the officers of State, including the Superintendent of Public Instruction, by the suffrages of the people.

A majority of a select committee appointed in relation to a further reduction of the price of University lands, reported that the existing laws did not discriminate in *price* as well as *value;* that they considered the fund a sacred one, and the interests of the University a paramount object of legislation, but that at the same time the interests of all—the poor man struggling to make a comfortable home in a new country, as well of him whose previous efforts, or hereditary property have enabled him to give his offspring a collegiate education, should be promoted; that it was urged that enough was already realized for the competent support of the University, but that the committee knew nothing of the facts from the competent authority, as the report of the Regents had not been definite on the subject. They proposed an act authorizing an appraisment of the lands with reference to soil, situation, timber, &c.

The memorial of SAMUEL BARSTOW, GEORGE ROBB and L. BISHOP, a committee of the BOARD OF EDUCATION of the city of Detroit, was laid before the Legislature, respecting an amendment of the law relative to the public schools of that city. From this memorial, the following extract is subjoined:

The board of education of the city of Detroit was organized by a law passed in February, 1842, upon the petition of a large majority of the freemen of said city. By this law the whole city of Detroit was organized into a single school district, and the common council of said city was invested with the power to assess and levy a tax not exceeding one dollar for each child in the city, between the ages of five and seventeen years, for the support of free schools in said city.

Previous to the passage of this law the city was divided into eight school districts, and was in all respects, subject to the general school law of the State then in force. There was no power vested in the said city to levy any tax whatever for the support of schools, and the only fund for that purpose, was the proportion of the income of the State school fund, annually apportioned to this city, which up to that time had in no year exceeded $900, and had generally been under that sum. Besides, even this small sum had for a year or two previous been almost entirely lost by failures of banks with which it had been deposited. The consequence of this state of things was, that for several years previous, our city may almost literally be said to have been without common schools, or any public provision whatever for the education of its children. For two years previous to 1842, during a great portion of the time, no common schools were open in the city. In a portion of the eight districts, schools were kept open from four to six months in the year, but in some of them district schools were not opened at all. The schools they opened were kept in hired rooms by very incompetent teachers, and from the shortness of the time they were kept open, and their inadequate support, were almost worthless.

Such was the state of things when the law of February, 1842, was passed. In March of that year, the board of education was organized under it, and entered upon its duties.

It was found by said board that they had every thing to create, and that a degree of neglect beyond what they imagined possible, had existed, from the earliest period in the history of said city with regard to the all important subject of education. It was found by them that in a city where Congress had given the most unlimited power of disposition and arrangement, where in fact every foot of ground had been disposed of by the public authorities, and where the most unlimited power had existed to appropriate ground for public purposes—in a city which contained 10,000 people, which embraced great wealth, and which had been in existence nearly half a century, there was not a single lot reserved and vested in the public or district authorities for the purposes of education; that in the whole city there was but one school house, and that was a small and inconvenient building not worth over $400, erected upon a leased lot. Besides, there was no furniture, except a lot of old benches and desks not fit for the uses for which they were intended. A lot of depreciated bank paper, and a very poor school house on a leased lot—completed all the provisions which the city of Detroit in this enlightened age had provided for the support of public schools, and which came into the hands of the board of education from the old districts.

It became therefore at once necessary not only to establish and support schools, but to build school houses, and not only to build school houses, but to purchase lots on which to erect them. In short not only schools were wanting, but all the apparatus, furniture, buildings and property of every kind necessary to a system which should be adequate to the wants of so large a city. * * *

The number of children in the city of Detroit between the ages of five and seventeen, is 3, 506, as shown by the last school census. The city tax for the coming year will therefore be $3.506. If to this be added our portion of the income of the State school fund, which may be estimated at $1.000, the whole income of the board will be $4,506. Of this sum $500 will be required to close up the building and other accounts for the past year, leaving $4,006 as the net amount applicable to the support of the system for the next year.

In order to show how inadequate this amount is to support the schools, and also to appropriate any considerable amount to the purchase of lots and building of school houses, we state the following facts and estimates:

During the last year we have supported twelve schools at an expense of $2,800 for wages of teachers, of $250 for rents and insurance, of $150 for fuel, and an estimated sum of $200 for repairs, seats, and other school furniture and apparatus, making in all, $3,400.

These schools during the last quarter show a school list of 1,286, or about 107 for each school taught by a single teacher, a number entirely too great; thus showing the absolute necessity of increasing their number. But admitting that they are not too crowded, the increase in the city, which is over 200 per year, requires at least the addition of two schools, the expense of which will be, basing the estimate upon the same data with schools now in existence, $566 66, thus making an aggregate of $3,966 66, which will be required to keep up our system during the coming year, without appropriating a single dollar to school houses, or adding anything to the salaries of our teachers.

Of these twelve schools, four have been kept in hired rooms, very small and inconvenient. indeed entirely unfit for school houses; one has been kept in a room in an old market house, which had been abandoned by the city as a market house and had been fitted up with benches in order to use it as a school room; one in the building owned by the branch university, of the use of which the board may at any time be deprived; one in the basement of a church, the use of which is gratuitously given, and five in school houses erected for that purpose, there being at this time but four school houses in the city besides one now nearly finished, which will accommodate the two additional schools contemplated for the coming year.

The above facts are stated to show that the board of education has not and cannot have under the present laws the means to buy lots or build school houses at all adequate to the wants of the city, and the necessity of providing an additional fund for that purpose.

If, in addition, we consider the rapid increase of our city—that in the course of five years to come an increase of 1,200 to 1,500 will probably take place in the number of its children of school ages, which must render necessary a great increase in the number of our schools, and of course of houses for them to occupy, and recollect that the increase of tax on these 1,200 or 1,500 children would only be a sum sufficient to build school houses for two schools, even if it could be all applied for that purpose—it is apparent that our situation with regard to school houses will be constantly growing worse and worse, unless we resort to some other mode of getting them.

Another important view of this matter is, that vacant lots are becoming scarce and are increasing in value in the city, so that if school lots are not soon obtained, there will be great difficulty in getting them in convenient locations, and much higher prices will have to be paid.

The experience of all who have reflected upon this subject, will convince them that the goodness and efficacy of a school depends very much upon the convenience and comfort of the school house. This is particularly the case in cities; crowded rooms without yards or good ventilation, in buildings erected for other purposes, where boys and girls are thrown together without even the conveniences which decency requires, are not only unfit for the ordinary purposes of the school room, but they have a most injurious effect upon both the health and morals of children. We can never have a system of schools worthy of our city, so long as we are forced to occupy hired rooms instead of good, well ventilated and comfortable school houses, with convenient yards and out buildings attached.

In view of the facts above stated, we recommend that application be made to the Legislature, for the passage of a law authorizing the freemen of the city of Detroit to vote, and the common council to assess and collect a tax, not exceeding $1,500 in any one year, to be expended in the purchase of lots and the erection of school houses in said city, and also authorizing the board of education to borrow a sum not exceeding $5,000 to be expended for the same purposes. We can see no objection to vesting such a power in the people to tax themselves for an object not surpassed in importance by any other, and we are satisfied that it is the most sacred duty of the Legislature to co-operate with the people in the great work of universal education.

As a matter embraced within the department of literature, a letter of Mons. Vattemare was laid before the Legislature, suggesting "the indispensableness of placing the management of international exchanges in the hands of the Regents of the University."

A bill was reported in the House of Representatives to provide for teachers' institutes, and the committee on education were instructed to enquire into the expediency of imposing a penalty on Supervisors who neglected or refused to assess school, township and library taxes; but these subjects received no further action. Acts were passsed incorporating Adrian Seminary, White Pigeon Academy, and the Raisin Institute. An act was passed providing that in addition to the taxes already authorized, the common council of Detroit were empowered to levy and collect a tax, not exceeding $1,500 in any one year, to be expended in the purchase of lots in the city, for the use of the Public Schools, and in the erection and building a school house or houses, with the necessary out-buildings and fixtures on any lot or lots which may be so purchased, or any other lots owned by the board of education, or which they might acquire, the said tax to be devoted to no other purpose, and to be paid to the treasurer of the board of education. The board were authorized also to borrow such sums as they deemed proper, not to exceed $5,000 for the purposes above specified. This act was approved March 12, 1847.

The statutes of 1846, relating to schools were amended, so that the distribution of the income of the fund should be made by the first of May, or as soon thereafter as practicable. A joint resolution was passed authorizing the Superintendent of Public Instruction to compile so much of his annual reports for 1845 and 1846, as he deemed necessary for the purpose of giving general information relative to common schools and to distribute the same. An act was passed and approved, providing that so much of the annual State tax, on the several rail road companies within the State, as might be necessary, should be specifically set apart and appropriated for the payment of interest on such sums as are now due from the State, or hereafter may be due to the UNIVERSITY and PRIMARY SCHOOL funds. A joint resolution was passed and approved March 16, in relation to loans from the University and school funds.

1848.

EXTRACT FROM GOV. RANSOM'S MESSAGE.

There is no subject paramount in importance to that of common school education—none that has a higher claim to the fostering care of the government. I am not aware that further legislation is necessary in relation to our common school system, unless it be deemed expedient to provide for the establishment of Normal schools for the education and qualification of teachers. Such institutions when properly conducted, have been productive of great good, and no doubt is entertained but such would be the result of their introduction into our State, on being made to form a part of our educational system. By a joint resolution of the Legislature, approved March 4, 1847, the Superintendent of Public Instruction was required to compile so much of his annual reports for the years 1845 and 1846, as he should deem necessary for the purpose of giving general information relative to common schools That duty has been performed, and the "compilation" contemplated by the resolution has been made by that officer, and will be laid before you.

The number of townships from which reports have been received pursuant to law, is 425, somewhat exceeding the number by which reports were made last year.

The number of school districts, from which reports have been received, is two thousand nine hundred and fifty—being eighty-one more than reported last year; and the number of children reported, between the ages of four and eighteen years, is one hundred and eight thousand one hundred and thirty—showing an increase of ten thousand four hundred and seventy-two, upon the number returned in any former year.

The whole number that have attended common schools during the past year, as shown by the returns from the several counties, is eighty eight thousand and eighty; ten thousand two hundred and seventy-three more than are reported to have received such instruction the previous year.

For the year 1846, the primary school interest fund apportioned among the several counties and townships of the State, was $27,925 72—thirty-one cents to every child reported between the ages before mentioned.

The amount divided the present year is $31,250 54—thirty-two cents to each child entitled, by law, to participate in the distribution of the fund.

The amount expended in the State, during the year, for the support of common schools, was $130,531 80; $36,543 75 of which was applied to the building and repairing of school houses.

There are three hundred township libraries in the State, containing forty-three thousand nine hundred and twenty-six volumes, according to the returns of the past year, being thirty more libraries and six thousand nine hundred and thirty-eight volumes of books, more than were reported in 1846.

These libraries circulate through one thousand three hundred and forty-nine school districts, two hundred and sixty-eight more than have participated in their benefits in any former year.

The returns evince an increasing interest in all parts of the State, in behalf of common schools, and of education generally. In several villages, union schools houses have been erected at an expense varying from $800 to $3,000, and a greater willingness is manifested to employ competent teachers, and to pay an adequate compensation for their services.

The increasing usefulness and prosperity of the University cannot fail to be a source of gratification to every citizen of Michigan.

Of the twenty-six professorships contemplated by the organic law of the institution, seven have been already established by the Board of Regents and their chairs filled, by whom instruction is given in all all the branches of literature and science usually taught in collegiate institutions of the highest grade.

Of the seven professors appointed, there is one of the ancient languages—one of the modern languages—one of mathematics and natural philosophy—one of moral and intellectual philosophy—one of logic, rhetoric and the philosophy of history—one of botany and zoology, and one of chemistry and geology.

The library, consisting of about five thousand volumes, is believed to be one of the most valuable, of its extent, in the United States, embracing as it does, the most approved foreign works in the several departments of literature, science and the arts.

Its cabinet of natural history is, also, of great extent and value. The cabinet purchased of Baron Liederer, is a rare and rich collec- of foreign minerals. Besides which, it has an extensive collection of American minerals and fossils, together with suits of specimens, illustrative of the geology, zoology and botany of Michigan, affording altogether greater advantages to the student in natural history, than any similar institution in this country.

The success of the University thus far has exceeded the expectations of its most sanguine friends. The number of students now belonging to the several classes is, eighty-three, and that the number will be largely increased at the commencement of each succeeding collegiate year, there is every reason to expect.

The professors have been selected for their ability, learning, and high moral qualities, and, that they possess them all, in an eminent degree, is demonstrated by the manner in which they have discharged the varied, arduous and responsible duties of their respective stations.

The finances of this favored institution, are also upon a most satisfactory footing.

A debt was early contracted in its behalf, for a loan of $100,000 of the bonds of the State, which has been reduced, from time to time, by the sale of portions of its lands for warrants drawn upon the internal improvement fund, to $20,628 01, and the net amount of revenue derived from all sources. during the past year, and made available for its general use, after deducting interest due on the balance of its debt, will exceed $15.000, about half of which has been expended in the erection of an additional building for dormitories and lecture rooms.

Appropriations are no longer made by the Regents for the support of branches of the University, and instruction is continued only in those at Kalamazoo and Romeo.

REPORT OF SUPERINTENDENT.

In connection with the annual report, (being the twelfth annual report from the office,) the Superintendent laid before the Legislature, the compilation of his previous reports relating to the condition of primary schools. The report announces the formation of a State educational society, and includes its constitution and forms for county and township societies. He reports these associations as having been the means of doing much good. The incorrectness of the reports of school officers and county clerks is again alluded to, and explanations and instructions again given in relation to them. In relation to the relative progress of the primary and select schools, the Superintendent remarks:

While there has been a large *increase* in the number of scholars attending common schools, there has been a corresponding decrease, in the number attending select schools. Many parents who are anxious to afford their children every facility for improvement, have withdrawn their patronage from select schools, having become satisfied that under existing laws, with a proper interest intheir behalf, common schools may be made both *better* and cheaper than select schools generally are.

The report dwells at great length upon various important topics— Union schools, school houses, their location, architecture, size, construction, ventilation, furniture, seats, desks, and everything that relates to their external and internal arrangement. From the compilation is extracted the following interesting comparison, between the population of Michigan and other States of the Union, in regard to individual attainments in certain particulars, &c.:

According to the census of 1840, the total population of the United States, was, in round numbers, 17,000,000. Of this number, 550,000 were whites over twenty years of age, who could not read and write. This gives one white person over the age of twenty, to every thirty-one of the entire population of the United States, that is unable to read and write. The proportion varies in different states, from one in five hundred and eighty-nine in Connecticut, to one in eleven in North Carolina.

If we exclude all colored persons, and whites under twenty years of age, the proportion will stand thus: In the United States, one to every twelve is unable to read and write. The proportion varies from one in two hundred and ninety-four, in Connecticut, which stands the highest, to one in three in North Carolina, which stands the lowest.

In Tennessee, the proportion is one in four. In Kentucky, Virginia, Georgia, South Carolina, and Arkansas, each, one in five. In Delaware and Alabama, each, one in six. In Indiana, one in seven. In Illinois and Wisconsin, each, one in eight.

On the brighter end of the scale, next to Connecticut, in which the proportion is one in two hundred and ninety-four, is New Hampshire, in which the proportion is one in one hundred and fifty-nine. In Massachusetts, it is one in ninety. In Maine, one in seventy-two. In Vermont, one in sixty-three. Next in order comes Michigan, in which the proportion is one in thirty-nine. There are twenty states below Michigan, and only five above her.

But even this estimate, favorable as it is, does not allow our own State an opportunity to appear in her true light. It is well known that a great proportion of the illiterate population of this State, is confined to a few counties.

In Mackinaw and Chippewa counties, there is one white person over twenty years of age to every five of the entire population that is unable to read and write. In Ottawa, one in fourteen. In Cass, one in twenty-two. In Wayne and Saginaw, each, one in thirty-six.

On the other hand, there are eight entire counties in the State, in which, according to the census referred to, there was not a single white inhabitant over twenty years of age, that was unable to read and write. It is an interesting fact, that in Ohio, also, there are seven such counties, making fifteen in these two States, while in all New England there are but two—(Franklin in Massachusetts, and Essex in Vermont.)

There may also be selected, in this State, thirteen counties, viz: Allegan, Barry, Branch, Clinton, Eaton, Genesee, Ingham, Ionia, Kalamazoo, Lapeer, Livingston, Oakland and Oceana, in which, collectively, there is only one white person over twenty, in four thousand six hundred and five of the entire population, that cannot read and write. This is seven hundred and eighty-one per cent higher than the highest entire State in the Union.

In addition to these, in the three counties of Hillsdale, Jackson and Kent, there is but one in four hundred and twenty-five that is unable to read and write, which is forty per cent higher than any entire State in the Union, with the single exception of Connecticut.

But let us make the comparison in another respect, and see what proportion of the population of different States are receiving instruction in schools. Here to do justice to Michigan, we ought to take the census of 1845, and the school returns for that year, inasmuch as our school system had had in 1840, hardly an opportunity of going into operation since its adoption.

In 1840, one in seven of the entire population of the State attended school a portion of the year. In 1845, the proportion had increased, taking the census and school returns for that year, to one in four. In this respect, there are but three States in the Union, that, according to the census of 1840, rank higher than Michigan stood in 1845. Their names in order are Maine, New Hampshire and Vermont. In round numbers, the proportion of the entire population that attended school in each of these States, is one in three. In Michigan, Massachusetts, Connecticut, and New York, it is one in four. In Rhode Island, one in five. In Ohio and New Jersey, each, one in six. In Pennsylvania, one in eight. In no other State is the proportion more than one in ten; while in ten States, it is less than one in twenty-five. Here, again, we see that Michigan stands high on the list of States.

In two of the New England States, nineteen-twentieths of the scholars taught, are instructed in common schools. In New York, fourteen-fifteenths. In one of the New England States, only four-fifths, the remainder being instructed in academies and select or high schools.

In some of the Southern States, only two-thirds or three-fourths of the entire number in school, attend common schools. In Michigan, forty-six forty-sevenths of all scholars attending school, receive their instruction in common schools. This is a greater proportion than in any other State of the Union. Ohio ranks next, in this respect, thirty-six thirty-sevenths of her scholars being taught in common schools.

In the three thousand school districts of this State, there are upwards of one hundred thousand children to be instructed. The question naturally arises, How shall we provide competent teachers for this army of youth, to whom are to be entrusted the future destinies of the Peninsular State?

Two methods have been proposed. One is, to invite the redundancy of teachers at the East, and especially those of New England, to supply the educational wants of destitute portions of our State, through the agency of the "board of national popular education."

The other method is to *train up a supply of competent teachers at home.* Upon this, *only*, can we safely rely.

THE UNIVERSITY AND BRANCHES.

At a meeting of the Board of Regents in August of this year, the report of the committee on the branches showed but four of them in existence and they had, after a careful examination, come to the conclusion that appropriations could not be made for such as were in existence, or for the establishment of others, without seriously trenching upon the resources, and limiting, in a great degree, the usefulness, and even endangering the success, of the parent institution. Since this period, no appropriations have been made to any of the branches, with the exception of $10 00 to the Romeo branch, for the purpose of raising a question before the supreme court, as to the *constitutionality* of such appropriations. The reports of the State Treasurer and Commissioner of Land Office showed that on the 30th day of the preceding November, the debt of $100,000 had been diminished $79,371 99, leaving the sum of $20,62[illegible] only remaining of that debt.

It was found that the estimated income of the University, after payment of the regular current expenses, would leave a probable surplus of five thousand dollars, which could be applied to the erection of an additional building. More accommodation was needed for students, and a laboratory and recitation rooms. Urged by this necessity, the board resolved to commence the construction of a building similar to the one in use, and $5,000 was appropriated for that purpose, and Major Kearsley and John Owen, Esq., appointed to carry the resolution into effect. This had been done, the walls were up, the building enclosed, roofed, and covered with tin and otherwise completed at a cost not varying far from the appropriation. The funds justifying, an additional appropriation of $2,000 was made to cover other expenditures connected with the building.

A superintendent of repairs was appointed, who was to have general superintendence of the buildings and grounds. The Board announced that the institution was fulfilling its duties in a manner creditable to the Faculty, and highly useful to the public, and they looked forward with confidence to its increasing usefulness and future eminence.

REPORT OF VISITORS.

The report of this board, consisting of Rev. JOHN D. PIERCE, Hon. J. GOODWIN, Rev. C. T. HINMAN, and GEORGE E. HAND, having been made, in common with the other gentlemen, by the Rev. Mr. Pierce, (first Superintendent,) who had incorporated into the organic law, the provision for the appointment of such a board annually, it may be justly presumed to present a more perfect idea of the outline of their intended duties than had thus far been given to the public. For this reason, and for important suggestions it contains, which may be useful in the future, it is here given in full:

To the Superintendent of Public Instruction:

SIR—The board of visitors respectfully report that they assembled at the University in August last, for the purpose of being present at the public examination of the classes, preceding the commencement, and of examining into the state of the University, its wants, its progress and its prospects. The site of the University, being, as it is, a fine, high table of land, commanding varied and beautiful landscape views, with a fertile, dry soil, is well chosen. Unfortunately, the noble forest trees which formerly tenanted these grounds, (the only connection between the present and the past, in this new world,) had all been destroyed before the land was appropriated to its present use, and their stately compeers, a little way remote, only seem to admonish us of how much we have lost by their untimely fate. That which first most strongly arrests one's attention upon approachng the University grounds, is the almost total absence of shade and ornamental trees. This is not surprising in a new institution, but it demands immediate attention—prompt action. The soil is strong, and well adapted to the production and growth of trees, as the neighboring forests attest. In the same forests, and in convenient proximity, are found in almost every variety, the trees indigenous to the climate. A little considerate attention now given to ornamenting the grounds with trees will, in a few years, yield an ample harvest of security, comfort and protection. A considerable number of trees have been recently planted, but we were sorry to observe that nearly all of them were comprised in two or three varieties, more distinguished for their rapid growth and precocious development, than for symmetry of proportions, beauty or permanence, and which will in regular course reach the "sere and yellow leaf" of their existence, sooner than the youth who assisted to plant them. A portion, at least, of the trees planted, should be of the most durable, stable and stately kinds. How much of interest, comfort and enjoyment, trees grown venerable with the Universities they surround and protect, add to college grounds and college life, all can attest who are conversant with the older and more eligible literary institutions of the country. Cambridge and Yale, stript of their fine old shade trees, would be shorn of half their attractions. The pursuit of learning, science and literature, much of which is laborious and exhausting, should be made attractive by the highest garniture of nature and of art. The highway of thought, and intellectual development and progress, much of which is parched and rugged, should, so far as may be, be refreshed with fountains and strewn with flowers. One of the appended resolutions of the board, embodies their views on this not unimportant subject.

The philosophical and chemical apparatus are evidently quite inadequate to the wants of those departments. Some of the most common and important experiments cannot be made for want of suitable apparatus. This deficit should, we think, receive early attention and remedy. However important buildings may seem, needful apparatus and books are even more so. The brick and mortar, of which are reared the stately walls, can be of little avail, without intelligent minds within, and the proper appliances for communicating that intelligence to others.

The library, very considerable and creditable in extent, is valuable and excellent—but further additions are needed to keep pace with the rapid progress of the age.

The suits of specimens in mineralogy and geology are uncommonly full and splendid, and the other departments of natural science are very rich in preparations and specimens.

The board have the satisfaction of saying that the examination was generally well sustained, and the performances on the day of commencement, were in most instances of a high order, creditable alike to the young gentlemen who participated in them, and the professors who had been charged with their education and instruction.

The board had of course but little opportunity to know or judge of the discipline or details of the government of the University; but have reason to believe that it is discreet, prudent and salutary. In every institution of learning, there must be system, order, rule, subordination, compliance with the regulations, cheerful acquiescence in what is enjoined. Whilst there is much occasion for watchful solicitude, considerate kindness and charitable forbearance on the part of those who are charged with the immediate administration of the affairs of a College or University, they are also sometimes required by a duty which their responsible position imposes, a duty which they owe to the public, to the parents who have entrusted to them the education of their sons, and to the youth, whose future hopes and prospects greatly depend upon their careful training at this period of life—to adopt strong measures, and perhaps, in some rare instances, almost bordering on severity.

Men who are fit to be placed in such highly responsible stations, themselves, upon the ground, will act wisely, and a healthy public sentiment will sustain them in their action. The young gentlemen gathered into an institution of learning, should feel that they also have duties and responsibilities; their own sense of propriety will dictate consideration and regard for the hopes and expectations of their parents and friends, and gratitude for the sacrifices and exertions of those who are expending their hard earned money on their education, will prompt them to peaceful and quiet demeanor, to punctuality and promptness in their lessons and recitations, to deference and respect for their teachers, and to a general and cordial co-operation in sustaining a wholesome police and good order, so essential to the well being of every community, whether social, civil or literary. Anarchy in State is worse than the worst government; anarchy in institutions of learning is more destructive, more fatal to progress, than any other, we had almost said, than all other evils put together. These remarks might seem uncalled for, but can scarcely be deemed out of place when it is remembered that every institution is liable to such trying exigencies, that almost all have encountered them to a greater or less extent, and it is well to promote a healthful public sentiment on a subject so intimately connected with the welfare, not only of our University, but also of our seminaries, academies and common schools.

The board wish to call attention to the great importance which they attach to the rank which our University shall take and maintain amongst like institutions in our country. That its rank and position should be high amongst the highest, all will admit; to that proposition every man will assent. State pride, our personal wishes, the interest which all must feel in the training and development of those who are to become our religious teachers, who are relied upon to heal our bodily ailments, who are to make and administer our laws who are soon to manage our public affairs, all combine with oppressive force to show the great and absorbing importance of this matter. Why, then, it may be asked, do we dwell upon it? Because, that though theoretically admitted by all, it is, we fear, practically overlooked by many. On the one hand, we wish to call the attention of all who are immediately connected with the University, to the fact that we expect much, very much, from them. The institution is well endowed, if not just now, certainly prospectively, with moderately good management of its funds. It is eligibly situated; it has started in its eventful career under favorable auspices; its position is in a fine region of country, in a temperate latitude, in a healthful climate. What Yale is to the States east of the mountains, the University of Michigan should be to the Western States. We hope for much, we expect much—have we not a right to expect much? Let the standard be fixed at once, so that the proudest institution in the country shall not be ashamed to fraternize with us as equals; so that our sons shall have no occasion, through aspirations for higher attainments or higher honors, to leave the halls of our own University for those of any other whatever. We call upon the Regents, the Faculty, the professors, to make it such an institution. But to make it and keep it such, much care and attention are requisite. The Regents must be vigilant in looking to the capacity, the attainments, the reputation, the character, the manners, the habits, the physical vigor, the intellectual development, of those whom they shall select for instructors.

We call upon the Faculty and professors in the University, and doubt not that our appeal will meet a cordial response, to bear in mind the important position they have taken, the duties of vital interest which they have assumed to discharge, the intimate relations they bear to the honor or dishonor, the weal or woe, of this commonwealth. It is but reasonable to presume, when such momentous results hinge on their action, that they will cheerfully devote their whole time, their best energies, their undivided attention, to instructing, enlarging, developing, giving energy to the minds and intellects of those placed in their charge. We expect them to make our University a distinguished seat of science, learning, literature, refinement and taste—a blessing to our people, a proud monument to themselves--an honor to the State and Nation.

But to have the University accomplish all its high destinies. the State also has solemn duties to perform; it must faithfully discharge the solemn trust committed to it by the general government; it must preserve strict good faith with the University; it must husband its resources and revenues; it must, in no case, allow political considerations to make merchandize of the interests of the University, and of the people's birthright, the privilege of a free and gratuitous education of their sons in its halls. For that purpose the people of the nation have nobly endowed the University; for that purpose and that only, let that endowment be appropriated and stand. Let the hand that for sinister purposes would lay hold of that or any other fund set apart to the education of our youth, be palsied in the touch; let the tongue of him who would thus betray his trust and his country, cleave to the roof of his mouth.

The board take occasion to remark upon the great importance of a full and thorough preliminary preparation of the students before being entered at the University, and that the standard of scholarship required of those who enter the University, should be elevated, as a prominent means of elevating, not only the character of the University itself, but also that of inferior schools throughout the State, which look to it as a model, and grade their literary character according to the rank of this, the leading institution of the State. It was very apparent from the examination of the lower classes, that the young gentlemen composing those classes, had entered upon their common career at the University, with very unequal degrees of preparation.

Some evidently had been but ill prepared to enter upon their college course, and encounter its severe and rigid routine of study, and in addition to the discouragement and mortification ever attendant upon inferior scholarship, and the danger of overtasking themselves to make up their deficiencies, would realize in but an imperfect degree, the benefit and advantages of a thorough education. This subject can hardly receive too much attention. It enters largely into the essence of the lives and fortunes of educated men. A crude and imperfect preliminary education, of which the student is himself probably ignorant at the first, is often the occasion of embittering his hours of study, breaking his spirits, and in long after years is fruitful of vain regrets that his happiness and fortunes for life, have been marred through the ignorance or stupidity of his early instructors. The evil of which we are speaking is wide-spread in the Western States. It is a matter of common remark in the Eastern Colleges, in reference to students from the west. It is an evil which cannot be too promptly remedied. In vain do you fill your professors' chairs with men of the highest eminence, if the youth who resort to them for instruction, must be fed with milk instead of meat. In vain may we look for a high standard of attainment in the graduating classes, if the standard of preparation for entering upon the college course is a low one—in vain shall we expect to see the Alumni of our University, when they meet and mingle with, or confront those of other Universities, stand erect with arched brow and bold front, conscious of the plentitude of their intellectual stature and developement—if the student is to spend half his time at the University, in learning what he should have known when he entered it. Let parents and guardians, if they wish their sons and wards to reap the full benefit of a liberal education, see well to it that they are properly and sufficiently prepared at the outset, and that they lose as little time as possible by absence during the college course It is said, and without doubt, truly, that many portions of the State are destitute of proper schools and seminaries for training and preparing students for the University. But the absence of such schools and seminaries, however prejudicial and deeply felt in the University, has much more wide spread and deplorable results, in the destitute districts themselves; and it is seen in the very imperfect education and lack of intelligence in the more favored, and almost absence of education among the less favored, in such communities. There, also, the common school, (that nursery of thought and intellect, which we should all assiduously cherish,) droops and languishes, and the munificent provision made by the State, for the education of the whole rising generation, serves little other purpose than to pay blockhead teachers for entailing their own ignorance and stupidity upon their pupils. What an evil—what a calamity—how widespread—how diffusive—how frightful. How can it be remedied—how prevented? If our common schools are to work their perfect work in rearing up generation after generation of intelligent, educated and virtuous men and women, who shall be ornaments to society, and appreciate and perpetuate the blessings and privileges which they enjoy, the teachers in those schools must be themselves intelligent and properly educated. The teachers cannot be so educated without the aid of good grammar schools, academies, seminaries, or branches of the University, to fill the wide intervening space between the common school and the University. Schools of this high order should be found in every county—yea, as far as may be, in every town—that they may be accessible to the whole population, male and female. In New England, such schools and seminaries are found in almost every town and village. Is it wonderful that a population, reared under such auspices, should be intelligent, effective and prosperous?

New York has for many years past, emulated New England, in its liberal and varied provisions for diffusing education and knowledge among the masses of her multitudinous population. She has also within a few years past, established a State Normal School, which has excited the strongest interest and countenance throughout that State. Michigan need not be far behind her elder and more advanced, but not more forward sisters. She has accessible and quite within her reach, an ample fund to supply the wide chasm in her educational system, now found to exist between her common schools and the University. It is not by abstracting from either the common school or the University funds; neither of these are more ample than are needed in their appropriate and respective spheres, and to accomplish the objects for which they have been respectively appropriated and designated by the munificent donor, the General Government. But we have certain salt spring lands, which though not now subject to sale, no doubt Congress would cheerfully authorize us to sell and appropriate for this purpose. We confidently believe that in no other way could those lands be so wisely or usefully appropriated; and in that faith we have, in a subjoined resolution, recommended that the Legislature take immediate measures to appropriate the State salt spring lands to that object. No other appropriation of those lands could effect such wide-spread and continuing results—could do so much to humanize and elevate society in our midst—to give a healthful and vigorous tone to the intellectual development of the masses of our community. We propose that they should be appropriated to the support and assistance of a State normal school, branches of the University, academies, high schools and other seminaries of learning, of a high order, throughout the State. A large fund in the State of New York, is so distributed and appropriated annually, and with the best results. The normal school should be a model institution, for the training and preparation of teachers for the inferior schools. With this assistance and encouragement, the branches of the University which have languished or become dormant, would be speedily revived—high schools, academies, and other seminaries for instruction in the higher branches would spring up, and give a new impulse to education and mind, throughout the State. There would be no lack of suitable schools and seminaries for training and preparing the sons of our soil for the University, in such manner that they may there pursue the liberal arts, with pleasure to themselves and credit to the State; and thus shall a race of men spring up from our midst, who, whether in the pulpit or at the bar, or in the professor's chair, or in the halls of Congress, shall sustain the honor of the State, and proudly manifest the high tone and character of our institutions of learning. Such demonstrations can never fail of producing conviction. And it is thus we must raise up, educate and qualify our youth for public life, if we would be respected by others, or successfully maintain our own rights and dignity. And while these branches of the University, high schools and seminaries, would spring up thickly throughout the State, supplying the University liberally with students, the University on its part, would furnish its supply of finished scholars for preceptors and instructors in those branches. Seminaries and high schools, which in their time, would raise up, train and prepare large numbers of competent and highly educated teachers for the common schools, which would constantly keep that first and most important department of popular education, in healthful activity and vigor.

Thus the reflex influence of the common schools on the University, and the University on the common schools, would be beautifully illustrated, and constantly seen and felt. No one, because his son was not at the University, would feel that he was not receiving any benefit from it, since any man who had children in the common scho ol, would be receiving an annual installment from the University fund.

In the intermediate schools and seminaries, also, our youth in large numbers, whose circumstances would not permit them to enjoy the higher instruction of the University, (Scot-free, as it is to all the sons of Michigan, who will come and partake of it,) might obtain, if not a finished, certainly a highly valuable and practical education in almost all departments of instruction—and these privileges would be extended alike to male and female. Education of a higher order and refinement would thus be diffused through our whole population. What a contrast would such a picture present to the state of things we now see around us. Then might the Peninsular State boast a system of public and popular education within her limits more perfect in itself, more munificently endowed and more liberally administered than any other in these United States.

A few years of progress and development, under such a system, would make Michigan one of the noblest States of the Union.

LEGISLATION.

Various propositions came before the Legislature for legislation relating to schools, among which was one for establishing a separate department at the University for teachers; also for providing for the instruction of the deaf, dumb and blind; also for amending the laws so as take off all restrictions as to the raising of money for building school houses; for establishing temporary Normal schools or teachers' institutes; for a change of the law so that the mill tax might be raised by vote of townships. The Senate passed a bill providing that one of the branches of the University should be established as a State Normal school; but none of these became laws, except that providing for an asylum for the deaf and dumb. A charter was granted to Howell Academy; to Leoni theological institute; to Leoni seminary; to Olivet institute.

The school law was amended so that the qualified voters of any district might, at their annual meeting, raise by tax upon the taxable property of the district, a sum not exceeding a dollar a scholar for every scholar in the district between the ages of four and eighteen year, for the support of schools, to be levied and collected like other township taxes.

1849.

EXTRACT FROM GOV. RANSOM'S MESSAGE

The laws by which our common schools are regulated, it is believed, require no change. None perhaps could be devised which would more effectually secure the great object in view. than those now in force. The report of the Superintendent of Public Instruction, in which most of the important and interesting topics connected with our educational system are fully discussed, will be laid before you in due time.

No subject should more earnestly engage your attention than that of common school education.

The number of children reported between the ages of four and eighteen years, is 117,952, being 9,822 more than have been returned in any previous year. The whole number that have attended common schools during the year is 98,044, nine thousand nine hundred and sixty-four more than attended last year.

The amount of the primary school interest fund apportioned among the several counties and townships of the State for the past year, was $32,605 20, thirty cents to each child reported between the ages of four and eighteen years.

The amount of the mill tax for the township libraries, and the support of schools, was $15,020 44, which is more than double the amount heretofore raised for that purpose in any one year.

The amount of money raised by vote of the people for the support of schools at the last annual township meetings was $11,346 11, nearly three times the amount hitherto raised for such purposes.

The amount of money actually distributed among the several counties and townships of the State, for the support of schools during the past year, from the three sources mentioned, was $11,970 14 *more* than for any preceeding year.

The sum total of all school lands sold up to this time, reported by the Commissioner of the Land Office, was 111,126 acres. Over one-fourth of this had been sold during the last two years.

The total amount of all University lands sold up to this date was 20,309.54 acres, which taken from the whole amount selected (44,-416.31 acres,) left a balance on hand subject to sale of 24,106.77 acres.

REPORT OF SUPERINTENDENT.

The report of the Superintendent states that during the current year, he had spent the greater portion of the time in active labors abroad, attending educational meetings, conducting teachers' institutes, and co-operating with the friends of education. He speaks of these labors as being highly useful, and that increased interest had been aroused by these means, by the labors and zeal of the christian ministry, by educational societies, and by the influence of the press. He again recommends the establishment of an educational journal.

In relation to that part of the system which embraces the duties of county clerks, he observes that these officers have repeatedly expressed the hope that the Legislature would provide for the regular annual distribution of the reports of this office, to county clerks school inspectors, and directors of school districts. It was thought to be more necessary inasmuch as in the absence of an educational periodical, the annual reports constitute the principal and well nigh the only medium through which the Superintendent could communicate with local officers, as well as the source from which they hope to derive information in relation to the wishes and recommendations of the Superintendent, and the progress of education in different parts of the State. The following extract shows the progress of the schools.

STATISTICAL INFORMATION.

Under this head, in the reports from this department for former years, are statements which show a marked improvement, from year to year, in the condition of our schools, the number of scholars that attend them, the number of visits they receive from district and township school officers, the number and size of township libraries, the extent of their circulation, etc., etc.

By examining the reports received at this office for the last school year, and comparing them with the reports for preceeding years, it will be seen that our system of public instruction is still gaining upon the confidence of the public and rapidly increasing in usefulness.

The number of townships from which reports have been received for the past school year, is 442—17 more than reported the preceeding year. The number of school districts reported, is 3,671, which is 129 more than have reported in any former year. Of this number, 2,548 have maintained schools taught by qualified teachers, the constitutional term. This shows an increase of 177 over former years. The number of children reported between the ages of four and eighteen years, is 117,952, the same being 9,822 more than have been reported for any former year. The whole number that have attended school during the year, is 98,044, which shows an advance of 9,964 over all former years.

While there has been an *increase* in the wages paid "qualified teachers," there has, at the same time, been a *decrease* in the number of months the schools of the State have been taugnt by unqualified teachers, amounting, in the aggregate, to more than *eleven years;* and a corresponding decrease in the wages paid them.

The interest of the primary school fund apportioned to the several counties and townships of the State in May last, was $32,605 20, the same being 30 cents to every child reported within the legal ages, and an increase over former years of $1,330 46. For the preceding year, the apportionment was 33 cents to every child reported between the ages of four and eighteen years. This shows a falling off of two cents in the amount apportioned to each scholar, which was caused by a greater proportionate increase in the number of scholars, than in the amount apportioned from this fund—a circumstance which it is not probable will ever occur again; for there can be but little doubt that the annual increase of the primary school interest fund will be eight or ten thousand dollars a year for several years to come.

The amount of the mill tax for township libraries and the support of schools, is $15,020 44, which is more than twice the amount heretofore raised in any one year.

The amount of tax voted by the people for the support of schools, at the last annual township meetings, is $11,346 11, which is nearly three times the amount heretofore raised for said purpose.

The amount of public money actually distributed among the several counties and townships of the State for the support of schools during the past year, from the three sources just named, is $11,970-14 *more* than for any former year.

It was stated in the last annual report from this Department, that while there had been a large *increase* in the number of scholars attending *common schools*, there had been a corresponding *decrease* in the number attending *select schools*. This fact shows that while our common schools are gaining rapidly upon the confidence of the public, our select schools are losing patronage.

This two-fold method of showing the superiority of common schools when judiciously managed and properly improved, over select schools as they ordinarily exist, is now still more manifest than ever before.

During the last year, the *increase* in the number attending common schools has been nearly *ten thousand*, as we have already seen; and the *decrease* in the number attending select schools, has been upwards of one hundred.

The reports show that there are 245 township libraries in the State, containing in all, 58,203 volumes, which is an increase of 45 townships, and 14,277 volumes, during the past year.

Amendments to the school laws were proposed, in relation to the supply of fuel, so as to authorize the districts to vote a tax therefor; it was recommended that districts should be authorized, where there were one hundred or more scholars, to raise any amount of tax they please for the purchase of apparatus, such a provision being, in the opinion of the Superintendent, necessary to meet the wants of UNION SCHOOLS. It was further recommended that section 137 of the law, should be repealed. It was also the recommendation of the Superintendent, that with our age as a State, and the advancement we had made in the department of Public Instruction, that teachers' institutes, under the circumstances, were preferable, to the establishment of a single State normal school. For the holding of such institutes, it was suggested that the expenses attending them should be provided for. The Superintendent (Mr. Mayhew,) says:

Some have proposed raising it by contributions from the citizens of places where sessions may be held. But this would be a heavy tax; and especially where the citizens of a place offer to board the teachers in attendance. Gratuitous board, as has been offered in several places, is all that could be desired, and more than could ordinarily be expected. Others have proposed that the teachers in attendance be required to pay a specific sum. But this might exclude many worthy persons who are unable to spare the necessary amount from the small sum they have received for their services as teachers. Others still propose to raise the necessary sum to meet the expense of maintaining an Institute in each county, by a county tax. But if this method were desirable, it is not practicable. The number of teachers that would attend would be hardly sufficient to justify such an undertaking in some of the new counties. It would moreover be difficult, if not impossible to secure the services of a sufficient number of competent persons to carry forward so many Institutes at the same time. The plan proposed is a medium between county institutes and a State normal school, combining to a great degree the advantages of both, without the inconveniences of either. I would recommend that the expense of providing a board of instruction, be met in this way: Authorize the Superintendent of Public Instruction to draw a warrant upon the State Treasurer, for the necessary sum, to be paid from the annual income of the primary school fund.

A circular was issued, proposing the holding of a series of institutes very nearly on this plan, in reply to which, the Superintendent received very encouraging communications. Several sessions were subsequently held. The Superintendent thus speaks of UNION SCHOOLS:

This deservedly popular, and eminently useful form of common school organization, was dwelt upon at considerable length, in the last annual report from this department, commencing at the one hundred and first page. Their nature and advantages are there somewhat fully presented. This class of institutions, which may be made to constitute a connecting link between the ordinary common school and the State University, is fast gaining upon the confidence of the public. Those already established, have generally surpassed the expectations of their founders. Some of them have already attained a standing rarely equalled by the academical institutions of the older States. Large, commodious, and beautiful edifices have been erected, in quite a number of villages, for the accommodation of these schools. These school houses frequently occupy the most eligible sites in the villages where they are located. I am happy in being able to state, in this connection, that the late capitol of our State having been fitted up at much expense, was, in June last, opened as a common school house; and that, in that house, is maintained a free school, which constitutes the pride and ornament of the city of the Straits.

The Superintendent concludes this, his last report to the Legislature, as follows:

The citizens of our State may well be proud of the unparalleled success of our system of public instruction. The doors of our improved, and rapidly improving common schools, are open to all. The number in attendance at these institutions, increases several thousand from year to year. In round numbers, *ten thousand more* of the youth of our State drank at these fountains of intellectual and moral culture—of domestic and social happiness—of State and national prosperity—during the last year, than in any former year. At the same time, the blessings of our State University, which, like our common schools is alike open to all, are sought and enjoyed by an increasing number of the young men of our State, who may, at home, enjoy well-nigh all the literary privileges afforded in the older States.

REPORT OF REGENTS.

This report embraced the condition of the UNIVERSITY, as to its expenditures, in detailed nnd tabular form, the whole amount expended for building purposes, from January 8th, 1847, to October 3d, 1848, being $16,350 00.

MEDICAL DEPARTMENT.

The Board announce that incipient measures had been adopted for the organization of a MEDICAL DEPARTMENT, by constituting three professorships, viz: one of ANATOMY, charged with the duties also appertaining to special and surgical ANATOMY—one of MATERIA MEDICA, charged also with the duties appertaining to PHARMACY and MEDICAL JURISPRUDENCE—and one of the PRACTICE OF PHYSIC, charged also with recitations in obstetrics and diseases of women and children. Dr. DOUGLASS had been designated to fill the professorship of MATERIA MEDICA, and Dr. ABRAM SAGER that of the theory and practice of medicine, but without any additional expense to the University.

The number of students in the department of literature, was thirty-eight. The estimated receipts of the University were $13,000 00 for the next year. The Board remark that the financial system of the University had been matured by the experience of past years, and seemed now to be conducted with as rigid a regard to economy as the interests of the several departments will allow.

The report of the FACULTY embraced a new code of laws for the local government. They say:

On the introduction and enforcement of a new code of laws, there might naturally be expected some friction, yet the Faculty are happy in being able to assure the Board that the enforcement of these laws has been wholesome, and unattended by any serious difficulty. Although one dismission, and a few cases of suspension have occurred during the year, our quiet has not been disturbed by any rebellious spirit, nor by any very high misdemeanors. The Faculty will, however, take the liberty of suggesting a few amendments of the existing code of laws, principally the result of experience. They beg leave, also, to recommend a slightly modified course of studies. The suggested amendments will be found in the accompanying copies of the catalogue and statutes.

As some difference of opinion has existed in the Board, in respect to the propriety of a law prohibiting certain societies in the University, the Faculty herewith present for your consideration a special report on that subject, accompanied by a correspondence with the presidents of the principal colleges in our country.

If the Board will appropriate means for carrying out their intentions in regard to prizes, as expressed in the last section of the laws, the Faculty will announce the subjects for the present graduating class.

We also ask to be authorized by the Board to expend the whole amount of the special appropriation of one hundred dollars, to be made this year, we presume, as last, in the increase of the library, in the departments belonging to the several professors; except so much as shall be necessary for the purchase of Silliman's Journal, and of the four reprints of foreign journals.

The course of study has been pursued and accomplished in the several departments, except that of languages. Here, the failure has resulted from the impossibility of accomplishing the whole, under the existing arrangement.

REPORT OF BOARD OF VISITORS.

This report, signed by Rev. Dr. DUFFIELD, as chairman of the board, is so valuable in its suggestions and statements, that notwithstanding its length, it is deemed essential to the objects of this historical sketch of the affairs of the University to give it in full:

The organic law "of the University (of the State of Michigan) and its branches," agreeably to whose provisions we have been appointed by you, during this current year, as "a board of visitors, declares, that our "duty shall be, to make a personal examination into the State of the University in all its departments, and report the result to the Superintendent. suggesting such improvements as (we) may deem important."—*Sec.* 15.

In pursuance of your request, a majority of the board of visitors repaired, in July last, at the time named, to the University in Ann Arbor; and, having made their examination to some extent, in the absence of two members of the same, adjourned to hold a future meeting in the same place; which, after due notice given, was accordingly done; and the following report adopted, by the members present:

The departments of the University, as prescribed by the organic law, are—FIRST, "of literature, science, and arts; SECOND, "of law;" and THIRD, "of medicine." In the first department, the law contemplates FIFTEEN professorships, viz: one each, and severally—1st, of ancient languages; 2d, of modern languages; 3d, of rhetoric and oratory; 4th, of the philosophy of history and logic; 5th, of the philosophy of the human mind; 6th, of moral philosophy; 7th of natural theology; 9th of mathematics; 10th of natural philosophy; 11th, of chemistry: 12th, of geology and mineralogy; 13th of botany and zoology; 14th, of fine arts; 15th of civil engineering and drawing.

This department has been organized since 1841, and has not yet been perfected; but agreeably to the provisions of the organic law, the professorships have been created, as the number of students, their progress in study, and other exigencies required. Seven professors have been appointed, who discharge the duties of *eleven* professorships; viz:

1. GEO. P. WILLIAMS, professor of natural philosophy and mathematics.

2. ABRAHAM SAGER. professor of botany and zoology.

3. ANDREW TEN BROOK, professor of moral and intellectual philosophy.

4. Daniel D. Wheedon, professor of logic, rhetoric and history.
5. John Holmes Agnew, professor of Latin and Greek languages.
6. Silas H Douglass, professor of chemistry, mineralogy and geology.
7. Louis Farquelle, professor of modern languages.

The examination of the students, which we witnessed to some extent, on two different occasions, furnished evidence of the zeal, fidelity and ability of the professors, in their respective departments of science, and of the success and diligence of the students, generally.

The resources of the University, and the pressing exigencies in this early stage of its organization, will not admit, at present, of the appointment of any greater number of professors; nor is it, with the present number of students, at all necessary—that number ranging somewhere between eighty and ninety. The Regents have wisely arranged the combination of professorships, and distributed the duties of the same among the existing professors, so as to embrace the entire range of studies pursued in our best conducted eastern colleges, with the exception of the subject of political economy. It deserves to be particularly noticed, that they have introduced a system of extensive and efficient study in the modern languages, running through the whole course, which will make all the students acquainted with most of the modern languages of continental Europe, and particularly the French, Spanish, Italian and German. In eastern colleges, the modern languages are but an incidental study, during one or two terms of certain classes; and that by students only who elect them in preference to other branches. In this respect our University possesses superior privileges; and meets, more extensively and efficiently, the wants of our educated youth, than any of our older colleges. It is a new feature in college studies, and particularly appropriate to our Western States, filling up with a foreign population from nearly all the different nations of Europe.

It is suggested, whether a much more practicable and economical permanent arrangement, than that contemplated by the organic law, and that which the Regents have thus far, "in the first organization" adopted, is not in every way preferable; and therefore, whether such amendments might not be made to the statute, as shall give to them full power to provide, at any time hereafter, for the full range of study contemplated in it, without employing more professors than may be actually needed. The duties of several of the professorships, may occasionally be better distributed and provided for, at the discretion of the Board of Regents, who may consult the convenience, qualifications and taste of the different professors whom they may elect, and the relative importance and value of the branches of study, than by being required to appoint so many distinct professors, and one severally for each.

It is suggested, also, whether the employment of tutors might not be provided for, so as to meet certain interests of education and government, as efficiently, and more economically than by the multiplication of professors. Where the duties of instructors must be discharged by means of public lectures, it is essential that competent professors should be secured for that purpose. But where the nature and routine of study require a closer inspection, and severer drill and discipline of mind, than are requisite in the natural sciences, as in the languages and mathematics, somewhat of the labor, especially in the inferior classes, may be wisely and advantageously allotted to tutors, while the professors' time may be occupied with the higher, more difficult, more erudite, and more abstruse studies, appropriate to the more matured years and judgment of the superior classes.

The general experience of Colleges, if not the universal voice of those whose students reside not in parent's houses, commends, both for economy and efficiency, the employment of young unmarried men, recently graduated, who, being associated with the professors, may render important services, in various departments of science, and for general purposes of necessary government. There is no tutor at present associated with the Faculty. The consequence is, that the professors, having families, and separated in their dwellings from the students, are totally unable to exercise the necessary *surveillance* for all purposes of moral and physical safety and welfare.

The Board of Regents have wisely abstained from requiring, as is done in other colleges, the students to board in commons. They have left each at liberty to procure, in respectable families in the village, such accommodations in this respect, as may best suit their means and inclinations. When students come from abroad, and have no guardians and friends with whom to lodge, in the village, they are congregated in buildings erected for the purpose of affording conveniences for dormitories and studies. Two large edifices, four stories high, have been constructed for this purpose, and the great body of the students are lodged in them. These buildings are without any officer of college residing or lodging in them. There is no one whatever, dwelling in any of the suites of dormitories, to watch over and guard, during the hours of evening and night, the general interests of a large number of youth.

In all colleges there are many young men, especially in the two superior classes, whose sense of propriety, honor and duty, will always be sufficient to restrain and direct them. But perhaps a large number will most frequently be found in the inferior classes, whose tender years and limited experience, often render them liable to imposition and severities attempted by others older than themselves. Moreover, there is a ready, easy and frequent opportunity of access to instructors, both for purposes of directing and facilitating study, and of consultation in other matters, which it is important should be furnished in official guardians, and not be left at hazzard, and which can only be fully secured by the appointment of suitable tutors to take cognizance night and day, of the youth lodging in the several sections of the dormitory buildings subjected to their care.

The buildings which have been erected by the Regents for dormitory purposes, are admirably finished, after the most approved plan, the result of long experience and observation on the part of college officers.

Should the appropriate buildings be erected for lecture and recitation rooms, agreeably to the plan of the Regents, and the present edifices, conformably with the original design of their construction, be wholly occupied for dormitory uses, each of the two stately edifices now on the ground, would afford just such ranges or suites of rooms as four double four story houses would furnish, viz: 16 study rooms, and 32 separate chambers—in all, 64 of the former, and 128 of the latter, with necessary wood, and other closets. One-fourth of each building, however, of necessity has been appropriated for lecture rooms, recitation rooms, chapel library, mineralogical cabinet, and society halls. The buildings have been so constructed, that there is no possible communication from one section to the other, although both are included under the same roof, without having to pass outside. The studies and chambers in each section all communicate with one common stair-way, commencing on the entry of the lower floor. A tutor for each section containing 16 studies and 32 chambers—should he take a student into his own apartment with him, and having his room on the first floor, at the commencement of the stair-way, would have the watch and guard of thirty-one young men. He would thus prevent the ingress of improper persons to the building, and the egress of the students at improper hours and for improper purposes, while a much more efficient drilling in their studies, of the inferior classes might be secured. The want of such a class of offices, must necessarily operate to the detriment of the students, both in respect of study and the necessary *surveillance*. The Faculty have earnestly recommended to the Board the adoption of this feature into their system, and we accord with them in their suggestions in this respect. If the Regents have not power, under the existing organic law, to appoint such officers, it would be proper that it be so amended as to authorize them to make such arrangements, economical and otherwise, as may in this respect be found most advantageous.

Beside the fifteen professorships contemplated in the organic law, it provides also for the appointment of a chancellor. This officer has not been appointed, and for reasons which we deem abundantly sufficient. The law defines not, nor in any degree aids in determining what are the powers and duties of the chancellor. If the import of the name and the usages of the English institutions, whence the title has been borrowed, or the nature of courts of chancery, in which the chief judge is called chancellor, are to be taken into view in estimating his duties, there appears to be no ground of analogy that would enable us to do so.

A chancellor is supposed to have originally been a notary or scribe under the Roman Emperor, named CANCELLARIUS, because he sat behind a lattice, balister or railing, called CANCELLUS, to avoid being crowded by the people. Naude says it was the Emperor himself who sat in the "*Chancel,*" and rendered justice from within, while the chancellor attended at the door of the same, and thence obtained his title. Others allege that it is derived from the word CANCELLARE, signifying to erase or cross out, and that he took his name from the fact, that, through him, all letters, addresses, petitions, are passed to the king, and being first examined, were *cancelled* by him, if amiss. Coke says he had his title, because all patents, commissions and warrants coming from the king were examined and *cancelled* by him, when granted contrary to law. Others, because he *cancelled* and annulled the sentences of other courts. Others, still, have conjectured different reasons for the appellation; but it is certain that the name of chancellor was known in the *courts* of the Roman Emperors, and denoted a chief scribe or secretary, invested with judiciary powers, and a general superintendency over the other officers. Gibbon has noticed that under the Emperor Carinus, one of his door-keepers, with whom he entrusted the government of the city, was denominated *Cancellarius*, from which humble original, he says, the appellation of chancellor, has, by a singular fortune, risen into the title of the first great office of state in the monarchies of Europe. From the Roman Empire it passed into the Roman church, and hence every bishop has his chancellor, the principal judge of his consistory.

The modern nations of Europe, which grew up on the ruins of the Roman empire, have nearly all preserved its chancellor, with different jurisdictions and dignities, according to their constitutions. In all he seems to have had supervision of all charters, letters patent, and such other instruments of the crown, as were authenticated in the most solemn manner; and from the time that seals came into use, to have had the custody of "the king's seal," just as he was said, while an ecclesiastical officer near his person, for his aid in casuistry, to have had "the keeping of the king's conscience." The Lord High Chancellor of England is the first dignitary after the king and princes of the realm, being the chief administrator of justice near the sovereign, judge of the court of chancery, having the appointing power of all the justices of the peace in the kingdom, being general guardian of all infants, idiots, and lunatics, and having the general superintendence of charitable uses, and being assisted by twelve coadjutors, or inferior officers, once called *Clerici*, as being in "holy orders," but were *masters in chancery*, and the *master of the rolls*.

The chancellor of an University, is he who seals the diplomas or letters of degrees, provisions, &c., given the University. The chancellor of Oxford is their chief magistrate, *elected* by the students themselves. His office *durante vita* is, to govern the University, preserve and defend its rights and privileges, convoke assemblies, and do justice among the members of his jurisdiction. Under him is the vice chancellor, nominated by him, and elected by the University in convocation, whose business is strictly *vicarious*—acting in the absence of the principal. Four *por vice* chancellors are chosen by him out of the heads of colleges, to one of whom he deputes his power in his absence.

The chancellor of Cambridge is in most respects like that of Oxford, only he holds not his office *durante vita*, but may be elected every two years. The vice chancellor is chosen annually, by the collegiate senate, out of two persons nominated by the heads of the several colleges and halls. The word University, is a collective term applied to an assemblage of several colleges established in a city or town, having faculties of theology, law, medicine and the arts and sciences. In Oxford there are twenty distinct endowed corporations, termed colleges, and five are called halls, or buildings appropriated for the residence of students. In Cambridge there are thirteen colleges, and four halls. Over the several faculties and officers of these different colleges, the officer called chancellor, is the supreme judge and administrator in the University, or cluster of colleges.

There is nothing answerable to this state of things in our American institutions, and the word University is used rather by accommodation or anticipation, where separate faculties for law, medicine, theology and science exist, or may be contemplated. The original law of our institution contemplates the organization of three distinct colleges.

The government of our American colleges needs no such office as a chancellor. It is a title totally unsuited to democratic simplicity. Such an officer, to be appointed by the Regents, with such a title and no well defined duties, would either be a perfect sinecure, or excite jealousies and prove a cumbrous clog in the operations of our Unisity. We cordially approve of the policy and views of the Board, therefore, in abstaining from the appointment of a chancellor.

The Faculty of the arts and sciences, comprises the existing professors actually engaged in the business of instruction; several of the same being occupied in this way only a portion of each year. From the professors engaged regularly in the business of instruction during the whole year, one, according to an established law of rotation, becomes the president of the Faculty, and the acting principal of the University for one year; performing all the duties—in the way of convoking the Faculty, presiding at its meetings and administering the government—which are commonly discharged by what are called the president of the college. Thus far, the experience of our University commends the wisdom of the Regents. A similar arrangement, we understand, exists in the University of Virginia. We therefore suggest, that the organic law be amended, so as to strike from it the exceptionable, and somewhat monarchical feature of a chancellor, as contemplated by its existing provisions, and extend to the Regents the appointment of officers, and the arrangement and distribution of their duties. The direct responsibilities and practical wisdom, the constant watch and minute knowledge of the wants and interests of the institution, which pertains to the Regents, qualify them for this much better than any theoretic legislation can do.

At the same time, and appropriately in this connection, we take occasion to suggest a general revision of the organic law, and such further legislation as may have been rendered necessary or desirable by the past experience of the Board, and may be best caculated to promote and secure the uniform, persevering and regular administration of a system thus far so happily designed, and developing itself so advantageously and successfully. The knowledge which, through their observations and experience the Regents—who have been constantly and actively engaged in the management and prosecution of the interests of the University, and thus better enabled to acquire—will possess a practical value superior to all that may be had by those who merely look on from a distance, and are not particularly and personally conversant with its affairs. The University is a blessing and an honor to our State. We may well be proud of it. It gives us a name abroad, and is already affording rich hopes of promised good to be very speedily reaped among ourselves, in the high tone of education, that will characterize, at no distant day, the young men passing from it into actual life. Its influence is already felt on the other side of the globe. We know not that there is, in any other State in the confederacy, an institution which furnishes, as does our University, such an amount and means of instruction, free of all charge. As in our admirable system of free schools, so is it in our University, instruction "without money and without price" is provided for any and every youth that enters it. While the price of board, which varies from $1 25 to $1 75 per week, can be had in families in the village, and opportunities are afforded to those that are necessitated to teach, or labor, or industriously occupy themselves for a portion of their time, in order to meet their expenses of boarding and clothing, &c., few, if any of our young men, desirous of receiving a liberal education. need be deterred from seeking it. If the standard of education in our schools should be elevated, so as to embrace the full course of ordinary high schools or academical study, comprising the Latin and Greek languages, and such branches of mathematics as are included in the preparations for entering college—which extension and improvement we hope shortly to see accomplished by means of "Union Schools," and of the interest that you, sir, as Superintendent of Public Instruction have been instrumental in exciting—we may expect very soon to see a much larger proportion of our youth availing themselves of the advantages afforded by the University for the procurement of a liberal education. A monopoly of learning should, by all means be guarded against, and that as seduously as any of the monopolies toward which the tide of popular prejudice is justly directed. But this can only be done by fostering our University, and endeavoring to diffuse the benefits it affords, and place them equally within the reach of all. May nothing occur to embarrass or frustrate the plans of the Regents thus far so successfully prosecuted.

It is a happy circumstance, that since the commencement of the labors of the Regents, nearly cotemporaneously with the organization of our State itself, there has not been any thing to distract public attention, to excite political or denominational jealousies, or to secure unwise interference with the management of its concerns by its officially constituted guardians. The transactions of the Board have been free from sectarian influences, and the wise and judicious course pursued by the Regents, in selecting, as far as possible, their professors from different religious denominations, and in appointing those who would be generally acceptable to the community, has conciliated general confidence. It is also a theme for congratulation, that—while in other States, where Legislative interference, prompted by political and religious jealousies, has dictated to and controlled those who have been immediately and personally responsible as Regents or directors, or trustees of some institutions receiving State patronage, and while the history of such colleges has been but a series of disasters and confusion, revolution and disorganization, rendering them sometimes a by-word and reproach, and necessitating religious denominations to organize, endow and patronize their own peculiar means for the education and preservation of their youth—the University of Michigan has been subjected to no such hostile influences, The guardian genius of Christianity, broad and free—noble and grand as the Bible. has nevertheless been cherished and appreciated; and the Regents have been permitted, unmolested, to develope their measures for the education of our youth.

The several chief magistrates of our commonwealth, who, by the organic law, are ex-officio presidents of the Board of Regents, have manifested a liberal and disinterested regard for the best welfare of the interests of education, following the example of Governor Mason, who devoted much of his time and thought to the University, and contributed, by his zeal and his enlarged views of the wants of our State in this respect, to give character and shape to the early movements, and the very laborious efforts of the Regents in the initiatory processes of its organization. The relation of our University to the State is somewhat peculiar, and different from some of the State institutions whose history has been so disastrous. The State being constituted the trustees in fact, to promote the great ends of the Federal Government, in their liberal endowment of the University, by the grant of seventy-two sections of land, have endeavored to execute that trust, agreeably to the provisions of the organic law enacted for this purpose, by means of a certain number of gentlemen, twelve in all, to be appointed by the Governor, with the consent and approbation of the Senate, associating with them the Governor, Lieutenant Governor, the chancellor of the State, and the presiding judges of the several district courts as ex-officio members of the Board. The members of the Board of Regents, appointed by the Governor and Senate, serve for four years, three only being appointed each year. Their duties have been discharged without fee or reward; and on them mainly has been devolved the chief care and labor of carrying out the necessary details, and of executing the plans of the Board. The sale of the lands, the investing of the proceeds, the collecting the interest, and the general management of its fiscal concerns, are confided by existing laws to the commissioner of the State land office and the Superintendent of Public Instruction, and the avails thereof reach the Board through the State Treasurer. What the resources of the Board will be, from year to year, they can never tell directly themselves, having no officer of their own, or responsible to them, whom they may direct, to give them information, they are, always and wholly dependent for it on the State officers, viz: the Treasurer and Superintendent, who by writing furnish it. This has been, and may yet be more seriously, the occasion of embarrassment. The Board having sometimes been led to expect that means would be at their disposal, sufficient to justify them in incurring various expenses necessary for the extension of their system of instruction, eventually have been disappointed.

There is a building necessary for a laboratory and the delivery of chemical and other lectures, which it was supposed, a year ago, the funds available would be adequate to meet; and an appropriation was prospectively made accordingly. But the actual state of the finances, as paid into the treasury of the Board rendered it necessary to suspend furtner operations. Happily, the prospective deficiency was suspected and discovered by the fiscal officers of the Board, before the contracts authorized had been made by the committee appointed for the purpose.

It is greatly to the credit of the Board, that, placed as they are by the organic law, in this anomalous, and sometimes perplexing condition, they have, nevertheless, thus far, so judiciously conducted the disbursement of moneys put into their hands—that they have erected four houses for professors' dwellings, two large, handsome and commodious halls, four stories high, for dormitory purposes and for students—for a season, reared and fostered branches, till they were able to sustain themselves,—organized a Faculty, and sustained the professors—while the debt incurred in 1838, by the loan of $100,000 on State bonds granted for that purpose by the Legislature, has been so far reduced, by the payment and discharge of principal, agreeably to a wise specific legislation for the redemption of said bonds, so as to leave but about $20,000 remaining, to be liquidated.

It is suggested whether some change in the organic laws, on the subject of the University funds, might not be beneficially made on a revision of the same, by the competent authorities. The future and permanent welfare of the University depends upon the prudent and careful management of its funds. It would seem but reasonable, that the Regents, who are held immediately responsible to the public in all matters pertaining to the interests of the University, should have some way of being heard and acting in relation to the preservation and promotion of its financial interests.

There are certain interests of the University that require speedy attention. There is no philosophical apparatus, nor are there any mathematical instruments at all appropriate to the wants of the institution. There is not a telescope, or sextant, or orrery, or transit instrument, or any whatever for astronomical uses or celestial observations, belonging to the Board; nor have they any of the important and necessary means and facilities for demonstrating and illustrating the great laws of electricity, of galvanism, of magnetism, of pneumatics, of hydraulics, of hydrostatics, of optics, and of the mechanic powers, except a few limited appliances, that have been picked up by the merest accident. Not an instrument, even, for meteorological purposes, is to be found in their inventory, notwithstanding the subject is becoming every year one of increasing interest to the scholar and practical man, and awakens the attention of our national and other Legislatures.

The organic law authorizes the Board " to expend as much of the interest arising from the University fund, as may be necessary for the purchase of philosophical and other apparatus, a library, and cabinet of natural history," &c.—Sec. 18. A mineralogical cabinet, and to some extent, geological collection, of great value, have been procured. There is also a tolerable collection in other departments of natural history; and especially of the birds, animals, reptiles and flowers of our own State. A valuable and extensive library, too, has been procured, which is rich in historical collections, but which is deficient in classical literature, in that of the modern languages of Europe, in standard works of philosophy, and of the various exact and physical sciences, with the exception of geology and mineralogy, and in other important, especially modern publications, that should be within the precincts of every college.

The organic law provides for the appropriation of the initiatory fees of the students, which is the only charge allowed to be made of them, for the necessary repairs of buildings, and for the increase of the library. Hitherto, little or nothing available, or of much account, has been derived from this source, for the increase of the library.

The surplusage of the last two years in the revenue of the Board, has been absorbed by the erection of an additional suite of dormitories, which had become indispensably necessary for the accommodation of students, and which has been provided in a new symmetrical, substantially built, and well finished edifice, corresponding with the one previously on the ground. That of the coming year will be absorbed, in all probability, by the erection of a chemical laboratory, and lecture rooms, connected with it, which have become as indispensably necessary. But it is suggested, that however important such demands may be, the interests of the University require the procurement of a philosophical and other apparatus as speedily as possible.

The building about to be erected is intended to afford accommodations for, and facilitate the operations of a Faculty for a medical school or college, which, during this current year the Board have undertaken to organize. In as economical a method as practicable, the professors of chemistry and geology, mineralogy, and of botany and zoology, in the college of literature, science and arts, have been appointed to professorships in the medical college, of which they now form the Faculty. The former assumes the title, and performs the duties also, of professor of *materia medica*, of professor of pharmacy and medical jurisprudence; the latter of professor of the theory and practice of medicine, and performs the duties also, of professor of obstetrics, and the diseases of women and children. A third, it is expected will be appointed as soon as arrangements can be completed for opening this department. The organic law contemplates six professorships in this college: 1st, one of anatomy; 2d, of surgery; 3d, of pathology and physiology; 4th, of the practice of physic; 5th, of obstetrics and the diseases of women and children; 6th, of materia medica and pharmacy, and medical jurisprudence. The professor to be appointed next will assume the title of professor of anatomy and discharge the duties of professor of spinal and surgical anatomy.

The Regents have had regard to the provision of the organic law, in this as well as the other department, which directs them so to arrange the professorships as to appoint such a number only as the wants of the institution shall require. By the organization of this department, it is expected at an early period to afford advantages at home, to at least one hundred youth of our own State, who it is estimated have to seek them annually abroad in the prosecution of their medical studies.

The board ot visitors are happy, in the conclusion of their report, to express their entire approbation of the zeal and fidelity with which the Regents and Faculty execute the high trusts reposed in them. The watchful preservation of its funds—the prudent management of its affairs, by gentlemen that appreciate the value of a liberal education, and in their patriotism and religion rise above the jealousies and prejudices of sect and party, the steady and uniform perseverance in carrying out and perfecting the system already adopted—and the blessing of a benignant Providence, will not fail, at no distant day, not only to render the University of Michigan, of inestimable benefit to our State, but to make it rank among the highest and oldest of the literary institutions of our country, in respect to the extent, liberality, elevated standard and efficiency of its course of study, the talent and reputation of its Faculty, the character and usefulness of its students, the industry and disinterestedness of its Regents, and the wisdom and care of a fostering legislature.

INCORPORATED INSTITUTIONS.

This class of literary institutions had not previously received the notices of the Superintendents in their annual reports. The Superintendent this year, says of them: "that by examining the session laws as far back as 1841, there appears to be seventeen in number." Five of them were subject to visitation by the Superintendent, and were required to make an annual report to him. Three were required to make an annual report, and eight neither subject to visitation nor required by their charters to make a report. One it was made the duty of the Superintendent once in each year, to attend the examinations of, and to report its condition and prospects to the Legislature. No reports had been received from any of them, with the exception of Michigan Central College, which institution was represented to be in a flourishing condition, owning real estate, with two college buildings substantially built of two stories, containing rooms for recitations, apparatus, libraries &c., and for the accommodation of from forty to fifty students, and possessing a library of

1,500 volumes valued at $1,200, and a chemical and philosophical apparatus worth $1,000. The course of study embraced college, preparatory, English or teacher's course, and ladies course.

The plan of the institution embraced sooner or later the following professorships: a president and professor of moral philosophy, a professor of philosophy and logic, one of ancient languages, one of modern, one of mathematics and natural philosophy, one of rhetoric and belles letters, one of political economy, one of chemistry, botany and physiology, one of geology and mineralogy, and a principal of the preparatory department. Of these, six had been chosen and accepted their appointments, and a lady eminently qualified was at the head of the female department.

LEGISLATION.

A petition was presented to the Legislature from an incorporated institution asking a loan from the school fund, and a report adverse to the prayer of the petitioners, was made by the chairman of the committee on education, Dr. O. C. Comstock, stating the settled policy of the State to be against the principle of loaning the fund or revenue derived from it.

A communication was received from the Regents through the executive committee, J. Kearsley, Esq., Hon. E. Farnsworth, Hon. J. Goodwin and Dr. Pitcher, asking the passage of a law requiring the commissioner of the land office to report the sales of the University lands. They say:

The Regents are required by law to make an annual report, and the public has a right to expect a correct account of the University receipts and expenditures, in such report. Yet under existing laws, the Regents have no official information of what University lands have been located—whether the whole of the grant or not—how much has been sold and at what prices—how the money has been disposed of, and what may be expected or relied upon in future.

The Regents now receive, like a child under guardianship, what the State authorities give them, and are compelled for want of anything else, to make this the basis of action, without knowing officially how the fund itself is managed or the income derived, and without the information that is necessary to make the financial entries of the State and University treasury a counter-check and corrective of each other.

We believe that we should have the means always within our own control of showing to the country what has been done with the University lands. We believe it was the purpose of the law to confer upon the Regents a higher and more important trust than the mere expenditure of money placed in their hands by the State. We feel that it is required of us to know the actual income and insist upon its rightful appropriation, and we then ask the means of doing accurately and authoritatively our whole duty as Regents. This cannot be done, as we believe, under existing laws, and we therefore present our views to the Legislature, and ask such action as will best secure the faithful execution of the important trust committed to the government of Regents in making the University grant most available to the cause of education.

At this session, the present incumbent was nominated and confirmed as Superintendent of Public Instruction. Its legislation gave to Michigan an act for the establishment of a STATE NORMAL SCHOOL, providing for its endowment, and building and other purposes, twenty-five sections of salt spring lands. Its object was defined to be the instruction of persons, both male and female, in the ART OF TEACHING, and in all the various branches that pertain to a good common school education; also to give instruction in the MECHANIC ARTS, and in the ARTS OF HUSBANDRY and AGRICULTURAL CHEMISTRY, in the FUNDAMENTAL LAWS OF THE UNITED STATES, and in what regards THE RIGHTS AND DUTIES OF CITIZENS. It was placed under the direction of a BOARD OF EDUCATION, three of whom were to be appointed by the Governor by and with the advice and consent of the Senate. The Lieut. Governor and Superintendent were to be members by virtue of their office, and the latter to be Secretary of the Board, and to communicate such reports to the Legislature as were required. This act was subsequently amended and consolidated.

The powers of school district boards were enlarged by an act approved March 31, 1839. OAKLAND FEMALE SEMINARY was incorporated; also the Tecumseh Literary Institute. A joint resolution was passed authoriziug a sufficient number of the last report of the Superintendent to be printed to enable the county clerks to distribute copies to the boards of school inspectors and directors of districts. Two fractional school districts were *dissolved*, and local legislation had for various separate school districts. The primary school law, in its general provisions, remained unaltered.

1850.

EXTRACT FROM GOV. BARRY'S MESSAGE.

The University is represented to be in a prosperous condition. Its catalogue presents a list of 7 professors and 72 students. In addition to the department of science and arts, the board of regents have organized a department of medicine, in which a course of instruction will commence in the Autumn of the present year. A laboratory has been built on the eastern side of the University grounds, and is designed to accommodate the medical department, for which purpose it is amply sufficient. The receipts for the present year are estimated at $12,000 00, of which $1,000 are from room rents and admission fees, and $11,000 00 from the University interest fund. The board of visitors recommend the re-establishment of branches as soon as the condition of the funds will permit.

The whole necessary aunual expense of a student in this institution does not exceed $100, and by practice of strict economy, may be reduced to $70. Tuition is gratuitous, and a small sum only required for room rent and admission fees. While the expenses are so moderate, it is believed the advantages offered to students in the University of Michigan are scarcely excelled in similar institutions, longer established and more favorably known.

The system of common school education, adopted in the State, continues to produce favorable results. No essential change in its provisions are at this time deemed necessary or advisable.

The number of children reported, between the ages of four and eighteen years, is 125,218, and the whole number that have attended primary schools the past year is 102,871.

The amount of money appropriated from the primary school interest fund, is $39,382 95, and the amount of mill tax, $17,830 13. The whole amount raised for all purposes, including the mill tax and taxes for the construction and repair of school houses, was $73,804 97, which added to the sum distributed from the school intesest fund, makes the large amount of $113,187 92 expended in the State the past year for the promotion of common school education.

The board of trustees of the Michigan asylum for the education of the deaf and dumb and blind, and of the asylum for the insane, report that they have located the former at Flint, in the county of Genesee, and the latter at Kalamazoo, in the county of Kalamazoo, and from the citizens of those counties respectively, have received donations of $3,000 and $1,500 in aid of the institutions, and also lands suitable for the erection of requisite buildings.

The board of trustees also report that as the proceeds of the sale of the salt spring lands granted, and the donations made, will all be required for the erection of necessary buildings, these institutions, having strong claims upon public bounty, will still be destitute of sufficient endowments to afford that degree of usefulness desired and expected from their establishment.

The government of these asylums is vested in a board of trustees consisting of five members elected annually by the legislature in joint convention.

The board of education, under the law establishing a State Normal school, early in the year, selected twenty-five sections of land granted for that purpose, but of the selections made twelve sections were lands erroneously confirmed to the State. * * *

The Normal school has been located at Ypsilanti, in the county of Washtenaw, upon condition that the sum of $17,000, subscribed by its citizens, be satisfactorily secured ; of which sum $7,000 may be discharged by conveyance in trust to the board of a site and building thereon, designed and deemed suitable for the purpose of the school.

REPORT OF SUPERINTENDENT.

This report embraces the following subjects: the condition of the University, the statute duties of the office, a list of the literary institutions incorporated since the organization of the State government, the correspondence of the the office, the Normal school, free schools, and a partial sketch of the history of the school fund, and the usual reports of the Regents and visitors for the year. The branches were commended to the Legislature as an important part of our educational system. The great defect of the system was believed to be the want of an intermediate grade of institutions between the University and the primary schools. It was suggested whether some aid might not be afforded to incorporated literary institutions, without detriment to the University, upon their preparing students for admission to it. It was also believed that UNION SCHOOLS might probably at a future time supply in some degree the deficiency now felt in the system. As an important object connected with the promotion of science, it was recommended that METEOROGICAL OBSERVATIONS under the system adopted by the Smithsonian institute, should be made at the University. A system of observations had been established in the University of the State of New York and in their academies. It was conceived to be an object of importance to the State, situated as it was, in a region of country bordering upon the great Lakes, where such observations would add to the common stock of knowledge and lead to important results connected with agriculture and commerce, and it had been enjoined upon the Legislature to foster scientifical improvement.

The amount of school moneys apportioned to the townships this year, was $39,057 67. The whole number of children apportioned to, 118,223.

The official correspondence of the office was reported as increasing in volume and importance, and it was urgently recommended to the Legislature to make the decisions of the Superintendent in cases arising under the school law, final.

The importance of teachers' institutes was acknowledged as an efficient means of improvement among teachers. A list of books which formed the nucleus of a library for the office of Superintendent was reported, and a list of text and library books recommended to schools and school districts. A change was recommended in the system of reports—providing for the transmission of the reports of school inspectors directly to the Superintendent. Previous to this time, the reports of these officers were transmitted to the county clerks, whose duty it was to make abstracts of the same and forward to the Superintendent. This officer had no means heretofore of inspecting them, while for years complaint had been general, that they were defective and loosely made out. Errors of magnitude were discovered relating to reports of fractional districts, which had been alluded to during the administration of the office by Franklin Sawyer, Jr., but for which no remedy had been provided. Instances were given showing the practical operation of the law, and as nearly as could be ascertained an inequality in the distribution was unjustly taking place to the amount of over $2,000 annually.

Although the doctrine had been substantially recognized in the State that the "property of the citizens should educate its children," the expediency of adopting a system of FREE SCHOOLS was suggested as a subject for consideration.

The whole number of townships reporting was	448
" " districts "	2,536
" " children attending school	102,871
" " " drawing public money	125,218
Number of volumes in township libraries	67,877
" of qualified male teachers	1,435
" " female "	2,618
Average wages to male teachers	$14 00

Average wages to female "	$6 00
" months schools taught	5
Amount paid in rate bills	$29,717 88
" raised for school houses, repairs and sites,	51,085 26

REPORT OF THE REGENTS.

The number of students in the University was 84. The estimated expenses for the year, $11,289 41. Estimated receipts, $12,000. The Regents announced that the edifice designed for a Medical Department was nearly completed, so that at no distant period the pressing claims and necessities of the State in this respect would be supplied. The building committee report outstanding items of indebtedness amounting to $700.

UNIVERSITY INTEREST FUND.

There was received to the credit of the University interest fund for the last six fiscal years, as follows:

In 1843	$5,427 03
" 1844	8,752 90
" 1845	9,467 99
" 1846	10,013 51
" 1847	11,077 19
" 1848	10,829 44

REPORT OF BOARD OF VISITORS.

This board consisted of the following gentlemen: Isaac E. Crary, A. M., Ross Wilkins, A. M., David Noble, A. M., Rev. Joseph Penney, D. D., Rev. Samuel J. Graves, A. M. The following extract embraces their views in relation to the University:

To Francis W. Shearman, Esq.,
Superintendent of Public Instruction:

Sir—The undersigned, a majority of the board of visitors, appointed by you to make a personal examination into the state of the University in all its departments, for the year 1849, respectfully report, that they as a board, visited the University on the 18th and 19th days of August last. One of their number was in attendance on the 15th and 17th of the month, and witnessed the examination of the sophomore and freshman classes in a portion of their studies for the year. The Rev. Mr. Graves was present at the commencement of the examination of the senior and junior classes—but was unable to remain in attendance, on account of ill health.

The examination as far as attended, and the commencement exercises of the graduating class, afforded evidence of skill and fidelity in the professors as well as of diligence and talent in the students.

The aim of both evidently had been the cultivation of a vigorous intellect. The compositions and elocution were characterized by good taste, and a methodical mental discipline. They were free from the mannerism of mechanical drill, and preserved under the uniform that assimilates educated men, the distinctive qualities of the individual mind.

But on no other point were the visitors more highly gratified than the noble sentiments of morality and religion with which the students seem to be imbued, and considering that these are not elicited by the requirements of an institution expressly religious, and therefore devoted to some one denomination—but the spontaneous fruits of the re-union of all, under the impartial protection of the civil government, they cannot but regard it as a strong presumption in favor of the principles on which the University is founded as well as a merited testimonial to the character of its present instructors.

The library is a valuable collection, and seems to be kept with care.

The cabinets of natural history are excelled but by few in the U. States. In the departments of geology and zoology an appropriation is needed for the arrangement and better preservation of a vast collection of valuable specimens. The apparatus for chemical illustration, and still more for the various branches of natural philosophy, require many additions.

The imperative demands of the age have placed all the higher institutions of education, into a perplexing dilemma. The natural and mathematical sciences in their present extensive applications to agriculture, manufactures, and the mechanic arts, together with the political and economical sciences in aid of our free institutions, make so large and so just a claim on academic time, as is hard to reconcile with the acknowledged rights of classical and belles letters studies. The only safe and practical expedient that presents itself to the board, is transferring a part of what is now included in the college course, to the requirements of the preparatory course. Many advantages, besides the one chiefly contemplated, would result from the measure. A higher standard, and a more elevated character would be given to the preparatory schools, and their sympathy with the University increased. The age at which students would enter the University and consequently leave it, would be more advanced, and thus would be secured a maturity of mind more favorable to a thorough and permanent education.

An order of studies which necessity originated, and custom has continued in many of our older colleges is happily in part corrected, and should be wholly so, in the University. We refer to the arrangement whereby rhetoric and logic, which should be practically applied in every composition and debate, during the whole course, are placed at the end of the course in the senior year.

The design of diffusing the stimulus as well as the benefits of education, among the whole people by branches of the University in differents parts of the State, embodies a principle which neither justice nor good policy will permit to be abandoned or neglected. The organic law of the University makes it the duty of the Regents to establish such branches; and although their efforts have heretofore been unsuccessful, from the immaturity of the settlements and a badly devised system of rules and regulations, yet the best interests of the whole people call for further effort and renewed exertion on the part of those to whom is entrusted in an especial manner "the promotion of literature, the arts and the sciences." The fund at their control may not be sufficient to accomplish the whole design. But something should be done that the University may represent itself in the different sections of the State. Branches should be established and fostered, or their places will soon be supplied by sectarian colleges.

In the opinion of the board, it would conduce to the best interests of education, and the usefulness of the University to confer its honors in all their grades, from the lowest to the highest, upon all candidates who, wherever and however prepared, pass a good examination before the officers of the University, at an appointed time and place on the corresponding parts of the University course; and to recognize in each organized county, or senatorial or judicial district of the State, as a branch of the University, that institution which actually prepares the greatest number of such candidates, and at the same time yields a strict compliance with such requisitions as may be prescribed by the Regents for the promotion of some one or more of the natural sciences.

The board are not satisfied that the government of the University act wisely in withholding all inducements to application, except such as arise from the love of books and the hope of future usefulness. Many a student may "trim his midnight lamp and watch his lone taper till the stars go out" from such high incentives—but many more will be found to flag in their onward course to the summit of the hill of science. To many of the latter, competition for the prizes of a college course furnishes constant stimulus to honorable action, and when those prizes are won, the distinction feeds ambition with further desire. Such prizes may have been improperly bestowed in other literary institutions—but this furnishes no good reason for their entire omission. Only let the Regents devise a judicious system for the distribution of such prizes, and they will soon discover their salutary effects upon the students, by a more peculiar attendance at the University, and general application to study.

The object of the University is to provide the inhabitants of this State with the means of acquiring a thorough knowledge of the various branches of literature, science and the arts. In the main this object seems to have been kept in view, as well by the Regents in most of their enactments as by the Faculty, to whom is entrusted the immediate government. A portion of the board, however, think that there has been a departure from the strict line of duty, both by the Regents and the Faculty, in attempting to proscribe the existence of secret societies among the students. Some of these societies have a name coming down from a remote antiquity; and all of them are designed to promote either intellectual. moral or social improvement.

Their proscription at this late day, can be attended with no good results, and may be fraught with evil consequences. If the Legislature of the State not only suffers societies of like character to exist, but gives them charters of incorporation, it behooves the government of a Universiıy, founded upon the principles of that of Michigan, to deliberate with great care, before they issue an ukase proscribing any set of students for belonging to secret societies. In the opinion of some of the board, it would be such an encroachment upon privileges that ought to belong to individuals, as should not be made, unless such privileges are clearly shown to be detrimental to the literary pursuits of the students, and subversive of their good morals.

The board made no examination of the books and papers of the secretary of the Regents. No opportunity was presented while they were in session; the office of the Secretary being at Detroit, and his books and papers, while at the University, not convenient for inspection and examination. By attendance at one of the meetings of the Regents, the board came to the conclusion that the affairs of the University for the past year, had been managed so as to promote the best interest of the institution.

REPORTS OF INCORPORATED LITERARY INSTITUTIONS.

Under a law of 1837 in force, reports were received from several of these institutions. The trustees of OLIVET INSTITUTE reported

That the patronage the Institute has received during the past year, and its present prospects, afford them much encouragement to persevere in their efforts to promote the cause of popular education.

During the year ending July 1st, above one hundred youth, of both sexes, received instruction in the Institute. Of these, two have entered the University of our State, as members of the present junior class; one has entered college in Ohio; and some fifteen others have pursued the classical course of the Institute to some extent, several of whom contemplate a collegiate course. Four instructors have been regularly employed in the Institute, and an additional assistant during part of the year. Instruction has been given to classes in the ancient classics, and in all the higher branches of mathematics, including natural philosophy and astronomy. Physiology, and intellectual and moral philosophy have also received some share of attention. A teachers' class was formed at the beginning of the fall term, and continued for seven weeks, during which the members were taken through a thorough course in all the branches usually taught in common schools, accompanied with lectures on various practical topics connected with school teaching. Such a class will be formed at the commencement of the fall term each year, and is designed especially to fit teachers of common schools for their employment.

The Institute has no endowments, and no permanent source of revenue. The trustees are in possession of about 150 acres of land, of which only a few acres are under improvement. The building hitherto occupied for school purposes, is owned partly by the district, and affords but two rooms for the use of the Institute. The part thus occupied is valued at about $300. We have now in process of completion, a three story edifice, designed to accommodate nearly forty students, and furnish four convenient rooms for recitations, library, apparatus, &c. A part of this will soon be ready for occupancy. The cost, thus far, is near $2,000.

The library of the Institute consists of about 700 volumes, many of which are of an excellent character, and of considerable value. The whole may be valued perhaps at $500.

The Institute is but partially supplied with apparatus for illustrating the various branches of natural science—a lack which the instructors deeply feel, but have not the means of supplying, without aid from some legislative or charitable source. The founders of the Institute, seeing the embarrassment to which the incurring of large debts has subjected many other similar institutions, adopted the principle of incurring no debts beyond their visible means. In consequence of adhering to this policy, and of receiving very little aid beyond the contributions from the few who compose our own community, our buildings and other improvements have progressed very slowly—too slowly for the accommodation of the large number who have applied for instruction. We have deemed it better and safer, however, to adhere to this policy and suffer the inconvenience, than to encumber ourselves with debt.

One feature of our Institute commends it to the indigent and self-dependent youth of our State, viz: the incorporation of *manual labor* with intellectual training. By the pecuniary advantage thus offered, many of our students have been able to continue their studies a great portion of the year, who otherwise would have remained only a few months, or perhaps would not have entered the Institute at all.

In conclusion, we would respectfully suggest, whether a small portion of the ample school fund of our State can be more judiciously applied for the promotion of education, than in furnishing such auxiliaries as ours throughout the State, with a suitable outfit of maps, charts and apparatus. Such a grant, though small in value, would greatly encourage such institutions, and essentially enhance the interest among the hundreds of youth annually assembled in them for instruction.

The VERMONTVILLE ACADEMICAL ASSOCIATION, reported 36 scholars. The WOODSTOCK MANUAL LABOR SEMINARY, reported between 60 and 70 students. The property of this institution was reported to be estimated at $5,000. Its indebtedness about $2,000. Its library consisted of 1,500 volumes. Buildings partially completed.

The BOARD OF EDUCATION of the city of Detroit, reported 18 schools in operation, four of which were under charge of teachers at the rate of $400 per year, each; twelve under female teachers at $200 per year, each; and a colored school under charge of a female teacher, at the rate of $200 per year. These schools had been open during the year, with the exception of four weeks in summer.

STATE NORMAL SCHOOL.

In accordance with the act establishing this institution, the following members of the board of education were nominated by the governor and confirmed by the Senate, viz: SAMUEL BARSTOW, RANDOLPH MANNING, and REV. SAMUEL NEWBURY, who constituted the board, together with the LIEUTENANT GOVERNOR and SUPERINTENDENT OF PUBLIC INSTRUCTION, the latter of whom transmitted, in behalf of the board, their first report to the Legislature. The following extract gives their proceedings up to this time:

The board organized and held their first meeting in the month of May last, at the city of Detroit, and appointed Samuel Newbury president. Provision was made for carrying the law into effect, by the location of lands granted for the purposes mentioned therein; and the president was directed to discharge the duties enjoined upon him, in visiting various places of importance in the State, by receiving donations and obtaining propositions for the establishment of the school at an early day as practicable, and report to the Board.

The second meeting of the Board was held in the month of September last, at which time the report of the president, embracing the propositions received from various villages, and of the committee to locate the lands required in the act, was submitted. Propositions for the location of the school were received from Ypsilanti, Jackson, Marshall, Gull Prairie and Niles.

The location of the school has been a duty of great delicacy and no small difficulty. Each of the places mentioned proposed to furnish a site for the building, and tendered large subscriptions in aid of the institution, to be paid in money. After a full investigation and examination of the various proposals, and taking into view all the objects to be attained by the location, the board finally fixed upon the village of Ypsilanti, which was conditionally designated as the location of the Normal school. The condition was the furnishing satisfactory security to the board for the performance of the terms offered by the citizens of that place. The advantage of this site, in point of health, accessibility and locality, were deemed, under all the circumstances, not second to any other, while the proposition to the board was by far the most liberal. In view of the limited means, also, at the disposal of the board, and its small prospective income from a speedy sale of the land, the proposition was of such a character as to furnish decisive reason for its action. The proposition made by the citizens of that place included the offer of an eligible lot of ground for the site of the proposed school, a subscription of $13,500, well secured, payable one third September 1, 1850, and the balance in one and two years thereafter, the use of temporary buildings for the Normal and Model schools, until a suitable building could be erected, and the payment of the salary of the teacher of the model school for five years. Such a proposition was deemed by the board satifactory evidence not only of the liberality and public spirit of that place, but of the existence of interest in the general subject of education, which can not be less important to the institution in the future, than the liberal offer which it induced. The places in competition for its location, exhibited a like enlightened and generous liberality, which, while it increased the difficulty of action on the part of the board, finally induced them, while there seemed to be in fact so little choice of locality between the various places, so far as the interests of the State were to be subserved in the location of the school, to yield a preference to that place whose offer was the most liberal and advantageous. The site selected is convenient of access to all parts of the State, The village of Ypsilanti is sufficiently large to furnish every facility for boarding pupils, and the character of its population, and the deep interest manifested by them upon the subject of education, cannot fail to surround the institution with good influences.

A selection has been made for the site of the building, situate on a rise of ground on the north western border of the corporate limits of the village—a deed of which has been executed and delivered, free of expense, to the board. A guarantee, the draft of which, was submitted to the Attorney General, securing the payment of $13,500, has been executed and delivered to the board. There has been a compliance with the terms submitted by the citizens to the board, by the execution of the additional securities and agreements, which, together with the guarantee above mentioned have been received by the board as the fulfilment of the condition upon which the State Normal school was located at that place.

The location of the lands required by the act, was made at an early day after the organization of the board. They were made from the descriptions of salt spring lands as shown on the books of the State Land Office to be the property of the State. Due notice was given to the Commissioner, and a proper deseription of the lands so located, delivered to him to be filed in his office. After the locations were made and notice given to the Commissioner of the State Land Office, the board were notified by the Commissioner that it had been ascertained that a portion of the lands were not the property of the State and that they had been erroneously confirmed to the State by the general government; and that said lands had in fact been sold or disposed of by the United States previous to the confirmation of them by the secretary of the treasury.

Accompanying this report, in joint document No. 14, is to be found a list of the lands selected by the board, laying in the counties of Macomb, Kent, Ottowa, Washtenaw and Ionia.

LEGISLATION.

The MEMORIAL of ANDREW M. FITCH, JOHN A. 'BAUGHMAN, CLARK T. HINMAN and ELIJAH H. PILCHER, was presented to the Legislature, petitioning for the grant of a charter for a FEMALE COLLEGIATE INSTITUTION, in connection with the Wesleyan Seminary, at Albion. The application is briefly set forth, as follows:

We would respectfully set forth that the said Seminary has now been in successful operation for more than five years, and has sent forth a large and healthful influence in the cause of education. Still there is wanting an institution in this State, which will meet the highest wishes and literary aspirations of the females of our growing and highly prosperous State. In granting what is here prayed for, you will in no manner interfere with any institution now established under your fostering care.

Comparatively nothing has been done to cultivate, enlarge and properly direct the intellectual powers of those who are to give the first direction to the thoughts of those who are to succeed us on the great theatre of life, and to whom is to be entrusted the perpetuation of our free institutions.

What is petitioned for, is properly an enlargement of an existing charter, so as to meet the exigency of the case.

By granting our petition we are fully persuaded you will confer a great public benefit.

A MEMORIAL was presented relative to agriculture, by Bela Hubbard, Titus Dort and J. O. Holmes. representing that the committee of the State Agricultural Society had had in consideration a subject of great importance, viz: the establishment of a CENTRAL AGRICULTURAL OFFICE, and an appropriation was deemed desirable for a LIBRARY. Of this subject, in connection with the UNIVERSITY, the agricultural committee say:

In the organization of our State University, it was contemplated, (as appears by section twenty-six of the act,) that "in one of the branches there should be a department of agriculture, with competent instructors in the theory of agriculture, including vegetable physiology, agricultural chemistry, and experimental and practical farming and agriculture." Such a department, it is plain, to be vigorously and practically carried out, must have its more immediate and vital connection with the State Agricultural Society and its institutions. With an agricultural college should also be associated a model and experimental farm, a botanical garden, and perhaps a veterinary establishment.

By these means will the farmers of our State—its great leading class—be furnished with institutions peculiarly theirs. They will be provided with the means of educating their youth in every practical and scientific detail necessary or useful to that most important of all occupations, to as full an extent as is now afforded by the higher colleges of our land, to candidates for the so-called "learned professions."

On the 21st of January, the Senate adopted a resolution in relation to the management of the loan of $100,000 and to a certain claim, arising out of the same, which it is only deemed necessary here to refer to, and which is to be found in Senate document No. 11, of the session, (1850.)

This document contains the reply of the Secretary of the Board, extracts from the journal of the Regents, copy of the bond given by Major Kearsley, and also by the Bank of Michigan, the report made by Major K. of his proceedings in July, 1838, and also a statement of his claim.

The memorial of G. M. Barber and other students, relative to the proceedings of the Regents and Faculty as to secret societies, was presented to the Senate. A report was made in relation to the same subject by a committee of the Board of Regents, and also by the Faculty. All the documents relating to the controversy may be found in the journal of the Senate, being documents number 15, 16, 11, 37 and 38. As they do not relate to the legitimate object of this compilation, they are here referred to, simply as a matter of reference to those whose duty it may be to examine them, if a similar question should be raised in the future, in the local government of the University. As this is not anticipated, the subject is not of importance otherwise, in the history of its affairs.

Another memorial from the State Agricultural Society was presented to the Legislature, praying for the establishment of a STATE AGRICULTURAL COLLEGE. As to the character and scope of such an institution, the memorial says:

The first and most important consideration is, that the institution would be a *labor school;* in which the actual work performed by the pupils would be passed to their credit, in the account for their instruction. Thus the expense would be greatly diminished if not altogether paid. The very act of labor would be a practicable application of the precepts taught, and the poor would enjoy equal privileges with the rich.

The institution should be attached to, or form a *branch of the State University,* as is contemplated by the charter of that institution, and having the benefit of lectures from the professors, and such other sources as may be expedient, resident professors, with expensive salaries, would not be necessary.

There should belong to the institution a *Farm,* of sufficient capacity to embrace a variety of soil and surface, upon which all the operations of agriculture, connected with tillage, the culture of all the useful grains, grapes and roots, the raising of stock, &c., could be conducted to the best advantage, and where the operations of draining, and the treatment of different soils, could be thoroughly exhibited—in fact, a farm which, under the superintendence of practical and scientific masters, should become a *Model* for the farms of our State.

There should also be attached a *Botanical Garden*, to be under the charge of the professor of Botany of the University, in which should be cultivated specimens of the trees, shrubs and plants indigenous to our State, as well as all plants and weeds, a knowledge of the properties and habits of which is useful to the farmer.

The *studies* taught at this college should be of an eminently practical kind. Bende's agriculture in its details, mathematics and the keeping of accounts, mechanics, natural philosophy and the natural sciences, with their applications to agriculture. With these could be profitably associated Anatomy, so far as connected with the structure and diseases of animals, and the study of insects and their habits, and, to some extent, engineering, architecture, and landscape gardening. Nor should the claims of literature and the fine arts be wholly neglected, as tending to polish the mind and manners, refine the taste, and add greater lustre and dignity to life. In fine, those branches of education which will tend to render agriculture not only a useful, but a learned and liberal profession, and its cultivators not the "bone and sinew" merely, but the ornaments of society.

One prominent advantage possessed by the pupil in such an institution should not be overlooked, in the judicious combination of labor and study; resulting in confirmed health, and thence increased mental as well as bodily vigor.

But the importance of the plan proposed will weigh little, unless it shall be proved to be *practicable.* The only obstacle that can be reasonably supposed to exist, is the expense of founding and conducting such an establishment. In the communities of the old world, this obstacle, serious as it is under their circumstances, has been overcome, and with triumphant results. Probably no community in the world possesses greater facilities for the experiment, if it be deemed such, than ours. On the plan suggested, no large endowment is necessary. The connection with the University would furnish a large part of the means for instruction, at comparatively little cost to the institution.

No where, in a settled community, is *land* so cheap, at the present moment, as in this State. No State is more amply provided with landed and other means for the promotion of education. May not a part of this fund be as legitimately applied to this object as to other plans of educational improvement?

In the House of Representatives, the committee on education, through Hon. Hovey K. Clarke, their chairman, made a report in relation to the establishment of Free Schools and other matters embraced in the report of the Superintendent. The following extract contains substantially the views of the committee:

The committee on education, to whom was referred the annual report of the Superintendent of Public Instruction, respectfully report:

That in the judgment of your committee none of the topics presented in the report of the Superintendent which would seem to invite the action of the Legislature, can be considered of greater importance than that which relates to the establishment of FREE SCHOOLS throughout the State. The voice of the public press, the petitions which have been presented to the Legislature at the present session, and the generally expressed desire in many parts of the State, that the public should assume in practice the duty, which in theory has long been acknowledged, namely, the education at the public cost of the children of the State, have induced your committee to examine this question with a view to ascertain its present practicability.

The example of other States is undoubtedly operating extensively among the people of this State as a stimulus to the establishment of free schools. And the fact, that three of the States formed out of the ancient North-West Territory, have already preceded us in this step upon a higher level of educational effort than we have yet attained, ought to commend our earnest attention to a subject of such paramount importance. Michigan has thus far maintained an honorable pre-eminence in the education, intelligence and general cultivation of its people. But these qualities will cease to be our characteristics, unless earnest and well directed efforts be made to extend the influence, and to elevate the standard of education among us. As a means of elevating this standard, the recent legislation of the State, providing for a supply of competent teachers, through the agency of the Normal school, may be regarded as a measnre at once liberal and wise. And as a means of extending the influence of education, a system of free schools, if conducted by competent teachers, will undoubtedly be found to be the wisest and most efficient policy. Yet all this involves an inquiry into the present ability of the State to sustain them without imposing an onerous burden of taxation upon the people.

This question is obviously one which should be carefully pondered; for there is, perhaps, some danger that a premature effort to accomplish an object so eminently desirable might react with mischievous effect. This danger should be considered, that it may be well understood, and the means to avoid it may be wisely chosen.

It is very much to be regretted that the only means we have to ascertain the present expense of supporting our common schools, do not afford perfectly reliable data. The provision of law which requires the annual levy of a tax of one mill upon the assessors' valuation for the increase of township libraries and the support of schools, ought to have produced for these objects, for the year 1849, upon the valuation of 1848, the sum of $29,908 76. Yet the returns to the Superintendent of Public Instruction show an aggregate of only $17,-830 13 for this purpose, by which it would appear that the school funds were deprived of over $12,000 for the last year. The law which requires the levying of this tax is positive in its terms—absolutely requiring the supervisors to levy it; and yet it seems to have been disregarded, to a certain extent, in all parts of the State alike. A comparison of the aggregate valuations of the counties, as exhibited on page 43 of the Auditor General's report, with the amount of the mill tax, as appears on pages 72 and 73 of the Superintendent's report, shows to what extent this duty has been neglected by the supervisors of townships.

So also the attempt to ascertain the amount raised by tax which the districts are authorized to raise *per capita*, is baffled by the neglect of some six or seven counties to make any return under this head; and many others, and some of them large counties, return such inconsiderable sums, that great doubts are suggested of the accuracy of the reports.

Taking these reports, however, as true, it would appear that the amounts actually expended for tuition in the primary schools during the past year, are as follows:

Raised by tax:		
The mill tax,	$17,830 13	
Deduct for library purposes in 448 townships, reporting at $25 each	11,200 00	
Leaving of this tax applicable to the payment for tuition,		$6,630 13
Per capita tax, not exceeding $1 per scholar,		4,624 56
Total raised by tax for tuition,		$11,254 69
Distributed from primary school fund,		39,052 67
Total of public moneys		$50,312 36
Collected upon rate bills,		29,717 88
Total cost of tuition in primary schools		$80,030 24

The sum of eighty thousand dollars must be assumed as the nearest approximation we can make from the reports to the actual cost of tuition in the primary schools during the past year. It is not unlikely, however, that a much larger sum was collected upon the rate bills than the reports exhibit. And it is possible that this sum should be further increased, in fact, by the portion of the mill tax levied and collected but not reported. It is quite impossible to ascertain the degree of allowance which should be made for such inaccuracies; your committee are therefore obliged to assume from the returns to the Superintendent, that the tuition of 102,871 scholars for five months in the year, has cost an average of about eighty cents each.

Your committee, however, desire to repeat, that they are by no means satisfied that the conclusion thus announced may be relied on as true. It is the nearest approach to truth which, under the circumstances, they can make. If it could with certainty be relied upon, your committee would not hesitate to recommend, and rejoice in the recommendation that the school houses of Michigan should be declared "open to all who may choose to enter." But, while they dare not do this upon such imperfect data as they have by which to ascertain the expense that would thus be cast upon the people, they feel bound to recommend some action looking to the same desirable end. And they believe that if the present law, which allows the levying, by the vote of any school district, of a tax not exceeding one dollar for each scholar within the required ages, upon the property of the district, be repealed, and the present mill tax be increased to two mills, that greater equality in the assessment of school taxes will be secured, and it is hoped, a fund sufficiently large will be obtained to make the primary schools of the State substantially free. At any rate, if this much desired object be not the result, the increase of taxation thus provided for, of a known and limited amount, cannot be regarded as oppressive, and future legislation upon more accurate data, may complete the work, towards which, we now desire by cautious and prudent measures to advance.

The prosperous condition of the University, as appears from the report, and the report of the board of visitors, annexed thereto, attracts the notice of your committee, who rejoice to learn that this institution is laying a foundation for the highest usefulness of the rising generation of our State. The establishing upon a basis, indicating present and increasing prosperity, of a collegiate institution, even when sustained by an ample endowment, is ordinarily the slow and toilsome work of years. And the establishment of such an institution, under the control of the public authorities of a State government, has been a problem of so much difficulty and doubt, that even a moderate degree of success affords ample occasion for grateful remembrance of the labors and services of those by whose care and watchfulness such a measure of success has been achieved. And perhaps no higher praise can be awarded to the management of the University, than is borne by the universal testimony to the character and scholarship of the classes which have thus far been graduated. On this point the report of the board of Visitors holds the most unequivocal language of approbation of the "skill and fidelity in the professors, as well as of diligence and talent in the student. * * *

The department of Public Instruction ought to be regarded as second to none in the State government. The duties of it follow every family in the State to its very fireside, and invite them to an interested co-operation in labors of great importance to the well being of the State. The performance of such duties by the head of such a department, demands the employment of talents of a high order and of the utmost business activity. The report of the Superintendent shows a diligent attention to a great variety of duties, and which must have involved an amount of labor for which the compensation allowed by law is a most inadequate remuneration. Your committee therefore take leave to express the hope that this injustice will be suffered to exist no longer; but that a greater efficiency in the office may be secured by placing it, in regard to compensation of the incumbent, on the same level with other State officers, whose duties are neither more important nor onerous. It is hoped that the head of a department so important as this will no longer be regarded as a clerkship, of little responsibility and but inconsiderable labor.

Such an increase of compensation is, moreover, urged in view of a proposed increase in the duties of the Superintendent's office. The mischiefs which arise from the present mode of reporting the annual statistics of the school districts are forcibly set forth in his report, and the means to obviate them are there suggested. Your committee agree entirely in the recommendation, that the township inspectors be required to transmit directly to the Superintendent their annual reports, and thus dispense with the abstracts which the county clerks are now required by law to make. This recommendation is made not only as a matter of economy, which will effect a considerable saving in the sums paid to the county clerks for making these reports, but because the labor of arranging and combining them may be done in the Superintendent's office with much greater certainty of its correctness in view of all the interests to be affected by it.

To carry into effect the foregoing recommendations, I am instructed by the committee to report a bill to amend chapter fifty-six of the revised statutes, and a bill to amend chapter fifty-eight of the revised statutes.

LEGISLATION.

The school law was amended, in pursuance of the recommendations of the Superintendent, so as to bring the report of the school inspectors directly to his office, and the duties heretofore devolving upon the county clerks, so far as the making of abstracts and returns were concerned, abolished. Various other amendments were made, which, as they are now in force, will be found in the primary school law, as published in this document. The law regulating the duties of Superintendent was also changed, and will be found in a subsequent part hereof. The mode of electing members of the board of education was changed by an act of March 29, 1850. An act was passed, enlarging the powers of the trustees of the Wesleyan Seminary, at Albion, and authorizing them to establish at Albion, a FEMALE COLLEGE, as a branch of the Seminary. It was made subject to visitation by a board, to be appointed by the Superintendent, and the trustees required to make a report annually to that officer.

An act was passed to incorporate the Young Ladies' Seminary of the city of Monroe. It was made the duty of the trustees to submit to the Superintendent an annual report, exhibiting its condition in all its departments. The St. Mary's Academy, at Bertrand, in Berrien county, was incorporated; also, the Clarkston Academical Institute; also, the Clinton Institute; the Lawrence Literary Institute Association; the Michigan Central College, at Spring Arbor; St. Mark's College, at Grand Rapids. An act was passed and approved April 2, relative to the support of schools, and the custody of township libraries. The free school law of the city of Detroit was also amended.

THE CONSTITUTIONAL CONVENTION.

This was an important year in the history of public instruction in Michigan, inasmuch as the act was passed by this Legislature, in conformity with the previous votes of the people, to provide for a REVISION OF THE CONSTITUTION. For fifteen years the provisions of the first constitution, relating to education, had stood the test of time and trial—had been the means of securing constant progress, and achieved for Michigan, what had not been accomplished by the provisions of the constitution of any other State of the Union, for the same length of time. The history of our educational affairs, as detailed in this document, presents an array of facts, and develops marks of constant improvement, which, while it exhibits the struggles through which we have passed, must be a source of gratification to every citizen of the State. Upon the subject of education, none can accuse the State of Michigan of apathy or indifference. It is a subject that has been constantly kept before the people, and appreciated by them; and amidst vicisitudes of no ordinary character, its educational resources and institutions have been secured, preserved and cherished. The first fifteen years of our educational history, under the first constitution adopted by our people, constitutes an epoch, to which we may proudly look back and refer, and from which may be derived a light and a lesson for the future. But with a knowledge of what had been thus far achieved, and with a consciousness of attaining a yet higher standard of improvement, the organic law was cheerfully and with hope, subjected to a revision, from which it was believed still higher and greater results were yet to be accomplished.

The article upon education proposed to the convention, was submitted on the 15th day of June, by Mr. Walker, of Macomb. The committee consisted of the following gentlemen, viz: Messrs. Walker, Van Valkenburg, Butterfield, Eastman, Desnoyer, J. D. Pierce, Barnard, Williams and Edmunds.

Section 1 provided for the election of a Superintendent of Public Instruction, by the electors, who should have general supervision of public instruction, whose duties should be prescribed by law, and whose term of office should be two years.

Section 2 provided that the proceeds of the sales of all lands granted for school purposes, should remain a perpetual fund, the interest of which, with the rents of all unsold lands should be inviolably appropriated to the support of primary schools throughout the State, and distributed annually on such fair and equitable terms as should be provided by law.

Section 3 provided that the Legislature should establish by law, a system of primary schools, by which such schools should be kept in each and every district for at least three months in every year, FREE AND WITHOUT CHARGE FOR TUITION, to all children between the ages of four and eighteen years, and should provide *that any deficiency that may exist after the distribution of the primary school interest fund, shall be raised in the several townships and cities, by a tax upon the whole taxable property in such townships and cities respectively. The English language and no other should be taught in such schools.*

Section 4 provided for the election by the people of six Regents of the University—two for six years, two for four, and two for two years; after which there was to be two Regents elected at each subsequent election, to hold their offices for six years.

Section 5 made it the duty of the Regents at their first meeting, to elect a PRESIDENT of the UNIVERSITY, who was to be a member of the Board, and the principal executive of the University. The Board to have direction and control of all its expenditures, and general supervision of the institution.

Section 6 appropriated the sales of all lands granted, or to be granted for University purposes, as a perpetual fund, the interest of which, with the rents, should be inviolably appropriated to the support of the University, and with such branches as the public good required, for the promotion of literature, science and the arts.

Section 7 provided for the election of three members of the board of education, who, together with the Superintendent of Public Instruction, were to have general supervision of the STATE NORMAL SCHOOL.

Section 8 secured the proceeds of sales of lands appropriated to the normal school, in the same manner as University and school lands.

Section 9 provided for the encouragement and promotion by the Legislature, of intellectual, scientifical and agricultural improvement, and for the establishment of an agricultural school, with a model farm; also for the establishment of libraries, one at least in each township, to the support of which, moneys paid for exemptions from military duty, and all fines assessed for breach of penal laws, were to be exclusively applied.

The article as reported, was taken up in convention, on the 26th of June. A substitute for section 3, was offered by Mr. FRALICK, of Wayne county, who was in favor of raising a tax upon the property, regulated by the number of scholars, if there was a deficiency after the distribution of the income of the school fund—that the Legislature should levy a tax on the whole taxable property of the township or city. Mr. MORRISON, of Calhoun, also proposed a substitute—that the Legislature should provide by law, that in the year 1855, and every year thereafter, a general tax should be levied in the State, for the support of primary schools, not exceeding three mills upon each dollar of the valuation of the taxable property of the State; such tax to be levied and collected in the same manner as the State tax for State purposes. Mr. LEACH, of Genesee, also proposed a substitute, which was as follows:

A primary school shall be kept in each school district in the State, at least ——— months in each year.

The right to attend such schools is guarantied to all persons between the ages of four and twenty-one years.

For the support of primary schools there shall be raised annually, a State tax of not less than ——— cents per scholar for each scholar returned to the office of the Superintendent of Public Instruction, and such tax and also the interest of the primary school fund shall be annually distributed among the several school districts in this State, in proportion to the number of scholars in each, as shown by their returns to the office of Superintendent of Public Instruction; and any deficiency that may exist in the districts, after the distribution of said moneys, shall be raised by tax on all the taxable property in such districts.

The substitute was opposed by Mr. J. D. PIERCE, for the reason that it would be found difficult to levy a tax upon the districts. It had been attempted and failed. He was in favor of free schools, and a State tax. Mr. RAYNALE was also opposed to the section and the amendments, being of opinion that it was safer left with the Legislature to establish by law a system of common schools. Mr. BAGG was in favor of free schools—free as the air we breathe—and proposed a further amendment, providing that the Legislature should establish a system of primary schools, such schools to be kept up at least three months free, without charge of tuition, to all children between the ages of four and twenty-one years. Mr. ALVORD thought that the spirit of the age made it obligatory on the convention to provide that schools should be kept up, and was in favor of a tax to pay for free schools. Mr. HANSCOM was in favor of obliging the Legislature to provide for a system of free schools, and of leaving the details to it. Mr. VAN VALKENBURG believed that the Convention was called upon to establish a system of free schools—was unwilling to leave it with the Legislature, except to manage the details. The chairman of the committee, Mr. WALKER, said the committee had discussed the proposition to raise a definite sum per scholar, throughout the State, but the difficulty was, if the sum was fixed, it must remain so until the constitution was amended. Mr. CORNELL offered an amendment, providing that the Legislature should establish free schools throughout the State and provide for their support, and that after applying the school and such other funds as shall be set apart for the support of such schools, the balance should be raised by a tax upon the taxable property of the State. Mr. WHIPPLE regarded this question as the most important one that had come before the Convention, and was of the opinion that the people were prepared for and wished a free school system. The chairman of the committee thought the proposition of Mr. Leach, of Genesee, was of the same character as that adopted in New York, and which contained the elements of discord. He had been advised by a letter of the Superintendent of schools of that State, that if any attempt should be made to change the school system of Michigan, we should avoid raising any portion of the tax in the school districts.

Another amendment was offered by Mr. Fralick, as follows:

Sec. 3. The Legislature shall provide by law for a system of primary schools, by which such schools shall be kept up and supported in each school district, at least three months in every year; and any school district neglecting to keep up and support such a school, may be deprived of its proportion of the public funds; and a tax shall be levied on the several townships and cities of the State, upon the whole taxable property in such townships and cities respectively, for the support of such schools, provided such tax shall not exceed the amount of ———, in any one year, for all children between the ages of four and eighteen years, in any township or city, and the amount of such tax in each township or city shall be distributed to the several districts therein, keeping a three months' school, in proportion to the number of children between the ages of four and eighteen years, returned from said districts respectively.

The amendment was opposed by Mr. N. Pierce, who believed the greatest difficulty in New York had arisen from authority given to districts. He was in favor of imposing a tax upon the taxable property of the State, but that it should be limited to two mills upon the dollar, and the remainder should be collected by a tax on the district, or the persons sending to school, or the property of the town or district. Mr. Crary said, substantially, that the school system now in operation was as good a system as ever was devised, and had been copied by several States. It took from 1843 to the present time to perfect it, and the Convention had better leave it to the action of the Legislature, to provide for free schools by such a system or mode as it thought best, either by general taxation, or tax levied in districts, counties or township.

The difficulty in New York was the inequality of taxation. The committee on education had, however, neglected an important feature—they made no provision for a forfeiture of the public money, if a district neglected to keep a school for a certain time. If we were going to have a system of free schools, there should not only be a forfeiture of public money, but a penalty for neglecting to comply with the law. He was willing to leave it to the Legislature, as long as a public officer was kept, whose business it was to attend to the cause of education—he believed that such an officer was requisite to sustain and forward the cause of education, and that it was necessary that each State should employ one; but that if such officer was dispensed with, he should consider the cause of education in danger;

while with such an officer, the subject would be kept before the people, and the cause would flourish. Mr. MOORE was in favor of establishing the system of free schools upon a thorough basis, and wished to see it immediately adopted. Mr. TIFFANY thought the Legislature would adopt the system when the people demanded it. The question being taken on Mr. LEACH's substitute as amended, it was not sustained. Mr. BUSH was in favor of leaving the establishment of a system of free schools to the Legislature, and was opposed to the provision reported by the committee. The following extract contains the substance of his argument:

The provision as reported gives the power to raise revenue sufficient to make schools free: first, to the township, and in case of deficiency, the deficit to be raised by the school district. Experience has shown us that great inequality in taxation will exist in different locations of the State; it but proposes to make permanent in the constitution the system that was commenced under the liberal provisions of our present constitution by the statutes of 1838. The Legislature then, actuated by the purest patriotism, provided that any deficiency that might exist, after using their proportion of the primary school interest fund, might be raised upon the taxable property of the school district. The inequality that existed in the districts was so great, and so apparent, that the system fell at once into disrepute. One district would, by economy, cause a school to be kept up without resorting to oppressive taxation; another, perhaps in the same township, by prodigality and extravagance, levied a tax upon the property of their district, ostensibly for the support of schools, which the property holders were neither able nor willing to bear. This evil existed in some portions of the State to so great an extent as to affect the relative value of real estate, and necessarily led to a modification of the law. I therefore am opposed to the provision as reported, believing that the same evils would result from its operation, and the consequences would be more disastrous from a constitutional provision, in consequence of permanency, than from a repealable law.

The amendment provides that a tax shall be levied upon the whole taxable property of the State, and shall, when collected, be distributed among the districts, in proportion to the number of scholars, in the same manner as the primary school fund is now distributed. As a friend of universal education, I go for this measure, believing that the whole property of the State should be taxed for the education of the children of the State. Under this system, schools may be free, and will be free, if wisdom characterize the action of those whose duty it becomes to carry out this principle. The only question with me is this: the amendment provides that the Legislature shall provide for levying a tax, &c. I would prefer the word *may* to the word *shall*, although probably the effect will be about the same. Action cannot be enforced until it is deemed expedient—an imperious mandate is no more *important* than a mere *permission*, unless sanctioned by the public will, and when so sanctioned, either is effectual.

Mr. Fralick moved to amend the section as follows:

Strike out all after "shall," in first line, and insert "provide for a system of primary schools, by which a school shall be kept up and supported in each school district, at least three months in every year; and any school district neglecting to keep up and support such a school, may be deprived of its equal proportion of the interest of the public fund. And the Legislature may levy a tax on the whole taxable property of the several townships or cities of this State for the support of said schools."

The amendment was opposed by Mr. Britain, whose views are evinced in the following extract from his remarks:

We should provide for two things: one is equal taxation—the other, that the rising generation shall be instructed. But it has been said that the Legislature had the power, and we are asked why they did not exercise that right. I answer, that the will of the people has been defeated by the talents of men like the gentleman from Wayne. Numerous petitions were received last winter by the Legislature, praying for free schools. Why was it not granted? Not because there was a feeling against it, but because those opposed to it pointed to the assembling of this Convention—that it had better be left until that time.

I am not satisfied with this amendment, because it surrenders the principle. If it cannot be established for six months, let it be for three; but I hope that we shall not be satisfied with any amendment short of that. Every collection of taxes by a district, is liable to be unequal.

This would be extremely unwise and unjust. The true theory of government, as understood at the present day, requires the whole property of the State to support the government of the State, instituted for the protection of said property. And no fact has been more satisfactorily established than the fact that the property of the State can more cheaply educate the people of the State, and maintain the government over an educated people, than it can support a government over an uneducated people; and that a tax for educational purposes is but an interest tax for the protection of property, and should be paid equally by all taxable property protected.

If these premises be true, the duty of this Convention must be apparent. It is alike bound by justice and sound policy *to provide by a tax* upon the whole people, for the most economical and perfect protection of the whole property, instead of leaving it subject to the payment of onerous taxes for the support of government, over a population but half educated by the limited means heretofore drawn with so much injustice from parents and guardians, who possess comparatively but a small share of the property of the State.

There is another argument in favor of free schools, which addresses itself to higher motives, and the soundness of which is perhaps quite as well established as the former. It is this: the children of the State are the property of the State, and entitled to support, education and occupation, whether their immediate guardians are able to give it to them or not.

This theory, resting upon the character, and resulting from the obligations of our civil compact, formed for the purpose of supporting, protecting and benefitting each other, claims that the present generation is bound by the strongest obligations of duty, to support, educate and qualify for self-government, the rising generation; and so many means are already provided by law for the accomplishment of these desirable ends, that to a discriminating mind, the only wonder is, that more direct, just and efficient means have not been adopted for the accomplishment of so desirable an object. But, Mr. Chairman, the most difficult questions connected with this subject are, the best method of raising the means, and of insuring their economical expenditure. If you raise the whole amount by a State tax, there may be difficulty in securing an economical expenditure, as the immediate interests of persons interested with the expenditure, will be to draw as copiously from the fund as practicable. If you raise a part of it by State tax, and permit the districts or townships to raise the balance by district or township tax, or a capitation tax, or by rate bills, as they may deem expedient, some will raise by district, some by township, and some by capitation tax, while others will collect by rate bills, from parents and guardians.

The property of a district supporting its schools exclusively by a tax upon property, would pay a higher tax than that of a township supporting its schools in part upon rate bills; dissatisfaction would inevitably be the consequence, and the system might be broken down by the crafty property-holder, before it received a fair trial. I think that all the burdens we impose should be imposed equally. That the best method of accomplishing this will be to raise a large portion of the school moneys by a State tax, and the balance by a uniform tax, as far as the interests of education will permit, beyond the control of the district. A school in every district should be free during a part of each year, to all scholars residing in the district, and made free from expense to all who are unable to pay; and also made as nearly free from expense to all as shall be consistent with a guaranty of an economical expenditure of the public moneys; and the tax for the support of such schools should, as far as practicable, be a State tax.

Mr. Crary said by the present system we have about 33 cents per scholar—the tax upon the district—the residue raised by a rate bill. We have thus three sources of revenue at the present time, and many persons are not prepared to go further than the method suggested by the substitute. Some wish to make it imperative, but I do not think that it is desirable to levy a tax, and I will give my reasons.

It is a pretty thing to have a beautiful theory, but sometimes the practice is very different. Difficulties will arise under the general tax system. If you levy a tax—a tax for the whole State—who will regulate the prices to be paid for teachers in the districts? If left to the district, what will they make the expenditure? They may pay their teacher forty dollars per month and have but a few scholars. There will not be that care which is required at present, and the chief expense will be thrown upon the more wealthy portion of the State. It would be best to leave it open; let the Legislature say whether it shall be by towns or counties, or by districts; making it imperative that in two, four or six years, a free system of schools shall be established. If we embody in the constitution, to take immediate effect, the substitute of the gentleman from Genesee, we shall not convince the people that we have done one thing towards lessening the expense, for we cannot carry his proposition into effect short of a tax of $100,000 for the State; it will probably be more, but I am taking a low estimate. Now, if in this constitution you impose a tax upon the people of this magnitude, how much will they thank you for it? They will say, we sent you to lighten our burdens; you have made them greater.

I think that it must be left to the Legislature. It is, I think, the voice of the Convention to have a free school system—it is my wish—but we must not impose too heavy a burthen to accomplish this object; for if we do, the people will not sustain our action.

Mr. C. moved to amend the amendment so as to provide that any school district neglecting to keep up and support a school wherein instruction in the English language is conducted for three months in each year, should be deprived of its equal proportion of the income of the fund, and the motion was agreed to.

Mr. WORDEN moved to amend by striking out of the amendment of Mr. FRALICK the words "several townships and cities of the State."

Mr WALKER thought the principle would operate very unjustly to the new portions of the State. He had made an examination in regard to the amount of the school fund distributed in the different counties in the year 1849, and of the amount required to be raised for school purposes. By an examination of the tables it would be found as an almost universal rule that the new counties would have to raise by taxation much more than the amount to be distributed to them out of the school fund. In some counties they would be obliged to tax two cents on the dollar on the basis of the distribution. On that account he thought there was something due to that section of the State. From the many inconveniences to which the new counties were subjected, by the sparseness of their population, and the great expense which was attendant on the support of their schools, he considered it but just that that they should have the benefit of the tax upon non-resident lands. It was known that a larger number could be educated in a thickly populated portion of the State, and for a longer period, than in those parts which were thinly settled. He would state, however, that the county of Wayne would raise by taxation more than it would receive from the general fund. It resulted from taxation on the increased valuation of property in the city of Detroit, over the farming sections of the country. Macomb county, on the other hand, would receive three or four hundred dollars more, under the distribution of the general fund, than she would be obliged to raise by taxation. The new counties ought to have the benefit of the tax on the non-resident lands, to be applied to the support of their schools. They would necessarily have to undergo many inconveniences from their situation—their schools would be small, and consequently would require much more to educate their scholars than in the older settled counties.

Mr. N. Pierce did not agree with the gentleman last up in what he said relative to the hardships to which new settled counties were subject. He thought such inconveniences as were alluded to, merely temporary. He wanted to know why a county with five hundred inhabitants must tax the whole non-resident land. He would like to be informed why a county should take his land, for instance, and tax it when he sent no children to school. He had yet to learn that the children of one county could not be as well educated as another. If Macomb county could not raise sufficient money, he would say take it from the State tax; so in regard to Calhoun or any other county. It was a State policy he desired to see adopted in this matter; one by which the blessings of education would be diffused amongst all.

Mr. Sturgis was in favor of raising a State tax for educational purposes, and not a county or township tax. There were many counties possessing a large amount of taxable property, that had in reality no more scholars to educate than those not possessing one-half that amount.

Mr. Williams desired to observe all courtesy towards gentlemen on this floor. He would be allowed to say, however, that there was such a thing as theory, and such a thing as practice. He desired to have a State tax, in order to have justice done to both the settled and the unsettled portions of the State. He would put it to gentlemen and ask, if we enjoined the people of the counties to assess themselves, would they get anything more than they would get under a State assessment? The people of each county sparsely populated would assess themselves just enough to educate their own children, and would let an immense amount of property go untaxed. Thus the whole State must lose.

There was one difficulty which occurred to him as conclusive on this whole matter of putting this tax upon any smaller district than the entire State. The matter was very fully discussed in committee of the whole. The difficulty was in effect this: in New York the system which was adopted, required that the schools should be supported largely by taxation of the individual, and enough raised to keep up a school for a given number of months in the year. What was the result? Simply this: the rich and the poor were arrayed against each other, and the childless were opposed to those who had children. How much money should be raised was a subject of fierce contention; sometimes one kind, and sometimes another kind of people resisting. Those who paid the least, generally resisted the most. As well as he recollected, the gentleman from Calhoun, [Mr. J. D. Pierce,] had had a letter from a distinguished friend of education, in which he referred to the difficulty then existing in the State of New York, in relation to this school question, and stated that the whole State was rife with these difficulties, creating almost universal excitement.

Here, then, were two objections fatal to the views advanced by the chairman of the committee on education. Any plan that was impracticable was not only unjust to that portion of the State for which all his sympathies were excited, but was also an injury to the whole State. He believed that the whole State should support every portion of its government, and necessarily to educate the whole people. He laid it down as an axiom that the whole property should educate the whole people.

Again, we could probably tax the whole property of the State on some uniform and general plan more economically, and distribute it in the already necessary distribution of the primary school fund, with less waste than upon any other plan whatever. Not only so, but if we left it to townships and counties, the administration would be always conflicting and unsatisfactory. If we had forty assessments, by forty counties for the school tax, we should have just as many different school systems.

He would go for any uniform system that reached every person in the State, and taxed equally all the property of the State; and in his opinion it was the duty of the committee to construct and organize a system that was efficient, just, comprehensive and more than all, perfectly practicable.

Mr. Fralick said, it appeared to him that the gentleman had misconceived the question. It appeared by his argument that this matter of taxation was to be left to the counties or townships. The gentleman was wrong there. It was to be a tax levied by the Legislature.

Mr. Williams—I was arguing a different question. The question now under consideration is whether you make it a local or a State tax.

Mr. Fralick (continuing)—thought he understood the gentleman's argument. It amounted to the same thing, for it was still a State tax; the only difference was as to the distribution of the money in the township. He did not desire to make a great State system whereby the money would have to go through a dozen toll gates, every man having something off it. He wanted to have the money available whenever it was required, for in fact the school fund went through so many operations now, that we got it when the teacher should have been paid five months previous. Instead of getting it in the winter, they did not receive it until June. What he particularly desired was, that the money raised in a township remain in it, so that it might be always available.

Mr. Hanscom was of opinion that both the systems proposed were wrong. He was in favor of leaving the Legislature to determine how this tax should be raised. Let them try one mode of taxation first, and if that did not work well, they could then try another.

Mr. Bush was in favor of having a tax imposed upon all the taxable property of the State, to be fairly and equitably distributed, so that every scholar should have his quota.

The amendment of Mr. Fralick was finally disagreed to. The question recurring upon the substitute of Mr. Cornell, providing that after the application of school moneys, and other funds set apart, the balance should be raised by a State tax. To this, amendments were offered by Mr. Gale and Mr. Hanscom. A substitute was offered by the chairman of the committee providing for free schools to be kept for three months of each year, and for making up any deficiency by a tax upon the whole taxable property of the State. This proposition was advocated by Mr. Van Valkenburg, who said that

No time is limited when the Legislature shall carry it into effect. The committee thought it best to leave the subject to them. If limited, and the time passed, they might say that the question is put to rest; therefore we thought it the best to leave it an open question, and thus meet the views as expressed in committee of the whole yesterday, and we were anxious to meet the views of the delegates and the requirements of the people. It is conceded that free schools are wanted, and should be supported by a universal tax throughout the State, and that free schools should be instituted as soon as practicable.

It has been remarked that schools should be free to all—that the children of the State were the property of the State—that the State was responsible for the education of its children. For that reason we think a State tax is the most proper, and would avoid many difficulties that would grow out of the levying of taxes on the towns and cities. It has been said that schools should be as free as the air we breathe, or the water we drink. Our sources of education should be like the rays of light, penetrating the darkness. If we adopt this system we shall see our State take an exalted position among our sister States of the Union.

It was opposed by Mr. Hanscom as being subject to two objections:

First, it says that all deficiencies that exist after the distribution of the income, shall be raised by a State tax. Now, sir, I would leave the Legislature to provide the taxation in the manner they deem best. We may get a donation of land from Congress; if so, it might be applied instead of a State tax. If they think that it is the best way, they will do it; but I do not think they should be bound or limited in the mode of raising a tax. It imposes no imperative duty upon the Legislature at all; it merely requires them to do it, without fixing a limitation when it shall be done.

Mr. MOORE advocated the adoption of the clause, engrafting the principles of free schools in the constitution. He said:

Mr. Chairman, this subject is one of the first importance, and I hope we shall not differ in principle or in the detail. The details I am not so particular about, if the result is arrived at. The grand effort for us, is to establish schools free or nearly so. The way or the details of the system I care little about, so the thing itself is accomplished. I would engraft in this constitution the principle of free schools. I would leave it to the Legislature to fix it at some future day. It is practicable now for us to lay the plan whereby the children of the State can be educated.

I have no objection to the amendment sent up by the gentleman from Calhoun, [Mr. Morrison.] It contemplates five years before this system can be brought about, and I have no disposition to delay this effort a day. This is the place and the time to provide for the system. I would not adopt the system of New England, although there, it is the best, and no other, perhaps, would do so well; but our country is new, and things are not yet regulated. We have many new and thinly settled districts, where town taxes could not be raised, and of course it would be unequal. New England raises her fund by a town tax on property, and distributes in the districts from the towns. * * I think, Mr. Chairman, we are pretty well agreed that a State tax is the plan for us to adopt; and two mills to the dollar added to our present fund, will furnish four months more free schooling in each district than we have now. We raise now by general fund $156,000, which affords a school five and a half months in the year. But it is not worth while to go into detail. I hope the committee will not let the disagreement about the plan to be adopted, defeat a measure so desirable and so just as this. It is just not only to the children growing up in the State, but to the citizens, and to the character of the State, which stands the sixth State in the Union for intelligence—in reading and writing—as reported in our last census.

What has made New England what she is but her common schools; her school system? And here let me say, when New England had 2,000,000 inhabitants she had between ten and twelve thousand schools—a school to every 200 persons.

Let me give some of the plain, simple reasons why we should establish free schools, or nearly free, so that, at any rate, every child would be free to go, and should go, and so numerous that a school house would be within the reach of all. The management, however, should be left to the districts themselves, so as to sustain the interest felt in the schools by all classes; and the fund should only be distributed to those that would try to avail themselves of its benefits. You lay it down as a principle, that the man who does not try to help himself, should not be helped. So in a measure with school districts; but by all means give them the opportunity; bring education to their door, to their very threshhold.

The tax should be on the property of the whole State, and distributed by the school officers of the State as the other fund is, and to those districts which will avail themselves of it; for, I say again, that unless the people themselves enter into it, all the money you give will not accomplish the object. The interest and earnestness with which the districts engage in it, is of as much consequence as the money appropriated. The tax, I say again, should be on property, so the poor would be saved from a burden which otherwise might be too heavy, and the rich secure the most ample protection on their property, by the diffusion of intelligence and morals among all classes.

1st. Every holder of property has a direct interest, in a pecuniary point of view, in educating the masses. For every law upon which the value of property or the peace of society depends, will, in a few years, be at the disposal of the children growing up in the State. The amount of vice and crime, and the expense of prosecuting and punishing criminals will be diminished in proportion to the intelligence of the community. Ignorance is idle and unthrifty; it is the father of vice. Uneducated mind is educated vice.

Intelligent labor is doubly as productive to the State as the tool of the ignorant. Witness New England; look at her manufactories, her mechanical labor, her inventions, in short, her innumerable commodities, with which she fills this whole earth. There is not, perhaps, a country on the globe where her arts have not been introduced. And why is it? Because she started with a universal system of free schools. Nothing else ever laid the foundation of her prosperity. And so let it establish ours. We have infinitely a better soil, abundance of water power, and every variety of climate, and can grow almost every variety of the world's products. Now, with all these advantages, let us engraft in the constitution such a system as will secure to the rising generation equal rights in education, as well as equal rights in political, civil and religious liberty. Then, I say, if all the property holders are to share in the advantages, they may well and fairly be asked to contribute to the result.

2d. It is the duty of the State to provide for the education of all its children. The existence and safety and wealth of the State depend upon it. It is the first duty of government to protect the lives and property of her people.

If the property and safety of society demand universal education, it is the duty of the State to provide for it. If she has a right to lay a tax for the suppression of crime and idleness, by erecting prisons and houses of correction, she certainly has a right to do the same for the prevention of crimes, by schools.

3d. These common schools are of exceeding value by way of bringing forward and cultivating minds of great worth, that had otherwise laid forever buried in the obscurity of poverty. They are like scientific surveys for the discovery of the mineral resources of the State. A large number of the very first men of New England would never have been raised to notice, but for the exploring system of common schools, where the rich and poor meet together without any degrading distinctions; and only mind tugs with mind all over the commonwealth, year after year. If there is one rare intellect in any corner of the State, it will be brought to light and developed; and many such, coming up from all quarters, will enhance greatly the literary character and wealth of the State.

4th. Free schools have a powerful influence in disseminating the principles of true *democracy*. Where on earth is there such a practical demonstration of the doctrine that "all men are born free and equal," as in the school house under a free school system—where every barefooted urchin may have the same teacher, the same books, and set on the same seat with the most fortunate heir in town—may stand at the head of his class and take precedence over all that wealth and rank can array against him, if only God has given him the better mind, or the more diligent disposition? It ennobles and encourages the poor boy, and fires him with such thoughts of the dignity of a human soul that tyrants can never after oppress him with impunity. It corrects, too, the thoughtlessness of the rich by the standard of mind, and teaches them to reckon rank by the Roman rule of merit.

5th. A general tax is on many accounts the best mode of providing public schools. When every man pays his money he will feel an interest, and the interest thus awakened all over the State, is worth the amount of the tax, to say nothing of the instruction given to the children. Besides, as men come to understand the doctrine upon which the right to thus tax them is based, and see the principle satisfactorily illustrated, they will discover also that they have in many other respects mutual interests; and so, public spirit, so necessary to general improvement, will be more and more promoted. This system, too, has the merit of providing for the education of the poor, without any of those personal distinctions that degrade.

6th. It is particularly incumbent upon Michigan to provide a system of free schools. She has invested a large sum already in such a way that much of its value and prospects to the State must be forever lost without a free school system.

* * * * That University will forever lose half its utility to the State, without the common school system to explore every opening and prairie, and kindle up the latent genius that is slumbering in log cabins all over the land. Such minds once taught, will, by comparison and competition with others, create the appetite for knowledge, and from the district school will find their way to the fountain your State has so munificently opened to all her sons. Michigan has built up one side of the most liberal structure for education in any State—it only remains to complete the other side, and so perfect the edifice.

Mr. Comstock expressed the opinion that the Legislature could better carry out the details of the measure, and was in favor of the proposition of Mr. Hanscom.

The debate was continued with deep interest, and evinces so much practical knowledge of the subject on all sides as to make it a very important portion of our educational history. The following is therefore extracted from the journal of the Convention:

Mr. Morrison offered the following as a substitute for section 3:

"The Legislature shall provide by law that in the year 1855, and every year thereafter, a general tax shall be levied in the State for the support of primary schools, not exceeding five mills on each dollar of the valuation of the taxable property in the State. Such tax to be levied and collected in the same manner as the general State tax for State purposes, and apportioned for the support of primary schools throughout the State, in the same manner as the primary school interest fund, and shall provide that during the time required to expend the amount thus apportioned among the several districts, a school shall be kept in such district, without any charge for tuition, to all scholars residing in such district between the ages of four and twenty-one years; and the instruction in such school shall be conducted in the English language."

Mr. M. said—The proposition is, that in 1855 the Legislature may fix a tax not to exceed five mills on the dollar. My object is to permit the people to feel the benefit of the reforms that we have made; for if we impose a heavy State tax, the burdens will be increased instead of diminished; therefore I wish the matter postponed until the year 1855. Yet, it does not prevent the Legislature from establishing schools earlier, if it is deemed expedient; nor does it prevent them raising a part of the tax, or the whole, before that time.

The amount of the interest upon the public fund was $52,000; the average time that schools were taught was nearly five and a half months; these, if taught by female teachers for three months, would cost $59,320, leaving only a deficiency of $6,320; if taught by male teacher, the amount would be $77,500. Now, by raising one mill upon the dollar, we shall raise a tax of $28,000; of two mills, $56,000; of three mills, $84,000; which would render every school in the State free for three months in the year. Supposing our property to be $30,000,000, a tax of five mills would be $150,000, a sum sufficiently large to keep the schools for four months in the year.

My object in proposing this substitute was, that as it appeared to be the wish of the Convention to raise it by a State tax, I knew no other way that it could be done, except by a specific tax—a mill tax, for instance; and after this, if the constitution provides that we shall have a State board for the purpose of equalizing property throughout the State, probably it would amount to $60,000,000; that would then amount to $300,000; and if came to $100,000,000, we shall have from this source an income of half a million; this, then, to be apportioned among the districts with the interest of the primary school fund; and thus the difficulties that have been raised in regard to the revenues would cease; it would then be the interest of no one to break down the primary schools. If the tax was levied three months before the public money was given, the money would have been paid, and men would build up the primary schools.

It will be for the interest of the districts to make the best terms they can with teachers, and keep them as long as they can. There may be sufficient to keep one school six months; it should then be applied to that, six months. To another three months. One may require double the salary for a teacher that another has to pay. The money received by the schools should be equal; and they should not employ teachers to whom they would have to pay a large salary.

Mr. WILLIAMS—It seems that there are almost as many different opinions as there are men in this Convention. In view of this fact, the chairman called the committee together. It was found that while the committee disagreed on some topics, there were some principles upon which all agreed, and these are embodied in the proposition now offered by the chairman. We agreed on "free schools—three months' term in all districts—no charge for tuition—the English language to be necessarily taught." In regard to taxation, the mode and manner, we could not agree; but we could agree that all the property of the State should be reached by taxation for this purpose, and should bear somehow its equal and just share of the burden. For himself, he believed that the tax should be levied by the authorities of the State. He would not leave the system, and the whole success of the system, at the mercy of either district, town or county.

The proposition of the gentleman from Oakland leaves it in discretion of legislation to say whether every locality should not assess the tax to suit its convenience. If each district can do as it pleases, it can destroy the efficiency of the system as applicable to itself. Now, if we need and want a free school system at all, we want it most for those districts that would meet its requisitions with the greatest reluctance. The most backward, the most ignorant, the most indifferent, are the very portion of the population we wish to enlighten. The State wishes to stretch its paternal arm around them. It wishes to educate all, willing and unwilling. To obviate all difficulties, for himself, whatever taxes are laid, he thought ought to be imposed and assessed by one authority, embracing the whole State.

With regard to the suggestion of the gentleman from Oakland, (Mr. Hanscom,) that the proposition of the chairman of the committee was deficient, because there might be other resources besides the income of the primary school fund, he did not think they had much force. If the Legislature can afford any sum at any time to increase the means, they can make them a part and parcel of that fund by legal enactment. If we should obtain lands from the general government—if justice long delayed should be meted to us, and the million or more of acres due, (the general government being as liberal to us as to our sister States,) is at last conceded, either to the demands of our delegation or to the prayer of the memorial of this Convention, now in preparation by the gentleman from Wayne, [Mr. Backus,] then such lands, or a part of them should, by the terms of the grant of Congress, be made a part of the primary school fund.

If he remembered the language of the substitute of the chairman, it was this: "Any deficiency that may exist after the distribution of the income from the primary school fund, shall be raised by a tax on the whole taxable property of the State." Thus fixing the principle that all the property of the State should be equally taxed, but leaving the mode and the distribution to be determined by the Legislature. Whatever his private views were, he felt bound to concur with the committee. He believed half the members of the House had plans drawn up, and to meet each man's views was impossible. On such a basis as the committee have conceded to, a system of free schools can certainly be created which will be efficient, practical and comprehensive.

Mr. ORR said—Mr. Chairman, I cannot, as the representative of one of the new counties, suffer this very important question to come to a vote without at least an expression of my opinion on a subject which so directly interests my constituents. I have the honor, sir, to hold a seat on this floor through the partiality of my immediate constituents in the county of Barry. But, sir, while I represent the county of Barry in this Convention, I claim as my constituency the undivided one-hundredth part of the people of this State. And, sir, as it has been my constant endeavor during our deliberations in this body to support such measures as would advance the great interest of the State at large, I must be permitted on this occasion to express my disapprobation of this or any other measure that would in the least degree be prejudicial to the new counties, and particularly to the county I represent in this Convention.

This proposition has for its object, sir, to rob the new and sparsely populated counties of this State of a portion of the money raised in such counties, for educational purposes, and give it to the older and more densely settled portions of the State. Gentlemen propose to raise a State tax of two mills on the dollar of the valuation of all the taxable property of the State. This tax they would raise on the basis of taxable property, making each county contribute to the general fund according to their several abilities. This, they say, shall constitute a State fund for the support of free schools. But, sir, they propose to make the distribution on a very different system. They would distribute this money among the several counties of this State, according to the number of children between the ages of four and eighteen, reported by the different county clerks to the office of the Superintendent of Public Instruction.

Now, sir, it must be remembered that the more populous counties return more scholars to the above office in proportion to their taxable property, than are returned by the new and thinly settled counties. Consequently, on this system they would receive more money than they contributed, while the new counties would contribute more money than they would again receive. The proposition now under consideration would have this effect, sir, and I believe it to be unjust and oppressive. I hope, sir, it will not prevail.

Mr. Chairman, it is claimed here by some gentlemen that this discrepancy in valuation, compared with the number of children reported to the office of the Superintendent of Public Instruction, arises in consequence of the great amount of non-resident land lying in some of the new counties. This, sir, is true; there being neither family nor scholars to represent this species of property. But is this the fault of the new counties? I think not, sir. The most of this non-resident land was located at a very early day; and being generally of the best quality, it is held at so high a price that the industrious poor man seeking a home in this State could not afford to purchase it. He was, therefore, absolutely compelled to buy government land at a cheaper price, wherever he could find it interspersed with large and numerous tracts of non-resident land. This state of things is very inconvenient to the actual settlers. The settlements are, in consequence of this, located in different parts of the county, entirely detached from each other, separated by large tracts of uncultivated land, and often by intermediate forests.

Now, sir, it will not be pretended that citizens of a new county, thus situated, can educate their children with the same facility or economy as those living in better settled and more populous counties. Therefore I hold, sir, that if this non-resident land interposes any obstacles to cheap and economical schools in the new counties, they should enjoy the exclusive advantage of taxing this kind of property for educational purposes.

There appears to be but very little difference of opinion, sir, in this Convention, about the propriety of providing in this constitution for the encouragement of primary schools. But gentlemen of this Convention seem strangely partial to the name of "*free*" schools. There is something fascinating, sir, even in the name. But if a system of free schools is not attainable—if such a system is not practicable—why pursue in such hot haste the empty name, and loose sight entirely of the reality? Why not be satisfied with giving suitable encouragement to our schools—such encouragement, sir, as the circumstances of our people will warrant? Why raise a great State tax? Why collect and gather it from different townships and counties of the State on the basis of taxable property, and in making your distribution parcel it out on a different basis, to wit: according to the number of scholars reported to the office of the Superintendent of Public Instruction? This, sir, is the proposition.

A three mill tax assessed on all the taxable property of the State, would, together with the annual interest of the primary school fund, afford pretty good encouragement. This should be assessed annually by the supervisor of every township in the State; and when the money is collected it should belong exclusively to the township in which it was raised, and should be appropriated religiously to the support of primary schools. This plan would give to every township its own money, and no more. This plan, sir, being reasonable and just, cannot fail of being satisfactory to all portions of the State.

Again, one dollar per scholar might support a free school for a term of three months in one of the older counties, such as Oakland, Washtenaw or Lenawee, while it would be totally inadequate in Allegan, Barry or Ionia. Therefore, I hold that it would be both unjust and oppressive to compel any one of the new counties to raise money to aid in support of free schools in the older counties, and that too, sir, when they already enjoy better facilities for education. But, sir, for the purpose of illustrating this subject more clearly and forcibly, I will here exhibit some statistics which I have prepared, on this subject. I have grouped together the counties of Allegan, Barry and Clinton, as a fair average of the new counties; and Jackson, Kalamazoo and Lenawee as a fair average of the old counties; and by calculation it will be seen, sir, that the first three counties would each contribute more than they will again receive, while the other three counties will receive more than they contribute.

By the State tax system, Allegan county would loose in round numbers, $795; Barry, $155, and Clinton, $553; while the other counties would each gain a proportionate sum of this money. For these reasons, I hope, sir, that some other plan will be agreed upon, which, while it encourages our primary schools, will be less oppressive and more equal in its operations.

Mr. N. Pierce—I think, sir, that the gentleman's reasoning goes to show that it is not equitable ground. If there are one hundred children to be educated in Barry county, and if there are four times that number in Lenawee county, with no more means to be taxed, then I say that the county of Barry should contribute her part; and I think that a different course would be improper and unfair. It has been said that there is a good deal of difficulty with regard to the words "free schools." The words "free schools," is like free government—like the word "democracy." What does that mean? It means a government by a people. But there are burdens to be borne, and we have actually to release a portion of a our liberty for the benefit of the whole. You cannot establish a prosperous free school system, except you collect some tax out of the interested parties—except you charge something upon the persons sending the children to school—charging them sufficiently to make them parties in the case. I have never seen it otherwise, and I don't believe it can be done.

I am unwilling that any sweeping clause should be placed in the constitution without being limited. I think it should permit a State tax; then limit it, and provide that the remainder shall be raised by towns or districts; I care not which. We are all agreed in favor of free schools, and it sounds well in theory; but in carrying out the details we find out the objections. I do not believe that the people will pay five mills upon the dollar My instructions are directly the reverse; that is, to lighten the burdens; and the present system of free schools is a good system; it has worked very prosperously. We have now a State tax of one mill, which, with the addition of the school fund, makes our schools to a certain extent, free; that is, it gives them the character of free schools.

Like every other member, I have my views, and I should like to strike out of section three, all after the word "provide," at the end of the third line, to the word "and," in the line following. That would double the present State tax, by leaving it in the power of the Legislature to double the present tax of one mill. That would render them as free as we ought to make the schools. Then let the balance be raised as the wisdom of the Legislature may direct. The whole property of the State should be taxed equally for the education of the children of the State. I cannot see any propriety in limiting it to one county. A county that has a large estate and no children, should contribute accordingly, as an individual who is wealthy and without children has to educate the children in the town or district. If his county is as well educated as others, it works no injustice; it is applied like the primary school fund.

Now, sir, the school lands where I live are worth $20 per acre; where he lives it is worth $4 per acre; the money is put together and equally divided, and there, of course, the new counties have the advantage. I think it will not be best for this Convention to direct the Legislature to impose a heavy tax. If the people should tell the House of Representatives not to do it, are we better than the next House of Representatives? I think not. Our system may be improved; but it is a good system. I think that there should be a State tax—a fixed amount, not entirely free for tuition. If the district spend $100, the parents or guardians should at least contribute $12. Otherwise there would not be economy; therefore I think it would be better. I think if schools are free of tuition, it will cause difficulty and trouble. It has operated badly and was changed.

Mr. VAN VALKENBURGH—My colleague tells you that it is putting it off for five long years. The committee came to the conclusion that the proposition of the gentleman from Oakland would put it off for five years. And if the Legislature refuses to obey the instruction, what will be the condition of the State? Will it not put off this question interminably—it may be until the formation of another constitution? He urges as a reason, that it will put off the system so long. Well, sir, when the question was upon the subject of pay, three dollors being inserted instead of two, he made a speech—one in which he said that his constituents would denounce him as a demagogue if he supported the measure. Well, sir, in conversation with me, he told me, forsooth, that the committee wanted to strike out three and insert four. That was his argument. Now, the argument is, we are putting it off for five years—not fixing a time. Now, we take the position that he is putting it off too long; we wish to have the provision incorporated in the constitution, and have it acted upon as soon as can be, consistently with the interest of the State.

The gentleman from Calhoun, [Mr. N. Pierce,] says that some little tax must be imposed upon the districts to make them interested. Will not a tax upon the whole, which every individual is bound to pay, make them interested? Will they not see that the money is properly appropriated, and is not his argument fully answered?

Mr. CHURCH moved to strike out in Mr. Hanscom's substitute, after "constitution," and insert "establish a system of common schools, in which the instruction shall be conducted in the English language, and shall be free of charge to pupils between the ages of four and eighteen years, at least three months in each year, in each school district in the State, and shall provide by law for the support of such schools by a tax or taxes upon property."

The difference in the two propositions, (said Mr. C.) consists in the latter clause. Mine goes further than that of the gentleman from Oakland, in this respect, that it provides for a tax or taxes upon property, but does not designate whether it shall be State, town, district or county tax. There can be no agreement about the kind of tax; there are objections to every plan—objections so serious that probably this Convention cannot be brought to agree to any proposed plan.

Mr. WILLIAMS—If he understood the gentleman from Kent, [Mr. Church,] he was willing to base a free school system on taxation in the districts, similar to the method in New York. Now, if the gentleman from Jackson, [Mr. Cornell,] had the evidence showing the almost fatal operation of that part of the New York system, he hoped it would be adduced. The jealousies, heart-burnings and obstinacy in districts had, he understood, rendered the New York system almost impracticable, and in that State they were about re-constructing their whole system. Yet the gentleman from Kent, he thought, was willing to risk the same experiment among ourselves.

Mr. WHIPPLE—I would ask whether the instruction shall be given exclusively in the English language.

The CHAIR read—"Instruction shall be in the English language."

Mr. WHIPPLE—By that term you would render it impossible for any language except the English to be taught in the common schools.

Mr. CHURCH—I do not understand the gentleman. Does he think that we are going to speak French, Spanish or Irish in the common schools?

Mr. WHIPPLE—Yes sir, I do. In the counties of Branch and St. Jeseph, not only the English, but German and French languages are taught; and it is a most valuable improvement of the common school system. I do not mean the dead languages, but the modern ones should be taught; and it seems to me that this amendment will put it out of the power of thousands of children to gain a knowledge of the French and German languages.

Mr. J. D. PIERCE—In some schools latin has been taught; I have taught it in a common school. I would not adopt any provision by which any knowledge would be excluded. I would make it imperative that the English language should be taught.

Mr. GOODWIN—I do not think that it excludes the other languages.

Mr. CHURCH—It means simply this: that no school shall draw the public money, in which the language used colloquially shall be other than the English.

Mr. J. D. PIERCE—We have so much distrust of future legislators that we cannot adopt a system that will be satisfactory. Do gentlemen think that all wisdom will die with us, or that the people will not send men to legislate, capable of taking care of their interests? All that we ought to do, is this: we should say the Legislature shall establish primary sshools. We cannot go into detail.

Mr. Goodwin would again remark that he did not think it prohibited the other languages being taught.

Mr. Hanscom—In all the colleges is not the instruction given through the medium of the English language?

Mr. Whipple—No sir. How could that be? I think it is impracticable, and that that mode of instruction will amount to nothing. I think it important that the great outlines of the system should be prescribed in this constitution. I have confidence in future legislators, but I wish their line of duty distinctly marked out. We have here a great deal of talent and practical experience, and it is proper that it should be brought to bear in the adjustment of this system; the time for which a school should be kept; the mode of instruction. I am opposed to confining a scholar to the use of the English language. We can as well determine these points as future legislators. The same reasons will exist then as now.

Mr. J. D. Pierce—I am willing that the first principles should be fixed; but we may adopt some principles that may not work with justice. If the Legislature adopts any measure, they can alter or amend it—we cannot.

Mr. Gale—The measure appears to me perfectly impracticable—to make it obligatory upon the Legislature to make schools free for even three months. Let us look for a moment at practical men carrying it out with practical experience. Let us have a school of fifteen scholars, and we know that in new counties there are many schools with not more than fifteen scholars, on account of the sparse population. Fifteen scholars require a teacher; if they pay him $20 per month for three months, ($25 would not be high,) and nothing has been said with regard to fuel or other incidental matters—we have $60 for fifteen scholars, which is at the rate of $4 per scholar. Another school in the same town or county, or State, may have 100 scholars, they may keep school the year round, and if they give their teacher $20 per month, that will only be $2 40; if they give $25, there will still be 100; yet, if we make a system of free schools, we should make them as nearly equal as we can, practically. We should give them as much per scholar as will sustain and support a school of 30, 40, or 50 scholars. But, sir, the school of 15 may require as competent a teacher as the school of 100. Now, I would ask, if the people will submit to legislation of this kind and character? I believe that they will not, and that we should fix no time that the schools should be perfectly free.

Gentlemen do not reflect upon the practicability of the thing. There are none more desirous than I am for free schools, if I thought it practicable. There are many things fine in theory, which cannot be practiced; and we should endeavor to avoid theoretical legislation. If you decide that all schools shall be perfectly free, they can then have a teacher. and pay him what they choose, draw upon the town or county for the sum, and the smallest will be entitled to draw as much as the largest. If you say that they may draw so much per scholar, you should give them some provision whereby they can make up the deficiency upon the taxable property in the district, or by some other means.

I am opposed to the substitute of the gentleman from Oakland, because it limits the ages from 4 to 20 years. Why not say 21? People are practically in the habit of sending their children until they are 21. It is the duty of a parent to provide education, even if a son is in his twenty-first year, and yet for that year he must pay.

Mr. HANSCOM thought that every system, according to the gentleman from Genesee, was perfectly impracticable. He manifests deep anxiety, but is unwilling to do any thing whatever. It would surely be possible for the Legislature to carry out the details of a system, and make the apportionment as nearly equal as possible. Every school might not be free; but it would be a near approximation to it. If we only looked to the dangers and all the possibly bad effects which, perhaps, have no real existence, we shall never be able to get a system at all.

Mr. CHAPEL—I think the proposition of the gentleman from Oakland is as near as we can fix it, except we go into detail. I think that details might be gone into that would satisfy every gentleman in this Convention. I cannot see the difficulty. The gentleman from Genesee tells us that it will be unequal. If the money taxed in each county can be distributed to each school in the county, giving the supervision to the supervisors in their own county, to so distribute, it cannot be liable to any serious objection. There are the records in the State offices to find out the number of scholars in each county, and get at the amount of property taxed for school purposes in the county; then add to that the amount they are entitled to receive on the school fund, and divide it equally. They have had their property taxed, they have had their schools returned, and it works equally. Then give the districts power to raise a tax, if they wish to go further. The difficulty seems to be to fix a proper time. I think three months is a proper time. Twenty-nine millions dollars, the value of the property of the State, with a tax of three mills, gives $87,000; the amount of public money, $52,305, making the sum of $139,305. There are 3,060 districts, containing about 100,000 scholars; divide the amount of money equally for the purpose of having a free school, and it will give $1 21 per scholar; and that will keep a school three months.

Mr. CORNELL—The gentleman from Genesee, (Mr. Gale,) has made a calculation, and upon that has expressed his belief that the people would not be willing to pay what was required. He forgets that in the small schools a teacher is employed, where compensation at the most is $2 per week; if a female teacher is employed only half the time, the estimate would fall far below his computation.

Mr. FRALICK—It appears necessary here to get up something new without going into detail or showing a good reason why we should do so. I am not satisfied or willing to vote for a change except it is evidently for the better; something better than merely a theoretical view. We hear a great deal of fault found with our present system, and at the same time, I do not believe there is a better system in the United States; and until we can get something better, we should keep what we have. The present system works well; the latest reports show that our schools are in as good a condition as any State in the Union, and the children are as well educated as in any other State. Yet our present system must be sacrificed to a mere theory —to the oft repeated cry that the children of the State are the property of the State, that they must all be taught, putting all in jeopardy and confusion by the experiments of a free education. Take the same ground on other questions. Are gentlemen willing to pay for the expense of trying criminals by a State tax? It would be a great saving to our county if they would. Wayne county has convicted half the criminals and paid half the expense of the State, in that respect. Do members wish to make it a State tax? If so, then I will also go for the system. I have heard no proposition that it shall be paid by a State tax. We have a large amount of paupers of the State to support in Wayne county, but I have heard no proposition about supporting them by a State tax, not a word. Upon the contrary, after we have convicted the criminals, then they make us bring them to Jackson; we pay the expense and they are silent; but when the question comes up that they shall take our property for the benefit of their schools, they are universally in favor of it, for it works to their advantage.

This will be injurious to every new county in the State. I have a small statement showing the result, or bearing of a State tax, as proposed in a three months' school:

Counties.	Loss.	Gain.
Allegan	$1,101 00	
Barry	317 00	
Berrien	175 00	
Branch		$633 00
Calhoun	320 00	
Cass		3 00
Chippewa	177 00	
Clinton	822 00	
Eaton		306 00
Genesee		550 00
Hillsdale		715 00
Ingham	282 00	
Ionia	192 00	
Jackson	121 00	
Kalamazoo		759 00
Kent	148 00	
Lapeer		390 00
Lenawee		701 00
Livingston		1,271 00
Mackinac	204 00	
Macomb		1,271 00
Monroe		582 00
Oakland		631 00
Ottawa	1,082 00	

Saginaw	873 00
Shiawassee	7 00
St. Clair	740 00
St. Joseph	52 00
Van Buren	546 00
Washtenaw	125 00
Wayne	1,904 00

Is it right that the new counties shall be taxed for the benefit of the older counties, which have the lands taken up and settled, and where it does not cost as much to keep a school, owing to the population being more dense?

I am not willing to adopt a new system because of the word "free," a theory which we cannot reduce to practice. The taxable property of the State will be about $100,000,000—a one mill tax will give us $100,000; that added to the school fund will give us a three months' school. I have heard not one word of complaint, except in regard to the districts; and we had better refer it to the Legislature to amend the present system by legislative enactment.

Mr. Bush—I rise to correct a statement of the gentleman from Wayne; he is generally very correct. He says he has never heard a proposition to pay for the conviction of the criminals of Wayne. The parents produce the children, feed and clothe them, the State educates them. The county of Wayne produces the criminal, tries and convicts him, and the State pays the expense of keeping him. I am satisfied that our opinions are so diverse, that we cannot adopt a system of detail. I am in favor of the measure proposed by the gentleman from Oakland, or something like it. One argument that should have great weight is, that the Legislature can alter and amend; they can profit by the light of experience, and remedy errors that may have been committed.

The question being on Mr. Church's amendment, it was lost.

The question then being on Mr. Hanscom's substitute, the substitute was lost.

The proposition then recurring upon the substitute of Mr. Walker, on motion of Mr. Woodman, "eighteen" was stricken out, and "twenty-one" inserted.

Mr. Crary moved to strike out all after "tax;" but the committee refused to strike out.

Mr. N. Pierce moved to strike out, "and without any charge for tuition."

Mr. Walker—Gentlemen attack the free school system indirectly; they do not say we are directly opposed to it, but they will bring every argument to bear indirectly against it. Now, I think this is indicative of the state of public feeling. The gentleman from Genesee, [Mr. Gale.] says that it is impracticable. The wisdom of Solomon, he said yesterday, could not devise the means of giving us a free school for three months. But the history of the New England States shows us that it can be so done. The difficulty is this, that certain things are by them considered to be part of the law, which this Convention does not. The gentlemen from Genesee, Wayne, Calhoun and Lenawee, all seem to think that the schools will not be entirely free--that there shall be some charge for tuition--it may approximate, but they shall not be established as free schools by the fundamental law of the land. They had rather that "the Legislature may,"—that the present system works well.

Let us look at the operation of this system upon the poor. In 1838 we had from the interest of the school fund, some $39,000; in '39, $42,000, for the benefit of the children of the State. It was the intention that all should participate; but this is not applied for the purpose of keeping the school for any length of time, free—it is turned in for the support of the school. The balance being raised by a tax, and the person who has not property sufficient to pay his school tax, although he may have four, five or six children, cannot send them for one day, except they come under the poor act. This is the practical effect; and thus the poor man is deprived of the liberality of the United States, which granted the land for the purpose of education.

We were told on a former occasion that the pride of a king was in the multitude of his people. I would ask, is not the pride of a Republic in the intelligence of its people? How long should we be a republican government if we were deprived of schools? Or, if a great portion are withdrawn, the necessary consequence will follow. There will be a great gulph between the two classes; wealth and intelligence on the one hand, ignorance and poverty on the other. If we refuse to adopt the principle that all the children shall be educated, we undermine the basis upon which our government is instituted. Can a republican government be sustained without intelligence? It may be attempted, but the pyramid is resting upon its apex, and the first political convulsion will overwhelm it into ruin. What has given the American people their success in government? Education; it has opened every avenue to industry; suppressed crime; expanded the energies of all; if it taxes wealth, it creates wealth in the community. Why should our roads be made by a tax upon property?

Mr. Church—Not a gentleman has opposed the tax upon property.

Mr. Walker—They have carried the bottle under the cloak. It might be said that the man who had ten children should work ten times the highway tax as the man who has no children. He travels the road ten times as much. So with poor houses; so with courts; so with prisons; for the wealthy, honest man, with no children, might say, I don't intend to commit crime; I want no poor house; I have no trials in the courts; let those pay for them that are poor; let them support them that may use them. This is the doctrine, if carried out. And I believe the support of all that I have named should be based upon property, because it is a general benefit to the whole community.

Mr. N. Pierce denied the charge that he was opposed to primary schools. He did not want any untried system, but that the Legislature might have power to improve or alter. He did not think that people should be charged with illiberality or hostility to a system because they did not choose to go through his machine.

Mr. Redfield moved to strike out the words "all the children between the ages of four and twenty-one years," and insert the word "persons;" but the amendment was lost.

Mr. Skinner—I deem it by far the most important topic that has occupied the attention of this body since its commencement, or that will before its close. All the wisdom of this Convention is needed to settle this matter rightly; and if not settled rightly, the evils may be incalculable. We are well agreed on general principles. We all seem to entertain this noble sentiment, that the children of the State are in a certain sense the property of the State; that they should, in some degree at least, be educated by the State. But how shall this be done? Various plans are suggested; but none of them are unobjectionable; none seem to meet the views of but a small portion of the Convention. That offered by the chairman of the committee of education is, in my opinion, preferable to the rest, and for this I shall vote, if nothing better is presented. I hope, however, that something less objectionable will be offered. I have not risen to express my own views, but to draw out the views of others, in whose opinions on this subject I should have much more confidence than in my own, and who have hitherto kept silent in this discussion.

The question recurring upon Mr. Walker's substitute,

Mr. Crary said, we have been some time discussing this subject, and as yet have come to no conclusion. There is such diversity of opinion that it seems impossible to arrive at a result that will meet the views and feelings of all. A portion are unwilling to believe that there can be any patriotism in our future Legislatures. They are disposed to tie everything down, supposing all the wisdom of the State to be concentrated here. Not fully believing this proposition, I am willing that the details of this subject should be left to the Legislature. We can mark out the outlines, and leave the rest to legislation; for we cannot satisfactorily fill up the details of the system.

We have before us the proposition of the committee, and from their respectability, their number, and the zeal with which they sustain these propositions, those of us who differ with them can scarcely expect to obtain a majority of the Convention in opposition to what they have laid before us as the unanimous result of their deliberations. Yet I do not believe that they have given to the subject all the attention which it demands, or looked at all the consequences which will follow the adoption of their report.

The language is: "Any deficiency that may exist after the distribution of the income of the primary school fund, shall be raised by a tax upon the whole property of the State." The tax shall be general throughout the State; the same in Oakland as in Barry; the same in Berrien as in Wayne. Now, sir, what will be the effect of this general legislation, without reference to the future action of the Legislature? Having apportioned the public money, amounting at present to thirty-three cents on the scholar, you have a deficiency in 3,060 districts to be reported somewhere, that the same for a three months tuition, may be made up by general taxation. The deficiency must be raised by general taxation in the State. Such a provision will lead to one universal scramble, to see who shall get the largest share of the money. This scramble can only be prevented by allowing the Legislature to fix the maximum and the minimum of the wages of the teachers. If the Legislature must do this much, why not leave all the details to them? Why not say the Legislature shall provide a system of free schools, leaving to them the plan of taxation, and the mode of applying it?

The committee proposed a mongrel system; for that was not a free school where there was any charge for tuition—not a free school where the poor man might have his child frozen to death for the want of wood, or the teacher starved for the want of board. In a free school, fuel, board, and implements for school house, must be provided; and these in some instances amount to half the expenses, especially in schools kept by females. New York has a four month's free school, and they covered the entire expenses, fuel, board, school books, and insurance for school house. What was the expense of that system? Fifty cents per scholar was received from the fund; then fifty cents tax per scholar from the county, and fifty cents more from the town. But this was not sufficient. A further tax was authorized to be levied upon the school district, and it was this last tax which seems to have ruined the system.

We propose to levy a State tax to make tuition for three months free. We propose to make it imperative; but if it be too expensive, or if it does not meet the wants and wishes of the people, you may insert it in the constitution, you may make it imperative, but it will be in vain. The people will overthrow the system if they do not like it, and there will be no remedy; it will be made a nullity, or the clause will be repealed. What we are attempting was tried by the State of Louisiana, and the system had to be changed. The State now gives annually $450,000 in aid of a free school system, and leaves the rest of the money to be raised by the locality. Delaware made a similar attempt; and she had to change her plan. N. York is about abandoning the system she first adopted, for one more suited to her circumstances. Yet we propose to uproot our present system and propose another that we know nothing about. We have a system that all admit to be a good system, although the gentleman from Macomb (Mr. Walker) made a side attack upon it. I do not say that it cannot be improved, but it works well. If the new system is adopted it may suit the people; and if it does not, you will not be able easily to change it if you fix the details in the constitution.

I would suggest that the amount of a mill or two mill tax be distributed to each school in proportion to the number of the scholars, or to their attendance, and then let the towns or school districts raise such amounts as they may deem proper. They will then have an inducement to use economy; they will then have no temptation to squander the money which, under the other system, they could. If we are to have a free school system, we had better give such a direction in the constitution, and let the Legislature manage the rest. We shall then have a system which can be adapted to our circumstances.

The question then recurring upon Mr. Walker's substitute, the committee refused to so amend.

Mr. MORRISON offered the following as a substitute to section 3:

"The Legislature shall provide by law that in the year 1855, and every year thereafter, a general tax shall be levied in the State for the support of primary schools, not exceeding five mills upon each dollar upon the valuation of the taxable property in the State. Such tax to be levied and collected in the same manner as the general State tax for State purposes, and appropriated for the support of primary schools throughout the State in the same manner as the primary school interest fund; and shall provide that during the time required to expend the amount thus apportioned among the several districts, a school shall be kept in each district, without any charge for tuition to all scholars residing in such district between the ages of four and twenty-one years; and the instruction in such schools shall be conducted in the English language."

Mr. M. said—The latter clause provides for all the difficulties in raising the funds and making it a free school—provides that the money so raised shall be expended, and during the time it is expended the school shall be free—that during that time no rate bill shall be charged. This will not prevent the inhabitants from employing the teacher a longer time, if they choose; and it will present no temptation to squander the money. I would move to strike out "charge for tuition." The motion was lost.

On motion of Mr. H. BARTOW, "five mills" were stricken out, and "two mills" inserted.

Mr. MOORE moved to strike out "1855" and insert "1852;" but the committee refused to strike out.

On motion of Mr. W. ADAMS, "exceeding" was stricken out, and "not less" inserted.

Mr. Morrison's substitute was then disagreed to.

Mr. N. PIERCE offered the following as a substitute for section three:

"The Legislature shall establish by law a system of primary schools, by which such schools shall be kept in each and every school district for at least three months in each year, free to all children between the ages of four and eighteen years, and shall provide for the levying of a tax not exceeding two mills upon the dollar upon all the taxable property in the State, for the support of said schools; and the English language shall be taught in such schools."

Mr. CHURCH moved to amend the substitute by striking out the words "and the English language shall be taught in such schools," and inserting the words "and all instruction in the said schools shall be conducted in the English language;" which was agreed to.

On motion of Mr. ROBERTSON, the words "and without charge for tuition," were inserted after "free."

Mr. N. Pierce's substitute, as amended, was then adopted.

Various propositions were offered in relation to sections four, five, six and seven, and the following was offered by Mr. Crary, to stand as section 9:

"Institutions for the benefit of those inhabitants who are deaf, dumb, blind or insane, shall always be fostered and supported, and the proceeds from the sale of all lands that have been or shall be hereafter granted or appropriated for the support of such institutions, shall be inviolably appropriated according to the terms and conditions of such grant or appropriation."

Mr. Soule offered the following as a part of section 9:

"And the twenty-two sections of salt spring lands now unapproted, or the money arising from the sale of the same, where such lands have been already sold; and any land which may hereafter be granted or appropriated for such purpose, shall be set apart for the support and maintainance of such school and farm. And the proceeds of the sale of all such lands that have been or that may be hereafter sold, shall be a perpetual fund, the interest of which, together with the rents and profits of such lands, shall be appropriated, for the support of such school and farm."

Mr. Crary offered the following to stand as section 11:

"Until the existing State debt is paid, all specific State taxes are set apart and appropriated to the payment annually of the interest that may become due from the State to the school and other educational funds, or so much thereof as may be necessary for such purposes, and from and after the payment of said debt, such taxes shall be inviolably appropriated annually for the support of primary schools."

Mr. Crary was aware that there would be some objection to the application of this money to the cause of education. I propose to have the interest of the primary school fund paid from year to year, and secured by sources about which there can be no question. I want it so that the Executive department cannot expend it; that the Legislature cannot expend it; that it shall be understood and known that it belongs to the cause of education; that it cannot be used for any other purpose. If left in the treasury, the first difficulty in legislation would probably be to authorize the use of the money. From time to time there may be a Legislature that will do injury to the fund. The general legislation may be right; but one Legislature may do an injury that we cannot recover from for a series of years. I propose to guard against the evils which one Legislature may do.

Mr. Whipple—The proposition of the gentleman from Calhoun is an important one. I understand that the specific taxes are derived from railroads, plank roads, banks, and any other moneyed corporation. I venture to predict that in a few years the fund from this source will be very large; perhaps in ten years it will amount to $100,000.

The gentleman from Calhoun says that the State is largely indebted to the educational fund, and that he wants some better security than the faith of the State. I want no better security than the faith of the State, and I think *that* being pledged, it is sufficiently ample for any security. But it must be recollected that in addition to being indebted to that fund, the State is indebted to private individuals to the amount of one and a half or two millions. While we are taking care of ourselves, we should not lose sight of our foreign creditors. I should have no objection to place it upon this fund if our State debt was liquidated; but while that remains, I am unwilling so to do, as we shall by so doing add to the burdens of the people of the State. I think, moreover, that it is the duty of this Convention to make some provision for the payment of this debt. I think it should not be left to the fluctuations of public opinion, or of legislation.

We are a young community—we are not poor—we are in comparatively comfortable circumstances; but we are a rapidly growing community, and we ought on that account not to place upon our own shoulders too great a burden, but to leave a portion to those who come after. I believe that the people of this State will not neglect to pay the interest of the primary school fund. But we must bear in mind that the principal of the State debt, as well as the interest, will in a short time have to be arranged. If we take our available means and divert them to other purposes, we may be the means of placing a burden upon this people, greater than they will be able to bear. We had better leave a portion to those who come after us; they will be more able to sustain it than we are.

After some debate, Mr. Crary withdrew his proposition.

Thus far the debates upon the subject were in committee of the whole. The Convention took up the article on the fifth day of August, being the forty-eighth day of the session. The action in Convention appears in the following extract from its journal:

On motion of Mr. WALKER, the article entitled "Education" was taken up.

The question being upon concurring in the amendments made in committee of the whole, section 1, as amended, was agreed to.

Section 3, as amended, was then read.

The question being on agreeing to the amendment,

Mr. GREEN moved to amend the original section by striking out all to and inclusive of the word "respectively," in the sixth line, and substituting as follows:

"Each of the cities and townships of this State shall, in the year ——, and in each and every year thereafter, raise by tax upon the real and personal estate in such cities and townships respectively, a sum equal to —, for each and every person residing in said cities and townships, between the ages of four and eighteen years, as shall appear by the returns of the school districts therein; which sum, together with the money apportioned to each of such cities and townships from the interest of the primary school fund, shall be apportioned pro rata among the several school districts therein, according to the number of persons between the ages of four and eighteen years, residing in each, as shall appear by the last annual reports of such districts, to be used by them in payment of teachers' wages therein. The amount so to be raised may be increased or diminished by the Legislature as they may deem right and proper; but such increase or diminution shall not exceed —— cents per scholar, as above named, at any one session of the Legislature."

Mr. GREEN said he did not desire to prolong the discussion upon this question. The uniform opposition which all the propositions offered on this subject had received, prevented his supposing that any proposition of his would obtain the unanimous support of the Convention. He thought, however, that his proposition presented advantages over any which had been as yet presented. He was of opinion that this would be better than any other, on account of the inequalities of some of the counties. It appeared to him to be unjust, where the authorities of a town had a right to make those districts as small as they pleased, and to give such salaries as they saw fit, to require another district to raise a sum, without reference to the size of the district. It would be better, he thought, to levy the sum upon the scholars. They would know when they employed teachers how many they would have to teach, and calculate their expenses accordingly. There would be then all the inducement possible for them to make their money go as far as they could. Small districts would be induced to alter their boundaries, so as to embrace more territory. He had objections to the article as amended; in fact certain persons would be excluded from the schools—those who were under four and over eighteen years of age. Such a provision would be very unwise. It sometimes happened that persons over eighteen desired to attend school. As to those under four, it was often very desirable to send them to school.

Mr. N. PIERCE observed that it seemed to him there was some difficulty about the proposition, [Mr. Green's.] The gentleman preferred collecting the tax in towns. He altogether preferred collecting the tax in the whole State; for, some towns would not have the same proportion in regard to the amount of scholars to be educated, as others; the tax then would be unequal throughout the State. The article as amended would suit him very well, if the words "between the ages of four and eighteen years" were struck out, and the words "that all children or persons attending schools," were inserted. This, he would much prefer to the proposition offered by the gentleman; but if the Convention should otherwise decide, he was content.

Mr. HANSCOM hoped the amendment reported from the committee of the whole would not be agreed to. He was willing to lay down by constitutional provision, some broad principle, so that the Legislature would have only to go on and establish this system at a subsequent period. It would be better, in his judgment, to leave the whole matter with the Legislature. They could try one mode of taxation or another. He was willing that the subject should be left for them to act upon as in their wisdom they saw proper.

Mr. Green had intended to have said, when up, that he was willing to leave the matter to the Leglslature; that would be his choice, and was, in his opinion, the best course to be pursued.

Mr. Green's amendment was not adopted.

Mr. Leach moved to amend the substitute reported by the committee, by striking out of lines three and four, the words "not exceeding two mills upon the dollar;" which was disagreed to.

Mr. Gale offered the following as a substitute for the one reported by the committee:

"The Legislature shall establish and provide for a system of primary schools within five years from the adoption of this constitution, in which the instruction shall be conducted in the English language; and as nearly free to all scholars residing in the several districts as may be deemed practicable."

Mr. Leach moved to amend by striking out "five," and inserting "two;" which was lost.

Mr. Gale—As the matter now stands, it is carried out too much in detail, yet it does not carry out what it bears upon the face of it. It declares that these schools shall be free schools; let any man carry it out in figures, and he will find it is no such case. He may calculate upon the taxable property of the State, and upon his two mills on the dollar, and yet he cannot carry out his free schools. It ought to be a little practicable; but it is entirely impracticable now. Take, for instance, a school of fifteen pupils—there are many that have but that number, and some as low as eight or ten—it is necessary they should be formed into a district, or else they cannot get an education; the settlements are so sparse that they cannot have a great number of scholars attending, on account of the distance they have to go to school; and they would have but $12 75 to sustain their school for three months! The whole thing appears to me to be entirely impracticable. I think it would be entirely the better course to leave the matter in the hands of the Legislature. Again, it is highly impolitic that we should inflict the system of free schools on the State without having investigated the whole matter, and knowing what it would be in its practical details.

Mr. Walker observed that these schools were not to be supported, according to the provision of the section, merely by a tax of two mills. The mode of taxation was optional, either by the two mills, or by a town tax, or by both.

The amendment presented by the gentleman from Genesee, [Mr. Gale,] was not adopted.

Mr. Hanscom offered the following substitute for the one proposed by the committee:

"The Legislature shall, within five years from the adoption of this constitution, provide for and establish a system of primary schools, by which such schools shall be kept free and without charge for tuition, for at least three months in the year, in each school district within the State."

Mr. Woodman moved to strike out "three months," and insert "four months;" also strike out "five years," and insert "three years."

A division was had, and the first branch of the amendment was lost.

The second proposition was also disagreed to.

The substitute offered by Mr. Hanscom was negatived.

Mr. BAGG offered the following as a substitute, which was rejected.

"The Legislature shall establish a uniform system of primary schools throughout the State, by levying a State tax upon the taxable property of the State."

The substitute reported by the committee of the whole for section three, was then concurred in.

Mr. SOULE proposed the following as a new section, to stand between sections three and four:

Any school district neglecting to keep up and support a school for three months in each year, shall be deprived of its proportion of the income of the primary school fund, and all funds arising from tax for the support of schools.

And the same was adopted.

AGRICULTURAL SCHOOL—IN CONVENTION.

Mr. WILLIAMS offered the following amendment:

The said school and farm shall be under the superintendence of the Regents of the University, who may locate the same on any of the University land which they may appropriate for that purpose, not exceeding 640 acres, or on any land donated for the purpose; and it shall be a branch of the University for instruction in agriculture and the natural sciences connected therewith.

And said—It may not be obvious why I have offered the amendment. I will briefly, therefore, explain. Placing the institution in question under the Board of Regents, obviates the necessity of creating a new board. My principal reason is, however, to connect the school with the University as a branch, in order that the school, which may be illy supplied with professors, may avail itself of those provided and paid for by the University. The professors of the natural sciences and the professor of anatomy and physiology can deliver full courses of lectures to the proposed school, with very little additional cost. It is to gain this great advantage that I want the disposition of the whole subject as contemplated by the amendment. It will be a responsible trust. The funds may be large, the experiment is new, and I know of no more fit repository of the trust than the Regents, highly fitted as I believe they must necessarily be.

Mr. McCLELLAND was somewhat in favor of the experiment of a model farm. But he would submit it to the Convention to say if it were proper to bind up those lands so that if this experiment failed, or the people became entirely dissatisfied with it, they were to be bound hand and foot in regard to the disposition of these lands. He did not like the idea of so fixing these twenty-two sections of salt spring lands, as to take them out of the hands of the people entirely, and place them beyond the action of the Legislature in any contingency. He would therefore vote against the amendment.

Mr. Walker observed that, instead of twenty-two sections, there were but about 2000 acres of unappropriated salt lands.

Mr. Williams went to the land office in order to ascertain the facts relative to these salt lands, and there learned that the whole number of acres granted us by the general government, was seventy-two sections; but we never received but 45,345 acres, being 735 acres less than 72 whole sections. Of these lands, fifty sections have been appropriated to the deaf, dumb and blind asylum, the insane asylum, and the normal school—equal to 32,000 acres; thus leaving, in fact, applicable to this subject, (acres,) 13,345

Of this quantity has been sold, (acres,)	3,721	
The general government has disposed of, which must be re-granted by government,	7,680	
Leaving unsold in office,	1,944	13,345

The quantity sold by the State has brought the sum of	$16,273 25
One quarter having been paid in hand. The balance, (9,624 acres,) should yield $4 per acre, if sold at the minimum valuation,	38,496 00
Total,	$54,769 25

The gross fund, therefore, if all the lands were sold, would amount to $54,769 25—a sum fully adequate to establish on a stable and respectable basis, the institution contemplated.

Mr. Crouse was opposed to the whole proposition, and would at the proper time move to strike out. He was entirely opposed to submitting the management of this proposed institution to the Regents of the University.

The question was then taken upon Mr. Williams' amendment, and was lost.

Mr. Warden moved to amend the amendment made in committee by striking out the words "and farm," wherever they occurred.

Mr. N. Pierce—The subject is one familiar to all here, although not farmers. I am not tenacious whether the amendment made by the committee should prevail or not, or whether the amendment to the amendment should prevail. I think the model farm is only a small part of the matter. I suppose the education is the principal thing on which reliance will be placed. Whether it is rational to apply some of the lands granted by the United States to this State, to this purpose, is a matter for the consideration of this Convention. It seems to me that the agricultural population have as much right to have a share in the education of the State as any other branch of the people; and I think it fair to apply the public funds to some extent to that purpose. But it will be an experimental matter. * * * I am not disposed, then, to take the revenues of the State and apply them unreasonably to any experimental matter whatever. If the Convention do not think it consistent with the present policy of the

State, they should not take these lands for this purpose; we ought rather to apply them to the reduction of our debt, or to other means of education.

Mr. Cornell did not know if this were the time at which to start an agricultural school. He was of opinion for many years that at least one quarter of the time was thrown away by reason of our students not being obliged to work at their studies; if they did, they would leave our colleges with stronger constitutions and sounder understandings. Six hours were as many as any man should study in a day. Was it not as well that our students should labor for a certain portion of time, as to be moping and lounging about the streets? What was the consequence of the present system? Men went through their different classes, and when they came out they were broken down in mind and body; and of the principles of the business they embraced, they knew nothing almost. If they were taught to labor, they would turn out something else. Every man should have more or less a practical education. The farmer had no need to know the dead languages; but he might the modern and the natural sciences. He should be taught every thing appertaining to the management of the farm. The gentleman last up did not attach any importsnce to the model farm—he (Mr. C.) did, for this reason: that when a man studied anything in the laboratory, he would go out a practical man, and apply the principle which he had previously studied. A man would thus become imbued with a spirit for the application of the sciences to agriculture, so that in after life, when he went upon a farm, he would understand thoroughly the theory and practice of farming. A great deal might be said on this subject; but he would simply say that he considered the model farm of importance, and if any portion of the proposition was retained that should be.

Mr. Britain thought that the best school in which men learned farming, was a practical one. The agricultural school the best adapted for making farmers, was the farm under the direction of the owner, whose interest it was to apply every facility for the better cultivation of his property. He would venture the opinion that if we gave $50,000 to the Regents of the University, or three other men, that farm would never be carried on as well as if it had received no government sustenance.

If the University was so fixed as to have the mechanical labor system connected with it, he would readily approve of it. But that was out of the question. If it should happen that the farm were located at some place far away from the University, the pupils would lose the advantages pointed out by the gentleman from Jackson, [Mr. Cornell.] He could not see how we were to attach a model farm to the University. Let farmers be taught geology, chemistry, &c., &c., and then go home and apply that knowledge. But he should like to know what farmer would think of sending his son abroad to be taught how to plow, reap, or sow, or to do anything connected with a farm in that way? He would venture to say that any practical farmer could teach these, or any professors, in everything relating to a farm. As to the benefits resulting from this proposition, he was entirely in the dark.

Mr. WILLIAMS—I am somewhat surprised at the remarks made, especially by the gentleman from Livingston, [Mr. Crouse.] Now, the design is exactly contrary. It is to take those who are certain to be skilled in manual labor, and teach them the general laws by which every thing grows and thrives; to illustrate to them, by practice, the newest discoveries in agriculture; to open their minds to the reception of every useful truth, come from whence it may; and more than all, relieve the young from the thraldom of any traditionary errors which may have clung to their fathers from generation to generation. Teach rich men's sons to work! To work with the hoe and the plow! Every boy in the country understands that. But the object of such a school is to teach a man how to promote and protect all his interests. I hardly know how to illustrate the subject. But, suppose the farmers of this State had, by a thorough education of the young wheat growers, increased the value of the wheat one cent per bushel. If we raise 7,000,000 bushels, it would make $70,000. If it could be increased in quantity ten per cent., it would make a difference in the production of the State for a single year, of $500,000. Bring sharpened intellects to every daily pursuit of the farmer, and produce, by the use of study, experiment and science, a corresponding increase of the productions of the State, and the cost of a hundred schools would soon be saved.

There are many branches of study that a farmer's boy ought to know, and which he does not learn in ordinary schools, which are rather calculated to fit a man for the counting room or college. I recollect a short time since, that I saw a man—a respectable and intelligent man—upon the point of losing quite a large a sum in a court, because he could not measure wood, piled in the shape of a section of a cone, for a coal pit. A man will find every day, in practical life, that he could save himself from expense and loss of time, if he had a knowledge of such matters. He ought to be familiar with the laws by which mechanical powers are applied. He ought to understand the readiest methods by which measurements of all kinds are made. I will put a case to the gentleman from Livingston: Suppose he and a neighbor had a large bin of wheat to measure, before they could settle or divide. An untaught man might measure it all over, and handle all. His boy, if taught rightly, could, in less than five minutes, calculate from the cubic contents, the number of bushels, and save the whole time and expense. These are the kinds of knowledge which he would have every farmer learn while young. But the great advantage of these schools was in the instruction which might be obtained in agricultural chemistry—a knowledge of the elements necessary to each crop; and that knowledge of physiology which would enable a man to propagate with success the finest breed of animals, or bring to the most perfect development, vegetable life. But the five minutes had expired, and he would not encroach on the rule, though he could pile up abundant proofs to show the advantages of such a school.

Mr. CROUSE remarked that he was as anxious as the gentleman [Mr. Williams] for farmers to have their sons educated. He believed that this article provided for their education, without a model farm. He certainly would be glad for his son to be able to calculate quantities. But, if he had a son who could not calculate the contents of an oat or corn bin, he certainly would sit up with him at night and teach him. He would not send him to a model farm or to the University to learn it. The article made such a provision that every child could be at school three months in every year, for fourteen years, or three and a half years in all. He would venture to say that nine-tenths of the people had never been within the walls of a school house for that period. The article also provided that the course of education should be pursued under competent teachers; and altogether it would afford sufficient facilities, under existing circumstances for the acquisition of a good education.

Mr. J. D. PIERCE concurred very fully with the gentleman from St. Joseph, [Mr. Williams.] To give a proper direction to knowledge in this department, (agriculture,) was of the utmost importance to mankind; for in fact the entire subsistence of the earth depended on it. Knowledge, and varied knowledge, was highly needed in farming. In Europe, they were ahead of us, in this respect. The reason was this; they turned their young men to farming, and sent them to farming schools. They raise in Europe as much as from sixty to seventy bushels to the acre; and in some instances we succeed in doing so in this country.

If the gentleman from Livingston, [Mr. Crouse,] or any other gentleman, hired a man who had been trained in one of these schools, and set him plowing along side of a man who had not been so educated, he would see that the former did twice the work of the latter. He [Mr. P.] had a man for some time, who had been two years in one of these schools, and in the sowing season he would not have a furrow that was not of equal length with the rest, and all straight.

Mr. ROBERTSON (interposing) inquired in what country in Europe farmers sent their sons to farming schools.

Mr. J. D. PIERCE, in reply, said that in Germany young men were sent to them, and in many parts of Great Britain such schools had been established, supported by private patronage. He saw no difficulty in carrying out the proposition, and would vote for it.

Mr. CORNELL observed it was well understood that when the law was passed establishing the State University, there was provision made for branches thereto, and one of them was to be an agricultural branch; the branches had been lopped off, and this proposition was only intended to carry out that provision. The utility of the plan, he thought no man acquainted with farming operations, could for a moment question; and that science should to some extent direct practice, and practice follow its teachings, none would deny. It was not claimed that the professors in this establishment were to be practical farmers; their business would be to show the best mode of applying scientific knowledge to agriculture. He would here refer to one simple matter—he would refer to our manures. Our lands are rich enough without manures now, but the time would come when they would require them. What sort of manure would a farmer apply to his lands unless he knew something of chemistry? If he did not know, he would guess at it. A man might apply a manure containing all the elements sufficient to raise forty bushels to the acre, yet, lacking one other element, it would not produce three bushels. Practical farmers knew that such was the case. He knew an instance of a farmer in North Carolina who had a farm that had been an excellent wheat farm; the quantity of wheat, however, decreased from year to year. The farmer manured his lands with all sorts of manures, but to no purpose. At length the farmers in his neighborhood said he should not sow wheat except once in three years, and they recommended certain descriptions of manure. The farmer, however, got nothing but straw, and about three bushels of wheat. Some of the farmers then recommended him to apply plaster; still he got but three bushels. Then they told him to put on lime and plaster, and still he got no more. Then a committee was appointed to investigate the case, and they finally stated the facts to the editor of an agricultural paper, described the manure applied, and it was found out that the manure lacked but one element, which, if the farmer had gone to the expense of twelve shillings or so, in procuring, he would have had twenty-eight or thirty bushels to the acre. The ingredient wanted was simply phosphoric acid; that which was found in bones. It was so that where a necessary element of a manure was lacking, the farmer received but very little return for his outlay.

Mr. Comstock expressed himself in favor of retaining the provision; he thought it due to the farming community that means for the acquisition of this very useful information should be afforded them.

Mr. Crouse said it was observed by the gentlemen from Calhoun, that they attained to greater perfection in Europe than we did here. In his part of the country there were farmers who had been brought up in England, and for his life he could not see that they were any better farmers than we were, and in some instances they were not as good.

The question was then taken upon Mr. Warden's motion to strike out. and was lost.

The question then recurred upon agreeing to the amendments reported from the committee of the whole.

Mr. McClelland moved to amend by inserting after the word "and," where it first occurred, the word "it shall be competent for the Legislature to appropriate;" and also to strike out "set apart," in the sixth line of the section as amended.

Mr. McClelland said his object was to prevent these lands being put beyond the reach of the Legislature, if there should be a failure in the farm. He had great confidence in the scheme, if it did not get into the hands of politicians. We had had a great deal of experience on this subject; for it had been found that wherever collegiate institutions were in the hands of State officers, they had generally become merely political machines, and turned out a failure.

Mr. WILLIAMS said he was opposed to the amendment. * * * * * * * Twenty-five sections of these salt lands, by sections eight and nine, had been created a perpetual and inviolable fund for the support of the State Normal School, and for the asylum for the insane, and for deaf mutes, and the blind. If we were satisfied with the expediency and importance of an agricultural school, there were no reasons bearing on the application of the fifty sections, which would not justify us in appropriating the last twenty-two sections, as inviolably as the other fifty.

Mr. McCLELLAND said—The Normal School plan has been most fully tested in nearly all the old States of the Union. But gentlemen must admit that in this country at least, this model farm or agricultural school, exclusively agricultural in its character, is an experiment. Well, if it be an experiment, I ask, is it judicious or wise in us to bind up forever these salt spring lands? Why does the gentleman mistrust the Legislature? If the people be in favor of appropriating lands for this purpose, the Legislature will act in accordance with their wishes, as a matter of course; and our making this provision will show them what we intend should be done with these lands. But if this experiment should fail, yet the gentleman [Mr. Williams] would make it imperative on the people to sustain this school in this way, and no other. But if it prove a failure, would it be reasonable to ask any man to support it? I should think it would not. * * * *

Mr. CORNELL observed that he was willing enough the amendment should be made. He thought that if the school failed, as remarked by the gentleman last up, the Legislature should have the control of these lands. The gentleman was mistaken in saying that this school was to be exclusively agricultural. Such was not the case; all the mechanical arts, and the various scientific matters would be taught in it.

Mr. BRITAIN hoped the amendment would be adopted. There was a feeling throughout the State to advance the cause of agricultural education. These lands would be safe in the hands of the Legislature; if the experiment should be found to be impracticable, the funds could then be diverted to some other channel.

The question was then taken upon Mr. McClelland's amendment, and was sustained.

The amendments reported from the committee of the whole, were then severally concurred in.

Mr. BRITAIN moved to amend section eleven by adding after the word "farm," in the eighth line, the words "until otherwise appropriated by law;" which was agreed to.

Mr. WILLIAMS moved to amend by inserting after "farm," in sixth line, "and it shall be competent for the Legislature to make the same a branch of the University for instruction in agriculture and the natural sciences connected therewith, and place the same under the supervision of the Regents of the University."

Mr. W. said—Though the Convention have refused to place the proposed school under the supervision of the Regents, yet, as they have left the creation of the school itself to the discretion of the Legislature, there can be no harm in leaving this subject also to their discretion. I only want the Legislature to have the power to connect the school with the University, by ever so slight a tenure. Surely there can be no more fit repository of the management of the institution than the Regents. They will be likely to be practical men, of wide experience, of integrity and public spirit. But I wish it made a branch for the reason stated before. An agricultural school would probably be placed under a farmer of great comprehensiveness of mind, and great practical skill, and a professor of agricultural chemistry, and such other teachers as may from time to time be required. There will necessarily be connected with the University, professors who have no very onerous duties, and who are employed but a portion of the year. It so happens that these were the very professors whose lectures and instructions would be invaluable to an agricultural school, which may be too poor to employ a separate corps. They would probably perform all the duties of both institutions, for the same, or very little additional compensation. The professor of anatomy and physiology could deliver a course of lectures, embracing that knowledge of general laws regulating health, life and growth, and the improvement and cultivation of both the animal and vegetable creation, and the preservation of the physical man of the students themselves. The professors of natural philosophy, geology, and natural history, could all be made valuable to the branch. The professor (if such shall be employed) of the application of science to the arts, and an illustration of the manner in which the wonderful discoveries and inventions of this wonderful age are put into daily practical use, would confer great benefits on the school by his occasional instructions. Now, if an agricultural school is ever organized, I wish to connect it by some tie that will enable it to avail itself of such valuable instruction, so nearly gratuitous as it must be, if these duties are imposed by the Regents on the professors of the University.

THE UNIVERSITY—IN CONVENTION.

Mr. Whipple offered the following substitute for section four of the article:

"There shall be appointed by both branches of the Legislature, in joint convention assembled, in the year 1852, eight Regents of the University; two for the term of eight years, two for the term of six years, two for the term of four years, and two for term of two years; and at each subsequent election two Regents shall be elected in the manner aforesaid, who shall hold their office for the term of eight years."

Mr. W. said—The number of Regents provided for in the article, as it now stands, I think, is too small; because we all know that the board of Regents perform their duties without any compensation—their labors are gratuitous. And it is very difficult, and will be found difficult, perhaps, in five cases out of seven, to obtain a full attendance at the board; and it may be very important, on occasions, that the board should be full. The Regents reside in remote parts of the State; that is, at places distant from that at which the meeting is to be held. In fact, sir, I am unwilling to trust the great interests of the University to a less number of my fellow citizens than six. The interests are of too much magnitude to be trusted to the control of less than six men. I therefore propose that there shall be eight Regents, under the impression that as a general rule they can obtain six at any called meeting of the board. And then, again, I am exceedingly anxious to multiply the number for another reason: if we select eight, (and I should prefer twelve,) your Regents will be distributed over every part of the State, and the public will thus obtain a knowledge of the character of this institution; for the Convention will observe that the concerns of this University are to be placed in the hands of the Regents. They will obtain very important knowledge in regard to this establishment, and the people among whom they live will become informed as to the nature of this institution, and will become interested in it.

As I said before, I should prefer twelve; six is too small. I know it has been said that a small board will effect more than a large one. That may be a very good rule; but I do not see the applicability of it to the case before us. I do not see how we can effect the object which we have in view, more effectually than by providing that there shall be eight Regents.

The second branch of my proposition proposes that instead of electing the Regents by the people at large, they shall be appointed by the Legislature in joint Convention. My object is this, to place the University beyond all political influence. There is no gentleman, I suppose, in this Convention, disposed to put this institution within the grasp of either political party of the State, or to bring it under any improper influence. Now, it is well known that since the organization of that institution, the Governor and Senate have selected from the different parts of the State the most distinguished and worthy individuals to fill this office, and the happiest results have been had. The difficulty in electing the Regents by general ticket, I take it, is this: one party meets to nominate State officers, among others six Regents of the University, or eight, if this amendment be adopted; the question then arises in my mind whether they will nominate all or part, by one party. What will be the result? It may be that the Regents will thus be thrown all in one portion of the State. I take it for granted that in electing Regents, men may or may not be governed by party predilections. The result might be this: when the eastern part of the State was represented by six Regents, the other portions of the State would be represented by but two.

I think that instead of leaving the appointment to the Governor and Senate as heretofore, it would be safer in the hands of the Legislature in joint convention. It appears to me that by adopting this course, we will accomplish the object that we all have in view, with more certainty than if we left it open to the ordinary party contests of the day.

Mr. McClelland—I would suggest to my friend from Berrien the propriety of having these Regents appointed by the Governor and Legislature. It would be better than leaving the appointment with the Legislature alone; because, if left to them, some of the difficulties suggested might arise. I think it would be much better to leave it to the Governor, to be approved by the Legislature in joint convention.

Mr. Whipple had no objection to so amend his proposition; and the substitute was then amended as suggested.

Mr. Bagg—I am opposed to the substitute offered by the gentleman from Berrien, [Mr. Whipple,] and the amendment suggested by the gentleman from Monroe. I am for having the people elect these men. I know no good reason why the people cannot as well elect these Regents as the Legislature. Sir, I believe the people have the good sense to make a proper selection in this matter. If there be any argument against the election of these officers by the people, it applies equally against their being appointed by the creatures of the people, the Legislature. I never desired to see them appointed by the Governor; but I prefer the substitute as modified, to the original proposition. However, I should desire to amend in this way: "there shall be elected at the first election after the ratification of this constitution, twelve Regents."

Mr. Walker said he had no great feeling on this subject. It was considered by the committee that the Board of Regents, as heretofore organized, was too large, and that more efficiency would be introduced by reducing the number. Their object in fixing upon "six," was to insure a more direct responsibility on the part of the Board. He believed, from knowing it was demanded that all officers should be elected by them, that those should also. He had no fear in leaving the election of the Regents to the people, and so making them directly responsible to the public.

Mr. N. Pierce observed that the government of the University was not such as it should be. With the large amount of funds which it had at its disposal, for the last fifteen years, it graduated only about twelve students in the year. This institution did not educate one-half the number that other chartered institutions in this State did; and this resulted merely from the goverment. In the Albion Seminary they graduated about fifty this year. There was something wrong about all this. He made these remarks merely to set forth some information which he received last year, as a member of the Legislature. He would much prefer that any sectarian religious society had care of this institution, than to have no one tanght in it. They taught no one—their rules and course of study were good, but still they did not get pupils. The University was surrounded by difficulties that should be looked into.

Mr. Church could not look with any complacency upon the idea of taking the Regents of the University into the two great caucuses of the political parties of the State, every two years. There, no doubt, they would be used as a sort of small change. He knew what sort of people there were in State conventions; and in settling between the different candidates of the State, the settlement for the smaller candidates, and the claims of one section of the State, would be made up in this way: "we will give you a Regent if you go with us for Treasurer." Such would be the case; they would certainly become "small change," if the plan of electing them by the people were carried out. He agreed with the delegate from Macomb, [Mr. Walker,] as to the number of Regents. He did not think it well to increase the number. But in view of the difficulty of collecting a small number from the different parts of the State, that fact would be sufficient to recommend the proposition of the delegate from Berrien, [Mr. Whipple.]

Mr. Leach expressed himself as being opposed to the substitute. He thought that the question in regard to the election of officers by the people, had been finally disposed of. The argument against the election of Regents by the people, he considered, held equally against the election of any other officers whatever. Education demanded that these men should be protected from all sectarian and party influence. If the appointment were left to the Legislature, would not the Regents be party men? He expected they would. If elected by a democratic Legislature, they would be democrats, and *vice versa.* He thought, from the history of the past, they would be political men. He would assert, that as a general thing, men nominated by the Legislature had been political men.

The question being upon the adoption of the substitute, [Mr. Whipple's,] the same was taken by yeas and nays—yeas 30, nays 28.

Mr. Whipple submitted the following, to stand as a new section, (5;) and the same was agreed to:

"The Regents elected pursuant to the provisions of the foregoing section, and their successors in office, shall continue to constitute the body corporate, known by the name and style of the "Regents of the University of Michigan."

On the 6th of August, Mr. Cornell moved to re-commit the article on Education to the committee, with instructions to strike out section 3 and insert: "The Legislature shall, as soon as practicable, establish a system of primary schools, the tuition of which shall be free throughout the State, and provide for their support." After debate, the vote being taken upon instructing, as proposed by Mr. Cornell, the result was yeas 45, nays 23, and the article was re-committed. The article was reported back on the same day. After some further amendments were proposed without success, the question being upon ordering the article to a third reading, it was lost by a vote of 33 to 28.

On motion of Mr. J. D. Pierce, the vote was re-considered, and the article laid upon the table. As remarked by Mr. Pierce, the system of free schools had the decided majority of the Convention, but a provision had been inserted which destroyed that principle.

On motion of Mr. J. D. PIERCE, the article was again taken from the table, and re-committed to the committee on Education. It was reported back by the committee on the following day, with section 3 as follows:

The Legislature shall, within five years from the adoption of this constitution, provide for and establish a system of common schools. Such schools shall be kept without charge for tuition for at least three months in each year, in every school district in the State.

Mr. BRITTAIN moved to add to the substitute: "and all instruction in said schools shall be conducted in the English language," which was accepted by the committee. A substitute was offered by Mr. FRALICK, which was not adopted, and the substitute as reported by the committee, was then concurred in. The section which related to the election of Regents was again discussed.

Mr. BAGG offered the following substitute for section four:

" There shall be elected at the first general election for judges in this State after the ratification of this constitution, twelve Regents of the University; four for the term of six years, four for the term of four years, and four for two years; and at each subsequent election for judges, there shall be four Regents of the University elected, who shall hold their office for the term of six years."

Mr. B. hoped the substitute just offered by himself, would prevail. * * * Gentlemen agreed that the Regents of this institution should be placed beyond the operation and effects of party, and therefore should be elected by the Legislature. Would this remove the objection? Would the Legislature be any less free from the machinery of party? Certainly not. That arena was as liable to be affected by party as the general election by the people themselves. The substitute proposed to elect the Regents of the University at the same time and in the same manner as the circuit judges. Were the Regents of the University of more consequence than your judges of the Supreme Court? Was not the judiciary at the very base of your government? Did not these judges adjudicate on the whole, ultimately? If so. was not what was applicable to one applicable to the other? He could see no difference.

After debate, the substitute was agreed to, yeas 44, nays 26.

The article was then ordered to a third reading, and the deliberations of the Convention resulted in the 13th article of the revised constitution, adopted by the people, and which is now the organic law of the State.

ARTICLE XIII.—EDUCATION.

Sec. 1. The Superintendent of Public Instruction shall have the general supervision of public instruction, and his duties shall be prescribed by law.

Sec. 2. The proceeds from the sales of all lands that have been or hereafter may be granted by the United States to the State for educational purposes, and the proceeds of all lands or other property given by individuals, or appropriated by the State for like purposes, shall be and remain a perpetual fund, the interest and income of which, together with the rents of all such lands as may remain unsold, shall be inviolably appropriated and annually applied to the specific objects of the original gift, grant or appropriation.

Sec. 3. All land, the titles to which shall fail from a defect of heirs, shall escheat to the State; and the interest on the clear proceeds from the sales thereof, shall be appropriated exclusively to the support of primary schools.

Sec. 4. The Legislature shall, within five years from the adoption of this constitution, provide for and establish a system of primary schools, whereby a school shall be kept without charge for tuition, at least three months in each year, in every school district in the State; and all instruction in said schools shall be conducted in the English language.

Sec. 5. A school shall be maintained in each school district, at least three months in each year. Any school district neglecting to maintain such school, shall be deprived for the ensuing year of its proportion of the income of the primary school fund, and of all funds arising from taxes for the support of schools,

Sec. 6. There shall be elected in each judicial circuit, at the time of the election of the judge of such circuit, a Regent of the University, whose term of office shall be the same as that of such judge. The Regents thus elected shall constitute the Board of Regents of the University of Michigan.

Sec. 7. The Regents of the University and their successors in office shall continue to constitute the body corporate, known by the name and title of "the Regents of the University of Michigan."

Sec. 8. The Regents of the University shall, at their first annual meeting, or as soon thereafter as may be, elect a president of the University, who shall be ex-officio a member of their Board, with the privilege of speaking, but not of voting. He shall preside at the meetings of the Regents, and be the principal executive officer of the University. The Board of Regents shall have the general supervision of the University, and the direction and control of all expenditures from the University interest fund.

Sec. 9. There shall be elected at the general election in the year one thousand eight hundred and fifty-two, three members of a State board of education; one for two years, one for four years, and one for six years, and at each succeeding biennial election there shall be elected one member of such board, who shall hold his office for six years. The Superintendent of Public Instruction shall be ex-officio a member and Secretary of such board. The board shall have the general supervision of the State Normal school, and their duties shall be prescribed by law.

Sec. 10. Institutions for the benefit of those inhabitants who are deaf, dumb, blind or insane, shall always be fostered and supported.

Sec. 11. The Legislature shall encourage the promotion of intellectual, scientific and agricultural improvement; and shall, as soon as practicable, provide for the establishment of an agricultural school. The Legislature may appropriate the twenty two sections of salt spring lands now unappropriated, or the money arising from the sale of the same, where such lands have been already sold, and any land which may hereafter be granted or appropriated for such purpose, for the support and maintenance of such school, and may make the same a branch of the University, for instruction in agriculture and the natural sciences connected therewith, and place the same under the supervision of the Regents of the University.

Sec. 12. The Legislature shall also provide for the establishment of at least one library in each township; and all fines assessed and collected in the several counties and townships for any breach of the penal laws, shall be exclusively applied to the support of such libraries.

THE FIRST AND THE REVISED CONSTITUTION.

A comparison of these instruments, the first of which will be found on page eighteen of this document, will show the points of difference and the improvements made in the latter.

The first article of the old constitution provided for a Superintendent of Public Instruction, who was to be appointed by the Governor, by and with the advice and consent of the Legislature, in joint vote.

The revised constitution, under article VIII; entitled "Of State Officers," provides for his election biennially, by the people, and he is to keep his office at the seat of government.

The first constitution provided that the funds accruing from the sale or rents of University and school lands, should remain a perpetual fund, &c. The revised constitution provides that the proceeds of the sales, and of all lands or other property given by individuals, or appropriated by the State for such purposes, should remain a perpetual fund, which, together with the rents, &c., shall be inviolably appropriated, and *annually applied to the specific* objects of the original grant or appropriation.

The revised constitution provides that all lands, the titles to which shall fail from defect of heirs, shall escheat to the State, and the interests on the clear proceeds of the sales, are to be exclusively appropriated to the support of primary schools. The first constitution had no such provision.

The first constitution required that the Legislature should provide for a system of *common schools,* by which a school should be kept up and supported in each school district at least three months in each year; and any school district that neglected this, was deprived *of its equal proportion of the interest* of the fund.

The revised constitution requires that the Legislature shall within five years, provide for and establish a system of *primary schools,* to be kept *without charge of tuition,* at least three months in every year, in every school district. and all instruction is to be in the English language; and any school district neglecting to maintain such school, for such time, is to be deprived not only of its proportion of the school fund. *but of all funds arising from taxes* for the *support of schools.*

The revised constitution provides for the election of Regents of the University. It provides for the election of the members of the board of education, to have charge of the Normal School, and it further provides that institutions for the benefit of the deaf, dumb and blind, and insane, shall be fostered and supported. It provides also for the establishment of an Agricultural school. The first constitution provided for none of these.

The first constitution provided for the establishment of libraries, one at least in each township, and appropriated for their establishment and support, *the money paid* for exemptions from military duty, and the *clear proceeds* of all fines assessed for breach of the penal laws.

The revised constitution provides that *all fines assessed and collected* in the several townships and counties for breach of the penal laws, shall be applied to the support of the libraries ; there being no longer any moneys required to be paid for exemptions from military duty.

Both enjoin upon the Legislature the encouragement and promotion of intellectual, scientific and agricultural improvement.

Under the head of "finance and taxation," the revised constitution further provides that all specific taxes except those received from the mining companies of the upper peninsula, shall be applied in paying the interest upon the primary school, University and other educational funds, and the principal of the State debt, in the order herein recited, until the extinguishment of the State debt other than the amount due to educational funds, when such specific taxes shall be added to and constitute a part of the primary school interest fund.

A comparison will show that the trust confided by the people to their delegates in Convention, was satisfactorily executed in relation to education; that if they did not wholly agree upon the details to be embodied in the article upon this subject, they established it, finally, upon a basis of wisdom and improvement. It proved to be satisfactory to the people; and it only remains for those who are charged with carrying its provisions into effect, to act with the same amount of industry, zeal and fidelity, to ensure to the people of Michigan and to their posterity, a system of public instruction and educational institutions, worthy of an enlightened and improving age.

1851.

EXTRACT FROM GOV. BARRY'S MESSAGE.

In view of the paramount interest of agriculture, the framers of the constitution, while they did not fail to provide for intellectual and scientific instruction, at the same time enjoined upon the Legislature the duty of promoting agricultural improvement, and the establishment of an agricultural school.

Opinions will be, perhaps, in some degree divided, whether the school contemplated shall be one of manual labor with farm attached, or one in which the theory and science of agriculture alone shall be taught. It will be the province of the Legislature to determine its character in this regard; but the object to be effected should be kept in view, and the best method of inculcating agricultural improvement adopted.

Of the salt spring lands, the Legislature is authorized to appropriate to this purpose twenty-two sections; but of these lands less than fifteen sections remain unappropriated, exclusive of the twelve sections mentioned in another part of this communication, erroneously confirmed to the State, after their sale, by the general government. The appropriation, therefore, must be limited to the sections on hand, at least until the action of Congress be obtained upon our claim for the remainder.

It may not be fruitless of results to inquire whether, by some appropriate legislation, with small expenditures, you may not put within reach of the husbandman a knowledge of the improvements made in the implements of agriculture, and also communicate to him the discoveries made by the application of science to this pursuit.

Universal education of the masses is the only sure guarantee of the permanency of a republican government. Without general intelligence, a people can neither know nor appreciate the benign influence of free institutions. If ignorance and consequent degradation characterize the mass of a nation, the despotism of a tyrant, or the worst despotism of anarchy, characterize its government. All history, whether ancient or modern, affords abundant and satisfactory evidence of this.

Common schools are designed for the education of the masses, and so beneficial is their influence that their discontinuance would not only work a great evil to society, but endanger even the permanence of our political institutions. In a government so complex and embracing relations so delicate as ours, greater intelligence and consequent moral power is required for its maintenance than in governments otherwise constituted; and these alone will secure, if any thing can secure, its indestructible perpetuity.

Few new States have exceeded Michigan in providing for the education of youth. The grant of every sixteenth section, as far as possible, in the settled portions of the State, has been made available, and further means have been provided by taxation, so that the whole amount expended for the promotion of common schools, including voluntary contributions, will favorably compare with the expenditures of other and older States for the same purpose.

One step more is required to secure to all the children of the State the benefits of a common school education, and that step is the establishment of FREE SCHOOLS. Though hitherto the charge of tuition has always been remitted to those not able to pay, yet, from a sentiment of delicacy or pride, the poor have not, in all cases, sent their children to school By provision of the revised constitution it is made the duty of the Legislature, within five years, to provide for and establish a system of primary schools, to be kept in each district of the State, at least three months in the year without charge of tuition.

A provision of this kind cannot but meet the cordial approbation of every patriotic individual and well wisher of his country. The taxation necessary to carry this into effect, will hardly exceed that of the last and previous years collected for the purpose of education; and the common schools will, in name and in fact, be free to all. Complaint of taxation, for the purpose of education, has scarcely ever been made, for the proprietors of estates, though without children to educate, have property to protect, and the tax paid is but a small premium advanced for insurance of its safety.

The number of children in the State reported between the ages of four and eighteen years, is 132 234, and the whole number that have attended school the year past, is 1[illegible]0,478.

After the liquidation of the public debt the primary school interest fund will be greatly increased by the addition thereto of all specific taxes collected in the State.

The number of students in the department of arts and sciences in the University, is 64; and the number in the medical department exceeds 80. The whole amount paid last year to the treasurer of the University, from the University interest fund. is $9,644 70.

The organic law of the University makes it the duty of the Regents to establish and maintain branches; but, from the insufficiency of the funds placed under their control, they have not been able fully to comply with this requirement. The consequence has been that, from the want of sufficient institutions to prepare young men to enter the University, the number of its students in the department of the arts and sciences, has been limited. Other causes have, doubtless, contributed to this result; but the main reason, I doubt not, may be found in the want of preparatory schools, constituting an intermediate grade between primary schools and the University. The means at the disposal of the Regents not being adequate, we must look for their establishment to some other source, as their existence, beyond doubt, is indispensable to the prosperity of the University, and the promotion of intellectual and scientific improvement made imperative on the Legislature. The Superintendent of Public Instruction suggests, as worthy of consideration, whether, in the absence of sufficient means to sustain the branches, we may not, with advantage, extend assistance to existing incorporated institutions of learning, on equivalent terms, and in such manner, as, working no detriment to the University, will make them tributary to that institstion, and prevent, ultimately, that antagonism and rivalry which otherwise might arise.

The advantages offered to the student, in the department of the arts and sciences, in the University of Michigan, are scarcely exceeded in the colleges of the older States; and the expenses of the collegiate course in the former are considerably less. And though the number of students are less, than with the advantages offered, we might have reason to expect, yet perhaps no other like institution, not longer established, has contributed more to the promotion of science.

The present class of students in the medical department, being the first formed, is unprecedentedly large. The inducements offered, will, I doubt not, secure the attendance of an increased number in succeeding years.

The Regents are hereafter to be elected by the people, and the first election is to be held on the first Monday of April next, at the time of the election of judges of the circuit courts. A State board of education is also to be elected at the general election in 1852. The requisite provisions of law should be passed at the present session.

The board of education have contracted for the erection of a suitable edifice for the State normal school, for $15 000; and of this sum $12,000 have already been paid the contractor, in notes and obligations donated by the citizens of Ypsilanti. Ample security has been taken for the completion of the contract by the 1st day of March, 1852, when it is expected the institution will be in readiness to receive pupils.

The board of trustees of the Michigan asylum for the education of the deaf and dumb and blind, and of the asylum for the insane, will, in due time, present a report of their proceedings. The means appropriated, it is believed, will be found entirely inadequate to effect the objects contemplated.

EXTRACT FROM SUPERINTENDENT'S REPORT.

The management and supervision of the University continues to be a subject of very general and deep interest. Its condition at the present time, as far as official information has come to this office, is derived from the reports of the Board of Regents, and the Board of Visitors, appointed in pursuance of the provisions of section 15 of chapter 57 of the revised statutes, to both of which the Legislature is respectfully referred. The estimated receipts for the coming year are calculated at $17,088 23. The estimated expenses, $16,263 33. The former exceeds the receipts of last year by $5,088 23, while the expenses are also increased $4,976 92. The sum of $6,010 00 is set apart in this estimate, to pay interest upon the loan of $100,000, and the balance for the support of professors, officers of the board, expenses of Regents, insurance and incidental expenses. It would be of no utility at this time, perhaps, to discuss the financial or general policy which has been adopted by successive Boards of Regents. The heavy loan early contracted, and the large amonnt invested in buildings, has proved a serious detriment to the interests of the institution, and will continue to embarrass its legitimate field of operations until effectual provision is made for sinking the debt. What provision has been made for this purpose is unknown to this department. Information in this respect was required from the Board of Regents, but not in season for that body to prepare and submit it at this time. It is believed, however, that the importance of relieving the University from this burden must be apparent to all. A heavy expenditure has been incurred in erecting the building for the medical department. According to the report of the building committee it has cost nearly $9,000, and the whole of this amount will be required to complete it. An increase has been made in the number of medical professors, and one professor has been transferred. The whole number of professors in the institution is ten; who are receiving a salary each of $333 33 per term, for the time actually employed—the academic year consisting of three terms. The importance of this branch of the University is fully appreciated, and it is justly remarked by the executive committee, that the "young men of our State who have heretofore in large numbers sought instruction in other institutions abroad, are now assured of at least equal advantage at home." The reputation of the medical corps of professors stands deservedly high, and in this respect the greatest inducement is afforded, not only for a large accession of students from our own, but from neighboring States. While it is gratifying that this department is now ready for service, it continues to be a question whether heavy expenditures for building purposes, or for objects collateral to the main department of the institution, and in some respects secondary in impartance, (though by no means to be neglected under better auspices,) will not still further embarrass and retard the progress of the main collegiate interests of the University. No misfortune has ever occurred to this institution equal in extent to that which has grown out of that system of policy which has permitted, or rendered necessary, perhaps, the abandonment of branches; and it would seem to be of the first importance, if the means of the institution will permit the outlay of a large amount of capital for any purpose, that it should be directed into this channel. It is the settled judgment of this department that so soon, at least, as the debt is extinguished, further effort and renewed exertion should be made, that the University "may represent itself in the different sections of the State through its branches." Reasons are multiplied, indicating this policy as the only sure means of filling up the institution, and guarding against the multiplication of sectarian colleges.

At this peculiar juncture of affairs in the educational world, when old usages and systems seem to be giving way to the onward march of intellectual, moral and physical progression, it becomes a matter of the deepest interest to the friends of our educational system, and the University especially, to investigate the means of keeping full pace with this advancing spirit. The change in the collegiate course and system, contemplated and adopted in pursuance of the recommendation of President Wayland, of Brown University, is attracting much attention, and giving rise to much favorable discussion. The views advanced in the report of the president of this institution commend themselves to the consideration of the friends of education, and may doubtless suggest in the future, important subjects of reflection connected with the University of Michigan.

The following views of President Wayland, in relation to the subject of collegiate education, develope the character of the change contemplated at Brown University. The President says:

To us it seems little option is left to the colleges in this matter. Any one who will observe the progress which, within the last thirty years, has been made by the productive classes of society, in power, wealth and influence, must be convinced that a system of education practically restricted to a class vastly smaller, and rapidly decreasing in influence, cannot possibly continue. Within a few years the manufacturing interest has wrung the Corn Laws from the aristocracy of Great Britain. Let any one recall the relative position of the professions, and of the mercantile and manufacturing interest, in any of our cities, twenty years since, and compare it with their relative position now, and he cannot but be convinced that a great and progressive change has taken place. Men who do not design to educate their sons for the professions, are capable of determining upon the kind of instruction which they need. If the college will not furnish it, they are able to provide it themselves, and they will provide it. In New York and Massachusetts, incipient measures have been taken for establishing agricultural colleges. The bill before the Legislature of New York provides for instruction in all the branches taught in our colleges, with the exception of languages. It is to be, in fact, an institution for giving all the education which we now give, agricultural science being substituted for Latin and Greek. What is proposed to be done for the farmers, must soon be done either for or by the manufacturers and merchants. In this manner each productive department will have its own school, in which its own particular branch of knowledge will be taught, beside the ordinary studies of a liberal education. A large portion of the instruction communicated, will thus be the same in all. Mathematics, mechanics, chemistry, rhetoric moral and intellectual philosophy, and political economy, will be taught in them all. The colleges teach precisely the same sciences, with the addition of Latin and Greek, in the place of the knowledge designed in these separate schools for a particular profession.

If the *prestige* of colleges should be thus destroyed, and it be found that as good an education as they furnish can be obtained in any of those other schools, the number of their students will be seriously diminished. If, by this dissemination of science among all the other classes of society, the tendency towards the professions should be still further arrested, the colleges will be deserted by yet larger numbers. They may become very good foundations for the support of instructors, but very few will be found to avail themselves of their instructions.

The objection that would arise to this plan would probably be its effect upon the classics. It will be said that we should thus diminish the amount of study bestowed on Latin and Greek. If, by placing Latin and Greek upon their own merits, they are unable to retain their present place in the education of civilized and christianized man, then let them give place to something better. They have by right, no pre-eminence over other studies, and it is absurd to claim it for them. But we go farther. In our present system we devote some six or seven years to compulsory study of the classics. Beside innumerable academies, we have one hundred and twenty colleges, in which, for a large part of the time, classical studies occupy the labors of the student. And what is the fruit? How many of these students read either classical Latin or Greek, after they leave college? If, with all this labor, we fail to imbue our young men with a love of the classics. is there any reason to fear that any change will render their position less advantageous? Is there not reason to hope that, by rendering this study less compulsory. and allowing those who have a taste for it to devote themselves more thoroughly to classical reading, we shall raise it from its present depression, and derive from it all the benefit which it is able to confer?

METEOROLOGICAL OBSERVATIONS.

This subject was earnestly commended to the attention of the Legislature.

The establishment of a system of observations upon the subject of meteorology, and more especially as connected with mean temparature, the direction and force of winds, state of the atmosphere, &c.,

was suggested in the last communication from this department, as an important object to all classes of our people, and more especially to our agricultural and commercial interest. The expense attending it would be trifling in comparison with the amount of good to be accomplished, and the work may be properly performed by the professors, without detriment to their other duties. This system of observations is becoming, and is now, in fact, national—both the general government and particular States alike interesting themselves is an object which is so nearly allied to the most useful pursuits and purposes of life. The most valuable information in this respect is disseminated by the Board of Regents of the New York University, who last year revised their system, and recommended that proper instruments be furnished to the principal towns and flourishing literary institutions. It would be an object of interest and profit, both in a scientific and pecuniary point of view, to all our citizens, to adopt a similar course in this State, and to furnish various institutions in different sections with a set of instruments, the cost of which for a set very well adapted to the purpose, does not exceed $32. The remarks of the board of trustees of the Romeo branch upon this subject, transmitted with their report, are commended to the attention of the Legislature.

REPORT OF THE REGENTS.

Since the last report, an increase had been made in the number of professors by the appointment of Doctors Gunn, Allen and Denton, and the transfer of Professor Sager to the medical department, which was now organized. The first announcement of the medical faculty was published this year.

In the department of arts and sciences, the whole number of students was 72.

The estimated receipts for the ensuing year were $17,088 23. The estimated expenses $16,263 33. The amount received to the credit of the University fund, from July 1, 1849, to June 1, 1850, was $10,682 47. The quantity of University land sold during the same period was 623.93 acres, amounting in all to $9,568 09.

The following is a statement of the course of studies, &c., pursued at the University:

ADMISSION.

Candidates for admission to the Freshman Class must not be less than fourteen years of age, and must sustain an examination in English Grammar, Geography, Arithmetic, Algebra through simple equations, first part of Krebs' Guide for the writing of Latin. Latin Reader. Cornelius Nepos, (Arnold's,) Cicero's Orations against Cataline, Virgils Æneid, Greek Reader to the poetry, the four Gospels, Latin and Greek Grammar, Keightley's Grecian and Roman History.

Candidates for an advanced standing, in addition to the preparatory studies, are examined in the studies to which the class they propose to enter have attended.

All applicants for admission must present testimonials of good moral character, with a letter from a parent or guardian; and students coming from other colleges, a certificate of honorable dismission.

No student is considered a regular member of the University, until after a probation of twelve weeks.

RECITATIONS AND EXAMINATIONS.

Each class attends three recitations or lectures daily, except Saturdays, when there is an exercise in Elocution. There are also frequent exercises in translation, composition and oral or written disputations.

Public examinations are held at the close of each term attended by the board of visitors, appointed annually by the Superintendent of Public Instruction, and by a committee of the Regents.

The following scheme exhibits the subjects studied in the several terms of each year:

FRESHMAN YEAR.—FIRST TERM.

Livy, (Lincoln's or Folsom's,) Roman Antiquities, (Eschenberg's Manual') Homer's Odyssey, (Owen's,) Bourdon's Algebra, Newman's Rhetoric.

SECOND TERM.

Livy, Ancient History, Grecian Antiquities, (Esch. Manual,) Homer's Odyssey, Algebra, Legendre's Geometry.

THIRD TERM.

Horace, Odes, Xenophon. Anab., (Owen's,) Geometry, Botany. Zoology.

Monday morning, throughout the year, Greek Testament, (Gospels.)

SOPHOMORE YEAR—FIRST TERM.

Newman's Rhetoric, Horace Satires, Xenophons' Anabasis, Plane and Spherical Trigonometry, Conic Sections.

SECOND TERM.

Analyt, Geometry and Calculus, Tacitus, Germania et Agricola, (Tyler's,) Demosthenes de corona, Isocrates.

THIRD TERM.

Sophocles, Cicero de Senectute et de Amicitia, French.

Monday morning, throughout the year, Greek Testament, (Acts.)

JUNIOR YEAR—FIRST TERM.

Wayland's Political Economy, Logic, French, Olmstead's Natural Philosophy.

SECOND TERM.

Tacitus, Historia, Euripides, Natural Philosophy, Chemistry, Mineralogy.

THIRD TERM.

German, Blair's Rhetoric, Olmstead's Astronomy.

Monday morning, throughout the year, Greek Testament, (Epistles.)

SENIOR YEAR—FIRST TERM.

Geology, Upham's Mental Philosophy, German.

SECOND TERM.

Upham's Mental Philosophy, (3d Vol.,) Whateley's Logic, Wayland's Moral Science, Natural Theology, Evidences of Christianity.

THIRD TERM.

Butler's Analogy, Plato's Gorgias.

Monday morning, throughout the year, Greek Testament, (Epistles.)

BOOKS OF REFERENCE.

Ramshorn's or Dumesnil's Latin Synonymes, Smith's Dictionary of Greek and Roman Antiquities, Anthon's Classical Dictionary, Mitchell's or Butler's Atlas Classica, Mitchell's Ancient Geography, Cousin's Psychology, Stewart's Philosophical Works, Locke on the Human Understanding, Edward's on the Will, Whewell's Elements of Morality.

EXPENSES.

The only charges of the institution are an admission fee of $10, and a sum, ranging from $5 to $7 50 a year, for room rent and the services of the janitor, a receipt for the payment of which, signed by the inspector of the University buildings, must be presented to the president of the faculty, before a student can be permitted to recite. Tuition is gratuitous. Including board, washing and books, the necessary expenses of a student, for a year, will range from $70 to $100.

GOVERNMENT.

In the government of the institution, the faculty ever keep in mind that most of the students are of an age which renders absolutely necessary some *substitute for parental superintendence.* It is believed that no college in our country can secure public confidence, without watching over the morals of its students, and making strict propriety of conduct, as well as diligent application to study, a condition of membership.

Considering, therefore, the government of the students as a substitute for the regulations of home, the Faculty endeavor to bring it as near to the character of *parental control* as the nature of the case will admit, and to attain the end, not wholly nor chiefly by constraint and the dread of penalty, but by the *influence of persuasion and kindness.*

But there may be in the college, as well as in the family, or community, perverse individuals, whom nothing but the fear of penalty will influence. In respect to such the faculty consider themselves bound, as standing in the place of parent or guardian, to see that the student be kindly and faithfully advised and admonished, and also that the parent be fully informed of any improper conduct in his son. If such correction prove insufficient, a regard for the best interests of such a young man, and certainly a proper care for the other members of the institution, require that he should be removed. He has forfeited all claims on the institution, by violating the indispensible conditions on which its advantages are to be enjoyed, and is, therefore, forthwith to be returned to his parent or guardian.

Parents are advised to appoint a guardian in Ann Arbor, to take charge of funds for the use of their sons.

No student shall be excused to return home, unless at the written request of his parent or guardian.

PUBLIC WORSHIP.

The students are required to attend prayers daily in the college chapel, and to attend public worship on the Sabbath, at such one of the churches in the village of Ann Arbor, as their parents or guardians may direct

LITERARY SOCIETIES.

There are two literary societies connected with the college, which hold weekly meetings during term time, and possess valuable libraries of select and miscellaneous books.

VACATION.

Vacations are as follows, viz:

From commencement, the 3d Wednesday in July—eight weeks.
From Wednesday next preceding the 25th December—two weeks-
From the 3d Wednesday in April—three weeks.

CALENDAR FOR 1850.

Jan'ry 3. Winter term begins.
April 10. Examinations commence.
" 17. JUNIOR EXHIBITION—term ends.
May 9. Summer term begins.
July 10. Examinations commence.
" 16. Annual meeting of Regents.
" 17. COMMENCEMENT—term ends.
" 18. Examination of candidates.
Sept. 11. Examination of candidates.
" 12. Fall term begins.
Dec. 11. Examinations commence.
" 18. PUBLIC DECLAMATION—term ends.

DEPARTMENT OF MEDICINE.

Arrangements are being made to commence a course of instruction in this department, in the autumn term of 1850.

The Board of Regents have adopted the plan of requiring attendance upon but one course of lectures, which, in consequence, will be extended through the academic year, and subject to the same vacations as in the department of science and arts.

The requirements for admission will be made to conform to those advised by the National Medical Convention, viz: "a good English education, the knowledge of natural philosophy, the elementary mathematical sciences, and such an acquaintance with the Latin and Greek languages, as will enable the student to appreciate the technical language of medicine, and read and write prescriptions."

EXTRACT FROM REPORT OF THE BOARD OF VISITORS.

The board consisted of the following gentlemen, viz: Rufus Hosmer, Esq., Hon. Ellsworth Walkley, Hon. Wm. Finley, Rev. L. Smith Hobart, Geo. C. Gibbs, Esq.

Of the board of visitors appointed to make a personal examination into the state of the University for the current year, Messrs. Gibbs, Walkley and Hobart were present at the exercises of commencement in July last; at which time they attended in part to the duty assigned them. The examination of the students was atttended only by the last named member. The examination, which commenced on the 11th ultimo and continued six days was attended throughout by Messrs. Hosmer, Walkley and Hobart, with the exception of a day each, in the case of Messrs. Hosmer and Walkley. Having endeavored to become as fully acquainted with the state of the University in all respects, as their opportunities would permit, the undersigned would respectfully submit the following report:

The addresses of the graduating class at *commencement*, evinced a good degree of talent and study. They were bold and manly in sentiment, generally marked by good taste in composition, free and vigorous in elocution. We were deeply impressed with the great need there is for more spacious accommodations for these exercises than have hitherto been enjoyed. Commencement at the University is the literary festival of our State. It is an occasion when large numbers from all parts feel disposed to meet at our ATHENS; many too whose presence adds to the interest, and stimulates a generous emulation among the candidates for collegiate honors. But it is known to this board that not a few are annually deterred from attendance by the probability that if they come to the place they may fail of gaining access to the crowded room where the exercises are held; or at best, witness them only from the midst of so dense a crowd as to deprive the occasion of all enjoyment. We think that not one-fourth the number of our citizens attend commencement that would *attend gladly* if they were sure of a favorable opportunity to witness the exercises. It is true, the plan of the University contemplates the erection of a chapel much more spacious than either of the churches now used on commencement occasions. But we suppose that a number of years *yet must* elapse before that can be done; and besides, we doubt whether, when erected, it will not then be found as inadequate to accommodate those who will desire to attend this literary anniversary, as the churches now used.

We suggest, therefore, as what seems to us a far preferable mode of meeting this want, the purchase of a large canvas tent. The one owned at Oberlin, Ohio, was procured and used on one occasion with great satisfaction. A tent of that descriptton, which will easily accommodate 2,500 persons, will cost about $500. Should a tent be purchased, the erection of a chapel might be deferred without serious inconvenience, for a number of years. So crowded are the churches now used, and so liable to damage, that it is with much and increasing reluctance that their use is allowed. Some of them, indeed, can no longer be obtained. We believe the best interests of the University demand that the proposed purchase should be made without needless delay.

The recent term was closed with *public declamation* by several members from each of the three lower classes. The speaking, with few exceptions, was highly creditable. Excellence, in this respect, is so important in our country, and its attainment may be so effectually encouraged, that we would strongly recommend the bestowment of a prize upon the best speaker in each of the classes. These prizes might very appropriately consist of books with suitable inscriptions, signed by the Faculty; and they would be sought, not so much for their intrinsic worth, which might indeed be small, as for the testimonial which they would afford of pre-eminence in elocution.

* * * * * * *

The Board have given some attention to the *course of instruction* pursued in the University. We suppose that the great aim of all intellectual culture is two-fold—the *discipline* of the mind and the *storing* it with knowledge. Of these, in a collegiate course, discipline is doubtless the more important; and yet, to a great extent, it must be sought in the use of means by which also knowledge may be acquired. There are doubtless some studies more largely conducive to mental discipline than others, and yet we judge that discipline will be the sure result, in some valuable degree, of all study, the pursuit of which is marked by *accuracy and self-reliance;* and here, in our view, is indicated the true work, to a great extent, of the instructor.

In regard to the knowledge to be imparted in a collegiate course, it is obvious then, that the aim should be not to *perfect* the pupil in merely a few branches of learning; nor, on the other hand, to furnish a little of almost everything; nor yet, to complete the details of either a professional or a practical education, but rather to *commence a thorough course,* and carry it as far as the term of collegiate study will allow; to be regarded, and to be in fact, the proper and substantial *foundation* of whatever superstructure, professional or practical, each man may see fit to rear upon it. In this view, it is clearly necessary, if a proper *symmetry* and *balance* of character is to be secured, that all the important faculties be brought duly into exercise. In selecting the subjects upon which the powers of the mind shall be employed, respect must be had to those kinds and degrees of knowledge which are properly fundamental to all professions and pursuits, and which may be compassed within the period of collegiate study; and then with a view to the attainment of that mental discipline indispensable to true scholarship, the subjects of study, judiciously selected, must be pursued with the spirit of manly self-reliance and critical accuracy.

How far this latter object is likely to be secured by the *manner* in which the business of instruction is conducted in the University, has been already indicated. In regard to the course of study adopted for the University, we believe it in the main to be good—that which the experience of our best institutions has shown to be best, both in the subjects and the authors. We learn, however, with regret, that the study of *History* has been dropped from the course. We would suggest whether, for reasons that surely need not be stated, it ought not to be restored. If so important a subject has been omitted for the want of time, we would suggest further, that the recitation in the Greek Testament, which now occupies every Monday morning throughout the whole course, and in which no examination is sustained by the students, and which we have reason to believe is nearly valueless, be stricken from three years of the course, and its place, or time equivalent, occupied by History. The exercise in the Greek Testament we would limit to one year, and require the class studying it to sustain a rigid examination, as in other studies.

We would also suggest whether the value of the course would not be somewhat enhanced by substituting for Botany and Zoology, an equal amount of instruction in Human Physiology, and the general principles of civil law. Not indeed, as introductory, or specially related to medical or legal science, but as affording knowledge eminently practical, and fundamental in all the pursuits in life.

We have given some attention to the *relative importance of the subjects* in the course of study, and to the amount of time which is in fact bestowed upon each. A careful examination shows that the aggregate of the recitations and lectures in the whole course of study, as it is arranged and exhibited in the catalogue for 1850, is 2,345, to which should be added 200, as the estimated value of the exercises in elocution and criticism, making a total of 2,545.

Of these, 330 are devoted to Latin,
630 " Greek,
495 " Mathematics, pure and mixed,
236 " Modern languages,
854 " all other subjects.

Now, to us, there has appeared no sufficient reason for giving to the Greek language in the curriculum the pre-eminence over the Latin. We are of the opinion that it holds no such pre-eminence in the best colleges in our country as it holds in our University, where it will be seen that Greek has nearly double the time that is assigned to Latin. We would suggest that at least 70 recitations should be added to the Latin, making its number 400; and that the Greek should be reduced to the same number. This would make the number representing the ancient languages, 800. Now, while we are not prepared to say that the Mathematics (including Natural Philosophy and Astronomy) should receive the same amount of attention as the languages, yet we are well persuaded, whether respect be had to the attainment of mental discipline or useful knowledge, that this department of study should occupy a larger place than either Latin or Greek alone. We would therefore recommend, without hesitation, that the number representing the mathematics be so far increased as to stand at five hundred. If it should be thought that the proposed limitation in respect to Latin and Greek will leave the graduate with too imperfect a knowledge of these languages, we can only say we know of no remedy for the evil better than that which was suggested by the board of visitors last preceding us. Let a larger amount of classical knowledge be required as a condition of membership in the University.

On the subject of *Modern Languages*, we concur with a former board of visitors, in saying that students in our University possess in this respect superior privileges; and that the provision made for them is particularly appropriate to our western States, filling up as they are with a foreign population from most of the European nations. We regret that the Regents have found occasion to strike from the course the Spanish and Italian languages, but especially the former. The extension of our territorial limits in the southwest, has made the demand for an acquaintance with that language by many of our people, somewhat more practical and urgent than formerly. But what we regret much more in relation to this subject, is that only two terms of study are allowed to each of the languages retained, the French and the German. Although much is accomplished, yet this brief period leaves the acquisition so imperfect, that it is felt, both by the student and the instructor, that there is great danger that all will be lost. So important has it seemed to the professor in this department that the instruction should be carried further, that we understand he has offered to instruct the classes in French and German another term in each year, gratuitously, if he might be allowed the opportunity. We therefore strongly recommend that the instruction in French and German be extended to two hundred recitations in each, that is, through the year, instead of being confined to two terms, as at present.

The board of visitors have been led to inquire whether the University may not be made more largely to promote the educational interests of the State, *by extending its advantages*, in part at least, to many to whom they are not now open. We think the number is considerable of those who, from the want of time or means, or a disposition, will never enter the University to pursue the full course of instruction as now laid down; who still, if it were allowed, would gladly avail themselves of the instruction imparted upon a part of the subjects of the course. Why, then, while the University shall continue to confer degrees only upon those who have finished the usual prescribed course, shall not other students who do not aim at the honors of the University, be allowed, under proper regulations, to attend on the instruction of the classes, as far as they shall choose? And, indeed, why may not the daughters of our citizens, as well as their sons, participate in the advantages afforded by the University, at least so far as to attend the various courses of lectures that may be delivered to the under graduates? This plan would afford the very best advantages to those who, from circumstances, wish for a limited education. And such an education must after all, be that which is acquired by the great body of our public and practical men. That the means of such an education should be abundant, and the encouragements every way adequate, none will deny. If there are any valid objections to the proposed extension of the advantages afforded by the University, they have not occurred to us; and we desire that the suggestion should receive a respectful consideration.

We wish distinctly to reiterate the suggestions of former visitors in regard to the employment of *Tutors*. We believe at least two to be greatly needed.

1st. That the so called professors may become professors in fact; that they may be relieved in part from the mere detail and drudgery of drill, and devote themselves to the preparation and delivery of courses of lectures, illustrating and enlivening the subjects of study in their several departments—lectures which shall, besides, answer some valuable end to the students as models of writing and effective elocution.

2d. Because, while on the one hand there is needed the experience of those who have been long resident at the institution, there is equal need on the other of the fresh and minute information of those who, having more recently mingled with students, have a distinct recollection of their peculiar feelings, prejudices, and habits of thinking. We doubt indeed, whether elementary principles are not generally more likely to be taught to the best advantage by the young than by those whose researches have carried them so far beyond the simpler truths that they come back to them with reluctance and distaste. Young men have usually more ardor than those more advanced, in communicating familiar principles, and in removing those lighter difficulties of the student which, not long since, were found lying across their own path.

3d. They are needed for purposes of police and salutary restraint. When so many young men, of every variety of character are assembled in collegiate halls, away from parental restraint, and the larger part of their time, both day and night from the oversight of their instructors, it would indeed be strange if there were not many improprieties and irregularities, greatly detrimental to the student's advancement in study, injurious to his physical constitution, and destructive to his morals. The desirableness of Tutors in respect to the restraint which they may exercise upon students—being always with them—not only during the business of the day, but in hours assigned to rest, may not be appreciated by some, simply from their not knowing how great and how constant the occasion is for such *surveillance*.

We have much pleasure in thinking that one of the important wants of the University is at length to be supplied. We refer to a *President*. By the eighth section in the thirteenth article of the new constitution the first Board of Regents elected by the people, are required at their first annual meeting or as soon thereafter as may be to elect a president of the University, who shall be its principal executive officer, and also a member of the Board of Regents. We believe that the accession of a president, who shall be worthy of the place—having a reputation already established, combining the essential qualifications of an efficient executive officer, and a successful instructor—will be a happy era in the history of the institution. *We hope the election of a president will take place at the earliest possible period.*

This board would call attention to the fact that the well tried and time honored system, nearly universal in the higher literary institutions of our country, of graduating the merit of the higher classes, and *awarding collegiate honors* at commencement and junior exhibitions, find no place in our University. This subject has been noticed in the reports of several former boards, and we shall cordially adopt the following extract from the report of last year: "The board are not satisfied that the government of the University act wisely in withholding all inducements to application, except such as arise from the love of books and the hope of future usefulness. Many a student may 'trim his midnight lamp and watch his lone taper till the stars go out,' from such high incentives—but many more will be found to flag in their onward course to the summit of the hill of science. To many of the latter, competition for the prizes of a collegiate course, furnishes constant stimulus to honorable action; and when those prizes are won, the distinction feeds ambition with further desire. Let the Regents devise a judicious system for the distribution of such rewards, and they will soon discover their salutary effects upon the students, by a regular attendance at the University, and general application to study."

In the opinion of this board, the interests of the University have been seriously neglected, in respect to *philosophical and astronomical apparatus.* Although the Regents have been fully authorized from the beginning, to expend so much of the interest arising from the University fund as might be necessary for the purchase of such apparatus; yet, up to the present time, there is nothing deserving the name. Six classes have been obliged to graduate without the important advantages afforded by even a moderate supply of apparatus, and for ought that appears, the prospect is no better for still other classes. We are aware that it will be alledged that the funds were all needed for the erection of additional buildings. We believe, however, that it was due to the young men who have graduated at the University—to the best reputation of the institution itself, and to the claims of thorough scholarship—that the erection of the last two buildings should have been deferred for one or two years longer, and the money appropriated to the purchase of such a supply of apparatus as would at least have met the more urgent wants of the University in that respect. We would strongly urge that this interest should receive immediate attention.

The *Mineralogical Cabinet*, which for the number of specimens it contains is believed to be unsurpassed in the country, appears to be in good condition, yet it seems to us that its utility is greatly circumscribed from the want of a catalogue containing an easy reference to every specimen, together with a concise description of each. The only catalogue of the Cabinet is a manuscript in the German language, prepared by the gentleman of whom the collection was purchased. Hence the Cabinet is nearly as unintelligible to the students through a large part of their course, as would be a volume of Chinese. The same is true of the numerous visitors to the University. A catalogue, which the professor of mineralogy has assured us he would cheerfully prepare without charge, (such is his sense of its desirableness,) and the printing of which might cost thirty-five dollars, would essentially aid the study of this important branch of knowledge, as well as add greatly to the pleasure and profit of our citizens, and of strangers who have occasion to visit the Cabinet. We judge it highly important, therefore, that an appropriation of the small sum necessary should be immediately made for the printing of such catalogue of the Cabinet as we have suggested.

The *Medical Department* of the University went into operation the first Wednesday in October last. Five professors are occupied in giving instruction at the rate of four lectures a day for nearly seven months in the year. The edifice which had been erected for this department, is elegant and commodious, and capable of accommodating a large class of students. The number of students now in attendance is eighty-eight, of whom nine are candidates for degrees.

With gratuitous instruction, with the ample material and means of illustration which will soon be possessed, and with a diligent and skillful Faculty, the prospect is flattering that this department will be highly prosperous.

By the law, (R. S., chapter 57, section 15) it is made the duty of the Superintendent of Public Instruction annually *to appoint a board of visitors*. "whose duty it shall be to make a personal examination into the state of the University in all its departments, and report the result to the Superintendent, suggesting such improvements as they may deem important, which report shall be transmitted to the Legislature at its next session." We suppose this law was intended to secure to the public a means of full and accurate information concerning the University, additional to and independent of all other means; and we believe the accomplishment of this object to be highly important, both to the people and to the University itself. If the people know that the institution is wisely managed and useful, it will possess their confidence and be sacredly cherished. If mismanagement and inefficiency are sure to be exposed, they will rarely exist. It ought however to be understood that the duties of a board of visitors, such as the law contemplates, cannot be properly performed by a mere attendance on commencement exercises, or by a few hours spent in witnessing the examination of students, or by a pleasant walk through the library and cabinet. It is demanded that they should prosecute their work in a business like manner, giving to it time enough to investigate thoroughly the condition of the University in all respects; and then to make a full report of the results—and to do this, even though it may sometimes occasion the sacrifice of personal feelings and interests for the general good. It has been alleged that the duties of the visitors have generally been performed in a superficial manner. This may be true; but it is pertinent to inquire whether it may not be traced, in part at least, to the fact that but few persons can be found who are willing to give not only their time and their labor to such an investigation, but also to bear their own expenses while thus employed.

The board of visitors had desired to make a full examination into the *financial condition* of the University. but the want of time. and an intimation that the Regents of the University had been called upon for a full and detailed statement of the financial affairs of the institution from its commencement to the present time. by the Superintendent of Public Instruction they are satisfied that information upon the subject referred to, long desired, and of much importance, will be furnished.

In view of the expenditure of about $85,000 in the erection of buildings and the purchase of books and apparatus, and the annual expenditure of about $10,050 as salaries of the professors, superintendent of building, and other incidental expenses, with an endowment sufficient to carry out all the benificent designs of its original founders, the inquiry naturally arises. *why is it that with such an expenditure the number of students actually in attendance should be so small?* The number of students actually in attendance, was ascertained to be fifty, besides five or six who were said to be absent teaching, but who are pursuing their studies. This number, it is believed, is about an average of the number for the past ten years, but less than an average for the past five years. The largest class which has graduated in any year numbered twenty-three. and the smallest, ten; and the whole number who have graduated is eighty-nine.

The institution was intended to be a free institution. and it is nearly so to the student. With an adequate number of professors and rooms sufficient to accommodate more than double the number of students in attendance, from some cause the inducements or advantages offered seem not to be sufficient. It has been said that the institution has not yet acquired a reputation, but we cannot learn when one will be acquired under its present management. An institution without a head that can command the confidence or respect of the community or students, with professors in some cases selected less for their scientific attainments and reputation as instructors than for other considerations, and without unity of feeling or action, it cannot be surprising that the expectations of the framers of the institution have not yet been realized, or that the institution has not yet acquired a reputation sufficient to fill its halls with students willing to be educated gratis.

Our State is not so destitute of young men of natural ability and ambition as a superficial view of the University would indicate. The original plan of the institution would not furnish accommodations sufficient for those who would ask to partake of its advantages, if it had a responsible head, with an established reputation sufficient to command respect and confidence, (as we are satisfied soon will be the case,) and the professors' chairs were filled with those not only competent to discharge the duties assigned them, but willing to act in concert for the advancement of the institution and the welfare of the students committed to their charge.

It is with mortification that we have felt compelled to speak of this subject, but our duty required it, and we have looked for no other rule to guide us.

In closing this report, we would express our strong hope that those who have predicted evil to the University from the change which is soon to take place in the manner of constituting the Board of Regents, will be thoroughly disappointed; and we are sure they will be if the friends of the University are duly active, and show themselves more anxious for its prosperity than for the gratification of their political preferences.

Let the University be preserved entirely free from party strife; let it be kept a common object of friendly and favoring regard among the several religious denominations of the State; let its ample endowment be vigilantly guarded, and all its expenditures made with a strict regard to wisdom and economy; let its Regents be educated men, men of broad and comprehensive views, practical and energetic, and devoted to the interests of the University; let its corps of instructors be able and earnest men skillful to teach, and wise and faithful in administering the discipline of the institution—and our University will indeed be the pride of the State, destined to hold a distinguished place among the varied agencies for diffusing useful knowledge among men.

STATE NORMAL SCHOOL.

The members of the board consisted of the following gentlemen, in addition to the Lieut. Governor, State Treasurer, and Superintendent of Public Instruction, viz: Isaac E. Crary, Samuel Barstow, and Elias M. Skinner. During the past year four additional acres of land had been purchased, a plan of building adopted, and a contract executed for the performance of the work, for $15,200, twelve thousand of which was to be paid by the citizens of Ypsilanti.

INCORPORATED LITERARY INSTITUTIONS.

The following is an extract from the report of the Superintendent, in relation to these institutions:

In pursuance of suggestions contained in the last report from this office, and of the statute various institutions have forwarded reports of their condition and course of study. All of these institutions are of a high grade, and situated in various parts of the State, are educating annually a large number of our youth. In these institutions it is not definitely known how many young men are preparing for the University. Some of them have the privilege of conferring degrees and granting diplomas under acts passed during the last session. This right granted to them in their charters, it would seem, forbids the hope that the young men attending them are to be graduates of the State institution. It was suggested heretofore by this department, that some system might be devised which would have induced these institutions to become tributaries to the University, and if it be considered a settled policy on the part of the Regents that branches are not eventually to be sustained, it is to be hoped that some inducement may be held out by legislation to effect the great object of filling up the halls of the University with students. The Union schools which are now beginning to be put into successful operation in our principal villages, may perhaps eventually become preparatory, and fill up the chasm which now exists in the system. Granting this, some system might nevertheless be adopted, and will, it is thought, become necessary, in order to excite proper emulation among them all, as well as among other institutions, to contribute to the welfare of the "University of Michigan," by bestowing to it each their full quota of pupils.

It was suggested in the report of this office to the Legislature of last winter, that the creation of the office of Superintendent of Public Instruction was intended to embrace the supervision of the entire system of *public instruction* in our State, including not only primary schools, but all other institutions. By this supervision, it was not intended to refer to any control over these institutions, but that they should be included in the general system of reports to this office. In this way information is accumulated and concentrated, and full means afforded of watching the progress of education in all its departments, and of forming a better and more accurate judgment as to the relative operations of the general system and of each incorporated institution. This is important to a full development of the educational means of our State, and the construction given of the original design of the framers of our first constitution, is fortified by the action of the framers of the recent organic law, who have defined the duties of the office, and ordained that it shall have a "a general supervision of *Public Instruction.*" With this view, it has from the first been an object of solicitude that full reports from all institutions, whether existing under the patronage of the State or not, should be received.

Reports were received from the Romeo branch of the University, the Wesleyan Seminary, Michigan Central College, Olivet Institute, Young Ladies Seminary at Monroe, Misses Clark's School at Ann Arbor, and St. Mark's College at Grand Rapids.

ROMEO BRANCH OF THE UNIVERSITY.

The whole number of students, 201, forty-three of whom were pursuing classical studies, nineteen French, and one hundred and twenty-seven the higher mathematics, and branches of English education. The following list of instructors was reported, viz:

Charles H. Palmer, A. M, Principal, and Instructor in Mathematics, Chemistry and Natural Philosophy; Charles C. Torrey, A. B., Instructor in Ancient Languages, Rhetoric and Moral Philosophy;

Mrs. B. A. Palmer, Principal of the Female Department, and Instructor in French, Botany and History; Miss Sarah J. Gillett, Instructor in Philosophy and Natural History; George A. Hoyt, Instructor in Vocal Music. The following is an extract from the report of the trustees for this year:

The Institution has been furnished with a cabinet of minerals and an extensive chemical, philosophical and astronomical apparatus, costing more than $500. This apparatus was purchased in Boston, of Mr. Weightman, well known as one of the most extensive manufacturers in the United States. The telescope is a fine achromatic, capable of showing clearly the moons and belts of Jupiter, and the rings of Saturn.

During the fall term, particular attention is given to a class of young ladies and gentlemen desirous of qualifying themselves for teaching. This class is reviewed in all the studies usually pursued in primary schools. Frequent lectures are given upon subjects connected with their profession, and no pains are spared to enable them to become able and efficient instructors. Those who are found qualified, are, if desired, furnished with schools. The number of students connected with this department was 57; who, during some part of the year, were engaged in teaching common schools. It is worthy of remark that the compensation paid teachers of primary schools, the present season, is more in accordance with the education and qualifications necessary to discharge faithfully the duties of a calling so responsible and important.

It is very much to be regretted that there is not some legislative provision in this State, or system adopted by the Regents, by which regular meteorological observations might be made at convenient places. This subject has not received the attention which its importance demands. Accurate meteorological tables, kept at different points, would do much towards correcting an erroneous impression in reference to the climate of the State, which its latitude is calculated to produce. On account of its proximity to the great lakes, the climate is much milder than is generally supposed; and, no doubt, these observations will show that the mean temperature of the southern half of this State is higher than that of the interior of Ohio. The meteorology of the region bordering upon the great lakes would possess a high, scientific value, and it would at the same time contribute greatly to show the congeniality of the climate to the most valuable agricultural products of the country, as well as to promote the safe navigation of the lakes, that add so much to the commercial importance of the State.

It seems very desirable that some plan be adopted by which the academies shall be placed under a general supervision, and made to share in a fund provided for that purpose, similar to the excellent system established in the State of New York. Such a system was commenced a few years since by the Regents, and this institution received from the University fund $200 for two years. This appropriation was afterwards discontinued, and no further aid was given till last winter $10 was appropriated by the Regents to this branch, the payment of which was refused, in order to test the legality of appropriations to branches from the University fund, by making a case for the Supreme Court. This case is now pending in that court. It is hardly perceived how any doubt could be entertained upon this point. The intention of Congress is so clearly expressed in the grants of University lands to the other north-western States, that the omission to particularize in the grant to this State could not lead to any ambiguity in reference to the design Congress had in appropriating these lands.

It can hardly be expected that the academies of the State will long continue, as at present, disconnected from its general plan of education The State has manifested its great interest in the education of every class, by its wise provisions for common schools, its liberal policy towards the University, and its benevolent regard for the blind, and the deaf and dumb, in commencing an institution for their instruction.

The primary school system of this State, and its primary schools, are decidedly in advance of any new State, and are not excelled by many of the old. The University, for the time it has been in existence, has met with abundant success. Such having been the course and progress of the State, it cannot be supposed that its academies, forming so necessary a part of the system—so necessary to supply its common schools with well qualified teachers—so necessary to furnish annually young men prepared to enter the University, will, much longer be permitted to remain without its fostering care and support.

There is an organized literary society in the institution, the members of which meet regularly, once a week, for the purpose of extemporaneous debate. Essays and addresses are occasionally delivered before the society, and all the proceedings are conducted in a manner well calculated to promote the improvement of its members.

WESLEYAN SEMINARY AT ALBION.

The departments in this institution consisted of the following branches: 1st. Moral and Intellectual Science; 2d. Natural Science; 3d. Ancient Languages and Elocution; 4th. Mathematics; 5th. Modern Languages; 6th. Belles Lettres; 7th. Primary English Literature; 8th. Fine Arts.

In addition to the course for male students, a department had been established for a Female Collegiate Institute, and a large and commodious building was about completed for this purpose. The design of this institution was to afford those who entered it, a thorough and systematic course of study, equal at least to the scientific course pursued in many of our colleges. The trustees say:

The question of the ability of the female mind to contend successfully in the scientific and literary arena, with the more favored sex, has been too long settled to require discussion; nor is the custom of granting the merited honors, without a precedent; but if it were, no apology could be required for bestowing what is fairly earned.

An Indian department had been established, the object of which was to furnish instruction in the several branches taught in the Seminary, to those Indians who expect to become preachers, interpreters, or teachers of schools, among their aboriginal brethren of the West. This department is purely missionary in its character, and believed to be the *first* and *only* one of its kind, in the West.

The institution was furnished with a valuable Planetarium, costing $600; a solar and compound microscope; a full pneumatic apparatus; a model steam engine; galvanic battery; electrical apparatus; air pump; mathematical instruments; optical apparatus; magic lantern; terruleum; globes, maps, &c., with suitable apparatus and tests for illustrating the principles of chemistry. The library contained about 700 volumes, to which was attached a reading room.

MICHIGAN CENTRAL COLLEGE.

The following extract from the report of the trustees, exhibits the condition of this institution in 1851:

COURSE OF STUDY.

The charter of the institution having been so amended at the last session of the Legislature as to confer upon it full college power, it is intended, from the beginning of the next year, (commencing Sept. 4,) to pursue a full college course as herein laid down, and those pursuing it will be entitled to the regular collegiate degree of Bachelor of Arts. But to meet the wants of a large class of young men who wish to obtain merely a thorough English education, another course of study is prescribed for those who prefer it. Those completing this course or its equivalent, will receive the degree of Bachelor of Science and English Literature.

The ladies' course is particularly adapted to those for whom it is designed; and is at least fully equal to that pursued in any female college in the country. Upon those who complete it, or its equivalent, the ordinary diploma will be conferred.

It is highly desirable in all the departments to pursue in the regular order, as laid down, the various studies. But where this is impracticable, as in many cases it will be, other arrangements will be made. In some branches of study it is found necessary to organize classes every term.

The method of instruction in the common and higher English branches, has constant reference to the wants of those who design to teach more or less; and during the first half of the fall term, a course of lectures on the instruction and management of common schools, is delivered by one or more of the Faculty, to such of the students as may choose to attend. In both winter and summer the demand for teachers in the vicinity is greater than the supply.

LIBRARY, APPARATUS, &C.

The college, though yet in its infancy, is furnished with a valuable library of 1,700 volumes, and a philosophical apparatus, superior to any other at present in the State; consisting in part of an electrical machine, with a three feet plate and its accompaniments, a powerful magneto-electrical machine, galvanic batteries, air pump, orrery, tellurium, magic lantern, with astronomical slides, microscope, globes, &c., &c. Also a chemical apparatus sufficient for most of the experiments in that study.

The reading room connected with the Institute is furnished with about thirty different periodicals, carefully selected, representing the different parties, sects and sections of the country.

MANUAL LABOR.

Manual labor has been furnished more or less to all the students who have desired it, and it is designed, as soon as practicable, to make arrangements for furnishing regular labor, that shall at the same time be healthful and profitable to all who may wish to spend a few hours a day in this way.

EXAMINATIONS, &C.

There is a public examination of the several classes at the close of each term, conducted in the presence and under the direction of an examining committee, invited to attend for that purpose.

CLINTON INSTITUTE.

This institution was incorporated in 1851. The trustees reported

That they have purchased a property in Mt. Clemens, and fitted up a building for educational purposes, estimated to be worth from one thousand to fifteen hundred dollars.

The institute has been in successful operation since the second Monday of September last, under the superintendence of Nathaniel Colver, Jr., A. B., of Boston, Massachusetts, late a graduate of Dartmouth College N. H., as principal; Miss Harriet P. Murdock, late a graduate of Jacksonville Seminary, Ill., as preceptress, and Miss Catherine Traver, teacher in the primary department.

Number of pupils last fall term, seventy five.

Number of pupils (present) winter quarter, seventy.

Salaries established as follows: for the principal, $500 per annum; for the preceptress, $250 per annum; for the teacher, $150 per annum. Total, $900 per annum.

There are six rooms in the building, the largest of which is 38 feet by 42 and the smallest 12 by 12; the main room is 14 feet high, well warmed and ventilated, and furnished with desks and chairs after a model from Barnard's School Architecture.

We have, as the property of the Institute, a piano for instruction in music, a small library, apparatus &c.

They would deem it very desirable to obtain a small cabinet of mineralogical, geological, zoological and botanical specimens from the collections of the late Dr. Houghton. some twelve or fifteen suits of which are now in the dormitories of the University buildings at Ann Arbor, entirely out of use, and fast going to destruction.

OLIVET INSTITUTE.

The board of trustees of Olivet Institute report that the institution is still in a flourishing condition. The number of students in attendance during the

Spring term,	30
Fall "	90
Winter "	95
Whole number, by terms,	219

Of this number, nearly fifty have been engaged in the business of teaching during a part of the year.

Five instructors have been employed regularly during most of the year, and three assistants during a part of the time.

The course of study pursued is designed to prepare those who shall complete it, to become eminent teachers, or those who may wish can pursue a course that shall fit them to enter the University, or any college they may choose, two years in advance.

Instruction has been given in the ancient classics, the mathematics, the natural. intellectual and moral sciences.

The teachers' class was formed, as usual, in the fall term of the school, and continued seven weeks, during which time a thorough review of the studies taught in common schools was completed; and in addition to this, a course of lectures was delivered before the class upon subjects connected with teaching.

The trustees are in possession of about 100 acres of land, a building two stories in highth, valued at $300. This building is used for a chapel, recitation room. reading room, &c. Another three story edifice is completed, which furnishes four recitation rooms. a library and apparatus room, and accommodates about forty students. The cost of the building is not far from $3,000. Additions have been made to the apparatus of the institution, so that it now possesses an air pump, with its accompanying fixtures, worth $100; an electrical machine, worth $100, and globes, with other apparatus, to the value of another hundred.

The library of the institute has been increased to more than 1,000 volumes.

The trustees feel determined to do all in their power to place this institution upon a permanent basis; and with the aid of friends and patrons, to make it worthy of the confidence and patronage of the public generally.

Thus far the success of the work has more than equalled the highest anticipations of its warmest friends. Should this success continue, we confidently hope that this Institute may yet become a great blessing to this our rapidly growing State.

YOUNG LADIES' SEMINARY AT MONROE.

The trustees of this institution made their first report.

The institution was opened for the reception of young ladies on the 13th of December last, with four teachers and fifty two pupils; since which time it has been on the steady increase, until over 120 young ladies have enjoyed its advantages.

The instructors are at present as follows:

Rev. E. J Boyd. A. M., principal, and instructor in ancient languages, mental and moral science; Mrs. Sarah C Boyd, principal and instructress in history; Miss J. E. Babbitt, instructress in mathematics; Miss J C. Tachaberry, instructress in instrumental music and drawing; Miss Kate Bennett, instructress in vocal music; Miss E. J. Walsh, instructress in French; Miss Helen Smith, assistant instructress in English branches.

During the past autumn, the trustees have erected, in addition to their previous buildings, a fine three story brick building 36 by 60, designed for school and lodging rooms, with a basement story for dining rooms, &c.; and when finished with its observatory, and piazza extending the entire length, this centre building, in connection with the others, will be truly an ornament to the city. The entire cost of the buildings and furniture will amount to more than $8,000.

The pupils have pursued the following studies, viz: In Latin, 12; French, 9; instrumental music, 17; drawing, 34; vocal music, entire school; algebra, 58; geometry, 9; chemistry, 15; natural philosophy, 25; moral science, 4; physiology and anatomy, 34; arithmetic, 133; astronomy, 20; geology, 9; grammar, 94.

It is furnished with maps, globes, and philosophical apparatus to some extent. It is intended to make it a seminary for young ladies, equal to any in the country, where all the solid as well as ornamental branches of a finished female education are pursued.

MISSES CLARK'S SCHOOL, AT ANN ARBOR.

The number of students in this institution was eighty-two. The following is a sketch of its history, progress and design:

At the request of some of the most respectable citizens, and an intimation that Ann Arbor demanded and could support an institution where young Ladies could receive a thorough and polite education, this school was commenced November 18th 1839. Up to the present time, it numbers 433 different pupils, of whom 94 have become teachers, principally in our common schools. Average attendance during the year, 80. The scholastic year embraces two terms, of two quarters each—eleven weeks in a quarter. Public examinations

occur uniformly at the close of each term, this being now the 21st examination.

Every member of a class is expected to be present at the examination of that class, unless excused by the principal, or on account of sickness, or other very sufficient cause.

There have been twenty nine graduates. None receive the certificate accorded to graduates but such as have passed a critical examination in the several branches of a solid English education, and who have been members of the school at least one year. This may be thought a brief trial, but testimonials are never promiscuously given, and always specifying for what received. It is also to be taken into consideration that the circumstances heretofore of most of our citizens, have precluded their children from a long continuance at school, and especially that not a few of our senior class are of those dependent upon their own exertions for an education, and who come to us with much maturity of mind, as well as of years—those who, if they have been debarred from the usual instruction, have ever been *thinkers* and close *observers* of Nature. Such are persevering students—acquit themselves well, leaving us with views enlarged by converse with science, and with that disposition for acquiring knowledge, which, when well disciplined, carries forward its own mental improvement.

Though the intellect be peculiarly our charge, mere intellectual advancement would be far from desirable, and productive only of an ill balanced mind; therefore, it is our endeavor closely to watch the *moral* culture of our pupils. With no *sectarian feeling*, but with a deep sense of religious responsibility, we would seek to give that tone to character which renders it practicably fitted for every station—yielding to duty, but firm to principle.

The intelligence of the present age expects the sound mind only in the sound body. Attention to health is a sacred duty. By every suitable means we would aim to secure it—inculcating strict observance of the physical laws—early rising and retiring—frequent outdoor exercise—equanimity, but cheerfulness of temper.

Twice in each week, in the season for walks, the School, accompanied by a teacher, make excursions into the neighboring country, in pursuit of minerals and flowers, for which there is no better field than Ann Arbor. In our State Geological Report, 1840, it is said that "the hilly region of Ann Arbor affords a fine locality for procuring every variety of granites quartz and hornblende, found in the State;" to which we may add, also, fossil remains of numerous species of crustaceans. To the stranger, the wild flowers of Michigan are ever a subject of admiration for their lovliness and beauty. These, in their luxuriance, deck our pleasant environs, and the Botanical Class being always required to collect specimens, we have herbariums of much value—individuals having often preserved several hundred specimens in a season.

The extensive library and cabinet of the University can be visited when it is desirable. Our own library, too, numbers 1,068 volumes, to which additions are constantly being made; we have also a good cabinet for the study of natural history; and the philosophical apparatus comprises electrical machine, globes, optical instruments, &c.

Situated in a pleasant and commodious building, in a healthy and convenient part of the town, no efforts or expense in our power have ever been spared to make this institution an agreeable and profitable residence to those entrusted to our care The young ladies under our particular supervision, are considered as constituting a family, looking to us as elder sisters, from whom is expected the kindest regard, and upon whose example and teachings, may, perhaps, rest their immortal hopes.

Though it would be impossible to enumerate all our rules—to prevent erroneous impressions, we would say, that the boarders are not allowed to attend public balls, or without permission accept invitations to walk, ride or visit; and unless from family friends, to receive calls, except on Friday and Saturday evenings, and then with the principal or vice principal. On Wednesday or Saturday afternoons they attend to their shopping, returning calls, &c., and on no other days, as it is not our desire to promote an undue love of society, unfitting alike for present duties and future usefulness; but an acquaintance with the courtesies of life—those observances resultant from the law of kindness and sound conventional rule.

Regular attendance at some place of worship is required; and as seats are provided in the different churches, it is requested that parents and guardians would designate their own preference.

As there are always some scholars from abroad, not resident with us, we would earnestly request the parents of such, to leave them under other than than their own control, for it is not possible to induce habits of study in the school-room, when the hours out of it, which should have been devoted to preparation for recitation, are passed in a manner destructive to that systematic and orderly arrangement of time, so important to be acquired by the young. * * * *

The catechetical mode of teaching we entirely discard. An analysis of the lessons is required in several classes, and in ALL the pupil is encouraged to think independently, and any errors corrected to the best of our ability by familiar lectures.

Recitations "in the words of the book" are not allowed, that being considered the work of mere memory, and not an exercise of the understanding.

ST. MARK'S COLLEGE, AT GRAND RAPIDS.

This institution had but recently been organized, but had already in attendance 160 students. It had adopted, as far as possible, the text books recommended by the Superintendent of Public Instruction. The trustees say:

The prospect of an increase of students is encouraging. Owing to the very recent establishment of the institution, a full body of professors had not been secured; additions will be made as soon as practicable.

The foregoing sketches develope an increasing field of usefulness, in this class of institutions, and also the fact, that an increasing interest is felt among the people, to extend to them a larger share of patronage. Although reports were not received as the law required, from all that had been incorporated, yet it will be seen, that in several of them, departments have been organized for the preparation and instruction of young men and ladies, as teachers of the primary schools, and others have been fitted for the University.

They receive no pecuniary support from the State, and are the result of the enterprise of individuals and communities in the several portions of the State, where they are located. The Legislature has granted acts of incorporation, and bestowed upon several, the power of conferring degrees. It is in the natural course and order of things, that these institutions will continue to grow up and increase in number and in influence. They are not deemed in any wise, as institutions antagonistical to the system established by the State, nor do they desire to become so. On the other hand, they are most important and praise-worthy auxiliaries to the great cause of education. They form a part of our system of PUBLIC INSTRUCTION, though receiving no aid from the funds of the State. Their progress and prosperity is none the less a subject of deep interest to the friends of education, and should be of watchful and fostering care on the part of every officer whose fortune it may be to be placed by the people at the head of the system.

FREE SCHOOLS OF DETROIT CITY.

The board of education reported nineteen schools in operation, and one colored school. The highest quarterly returns of scholars during the past year was 2,334, being an increase of 201 over the highest quarterly return of 1848, and being an average of 122 scholars for each school. It was estimated that in the course of the year, 4,000 scholars had attended the schools, being more than two-thirds of the shildren between the ages of five and seventeen. The total expenditures, including permanent improvements was $9,413.71. The total receipts, $9,014.34.

THE PRIMARY SCHOOLS.

The SUPERINTENDENT reported, in relation to primary schools, that the success of the system adopted in Michigan, had met, and indeed exceeded, the most sanguine expectations. The changes which from time to time had been engrafted upon it, as its defects were developed by trial and experience, had, as a general rule operated successfully, and tended to give greater perfection to the system in all its departments. To render it, if possible, still more perfect, and to give it full adaptation to the situation and wants of our people, is the chief duty of this department. With this view, in accordance with suggestions heretofore made, the Legislature of last winter engrafted radical alterations in the system of reporting to this office. In almost all other respects, with comparatively few exceptions, the school law was operating satisfactorily and successfully. But in this respect there appeared to be a necessity for amendment. Previous to the present year, directors of districts made their reports to the board of school inspectors—the inspectors to the clerks of the several counties; each of whom prepared abstracts, which latter were forwarded to this office. The reason for the change was founded upon facts, ascertained by an inspection of the reports of school inspectors, on file in the office of the clerks, that an erroneous and unjust distribution of the public moneys was annually taking place, from the wrongful action of fractional districts in making their reports. To correct the evil, it was deemed essential that the reports of the inspectors should come under the direct and personal inspection of the Superintendent. The useful results anticipated in this respect have not been fully attained, as yet, for two reasons: firstly, because the school officers in all sections have not fully described the fractional districts; and secondly, because sufficient time has not yet been afforded since their reception, to make a complete and full examination.

The result, however, cannot fail to be accomplished in the mode suggested, when accurate and full descriptions of these districts are obtained.

A critical examination of the reports of inspectors, which for the first time have come into this office since November last, has led to the conclusion that, for other important reasons, the change will result in benefit. The inaccurate and loose manner in which the reports of directors, especially, have been hitherto made, has been the cause of much complaint, both on the part of school inspectors and former incumbents of this office. In turn, the reports of inspectors have been imperfect, and as a natural consequence, the reports of county clerks defective. For this reason no certainty or accuracy has been or could be arrived at, and no data of a perfectly reliable character, upon which to base conclusions in relation to the operation of the system, or upon which practical calculations could be made. In addition to this, an inspection of the manner in which the blank forms are filled up by the proper officers, leads to the detection and correction of error, and to the perfection of the forms by this office. It is readily perceived that while this office was furnished with nothing but the abstract of the county clerks, no inspection of the manner in which local officers made up their reports could be had, without an examination of the reports in the various offices of the clerks, or the transmission by them of copies, which could not be practicable, or accomplished without great loss of time to the office or great labor to the clerks, and expense to the people. To give perfection to the system now adopted, it seems to be only necessary to revise thoroughly, and *simplify* the blank forms.

With the improvements that have been indicated, the school law in the main, will, it is thought. continue to operate successfully, without material amendment. While complaint is made by some, in relation to the operation of certain minor provisions and details, there is no part of the law which seems to meet with any general disapprobation. The law authorizing the voting of a tax of $1 per scholar, in many respects works unequally; but it is not believed to be so objectionable as to require repeal at the present time. The variety of constructions which are frequently given to sections of the school law, and the constant demand upon the office for its opinions, will be materially relieved by their publication. And as the demand for copies of the school laws with notes and forms, is becoming imperative, and the school laws having been materially amended during the last year, it is of the greatest importance that a new edition should be printed as soon after the adjournment of the Legislature as practicable.

The object of this delay would be to include such alterations as the Legislature may see fit to make at the present session, or which the people shall demand at their hands. Fortunately, the adoption of the provisions of the new constitution, "that the Legislature shall, within five years, provide for and establish a system of primary schools, whereby a school shall be kept without charge for tuition, at least three months in each year, in every school district," will not require any general revision of the present school law. The principle of free schools has been adopted by the voice of a large majority of the people of Michigan, affording renewed evidence of their liberal and enlightened views, and their willingness under any circumstances to contribute in the freest manner, to the education of all the youth of our State. This principle, therefore, so far as it is applied in the constitution to our own system, requires no argument. The trouble elsewhere, has been in getting at the detail of a law which will operate equally upon all the citizens of the State. The reports required by the law, which are essential to base our estimates upon, the provision especially which relates to the annual levy of one mill upon the assessors' valuation, for the increase of libraries and the support of schools, are not sufficiently reliable and certain to ascertain correctly the total cost of tuition in our schools.

As suggested by the chairman of the committee on education, to the House of Representatives of last winter, the mill tax for the year preceding, should have produced the sum of $29,908 76, while the returns show an aggregate of $17,530 12. The tax of one dollar per scholar, which is believed to be very generally voted, is not returned by many districts. For this reason, we can but approximate to what is the actual cost of tuition. The amount of mill tax reported this year is but a trifle over the amount reported last year, being $17,957 30. The nearest estimate that can be made under all circumstances, will not vary the total cost of tuition very far from the amount estimated by the House committee last year, viz: $80,-000. The true amount doubtless exceeds this sum. But no difficulty need arise from this cause at the present time. The most desirable and practicable method of adapting the law to the provisions of the new constitution is by a simple increase of the mill tax. This tax might be increased to two mills during the present session, and thus during the first two years we should approximate gradually towards the complete and full requirement of the constitution for free schools. The transition from the present system would be accompanied with no confusion, while with more reliable data accumulated hereafter, there would eventually be no difficulty in arriving at the actual amount required to support the schools free for tuition for three months in each year. It is respectfully suggested, therefore, if it is deemed advisable to legislate in relation to the subject, during this session, that the one mill tax now required by law be increased to two mills.

If we secure this, it will be an advance safely made towards the system contemplated by the constitution. It is agreed by all, that in legislating upon the subject, caution and safety in our action is far more desirable than a mere advancement without a full understanding of the probable effects of a change in the system, upon all the interests with which it is connected. When this is secured and the law, as changed, is in successful operation, the only remaining evil of which complaint may be justly made, and which arises in part from the great and wide spread *irregularity* in attendance upon our primary schools, should be remedied by a change in the basis of apportionment. An alteration in this respect, would be of great and immediate benefit to all our schools and to the system itself. It is therefore suggested, as the result of investigation and much reflection, that the apportionment of public moneys *shall eventually be based upon the actual attendance of scholars.* This will render it necessary that teachers should make returns relative to the subject in some proper way, and through some proper channel.

It must be apparent to those who have reflected upon the subject, that a distribution based upon the number of children *residing* in the district merely, cannot be sustained by any particular or sound reason. The principle of apportioning upon the number and according to the actual attendance, is evidently more just in itself, and the object to be secured by it apparent.

The number of children to whom the public money is now apportioned upon the basis of a mere residence in districts where schools have been taught for three months, is 135,234. The number actually in attendance upon all the schools is less than this by 21,756. A portion, doubtless, attend private and select schools. One effect of the change suggested would be, to induce the attendance of these at the primary schools. It is an important object of accomplishment that the large number of children in our State, who are not attending school, and who are growing up without the advantages which education affords, and who must eventually, if they continue to grow up in ignorance, add to the common stock of vice and crime, and become a burden to the public. should be in some manner brought within the refining and moralizing influences of early education. No greater stimulus could be given among the masses of the people of the State to accomplish this purpose, than to make the apportionment in the manner suggested. Such a system would give a new impulse to effort, by securing a general and regular attendance; and no object could be better adapted to secure the highest and most desirable results in our system of public instruction.

The suggestions thus advanced, constitute all of the most important which are thought proper, under the law requiring a report from this office, to present to the attention of the Legislature. It is believed, however, that teachers' institutes are the means of doing much good, and of eliciting much interest in behalf of the cause of education.

Without some aid on the part of the State they cannot be made as efficient as might be desirable. With some legislative aid they would, beyond question, be the means of advancing greatly the interests of education. The direction of these institutes might be properly submitted to the charge of the principal of the State normal school. The board of education, if the means at their disposal will permit, have in view the early appointment of this officer, who might well be employed in holding a series of institutes in various parts of the State, in making the acquaintance of the people, and exciting public interest in the normal school, which is calculated to be in readiness for pupils by the first of March, 1852.

STATISTICAL.

The whole number of districts reported, during the last year, is 3,097, being an increase of 37 over last year. The whole number from which reports have been received, is 2,525.

The number of children reported in each township between the ages of four and eighteen years, residing in districts where a school has been taught by a qualified teacher for three months, is 132,234, being an increase over the number reported last year of 7,016.

The whole number that have attended in all the schools is 110,-478, being an increase in attendance over last year of 7,607 scholars.

There has been an increase in the number of qualified male teachers, and a decrease in the number of female teachers.

Whole number of male teachers,......................1,475
" " female " 2,612

The amount of money reported as received from township treasurers and apportioned by township clerks, is $1,628 70. The amount of money raised by tax in all the townships during the last school year, was $81,392 44, being an increase of $7,587 45 over last year.

The amount paid on rate bills for teachers' wages, $32,318 75, being an increase of $2,600 87 over the preceding year.

There has been expended for the purpose of purchasing, leasing, repairing and building school houses, $46,797 00, which is less than the sum reported last year.

The amount of mill tax assessed by supervisors, as reported, amounts to $17,957 30, about the same as last year, and the returns evidently imperfect.

The number of children attending private schools is yearly diminishing, but slowly. They amount, according to the last returns, to 4,065 scholars.

The number of volumes in the township libraries have increased over last year, 16,946 volumes, the whole number reported being 84,823.

The following table shows the increase of scholars and the amount apportioned for the last six years, from the income of the primary school fund:

Years.	Scholars.	Am't apportioned.	Am't per Scholar.
1846	97,006	$22,113 00	28 cents.
1847	97,258	27,925 72	31 "
1848	108,130	32,605 20	30 "
1849	112,272	39,057 67	33 "
1850	125,866	42,794 44	34 "
1851	132,234	44,458 56	34 "

In concluding the report for the year, it was observed that:

It is considered a matter of great importance to publish in full, all the decisions which have been made, under the operation of our school laws, affording as they will to the various officers, greater facility in the proper discharge of their respective duties. As the annual report from this office does not go by law to the school officers, such decisions may, with greater usefulness, be embraced in the pamphlet edition of the school laws, which it is necessary to republish to meet the requirements of the people. As this cannot be done until the present Legislature shall have determined what amendments, if any, they will incorporate in it, or what additions will be required to the present law, it is respectfully suggested that the next annual report from this office be included in the pamphlet edition of the laws, and be distributed to the districts at as early a period as practicable. Although this will delay the re-publication of the school laws, it will nevertheless afford the best facility for the preparation of valuable statistical and other information, now greatly required by all who are connected with our system of primary school education. In such document, for the better information of the public, both at home and elsewhere, should also be included the laws and rules relating to the University, with more full information connected with all our institutions of learning, both academical and primary. In this way information will become general among our own citizens, and the people of other States will acquire that knowledge of our system of PUBLIC INSTRUCTION, which will enable them to appreciate its advantages, and realize the extent of educational achievement which the people of Michigan are destined to attain.

LEGISLATION.

An act was passed providing for the election of Regents, approved March 10, 1851. Also, an act approved March 28, providing that all former purchasers of University and school lands, who had annually paid their interest, but failed to pay 25 per cent. on the principal, might at any time prior to the first day of March, 1852, pay to the State Treasurer an amount which, together with the sums already paid, will make 25 per cent. of the original purchase.

By act No. 74, an amendment was incorporated into section 74 of the school law. (see school law.) An act was passed prescribing the duties of the Superintendent, and repealing chapter 56 of the revised statutes of 1846; also an act to provide for the election of Regent in the upper peninsula. The one mill tax was raised to two mills. An act was also passed to provide for the government of the University, and chapter 57 of the revised statutes of 1846 repealed. An act relating to the State library, was approved April 8, 1851, appropriating the State library room to the use of the Superintendent, for his office, and requiring the State Librarian to perform certain duties connected therewith.

At the extra session, an act was passed, directing the Secretary of State to send one copy of the annual report of the Superintendent to each school district, one to each township, one to each county clerk, and treasurer, ten to each city, one hundred and fifty to the State library, five hundred for binding, and one hundred for the use of the Superintendent. The sum of fifty dollars was appropriated for meteorological instruments, which have been purchased.

SKETCH

OF THE PUBLIC SCHOOLS OF THE CITY OF DETROIT.

OFFICE BOARD OF EDUCATION OF CITY OF DETROIT,
Detroit, October 25, 1851.

Hon. FRANCIS W. SHEARMAN,
Superintendent of Public Instruction:

DEAR SIR—In compliance with your request to furnish some facts relative to the rise, growth and present condition of the Free Schools of Detroit, I beg leave to transmit the following sketch, which is necessarily general in its character, and only regret my want of time to respond more fully upon the various topics in reference to which you inquire:

The cause of Popular Education in Detroit, has progressed slowly for a City that dates so far back towards the days of those noble Pilgrims, who, in their very first legislation, made sure provision for both the Free and Grammar School, by requiring every township of a certain number of householders, to build up these wells of learning in their midst. But the spirit of the Pilgrims blessed not the foundations of the city of the Straits. They were laid as early as 1701, but by very different hands from those which built upon the rock of Plymouth; and while we are compelled to acknowledge that with us this great cause is yet in its infancy, we nevertheless claim it to be an infancy which already foretokens a strong and vigorous manhood. Detroit, during the last four years, has been putting on the garments of a great Metropolis, and occupying as she does that peculiar position of a reservoir of the great tide of population and trade now rolling in upon her from the east, and the mouth-piece of the broad and fertile valleys that lie far behind her, and penetrate into the most remote regions of the west, no one can fail to see that the day is quite at hand when she must wield an influence more potent in its extent than any other city west of New York. How much depends upon the friends of popular education, in order to render that influence potent for good rather than evil, is already well known to yourself, and I trust appropriately felt by all those among us who have the best interests of their city at heart.

Previous to the year 1841, no such thing as a Free School was known in the city of Detroit, and the interests of general education consequently languished to such a degree, that the benevolent attention of a few gentlemen, interested in the subject, was at length excited to reform and check the evils which were rapidly springing out of this unfortunate state of things. Foremost among them, and the first to take any steps in the matter, was our much beloved fellow citizen, Dr. Zina Pitcher, long known for his untiring efforts in behalf of every interest connected with this important subject, and widely esteemed throughout our State, for his arduous labors in aiding to organize and perfect our State University; and associated with him was a no less devoted friend to education in our State, Samuel Barstow, Esq., who for many successive years continued to act as the presiding officer of the board of education, and still remains its most active and efficient member, and one to whom the city of Detroit must forever remain indebted for his generous and tireless devotion to this important interest. While acting as Mayor of the City, during the year 1841, Dr. Pitcher called the attention of the several members of the Common Council to the great need of common schools among us, and succeeded in obtaining some statistics on the subject which exhibited the condition of the community at that time in its connection with education. From these statistics disclosed at the time, it appeared that there were then in the City twenty-seven English schools, one French and one German school, but all of them exceedingly limited in numbers, and scarcely deserving the name of schools, except the one connected with St. Ann's (Catholic) Church, which embraced nearly all of the children of Catholic Families then resident in the city. The whole number of scholars in attendance upon these 29 schools at this time, was 700, and this in a city with a population of between 9 and 10,000 inhabitants!!

The average cost of tuition, as then estimated, was *seventeen dollars per year* for every scholar. It was likewise ascertained that there were more than 2,000 children of the proper school age, within the then limits of the city, all of whom, excepting the the seven hundred above referred to, were not in attendance upon any school whatever, while they were daily ripening into full grown citizenship, and hastening to take their places as Parents and Guardians in the community.

Speedy measures were then adopted by the gentlemen above referred to, in connection with others who came forward as fellow laborers in this good work, and by hiring vacant rooms and securing teachers, upwards of seven schools were soon opened in different parts of the city, and earnest efforts made to persuade various families whose children were then roaming the street, to send them to the daily schools thus established. Yet so great was the apathy and indifference felt by many on the subject, that when schools were thrown open for the instruction of their children at no cost to themselves, it still required the continued personal and individual effort of those interested to bring this portion of the community to see the great advantages they were able to derive for their families from the common schools.

Much difficulty, and embarrassment too, was felt from a certain other portion of our citizens, who, partially from a fear of increased taxation likely to result, in their opinion, from incompetency in the management of the schools, or a reckless and extravagant policy on the part of those interested in establishing the system, and also from a general want of interest on the whole subject of popular education, did not hesitate to array themselves in an attitude towards the new enterprise which savored much more of hostility than good will. This feeling pervaded the minds of a large portion of the older settlers, (although there were not wanting many honorable and distinguished exceptions among them who approved and smiled encouragingly on the project,) and so fettered and embarrassed the work at its very commencement, as to render it a matter of serious doubt for some time, whether it was destined to succeed or to be crushed in the bud. The friends of the system, however, still persevered in their laudable undertaking, and though often discouraged at the almost insuperable difficulties with which they were called to contend, never once thought of abandoning the noble enterprise in which they had engaged. Through their instrumentality an application was made to the next succeeding Legislature, for an act of incorporation, which was subsequently passed, and approved on the 17th of February, 1842.

This act incorporated the various schools of the city, which had just been established, into one district, under the style of "The Board of Education of the City of Detroit," and which is composed of two school inspectors from every ward in the city. Its officers consist of a President, Treasurer, and Secretary, who are annually chosen by the new board, at their first meeting. By the provisions of this act also, the common council are authorized once in each year, to assess and levy a tax on all the real and personal property in the city, which shall not exceed one dollar for every child between the ages of four and eighteen years, according to the last census taken and on file in the Secretary's office. By the same law, a further assessment of two hundred dollars per annum, for the benefit of the school library, is allowed, and generally collected. Subsequent legislation authorized the voting of a special tax by the freeholders of the city, of a sum not exceeding fifteen hundred dollars, whenever the same should be required, for the erection of school buildings, and this extra tax has been asked and granted in but two instances, since the organization of the schools.

This annual tax of one dollar for every scholar between four and eighteen, granted by the city, together with the proportion of moneys received each year from the State school fund, (and which for the last two or three years has barely exceeded two thousand dollars,) constitutes and comprises the only fund which supports the various schools of our city.

The board now have twenty-two schools in active operation, within the limits of the city, in which number is included one school exclusively appropriated to colored children, and their total annual expenditure in the support of these schools is about eight thousand dollars, of which sum more than six thousand are absorbed by teachers' salaries.

About three years after the schools were fairly started, and just as they commenced taking form and shape, the board were called to encounter a storm which came very near wrecking the whole system, and which, but for the prudent and temperate management of those then entrusted with the interests of the schools, must necessarily have resulted most disastrously to the permanent educational interests of our city. I refer to our first encounter with that perplexing, yet all important subject, the proper introduction of the Bible into the public schools. In a community as largely Catholic as was the city of Detroit at that time, it may be supposed that the opposition to the introduction of the Bible, *as a text book*, in the public schools, would be vigorously and earnestly contested, and it was so contested during a period of several months. The schools being then in their infancy, and the storm breaking upon them before they were fairly rooted, involved them in a peril from which it seemed at one time almost impossible successfully to extricate them. The religious feeling of the citizens was thoroughly aroused in reference to the matter, and the lines openly drawn between Protestants and Catholics. Petitions with innumerable names poured in upon the board, some asking positively for the introduction of the Bible as a text book in the schools, and others soliciting the very contrary, and insisting upon its total exclusion. So high did the excitement rise that many citizens on both sides of the question did not hesitate openly to declare, that unless their particular views were carried out in this matter, they would gladly see the entire school system broken up and swept away from our city. After this intemperate zeal of many had in a measure abated, the board proceeded to the discharge of their duty by calmly acting on the question; and about the third of February, 1845, peacably settled the whole difficulty, by the adoption of the two following resolutions, viz:

"*Resolved*, That it is the opinion of this board that there is nothing in their rules and bye-laws at all conflicting with the right of any teacher in the employment of this board, to open his or her school by reading without note or comment, from any version of the Bible they may choose, either Catholic or Protestant.

"*Resolved*, That any teacher who shall in any way note, comment or remark in his or her school, upon passages of Scripture, shall be removed from his or her school, upon the proof thereof being made to the committee of his or her school—the decision of said committee being subject, however, to review by the board."

Thus was this threatening peril avoided, the influence of the Bible fully preserved in the schools, and the school system itself saved from the ruin which seemed at first impending over it. From that time to the present, the policy set forth in the resolutions has been adhered to by the board, and all parties seem to have acquiesced in it as the most prudent, judicious and impartial mode of adjusting the difficulty. Nor are those now wanting among such as at first occupied respectively both extremes in the controversy, who have since come frankly forward and vindicated the course pursued by the members of the board at that time, as the wise and proper one; although, while standing in the breach, these gentlemen were exposed to shafts from both sides, and were sustained only by the consciousness of having rightly discharged their duty, and leaving the future to confirm the wisdom of their judgment. That future is already here, and their judgment stands approved by all who have traced the history of the schools from that day forward.

The twenty-two schools now in operation under the charge of the board, and already referred to, may be thus classified, viz: two Union schools, (the plan of which will be presently alluded to,) one in four, and the other in three separate departments; four middle schools, under male teachers, for scholars between the ages of five and eighteen years; eleven primary schools, under female teachers, for scholars between the ages of five and ten years, and one school for colored persons.

Our system of organization and discipline has grown up as it were under our own hands, and been adapted rather to our own peculiar circumstances and exigencies, than modeled upon any preconceived plan of those who confine themselves to one particular mode of conducting a school, and who regard it as the *one only method*, rejecting every thing else. We have preferred rather to be *eclectic* in our various organizations, and having first fully satisfied ourselves as to the character of our material, have then proceeded to adapt all that we found excellent and suitable in the numerous and varied systems that prevail throughout the country.

We are, however, exceedingly desirous of perfecting throughout our city, what we style the *Union School,* and which we find to be not only the most beneficial in all respects, but the most economical also. Our poverty as a board, and consequently our inability to erect suitable school buildings, delayed us a long time, before we were enabled to take the first step towards establishing such a school. Our city, (unlike the two on either side of us, Cleveland and Chicago, and mainly for the reasons already stated,) has never erected a uniform set of school buildings in the different wards of the city, and the only way in which we have to possess ourselves of buildings at all, is by taking advantage of the extra tax occasionally, of $1,500, and adding to it whatever we can manage, by the severest economy, to save from our annual receipts, and which you will readily see, from what has been stated, as to the amount of our receipts and expenditures, must be necessarily small.

Fortunately, however, for the cause of education among us, the large and commodious building formerly occupied as the State Capitol, in this city, upon the removal of the seat of government to Lansing, fell into the hands of the board of education and we were thus favored with an opportunity of establishing a Union school on a large scale, which was speedily done. This building now receives and shelters over five hundred children every day, and affords more comfortable school privileges than can be found in any other building dedicated to such purposes in the Union. Although now appropriated to much more humble pursuits than formerly, when its halls were used as the theatre of State legislation, yet we confidently hope that the State is deriving much more good from the work now accomplishing within its walls, than from that which was wont to be enacted there in earlier days. If no laws are now formally framed there, the future law-makers of the State are being made there daily, and it is hoped they will be fully qualified for their work when the time of their labor arrives.

The plan of the Union school, as adopted by the board of education, is briefly as follows: in the basement of the building is an infant school, where the children are familiarized with their alphabet and taught to spell. They are then elevated to the primary department, where they are still further instructed in the same studies, and also in the multiplication table, and somewhat in geography. They next pass into the lower or middle department, where the circle of study is enlarged, and they commence their work upon the text books, and are taught especially in Colburn's mental arithmetic, which has long been regarded with us as a *sine qua non* in our schools. The drill in this work is made very complete and thorough, and the pupil is not permitted to abandon it until he has mastered it all, from cover to cover. Having here qualified themselves for the upper or higher department, they are then transferred to the care of teachers, who conduct them through all the higher branches of study, and with whom they complete their course. These studies embrace the most finished style of reading and writing, grammar, geography, history, both ancient and modern, higher arithmetic, algebra, geometry, natural and mental philosophy, astronomy, composition, elocution, book keeping, surveying, music, &c. &c. The very highest attainment in all these studies is here reached, and the most difficult and abstruse mathematical and geometrical problems, as also the working out of eclipses may be seen in diagrams, as the work of the scholars, at every public examination.

The admission of scholars into these various departments is sought to be regulated, as far as possible, by age, although it is found that their respective attainments in a knowledge of the studies prescribed, is the safer and perhaps the better rule by which to advance them in their course.

The primary departments are under the care of female teachers exclusively, and the middle and upper departments are under the conjoint care of both a male and female teacher. Both sexes attend to the same studies, and are instructed in the classes, except as portions of them are occasionally withdrawn under the charge of the female teacher into the recitation rooms attached to the middle and upper departments; and in all matters of discipline, the male teacher of the upper department exercises full jurisdiction, not only over his own, but likewise over all the inferior schools in his building.

In this progressive method under competent teachers, we find our scholars strengthen with every onward step, and by the time they have completed the whole course of the upper and final department, they are generally abundantly qualified for any responsible position in life, either as machinists, surveyors, or mercantile clerks, according as their tastes may have most inclined or regulated their studies. "*Fesina lente!*" has been the principle upon which we have sought to proceed in carrying out our system, and by *thorough drill* in each particular study, from the commencement, (although attended at first with some delay,) we find the scholar advances much more rapidly and intelligently in the higher branches, than where he is hurried along superficially, and with much more apparent rapidity through his preliminary studies. The latter course never can make a good scholar, the former invariably will.

At present we have but two large Union schools conducted on this plan; but we hope before three years have elapsed to add at least two more of this kind to our present number, and so go on increasing them until we finally absorb all of the primary and middle schools now scattered abroad through the city into *Union schools*, which result we regard as necessary to the perfection of such a system as our city needs, and as will prove most advantageous to its youth.

The study of the classics has not yet been introduced into these schools, not from any lack of a due appreciation of their importance by the board, but mainly because of our limited means, the present want of legal authority so to expend any portion of our moneys, and the overflowing numbers of those who demand, as of the first importance, a thorough education in the English branches. Were it within the range of their power and means, I doubt not the board would be glad to engraft upon their system the grand peculiarity of the Parish schools in Scotland, where the teachers employed are good classical scholars, and impart instruction in the languages to their pupils, who often time pass from the parish school to the University. It is in fact, to this, more than any other one cause, that Scotland owes her great superiority over England, and almost all other countries, in the great number of her highly educated sons. When, however, our means shall have increased so that we may expand as we ought, and we are enabled to secure competent teachers in these studies also, our common school system *at home in Detroit*, we hesitate not in saying, will not fall behind that of any other in the nation. We hope for the early arrival of this day, and at present can do nothing more than faithfully and fully prepare the way for its coming.

Our school year is divided into three terms; the first commencing on the second Monday after the third Saturday in April, and closes the fourth Saturday in July. The second term commences the fifth Monday after the fourth Saturday in July, and closes the Saturday next preceding Christmas. The third term commences on the first Monday after the first day of January, and closes the third Saturday in April. By this it will be seen that we have but one long vacation, which is generally the entire month of August, and a week's vacation at the end of both the other two terms.

It is somewhat difficult to arrive at the precise number of scholars in daily attendance upon our public schools in the course of the year; but it has been estimated by the board at 4,250 for the last year, which is more than two-thirds of all the children of the city between the ages of four and eighteen. According to this estimate the average cost of educating each scholar per year under our present system, instead of being *seventeen dollars,* as was estimated before the schools were organized, *now falls short of two dollars,* and the standard of education is infinitely beyond what it was in 1841. When, too, we deduct from this, one-third of the children which are not found, as is above stated, on our public school rolls, all such as are in attendance upon the numerous select schools throughout our city, and such as have already passed into the Store and Workshop, it will be readily seen that the proportion of youth who are not in attendance upon any school at all is exceedingly small, and that our system enjoys a very large share of public confidence.

Public attention is now much more generally attracted to the schools than formerly; and public sympathy, instead of being arrayed against them, as was the case at first, now rallies warmly around them and lifts up its voice in their praise. In every humble dwelling throughout our widely extended city, as well as in the splendid mansions of the rich, the free schools have now one or more earnest and interested advocates. Men who were first opposed to the whole system, have been insensibly won over to its support by witnessing the additional lustre of character and personal graces which their little ones receive under their refining influence; and those who at the outset embarked with fear and trembling in the support of this noble enterprise, can now enjoy the pleasure of seeing the free school already established as a permanent institution among us. Opposition has ceased its clamor, and confidence has bestowed her smile upon these precious nurseries of our nation's security; and the man who seeks at this late day to pluck them down over our heads, must be prepared, like Sampson of old, to perish in the ruin which his own hand hath wrought.

I know not whether the foregoing hurried and rather superficial sketch of our educational interests will be of any service to you, or afford even one particle of instruction to the student who gleans in this field of inquiry, but leave you to judge—we profess not to be of superior position in this matter, knowing that we have had, and still have much to contend with; but nevertheless, we feel ourselves deserving, at least, of that humble plaudit, "you have done what you could;" and I am sure that you will not be disposed to withhold it.

I am, very respectfully,

Your ob't servant,

D. BETHUNE DUFFIELD,

Secretary of the Board of Education of the City of Detroit.

1852.

THIRTEENTH ANNUAL REPORT OF THE REGENTS OF THE UNIVERSITY.

The Regents of the University, through their executive committee, submit herewith to the Superintendent of Public Instruction, the documents composing their thirteenth annual report:

1st. Report of the Treasurer of the University.

2d. Statement by the Secretary, of warrants drawn upon the treasurer during the year.

3d. Report of the Commissioner of the Land Office.

4th. Report of superintendent of grounds.

5th. Report of expenditures, from executive committee.

6th. Report of the Faculty of Arts.

7th. Report of the Medical Faculty.

8th. Memorial of Alvah Bradish, Esq., on fine arts, &c.

9th. A historical memoir, by Z. Pitcher, M. D.

The receipts and disbursements of the treasurer, which balance each other for the year, amount each to $12,543 79; his report showing that there were no funds remaining on hand, June 30, 1851. On comparing the statement of the secretary, of warrants issued during the year, with the treasurer's report, it appears that the Board have contracted a debt, in the form of outstanding warrants, which amounts to $4,775 11, which the revenues of the Board will be able to extinguish, if no extraordinary appropriations are made in one or two years. This indebtedness of the Board has mainly been contracted in the construction of a building to accommodate the Faculty and students of the College of Medicine, which also contains a laboratory suited to the wants of the department of arts.

The report from the executive committee shows the particular purposes for which the funds of the Board have been expended, and

from that of the superintendent of grounds you will see that the receipts for initiation fees and room rent, have amounted to $2,364 95
To this, add the amounts received by the treasurer, viz: 12,543 79

And you have the gross sum of.................. $15,908 74
received and expended, or accounted for during the last academic or University year.

You are referred to the reports of the respective Faculties for an account of the number of graduates in the two departments of the University, and to that from the Faculty of medicine for a detailed statement of the duties performed by the several members thereof.

For the memorial of Mr. Bradish, the Board of Regents ask special consideration, both on account of the elevation of its sentiment and the purity and chasteness of the style in which it is dressed. His opinions on the influence which a cultivation of the fine arts will exert over the manners and morals of a people, are commended to the careful perusal of all who are charged with the education of youth, or the supervision of institutions of learning.

The memoir by Dr. Pitcher was written at the request of the Board of Regents, for the purpose of bringing before their successors a *resume* of their acts and the reasons for the adoption of some of their more important measures, in such a form that it might serve as a guide for their action, or a beacon to warn them, according as those acts may be approved or regarded of doubtful utility. We invite special attention to what is said on the subject of branches of the University, and express our opinion that the organization of Union schools in the villages and cities of the State, will both more effectually subserve the purposes for which common schools should be established, and at the same time furnish more efficient auxiliaries to the University than its branches were during their existence. In proof of this, it is deemed proper to state that the Union school at Jonesville, under the direction of A. L. Welch, Esq., a graduate of the University, has furnished candidates for admission to the Freshman Class, prepared in the most satisfactory manner. This is an important fact, as it shows what kind of fruits the Union school may be made to produce, and what relation these two portions of our educational system may be made to bear to each other. Another motive for its preparation, originating in a desire to make some reply to an honorable committee of the House of Representatives, who, by its chairman, had pronounced the University a failure, and to furnish an answer to those citizens who had petitioned the Legislature to abolish the medical department of the University, unless certain professorships therein named should be engrafted upon the present system of instruction in that department of that institution.

The only occurrence which the executive committee can recall as having transpired within the past year, and not alluded to in the reports of the standing committees, is the resignation of the Rev. Andrew Ten Brook, who occupied the chair of mental and moral philosophy in the University of Michigan. The committee deem it improper to let this occasion pass without expressing their regret that so estimable a man, so capable a teacher and so devoted a friend of the University, should have found it necessary or expedient to withdraw from the institution.

Very respectfully, your ob't serv't,

Z. PITCHER,

In behalf of Ex. Com.

Detroit, Sept. 14, 1851.

REPORT OF THE MEDICAL FACULTY OF THE UNIVERSITY FOR 1850–'51.

To the Hon. the Board of Regents of the University:

The Faculty organized May 15th, 1850, choosing Prof. Abram Sager, President, and Prof. M. Gunn, Secretary. September 23d, the routine of lectures and recitations was arranged as follows, viz:

MONDAY, A. M.

Recitations followed by lectures.

Obstetrics, &c., by Prof. Sager. Materia Medica, by Prof. Allen.

MONDAY, P. M.

Recitations followed by lectures.

Theory & Practice, &c., by Prof. Denton. Chemistry, &c., by Prof. Douglass.

TUESDAY, A. M.

Mat. Med., &c., by Prof. Allen. Anatomy, Surgery, by Prof. Gunn.

TUESDAY, P. M.

Theory & Practice, &c., by Prof. Denton. Chemistry, &c., by Prof. Douglass.

WEDNESDAY, A. M.

Obstetrics, &c., by Prof. Sager. Anatomy, &c., by Prof. Gunn.

WEDNESDAY, P. M.

Theory & Practice, &c., by Prof. Denton. Materia Medica, &c., by Prof. Allen.

THURSDAY, A. M.

Obstetrics, &c., by Prof. Sager. Anatomy, &c., by Prof. Gunn.

THURSDAY, P. M.

Theory & Practice, &c., by Prof. Denton. Chemistry, &c., by Prof. Douglass.

FRIDAY, A. M.

Obstetrics, &c., by Prof. Sager. Anatomy, &c., by Prof. Gunn.

FRIDAY, P. M.

Materia Medica, &c., by Prof. Allen. Chemistry, &c., by Prof. Douglass.

SATURDAY.

Reading and examination of theses, attended by all the Faculty, and occupying from two to four hours. Theses being required only once in two weeks, the alternate Saturday to be occupied by the usual number of recitations and lectures, distributed among the Faculty as convenience and utility at the time dictated.

The course was opened the first Wednesday in October, 1850, by an introductory lecture by the President. With the exception of a few days, early in January, 1851, which were occupied in completing the arrangements for warming the lecture rooms, the exercises continued in accordance with the foregoing schedule, till the Saturday immediately preceding the annual commencement of the medical department.

Ninety-one regular matriculants were in attendance throughout the course, also five honorary members of the class.

It may be mentioned that a considerable number of clinical lectures were given in addition to the regular curriculum, practically illustrative of interesting points in pathology and therapeutics. Several of the capital operations in surgery were performed before the class, as also many of minor character.

In consequence of the large number of students engaged in practical anatomical study, the professor of anatomy and surgery found his duties so excessively onerous that he was obliged to employ an assistant to act as a demonstrator. The professor of chemistry has also been obliged to make use of an assistant.

Invitation having been extended to the junior members of the class to participate in the exercise of medical composition, a large number of them cordially responded, so that very considerable labor was thrown upon the Faculty in the critical examination of the numerous "theses" presented.

Frequent review examinations were conducted, both of the junior and senior classes, at irregular intervals, and during otherwise unoccupied hours.

Much time and labor have necessarily been employed by the Faculty in the preperation of *means of illustration*, which the limited appropriations at their disposal have prevented them from otherwise procuring. By this course, they have been enabled to elucidate many of the more important subjects of remark, although much additional exertion and expenditure will be necessary to place the several departments on a proper footing in this particular.

Near the close of the term, several gentlemen having duly announced their intentions, and having presented the requisite credentials, were admitted to an examination for the degree of Doctor of Medicine. Of these, *six* were found to possess the proper qualifications, and, on the recommendation of the medical faculty, were admitted to that degree at the meeting of the Board of Regents in April last, being the date of the annual commencement of the Medical Department.

Twenty-three students passed the examination, holden about the same time, preliminary to their being admitted as candidates for graduation the next ensuing term. These were severally graded according to their merits, as shown on examination; it being understood that this will influence to some extent the mode and degree of their final examination.

It was deemed expedient, in order still further to aid the efforts of the Board of Regents, to elevate the standard of Medical Education, by facilitating the means to establish a summer reading term, free to all the students in this department. This has accordingly been done. Daily examinations have been held by the Faculty in the various branches of medical study. The number in attendance the present term, from the lateness of the notice, is small; yet it is believed that when the advantages of this course shall be more fully known, a large number will annually avail themselves of its benefits.

The Medical Faculty cannot allow this opportunity to pass without expressing their sincerest thanks for the cordial co-operation of the profession throughout the State, as well as the public generally, in sustaining their efforts to build up and give character to this new institution. Nor is this without a reason—the conservation of the public health is second to no other object of public interest.

Whether we can look for a largely increased number of students in this department, the ensuing course, is a matter of some little doubt. It is true, the fees actually paid are small, in comparison with those of similar institutions; yet, it is to be recollected, that the extraordinary length of the lecture term, whilst it increases largely the opportunities of the student, involves at the same time an increase of personal expenditures, so as very nearly to balance the amount. The examination upon preliminary branches, it appears, has also repulsive features to many students. From these causes mainly, it is thought, that although a large majority of the late medical class were residents of this State, yet still the catalogues of foreign institutions show that many students from this State were abroad. The extended term and the strict enforcement of the rules of examination are, however, it is believed, paramount to mere numbers, and should in any event be sustained.

The medical faculty are gratified in being able to report to the Board, that there are but few particulars in which further action of their body is deemed necessary. The plan of the institution, they are happy in being able to state, has been submitted to many of the most distinguished members of the medical profession throughout the country, and has met with their decided approval. It is essentially the one which has been recommended by that learned body, the American Medical Association.

It would largely facilitate the course of instruction in this department, were it more adequately supplied with appropriate apparatus, plates, drawings, models, &c. It is hoped, however, that the proceeds of the matriculation fees, which have been appropriated by vote of the Board to this object, will, if scrupulously devoted to that end, soon relieve the institution from the great disadvantages under which it at present rests from their deficiency.

To defray the expense of the diplomas granted, and still further to augment the contingent fund, it is recommended that a small fee be charged on each diploma which may be issued from this department.

The medical faculty was re-organized June 5th, 1851, by choosing Prof. Denton, President, and Prof. Allen, Secretary.

All which is respectfully submitted.

By order of the Medical Faculty.

J. ADAMS ALLEN, Secretary.

The following MEMOIR, embracing an epitome of the transactions of the Regents of the University, with some reasons for the adoption of their more important measures, from 1837 to June 30, 1851, has been prepared by Dr. Pitcher, and, having been adopted by the Board of Regents, was transmitted to the Superintendent with the report for the past year:

MEMOIR.

Being required by the Revised Constitution of the State, which prescribes a new mode of appointing, and changes the tenure of office of the Regents of the University, to surrender the trust hitherto committed to the present members, the Board of Regents, deeming it to be appropriate to add to a careful recapitulation of their receipts and expenditures, a succinct history of their administration, assigning the motives for their action and the reasons for the policy they have pursued, directed the following memorial to be prepared as a part of their annual report:

When the members of the Board were first called together by Stevens T. Mason, then Governor of Michigan, whose short and brilliant career constitutes an epoch in the history of the State, the important duties of selecting this site, which will remain sacred to letters, to science and the arts, so long as intelligence and virtue shall hold their seat in the affections of the people, and of providing the means by borrowing the credit of the State to adorn and improve it, were the subjects first presented for their consideration. The manner in which they performed these duties has become a matter of history. As such, it may be seen and read of all men. Of the judgment which the present or the future may form in relation to these transactions, the Board feel no apprehension and manifest no concern.

Having selected the site of the University, secured the means of erecting the buildings, purchasing the library, and of doing other things necessary to lay its foundation, it became apparent that the materials for the construction of the living edifice were not at hand. The blocks for the statuary were in the quarry, but there were no hands to hew them into form. Our political and social institutions were yet in a transition state. The common schools were then in chaos, and our whole system of Public Instruction in the State, at best, of inchoation. Believing that the attempt to establish or organize the University at this stage of our political existence, in this condition of the other educational institutions of the State, would prove abortive, the Regents resolved (as the constitutional authority or warrant for so doing had not then been questioned,) to invert the order of things contemplated in the organic law, and proceed at once to the establishment of *branches* as a means of furnishing the elements necessary to give vitality to the central institution, when the time for appointing its Faculty should arrive.

In order to carry this purpose into effect, the committee on branches were authorized to employ an agent to visit the different sections of the State and engage the co-operation of citizens living at such points as seemed most suitable for the establishment of branches, and report his doings to the Board. This agent, who was restricted to eight localities, reported in favor of locating a branch at Pontiac, Detroit, Monroe, Tecumseh, Niles, Grand Rapids, Palmer and Jackson, the citizens of which were required to furnish the site and the edifice necessary for the accommodation of the pupils. On the fulfillment of these conditions, branches were organized at Monroe, Tecumseh, Niles, White Pigeon, Kalamazoo, Pontiac, Romeo and Detroit. A department for the education of females was added to the branch at Monroe, Tecumseh, White Pigeon, Kalamazoo and Romeo. Branches were also located at Mackinac, Jackson, Utica, Ypsilanti and Coldwater, but no appropriations were ever made for their support.

On the first organization of the Board of Regents, it included no clerical members. For this reason, the University, then in futuro, was stigmatized as an infidel affair, which, it was predicted, would fail to perform the functions for which it had been endowed. This prediction was uttered with much confidence in certain quarters, and an act for the incorporation of a sectarian college was urged through the Legislature, partly by the force of an appeal to the religious feeling of the members, based on this accusation. Partly with a view to disarm that kind of opposition, and more especially because they believed it to be a duty, irrespective of it, the Board was careful to introduce the elements of religion into the branches, which they did by the appointment of clergymen of the different denominations as principals thereof.

In the adoption of rules for the government of the branches, special care was taken to guard the common school interest from injury, by requiring candidates for admission to undergo a preparatory examination. Tuition was to be paid in advance. A treasurer was appointed for each branch, who was required to make a report of the funds in his hands, at the close of each term. The course of study to be pursued therein was prescribed by the Board of Regents, which embraced the preparation of the pupil for college, his qualification for business, or for teaching, as he might himself elect.

With the design of inducing young men who had been educated at the branches, to engage in the business of instruction, a regulation was adopted which authorized the treasurer to refund the money paid for tuition, to all such persons as should furnish to him evidence of having been engaged in teaching, having regard to the time they had been thus employed. A board of visitors was also appointed for each branch, to whom such powers were delegated as seemed necessary to the practical working of the system.

Notwithstanding the pains taken to adapt these institutions to the public exigencies, so that their legitimate functions could be performed without infringing upon another portion of the educational system, they soon began to decline in popular estimation, because they were not able at the same time to perform the functions of a common school as well as a branch of the University. A feeling of jealousy was awakened in the minds of those whose children were excluded from them, either from want of age or qualifications. Consequently they were soon regarded as places for the education of the (so-called) *aristocracy* of the State, and the University, through the influence of the branches, began to be spoken of as an enemy to popular education. If an opinion may be formed of public sentiment by the tone of certain official papers, it would appear that that feeling, instead of becoming extinct, has only changed the mode and place of its appearing.

Finding that the branches were drawing largely upon the fund designed for the construction of the University buildings, and that they were not satisfactorily accomplishing the end for which they had been established, the Board of Regents, after mature deliberation, being fully assured that the expense of keeping them up was greatly disproportioned to the benefits accruing thereform, suspended, in 1846, all appropriations for their support, after more than $30,000 had been expended in trying to sustain them.

Whilst this trial was being made of the utility of branches, Professor Gray was in Europe selecting the library of the University, and Dr. Torrey, of New York, was negotiating the purchase of the Lederer cabinet of foreign minerals, which now constitutes the principal sources of attraction to persons visiting this institution.

From this experimental though abortive effort to build up and sustain branches of the University, the Board have learned, and they deem the lesson of sufficient importance to leave it on record, that local institutions of learning thrive best under the immediate management of the citizens of the place in which they are situated, and when endowed or sustained by their immediate patrons.

When the time arrived for the organization of the College of Arts, the Board were not forgetful of the truth that man is not merely an intellectual but a moral being—a being meant for virtue as well as for reasoning, and partly as the result of his reasoning. And in order that the youth who should resort thither for instruction in science, letters, and the arts, might also imbibe correct ideas of moral truth, and just conceptions of their relations to other men, as well as their Maker, they appointed a clergyman from the Presbyterian, Baptist, Methodist and Episcopal churches, respectively, to the professorships of ancient languages, moral and mental philosophy, the philosophy of history, and mathematics, with natural philosophy. In supplying the Chairs of chemistry and mineralogy, botany and zoology, and the modern languages, although the gentlemen occupying these places are unexceptionable in moral character, regard was more especially had to their other qualifications for these positions, than to the religious influence they might exert over the minds of the young men entrusted to their charge. In order to avoid the appearance of sectarian predominance in the institution, a regulation was established by which the four first named professors were required, in turn, to act as President, for one year from the time of his accession to the office. The inconveniences of this plan of rotation in the office of President, to which the state of the finances compelled the Board to adhere whilst erecting the buildings necessary for the two departments now in successful action, were not so sensibly felt until the medical department was established during the past year. Since then, the necessity of a common head has become daily more apparent.

The Board are aware that the wisdom of their action, in selecting so many of their faculty from the clerical profession, has been called in question; still they are so strongly impressed with the importance to youth, of correct moral training, during the period of college life, and of the necessity of a sense of religious responsibility, to insure fidelity in the instructor, that no present consideration would tempt it to found a collegiate institution, without its materials were cemented by religious belief, and its durability guarantied by the hopes which Christianity alone can inspire or impart. Whether these ends can be as well secured by other instrumentalities, is a matter which they seriously commend to the consideration of their successors in office.

In arranging the course of study for the under-graduates of the University, the Board of Regents, aided by the members of the faculty, have expended much patient, laborious and anxious attention. They have striven to adapt their legislation to the demands of an active age, so as at the same time not to be instrumental in confirming the idea that it is not an age of reflection as well as of action. With this view they have required candidates for academic honors to study the humanities of the older schools, as a means of acquiring elegance in diction and an easy and happy command of style in composition, whilst they have afforded them the means of acquiring the modern languages, and the elements of natural history, including both organic and inorganic nature.

The Board have not been unmindful of the tendencies of the age. They are aware of the growing impatience of youth to put off subjection to parental control, and to put on manhood—of the ardent desire of the young man to become rich, rather than wise—of the increasing disposition in all classes to despise precedent, to reject whatever is old, for that reason, rather than because it has become effete; and have labored, not so much to minister to the gratification of this morbid relish for unregulated liberty, as to cultivate in their course of study and system of discipline, a conservative sentiment which should restrain, guide, enlighten and direct the young men who may resort thither for mental improvement. They desire, with great humility, to acknowledge their submission to an all-sufficient Creator. They observe in His works an order of progression, a plan of development which illustrates His attributes, and demands their profoundest admiration. In the origination of matter they recognize His power; in the development of organic existences, His wisdom; in the creation of sentient beings, His goodness; and in the existence of man, His power, wisdom and goodness combined. In His scheme of creation alone, they find inscribed the law of progress.

They learn from His word, that man was created in His own image; that since his fall he is left with powers susceptible of enlargement by cultivation, but find no warrant for the belief that any new faculty or power can be added or developed by his own exertion. Man may therefore improve, but cannot progress. They further learn from experience, a truth long since uttered by a Jewish Rabbi, that wisdom cannot be devised: and they infer from these truths, the law, that each generation of men must learn wisdom by its own experience, and that every individual mind must be improved by the exercise of its own powers. In conformity to these laws, and to effect these ends, the course of study in the University has been regulated. The special objects being to teach youth how to study; to prepare them for professional reading or for becoming intelligent artisans or business members of society. Not being of the opinion that the untutored youth is the best judge of what he ought to learn, nor that the admission of pupils to an irregular course of study along side of those of whom a more thorough drilling is required, would have a favorable effect upon scholarship, the Board have required all candidates for academic honors to study the elegant and antique models found in the Greek and Roman classics, to submit to daily recitations and the moral restraints of a college faculty. They know that in the hurry of men to accumulate wealth or acquire power, they will forgo the advantages and pleasures derived from patient mental culture—resign the sceptre of mind for the gilded mace, or the delusive and transitory exercise of political authority—and knowing these things, they have felt it to be their duty to strive to establish another umpire than that of Mammon, and to tempt young men, by protracting their course of study, to look for distinction out of the counting room or the political arena.

It is admitted that the number of students in the University could be greatly increased, if there were no prerequisites to their admission; and they believe at the same time that a system which should look merely to the augmentation of numbers, would have a fatal effect upon scholarship, and subvert the object of the grant, the end and purpose of the endowment.

Since the foregoing was written, a national educational convention has been held at Cleveland, in Ohio, in which the expediency of expelling the classics from our colleges became the subject of discussion. One of the gentlemen who took part in this debate, having been at one time a Regent of the University of Michigan, included in his remarks an admirable defence for his colleagues, in the adoption of the course of study required of their under-graduates. I take pleasure in incorporating it into this memoir, although it adds essentially to its length. It is gratifying to add, that that respectable Body set the seal of its disapprobation upon the attempt to make it the medium of disseminating so pernicious a sentiment:

The Board adopted in the organization of the collegiate department of the University, the general system and plan of studies which have been approved for centuries in Europe, and almost universally by the directors of colleges in these United States. The curriculum is equally full and extensive with that in any collegiate institution in this country, intended mainly, though not exclusively, for the education of minors. It would have been as disastrous in its results, as certainly a breach of trust in its very nature, had the Board, with the commencement of the collegiate department of the University of Michigan, projected any novel system of education which had not been put to the test of time and experience. The collegiate course of studies in the United States, as in the different colleges of the Universities of Oxford and Cambridge, in England, and the Gymnasiums of Germany, is intended for a specific purpose, and wisely adapted to it. The history and experience of centuries have stamped it with the seal of approbation, and it is questionable, especially after several abortive experiments already made in this country, whether any other equally, not to say more, efficacious can be devised.

The design of collegiate education is not immediately to impart the knowledge of the sciences and the arts—not to fill the memory and minds of youth with mere information. This is the work of life. It is utterly impossible that in the course of four years, any person, whether a minor or of maturer years, can range through the whole circle of the sciences, the whole field of human knowledge. In many of the natural sciences, especially in chemistry, geology, mineralogy, and various departments of natural philosophy, the continual development of new facts and new discoveries, render it indispensable, even for the most learned professor, to be a diligent student, if he would keep pace with the progress of knowledge in his own department. The same remark may be made in relation to the moral sciences and ethics, economics and politics. Nor can the professor of mathematics, without continual study, long maintain his position and reputation as an instructor in the exact sciences.

Whoso would think of requiring from boys, in a course of four years training, to compass the entire range of the natural and other sciences, only betrays his own ignorance of the wide field of human knowledge. The course of collegiate study and its peculiar advantages, have already suffered much from attempts to enlarge the course of study, so as to embrace a wider field than can be perfectly or even profitably cultivated by youth generally, or by any one in so short a period as four years. Yet the demand of popular feeling has been for the enlargement, rather than for the curtailment of the studies of a college course; and institutions, depending on popular favor for the means of their existence, have been forced to meet and gratify, to some extent, that demand. The Board have not been insensible of this state of public feeling, and have felt the necessity of respecting it, as far as it could be done with safety to the real interests of college education. They have introduced into their schedule, as full a course of study in the exact and natural sciences, as is to be found in most colleges. They have far exceeded most in the provision made for the study of the modern languages, and they have manned their Faculty with talents and attainments inferior to few. It is not without the conviction, however, produced by their observation and the history of the University, that this extension of the collegiate course has tended to embarrass the student somewhat in the prosecution of his studies in the Latin and Greek classics. This has been matter of deep and serious regret with the Board. For, although there has been a studied attempt, in certain quarters, to disparage the study of the learned languages, as they are sometimes called, and although much interest has been manifested in decrying the Latin and Greek classics, and in demanding the substitution of various natural sciences and arts in their place, yet the Board hope that the day is far distant when any revolution will be wrought which would exclude them from a course of collegiate education, or deprive them of that prominence they have heretofore had and continue to possess. Objections against their study are generally founded in ignorance of their uses and design, or the true reasons which have determined the instructors of youth for centuries in giving them such a conspicuous position. It is not the amount of information obtained from classic sources, which commends them so much for the study of youth, as it is the admirable aid the Latin and Greek languages furnish for the discipline of the mind, the development of its powers, and the formation of habits of close thought and accurate discrimination, for the cultivation of a refined taste, and for securing a better, more accurate, and thorough knowledge of our own English tongue. It is not to be denied that some of the loftiest ideas of Liberty and Patriotism are derived from the Greek and Latin poets, historians, orators and statesmen, and that the benefits of ancient civilization may thence be secured for the purpose of modern advancement. But these and other kindred advantages are only secondary compared with the value of the Greek and Latin languages, especially the latter, to the English scholar, as they are the fountain of so large a portion of our own tongue. No man can be fully at home, in the knowledge of his own English, who is not acquainted with Latin.

The experience of past ages in Europe, and of nearly two centuries in our own country, has proved their importance and value as the means of mental drilling, and the easiest and best means of so cultivating the powers of his mind as to enable a young man easily to adapt himself to and become useful, not only in any of the learned professions, but in general for social influence in any vocation in life. It is true that there are men whose names are an honor to their country, and their age, who have been self-taught—who have struggled through all the disadvantages resulting from the want of an early education, and who, notwithstanding that they have never had a collegiate course, nor studied the Latin and Greek, have distinguished themselves, and greatly benefitted their fellows. But these are exceptions to the general rule. What would not their towering minds, rising above such disadvantages, have been, if they had but enjoyed the full benefit of a collegiate course? And what would multitudes of more moderate talent have failed to be, had they never been subjected to the college drill? They are the liberally educated minds who generally direct public sentiment, and possess the power to do so. Our legislative halls furnish abundant examples of the superiority which the liberally educated have over the uneducated, in the transaction even of the ordinary business of public bodies.

On the value and necessity of the study of the Latin and Greek classics, the Board have never entertained any doubts. In resigning their place to their successors, they feel that they would be unfaithful to themselves and to the University, did they not give their public testimony to what they believe to be essential, absolutely indispensable in a thorough course of liberal education.

Any attempt to derange the course of collegiate instruction, by a general provision for extensively introducing irregularities, by adapting it rather to men of mature years than to minors, by leaving the different subjects and parts of study to the selection or choice of students, and by requiring services from the professors accordingly, must prove disastrous to the University of Michigan. It will be but the signal for the commencement of collegiate institutions, under the care of different religious sects, and the sure means of destroying the confidence and attachment now felt towards the University, by the different religious denominations in our State. There is no short hand, patent road to learning; and students who are averse to a four years' course of laborious and assiduous application, under the care of competent professors, can never justly expect to become proficient in literature or science. Where so much time, however, cannot be given, as by those who may commence study after having passed their majority, or where facilities are denied for pursuing one or more branches of science, as of chemistry, mineralogy, or other of the natural sciences, and of their application to various arts, as of agriculture, mining, metallurgy, and the trades, or of the mathematics for purposes of engineering and mechanism, we feel that it is all-important to provide them as soon as practicable. But schools for such purposes will require separate lecturers and faculties, and funds beyond what the University at present would be competent to meet. They might well be associated with or clustered around the collegiate faculty, and form part and parcel of a great system, whose various branches strictly and properly constitute the University. But as Rome was not built in a day, nor in an age, so it must be the work of time, as means and students multiply, and wisdom and experience are had, to enlarge or add to what has already been begun. To destroy or revolutionize what has been done, will only be to drive many of our own youth to other States, to waste the public funds, to postpone to a later period, if not fatally to frustrate, the best interest of education in our commonwealth. Our whole system of free schools is capable of being carried out and up to any extent for popular education, and district and union or high schools may be readily engrafted on it, affording educational advantages abundant as needed, and near to every man's door. But the collegiate system and the course of studies particularly adapted to the learned professions, for establishing which the U. S. Government have endowed the University of Michigan, is as totally different and distinct from the common school, as is the appropriation of the sixteenth section in each township, from the seventy-two sections made for specific purposes. The Board have ever felt it their duty to guard the funds put at their disposal, and to use them in accordance with the design had by the U. S. in the endowment of the University of Michigan."

The failure of the University to arrest the public attention, by the display of numbers in its annual catalogue, is owing to extrinsic causes, and not to any inherent defect in its organization, or want of talent in its Faculty. There is yet a lamentable deficiency in the number of preparatory schools in the State, and notwithstanding this deficiency the ratio of college students to the population of the State is equal to that of any other State of similar age, and the institution itself is as prosperous as any other in the country, its equal in age and surrounding circumstances.

By an examination of the catalogues of the various medical schools in the surrounding States, it was ascertained that in 1848, from seventy to eighty students of medicine, citizens of Michigan, were attending lectures out of the State, and it was estimated that an equal number were reading in the offices of physicians at home. These statistics induced the Board to commence the erection of a laboratory, which should be spacious enough to afford the requisite accommodation for the medical department. In doing this, they found it necessary to expend more than their current income, both in '49 and '50. By doing this, they were enabled, having appointed a medical faculty, to open that department for the admission of students in October, 1850. A catalogue of that faculty and the regulations of the department, are hereto annexed.

In an age elated by its notions of progress, characterized by desire for change, impatience of authority, disregard for precedent, and even contempt of law, it may be deemed proper for this Board to give some reasons why, in their organization of the college of medicine, they have paid so much deference to the authority of antiquity and so little respect to revelations of the present day. By reference to the catalogue of the medical faculty, it will be seen that they have made provision for instruction in anatomy, or a knowledge of the structure, form and relation of the parts of the human body—physiology, or a knowledge of the functions or uses of the organs—pathology, or the changes produced therein by disease—practical medicine and surgery, which include the directions for arresting morbid action, removing its products and repairing the injuries arising from accident—materia medica, or a description of the remedies used for these purposes, with an account of their modus operandi—and obstetrics, embracing the doctrine of ovology—the theory of reproduction, including the development of the fœtus in utero, and its expulsion when arrived at maturity. To these, as a means of qualifying the medical student for the discharge of certain duties. which the public authorities may call upon him to perform, the Board have added a professorship of chemistry and medical jurisprudence.

The foregoing is a synopsis of the curriculum or course of study required of candidates for medical degrees in the University of Michigan.

The Board of Regents, at the time of adopting this curriculum, were fully aware that there existed a sect who believe "that nothing can be perceived of the internal operations of the animal frame where life is disturbed by disease—who teach that it is only by means of the spiritual influences of a morbific agent that our spiritual power can be diseased—that the causes of disease cannot possibly be *material*, but that they originate in a dynamic (spiritual) immaterial cause, and can only be destroyed by dynamic (spiritual) power; that even the different species of worms are found only in patients laboring under a psoric (itch) affection—that the symptoms of disease are only the expressions of agony in the immaterial part of our nature, on which the curative remedies act by virtue of their spiritually countervailing agency—that behind these symptoms there is nothing to be learned of disease—that nothing can be learned of the effects or properties of medicines except from the morbid appearances which they excite in health—that a dynamic (spiritual) disease is extinguished by another more powerful, bearing a strong resemblence to it, a fact which they assert is confirmed by biology—that the medicinal disease must hence be more powerful than the one it proposes to cure—that natural diseases cannot be overcome by the unaided vital energies—that any real medicine (Homeopathic) will at *all* times and under *every* circumstance, work upon *every* living individual—that notwithstanding the assertion that medicinal diseases expire, as it were, by virtue of a statute of limitations, and that both natural and medicinal diseases are spiritual dynamia, declare that the chronic affections arising from the use of bark, opium, mercury, silver, iodine, digitalis, sulphur, leeches and setons, effect changes in the organization, destructive to life, for which there is no remedy; that all chronic maladies, not the results of malpractice, on the part of old school physicians, arise from the miasm of syphilis, sycosis, and psora (itch;) that the latter (itch) is the sole true and fundamental cause that produces all the other countless forms of disease which, under the name of debility, hysteria, hemicrania, hypochondriasis, insanity, melancholy, idiocy, madness, epilepsy, rickets, caries, fungus haematodes, gravel, hemorrhoids, jaundice, dropsy, amenorrhœa, epistaxis, asthma, impotency, sterility, deafness, cataract, amaurosis, paralysis, and pains of every kind which appear in our pathology as so many distinct diseases—that neither the skill of the physician nor the powers of nature had ever been able to cure a disease by an antipathic remedy—that a primary psoric (itch) eruption may be cured by ten globules of sulphur, if one be given in seven days—that where the remedy had been abused even years before, the smelling of one globule moistened with mercury, and allowed to operate nine days, will again render the vital powers susceptible to its operation—that one dose of mercury (X°) is sufficient to cure syphilis—that the professors of homœopathy propose to develop the immaterial (dynamic) virtues of substances not inherently medicinal, by mere manipulation, such as trituration with sugar, or dilution in alcohol—that the remedy can never be so small as to be inferior to the disease—that it effects exclusively the organism already suffering—that all that is curable by homœopathy may, with the utmost certainty, be cured by inhaling the aura of one globule of sugar, of which one hundred weigh a grain, moistened with the remedy proposed to be used, even if the organ to which it is applied be in a state of paralysis—and that internal hemorrhages, threatening death, may be cured by magnetism, which recalls to life persons who have remained in a state of apparent death during long intervals of time, a species of resurrection of which history records many examples!"

But the Board itself held to the doctrine that man's *material* as well as his spiritual nature, is the subject of disease when he violates a law of its being, and that the diseases of the latter are only curable by the blood of the atonement. His physical system being formed of numerous elements, such as sulphur, soda, lime, iron, phosphorus, carbon, nitrogen, oxygen and hydrogen, either chemically or mechanically combined, it may become disordered if either of them become deficient or exist in excess. Some of its diseases must of necessity arise from material causes, which will require remedies of a like material nature for their removal. This belief leads necessarily to a conviction of the importance of knowing man's structure, the uses of his organs, as well as his relation to the objects by which he is surrounded; the medium in which he moves, the atmosphere he breathes, and the chemistry of the food on which he subsists.

As an intelligent exposition of the symptoms of disease requires an intimate knowledge of the nervous system, the students of the Medical Department of the University have been required, in order to ensure familiarity with the separate and related functions of the cerebrum, cerebellum, medulla oblongata, medulla spinalis, the par vagum, external respiratory or nerves of respiration, the offices of the different branches of the fifth pair, and the distinction between the afferent and efferent nerves, to study the works of such men as Bell, Hall, Lolly, Flourens, Majendie, Todd, Bowman, Bischoff, Philip and Lassaigne. To learn the properties of the gastric juice, they are referred to the experiments and writings of Spallanzani, Beaumont, Blondlot and Ch. Bernard. In order to be able to comprehend the consequences of the act of respiration, they are required to investigate the writings of Müller, Magnus, Bischoff, Edwards, La Grange, Hassenfratz, Collard de Martigny, Leibig, Crawford, Reid and Davy; and in order to a right understanding of the changes wrought by disease, and the proper use of remedies for morbid action, they are directed to study such post mortem explorations as were commenced by Bailey, and have been continued by Martinet, Hodgkin, Williams, Prout and Bright.

With all becoming regard for the opinions of such of our fellow citizens as have been led, by a belief in a dogma of the day, to petition the Legislature for the repeal of the statute regulating the practice of medicine and for the abolition of this department of the University, we would ask, in the name of the Board of Regents, what there remains to be taught the medical student to fit him for the discharge of the duties of his profession, which they have not made provision for? Is there any other way for the medical neophyte to acquire such knowledge as will admit him to a seat in the temple of the Coan sage than that pointed out, rugged though it be, in the University course? Or shall the accumulated results of three thousand years of experience be laid aside, because there has arisen in the world a sect which, by engrafting a medical dogma upon a spurious theology, have built up a system (so-called) and baptized it

Homœopathy? Shall the High Priests of this spiritual school be specially commissioned by the Regents of the University of Michigan, to teach the grown up men of this age that the decillionth of a grain of sulphur will, if administered homœopathically, cure seven-tenths of their diseases, whilst in every mouthful of albuminous food they swallow, every hair upon their heads, and every drop of urine distilled from the kidneys, carries into or out of their system as much of that article as would make a body, if incorporated with the required amount of sugar, as large as the planet Saturn? Shall they be appointed by this Board to tell men, whose skeletons contain twenty per centum of phosphorus, that this article, when its "spiritually dynamic power" is developed by trituration, will cure disease, if the patient inhale the aura from the pellets over a paralyzed surface, or apply them to the membrane of the intestinum rectum, at the same time that every kernel of wheat which goes to make up his daily food, if exalted by dynamic division, would furnish poison enough to destroy the Chinese Empire?* So of lime, which furnishes the foundation of his bony system; and so of carbon (charcoal) which constitutes a large proportion of the softer solids of his body.

Now, as this Board have been taught that man is a material reality, originally formed of the dust of the earth, that he possesses the faculty of assimilating materials necessary to his growth, that he is liable to disease when operated upon by causes which disturb the laws of his being, that his body is the subject of death and will be of a resurrection, that as it is developed and sustained by the incorporation of material elements introduced from without, so its abnormal condition is to be removed by agents having physical properties capable of exalting the vital actions when depressed, and of repressing their force when unduly excited.

Respectfully submitted.

Z. PITCHER.

Ann Arbor, July 15, 1851.

---

*NOTE.

In order that the foregoing may not appear to be merely a *figure* of speech, I have copied the following mathematical view of the results of homeopathic trituration and solution, from Professor Lee's edition of Paris' Pharmacologia. The reader will please to recollect that only one grain of medicine is employed for all the dilutions, no matter how inert the substance may be, as sponge. sulphur, charcoal and lime, and that the higher the dilution, the more potent the article becomes.

Cubic feet of water, weight 62.5 lbs. to the foot. (Decimals rejected.)

DILUTIONS.

5th. 22 587.
10th. 228,571.428 571,428.
15th. 2,285.714,285.714,285,714.285,714.
20th. 22.857,142,857.142,857,142,857.142,857,142.857.
25th. 228,571,428,571,428,571,428,571,428,571,428,571,428, 571,428.
30th. 2 285,714.285,714,285,714,285,714,285,714,285,714,285, 714.285,714,285,714.

Cubic feet of sugar—specific gravity, 1.6. (Decimals rejected.)

DILUTIONS

5th. 14,285.
10th. 142,857,142,857.142.
15th. 1.428,571.428 571 428 571.428,571.
20th. 14,285 714,285,714.285 714,285.714,285.714,285.
25th. 142,857,142,857,142 857,142,857,142,857,142,857,142,-857,142.
30th. 1,428 571,428,571,428,571,428,571,428,571,428,571,428,-571 428,571.428,571.

Diameter in feet and miles of a sphere of sugar whose solid contents are equal to the quantity in the preceding calculations. (Decimals rejected.)

DILUTIONS.

	Feet.	Miles.
5th.	30	
10th.	64.850	12
15th.	139,733,576	26 464
20th.	301 046,863,589	57,016,451
25th.		
30th.	1,397,335,762,135,022,914	264,646,924,646,784

Cubic miles of water. (Decimals rejected.)

DILUTIONS.

5th. ....
10th. 1,552.
15th. 15.528,166 354.612.
20th. 155,281,663.546 126,356,043.711.
25th. 155,281.663 546,126 356 043.711.416 427,470,7.
30th. 155,281,663 546 126,356,043,711,416,427,470,792,147,-007,20.

COMPARATIVE ILLUSTRATIONS.

	Miles.
Longest diameter of the orbit of the comet of 1680	13 000,000,000
do do do Halley's comet	3,420,000,000,000

	Miles.
Distance of the nearest fixed star	20,140,000,000,000
Greatest distance of the earth from the sun	97,118,538
do do do do Herschel	1,918,089,022

Thus it appears that the 20th dilution would require a sphere of *sugar more than half the diameter of the Sun's distance from the Earth,* and a sphere of *water* about equal in diameter to the same distance; while the 30th would require a sphere of *sugar* in comparison with the diameter of which, the distance of Herschel from the earth would form but an infinitely small fraction! Hahnemann, however, recommends that the dilution in certain cases be carried as high as the 1500th, and remarks, "*experience has proved that it is impossible to attenuate the dose of a perfectly homœopathic remedy to such a degree that it will not produce a decided amelioration of the disease.*" (Stratten's Trans. of Organon, p. 274.) Again, all the fresh water lakes in North America, including the great lakes at the North, are estimated to contain fourteen thousand cubic miles of water; but the *eleventh dilution* would require more than ten times this quantity of fluid. A grain of antimony dropped into Lake Superior, would therefore suffice for centuries to medicate its waters; so that a teaspoonful, taken at the Falls of Niagara, would constitute a much stronger dose than the homœopathists usually administer. It is demonstrable that a single *rose*, growing on the surface of the earth, or even on the planet Herschel, would be likely to effect each inhabitant on our globe, by its aroma, more powerfully than any homœopathic medicine whatever, at the 30th dilution. (Am. Ed.)

The composition of bone, urine, &c., having been referred to, I give the results below, for the information of the non-professional reader:

CHEMICAL ANALYSIS OF BONE.

Organic matter,	32.56	parts in	100.
Phosphate of lime,	52.26	"	"
Carbonate of lime,	10.21	"	"
Oxide of iron & magonese,	1.05	"	"

Magnesia, soda, &c., omitted.

Iron abounds in the red blood of animals. Phosphorus exists in the white and yolk of eggs, and in milk, and also in the seeds of grasses, as wheat, rye, oats, &c. Sulphur is found in flesh, in eggs and milk, and in small quantities in potatoes, cabbage, peas and cucumbers. Lime is universally diffused, and exists largely in the seeds of grasses, especially wheat flour.

MEMORIAL OF ALVAH BRADISH.

To the Hon. the Board of Regents of the University of Michigan:

I beg to offer for the consideration of the Regents, some observations on the principles of the *fine arts* and on taste; showing the advantages that would accrue to the University by the early introduction of their culture into that institution.

In our country the fine arts are already acknowledged to be an important branch of education, though they have not been so generally adopted in our seminaries as educated men feel to be desirable. For the short period of our political existence, we have made very great progress in the production of fine works of art; and the estimate of the value of art has been greatly extended; while the love and respect for the labors of the pencil and chisel have taken a strong hold on popular favor.

At an early period in our history, we were not deficient in distinguished names in art, such as West, Trumbull, Copley and others. These names commanded a respect wherever high art was reverenced, and in Europe, long before our literature and public men found favor, our distinguished artists and their productions were the medium of begetting for us among their philosophers and patriots a kindly and respectful consideration. In the mean time this talent has been enhanced among us in proportion to the growth of other elements of prosperity, till our artists are now known to every metropolis of the old world, and their productions will vie with the greatest that have been produced in modern times. This has been brought about, too, without the aid of princely patronage, without governmental protection, without State grants. American artists acknowledge the sound doctrine that the direct patronage of the State is not so safe a dependence as a popular love, founded on knowledge and general enlightened taste. We do not seek State patronage, but we are persuaded that art should be taught in our schools and seminaries, that the public may be provided with the means, and possess the previous training to build up in the mind intellectual taste, and a sound judgment in works of art as well as in poetry and literature.

It cannot be doubted that a wide diffusion of good works of art will promote the cause of morals, religion and manners; nor will it be necessary for me to offer to your body the names of distinguished writers who have cordially commended a cultivation of the arts, and enforced a consideration for them by showing their adaptation to our natural and virtuous impulses, and their high value to the well being of society.

Indeed, a cultivation of a pure taste has so direct and invariable a tendency to render persons more happy and better members of society, securing images and monuments for our respect, veneration and affection, that all educated persons are solicitous for the extension of this tate

The *fine arts* are the especial objects of intellectual taste; and though some degree of pleasure may be derived from the sight of art without the highest cultivation, yet the advantages of a sound taste, as applied to *art*, as well as to literature and the conduct of life, are too manifold, and I trust too obvious, to require argument. It may well be said, doubtless, that to the man who resigns himself to *feeling*, without interposing any judgment or sound taste, poetry, music and painting are but pastimes, and but little better than trifles. It is by studying the *great principles* of the fine arts, and exalting our taste to the dignity of a *judgment*, that we make them sources of refined and noble enjoyment. Nor, in my judgment, can this culture commence too early; for there is every reason that a just taste and correct eye shall commence at the same time with the teachings of morals and manners; and if they be combined, the intellectual powers will grow into greater harmony, and the harshness of a crude culture be taken from our minor morals and deportment.

This improved, refined taste begets a higher relish for the simple habits of life, in unison with republican tendencies. It deepens our love of Nature, and carrying its empire far into the principles and practice of ethics, subjugates natural impulses and elevates all our desires. The practice of reasoning on these interesting themes becomes a habit at last, and the habit strengthening the reasoning powers, gives that dignity to the arts which properly belongs to them, while the discipline is favorable to the investigation of the still more abstruse subjects of mental philosophy.

Purity of taste tends to invigorate the social affections, and to moderate those that are selfish. It makes us averse to coarse language and ungenerous conduct, while it encourages a sympathy with whatever is lovely, excellent and magnanimous. So closely allied, I repeat, to morality, is intellectual taste, that no one can doubt that a fine relish of what is beautiful, proper and elegant in writing, painting and architecture, is a most rational preparation for the same just relish of these qualities in character and behavior. A philosophical inquiry into the principles of the fine arts inures the reflecting mind to that most enticing sort of logic. The science of criticism, as applied to the arts, to composition and literature, may be considered as a sort of middle link that connects the different parts of education, harmonizing all. The student proceeds from the more agreeable and simple method, until custom improves his faculties, and he learns by this easy mastery to grapple with the intricacies of a deeper philosophy.

It has been remarked by a distinguished philosopher, that mathematical and metaphysical reasoning do not usually enlarge our knowledge of man; they not being so applicable to the common affairs of life, however valuable for the discipline of thought, while a just knowledge of the fine arts, derived from rational principles, furnishes elegant subjects for conversation, sharpens our sense of the beauty and strength of language, and prepares us for acting in the social state with dignity and propriety.

From these considerations, therefore, I trust it cannot be doubted that the inculcation of the principles of the fine arts will be acceptable to the present faculty of the University, as it will be genial and valuable to every department of study. It will not interfere in any way with the time allotted to any of these studies, as it is proposed that the professor of art shall impart the knowledge and gradually form the taste, by familiar lectures, by conversations, and by frequent reference to examples of fine art. These shall consist in drawings, in engravings, in paintings, and in casts from the antique. The professor of Greek must feel a lively interest, it is confidently believed, in a collection of those marbles which illustrate the text books that are put into the hands of his classes—such, for instance, as the Elgin marbles, from the Parthenon, or some noble busts of Euripides, Xenophon or Thucydides. These are eloquent and palpable; and the marble groups often possess a spirit and purity of sentiment far beyond the language of the poet or historian. The spectacle of these precious memorials of a past classical age, will impart increased interest to their studies and stamp on the memory of ardent youth, images of delicacy and heroism that will continue to warm his fancy in the toil of life.

The student of Virgil who pores over, it may be, the death of Lacoon, and perhaps with difficulty makes out the meaning of the poet, will find his imagination excited, by having at his command a cast of that exqisite group in marble, by which his memory will be sharpened and his taste improved. Especially should this union be encouraged, considering that in this instance it is yet an unsettled question whether the poet or the sculptor be the original! The subject of the fine arts and aesthetics, as has been remarked, connects itself with intellectual and moral philosophy; and that lectures and conversations on themes so agreeable would commend themselves, there can be no doubt, both to the classes who pursue these studies, and to the professor who presides over them. The able discussions of Stewart, of Reid, of Kaimes, Allison and Mills, of Burke and Knight, on the principles of the fine arts, on criticism and on taste, show how important they are considered in any general course of instruction; how they are connected with other branches of philosophy, and how deeply they teach the joys and welfare of society.

It is doubtless a matter of just regret that the seminaries and colleges of this country have not more generally provided departments of the *arts*. Unfortunely, we have copied too much after the English universities in this respect. But, as this oversight in the early foundation of these great institutions is generally lamented by the most liberal minds of England, as a source of great evil, and one, if it were possible, they would gladly see rectified, it certainly will be the part of wisdom for us, in laying the foundation of new institutions, to make ample provisions for this deficiency. The absence of this provision in the national schools of England, had its origin in illiberal, contracted views, similar to that spirit which at this day would exclude the study of the natural sciences.

Oxford and Cambridge have done nothing either for art or the natural sciences; and the low state of public taste in that country is little creditable to the character of institutions so powerful and opulent. This is generally acknowledged.

Is it not extraordinary that neither of these universities possess a school in which the theory or practice of any branch of art is taught; and has not even a course of lectures, nor any means by which a young man may be either taught or can acquire the requisite knowledge on this class of subjects? What they have inherited from the dark ages, they have tried to preserve, without, if possible, ever going beyond what then existed.

The time is speedily advancing, we may predict, when public taste and general refinement in this country will be in advance of that of England, notwithstanding the wealth and patronage that have been lavished on art there for the past one hundred years. But with us, this must be greatly aided and promoted by the introduction of this culture into our schools and colleges.

Even schools of design and academies expressly established for this purpose, may not, in my opinion, do so much towards building up taste and the diffusion of art, as the establishment of professorships in the higher seminaries, colleges and universities of the land, where their culture shall begin jointly with other academical studies, and where the theory of art shall be combined with and illustrated by the palpable productions of the chisel and pencil.

An able English writer in Blackwood's Magazine indulges in these sound remarks: "We should say decidedly that the best consideration for art, and the best patronage too, that we would give it, would be to establish it in the universities of Cambridge and Oxford. In these venerated places, to found professorships, that a more sure love and more sure taste for it may be imbedded with every good and classical love and taste in the minds of youth."

I should not omit, however, to call your attention to the fact, that the new university of London is an exception to this; and being founded in the spirit of the age, seems inclined as far as possible to rectify the error of the older institutions, and to restore the *faculty of the arts which has perished there;* and for this purpose has established lectures on the different branches of the arts.

The University of Michigan has taken higher ground—wider and better views than almost any institution in this country. She includes the natural sciences as too obviously in accordance with the spirit of the age. She has provided also emphatically for the *fine arts*. She has established a department of *arts,* which may be seen by a reference to the organic law creating this noble institution.

Chap. 2, *Sec.* 2—"The objects of the University shall be to provide the inhabitants of the State with means of acquiring a thorough knowledge of the various branches of literature, science and the *arts.*"

Sec. 9—"There shall be *three* departments: first, that of literature, science and the *arts*." "There shall be established a professorship of the *fine arts*."

I trust that this paper may not be deemed prolix, if I affix to it some considerations that would demand the attention of the professor of art, and a general scheme of action and duty that he would be glad to see carried out. All the objects included in such a scheme could not be realized at once; but it is confidently believed that he would be able very speedily to impart interest to this new feature in the University, and to awaken in its behalf a deep sympathy with the student and faculty; and I cannot doubt this interest and sympathy would in no long period of time spread to different parts of the State, and that he might be the medium, through the peculiarly attractive and genial nature of art, to render substantial and lasting benefit to this Institution. Some of these considerations and duties I have placed under separate heads, for the greater convenience of reference, and that the whole scheme may be more readily comprehended, as well as that its practical bearing shall be more easily seen.

Department of the Fine Arts in the University of Michigan—some of the duties, and general course indicated, which might devolve on and be pursued by the professor of such department.

1. Lectures on *intellectual taste*—lectures on the *theory of art*—general idea—lectures on the principles of the different branches of art—painting, sculpture, architecture, music, &c.—their relation to each other—intimately united to poetry—the influence of the fine arts on the feelings, on the manners, on morals and literature, on civilization, and on the sciences.

2. Show the value of art to classical studies—illustrate these studies by busts of those distinguished in eloquence, poetry or statesmanship—by coins, medals and inscriptions, so valuable also to elucidate the history and antiquities of Rome and Greece—its union with Greek literature—impossibility to appreciate Grecian history, eloquence and poetry, without an intimate knowledge of Greek art; one is the exponent of the other; have a collection of the casts from the Elgin and Phygalian marbles, from antique busts, and from exquisite groups, such as the Psyche and Laocoon, say half the size of life.

All these can be obtained at small expense, and they would prove invaluable memorials of the heroic ages of literature and art.

3. Copies from some of the best paintings, to illustrate *composition* in painting, to illustrate the principles in coloring, and *light and shade;* good engravings from celebrated paintings. These will constitute a collection permanently belonging to the University. To this collection might be added such portraits of the professors, chancellors, and other distinguished persons who have been connected with the institution, as might be induced by invitation, or otherwise, to leave them. Art preserves a memory of the past and is conservative.

4. Students who wish can take lessons in *drawing, in perspective, in coloring, in composition.* This department will thus have a direct, practical bearing on the acquirements of the students, aside from the refined taste its teachings will inculcate. The services of the professor might be made useful to the medical department. The study of the natural sciences will be greatly facilitated by drawings, diagrams, and transparencies. It cannot be doubted that *art* will foster an attachment to the University.

5. It is believed that in all the German Universities the *fine arts* are represented by a professor. Lectures prevail there as a mode of teaching, more than in the English. The German is far more liberal. A well educated German is thoroughly acquainted with music, with the theory of the arts, and often with the principles of each.

6. We have already some examples—Columbia College, New York, has a professor of *fine arts,* a young man of that city. West Point has a professor of *fine arts.* Cambridge has a collection of pictures, and inculcates the fine arts as a branch of her teachings. New Haven College has erected a separate building for the reception of Col. Trumbull's pictures, and has thus an admirable series of works to illustrate art. It is there lessons of patriotism may be first imbibed; it is there the student will first contemplate the noble designs of the "Battle of Bunker Hill," "signing the Declaration of Independence," "Washington's resignation of his commission to Congress," with many others of a National interest.

The Smithsonian Institute has already purchased one valuable work of art, and is in treaty for Power's Greek Slave; showing that the arts will be included in the legitimate objects of an institution that proposes to diffuse knowledge among mankind. This does not pro-probably name all the institutions in our country that have provided for the teachings of art in the course of their studies. Several societies and institutions in Boston, New York, Philadelphia, Albany, Cincinnatti, established expressly to encourage a taste for art, and cordially sustained by the public, are not mentioned.

7. Every step taken in this country to sustain art, by whatever method, whether by societies, State legislatures, or Congress, has been promptly met by the public, showing that the public sentiment is quite ready to sanction the boldness or liberality of those whose province it is to take initiatory steps in such encouragement. Very many instances of this can be adduced.

8. Michigan has taken the lead in the liberal basis on which her educational system is founded. Is not this fact a strong reason that *now*, while the course of instruction is *falling into permanent methods*, that a department so important, so essential to the best and the most liberal culture as that comprehending the *fine arts*, should not be omitted or postponed, but immediately and with confidence incorporated with her more obviously practical branches.

Without venturing to extend the argument embodied in this paper, the whole subject is respectfully submitted to the wisdom and consideration of your honorable body.

ALVAH BRADISH.

PART II.

THE PRIMARY SCHOOL LAW OF MICHIGAN,

WITH

NOTES, FORMS, AND INSTRUCTIONS

FOR CONDUCTING PROCEEDINGS.

The law does not impose upon the Superintendent the duty of deciding questions arising under the operation of the school laws. It is, however, a matter of necessity that it should be done—the interest of the schools requires it, and the school officers seek for and demand such decisions. The consideration of all the questions which arise in the townships and districts, which are submitted to the office for its advice and decision, involves an amount of labor which is not generally conceived. Many of these questions are the more important, because they are intricate. They require examination, reflection, a knowledge of the general principles of law, and also a practical acquaintance and familiarity with the operation of the system. Great pains, thought, and labor have been bestowed upon this part of the subject, and it is believed the notes will be found to meet all, or nearly all, of the questions that are generally raised in the districts. The decisions given have been based upon queries of officers, embraced in their correspondence. Should this document not be swelled to a size which forbids it, abstracts of this correspondence will be presented, showing for themselves the difficulties which surround and embarrass school officers in the discharge of their duties, and in relation to which they require the advice of the Superintendent.

The law embraces all amendments made up to 1852. Those portions which are in brackets are amendments. The number of sections are the same as in the revised statutes of 1846. The decisions here made are not intended to infringe upon the province of any legal department or tribunal of the State. They are confined to questions arising under the operation and in the administration of the school law. In cases where the district stands in the light of a contracting party, or where the school officers have subjected themselves or the district to a controversy in a court of law, it is neither the duty or the province of the Superintendent to determine what are, or what are not, the legal rights of the parties. Provisions exist in the State of New York, and in some other States, conferring a more extended jurisdiction in cases arising under the school laws; and the decisions being made final, have saved a vast amount of litigation, expense and difficulty. A provision to this effect has been recommended in Michigan by each successive Superintendent. In his remarks upon the school law of Rhode Island, Mr. Barnard recommended it as leading to a cheap, speedy and amicable settlement of numerous controversies which unavoidably spring up in the local administration of the system, which were previously carried into the courts, or the Legislature, involving much expense, much delay, and not unfrequently bitter, wide spread and lasting dissatisfaction.

The laws of the State of New York authorize any person feeling himself aggrieved in consequence of any decision made by a school district meeting, or by the town superintendent, in forming, or altering, or in refusing to form or alter a school district, or in refusing to pay any school moneys to any such district, or by the trustees in paying any teacher, or refusing to pay him, or in refusing to admit any scholar gratuitously, or concerning any other matter under the law relating to schools, to appeal to the superintendent, who is required and authorized to examine and decide the same, and the decision is final and conclusive.

—

OF PRIMARY SCHOOLS.

DISTRICTS.

SECTION 1. Whenever the board of school inspectors of any township shall form a school district therein, it shall be the duty of the clerk of such board to deliver to a taxable inhabitant of such district, a notice in writing, of the formation of such district, describing its boundaries, and specifying the time and place of the first meeting; which notice, with the fact of such delivery, shall be entered upon record by the clerk.

1. The power to form school districts is vested in the board of school inspectors by section 71. In proceeding to divide the township, as this is the first step to be taken, a full record should be kept, showing not only the number of each district, but accurately describing the boundaries of each, in order that the clerk of the board, under this section, may be accurate in his description to be delivered to a taxable inhabitant. The following form of the notice required, is prescribed:

To A.—— B.——, a taxable inhabitant of school district No.——:

SIR—You are hereby notified that the school inspectors of the township of ———, on the —— day of ———, 185 , formed a school district in said township, which they numbered school district No. ——, and which is bounded as follows: [Insert the boundary as copied from the record.] The first meeting of said district will be held at ————, on the—— day of ———, 185 , at — o'clock in the ——noon: You are hereby directed to notify every qualified voter of said district, either personally or by leaving a written notice at his place of residence, of the time and place of said meeting, at least five days before the time appointed therefor, as above; and after so notifying every qualified voter within the boundaries above described, you will endorse on this notice a return, showing such notification, with the date or dates thereof, and deliver the same to the chairman of the meeting, to be held at the time and place above mentioned.

Given under my hand, this —— day of ———, A. D. 185 .

(Signed,) ————————,

Clerk of the Board of School Inspectors.

For form of endorsement upon this notice, see note to section 3.

2. A taxable inhabitant receiving the notice mentioned in this and the following section, who neglects or refuses duly to serve and return the notice required, is liable, by the provisions of section 129, to forfeit a penalty of five dollars.

3. The time and place of meeting is to be fixed by the inhabitant who is served with the notice.

SEC. 2. The said notice shall also direct such inhabitant to notify every qualified voter of such district, either personally or by leaving a written notice at his place of residence, of the time and place of said meeting, at least five days before the time appointed therefor; and it shall be the duty of such inhabitant to notify the qualified voters of said district accordingly.

1. To save question as to the sufficiency of time in giving the notice, five full days, without any fraction of a day, should be given before the day of meeting.

2. The written notice required by this section, need not contain a description of the boundaries of the district. It is sufficient if it specify the time and place of meeting, and if it is served at least five days before the meeting.

The following form may be used, viz:

To A—— B——:

SIR—School district No. ——, of the township of ———, having been formed by the inspectors, you are hereby notified, as a qualified voter therein, that the first meeting thereof will be held at ———, on the —— day of ———, A. D. 185 , at —— o'clock in the ——noon. Dated this —— day of ———, 185 .

(Signed) ——— ———.

3. If in notifying the qualified voters, by any unavoidable accident, or in consequence of the fact that a single person has not been notified, or several persons, who were not believed to be a resident or residents of the district, or by reason of an impossibility to notify such person or persons, from the absence of himself, or the want of a place of residence temporarily, such want of notice does not affect the validity of the organization by the majority of the qualified voters. The law is imperative upon the inhabitant serving the notice, to notify every qualified voter, and the failure to do so affects him personally, and the proceedings of the district also, only where the omission has been *wilful or fraudulent.* See section 14.

SEC. 3. The said inhabitant, when he shall have notified the qualified voters as required in such notice, shall endorse thereon a return, showing such notification, with the date or dates thereof, and deliver such notice and return to the chairman of the meeting.

The following FORM OF ENDORSEMENT is recommended. If the qualified voters are all notified in one day, the form may be varied, but it will be found to be more satisfactory, and often save trouble, to give the names and dates of notification according to the form, and also for the greater facility it will afford to the director to record it, as required by section 4:

I, A—— B——, hereby return the within (or annexed) notice, and have notified the qualified voters of the district as follows:

NAMES.	DATE.	HOW NOTIFIED.
A—— B——,	January 1, 1852.	Personally.
C—— D——,	do do	Written notice.

Dated at ———, this —— day of ———, 185 .

(Signed) D——— E———.

1. Every chairman of the first district meeting, who wilfully neglects or refuses to perform the duties enjoined on him in this and the following sections, or in the chapter relating to primary schools, shall forfeit the sum of $5. See section 129.

2. The meeting must organize by the appointment of a chairman; and must then choose its district officers. The acceptance of any two of the officers elected duly organizes the district, and these may be filed forthwith, in pursuance of section 6. Section 130 imposes a penalty for neglect or refusal, without sufficient cause, to accept any such office, and serve therein. If the notice has not been given, or the qualified voters fail entirely to attend, when notified, the notice must be renewed, but no particular number is requisite to enable the district to effect its organization, after proper notice.

SEC. 4. The said chairman shall deliver such notice and return to the director chosen at such meeting, who shall record the same at length in a book to be provided by him at the expense of the district, as a part of the records of such district.

1. By section 9 the record here required is made *prima facia* evidence of the facts set forth, and of the legality of all proceedings in the organization of the district, prior to the first district meeting. It is important that it should be correct and complete. In case of the want of this record, its destruction or loss, it cannot be supplied. But if the district has exercised the franchises of a district, that is, elected officers, voted tax, employed teachers, made reports, &c., for two years, (section 10,) its organization is presumed to be legal.

SEC. 5. The qualified voters of such district, when assembled pursuant to such previous notice, and also at each annual meeting, shall choose a moderator, director, and assessor, [who shall be residents of such district, and] who shall, within ten days after such meeting, severally file with the director a written acceptance of the offices to which they shall have been respectively elected, which shall be recorded by said director.

1. The qualified voters at this meeting, after having elected district officers, cannot proceed to transact any other business, by voting a tax, or for any other purpose than the *organization* of the district. This is a meeting to choose a moderator, director and assessor. An addition to section 92 provides that in districts containing more than one hundred scholars between the ages of four and eighteen, the district board may be enlarged by adding thereto four trustees, provided the district determine to do so, at any *annual meeting*, by a two-thirds vote. This vote cannot be taken at the first meeting of the district.

2. The law is not definite as to the form of the acceptance. It must be in writing, and filed with the *director* within ten days after the meeting. Every acceptance should specify the office to which the person has been chosen. Each should be filed separately, to avoid confusion and error. The *fact* of the filing by the person elected to a given office, and the *date* of filing, are matters of record, to be made by the director. A mere *clerical* error, in the acceptance, will not vitiate it. If it is not in the precise words of the prescribed form, it is not the province of the director to decide upon its sufficiency or insufficiency, in case of question. In case of doubt, however, it would be a safe course for the person chosen to the office to decline serving, for the reason that if he has not filed his acceptance legally, he could not bind the district by his acts, but would himself be bound by his own acts.

3. After filing acceptance, the new officers supercede the old ones at once. District officers are not required to file an oath of office. Section 130 imposes a penalty for neglect or refusal of district officers to serve without sufficient cause, or for neglecting or refusing to perform any duty required by virtue of their offices.

4. If a newly elected district officer fails to file his acceptance, the previous officer holds over, and there is no *vacancy* to fill, unless the previous director has been in office ten days beyond the time of a second annual meeting after his election or appointment.

FORM OF ACCEPTANCE.

I accept the office of ——— of school district No. ——, of the township of ———. Dated this —— day of ———, 185 .
(Signed) A——— B———.

On the back of this should be endorsed: "Filed this —— day of ———, 185 . C——— D———, Director."

SEC. 6. Every such school district shall be deemed duly organized when any two of the officers elected at their first annual meeting shall have filed their acceptance as aforesaid.

SEC. 7. In case the inhabitants of any district shall fail to organize the same in pursuance of such notice as aforesaid, the said clerk shall give a new notice in the manner hereinbefore provided, and the same proceedings shall be had thereon as if no previous notice had been delivered.

SEC. 8. Every school district organized in pursuance of this chapter, or which has been organized and continued under any previous law of the State or Territory of Michigan, shall be a body corporate, and shall possess the usual powers of a corporation for public purposes, by the name and style of "School District number ———, (such number as shall be designated in the formation thereof by the inspectors) of ————," (the name of the township or townships in which the district is situated,) and in that name shall be capable of suing and being sued, and of holding such real and personal estate as is authorized to be purchased by the provisions of this chapter, and of selling the same.

SEC. 9. The record made by the director, as required in the fourth section of this chapter, shall be *prima facia* evidence of the facts therein set forth, and the legality of all proceedings in the organization of the district prior to the first district meeting; but nothing in this section contained shall be so construed as to impair the effect of the record kept by the school inspectors, as evidence.

SEC. 10. Every school district shall, in all cases, be presumed to have been legally organized, when it shall have exercised the franchises and privileges of a district for the term of two years.

The last above five sections, in addition to those which precede them, relate entirely to the formation and organization of school districts, each step being carefully taken. Section 8 provides that the district shall be a body corporate, possessing also the powers of a corporation for public purposes, and capable, under the name and number designated by the inspectors, of suing and being sued, and holding real and personal estate, and selling the same, as provided in this chapter. The statute nowhere contemplates the dissolution of a school district, nor does it directly confer upon any board the power to dissolve the body corporate. Nor can the board of inspectors, under the provisions of section 71, which authorize them "to divide the township into such number of school districts as may from time to time be necessary; (the boundaries of which districts they may alter and regulate, as circumstances shall render proper,") take any action in relation to the *dissolution* of a district, so as to work any change of the previous liability of the district, except in the manner pointed out in the formation of a new district, by sections 75, 76, 77 and 78. In 1843, the *possible dissolution* of a district was sought to be guarded against, and to prevent it in any way, penalties were sought to be and were subsequently imposed upon school officers who neglected to perform, or refused to do their duty, or serve in the offices to which they were chosen. Applications to dissolve these corporate bodies have in several instances been made to the Legislature, which has acted specifically upon them, but which has not conferred upon the board of school inspectors such a power. The revised constitution has provided that the Legislature may confer upon townships, cities and villages, and boards of supervisors, such powers of a local, legislative or administrative character as it may deem advisable; but the Legislature not having seen fit to enact any law upon the subject, the power of dissolving school districts is still vested in the Legislature.

The division of a township by an act of the Legislature, when no provision is made otherwise, does not dissolve nor alter the boundaries of a school district. The imaginary township line changes no residence of the district officers, but upon such division of townships or counties, single or whole districts are by operation of law transformed into *joint* school districts, and become of necessity subject to the provisions applicable to such districts. But a single instance of this kind is believed to have occurred, however, in this State.

DISTRICT MEETINGS.

SEC. 11. The annual meetings of such *(each)* school district shall be held on the last Monday of September in each year, and the school year commence on that day.

1. The annual meetings of school districts are the most important occasions which the law provides for the regulation of all matters pertaining to the schools. It has been justly remarked that "the opportunities afforded by the coming together of the inhabitants of each district, for deliberation and consultation in relation to their schools, and the various interests connected therewith, are calculated to exert a most beneficial influence in favor of education; to promote union, harmony and concert of action in the several districts; and to cement the ties of friendly, social intercourse between those having a common interest in the moral and intellectual culture of their children. It is therefore of the utmost importance that they should not be neglected; that the inhabitants should be prompt and uniform in their attendance, and that the proceedings should be invariably characterized by that order, regularity, dignity and decorum which can alone command respect and efficiently attain the objects to be accomplished."

The powers of the qualified voters at the annual meetings, are fully prescribed in sections 19, 20, 21, 22, 23, 24, 25, 26 and 27. The moderator presides at all meetings when present, and sections 30 and 31 give to the moderator, or person presiding, (see section 29,) the power to preserve order and prevent disturbance. Section 37 makes the director clerk of the meeting, but in his absence the qualified voters appoint a clerk, who is to certify the proceedings of the meeting to the director. It is the duty of the latter to preserve copies of all reports, and *preserve and keep* all books and papers belonging to his office.

FORM OF NOTICE OF ANNUAL MEETING.

NOTICE is hereby given that the annual meeting of school district No. ——, of the township of ———, for the election of school district officers, and for the transaction of such other business as may lawfully come before it, and deemed to be necessary, will be held at ———, on Monday the ——— day of ———, A. D. 185 , at —— o'clock in the —— noon.

Dated this ——— day of ———, A. D. 185 .

(Signed,) A—— B——, *Director.*

This notice must be posted in three of the most public places in the district, at least six days before the time of such meeting. [Six *full* days without any fraction of a day.]

1. Annual meetings may be adjourned from time to time, as may be necessary, in which case the following form of notice should be posted, as above required:

Notice is hereby given, that a meeting of the qualified voters of school district No. ——, of the township of ———, will be held at ———, on the ——— day of ———, 185 , at ——— o'clock in the —— noon of said day, pursuant to adjournment of the annual meeting. Dated this —— day of ———, 185 .

(Signed,) A—— B——, *Director.*

2. The qualified voters present at *any* meeting lawfully assembled, may re-consider, rescind, alter or modify any proceeding, action, or vote taken at an annual meeting, *provided* no obligation has been incurred under such previous proceedings, votes or resolves.

2. The proceedings of a district meeting, either annual, adjourned or special, are not to be deemed illegal for want of due notice, unless it appears that the omission was wilful and fraudulent.

3. Trouble is sometimes made by the failure of the qualified voters present to exercise discretion in relation to organizing the meeting. Due allowance should be made for variation in time, and a reasonable time should be given for all the voters to assemble before proceeding to business. Fifteen minutes or half an hour, according to circumstances, might not be unreasonable. Any number, however few, may then proceed to the transaction of the business of the district, or they may, if they think proper, adjourn. The latter, in many instances, might be the prudent course. If the meet-

ing is unanimous in favor of the officers to be chosen, it will oftentimes save trouble by offering a resolution in writing, designating the officers and offices; but if a difference of opinion exists, it would be well to vote by ballot. All other business should be done by written resolutions, and if the result of the vote cannot be ascertained in the ordinary manner, it should be done by count or by taking the ayes and noes. For this purpose the clerk of the meeting should prepare a list of the legal voters of the district in a tabular form, embracing all the subjects voted on, similar to the following:

NAMES OF VOTERS.	TO CHANGE SITE.		TO BUILD SC. H'SE		TO RAISE TAX.	
	Ayes.	Noes.	Ayes.	Noes.	Ayes.	Noes.
A—— B——,						
C—— D——,						
TOTAL, ...						

The clerk should keep his minutes so that, before the meeting adjourns, they may be read and corrected, if necessary, and approved by the meeting; and after being signed by the moderator and clerk, they should be recorded in the record book of the district. These minutes should be in form as follows, varied to suit the circumstances:

FORM FOR MINUTES OF PROCEEDINGS TO BE KEPT BY THE DISTRICT CLERK.

At an annual, special, or adjourned (as the case may be) meeting of the qualified voters of school district No. ——, of the township of ———, held at the ———, on the —— day of ———, A. D. 185 , pursuant to public notice, the moderator presiding, (or A—— B—— was chosen to preside, the moderator not being present,) and C—— D—— was present as clerk, (or E—— F—— was appointed clerk, in the absence of the director:)

Resolved, &c., [here insert the resolutions as passed,] If the vote was unanimous, *Resolved, unanimously*, &c.

In case of a vote to designate or to change the site, *two thirds* of the qualified voters present are necessary. In this case, after taking the vote as indicated above, the record should state substantially as follows:

It having been moved and seconded that the present site of the school house in the said district be established, (or changed,) or that the same shall be, &c., [here describe the locality and premises, accurately,] and the question being taken by ayes and noes, (or by ballot or otherwise,) it was carried, two-thirds of the voters present voting therefor, as follows: Those who voted in the affirmative were as follows [Here insert names in full:] Those who voted in the negative were as follows: [Insert names.]

Ayes, ——; Noes, ——; Total, ——.

The above form is given as a general guide, and of course may be varied as the director finds it necessary.

SEC. 12. Special meetings may be called by the district board, or by any one of them, on the written request of any five legal voters of the district, by giving the notice required in the next succeeding section; and in all notices of special meetings the object of the meeting shall be stated.

1. The *district board* may call a special meeting without the written request required in this section. Any *one* of the district board may call a special meeting on such written request. A form of notice will be found below, in which it is provided that the object of the meeting shall be set forth in the *request*, so that any member of the board calling such meeting, may incorporate it, verbatim, in his *notice*. It is not optional with the member or members of the district board, to call a meeting or not, but they are bound to do so, upon the request of five legal voters.

FORM OF WRITTEN REQUEST.

To the district board of school district No. ——: [*or to A—— B——, &c., one of the district board:*]

The undersigned, legal voters of school district No. ——, of the township of ———, request you, in pursuance of section 12 of the primary school law, to call a special meeting of said district, for the purpose of ——— ———, [Describe the objects of the meeting.]

Dated this —— day of ———, A. D. 185 .

(Signed,) ——— ———,
——— ———,
——— ———,
——— ———,
——— ———.

SEC. 13. All notices of annual or special district meetings, after the first meeting has been held as aforesaid, shall specify the day and hour, and place of meeting, and shall be given at least six days previous to such meeting, by posting up copies thereof in three of the most public places in the district: and in case of any special meeting, called for the purpose of establishing or changing the site of a school house, such notice shall be given at least ten days previous thereto.

FORM OF NOTICE OF SPECIAL MEETING.

SCHOOL DISTRCT NOTICE.—Notice is hereby given to the taxable inhabitants of school district No. ——, of the township of ——, that in pursuance of a written request of five legal voters of said district, a special meeting of said district will be held at ——, on —— the —— day of ——, A. D. 185 , at —— o'clock in the —— noon of said day. The object of said meeting is ——. [Here describe the object in full.]

Dated the —— day of —— 185 .

(Signed,) A—— B——.

The written request to the board, or any one of them, should be filed with the clerk and made a part of the record. The number of days designated for posting up the notice, either six or ten, as specified, should be *full* days.

1. A special meeting may adjourn from time to time, in which case like notices should be posted as are required in case of adjournment of annual meetings. When a special meeting has been called, and adjourns to a specified time and place, and at such time and place acts upon questions properly before it, under the notice, and again *adjourns* without day, or without specifying further time and place, the inhabitants cannot afterwards re-organize the meeting under the notice.

2. If a portion of the qualified voters, without reference to their number, at any meeting, assemble at the proper time and place, as designated in the notice, they may proceed to business. If they adjourn after transacting the business before them, and another portion of the qualified voters assemble after the vote to adjourn has been taken and carried, they cannot hold a subsequent meeting, re-organize, nor pass any vote, legally binding on the district, under the same notice. If, however, after the meeting has proceeded to business, there is an accession of legal voters, before an adjournment, any vote or resolution previously taken at the same meeting, may be reconsidered or rescinded, and the meeting may proceed to transact their business as a majority present shall determine.

3. The $1 tax, provided for in section 140, may be voted at a special meeting called for that purpose; but the district board cannot return such tax in any year to the supervisor, *for such year*, if voted after the annual meeting. The tax may be voted after the annual meeting, but it must be returned to the supervisor of the *next suc-*

ceeding year. This vote would be subject to be rescinded at the subsequent annual meeting. If it is not rescinded, it would be the duty of the district board to return the amount to the supervisor, as required in section 56.

4. A special meeting called for that purpose, may make a disposition of the public moneys, although the subject was acted upon at the annual meeting, under the same restrictions as the reconsideration of any other vote. If any obligation has been incurred, under the previous vote, the special meeting could not legally interfere with their former action in the premises.

5. A contract made with a teacher, by a director, as the law provides, (section 39,) cannot be annulled by vote at a special meeting.

6. A special meeting cannot determine any of the matters embraced in section 24. This duty is vested exclusively with the district board.

7. The qualified voters, at a special meeting, called under a notice specifying the object of the meeting to be to take measures to build a school house, have no power to designate a site. The object or objects of the special meeting must be fully and definitely stated in the notice.

Sec. 14. No district meeting shall be deemed illegal for want of due notice, unless it shall appear that the omission to give such notice was wilful and fraudulent.

1. A change of the usual hour of holding a district meeting, for instance, a notice fixing the time at 5 o'clock P. M., instead of 6 o'clock, (the usual hour,) will not invalidate the proceedings of the meeting held under it, unless the qualified voters have previously designated some other hour than that mentioned in the notice, for the hour of meeting, and the notice was wilful and fraudulent. There is a customary hour, but the district board may fix the time and place of the meeting, and the inhabitants are bound to *notice* the time as affixed in the call posted up according to law.

2. As the proceedings of the district meeting may be called in question, in the course of legal proceedings relating to taxes, or contracts, or other matters of importance to the district and to individuals, the qualified voters should not transact business, if there is any reason to believe that the omission to give the notice was wilful and fraudulent. The only safe course is to run no hazard whatever, under such circumstances.

SEC. 15. Every white male inhabitant of the age of twenty-one years, residing in the district, and liable to pay a school district tax therein, shall be entitled to vote at any district meeting.

1. Every white male inhabitant of the age of twenty-one years, *whether alien or citizen*, residing in the district, *having personal or real estate* assessed to him, or *subject to be assessed to him in the district*, is a voter at a district meeting. The property not subject to assessment and taxation is specified in Act 94 of the session laws of 1849. It exempts,

1. Household furniture, including stoves put up in any dwelling house, not exceeding in value one hundred dollars. 2. All spinning wheels and weaving looms and apparatus, not exceeding in value fifty dollars. 3. A seat, pew or slip occupied by any person or family in any house or place of public worship. 4. All cemeteries, tombs and rights of burial, while in use as repositories of the dead. 5. All arms and accoutrements required by law to be kept by any person or family; all wearing apparel of every person and family. 6. The library and school books of every individual and family not exceeding in value $150, and all family pictures. 7. To each householder, ten sheep with their fleeces, and the yarn or cloth manufactured from the same, two cows, five swine, and provisions and fuel for the comfortable subsistence of such householder and family for six months.

SEC. 16. If any person offering to vote at a school district meeting shall be challenged as unqualified, by any legal voter in such district, the chairman presiding at such meeting shall declare to the person challenged the qualifications of a voter, and if such person shall state that he is qualified, and the challenge shall not be withdrawn, the said chairman shall tender to him an oath in substance as follows: "You do swear (or affirm) that you are twenty-one years of age, that you are an actual resident of this school district, and liable to pay a school district tax therein;" and every person taking such oath shall be permitted to vote on all questions proposed at such meeting.

By reference to the note under the last preceding section, the chairman will readily see what qualifications are necessary for a voter at a school district meeting, viz: He must be a white male inhabitant of the State, of the age of 21 years; he must be a resident of the district; he must be liable to pay a *school disirict tax*. Every such inhabitant is liable to pay such a tax, whether he is an alien or a citizen, if he has either personal or real estate which has been assessed to him, or which is liable to be assessed to him, in the district. The property not subject to taxation is described under the previous section.

SEC. 17. If any person so challenged shall refuse to take such oath, his vote shall be rejected; and any person who shall wilfully take a false oath, or make a false affirmation, under the provisions of the preceding section, shall be deemed guilty of perjury.

SEC. 18. When any question is taken in any other manner than by ballot, a challenge immediately after the vote has been taken, shall be deemed to be made when offering to vote, and treated in the same manner.

SEC. 19. The qualified voters in such school district, when lawfully assembled, shall have power to adjourn from time to time, as may be necessary; to designate a site for a school house by a vote of two-thirds of those present, and to change the same by a similar vote at any regular meeting.

1. For manner of voting, &c., see note to section 11.

2. In some instances, districts have been unable, after designating a site, to procure a conveyance or title to the property, the owner or owners refusing to give a deed of the premises. Section 2 of article 18 of the revised constitution, provides for taking property for such purposes; but as the Legislature has not prescribed the manner in which it shall be done, no remedy is afforded by law in such cases.

3. The site for a school house should be designated with exactness and precision, either by metes and bounds, or by some defined and known landmarks. The safe rule is to make such a description as would be required in a deed of the premises. In designating a site, sufficient land should be procured for a school yard, play ground, necessary out buildings, and wood house, &c.

4. In case of sale of the site, (see section 59,) the district board may, if not otherwise directed by vote of the district, execute a conveyance of the same, in the corporate name of the district. In most instances, deeds of the site are executed with the right of reversion to the owner, when it ceases to be occupied for school purposes. In such cases, of course, the district cannot dispose of the site. When it does not revert to the owner, and the sale is directed under section 26, the district may appropriate the money arising from the sale, as they shall deem best, for *school purposes*.

5. The qualified voters cannot authorize the school inspectors, or any other person, to designate the site, *in the first instance*. They must establish it, if they can. If, after taking action, they fail to obtain the legal majority necessary, (two-thirds of those present,) the inspectors may designate under the provisions of section 20.

6. This section provides that the qualified voters may, by a two-thirds vote of those present, *change* the site. This can be done either before the school house has been built, or afterwards; but in the latter case, upon assuming the responsibility of paying full damages for any violation of contract which may have been previously entered into, and a *forfeiture* of the site, if the conveyance thereof was originally made for school purposes.

7. In purchasing a site, or selling, a sufficient sum may be lawfully voted to cover the expenses of procuring or perfecting the title. If it has not been voted, the district board may procure the necessary legal or professional assistance at the expense of the district. [See section 59.]

SEC. 20. When no site can be established, by such inhabitants as aforesaid, the school inspectors of the township or townships in which the district is situated, shall determine where such site shall be, and their determination shall be certified to the director of the district, and shall be final, subject to alteration afterwards by the inspectors only, if necessary.

1. The failure of the inhabitants to establish the site should be certified to the board of inspectors of the township; or in case of fractional district, to the joint boards, by the clerk of the meeting, or a certified copy of the proceedings and vote delivered to them or to their clerk, which should be kept of record. Their determination is to be certified to the director of the district in some form similar to the following:

The board of school inspectors (or a majority thereof) do hereby certify to the director of school district No. ——, of the township of ———, (the inhabitants of said district, at a legal meeting of said district, having failed to establish a site for the school house in said district by a legal majority thereof,) that the said inspectors have determined that the said site shall be as follows: [describe as in a deed.]

Given under our hands this —— day of ——— A. D. 185 .

A—— B——,
C—— D——,
E—— F——,
Inspectors.

SEC. 21. The said qualified voters shall also have power at any such meeting to direct the purchasing or leasing of an appropriate site, and the building, hiring or purchasing of a school house, and to impose such tax as may be sufficient for the payment thereof, subject to the limitation contained in the succeeding section.

1. A vote to purchase or lease a site, or to build, hire, or purchase a school house, does not carry with it any authority for the district board to purchase, hire or lease, or to build a school house, or to

purchase material, or contract for the building, without a further *direction to that effect.* (See section 59.)

SEC. 22. The amount of taxes to be raised in any district for the purpose of purchasing or building a school house, shall not exceed the sum of two hundred dollars in any one year, unless there shall be more than thirty scholars residing therein, between the ages of four and eighteen years; and the amount thereof shall not exceed three hundred dollars in any one year, unless there shall be more than fifty scholars residing in the district between the ages last aforesaid; and no sum shall be raised exceeding one hundred and eighty dollars for the purpose of building or purchasing a school house of less dimensions than twenty-four feet by thirty feet, and ten feet between floors; nor exceeding seventy-five dollars for the purpose of building or purchasing a school house, constructed of round or hewn logs.

1. Although but two hundred dollars can be raised in any one year, in a district, in which there not more than thirty scholars between the ages of four and eighteen years; and but three hundred dollars where there is not more than fifty scholars, between these ages, yet the district, if they desire to build a more costly house, may lawfully raise either of these sums *annually,* until a sufficient sum is raised to meet the wants of the district. In case there are over fifty scholars, the sum which may be raised is not limited, except as to the amount to be expended for buildings of the different *dimensions* specified in this section. The operation of this section is in a measure controlled by section 79, which forbids the district board, in purchasing or leasing a site, (such as shall be designated by the district,) or in building, hiring or purchasing a school house out of the fund provided for that purpose, from building any *stone* or *brick* school house on any site, without having first obtained a title in fee, or a lease for ninety-nine years; and from building any frame school house upon any site for which they have not a title in fee, or a lease for fifty years, *without securing the privilege of removing* the house, when lawfully directed so to do by the qualified voters, at any annual or special meeting.

2. Any lawfully organized school district, *which has kept up its organization,* can vote at any meeting regularly called, in pursuance of preceding provisions, *not to exceed* $200 in any one year, for the purpose of purchasing or building a school house, unless the district has more than thirty scholars residing in it, between the ages of four and eighteen years. If the number between these ages is no more than fifty, the district can vote *not to exceed* $300 in any one year.

Suppose there is forty scholars between these ages—the district can raise $3J0 and no more. Suppose there is fifty-one scholars, or over—the amount which can be raised is not then limited. The latter clause of the section limits the amount so far *as buildings of certain dimensions* are constructed.

A district may raise the sum of eighty dollars annually to build a frame house of *greater* dimensions than 24 by 30 feet; but no sum can be raised in any series of years exceeding one hundred and eighty dollars for a school house of *less* dimensions than this. The object of the law is to prevent a wasteful or extravagant expenditure of money upon a building of comparatively small size.

3. In order to raise money for these purposes, so as to have it collected in the assessment roll of the same year, the vote must be passed at the *annual* meeting for that year. In order to have the money collected in the assessment roll of 1852, for instance, the vote must be taken at the annual meeting of 1852. This is on the last Monday of September. By the second Monday of October following, the district board report the amount to be raised to the supervisor, and the supervisor puts it into his assessment roll by the 15th of November following.

4. The qualified voters, after voting a tax to build a school house under the restrictions of sections 22 and 59, may in directing the board, authorize them to contract with a third person or party, to build an additional story to the school building at the expense of such party, but on the condition that it shall never interfere in any way with the rights of the district or the purposes of the school or school house. The district cannot form a *partnership* with a third party in purchasing site or building the house. The site must belong to the district, or the lease vest in the district alone. Such contracts can only be viewed in the light of a *privilege*, granted by the inhabitants of the district, the use of which is not in any way to interfere with the legitimate purposes for which the building was erected, viz: for a school house. With these restrictions and this understanding, there can be no valid objection to such an arrangement. Without detriment to the school, or a disturbance of its functions and arrangements, additional taste may be displayed in the architecture of the school house, and some useful purpose of an in-

dividual or society subserved. For the protection of all parties in such cases, writings of the proper character should be carefully and legally drawn.

5. District officers, when directed by the district to contract for building the school house, should not let the contract to themselves. They may, *when so directed by the district*, proceed to procure materials and build the house under their own control and management, and in such manner as shall be for the interest of the district. The district may, if the voters see fit, appoint a building committee. The directions of the district to the board, or to the committee, may either be general or specific.

SEC. 23. Such qualified voters, when assembled as aforesaid, may from time to time impose such tax as shall be necessary to keep their school house in repair, and to provide the necessary appendages, and to pay and discharge any debts or liabilities of the district lawfully incurred: and in districts containing more than fifty scholars between the ages of four and eighteen years, may raise a sum not exceeding twenty dollars in any one year for the purchase of globes, outline maps, or any apparatus for illustrating the principles of [astronomy, natural philosophy and] agricultural chemistry or the mechanic arts.

1. The effect of this section is to limit the power of school districts having less than 50 scholars. In districts having less than that number, a tax cannot be raised for the purposes mentioned in the last clause. This provision is a useful and important one. Outline maps, globes, apparatus, &c., for illustrating the studies pursued, are important and indeed indispensable elements of success in teaching and in learning. The views of the Deputy Superintendent of the State of New York (Mr. Randall) meet with the hearty concurrence of this department of public instruction. He says, with truth, that "the principal facts in Geography (for instance) are better learned *by the eye* than in any other manner, and there ought to be in every school room, a map of the world, of the United States, of the State, and of the county. Globes are also desirable, but not so important as maps. Large black boards in frames or plaster are indispensable to a well conducted school. The operations in arithmetic performed on them, enable the teacher to ascertain the degree of the pupil's acquirement better than any results exhibited on slates. He sees the various steps taken by the scholar, and can require him to give the reason for each. It is in fact an exercise of the entire class; and the whole school, by this public process, insensibly ac-

quires a knowledge of the rules and operations of this branch of study."

2. The above views are earnestly commended to district officers, as philosophical and sound. The object had in view by the Legislature, in enacting this clause of the school law, is worthy of more attention than it has hitherto received. The subjects of agricultural chemistry and the mechanic arts are yet destined to become more important branches of instruction in our primary schools. Public attention is directed to them with greater earnestness, as they constitute, and will continue to constitute, the foundation of the two great practical pursuits of the citizens of this country.

3. Under this section a tax may be voted and raised for a fence, woodhouse, and necessary out-buildings, for a bell, if the voters desire to have one, for water-pail, cup, for washing apparatus, sink and drain; and in short, for all such appendages as are necessary to secure the health, comfort and convenience of the children while attending school, and to afford the usual and best facilities which can be afforded for keeping a good school, in all respects.

Sec. 24. They may also determine, at each annual meeting, the length of time a school shall be taught in their district during the ensuing year, which shall not be less than three months; and whether by male or female teachers, or both; and whether the moneys apportioned for the support of the school therein shall be applied to the winter or summer term, or a certain portion of each.

1. The month, as fixed by the laws of the State, is to be construed to mean a calendar month. This gives four and one-third weeks, or twenty-six days for a month, exclusive of Sundays. By a custom which is time-honored and nearly universal, the teacher should be permitted to dismiss his school on the afternoon of every Saturday, or all day every other Saturday, *without loss* of time. He should also be allowed to dismiss his school upon all holydays—on the 4th of July, New Year's, Thanksgiving, Christmas, days of fasting and prayer, set apart by the Chief Magistrate, Washington's birth day, and general biennial election days, without loss of time. (See note to section 39, and the form of contract for teacher.)

Sec. 25. In case any of the matters in the preceding section mentioned, are not determined at the annual meeting, the district board shall have power, and it shall be their duty, to determine the same.

1. The determination of the board is binding on the district until the next annual meeting.

SEC. 26. Said qualified voters may also, at any regular meeting, authorize and direct the sale of any school house, site, building, or other property belonging to the district, when the same shall no longer be needed for the use of the district.

1. See note 4 to section 19, page 351.

SEC. 27. They may also give such directions, and make such provisions as they shall deem necessary, in relation to the prosecution or defence of any suit or proceeding in which the district may be a party or interested.

1. The qualified voters may, under this section, employ counsel, and vote a tax to pay for such services, if they do not choose to leave the control of such matters to the officers designated by the law to attend to them.

DISTRICT OFFICERS—THEIR POWERS AND DUTIES.

SEC. 28. The officers of each school district shall be a moderator, director and assessor, who shall hold their respective offices until the annual meeting next following their election or appointment, and until their successors shall have been chosen and filed their acceptance, but not beyond ten days after the time of a second annual meeting after their election or appointment, without being again elected or appointed.

1. District officers cannot hold over their offices beyond ten days *after the time* of a second annual meeting after their election or appointment. If, after the district officers are once chosen, the district neglects to hold its next annual meeting, and holds its subsequent *second* annual meeting, without electing officers, or adjourns its meeting beyond *ten days* after the time of the last meeting, the terms of the old officers then expire, and the district is without officers. The mode of procedure under such circumstances is the same as that which is required in the formation of a new district.

MODERATOR.

SEC. 29. The moderator shall have power, and it shall be his duty, to preside at all meetings of the district, to sign all warrants for the collection of rate bills after they shall have been prepared and signed by the director, and to countersign all orders upon the assessor for moneys to be disbursed by the district, and all warrants of the director upon the township treasurer for moneys raised for district purposes, or apportioned to the district by the township clerk; but if the moderator shall be absent from any district meeting, the qualified voters present may elect a suitable person to preside at the meeting.

1. The person *appointed* to preside at the meeting has only the power to act for that meeting. It will not vitiate the proceedings of the meeting if such person prove to be a *minor*. This question has been repeatedly raised, but it would be well to avoid the raising of the question, by appointing a person who, beyond any exception which may be raised, has the legal qualifications of a voter.

2. The moderator is not bound to countersign orders drawn by the director, where they are not drawn in pursuance of law, or where they are drawn for any purpose other than the objects for which the money raised was appropriated. He would not render himself liable for refusing to countersign an order drawn by the director, to pay the "public money" to a teacher who is not a *qualified* teacher, such as the law requires. Instances have come to the notice of this department, where orders have been drawn by directors to pay teachers who were not "qualified teachers." The moderator in such cases may, and should, refuse to countersign the order. He, however, should be careful, to ascertain that the teacher is in fact not a "qualified teacher." It should appear clearly and legally that he was not so, to authorize the moderator to refuse his counter-signature.

SEC. 30. If, at any district meeting, any person shall conduct himself in a disorderly manner, and after notice from the moderator or person presiding, shall persist therein, the moderator or person presiding may order him to withdraw from the meeting, and on his refusal, may order any constable or other person or persons to take him into custody until the meeting shall be adjourned.

SEC. 31. Any person who shall refuse to withdraw from such meeting, on being so ordered as provided in the preceding section, or who shall wilfully disturb such meeting, shall, for every such offence, forfeit a sum not exceeding twenty dollars.

ASSESSOR.

SEC. 32. The assessor shall pay over all moneys in his hands belonging to the district, on the warrant of the director, countersigned by the moderator; and shall collect all rate bills for tuition and fuel, in obedience to the command contained in the warrant annexed thereto.

1. In collecting the rate bill, the assessor proceeds in the same manner as the township treasurer does in the collection of other taxes.

2. When a *judgment* is obtained against a school district, it is the duty of the assessor to notify the supervisor of the amount. (Section 125.)

SEC. 33. In case any person shall neglect or refuse to pay the amount on such rate bill for which he is liable, on demand, the assesser shall collect the same by distress and sale of any goods or chattels of such person, wherever found within any county in which the district, or any part of it, is situated.

1. The form of procedure under this section, in case of neglect or refusal, is similar to that of a constable upon sale and execution. Notice should be given in the same way; and property may be sold

as it is in the collection of any other *tax* assessed and collected by law.

SEC. 34. The assessor shall give at least ten days' notice of such sale, by posting up written notices thereof in three public places in the township where such property shall be sold.

SEC. 35. At the expiration of his warrant, the assessor shall make a return thereof, in writing, with the rate bill attached, to the director; stating the amount on said rate bill collected, the amount uncollected, and the names of the persons from whom collections have not been made.

1. For form of warrant see section 45. The return, which should be made upon a separate sheet of paper, with warrant and rate bill attached, may be in the following form:

I, A—— B——, assessor of school district No. ——, township of ——, do hereby make this my return of the annexed warrant with rate bill attached, and certify the amount collected on said rate bill to be the sum of —— dollars and —— cents; the amount uncollected, —— dollars and —— cents; and that the following are the names of persons from whom collections have not been made, and the amounts which are uncollected from each person:

NAMES.	$	
A—— B——,		
C—— D——,		

Dated this —— day of ——, A. D. 185 .

(Signed,) A—— B——, *Assessor.*

The assessor's warrant runs from the time it was placed in his hands for collection. In case the assessor fails to execute his bond, see section 67.

FORM OF ASSESSOR'S BOND.

Know all men by these presents, that we, A—— B——, (the assessor of school district No. ——, in the township of ——,) C—— D—— and E—— F——, (his surety,) are held and firmly bound unto the said district, in the sum of [here insert a sum of double the amount to come into the assessor's hands,] to be paid to the said district; for the payment of which sum well and truly to be made, we bind ourselves, our heirs, executors and administrators, jointly and severally, firmly by these presents. Sealed with our seals, and dated this —— day of ——, A. D. 185 .

The condition of this obligation is such, that if A—— B——, assessor of said district, shall faithfully apply all moneys that shall come into his hands by virtue of his office, then this obligation shall be void; otherwise of full force and virtue.

A—— B——, [L. S.]
C—— D——, [L. S.]
E—— F——, [L. S.]

Signed, sealed and delivered in presence of [two witnesses.]

SEC. 36. The assessor shall appear for and on behalf of the district, in all suits brought by or against the same, when no other directions shall be given by the qualified voters in district meeting, except in suits in which he is interested adversely to the district, and in all such cases the director shall appear for such district, if no other direction be given as aforesaid.

1. See note to section 27. See also section 123.

DIRECTOR.

SEC. 37. The director shall be the clerk of the district board, and of all district meetings, when present; but if he shall not be present at any district meeting, the qualified voters present may appoint a clerk of such meeting, who shall certify the proceedings thereof to the director, to be recorded by him.

1. See note 3 to section 11.

SEC. 38. The director shall record all the proceedings of the district in a book to be kept for that purpose, and preserve copies of all reports made to the school inspectors, and safely preserve and keep all books and papers belonging to his office.

1. The question has arisen whether if the record here provided for has not been kept, or is destroyed or lost, whether the district is *entitled to its share of the income of the primary school money.* Every school district from which a report has been made according to law, and showing that a school has been kept therein for three months, by a qualified teacher, is entitled to its share of the public moneys. See note 1 to section 4.

SEC. 39. By and with the advice and consent of the moderator and assessor, or one of them, the director shall contract with and hire qualified teachers for, and in the name of the district; which contract shall be in writing, and shall have the consent of the moderator and assessor, or one of them, endorsed thereon, and shall specify the wages per week or month as agreed by the parties, and a duplicate thereof shall be filed in his office.

1. The director must contract with and hire such persons as are *qualified* teachers—such persons as have offered themselves as candidates for teachers of the primary schools before the board of inspectors, and who, having been duly examined by them, or a majority of them, in regard to moral character, learning and ability to teach school, have received from such inspectors a certificate signed by them, or a majority of them, in such form as may have been prescribed by the Superintendent of Public Instruction. No person, who has not such a certificate in force, is legally *a qualified teacher;* and, by the operation of section 60, no public money can be paid to any teacher who shall not have received such a certificate, *before the commencement of his school.*

2. Every certificate given by the board of inspectors continues in force for two years, within the township. There is no authority for granting a certificate for a longer or shorter period. But a certificate may be annulled under section 90.

3. The contract with the teacher must in all cases be *in writing.* A contract made in any other way, is against the express provision of the law, and cannot be made binding on the district. If the director hires a teacher without following the requirements of the law, he makes *himself* liable to the teacher for the amount of wages contracted to be paid.

4. Unless the contract has been violated in its terms by the teacher, or unless his certificate is annulled by the Inspectors, the district officers cannot dismiss the teacher, without paying him the wages contracted for. Under a written contract, a district cannot withhold pay, to a qualified teacher, if he has not perfomed the services of a teacher, by reason of the neglect or refusal of the inhabitants to send their children to school. The teacher cannot, in this way, be deprived of his pay; nor for *such cause*, can the district officers *dismiss* the teacher, so as to affect his pay according to the terms of his contract.

5. It is the business of the *director* to contract with and hire teachers; but he must do so with the advice and consent of the moderator or assessor, or one of them, and of two trustees in districts having one hundred scholars or over; which consent must be endorsed on the contract. The moderator and assessor have no authority in any other way to employ a teacher, and can not do so, without the action of the director as required in this section.

6. The distribution of the increase of the school fund by the Superintendent is based upon the annual report made by the director. If the report is in conformity with law, the school money is distributed to the township, and the question as to whether the teacher has been legally employed, as for instance by a director who has not filed an acceptance, does not affect the distribution of the public moneys to the township if the school has been kept for the regular term by a qualified teacher.

7. No person, except the proper district officers, has any right to interfere with the management and supervision of the schools, or to

interfere with the authority of the teacher, except as he may do so through such officers: but any person who is liable to pay a school district tax, and possesses the qualifications of a voter therein, may speak and vote at any meeting, whether he has children to send to the school or not.

8. It is the business of the director, with the advice and consent of the other district officers named in this section, to provide a teacher for the school. No district meeting possesses the power to relieve them from this requirement of the law. Under section 24 the district meeting may determine as to the *length* of time a school shall be kept, &c.

9. If the district officers continue the teacher after a notice that his certificate has been annulled by the inspectors, it would operate as a continuation of the contract with such teacher.

10. The following form of contract is recommended to the directors of districts, in which it is stipulated that the teacher is to have a certain sum per month, or week, (as the parties agree,) in full of the teacher's services and board. The practice of "boarding round," as it is termed, has been found by experience often to be a source of difficulty, trouble and annoyance. There is no authority of law binding the inhabitants to board the teacher; and although it may accommodate and suit the views of some districts, it is believed, in most instances, to be a better course to give the teacher a specific sum and let him board himself.

This form is not compulsory. It is recommended as being that best adapted to subserve the interests of the school. It may be varied to suit the wishes of the districts; that portion which relates to the holy-days may be omitted if it does not suit the views of the inhabitants, or the district officers. Whatever may be the *terms* of the contract, the *manner* in which the form is drawn, is in conformity to law, and should be substantially observed.

FORM.

CONTRACT, entered into this —— day of ———, 185 , between SCHOOL DISTRICT No. —— of the township of ——— in the county of ———, State of Michigan, and A—— B——, a qualified teacher in said township; the said A—— B—— contracts and agrees with the said school district, that he will teach the primary school in said district for the term of ——— months, [or weeks] commencing on the —— day of ———, 185 , for the sum of —— dollars per month, [or week] which shall be in full for his services and for board.

In consideration of the premises, the said school district agrees with the said A—— B——, to pay said A—— B—— the sum of —— dollars per month, [or week] as follows: ————————————————————.

It is understood between the said A—— B—— and the said district that a month shall consist of twenty-six days, exclusive of Sundays; but that the said A—— B—— shall not be required to teach said school on each alternate Saturday, or in lieu thereof, on the afternoon of every Saturday, at his option; nor on the 4th day of July, the 22d day of February, New Year's, Christmas, Thanksgiving, or on the days of general biennial elections, as provided by law.

(Signed,) A—— B——, *Director.*
C—— D——, *Teacher.*

Approved:
E—— F——, *Moderator.*
G—— H——, *Assessor.*

In districts containing more than one hundred scholars, between the ages of four and eighteen years, (see section 92,) in addition to the assent of the moderator and assessor, or one of them, the law requires the approval of at least two of the trustees. The contract should be drawn in duplicate, one for the use of the district, and one for the teacher. If a contract is made with a teacher, and at the expiration of the time for which he has contracted to teach the district is without money, the teacher may sue the district. Whenever it is thought advisable, provision may be made in the contract saving the district from this difficulty.

Sec. 40. He shall ascertain, as near as practicable, before the commencement of each school term, the just proportion which each person having scholars to send to the school, ought to furnish of the fuel for such term, and give each such person at least five days' notice of the time within which he is required to deliver the same at the school house, and if any person shall not deliver his proportion as required, the same shall be furnished by the director, and the amount thereof shall be assessed on the rate bill, to the person neglecting to deliver his proportion as aforesaid.

1. A tax cannot be voted for fuel. This section of the law requires amendment. The mode of ascertaining, *as far as practicable*, before the commencement of each term, the *just proportion* which each person, having scholars to send to school ought to furnish, is not uniform. The last census is sometimes taken as the basis. It appears to be impracticable for the director, previous to the commencement of each term, to visit and enquire of each person how many scholars he will send to school during the term. Many persons do not send till the term has partially expired, and others who

send at the commencement take out their children before the close of the term. The only practicable method would seem to be to allow the director to furnish the necessary supply of fuel, and let the amounts due from each person be subsequently assessed in the rate bill.

Every person who sends scholars to school, without reference to the age of the scholars, is liable on the rate bill. In whatever mode, however, fuel is furnished, it should be provided at the school house, cut up and prepared for use; schools have frequently been dismissed for the want of this care, and not unfrequently its preperation, cutting it up, &c., is left upon the hands of one or two persons in the district, upon the teacher or the scholars.

SEC. 41. Within ten days next previous to the annual district meeting, the director shall take the census of his district, and make a list in writing of the names of all the children belonging thereto between the ages of four and eighteen years.

1. The construction heretofore given by this department in relation to who are to be included in this census, has been that it embraces all children resident in the district, whether the children of native born citizens, aliens, colored persons, or Indians. All these have a right to participate in the benefits of the school system, except where there has been special legislation, as in the city of Detroit, where a colored school is organized separately. The children who are at the county poor houses may be included in the census.

2. The ages of four and eighteen are fixed upon in taking the census, for the purpose of arriving at some proper basis for apportioning the public money. It is not the law, nor the policy of the law, to exclude those of all other ages from a participation in the benefit of the schools. Those of all ages have the right to attend them as scholars.

3. Section 130 imposes a penalty upon a director who refuses or neglects his duty under this section.

SEC. 42. He shall furnish a copy of such list to each teacher employed in the district, and require such teacher carefully to note the daily attendance of each scholar, and to make return thereof to him, including the ages of all scholars whose names are not on such list; and such teacher shall also certify and return, according to his best information and belief, the name of the person liable for the tuition of each scholar.

SEC. 43. In case the director shall not have furnished such list as aforesaid, the teacher shall keep a list of all the scholars attending school, and the number of days each scholar shall attend the same, with the age of each, and the name of the person liable for the tuition of each, according to his best information and belief, which list he shall return to the director as aforesaid.

1. Under these sections various questions have arisen, pertaining both to the director and the teacher. No time is fixed for the *return* from the teacher to the director. The return without *certification* is not a legal return. If a teacher neglects to make the certificate until after the term of the director in office at the time his school closed, has expired, but makes it to the director subseqently chosen to office, it is the duty of such director to make out the rate bill in accordance with the provisions of section 45.

2. The list required to be kept is the basis upon which the rate bill is to be made out, and the effect of carelessness or error in keeping it, will, to a greater or less extent, be felt throughout the district. The teacher should regard it his special duty to keep it with care. To carry out properly these provisions of law, a convenient and proper form should be had. This form, as filled up, besides being the basis of the rate bill, has been found by teachers to be useful and necessary in order to keep a correct account of the attendance of the scholars. A register, adapted to this purpose has heretofore been much used in the schools at the east, called "Wickham's School Ledger," and if the districts feel able to afford the expense, which is not great, it is strongly recommended to them to procure it. No form so well adapted to the requirements of the law, can be prescribed in this edition of the laws, for want of the proper space. What, in addition is required in the register, to use the words of the author himself, "will please the scholar and parent, interest the visitor and inspector, and be valuable and satisfactory to all." For the rate bill, it will furnish a correct guide; for the parent, a test of the teachers fidelity; and an evidence to both, of the scholarship and deportment of the pupils. The use of it in the schools will add materially to their means of usefulness.

The following form of a list will answer the purposes of both director and teacher, under section 42, at least so far as to furnish a guide, in the absence of a printed register:

FORM.

LIST, containing the names of all the children between the ages of four and eighteen years, belonging to district No. ——, of the township of ———, taken by the director previous to the annual district meeting for the year 185 .

To the Teacher:

In pursuance of section 42 of the school law, you are furnished with the annexed copy of a list of names of all the children belonging to the district, between the ages of four and eighteen years. You are required carefully to note the daily attendance of each scholar, and to make return thereof to the director, including the ages of all scholars whose names are not on the annexed list, and to certify and return, according to the best of yonr knowledge and belief, the name of the person liable for the tuition of each scholar.

Dated, —— day of ——, 185 . A—— B——, *Director.*

Names of children between four and eighteen years belonging to the district.		Time of entrance.	Whole No. of days attendance of each.	Name of person liable for tuition of each scholar.
A—— B——,		Jan. 1, 1852.	90	B—— H——,
C—— D——,		" 9, "	75	G—— N——,
E—— F——,		Feb. 1, "	45	F—— M——,
Name and age of each scholar who has attended school which are not on the directors list, to be furnished by the teacher in pursuance of section 42.				
NAMES.	AGES			
A—— B——,	19	Jan. 2, 1852.	70	E—— F——,
C—— D——,	15	8, "	55	L—— B——,
E—— F——,	17	Feb. 7, "	34	C—— R——,

I hereby certify and return that the foregoing is a true statement of the facts contained therein, and that to the best of my knowledge and belief, the list of names of the persons liable for tuition of each scholar is correct.

A—— B——, *Teacher.*

The foregoing form will answer the requirements of the law, so as to enable the director when it is properly filled up, to make out his rate bill; but in order to note the daily attendance, the teacher will be under the necessity of keeping a day or check roll. As a guide to the teacher in this respect, the forms and instructions of the Superintendent of New York, (Mr. Randall,) are well adapted to this purpose, and are herewith subjoined and recommended to the teachers of this State. Where no list is furnished by the director, this list kept by the teacher, must be certified to, as in the foregoing form, and returned to the director:

At the time any pupil enters the schools, the teachers should immediately insert the date and the name of the scholar. At the close of the quarter, the whole number of days that each pupil attended is to be ascertained, from the check roll, and entered in the third column.

Each teacher, at the commencement of every quarter, must provide a day or check roll, in which the name of every scholar is to be entered. It should be ruled so as give six columns, corresponding to the number of days in the week. The number attending should be ascertained each half day, and pencil marks made in the column for the day opposite to the name of each one present. At the end of the week, the number of days each pupil has attended during the week should be summed up and entered on the weekly roll. Each half day's attendance should be noted, and two half days should be reckoned as one day. The pencil marks on the day roll may be obliterated, so that the same roll may be used during the quarter. The weekly roll should be formed in the same manner, so as to contain the names of the pupils, and thirteen columns ruled, corresponding to the of number weeks in the quarter. In each of these columns is to be entered the result of the daily check roll for each week, in the following form:

WEEKLY ROLL.

Attendance of Pupils in District School of District No. ——.

Names of Pupils.	1st week.	2d week.	3d week.	4th week.	5th week.
J. Thorn,....	6 days.	4 days.	5 days.	6 days.	5½ days.

SEC. 44. The director shall ascertain from the return of such teacher, the number of days for which each person not exempted shall be liable to pay for tuition, and the amount payable by each.

SEC. 45. Within twenty days after receiving such list and certificate from the teacher, the director shall make out a rate blll, containing the name of each person so liable, and the amount due him for tuition and fuel, or either, adding thereto five cents on each dollar of the sum due, for assessor's fees, and shall annex thereto a warrant for the collection thereof, to be signed by him and the moderator.

1. Under section 58, it is the duty of the district board to exempt from the payment of teacher's wages and from providing fuel, all such persons residing in the district, as in their opinion ought to be exempted, and to *certify* such exemption to the directors. (See section 58.)

2. In order to ascertain the amount of tuition to be paid by each person who has sent to school, the amount of the public money should be deducted from the teacher's wages, and the remainder should be apportioned to those who have sent to school, according to the time sent by each. If but one person has sent to school, that person is liable for the *whole amount* of teachers' wages, after deducting the public money, and it may be collected of him by rate bill.

3. Scholars sent from one organized district and boarding there, stand on the same footing in relation to the rate bill, and the public moneys, as residents of the district. The person with whom such scholar boards may be made liable, and the rate bill should be made out against such person for tuition and fuel.

4. When two schools are kept in the same district, a rate bill should be made separately for each school.

5. A rate bill cannot be made out for any other purposes than for tuition and fuel.

6. A taxable inhabitant of a school district is not shielded from payment of a rate bill if he has sent to school, for the reason that the district board has admitted scholars from another district.

7. Persons residing within the district, sending the children of others to the school, are liable on rate bill for tuition and fuel.

8. A private claim or demand against the teacher can not be set-off against the amount due on the rate bill.

9. The *exemption law* does not apply to the rate bill.

FORM OF RATE BILL AND WARRANT.

Rate bill containing the name of each person liable for teachers' wages, in district No. ——, in the township of ———, for the term ending on the —— day of ———, 185 , and the amount for which each person not exempted from the payment thereof is so liable, with the assessors fees thereon:

Names of persons sending to school.	Whole No. of days sent.	Amount of school bill.	Assessor's fees thereon	Amt. for fuel.	Whole am't to be raised.
Peter Parley,	104	$1 04	$0 05		$1 09
Richard Roe,	104	1 00	05	$0 50	1 62
Total..........		$	$	$	$

To the Assessor of school district No. ——, of the township of ———:

In the name of the people of the State of Michig an: You are hereby commanded to collect from each of the persons in the annexed rate bill named, the several sums set opposite their names, in the last column thereof, within sixty days after the date and delivery hereof; and upon collecting the same, or any part thereof, at the expiration of the time allowed therefor by law, to pay over the amount so collected by you (retaining five per cent for your fees) to the or-
the director of said district, countersigned by the moderator

thereof; and in case any person therein named shall neglect or refuse on demand, to pay the amount on said rate bill for which he is liable, you are to collect the same by distress and sale of the goods and chattels of such person or persons, wherever found in the county or counties in which said district is situated, having first published said sale at least ten days, by posting up notices thereof in three public places in the township where such property shall be sold.

Given under our hands this —— day of ——, A. D. 185 .

A—— B——, *Director.*
C—— D——, *Moderator.*

SEC. 46. Such warrant shall command the assessor that within sixty days he collect of the persons named in said rate bill the amount set opposite their respective names, and that if any person shall neglect or refuse, on demand, to pay the amount on said rate bill for which he is liable, he collect the same by distress and sale of the goods and chattels of such person wherever found in the county or counties in which the district is situated, first publishing such sale at least ten days by posting up notices thereof in three public places in the township where such property shall be sold.

1. The annulment of a teacher's certificate by the board of inspectors does not affect the collection of a rate bill for the time the teacher taught under his certificate.

2. No rate bill can be collected after the time fixed in the warrant, except the time has been extended under section 47, and such extension cannot exceed thirty days.

3. Rate bills can not be collected from persons residing out of the district, except such as pay taxes in the district for which the rate bill is made out and who send scholars to school therein. (See section 137.)

4. No person can be *sued* for an amount due on the rate bill.

5. The public money is in reduction of the tuition of all the children who have attended school *without regard to their ages.*

6. All the children who attend the school must be charged at the same rate for tuition, without regard to the studies they have pursued, except in cases where the district officers have classified the scholars as provided in sections 92 and 93.

7. Persons who pay the teacher, voluntarily, such sums as he may require, may, by taking his order therefor upon the director, be entitled to receive the amounts from him, from the moneys raised for the teacher by rate bill, but the rate bill is to be made out in conformity with the teacher's return. If the rate bill and warrant is legal on its face, the assessor would not be liable for proceeding to

collect and enforcing collection according to his warrant. The director is to make out the rate bill in strict conformity with section 45. All the proceedings in the course of making out the rate bill and collecting it should be in strict pursuance of the law. The private dealings and business of the teacher should not interfere with the duty of the director in making out his rate bill as the law requires.

FORM OF NOTICE OF ASSESSOR'S SALE.

Notice is hereby given, that by virtue of the warrant annexed to a rate bill for school district No. ——, of the township of ———, bearing date the —— day of ———, 185 , I have levied on the goods and chattels of ——— ———, and shall expose the same for sale at public auction at the house of ——— ———, in the said school district, (or wherever the property may be,) in the township of ——— and county of ———, on the —— day of ———, 185 , at the hour of —— o'clock in —— noon of said day.

Given under my hand at ———, this —— day of ———, 185 .

A—— B——,
Assessor of said District.

This notice should be posted up ten full days before the day of sale, in three of the most public places *where* the property is to be sold.

SEC. 47. In case the moderator and director shall deem it necessary, they may, by an endorsement on such warrant signed by them, extend the time therein specified for the collection of such rate bill, not exceeding thirty days.

FORM OF ENDORSEMENT.

We hereby extend the time specified in the within warrant for the collection of the rate bill attached, for the further period of ——— days Dated the —— day of ———, 185 .

A—— B——, *Director.*
C—— D——, *Moderator.*

1. Sixty days is sufficient time for the collection of the rate bill in most cases, and it is better as a general principle to collect the rate bill promptly within the period first specified in the warrant.

SEC. 48. The director shall provide the necessary appendages for the school house, and keep the same in good condition and repair during the time a school shall be taught therein, and shall keep an accurate account of all expenses incurred by him as director.

1. The duty of directors under this section is special. The *care and custody* of the school house, and other property of the district, except so far as this section directs, belongs to the district board. The power of the director here given, extends to the supervision of the building, so far as it needs appendages and repairs; and to keep it in

good condition. He may and should see that the school house is provided with a good lock and key, whether he has been directed or not to procure it. The windows and doors should be guarded in the winter season to secure the scholars from the inclemency of the weather; broken panes of glass at all times removed, and new ones substituted; the stoves properly secured; the house sufficiently warmed; the desks, seats and school house protected from injury; the school house yard and out houses attended to and kept neat and clean. To defray these expenses a tax may be voted, and the director is entitled to compensation for his services, out of moneys collected by tax for the support of schools, or by special vote.

2. The health and comfort of children, the success of the teacher, and the welfare of the school depends greatly upon the manner in which the director attends to his duty.

3. As the director must necessarily incur expense, it may be well for the district to vote a specific sum, to cover the estimated amount required, in advance.

4. A director may charge for his time in hiring teachers—and in making out rate bills, but not for conveying teachers to be inspected, or taking them home.

SEC. 49. He shall present said account for allowance to the qualified voters of the district, at a regular meeting, and the amount of such account, as allowed by such meeting, shall be assessed and collected in the same manner as other district taxes; but no such account shall be allowed at a special meeting unless the intention to present the same shall be expressed in the notice of such meeting.

SEC. 50. He shall give the prescribed notice of the annual district meeting, and of all such special meetings as he shall be required to give notice of in accordance with the provisions of this chapter, one copy of which for each meeting shall be posted on the outer door of the district school house, if there be one.

SEC. 51. The director shall draw from the township library the proportion of books to which his district may be entitled, and return the same to the township library at the expiration of three months, and shall continue to draw books in like manner, at the expiration of every three months, and to return the same as aforesaid.

1. This last provision does not efficiently aid in carrying out the wishes of the people and the intention of the Legislature, in the establishment of libraries. It needs amendment. Directors are frequently delinquent in drawing and in returning books. In some cases they live at such distance from the township clerk, that it is inconvenient to draw them, and oftentimes it is rendered quite as inconvenient for

the inhabitants to obtain them of the director. (See note to section 115.) Directors in some instances have refused to draw books, in which case they are liable for neglect of duty. In this event, however, the law does not provide who shall draw them.

SEC. 52. He shall distribute the books drawn out by him to the parents or guardians of the children of the district of the proper age, for the time and under the restrictions contained in the rules prescribed by the board of school inspectors.

1. The township libraries are the property of the township. The parents and guardians of all children between the ages of four and eighteen years are permitted [section 114] to use books from such library *without charge*, being responsible to the township for the safe return thereof, and for any injury done thereto, according to such rules and regulations as are or may be prescribed by the board of school inspectors. The books in such library are once in three months to be distributed by the township librarian among the several school districts of the township in proportion to the number of children in each between the ages aforesaid, as the same shall appear by the last report of the director. [Section 115.] Inhabitants of the district not parents or guardians of children between the ages mentioned, should have access to the books of the library, and may do so under regulations made by the inspectors.

2. The revised constitution provides for the establishment of at least one library in each township, and that all fines assessed and collected in the several counties and townships for any breach of the penal laws shall be exclusively applied to the support of such libraries.

3. The school inspectors make themselves liable if they appropriate the library money to any other purpose than for the support of the library.

4. For library purposes $25 of the two mill tax is assessed under section 107. This cannot be diverted from the objects specified in the law.

SEC. 53. He shall draw and sign all orders upon the assessor for all moneys to be disbursed by the district, and all warrants upon the township treasurer for moneys raised for district purposes, or apportioned to the district by the township clerk, and present the same to the moderator to be countersigned by him.

FORM OF ORDER UPON ASSESSOR FOR MONEYS TO BE DISBURSED BY SCHOOL DISTRICTS.

Assessor of School District No. ——, *of Township of* ——:

Pay to the order of —— ——, the sum of —— dollars and —— cents out of any moneys in your hands belonging to said district. Dated this —— day of ——, 185 .

[COUNTERSIGNED] A—— B——, *Director.*

C—— D——, *Moderator.*

FORM OF WARRANT UPON TOWNSHIP TREASURER FOR MONEYS BELONGING TO SCHOOL DISTRICTS.

Treasurer of Township of ——:

Pay to the order of —— —— the sum of —— dollars and —— cents, out of moneys in your hands belonging to said district, and raised for the purposes of —— —— ——.

Given under my hand this —— day of ——, 185 .

[COUNTERSIGNED.] A—— B——, *Director.*

C—— D——, *Moderator.*

1. If orders legally drawn by the director and countersigned, are not paid on presentation at the proper treasury, the district is liable for the amount, and may be sued therefor. If the district officers have complied with the law, they are not liable *individually*, for orders drawn by them officially. If they have performed the duty which the law imposes on them, in order to raise the tax, they may presume the money is in the treasury after the time fixed by law for its collection has expired.

SEC. 54. The director shall also, at the end of each school year, deliver to the township clerk, to be filed in his office, a report to the board of school inspectors of the township, showing,

1. The whole number of children belonging to the district, between the ages of four and eighteen years, according to the census taken as aforesaid:

2. The number attending school during the year, under four, and also the number over eighteen years of age:

3. The whole number that have attended school during the year:

4. The length of time the school has been taught during the year by a qualified teacher, the name of each teacher, the length of time kept by each, and the wages paid to each:

5. The average length of time scholars between four and eighteen years of age have attended school during the year:

6. The amount of money received from the township treasurer, apportioned to the district by the township clerk:

7. The amount of money raised by the district, and the purposes for which it was raised:

8. The kind of books used in the school:

9. Such other facts and statistics in regard to schools and the subject of education, as the Superintendent of Public Instruction shall direct.

1. The provisions of the law regulating the duties of the Superintendent, and authorizing the correction of errors, approved April

4, 1851, do not extend to the reports of the directors. Hence, great care should be observed to perfect their reports. Blank forms for directors are annually forwarded to the county clerks, for all the districts of the State.

2. When a district loses its proportion of the income of the primary school fund and of all funds arising from taxes for the support of schools, by neglect of the director to make out and deliver his report to the inspectors, such director is liable to the district for the amount, of which it has been deprived by his neglect; and he is also liable to the forfeiture as provided in section 130.

3. Suit may be commenced for such forfeiture within two years from the time the forfeiture was incurred.

DISTRICT BOARD.

Sec. 55. The moderator, director and assessor shall constitute the district board.

1. By an additional act [section 92] it is provided that in districts containing more than one hundred scholars between the ages of 4 and 18, the district board may be enlarged by adding thereto four trustees, provided the district determine to do so by a two-thirds vote, at any annual meeting. In such districts the district board would consist of a moderator, director, assessor and four trustees.

2. A district board elected at the annual school meeting, and filing their acceptance forthwith, supercede the old officers at once, and may (or any two of them) notify the supervisor of the amount of taxes voted at said meeting.

Sec. 56. Said board shall, between the last Monday of September and second Monday of October in each year, make out and deliver to the supervisor of each township in which any part of the district is situated, a report in writing under their hands, of all taxes voted by the district during the preceding year, and of all taxes which said board is authorized to impose, to be levied on the taxable property within the district.

FORM OF REPORT BY THE DISTRICT BOARD TO THE SUPERVISOR.

To the Supervisor of the Township of ——:

The undersigned, district board for school district No. ——, in said township, do hereby certify that the following taxes have been voted in said district, during the school year last closed, viz: [Here specify the amount of each tax voted, and the purpose to which it is appropriated: also, the amount of taxes imposed by the district board, and give the sum total of the whole:] which you will please assess upon the taxable property of said district, as the law directs.

Dated at ———, this ——— day of ———, A. D. 185 .

A—— B——, *Moderator.*
C—— D——, *Director.*
E—— F——, *Assessor.*

1. The amount which would have been payable for fuel and teachers' wages, by persons exempted from payment thereof by the district board, must, by said board, be included in their report of taxes to the supervisor, to be by him assessed on the property of the district. The amount paid for school books for children, admitted free of charge, and all sums which could not be collected on the rate bill, are also to be included in their report by the provisions of section 57.

2. A report made out and delivered either on the last Monday of September, or on the second Monday of October, is in compliance with the law.

3. A district board should not report a tax to the supervisor unless a vote has been taken finally upon it. If the meeting adjourns to a time after the second Monday of October, and the question is pending, the board should not report a tax.

4. If the board include it in their report to the supervisor, and he levies it on the property of the district, it is illegal.

SEC. 57. The district board may purchase, at the expense of the district, such school books as may be necessary for the use of children admitted by them to the district school free of charge, and they shall include the amount of such purchases, and the amount which would have been payable for fuel and teachers' wages by persons exempted from the payment thereof, together with any sums on the district rate bills, which could not be collected, in their report to the supervisor or supervisors, to be assessed as aforesaid.

SEC. 58. Said board shall exempt from the payment of teachers' wages, and from providing fuel for the use of the district, all such persons residing therein, as in their opinion ought to be exempted, and shall certify such exemptions to the director; and the children of such persons shall be admitted to the district school free of charge during the time of such exemption.

1. The object of sections 57 and '8 is to make the primary schools accessible to all; the children of the poor as well as of the rich; and in the exercise of the power conferred on the board, a principle of liberality should be observed. Every reasonable facility should be afforded for the education of all children whose parents are in any way unable to afford the expense of the schools.

SEC. 59. They shall purchase or lease a site for a school house, as shall have been designated by the district, in the corporate name thereof, and shall build, hire or purchase such school house out of the fund provided for that purpose, and make sale of any site or other property of the district, when lawfully directed by the qualified voters, at an annual or special meeting: *Provided*, That the district board shall not in any case build a stone or brick school house upon any site, without having first obtained a title in fee to the same, or a lease for ninety-nine years; and also that they shall not in any case build a frame school house upon any site for which they have not a title in fee, or a lease for fifty years, without securing the privilege of removing the said school house when lawfully directed so to do by the qualified voters of the district, at any annual or special meeting.

FORM OF A DEED.

Know all men by these presents, that A—— B—— and C—— B——, his wife, of the township of ———, in the county of ———, and State of Michigan, party of the first part, for and in consideration of the sum of ——— dollars, to them paid by the district board of school district No. ——— of the township, county and State aforesaid, the receipt whereof is hereby acknowledged, do hereby grant, bargain, sell and convey to school district No. ———, the party of the second part, and their assigns, forever, the following described parcel of land, namely:

[Here insert description.]

Together with all the privileges and appurtenances thereunto belonging, to have and to hold the same to the said party of the second part, and their assigns, forever. And the said party of the first part, for themselves, their heirs, executors and administrators, do covenant, grant, bargain and agree, to and with the said party of the second part, and their assigns, that at the time of the ensealing and delivery of these presents, they were well seized of the premises above conveyed, as of a good, sure, perfect absolute and indefeasible estate of inheritance in the law, in fee simple, and that the said lands and premises are free from all encumbrances whatever; and that the above bargained premises, in the quiet and peaceable possession of the said party of the second part, and their assigns, against all and every person or persons lawfully claiming or to claim the whole or any part thereof, they will for ever warrant and defend.

In witness whereof, the said A—— B—— and C—— B——, his wife, party of the first part, have hereunto set their hands and seals, this ——— day of ——— A. D. 185 .

A—— B——, [SEAL.]
C—— B——, [SEAL.]

Signed, sealed and delivered in presence of
H——— I———,
J——— K———.

The deed should have of course the usual acknowledgement, and should then be recorded.

FORM OF LEASE.

Know all men by these presents, that I, A—— B——, of the township of ———, county of ———, and State of Michigan, of the first part, do hereby lease unto school district No. ——, in the township of ———, in said county, of the second part, the following piece or parcel of land, viz: ——; with all the privileges and appurtenances thereunto belonging; to have and to hold the same for ninety-nine years from the date hereof, [or fifty as the case may be,] for the purposes of a site for a school house in said district, and for no other purpose whatsoever; and in case of said piece or parcel of land being no longer used for the purposes aforesaid, the same shall revert to the said party of the first part, his heirs, assigns, or legal representatives. And in consideration of the premises, the said school district, party of the second part, covenants and agrees to and with the said party of the first part, to pay said party of the first part for the said premises, the annual rent of —— dollars, to be paid as follows: [Here describe when the same shall be paid, and how, if necessary.]

In testimony whereof, the said parties have hereunto set their hand and seals, this —— day of ———, A. D. 185 .

A—— B——, [L. S.]
Lessor.

C—— D——,
E—— F——, [L. S.]
G—— H——,

District Board of School District No. ——, *of the aforesaid township.*

Signed and sealed in the presence of
I—— J——,
K—— L——.

1. The lessor will probably want a copy of the lease. If so, a duplicate should be made out and signed as above, and placed on file with the director, to be delivered with other papers of his office to his successor.

2. By the latter clause of section 59 no district board can build a stone or brick school house on any site, without having a title in fee, or a lease *for ninety-nine years;* nor can they build a frame school house on any site for which the district has not a title in fee, or a *lease for fifty years,* without securing the privilege of removing the house. In case, therefore, a lease is taken for a shorter period of time than specified in these clauses, the following condition should be added in the lease, before the concluding paragraph:

And it is agreed between the parties of the first part, and the second part hereto, that the district board of said district may at any time hereafter, whenever they shall be lawfully directed so to do by the qualified voters of the district at any annual or special meeting, remove the school house erected, or to be erected on said site.

3. When a lease of a site is given for the full term of years, on condition that it shall be used for a school house, and the house is sold or removed for the purpose of erecting a better house, such sale is no violation of the terms of the lease. The district may safely proceed to erect another building thereon.

4. The district board has no authority to do any of the acts specified in section 59, except when they are lawfully directed by the district.

5. A contract to build a brick school house on a site, leased for a less term than the law provides, is in contravention of law.

SEC. 60. The district board shall apply and pay over all school moneys belonging to the district, in accordance with the provisions of law regulating the same, as may be directed by the district; but no school moneys apportioned to any district shall be appropriated to any other use than the payment of teachers' wages, and no part thereof shall be paid to any teacher who shall not have received a certificate as required in this chapter, before the commencement of his school.

1. If the district is not in funds when the teacher has fulfilled his duties under his contract, he must wait until the tax is collected for his pay, if the director has made a contract to that effect. If the contract does not provide, the teacher may sue the district, and if he does, it must be collected as provided in section 125.

2. District officers cannot draw money from the township treasury as an advance of money to be collected by rate bill. There is no authority of law for any such arrangement.

3. The provisions of this section are *imperative* in relation to teachers who have no certificate. It is not material, how well qualified the teacher may have been, how many certificates may have been previously granted to him, if he has not a certificate *in force* at the commencement of his school, no money apportioned to the district can be paid to him.

4. The inhabitants of districts have in some instances withdrawn children from school to get rid of the teacher. If a teacher is a qualified teacher, and has a written contract in conformity to law, to teach for a given length of time, he may collect his pay for the whole time, whether he has had scholars or not, provided he has held himself ready at all times to fulfill his contract.

SEC. 61 The moderator and director shall require of the assessor, and the assessor shall execute to the district, a bond in double the amount of money to come into his hands as such assessor during the year, as near as the same can be ascertained, with two sufficient sureties to be approved by the moderator and director, conditioned for the faithful application of all moneys that shall come into his hands by virtue of his office.

For form of this bond, see page 359. Such bond should be approved by the moderator and director.

SEC. 62. Such bond shall be lodged with the moderator, and in case of any breach of the condition thereof, the director shall cause a suit to be commenced thereon in the name of the district, and the money, when collected, shall be paid into the township treasury, for the use of the district, subject to the order of the proper district officers.

SEC. 63. Said board shall present to the district, at each annual meeting, a report in writing, containing an accurate statement of all moneys of the district received by them, or any of them, during the preceding year, and of the disbursements made by them, with the items of such receipts and disbursements.

SEC. 64. Such report shall also contain a statement of all taxes assessed upon the taxable property of the district during the preceding year, the purposes for which such taxes were assessed, and the amount assessed for each particular purpose, and said reports shall be recorded by the director in a book to be provided and kept for that purpose.

SEC. 65. The said district board shall have the care and custody of the school house and other property of the district, except so far as the same shall be specially confided to the custody of the director, including all books purchased for the use of pupils admitted to the school free of charge.

1. The district board in most of the districts of the State have received and will continue to receive applications for the use and occupation of the school house for purposes other than that for which it was built. The school house is the property of the district and the legal voters may take such action as they see fit to forbid its use for any other purpose than for teaching a primary school. They cannot divert the object for which it was built. or allow the use of the house for any other purpose while the school is kept therein. When the action of the district board in granting its use for other than school purposes is likely to create feeling or lead to difficulty or complaint, the expression of the inhabitants of the district should be obtained by a special meeting. There are many objects nearly allied to the cause of education and the progress of our children in the schools, both physicaly, intellectually and morally, for which the doors of the school house should be thrown open. In most instances the school house in our country is the first, and in all cases among the first buildings erected of a public character. If a majority of the qualified voters assent to it, it is in close proximity with the main design of the school house, to permit its use (when not occupied by

the school) for any object of social, moral or religious improvement; for the worship of God upon the Sabbath; for a Sunday school on the same day, for lectures, debates, and for any literary, moral, useful or scientific purpose; and for any public purpose connected with the general welfare of the inhabitants. These are matters of toleration however, to be determined by the qualified voters.

SEC. 66. The said board shall have power to fill, by appointment, any vacancy that shall occur in their own number, and it shall be their duty to fill such vacancy within ten days after its occurrence.

FORM OF APPOINTMENT.

The undersigned, members of the district board of school district No. ——, township of ——, do hereby appoint A—— B——, —— of said district, to fill the vacancy occasioned by [the removal, death or resignation] of C—— D——, the late ——.
Dated this —— day of ——, 185 .

E—— F—— } *District*
G—— H——. } *Officers.*

1. Persons appointed to fill vacancy, should file their acceptance in pursuance of section 5, and the director should make record of the appointment, and date thereof.

2. See note to section 28.

3. A majority of the district board can act, in order to fill a vacancy.

4. Section 95 provides that if the district board fail to supply any vacancy that shall occur in their own number, within ten days after the time of its occurrence, the school inspectors shall fill the same by appointment.

5. The *temporary* absence of a district officer, in consequence of his being in attendance as a member of the Legislature, or for any other cause, does not create a vacancy.

SEC. 67. If the assessor shall fail to give bond as is required in this chapter, or from sickness or any other cause, shall be unable to attend to the duty of collecting any district rate bill, the said board shall appoint an acting assessor to collect the same, who shall possess all the powers of the district assessor for that purpose, and shall before proceeding to the collection thereof, give bond to the district in double the amount of money to be collected, in the same manner, and with the same effect as the district assessor is required to give such bond.

1. If the circumstances, whether arising from sickness or other cause, which created the necessity for the appointment of an acting assessor, have ceased to exist, it will not affect the collection of the tax by the acting assessor, if he has entered upon that duty and

filed his bond. The acting assessor should go on and collect the rate bill. The bond may be given at *any time before* he proceeds to collect.

The following is a clause of the law passed in 1850, and is here in its proper place, but is not numbered as a section:

[Every school district office shall become vacant upon the incumbent ceasing to be a resident of the district for which he shall have been elected, or upon the happening of either of the events specified in section three of chapter fifteen of the revised statutes of 1846.]

Section 3 of chapter 15 of the revised statutes, as amended by an act of June 27th, 1851, enacts that every office shall become vacant on the happening of either of the following events, before the expiration of the term of such office:

1. The death of the incumbent:
2. His resignation:
3. His removal from office:
4. His ceasing to be an inhabitant of this State; or, if the office be local, of the district, county, township, city or village, for which he shall have been elected or appointed, or within which the duties of his office are required to be discharged:
5. His conviction of any infamous crime, or of any offence involving a violation of his oath of office:
6. The decision of a competent tribunal, declaring void his election or appointment; or,
7. His refusal or neglect to take his oath of office, or to give or renew any official bond, or to deposit such oath or bond in the manner and within the time prescribed by law.

TOWNSHIP BOARD OF SCHOOL INSPECTORS.

SEC. 68. The inspectors elected at the annual township meetings, together with the township clerk, shall constitute the township board of school inspectors; and the inspector elected at the annual township meeting having the shortest time to serve, shall be chairman of said board, and the said township clerk shall be the clerk thereof.

1. The new constitution has provided that there shall hereafter be elected in each organized township, one township clerk who shall be ex-officio school inspector, and one school inspector. This provision, however, will not be effective, until the present law, which provides for the election of two inspectors, is repealed, and a law passed conformable to and to carry out such constitutional provision.

2. The township clerk has a vote in the decision of the board, and possesses all the right and privileges of either of the elected officers as members of the board.

SEC. 69. The chairman of said board shall be the treasurer thereof, and shall give bond to the township in double the amount of library moneys to come into his hands during his term of office, as near as the same can be ascertained, with two sufficient sureties to be approved by the township clerk, conditioned for the faithful appropriation of all moneys that may come into his hands by virtue of his office.

FORM OF BOND TO BE GIVEN BY THE CHAIRMAN OF THE BOARD OF SCHOOL INSPECTORS.

Know all men by these presents, that we, A—— B——, (the chairman of the board of school inspectors of the township of ——) and C—— D——, and E—— F——, (his surety) are held and firmly bound unto the said township, in the sum of [here insert the sum of double the amount to come into said chairman's hands, as nearly as the same can be ascertained.] for the payment of which sum well and truly to be made to the said township, we bind ourselves, our heirs, executors and administrators, jointly and severally, firmly by these presents.

Sealed with our seals, and dated this —— day of ——, A. D. 185 .

The condition of this obligation is such, that if A—— B——, chairman of the board of school inspectors, shall faithfully appropriate all moneys that may come into his hands by virtue of his office, then this obligation shall be void, otherwise of full force and virtue.

A—— B—— [L. S.]
C—— D——, [L. S.]
E—— F——, [L. S.]

Signed, sealed and delivered in presence of
W—— G——,
M—— W——.

Remark.—This bond should be endorsed as follows:

"I approve the within bond."
(Signed) G—— H——, *Township Clerk.*

SEC. 70. Said bond shall be filed with the township clerk, and in case of the non-fulfillment thereof, said clerk shall cause a suit to be commenced thereon, and the moneys collected in such suit shall be paid into the township treasury for the benefit of the township library.

SEC. 71. The inspectors shall divide the township into such number of school districts as may from time to time be necessary, which districts they shall number, and they may regulate and alter the boundaries of the same as circumstances shall render proper: but no district shall contain more than nine sections of land, and each district shall be composed of contiguous territory, and be in as compact a form as may be; but no land shall be taxed for building a school house, unless some portion of every legal sub-division of said land shall be within two and one-half miles of said school house site.

1. The division of the townships into school districts, the initiatory step in the establishment of the schools, is a matter which rests solely with the inspectors. There is no appeal from their decision, and in all cases involving the expediency of their acts, they are only responsible to the source of their power—the people. The duty

confided to them is not only one of the most important devolving upon school officers, but often times the basis and a fruitful source of difficulty.

The following notes are taken from the pamphlet edition of the school law of 1848:

2. School inspectors, by examining section 71 alone, sometimes proceed to district a township, and to alter the boundaries of districts already established, without giving any notice thereof. Great dissatisfaction is frequently and justly the result of such a course. The school inspectors may not be able to please every person residing in districts they are required to establish. This, indeed, might often be incompatible with the conscientious discharge of their official duty. They should, nevertheless, do what they reasonably can to harmonize conflicting interests; and in order to do this, they must give aggrieved individuals, and all others interested, a reasonable opportunity for a hearing. This they may do by giving the notice required by sections 86 and 91, which should invariably be done.

2. The Superintendent would caution inspectors against subdividing districts any farther than becomes actually necessary to accommodate the citizens of a township. Large and populous districts are able to build good school houses, and employ well qualified teachers; while small and feeble districts sometimes feel necessitated to occupy unsuitable houses, and to depend upon the services of incompetent teachers. It is better to go a mile and a half, or even two miles, if need be, to reach a good school, than to reside within half a mile of an indifferent one.

3. When a regularly organized school district, in which a school has been taught the time required by law, is divided so late in the school year, as not to allow time for a school to be taught three months before the expiration of the year, does the part set off lose its school money for the ensuing year?

4. If the division takes place after the annual report is made, and before the school money is received, does the original district receive all the public money, or is the part set off entitled to a portion of it?

5. Is the part set off entitled to draw books from the township library, before the beginning of a new school year; or, in other words, until after the director makes his annual report to the school

inspectors? or can the original district claim and receive, to the end of the year, all the books it would have been entitled to, had there been no division?

The opinion of the office heretofore given in relation to these several questions, is as follows:

"1st. Whenever a school district is divided, each of the districts formed from it has a right, in making its annual report, to embrace the time a school was taught between the commencement of the school year, and the time the division was made, and to add thereto the time a school has been taught in said district subsequently to the division. If each district, reckoning time thus, is enabled to report a school taught three months or more, by qualified teachers, each is entitled to draw public money. But if either district, reckoning time thus, is unable to report a school taught three months by qualified teachers, said district is not entitled to draw public money.

"2. In the distribution of school moneys to said districts, the same sum should be apportioned to the two, that the original district would have been entitled to receive had there been no division. This sum should be divided between them according to the rules of justice and equity. If the division of a district takes place immediately after the commencement of a school year, and before a school has been opened, the money should be apportioned to the new districts in proportion to the number of scholars within the legal ages residing in each of them at the time of the division. But if the division is made after the close of the winter school, and two-thirds (more or less) of the public money has been apportioned to said school, in which both of the districts were entitled to share equitably, the remaining one-third should be apportioned as in the first case named.

"3. Whenever a district is divided, the part set off, when duly organized, is entitled to draw books from the township library at the time for quarterly distribution among the districts of the township, provided the director files with the township librarian a statement of the number of scholars within his district at the time the division was made. The director of the other district should do the same. The original district has no advantage over the one set off in relation to the use of the library, nor in any other respect.—[*School Law and notes of* 1848.

1. If land is so situated that every legal subdivision of it is within two and a half miles of the school house site, in the district where the land lies, the same is subject to a school tax, or any other tax for school house purposes, notwithstanding the same land may have been before assessed and taxed in another district. If a new district is formed, the inspectors should ascertain the amount justly due to the new district, as provided in sections 75, 76, 77 and 78. If this duty is neglected, it can have no bearing on the tax.

2. There is no provision of law by which lands in an *adjoining* township, and not in any organized school district, may be added to a school district which does not contain nine sections of land. The inspectors of both townships may proceed and create a joint district, however.

3. When a district is divided, regulated or altered, it should be done by resolution accurately describing the change and boundaries. Such alterations and regulations will continue doubtless to be necessary to adapt our school system to the increasing population and settlement of the State, but they are only to be made as circumstances shall render proper. The resolution, in case of forming a district, should be similar to the following, viz:

Resolved, That a new school district be formed in this township, to consist of the present districts No. 1 and No. 2, or of the present district No. 1 and part of district No. 2, (or whatever it may be,) which said district shall be numbered (insert the number) —— of the township of ———. And the said district shall be bounded as follows: on the north by the township line, on the east by the easterly line of the farm owned by A——— B——— and occupied by J——— L. ———; on the south by the south line of lots owned by L——— K——— and numbered 26 and 27; and on the west by the westerly line of the farm owned by D—— H——, &c.

The above is given merely as a guide; the description must be made according to the circumstances of the country and the settlement of the township, but it should be in form, and some such resolution as the above should be had and carefully recorded. And the same form of resolution should be used in regulating and altering the boundaries of the district. The new boundaries caused by the alteration should be given. [See section 138.]

4. The inspectors should not in regulating or altering the boundaries of a district, leave any portion of the inhabitants included in the former district or districts, unprovided for, or cut off any portion from the advantages of a school.

5. "The great aim of the officers to whom this duty has been confided should be to form, as far as may be practicable, permanent and efficient districts, competent both in respect to taxable property and number of children, to maintain good schools and affording all requisite facilities for the regular attendance of all the children entitled to participate in the benefits of the school."—*N. Y. Regulations.*

6. Districts should not be any smaller than the necessity and circumstances of the country will permit. The remark made by an officer of the school system of New York, that "in feeble districts—cheap instructors, poor and ill furnished school houses—and a general langour of the cause of education are almost certain," will be found to be true here.

SEC. 72. They may attach to a school district any person residing in the township, and not in any organized district, at his request; and for all district purposes, except raising a tax for building a school house, such person shall be considered as residing in such district; but when set off to a new district, no sum shall be raised for such person as his proportion to the district property.

1. Inspectors may perform their duty under this section without a meeting of the board, (in case it is impracticable for them to meet together,) by preparing a proper statement showing the fact that they have attached such person or persons to the district, which statement should be recorded by the township clerk after being signed by the inspectors or a majority of them. The law makes it necessary for the inspectors to act upon the request of the person wishing to be attached, but it is in the discretion of the inspectors whether to attach him or not. If they do so, the inhabitants of the district have no remedy but to acquiesce. If such person is attached, he stands on the same footing as a resident except so far as he is *restricted* by this section. There is no authority given to the Superintendent to interfere in these cases.

SEC. 73. The inspectors shall apply for and receive from the township treasurer, all moneys appropriated for the township library of their township, and shall purchase the books, and procure the necessary appendages for the township library, and make such rules for the regulation thereof, and the preservation of the books contained in it, as they may deem proper.

1. It is made the duty of the Superintendent to recommend rules for the government of the libraries. This provision was intended as a guide or assistance to inspectors, and to secure a uniform system; but the inspectors may adopt such rules as they may deem proper.

2. The inspectors may make a rule imposing a fine upon a director neglecting to return the books, drawn quarterly by him.

3. A majority of the board may make purchase of books, or they may designate one of their number or some other person, to make purchases, under their direction. The chairman of the board has no authority, without the concurrence and consent of the other inspectors, or one of them, to purchase or pay for books.

The authority to purchase books is one of the greatest importance, involving the whole question of the subsequent utility of the library. If the books purchased are not such as they should be—if they have not been selected with great care and consideration, and with a view to their adaptation to the great end proposed in the establishment of the libraries, the rules and regulations which may be made, will be of but little consequence. It was a subject of deep importance with the framers of our constitution, to secure the permanent establishment of these libraries, beyond the reach of dissolution and destruction, and it has been the aim of our legislators to make them in the highest degree, means of usefulness to our citizens and our children.

4. The inspectors cannot make a rule in contravention with the provisions of section 51.

5. Text books for the schools cannot be purchased as library books.

6. The inspectors should invest the library money so as to procure books of a varied character, historical, philosophical, agricultural, educational, poetical, &c., &c., but works of a merely sectarian or controversial character should not be purchased. No work of an immoral, or fictitious character should be purchased, and such works as "the celebrated trials of all countries," "lives of pirates," and the light reading of the day, are certainly not the works to prove useful to our people or our children.

SEC. 74. They shall appoint one of their number to visit each school in the township having a qualified teacher, at least once in each school term in which a school is taught, who shall inquire into the condition of such schools, examine the scholars, and give such advice to both teachers and pupils as he may think benefical.

1. If the opinions of the best and most experienced writers on primary education are not entirely fallacious, and if all the results of experience hitherto are not deceptive, the consequences of a vigorous system of inspection will be most happy. The teachers and pupils will feel that they are not abandoned to neglect; the apprehension of discredit will stimulate them to the greatest effort, while the suggestions of visitors will tend certainly to the improvement of schools, and they will themselves be more and more enabled to recommend proper measures from their better acquaintance with the subject.—[*Spencer, Superintendent of N. Y.*

2. When the schools are visited by the inspector appointed to do this duty, it is recommended that he invite parents and others to accompany him. For his services, he is entitled to his per diem pay.

3. "Section 74 makes it the imperative duty of the board of school inspectors to "appoint one of their number to *visit each school in the township* having a qualified teacher, *at least* ONCE *in each school term* in which a school is taught, who shall inquire into the condition of such schools, examine the scholars, and give such advice to both teachers and pupils as he may think beneficial."

4. "If the citizens of townships throughout the State, would, at their annual township meetings, select good practical men for school inspectors—the men best qualified to discharge the duties of the office, without any regard to personal or political considerations--and if the inspectors would be faithful in the discharge of this duty, there can be little reason to doubt that the schools of the State would advance *twenty per cent.* in excellence."

5. "The inspectors should, at their first meeting every year, appoint the best and most practical and efficient member of the board, a VISITOR; and he should visit *every school* ONCE at least, as the law directs. It would be well for inspectors to invite the citizens of districts, so far as practicable, and especially district boards, to accompany them in their visits."

6. "The visiting of schools is very commonly neglected, from the mistaken impression that inspectors are not entitled to pay while engaged in the discharge of this duty. But section 91, limiting the

meetings of the board of inspectors at the expense of the township to six, has exclusive reference *to meetings of the board.* This is a service not contemplated in that limitation. School inspectors engaged in visiting schools are entitled to pay for their services, as when engaged in the discharge of other official duties."—[*Notes of* 1848, *on School Law.*

SEC. 75. When a new district is formed, in whole or in part, from one or more districts possessed of a school house, or entitled to other property, the inspectors, at the time of forming such new district, shall ascertain and determine the amount justly due to such new district, from any district out of which it may have been, in whole or in part, formed, as the proportion of such new district, of the value of the school house and other property belonging to the former district at the time of such division.

1. When part of a district possessed of a school house and other property, is detached and attached to another district possessed of like property, the detached portion does not draw from the former district its proportion of the value of the district property. This is only the case where a *new* district is formed. Such a case might arise under section 71, providing for altering the boundaries and not under the provisions of this section.

2. See section 138 for mode of procedure in case of a tax for district purposes, when any portion of a school district has been organized into a new district after a tax for district purposes other than the payment of the debts of the district, shall have been levied but not collected.

SEC. 76. Such proportion shall be ascertained and determined according to the value of the taxable property of the respective parts of such former district, at the time of the division, by the best evidence in the power of the inspectors, and such amount of any debt due from the former district, which would have been a charge upon the new, had it remained in the former district, shall be deducted from such proportion. [*Provided,* That no real estate thus set off and which shall not have been taxed for the purchase or building of such school house, shall be entitled to any portion thereof, nor be taken into account in such division of district property.]

SEC. 77. The amount of such proportion, when so ascertained and determined, shall be certified by the township clerk to the supervisor of the township, whose duty it shall be to assess the same upon the taxable property of the district retaining the school house or other property of the former district, in the same manner as if the same had been authorized by a vote of such district, and the money so assessed shall be placed to the credit of the taxable property taken from the former district, and shall be in reduction of any tax imposed in the new district on said taxable property for school district purposes.

SEC. 78. When collected, such amount shall be paid over to the assessor of the new district to be applied to the use thereof, in the same manner, under the direction of its proper officers, as if such sum had been voted and raised by said district for building a school house or other district purposes.

[SEC. 79. Between the first and fifteenth days of October in each year, the inspectors shall make out and deliver to the township clerk, duplicate reports to the county clerk, setting forth the whole number of districts in their townships, the amount of money raised and received for the township library, together with the several particulars set forth in the reports of the school directors for the preceding year.]

1. The necessary forms required under section 79 are annually forwarded to the proper officers, by the Superintendent. The inspectors will perceive that the law is here materially changed since the pamphlet edition of 1848 was printed. They now cause to be made out two copies of their annual report—which are to be transmitted to the county clerk, and one should be kept by the township clerk in his office. This change was made so as to bring the reports of inspectors directly to the office of the Superintendent for his inspection, and to prevent errors in apportioning the income of the school fund. By this means the Superintendent is enabled to ascertain the manner in which the school inspectors perform their duties, as well as to receive such suggestions as they may see fit to make to him directly, in relation to the operation of the school system. The inspectors may afford material assistance in this way, to a proper understanding and development of the school system, and enable the Superintendent to suggest practical considerations to the Legislature for the improvement of the schools and the perfection of the system.

SEC. 80. The board of inspectors, before making their annual reports to the county clerk, shall examine the record of teachers to whom certificates have been given by them, and if in any school district a school shall not have been taught for three months during the preceding school year by a qualified teacher, no part of the public money shall be distributed to such district, although the report from such district shall set forth that a school has been so taught; and it shall be the duty of the board to certify the facts in relation to any such district in their report to the county clerk.

1. If a district has employed a teacher, who by reason of sickness, accident, or other cause, has been unable to teach for the term contracted, and by reason thereof, a school has not been taught for three months during the preceding school year, the district cannot receive its share of the public money. It may be paid to the teacher for the time he has taught; but if a three months' school has not been kept, the *district* can receive no public money.

SEC. 81. Whenever it shall be necessary or convenient to form a district from two or more adjoining townships, the inspectors, or a majority of them, of each of such adjoining townships, may form such district, and direct which township clerk shall make and deliver the notice of the formation of the same to a taxable inhabitant thereof, and may regulate and alter such district as circumstances may render necessary: [The director of such district shall make his annual report to the clerk of the township in which the school house is situated.]

1. "In the formation of a fractional school district, the concurrence of a majority of the inspectors from *each* of *all* the townships from which it is formed, is necessary. Suppose it is contemplated to form a fractional school district embracing a portion of the territory of three townships; and suppose *all* of the inspectors from two of the townships, and but *one* from the third were in favor of its formation, said district could not be formed."

2. "Whenever and wherever a fractional district exists, said district cannot be dissolved, nor its boundaries be in any way modified, without a general consent, viz: the consent of a majority of the school inspectors of *each township* from which the district is in part formed. The propriety of avoiding their organization, when it can be done without special inconvenience, is hence manifest."—*Notes of* 1848.

3. "It is the duty of the director to "report to the clerk of each township in which the district is in part situated, the number of children between the ages of four and eighteen years in that part of the district lying in such township, and books shall be drawn from the library of each township for the use of such district; but the district shall have access to but one such library at the same time, and the said inspectors shall establish the order in which books shall be drawn from each township library." Hence arises another inconvenience connected with fractional districts. They are entitled to draw books from the libraries of both or all of the townships in which they are in part situated, and hence have access to a greater number of books, it is true; but still, they are not, according to the provisions of the section under consideration, (82,) entitled to draw so many books at a time as single districts of the same size. Suppose a district is situated in part, in each of three townships, having in the township A—— 40 scholars between the ages of 4 and 18 years, and the townships B—— and C—— each 20, making 80 in all. The year the district draws books from town A——, they are enti-

tled to receive but *one-half* (40 is ½ of 80) of their equitable quota of books; and the years they draw from townships B—— and C—— but *one fourth* (20 is ¼ of 80) their equal proportion. Whatever might have been the intention of the legislature, this is the only construction the language of the section will warrant."

"Some school inspectors will not allow books drawn from their township library to circulate in those parts of fractional districts situated in other townships. The statutes of the State provide that the libraries of each of the several townships in which a fractional district is in part situated, may circulate throughout said district; and this provision inspectors consent to, whenever they form a fractional district. The only way of restricting the circulation of township libraries to the townships to which they belong, (in harmony with existing provisions of law,) is, to dispense with fractional districts."—*Notes of* 1848.

4. Teachers of fractional districts must be examined in the township to which the annual report is required to be made, which, as the law now directs, is the township where the school house is situated. Boards of inspectors, under the law of 1848, frequently neglected to designate the township to which the annual report should be made. This report must be made to the township where the school house is situated, *and to no other*. But the director, according to section 82, also reports to the clerk of each township in which the district is in part situated, the number of children between the ages of four and eighteen years, in that part of the district lying in his township. This latter report is the basis of the distribution made by the clerk of moneys raised in the townships. The annual report required to be made to the township where the school house is situated is the basis of the distribution of the public money.

5. See sections 142 and 143, as to duty of supervisor and township treasurer.

6. The inspectors can neither in the case of fractional or whole districts, act by proxy. They must be present at the meetings. They cannot give their assent or dissent officially, to any act of the board without being present. The preceedings of joint boards, should be sent to the clerks of the respective townships, for record. The law does not provide for any clerk for joint boards of inspectors.

7. Joint boards of inspectors may attach to a fractional district any person who requests to be so attached. They may also fill vacancies in such fractional districts.

8. The law does not provide specially for notices of meetings of the joint boards; but it would seem to be wise to pursue the same course as the law requires of whole districts, as far as it can be done, where the law has made no provision.

9. The law has made no provision in regard to moneys in the hands of township treasurers, which have accumulated by reason of the directors of fractional districts having heretofore made reports to several townships, of the number of scholars residing in such districts.

10. The Superintendent has no authority officially, to review the proceedings of the boards of inspectors either of whole or fractional districts, or the proceedings of the district boards.

11. Fractional districts have the same power as whole districts, and their proceedings are the same in all cases, where the law does not direct otherwise.

12. A fractional district may be formed out of two adjoining townships, in two adjoining counties.

13. For manner of apportioning the income of the primary school fund, and moneys raised in the township, see section 139. The public money is to be distributed to the townships to which the annual report is to be made. The other moneys raised in any one of the townships, to the districts and parts of districts therein, in proportion to the number of children in each, of the proper age.

Sec. 82. The director of every district, formed as provided in the preceding section, shall also report to the clerk of each township in which the district is in part situated, the number of children between the ages of four and eighteen years in that part of the district lying in such township, and books shall be drawn from the library of each township for the use of such district; but the district shall have access to but one such library at the same time, and the said inspectors shall establish the order in which books shall be drawn from each township library.

Sec. 73. Such school districts already formed from two or more townships, shall continue to be governed by the regulations established according to law, in relation to the annual reports, and the drawing of books from the township libraries, subject to such changes as may be made in respect thereto by the said inspectors, in conformity with the preceding provisions.

Sec. 84. The full amount of all taxes to be levied upon the taxable property in such districts, shall be certified by the district board to the supervisor of each of such townships, and each of said supervisors shall certify to each other supervisor within whose township such district is in part situated, the amount of taxable property in that part of the district lying in his township; and such supervisors shall respectively ascertain the proportion of such taxes to be placed on their respective assessment rolls, according to the amount of taxable property in each part of such district.

SEC. 85. It shall be the duty of the inspectors to examine annually, all persons offering themselves as candidates for teachers of primary schools in their townships, in regard to moral character, learning and ability to teach school; and they shall deliver to each person so examined and found qualified, a certificate signed by them, in such form as shall be prescribed by the Superintendent of Public Instruction; which certificate shall be in force for two years from the date thereof, unless annulled within that time; and no person shall be deemed a qualified teacher within the meaning of this chapter, who has not such a certificate in force.

1. This duty the law contemplates shall be performed by all three of the inspectors, but a majority may act, examine candidates, and sign certificates, the township clerk having the same power and authority as either of the inspectors.

2. The examination is to be public, and no certificate is to be given unless the inspectors are satisfied that the applicant possesses a good moral character and a thorough and accurate knowledge of the several branches of study usually taught in primary schools, and is in other respects competent to teach and govern a school.

3. If the applicant is found to be qualified, the inspectors deliver to him a certificate in the form prescribed by the Superintendent of Public Instruction. This certificate, by the express terms of the law, continues in force two years, unless annulled according to section 90. No certificate can be legally given in any other form, or for a longer or shorter time. There is no discretion vested with inspectors to adopt any modified or qualified form of certificate. It should be made out and delivered to every person found to be qualified, immediately after examination, and should be in the possession of the teacher when he commences his school, or he is not entitled to public money.

4. The law makes no restriction as to who shall be examined. It is the duty of the inspectors to examine all persons who offer themselves as candidates for teachers in their township. A school inspector may be examined as a teacher, but when he presents himself as a candidate, he must cease to act as an inspector. He must stand before the other members of the board like any other appli-

cant. He cannot sign his own certificate with one other member of the board. It must bear the signature of the other two inspectors, or it is not valid, and he can not be deemed a qualified teacher under the law.

5. In no instance can the requirements of the law for the examination of teachers be dispensed with. Every person offering himself as a candidate, must be examined in the manner and upon the points specified in the law. Such examinations must be had regularly at a meeting of, and before the board, and not before one of the inspectors at a time. When there are several persons offering themselves, the better way is to examine them as a class.

6. An inspector cannot authorize another member of the board to act for him on the examination of a teacher, or to sign a certificate for him, without his having participated in the examination.

7. A certificate is valid when two of the inspectors sign it after having had an examination as the law prescribes under section 86. The township clerk should give the notice under section 87; but there is no provision for public notice.

8. The inspectors cannot refuse to examine any person who offers himself before them at the time specified in section 86. In relation to the moral character of the applicant, they may act upon their own knowledge, or upon any satisfactory evidence adduced before them.

9. The general jurisdiction given by law to the inspectors is not affected in any way when the district has not employed a qualified teacher. A school kept by such teacher is subject to the inspection and visitation of the inspector appointed to do that duty.

FORM OF CERTIFICATE TO BE GIVEN BY SCHOOL INSPECTORS TO QUALIFIED TEACHERS.

The undersigned, inspectors of primary schools for the township of ———, in the county of ———, having personally examined A—— B——, at a regular meeting of the board, called for that purpose, and having ascertained his qualifications in respect to moral character, learning, and ability to instruct a primary school, DO HEREBY CERTIFY, that he is duly qualified for that service, and accordingly he is hereby *licensed* to teach primary schools in said township for *two years* from the date hereof, unless this certificate shall, before that time, be annulled according to law.

Given under our hands this —— day of ———, A. D. 185 .

C—— D——, }
E—— F——, } *School Inspectors.*
G—— H——, }

SEC. 86. For the purpose of making such examination, the board of school inspectors shall meet on the second Saturday of April, and first Saturday of November in each year, at the office of the township clerk, or at such other place as they shall designate; of which meetings the township clerk shall give at least ten days' notice in writing, by posting up the same in three public places in the township.

FORM OF NOTICE.

Notice is hereby given, that for the purpose of making an examination of all persons who may offer themselves as candidates for teachers of the primary schools of this township, the board of school inspectors thereof, will meet at the —— of —— ——, at the hour of —— o'clock in the —— noon of the —— day of ——, A. D. 185 .

A—— B——,
Township Clerk.

SEC. 87. The inspectors may make such examination at such other times as they may designate for that purpose, but shall make no charge against the township for examining teachers at any other times than those specified in the preceding section.

1. This section forbids the inspectors from making any charges against the township for their services under this section. It is reasonable however, if the candidate has failed to be present at the regular time of examination, that he should himself pay the inspectors if they demand it. They are not bound to make the examination if the candidate will not assent to this tax.

2. A teacher who receives his certificate at the examination had on any other than the days specified in section 86, is a qualified teacher and entitled to receive pay for his services out of the income of the school money.

SEC. 88. The examination of teachers shall be public, and no certificate shall be given by the inspectors unless they are satisfied that the applicant possesses a good moral character, and a thorough and accurate knowledge of the several branches of study usually taught in primary schools, and is competent in other respects to teach and govern a school.

For the mode and character of the examination which ought to be required under this section, see under head of "Examination of Teachers," in a subsequent part of this document.

SEC. 89. When a district is situated in two or more townships, the teacher for such district shall be examined by the inspectors of the township to which the director is required to make his annual report.

This report is made to the township where the school house is situated, in all cases.

SEC. 90. Whenever the inspectors shall deem it necessary to re-examine any teacher of a primary school in their township, they shall give five days' notice to such teacher of the time and place of such re-examination, and of their intention to annul his certificate if they find him deficient in the requisite qualificatiens; and at the time and place specified in the notice, if the teacher shall not appear and submit to such re-examination, or if he shall be found deficient as aforesaid the inspectors shall annul the said certificate.

FORM OF NOTICE.

To A—— B——:

SIR—You are hereby notified that the undersigned, school inspectors for the township of ———, will hold a meeting at —— ——, on the —— day of ———, at —— o'clock — M. You will please appear before them at the time and place aforesaid, for re-examination. It is our purpose to annul your certificate if you are found deficient in the qualifications requisite for a primary school teacher.

C—— D——,
W—— J——,
L—— M——,
School Inspectors.

Dated ———, 185 .

This notice may be signed by the township clerk, as clerk of the board. In case the board determine to annul the certificate, the clerk should make entry of the vote or resolution of the board to that effect; and the district which has employed such teacher should be furnished with a copy. And in case the certificate shall not be returned by the teacher, notice may be posted or published, if the inspectors deem it advisable, in the following form:

NOTICE.

The undersigned, school inspectors of the township of ———, having given the notice required by law, have re-examined A—— B——, a primary school teacher, and found him deficient in the requisite qualifications: This is to give notice that his certificate granted heretofore on the —— day of ———, 185 , has been annulled.

C—— D——, } *School*
E—— F——, } *Inspectors.*

This notice may be signed by the township clerk, as clerk of the board, or he may publish the resolution of the board itself, in lieu of notice. When the teacher does not appear, that fact should be set out in the notice, instead of the fact that he was re-examined.

SEC. 91. The whole number of meetings of said board of inspectors during any one year, at the expense of the township, shall not exceed six; and whenever said board shall meet for the purpose of forming or altering school districts, they shall cause the like notice to be given as is required for meetings to examine teachers.

SEC. 92. Whenever the board of inspectors of any township shall deem that the interests of any of the schools will be best promoted by so doing, they may form a single district out of any two or more districts therein, and classify the pupils in such district into two or more classes, according to their proficiency and advancement in learning, and require that such pupils be taught in distinct schools or departments as classified by them, and such district may have the same number of school houses, if necessary, and raise the same amount of taxes which the original districts forming the same could raise if not united.

[1. In districts containing more than one hundred scholars between the ages of four and eighteen years, the district board may be enlarged by adding thereto four trustees: *Provided*, That the district determine to do so by a two-thirds vote, at any annual meeting.

2. The additional trustees first elected shall serve severally one, two, three and four years, to be determined by lot immediately on filing their certificate of acceptance with the director. After the first election, each trustee shall serve four years.

3. All vacancies that may occur in the office of trustee shall be filled according to existing provisions for filling vacancies in the district board.

4. Rate bills shall be collected and all moneys shall be drawn and applied according to existing provisions of law, but in the employment of teachers the director shall have the approval of the moderator or assessor according to provisions of law heretofore existing, and of at least two of the trustees; and the authority to classify pupils in such cases shall be transferred from the school inspectors to the enlarged district board.

5. The boundaries of districts that may avail themselves of this act, shall not be enlarged nor diminished without the written approval of a majority of the enlarged district board.]

Sec. 93. The said inspectors may also, on the application of the district board of any district, classify the pupils therein in the manner prescribed in the preceding section, and require that such pupils be taught in distinct departments, whenever they shall judge that the interests of the school will be best promoted thereby; and in case of any such classification as is provided for in this or the preceding section, as many teachers may be employed for each district, as there are departments in which teachers are required.

[The district board in any school district in which the scholars have been or may be classified as provided in section number ninety-two or ninety-three of chapter number fifty-eight of the revised statutes, and the act or acts amendatory thereto, shall have power to graduate the price of tuition according to the studies pursued by the scholars respectively, in such manner as the said board shall deem just.]

[Sec. 2. The rate bills made out in accordance with the graduation provided for in the preceding section, shall have the same force and be collected in the same manner as the rate bills in other cases.]

Sec. 94. It shall be the duty of the board of inspectors, to render to the township board, on the Tuesday next preceding the annual township meeting, a full and true account of all moneys received and disbursed by them as such inspectors during the year, which account shall be settled by said township board, and such disbursements allowed, if the proper vouchers are presented.

Sec. 95. Whenever any district board shall fail to supply any vacancy that shall occur in their own number, within ten days after the time of its occurrence, the board of inspectors shall fill the same by appointment.

FORM OF APPOINTMENT OF DISTRICT OFFICERS BY SCHOOL INSPECTORS.

The undersigned, school inspectors for the township of ——, do hereby appoint A—— B——, *assessor* of school district No. ——,

in said township, to fill the vacancy created by the ——— of C——
D——, the late incumbent.

E—— F——,
G—— H——,
I—— J——,
School Inspectors.

1. The board of inspectors of one township cannot fill a vacancy in the district board where the district is fractional. This requires the action of the joint inspectors of the several townships.

CERTAIN DUTIES OF TOWNSHIP CLERK.

SEC. 96. The township clerk shall be the clerk of the board of school inspectors by virtue of his office, and shall attend all meetings of said board, and under their direction prepare all their reports and record the same, and shall record all their proceedings, including the names of teachers to whom certificates shall have been given, with the date of each certificate, and the name of each teacher whose certificate shall have been annulled, with the date of such annulment.

1. An error of the township clerk, such as entering upon his record the words "township board," when it should be "board of school inspectors," may be corrected. Any omission on the part of the clerk to record the actual proceedings of the board, should be supplied at once. For this reason, the clerk should read to the inspectors his minutes of proceedings before they are recorded. A mere clerical error may always be corrected.

SEC. 97. On receiving notice from the county treasurer, of the amount of school moneys apportioned to his township, he shall apportion the same amongst the several districts therein, entitled to the same, in proportion to the number of children in each between the ages of four and eighteen years, as the same shall be shown by the annual report of the director of each district for the school year last closed.

1. The apportionment of the income of the primary school fund made from the office of Superintendent is to the different townships, in proportion to the number of children in each, between the ages of four and eighteen, as appears by the reports of school officers transmitted to his office. This money is apportioned to townships in which districts have not kept up a school for three months, if the number of scholars residing in such districts have been reported; but the money thus apportioned to the townships, goes to those districts only in which schools have been taught three months, by a qualified teacher. See section 119.

2. When money has been erroneously apportioned to a district in which no school has been taught for the prescribed time, and drawn

by the district officers, there is no statutory provision for rectifying the error. It should be restored to the treasury of the township, and distribution of it made to such districts as are entitled to it.

3. If the township clerk makes an error in his apportionment, by which a district is deprived of its money, the district may look to the clerk for the amount.

4. The statute vests no discretion with the clerk to make an equitable distribution to districts, different from what the reports of the director shows.

5. The omission to date a report, regularly made from a district to a moderator, will not deprive such district of its proportion of public money.

6. The public money may be apportioned to a district, when the school has been sustained by subscription, if the scholar has been taught by a qualified teacher for the time required by law.

7. The public money may be used to pay so much of a teachers' wages as may be due him, on the revocation of his certificate.

8. For the manner of apportioning to fractional districts, see section 139.

9. The public money is to be apportioned among the several districts, in proportion to the number of children in each, between the ages of four and eighteen, as the same appears *from the annual report* of the director for school year last closed. If children between these ages move into adjoining districts after the census is taken by the director, and the report is made, the district into which they have moved draws no public money on their account.

10. Moneys raised by tax for support of the schools, can not be apportioned to teachers who are not qualified teachers.

11. When interest has accumulated on moneys raised for building purgoses, it should be appropriated to the same purposes as the principal. There is no authority of law for loaning the moneys raised for school purposes, or building school houses.

Sec. 98. Said clerk shall also apportion, in like manner, on receiving notice of the amount from the township treasurer, all moneys raised by township tax, or received from other sources for the support of schools, and in cases make out and deliver to the township treasurer, a written statement of the number of children in each district drawing money and the amount apportioned to each district, and record the apportionment in his office.

Sec. 99. He shall receive and keep all reports to the inspectors from the directors of the several school districts in his township, and all the books and papers belonging to the inspectors, and file such papers in his office.

Sec. 100. He shall receive all such communications as may be transmitted to him by the Superintendent of Public Instruction, and dispose of the same in the manner directed therein.

Sec. 101. He shall transmit to the county clerk all such reports as may be delivered to him for that purpose by the inspectors, within the time limited in this chapter.

1. No time is here fixed for transmitting the return, but it should be done without delay. The distribution of public money is made annually in May.

Sec. 102. Each township clerk shall cause a map to be made of his township, showing by distinct lines thereon, the boundaries of each school district, and parts of school districts therein, and shall regularly number the same thereon, as established by the inspectors.

Sec. 103. One copy of such map shall be filed by the said clerk in his office, and one other copy he shall file with the supervisor of the township; and within one month after any division or alteration of a district, or the organization of a new one in his township, the said clerk shall file a new map and copy thereof, as aforesaid, showing the same.

Sec. 104. The clerk shall also certify to the supervisor the amount to be assessed upon the taxable property of any school district retaining the district school house or other property, on the division of the district, as the same shall have been determined by the inspectors, and he shall also certify the same to the director of such district, and to the director of the district entitled thereto.

Sec. 105. Said clerk shall also be the township librarian, and as such, shall have the custody of the township library; and he shall do and execute all such other acts and things pertaining to his office as may be required of him by the inspectors.

OF TAXES FOR SCHOOL PURPOSES.

Sec. 106. It shall be the duty of the supervisor of the township to assess the taxes voted by every school district in his township, and also all other taxes provided for in this chapter, chargeable against such district or township, upon the taxable property of the district or township respecttvely, and to place the same on the township assessment roll in the column for school taxes, and the same shall be collected and returned by the township treasurer, in the same manner, and for the same compensation as township taxes.

Sec. 107. The supervisor shall also assess upon the taxable property of his township, two mills on each dollar of the valuation thereof, in each year; and twenty-five dollars of the same shall be applied to the purchase of books for the township library, and the remainder thereof shall be apportioned to the several school districts in the township, for the support of schools therein, and the same shall be collected and returned in the same manner as provided [in the preceding section,] and all school taxes returned for non-payment, shall be collected in the same manner as State and county taxes. [See sections 141 and 142.]

1. In many townships heretofore, for various causes, it has been the practice for the supervisors to omit the assessment of this tax·

It is the basis of the school system, and the most important portion of the system of taxation, devised to support the schools and render them under the requirements of the revised constitution, free to all who choose to enter their doors. The neglect to assess this tax in the manner the law provides, renders the supervisor not only liable to a penalty, but such a neglect is a misdemeanor, and an indictable offence. The district cannot by any vote, waive its assessment; nor can the $25 appropriated to library purposes be otherwise disposed of than as provided in this section.

2. The townships have in some instances used the mill tax for township purposes. The officers who thus appropriated it, or suffered it to be thus appropriated, are liable for it, and should restore it without delay.

3. See section 142.

SEC. 108. The supervisor, on delivery of the warrant for the collection of taxes to the township treasurer, shall also deliver to said treasurer a written statement of the amount of school and library taxes, the amount raised for district purposes on the taxable property of each district in the township, the amount belonging to any new district on the division of the former district, and the names of all persons having judgments assessed under the provisions of this chapter upon the taxable property of any district, with the amount payable to such person on account thereof.

1. By the provisions of section 142, the supervisor of each township, on the delivery of the warrant, &c., is also to deliver to the treasurer a written statement, certified by him, of the amount of taxes levied under section 107, upon any property lying within the bounds of a fractional district, a part of which is situated within the township, and the returns of which are made to another township: and the treasurer pays to the treasurer of such other township the amount of taxes so levied and collected.

SEC. 109. The township treasurer shall retain in his hands, out of the moneys collected by him, after deducting the amount of the tax for township expenses, the full amount of the school tax on the assessment roll, and hold the same subject to the warrant of the proper district officers, to the order of the school inspectors, or of the persons entitled thereto.

SEC. 110. Said treasurer shall, from time to time, apply to the county treasurer for all school and library moneys belonging to his township, or the districts thereof; and on receipt of the moneys to be apportioned to the districts, he shall notify the township clerk of the amount to be apportioned. [See sections 142 and 143.]

CERTAIN DUTIES OF THE COUNTY CLERK.

SEC. 111. It shall be the duty of each county clerk to receive all such communications as may be directed to him by the Superintendent of Public Instruction, and dispose of the same in the manner directed by said Superintendent.

SEC. 112. The clerk of each county shall, immediately after receiving the annual reports of the several boards of school inspectors, transmit to the Superintendent of Public Instruction one of the duplicate reports of each of the said several boards, and the other he shall file in his office; and on receiving notice from the Superintendent of the amount of moneys apportioned to the several townships in his county, he shall file the same in his office, and forthwith deliver a copy thereof to the county treasurer.

SEC. 113 of the school law, as published in the revised statutes and pamphlet edition of 1848, is repealed.

1. Section 112 makes a material alteration in the duties of the county clerk, from the law as published in pamphlet form in 1848. The county clerks make no abstracts, but simply forward the reports of the inspectors to the Superintendent.

2. An act prescribing the duties of the Superintendent, approved March 29, 1850, provides that whenever the returns from any county, township or city, upon which a statement of the amount to be disbursed or paid to any such county, township or city, shall be so far defective as to render it impracticable to ascertain the share of public moneys which ought to be disbursed or paid to such county, township or city, the Superintendent shall ascertain by the best evidence in his power, the facts upon which the ratio of such apportionment shall depend and make the apportionment accordingly. It also provides that whenever by accident, mistake, or any other cause, the returns from any county, township or city, shall not contain the whole number of scholars in such county, township or city, between the ages of four and eighteen years, and entitled to draw money from the fund, and by which any such township, county or city, shall fail to have apportioned to it the amount to which it is justly entitled, the Superintendent shail apportion such deficiency in his next annual apportionment.

LIBRARIES.

SEC. 114. A township library shall be maintained in each organized township in this State, which shall be the property of the township, and the parents and guardians of all children therein between the ages of four and eighteen years, shall be permitted to use books from such library without charge, being responsible to the township for the safe return thereof, and for any injury done thereto, according to such rules and regulations as are or may be established by the board of school inspectors of the township.

SEC. 115. The books of such library shall, once in three months, be distributed by the township librarian among the several school districts of the township, in proportion to the number of children in each between the ages aforesaid, as the same shall appear by the last report of the director thereof, and said books shall be drawn and returned by the several directors for their respective districts. [See section 144.]

1. The law does not authorize any other person but the director to draw books, and he is responsible for their preservation and safety after having drawn them.

2. No provision of law exists, by which different townships can exchange books.

3. Section 144 authorizes the school inspectors to suspend the operation of this section whenever they are of opinion that the interests of the people require it, and to restore it again as they think best.

Sec. 116. The clear proceeds of all fines for any breach of the penal laws of this State, and for penalties, or upon any recognizances in criminal proceedings, and all equivalents for exemption from military duty, when collected in any county, and paid into the county treasury, together with all moneys heretofore collected and paid into said treasury on account of such fines or equivalents, and not already apportioned, shall be apportioned by the county treasurer between the first and tenth days of April in each year, among the several townships in the county, according to the number of children therein between the ages of four and eighteen years, as shown by the last annual statement of the county clerk on file in his office; which money shall be applied to the purchase of books for the township library, and for no other purpose.

1. The boards of supervisors have no anthority to remit fines imposed by courts of law, and all moneys collected or received by the county treasurers on fines, penalties and forfeitures of recognizances, must be applied to the purposes indicated in this section, and to these alone.

Sec. 117. In each district in which a district library has been established, the director shall, as the librarian of the district, distribute the books therein to the children of his district of proper age, and shall collect from the parents or guardians of such children, all such damages as they may respectively become liable to pay on account of any injury done to, or loss of, or neglect to return any of such books or any books belonging to the township library, pursuant to such rules and regulations as shall be prescribed by the board of school inspectors.

Sec. 118. If such damage shall have occurred by reason of any injury to, or loss of, or neglect to return any books belonging to the township library, they shall be collected in the name of the township, and paid into the township treasury for the benefit of such township library; and if the same shall have accrued by reason of any injury to, or loss of, or neglect to return any books belonging to the district library, the same shall be collected in the name of the district, for the benefit of the district library.

1. It is questionable whether the township clerk can justly withhold books from a director who has refused to pay a fine imposed upon him. It would be questionable policy to withhold the distribu-

tion of the books, and deprive the inhabitants and children of the benefit of them, for default of a director. The law relating to libraries is a subject of considerable complaint. Such complaint seems to arise partly from defects in the law, and partly from the selections of books made by the inspectors. This subject is referred to at length in another part of this document, in connection with which will be found rules for their regulation and management.

2. The libraries are designed for those who have completed their studies in the primary schools, and those who have not. They are intended for the use of all the inhabitants of the district.

3. The use of the books cannot be restricted to scholars attending school.

DISTRIBUTION OF THE INCOME OF THE SCHOOL FUND.

SEC. 119. The interest of the primary school fund shall be distributed on the first Monday of May, or as soon thereafter as practicable, in each year, for the support of primary schools in the several townships in this State from which reports have been received from the Superintendent of Public Instruction, in accordance with the provisions of this chapter, for the school year last closed, in proportion to the number of children in such townships between the ages of four and eighteen years; and the same shall be payable on the warrant of the Auditor General to the treasurers of the several counties.

SEC. 120. The several county treasurers shall apply for and receive such moneys as shall have been apportioned to their respective counties, when the same shall become due; and each of said treasurers shall immediately give notice to the treasurer and clerk of each township in his county, of the amount of school moneys apportioned to his township, and shall hold the same subject to the order of the township treasurer.

SEC. 121. Whenever the clerk of any county shall receive from the Superintendent of Public Instruction, notice of the amount of moneys apportioned to the several townships in his county, he shall file the same in his office, and forthwith deliver a copy thereof to the county treasurer.

OF SUITS AND JUDGMENTS AGAINST SCHOOL DISTRICTS.

SEC. 122. Justices of the peace shall have jurisdiction in all cases of assumpsit, debt, covenant, and trespass on the case against school districts, when the amount claimed, or matter in controversy shall not exceed one hundred dollars, and the parties shall have the same right of appeal as in other cases.

SEC. 123. When any suit shall be brought against a school district, it shall be commenced by summons, a copy of which shall be left with the assessor of the district, at least eight days before the return day thereof.

SEC. 124. No execution shall issue on any judgment against a school district, nor shall any suit be brought thereon, but the same shall be collected in the manner prescribed in this chapter.

SEC. 125. Whenever any final judgment shall be obtained against a school district, if the same shall not be removed to any other court, the assessor of the district shall certify to the supervisor of the township, and to the director of the district, the date and amount of such judgment, with the name of the person in whose favor the same was rendered, and if the judgment shall be removed to another court, the assessor shall certify the same as aforesaid, immediately after the final determination thereof, against the district.

FORM OF CERTIFICATE TO SUPERVISOR.

To the Supervisor of the Township of———:

I hereby certify that the following judgments have been recovered against school district No. ——, of said township, and that the date of such payments, the amounts thereof, and the name of the person in whose favor said judgments were rendered, were as follows:

NAMES OF PERSONS.	DATE OF J'DGM'T.	AM'T OF J'DGM'T.	
A—— B——,		$	
C—— D——,			
E—— F——,			
		———	———

Dated this —— day of ———, 185 .

G—— H——, *Assessor.*

1. If the judgments, or any of them, have been appealed, the assessor, under his signature and the date of the certificate, should certify as follows:

I also certify that the judgments above specified as having been recovered by A—— B—— and C—— D——, have been removed to another court, according to law.

2. Copies of the above certificates are to be given to the director. See the provisions of section 127 in relation to judgments against fractional districts.

Sec. 126. If the assessor shall fail to certify the judgment as required in the preceding section, it shall be lawful for the party obtaining the same, his executors, administrators or assigns, to file with the supervisor the certificate of the justice or clerk of the court rendering the judgment, showing the facts which should have been certified by the assessor.

Sec. 127. If the district against whom any such judgment shall be rendered, is situated in part in two or more townships, a certificate thereof shall be delivered as aforesaid to the supervisor of each township in which such district is in part situated.

Sec. 128. The supervisor or supervisors receiving either of the certificates of a judgment as aforesaid, shall proceed to assess the amount thereof, with interest from the date of the judgment to the time when the warrant for the collection thereof will expire, upon the taxable property of the district, placing the same on the next township assessment roll in the column for school taxes, and the same proceedings shall be had, and the same shall be collected and returned in the same manner as other district taxes.

PENALTIES AND LIABILITIES.

Sec. 129. Every taxable inhabitant receiving the notice mentioned in the first and second sections of this chapter, who shall neglect or refuse duly to serve and return such notice, and every chairman of the first district meeting in any district, who shall wilfully neglect or refuse to perform the duties enjoined on him in this chapter, shall respectively forfeit the sum of five dollars.

Sec. 130. Every person duly elected to the office of moderator, director or assessor of a school district, who shall neglect or refuse, without sufficient cause, to accept such office and serve therein, or who, having entered upon the duties of his office, shall neglect or refuse to perform any duty required of him by virtue of his office, shall forfeit the sum of ten dollars.

Sec. 131. Every person duly elected or appointed a school inspector, who shall neglect or refsue, without sufficient cause, to qualify and serve as such, or who, having entered upon the duties of his office, shall neglect or refuse to perform any duty required of him by virtue of his office, shall forfeit the sum of ten dollars.

Sec. 132. If any board of school inspectors shall neglect or refuse to make and deliver to the township clerk, their annual report to the county clerk, as required in this chapter, within the time limited therefor, they shall be liable to pay the full amount of money lost by their failure, with interest thereon, to be recovered by the township treasurer in the name of the township, in an action of debt or on the case.

Sec. 133. If any township clerk shall neglect or refuse to transmit the report mentioned in the preceding section, to the county clerk, as required in this chapter, he shall be liable to pay the full amount lost by such neglect or refusal, with interest thereon, to be recovered in the manner specified in the preceding section.

Sec. 134. Every county clerk who shall neglect or refuse to transmit the report required in this chapter to be made by him to the Superintendent of Public Instruction, within the time therefor limited, shall be liable to pay to each township the full amount which such township, or any school district therein, shall lose by such neglect or refusal, with interest thereon, to be recovered in the manner specified in the last two preceding sections.

Sec. 135. All the moneys collected or received by any township treasurer under the provisions of either of the three last preceding sections, shall be apportioned and distributed to the school districts entitled thereto, in the same manner, and in the same proportion that the moneys lost by any neglect or refusal therein mentioned would, according to the provisions of this chapter, have been apportioned and distributed.

Sec. 136. The township board of each township shall have power, and is hereby required, to remove from office, upon satisfactory proof, after at least five days' notice to the party implicated, any district officer or school inspector who shall have illegally used or disposed of any of the public moneys entrusted to his charge.

MISCELLANEOUS PROVISIONS RELATING TO PRIMARY SCHOOLS.

Sec. 137. Any person paying taxes in a school district in which he does not reside, may send scholars to any district school therein, and such person shall, for that purpose, have and enjoy all the rights and privileges of a resident of such district, except the right of voting therein, and shall be rated therein for teachers' wages and fuel, and in the census of such district, and the apportionment of moneys from the school fund, scholars so sent, and attending generally such schools, shall be considered as belonging to such district: [*Provided*, That a majority of the qualified voters attending at any regular meeitng in the district in which such person resides, shall have determined that no school shall be taught in said district for the year, or, provided such person shall not reside in any organized school district.]

1. Under the law of 1848, as published in pamphlet form, any person paying taxes in a school district in which he did not reside, could send scholars to any district school therein, as provided in the first portion of this section. The proviso was enacted by a subsequent Legislature.

2. A person paying taxes in *several* school districts in which he does not reside, may send to any district school in any and all of said districts, subject to the proviso contained in this section. The number of scholars that may be sent is not limited by the law.

3. The scholars that are so sent, are not limited to the *children* of such persons, but to all such as are in their employ as apprentices, and all children living with such persons, and subject to their care and protection. Such children may be rated for teachers' wages and fuel, and should be included in the census of such district and in the apportionment of the income of the school fund.

Sec. 138. Whenever any portion of a school district shall be set off and annexed to any other district, or organized into a new one, after a tax for district purposes, other than the payment of any debts of the district, shall have been levied upon the taxable property thereof, but not collected, such tax shall be collected in the same manner as if no part of such district had been set off, and the said former district, and the district to which the portion so set off may be annexed, or the new district organized from such portion, shall each be entitled to such proportion of said tax, as the amount of taxable property in each part thereof bears to the whole amount of taxable property on which such tax is levied.

Sec. 139. For the purpose of apportioning the income of the primary school fund among the several townships, a district situated in part in two or more townships, shall be considered as belonging to the township to which the annual report of the director is required to be made; but money raised in any one of such townships for the support of schools therein, shall be apportioned to the districts and parts of districts therein, according to the number of children of the proper age in each.

Sec. 140. The qualified voters of any school district may, by vote at their annual district meeting, raise by tax upon the taxable property of the district a sum not exceeding one dollar for every scholar in the district between the ages of four and eighteen years, for the support of common schools in the district, and such tax shall be reported to the supervisor of the proper township, and shall be levied, collected and returned in the same manner as townships taxes are levied, collected and returned.

Sec. 141. If any supervisor shall neglect or refuse to assess the taxes provided for in section one hundred and seven of chapter fifty-eight of the revised statutes, he shall be liable to pay to any school district the full amount lost to such district by such neglect or refusal, with the interest thereon, to be recovered by the assessor in the name of the school district, in an action of debt on the case.

SEC. 142. The supervisor of each township, on the delivery of the warrant for the collection of taxes to the township treasurer, shall also deliver to said treasurer a written statement certified by him of the amount of the taxes levied under section one hundred and seven of said chapter, upon any property lying within the bounds of a fractional school district, a part of which is situate within his township, and the returns of which are made to the clerk of some other township; and the said township treasurer shall pay to the township treasurer of such other township the amount of the taxes so levied and certified to him for the use of such fractional school district.

SEC. 143. Each treasurer of a township, to the clerk of which the returns of any fractional school district shall be made, shall apply to the treasurer of any other township in which any part of such fractional school district may be situate, for any money to which such district may be entitled; and when so received, it shall be certified to the township clerk, and apportioned in the same manner as other taxes for school purposes.

SEC. 144. The board of school inspectors shall have power to suspend the operation of section one hundred and fifteen of said chapter, whenever they shall be of opinion that the convenience or the interests of the people of their township will be promoted thereby, and to restore the same, as in their judgment they shall think best.

GENERAL NOTES.

So far as the reports of cases coming before the higher courts of our own State, have been published, there appears to be but a single case which has been adjudicated, arising out of the operation of our school laws. This case is copied from Douglas' Michigan Reports, and is as follows: [See page 343 of this document.]

DISSOLUTION OF DISTRICTS.

People *ex. rel.* Strong, *vs.* Davidson and others, school inspectors of the township of Greenfield.

Under the statute (S. L. 1840, page 215, Sec. 25,) empowering the school inspectors of any township "to divide the township into such number of districts, and to regulate and alter the boundaries of said school districts, as may from time to time be necessary, they may dissolve one organized district, and annex it to another."

MOTION for a MANDAMUS, commanding Davidson and others, school inspectors of the county of Wayne, to pay or cause to be paid to school district No. 12, in said township, such sum of money as the district may be entitled to by law, from the common school fund, and from the fund arising from the taxes of the township.

It appeared that November 22, 1842, the respondents divided district No. 4, in said township, into two districts, the new district being numbered 12—that on the first day of December following, the organization of the new district, under the statute, was perfected; and that on the 13th of the same month the respondents made an order, dissolving the new district, and re-annexing it to district No. 4. The question involved in the case was, whether the respondents had power to make the last mentioned order.

B. F .H. WITHERELL, in support of the motion. WHIPPLE J., delivered the opinion of the court.

The authority of the inspectors thus to dissolve district No. 12, and re-annex it to the old district from which it was severed, must depend upon the construction of the twenty-fifth section of the act entitled "an act to amend the revised statutes relative to primary schools," approved April 12, 1840. [Re-enacted by revised statutes of 1846, page 227, Sec. 71.] [Session laws of 1848, page 215.] By that section the inspectors are authorized "to divide the township into such number of districts, and to regulate and alter the boundaries of said school districts, as may from time to time be necessary."

It will be perceived that the number of districts in any township is to be determined from the language of the section, which confers authority to *divide* the township from time to time into such number of districts as may be necessary. If they may divide the township into twelve districts, why may they not divide it into ten by enlarging the boundaries of one or more of those in existence, or, which is the same thing, by annexing two or more, so as to constitute but one district, as may from time to time become necessary? The power could not perhaps be derived from the words "regulate and alter the boundaries," &c., but these words taken in connection with the authority to "divide" from time to time as may be necessary, justified *legally* the order made by the inspectors. That order may have been unwise; it may have been an abuse of the discretion with which the inspectors are clothed; but such abuse of discretion cannot authorize the interference of this court. We think it clear that the authority to determine the number of districts in each township, ought to be lodged in some responsible body. Unless it is conferred upon the inspectors, the power does not exist; and as the words of the twenty fifth section justify the construction we have given to it, we are bound to overrule the motion for a *mandamus*.

Motion denied.

The following notes, taken from the New York decisions, are applicable to the existing laws and state of things in Michigan:

MULTIPLICATION OF DISTRICTS.

One of the most formidable obstacles to the efficiency of our common schools is believed to be the unnecessary multiplication and subdivision of districts. In those portions of the State where the population is scattered over a large extent of territory, the convenience and accommodation of the inhabitants, require the formation of districts comprising a small amount of taxable property, applicable to the support of schools and a limited number of children. But where an opposite state of things exists, the interests of education will be most effectually promoted, by assigning to each district the greatest extent of territory compatible with securing to the children the requisite facilities for their regular attendance at the schools.—[*New York Decisions*.

Almost all the existing evils of the common school system have their origin in the limited means of the school district. The tendency is to subdivision and to a contraction of their territorial boundaries. This consequence must follow in some degree from the increase of population; but the subdivision of school districts tends to advance in a much greater ratio. The average number of children in our school districts is about fifty-five. * * * *

From the observations he has made, the Superintendent deems it due to the common school system, that no new district shall be formed with a much smaller number, unless peculiar circumstances render it proper to make it an exception to the general rule. In feeble districts, cheap instructors, poor and ill-furnished school houses, and a general languor of the cause of education are almost certain to be found.—*N. Y. Dec.*

QUALIFICATIONS OF TEACHERS.

The qualifications of teachers are left to the discrimination and judgment of the legal examiners. They must determine the degree of learning and ability necessary for a teacher. They ought to be satisfied that a certificate is given to those only whose learning and ability fit them in all respects to instruct common schools.—*Ib.*

In judging of the moral character of a candidate for teacher, if the examining officers know of any serious imputation or defect of principle, it is their duty to refuse to certify. A certificate may be annulled for immoral habits generally, notwithstanding the teacher may perform all his duties during school hours.—*Ib.*

In relation to the moral character of the teacher, much is left to the discretion of the examining officer. He must be satisfied that it is good, because he has to certify to its correctness. On this point what would be satisfactory to one man might be unsatisfactory to another. Every person has a right to the enjoyment of his own religious *belief* without molestation; and the examining officer should content himself with inquiries as to the *moral character* of the teacher, leaving him to the same liberal enjoyment of his religious belief that he asks for himself. If, however, a person openly derides all religion, he ought not to be a teacher of youth. The employment of such a person would be considered a grievance by a great portion of the inhabitants of all the districts.—*Ib.*

If the trustees or inhabitants are to determine what their district require, and the certifying officers are to be governed by their opinions and wishes, the officers themselves might as well be dispensed with. In his annual report to the Legislature for the year 1835, the

Superintendent of Common Schools (Gen. Dix) observes: "One of the most responsible and delicate trusts to be executed under the common school system is that of inspecting teachers and pronouncing upon their qualifications. If this is negligently conducted, or with a willingness to overlook deficiences, instead of insisting rigidly upon the requirements of the law, it is manifest that men without the necessary moral character, learning or ability, will gain a foothoold in the common schools, and present a serious obstacle to the improvements of which they are susceptible. This would be an evil of the greatest magnitude, and there is no remedy for it but a strict inspection of the candidates. It has been the practice in some instances for the inspectors to have a reference to the *particular circumstances of the cases* in giving a certificate. Thus they have sometimes given an individual a certificate with a view to a *summer school,* in which the children taught are usually smaller and require less of the teacher, when the certificate would have been withheld, if it was asked with a view to qualify the teacher for a *winter school.* But it is obvious that such a distinction is wholly inadmissible. A certificate must be unconditional, by the terms of the law. The inspectors must be satisfied with the qualifications of the teacher "in respect to moral character, learning and ability;" and the certificate when once given is an absolute warrant for the individual to teach, and to receive the public money, unless revoked; in which case it ceases to be operative from the date of its revocation. The standard of qualification for teachers, so far as granting certificates is concerned, is of necessity arbitrary. The law does not prescribe the degree of learning or ability which a teacher shall possess, but virtually refers the decision of this important matter to the inspectors, who have not, neither should they possess the power of relaxing the general rule with reference to the circumstances of any particular case, by departing from the standard of qualification which they assume as their guide in others."—*N. Y. Dec.*

The inhabitants of the district, and particularly parents who have children attending the school, should be invited to be present at the inspection; * * * * and trustees of districts are required, whenever they receive information of an intended visit, to communicate it as generally as possible to the inhabitants —*Ib.*

DISCIPLINE AND CONDUCT OF THE SCHOOL.

It can scarcely be necessary to remark on the importance of order and system in the schools, not only to enable the pupils to learn anything, but to give them those habits of regularity so essential in the formation of character. Punctuality of attendance, as well as its steady continuance should be enforced. Parents should be told how much their children lose, to what inconvenience they expose the teacher, and what disorder they bring upon the whole school, by not insisting upon the scholars being punctually at the school room at the appointed hour; and above all they should be warned of the injurious consequences of allowing their children to be absent from school during the term. By being indulged in absences they lose the connection of their studies, probably fall behind their class, become discouraged, and then seek every pretext to play the truant. The habit of irregularity and insubordination thus acquired, will be apt to mark their character through life.—*N. Y. Dec.*

TEXT BOOKS.

It is believed that there are none now in use in our schools that are very defective; and the difference between them is so slight that the gain to the scholar will not compensate for the heavy expenses to the parent, caused by the substitution of new books with every new teacher; and the capriciousness of change which some are apt to indulge on this subject, cannot be too strongly or decidedly resisted. Trustees of districts should look to this matter when they engage teachers.

One consequence of the practice is, the great variety of text books on the same subject, acknowledged by all to be one of the greatest evils which afflicts our schools. It compels the teacher to divide the pupils into as many classes as there are kinds of books, so that the time which might have been devoted to a careful and deliberate hearing of a class of ten or twelve, where all could have improved by the corrections and observations of the instructor, is almost wasted in the hurried recitations of ten or a dozen pupils in separate classes; while in large schools, some must be wholly neglected.—*Ib.*

CHANGE OF SITE.

Experience has shown that by far the most fertile sources of contention and difficulty in the various school districts, originate from the proceedings of the inhabitants connected with the change of the site of their school house. Such a measure should, therefore, only be adopted when the convenience and accommodation of the inhabitants will be essentially promoted thereby; when the altered situation of the district imperatively requires a change; and even then, the full and hearty concurrence not merely of a clear and decided majority of the district, but of the inhabitants generally, should be secured, before any final decision is made. There must always be a portion of the inhabitants, residing at the extremities of the district, who will experience more or less inconviences, at particular seasons of the year, in consequence of their distanae from the school house; but it is better that these partial inconveniences should be submitted to, than that they should be transferred to others and the whole district plunged into a contention respecting the site. But when, in consequence of the enlargement of the boundaries of the district, a change is indispensable, the inhabitants should come together in a conciliatory and friendly spirit, having no other object in view than the best interests of the district and the convenience of the greatest number; and their action should be deliberate and circumspect—reconciling, as far as possible, the interests of all, and rejecting every proposition calculated to sow the seeds of dissension or disturbance in any portion of the district:—bearing in mind that a mere numerical triumph, leaving a large minority dissatisfied and irritated, however gratifying to the successful party, for a time, is but a poor compensation for a divided and distracted district, and an embittered and hostile neighborhood.—*N. Y. Dec.*

There can be no partnership in the erection of a school house, which will prevent the district from controlling it entirely for the purposes of the district school.—*Ib.*

A tax cannot be laid to erect a building to be occupied *jointly* as a school house and a meeting house.—*Ib.*

A tax may be voted for the erection of a *fence* around the school house lot, and for a *bell.*—*Ib.*

RECONSIDERAION OF PROCEEDINGS.

The inhabitants of school districts may reconsider and repeal, alter and modify their proceedings at any time before they have been carried into effect, either wholly or in part. But the intention to do so, should be explicitly set forth in the notice of the meeting called for that purpose. When, however, contracts have actually been entered into, liabilities incurred, or expenditures of money had, in the prosecution of any measure directed by the district, a reconsideration will not be sanctioned, as no means exists to indemnify those who may be losers thereby.—*Ib.*

TAXES.

Where a tax is voted by the inhabitants for any purpose, the specific amount of the tax, and the particular purpose for which it is designed, should be fully and clearly stated. And where several objects of expenditure are to be provided for, the amount to be raised for each should be expressed in the resolution.—*Ib.*

CONTRACTS WITH TEACHERS.

The most fruitful source of difficulty in school districts, has been the looseness and irregularity with which these contracts have been made. In some districts the trustees are in the habit of agreeing to pay the teacher the whole amount of public money that should be received, be it more or less. This is unjust to the teacher or the district, and has almost always led to contention. The agreement should be to pay him a specific sum by the month or by the quarter, adequate to the value of his services. If the public money is not sufficient, [in Michigan, public money and other taxes voted for support of schools] the deficiency should be supplied by a rate bill. It is not to be believed that any intelligent citizens will consider that sordidness to be economy, which prefers that their children should be brought up in ignorance, or instructed in error, rather than contribute the mere trifle which secure them an education, sound and accurate, at least as far as it goes. When the rewards which other professions and avocations hold out to talent, knowledge and industry, are so liberal, how can it be expected that persons competent to the great business of instruction, should devote themselves to it for a compensation inadequate to their support?—*Ib.*

BOARDING TEACHERS.

A practice prevails to a very considerable extent among the several school districts, of trustees' engaging with a teacher that he shall board with the parents of the children alternately. There is no authority for such a contract, and it cannot be enforced on the inhabitants. This compulsory boarding gives occasion to constant altercation and complaint, which often terminate in breaking up the school. The best arrangement is to give the teacher a specific sum and let him board himself. But there are some districts so destitute that it may afford the inhabitants considerable relief to be permitted to board the teacher. In such cases the object can be obtained in another way. Let the trustees contract with the teacher at a specific sum per month, or by the quarter, and they may agree with him, that if he shall be afforded satisfactory board at the house of any of the inhabitants, he shall allow whatever sum may be agreed upon per week for such board.—*N. Y. Dec.*

TEACHERS' CONTRACT.

If a teacher's certificate is annulled, the trustees [district board] are at liberty to dismiss him, and to rescind their contract with him. They engage him as a qualified teacher, and the moment he ceases to be so, there is a failure of the consideration for the contract. If, however, the trustees continue him to the school after notice that his certificate has been annulled, it will be regarded as such a continuance of the contract that they will not be allowed at a subsequent period to dispute it.—*Ib.*

EXEMPTION OF INDIGENT PERSONS.

In the exercise of the power conferred upon the trustees, of exempting indigent inhabitants of their district from the payment of the whole, or of portions of their rate bills, the utmost liberality, compatible with justice to the district, should be indulged. Nothing can be more at variance with the benign spirit and intent of the school laws, than the compulsory distress and sale of articles of absolute necessity to an indigent family, for the purpose of satisfying the rate bill for teachers' wages. And yet cases of this kind are frequently brought to the notice of the department. Every reasonable facility should be afforded to the children of the poor, for the attainment of all the blessings and advantages of elementary instruction; and this should never be permitted to become in any degree burdensome to their parents. Where any inhabitant of the district in indigent circumstances cannot meet the rate bill for the payment of the teachers' wages, without subjecting himself to serious embarrassment, or his family to sensible deprivation, he should promptly and cheerfully be exonerated. A just feeling of pride may reasonably be expected to preclude any from availing themselves of this exemption, unless under the pressure of absolute necessity; and occasional abuses of the privilege so accorded, are productive of less disastrous results, than a prevailing impression among the indigent inhabitants of a district, that their children can partake of the advantages of common school education, only at a burdensome charge to themselves, and by a sacrifice of the ordinary necessities and comforts of their families. —*N. Y. Dec.*

As a general rule, *all* under the age of twenty-one years, and of a proper age to be benefitted by instruction, are entitled to admission. There must, however, be some discretion vested in the trustees, in regard to such admission. Children having infectious diseases—idiots—infants—and persons over twenty-one, may undoubtedly be excluded; and colored children, where their attendance is obnoxions to the greater portion of the patrons of the school, especially in cases where schools have been established for their separate benefit, within a reasonable distance from their residence.—*Ib.*

DISMISSAL OF SCHOLARS.

It is the duty of the trustees to co-operate with the teacher in the government of the school, and to aid him, to the extent of their power and influence, in the enforcement of reasonable and proper rules and regulations; but they have no right to dismiss a scholar, except for the strongest reasons; for example, such a degree of moral depravity as to render an association with other scholars dangerous to the latter, or such violent insubordination as to render the maintenance of discipline and order impracticable, in which case they may legally exclude him from the school, until such period as he may consent to submit to the reasonable rules and regulations of the teacher and trustees; and if after such exclusion he persists in attending, without permission from the trustees, and contrary to their directions, he may be proceeded against as a trespasser.—*Ib.*

LIBRARIES.

The object of the law for procuring district libraries is to diffuse information, not only, or even chiefly, among children or minors, but among adults and those who have finished common school education. The books, therefore, should be such as will be useful for circulation among the inhabitants generally. They should not be children's books, or of a juvenile character merely, or light and frivulous tales and remances, but works conveying solid information which will excite a thirst for knowledge, and also gratify it, as far as such a library can. Works imbued with party politics, and those of a sectarian character, or hostility to the Christian religion, should on no account be admitted; and if any are accidentally received they should be immediately removed. Still less can any district be permitted to purchase school books, such as spelling books, grammars, or any others of the description used as text book in schools. Such an application of the public money would be an utter violation of the law. * * *

The selection of the books for the district library, is devolved by law exclusively upon the trustees, (in Michigan upon the school insepctors,) and when the importance of this most beneficial and enlightened provision for the intellectual and moral improvement of the inhabitants of the several districts, of both sexes and all conditions, is duly estimated, the trust here confided is one of no ordinary responsibility. In reference to such selections, but two prominent sources of embarrassment have been experienced. The one has arisen from the necessity of excluding from the libraries all works having, directly or remotely, a sectarian tendency, and the other, from that of recommending the exclusion of novels, romances and other fictitious creations of the imagination, including a large proportion of the lighter liertature of the day.

The propriety of a peremptory and uncompromising exclusion of those catch-penny, but revolting publications which cultivate the taste for the marvellous, the tragic, the horrible, and the supernatural—the lives and exploits of pirates, banditti and desperadoes of every description—is too obvious to every reflecting mind to require the slightest argument. Unless parents desire that their children should pursue the shortest and surest road to ignominy, shame and destruction—should become the ready and apt imitators, on a circumscribed scale, of the pernicious models which they are permitted and encouraged to study—they will frown indignantly on every attempt to place before their immature minds, works whose invariable and only tendency is disastrous, both to the intellect and the heart.

The exclusion of works imbued to any perceptible extent with sectarianism, rests upon the great conservative principles which are at the foundation of our free institutions. Its propriety is readily conceded when applied to publications, setting forth, defending, or illustrating the peculiar tenets which distinguish any one of the numerous religious denominations of the day from the others. On this ground no controversy exists as to the line of duty. But it has been strongly argued that those "standard" theological publications which, avoiding all controverted ground, contain general expositions of Christianity—which assume only those doctrines and principles upon which all "evangelical" denominations of Christians are agreed, are not obnoxious to any reasonable censure, and ought not, upon any just principles, to be excluded from the school district library. There are two answers to this argument, either of which is conclusive. The one is, that the works in question, however exalted may be their merit, and however free from just censure, on the ground of sectarianism, are strictly *theological,* doctrinal or metaphysical; and therefore no more entitled to a place in the district library than works devoted to the professional elucidation of law, medicine, or any other learned professions. Their appropriate place is in the family, church or Sunday school library. The other answer is, that in every portion of our country are to be found conscientious dissenters from the most approved theological tenets of these commentators on Christianity; individuals who claim the right, either of rejecting Christianity altogether, (as the Jews,) or of so interpreting its fundamental doctrines, as to place them beyond the utmost verge of "evangelical" liberality; and this too, without in any degree subjecting themselves to any well-founded imputations upon their moral character as citizens and as men. The State, in the dispensation of its bounty, has no right to trample upon the honest convictions and settled belief of this or of any other class of its citizens, against whose demeanor, in the various relations of society, no accusation can be brought; nor can it rightfully sanction the application of any portion of those funds to which they, in common with others, have contributed, to the enforcement of theological tenets to which they cannot conscientiously subscribe. Any work, therefore, which, departing from the inculcation of those great, enduring and cardinal elements of religion and morality which are impressed upon humanity as a part of its birthright—acknowledged by all upon whom its stamp is affixed, however departed from in practice, and incorporated into the very essence of Christianity as its pre-eminent and distinctive principle—shall descend to a controversy respecting the subordinate or collateral details of theology, however ably sustained and numerously sanctioned, has no legitimate claim to a place in the school district library, nor can its admission be countenanced consistently with sound policy or enlightened reason.

The following general principles have been laid down in a special report on common school libraries, prepared under the direction of the department, by Henry S. Randall, Esq., County Superintendent of common schools of Cortland county, and may be regarded as the settled principles of the department in reference to this class of books:

"1. No works written professedly to uphold or attack any sect or creed in our country, claiming to be a religious one, shall be tolerated in the school libraries.

"2. Standard works on other topics shall not be excluded, because they incidentally and indirectly betray the religious opinions of their authors.

"3. Works avowedly on other topics, which abound in direct and unreserved attacks on, or defences of, the character of any religious sect; or those which hold up any religious body to contempt or execration, by singling out or bringing together only the darker parts of its history or character, shall be excluded from the school libraries.

"It is said that under the above rules, heresy and error are put on the same footing with true religion—that Protestant and Catholic, orthodox and unorthodox, Universalist, Unitarian, Jew, and even Mormon, derive the same immunity! The fact is conceded; and it is averred that each is equally entitled to it, in a government whose very constitution avows the principle of a full and indiscriminate religious toleration.

"He who thinks it hard that he shall not be allowed to combat, through the medium of the school libraries, beliefs, the sin and error of which are as clear to him as is the light in Heaven, will bear in mind that the library at least leaves him and his religious beliefs in as good a condition as it found him. If it will not propagate his tenets, it will leave them unattacked. If he is not allowed to use other men's money to purchase books to assault their religious faiths, he is not estopped from spending his own as he sees fit, in his private, or in his Sunday school library—nor is he debarred from placing these books in the hands of all who are willing to receive them. His power of morally persuading his fellow men is left unimpaired; nor will he, if he has any confidence in the recuperative energies of truth—if he believes his God will ultimately give victory to truth—ask more. In asking, or condescending to accept, the support of an earthly government, he admits the weakness of his cause, the feebleness of his faith. He leans on another arm than that which every page in the Bible declares all-sufficient. In what age of the world has any church entered into meretricious connection with temporal governments, and escaped unsullied from the contact? Any approximation to such connection, even in the minutest particular—any exclusive right or immunity given to one religious sect or another in the school library or elsewhere, is not only anti-religious, but anti-republican. As men, we have the right to adopt religious creeds, and to attempt to influence others to adopt them; but as Americans, as legislators or officials dispensing privileges or immunities among American citizens, we have no right to know one religion from another. The persecuted and wandering Israelite comes here, and he finds no bar in our naturalization laws. The members of the Roman, Greek, or English Church equally become citizens. Those adopting every hue of religious faith—every phase of heresy, take their place equally under the banner of the Republic—and no ecclesiastical power can snatch even 'the least of these' from under its glorious folds. Not an hour of confinement, not the amercement of a farthing, not the deprivation of a right or liberty weighing 'in the estimation of a hair,' can any such power impose on any American citizen, without his own full and entire acquiescence."—*N. Y. Dec.*

When it is considered that the foundations of education are laid during the period of youth, and that the taste for reading and study is, with rare exceptions, formed and matured at this period, if at all, the importance of furnishing an adequate supply of books, adapted to the comprehension of the immature but expanding intellect—suited to its various stages of mental growth, and calculated to lead it onward by a gradual transition, from one field of intellectual and moral culture to another, cannot fail to be appreciated. And even if the intellectual wants of many of the inhabitants of the districts, of more mature age, are duly considered, it admits of little doubt that a due proportion of works of a more familiar and elementary character than are the mass of those generally selected, would have a tendency not only to promote, but often to create that taste for mental pursuits which leads by a rapid and sure progression to a more extended acquaintance with the broad domains of knowledge. Those whose circumstances and pursuits in life, have hitherto precluded any systematic investigation of literary subjects, and who, if they possessed the desire, were debarred the means of intellectual improvement now brought within their reach, can scarcely be expected to pass at once to that high appreciation of useful knowledge, which the perusal of elaborate treatise on any of the numerous branches of science or metaphysics requires; and the fact brought to view by the annual reports of the county superintendents, that by far the greater proportion of the inhabitants of the several districts neglect to avail themselves of the privileges of the library, indicates too general a failure to supply these institutions with the requisite proportion of elementary books.

In the selection of books for the district libraries, suitable provision should be made for every gradation of intellectual advancement; from that of a child, whose insatiable curiosity eagerly prompts to a more intimate acquaintance with the world of matter and of mind, to that of the most finished scholar, who is prepared to augment his stock of knowledge by every means which may be brought within his reach. The prevalence of an enlightened appreciation of the requirements of our people in this respect, has already secured the application of the highest grade of mental and moral excellence to the elementary departments of literature; and works adapted to the comprehension of the most immature intellect, and at the same time conveying the most valuable information to more advanced minds, have been provided—wholly free, on the one hand, from that puerility which is fit only for the nursery, and on the other, from those generalizations and assumptions which are adapted only to advanced stages of mental progress. A more liberal infusion of this class of publications sanctioned by the approbation of the most experienced friends of education into our district libraries, would, it is confidently believed, remove many of those obstacles to their general utility, which otherwise are liable to be perpetuated from generation to generation.--Dix, *Sup't. N. Y.*

SUITS.

Officers required by law to exercise their judgments, are not answerable for mistakes of law, or mere errors of judgment, without any fraud or malice.—*Jenkins vs. Waldron*, 11*th Johnson's Reports*, 114.

A public officer who is required by law to act in certain cases, according to his judgment or opinion, and subject to penalties for his neglect, is not liable to a party for an omission arising from a mistake or want of skill, if acting in *good faith*.—*Seaman vs. Paten*, 2*d Caine's Reports*, 312.

But an officer entrusted by the common law or by statute, is liable to an action for *negligence* in the performance of his trust, or for *fraud* or neglect in the execution of his office.—*Jenner vs. Joliffe*, 9 *John. Rep.* 381.

The collector or other officer who *executes* process, has peculiar protection. He is protected, although the court or officer issuing such process have not, in fact, jurisdiction of the case; if, on the face of the process, it appears that such court or officer had jurisdiction of the *subject matter*, and nothing appears in such process to apprise the officer but that there was jurisdiction of the person of the party affected by the process—*Savacool vs. Boughton*, 5 *Wendell's Reports*, 170.—[*N. Y. Dec.*

TEACHERS.

A teacher may employ necessary means of correction to maintain order; but he should not dismiss a scholar from school without consultation with the trustees.—*Ib.*

Teachers, though not, strictly speaking, *inhabitants* of the district where they are located, should be allowed to participate in all the privileges and benefits of the district libraries.—*N. Y. Dec.*

The authority of the teacher to punish his scholars, extends to acts done in the school room, or play ground, only; and he has no legal right to punish for improper or disorderly conduct elsewhere.—*Ib.*

Where a teacher is dismissed by the trustees for good cause, he can collect his wages only up to the period of his dismissal.

The teacher of a school has necessarily the government of it; and he may prescribe the rules and principles on which such government will be conducted. The trustees should not interfere with the discipline of the school, except on complaint of misconduct on the part of the teacher; and they should then invariably sustain such teacher, unless his conduct has been grossly wrong.—*Ib.*

The *holydays* on which a teacher may dismiss his school are such as it is customary to observe, either throughout the country or in praticular localities; among which may be enumerated the Fourth of July, Thanksgiving, Christmas, New-Year's, &c.—*Ib.*

The teacher may also, unless restraineed by special contract to the contrary, dismiss his school on the afternoon of each Saturday, or the whole of each alternate Saturday, according to the particular custom of the district in that respect, or his own convenience and that of the inhabitants.—*Ib.*

The practice of inflicting *corporal punishment* upon scholars, *in any case whatever*, has no sanction but usage. The teacher is responsible for maintaining good order, and he must be the judge of the degree and nature of the punishment required, where his authority is set at defiance. At the same time he is liable to the party injured for any abuse of a prerogative *which is wholly derived from custom.*—*Ib.*

EXTRACTS FROM THE REPORTS OF THE SUCCESSIVE SUPERINTENDENTS OF PUBLIC INSTRUCTION OF THE STATE OF MICHIGAN.

The opinions of men who have successively held the position of Superintendent of Public Instruction, and whose labors and experience have been given to the cause of education and to the system of instruction, cannot but be deemed of importance. Their views upon the subjects embraced under the following heads should not be lost sight of, but are respectfully commended to the school officers and citizens of Michigan, as embracing valuable suggestions. Taken together, they form the opinions upon various subjects of all the officers who have been placed at the head of the school system of Michigan, so far as it has been deemed practicable to compile them for publication in this document.

IMPORTANCE OF THE PUBLIC SCHOOLS.

The Superintendent cannot but urge anew the vast importance of making the public schools fully adequate to the wants of the entire community, and furnishing them with teachers competent to discharge the duties of their high calling. If, as they should be, decidedly superior to all other schools, they will be patronized as well by the rich as the poor. No schools are so expensive as private schools. Thus in Cincinnati, where the greatest provision is made for common school education of any city in the west, fifteen hundred children are taught in private schools, at an annual expense of twenty-seven thousand dollars; while in the public schools about three thousand are taught at a yearly expense of twenty-five thousand dollars. And it is gratifying to learn that the best teachers are to be found in the public schools; and so judiciously are these schools managed, that they are fast superseding all private ones, and gaining the ascendancy in the minds of all classes. If those two sums could be united in the support of the public schools, the entire youth of the city would be adequately supplied with schools of the first order. No influence can be more salutary upon the public mind, than that going out from such institutions. It soothes and harmonizes the great community of the public, and forms a connecting link among its different classes. Says Mr. Lewis, in the address before quoted, "It is to be borne in mind that ours is a government of public opinion, and when manhood arrives, the most ignorant and depraved lad about your streets, will have as much positive influence as the most wealthy and intelligent; and their influence among their fellows is generally even greater, owing to the prejudice against the rich. Nor are all the wealthy wholly exempt from a prejudice on the other extreme; especially when educated in select schools and confined to select society.

"Establish common schools, and sustain them well, and you will most assuredly fix a place where all classes will in childhood become familiar, before the influence of pride, wealth and family can bias the mind. An acquaintance thus formed, will last as long as life itself. Take fifty lads in a neighborhood, including rich and poor, send them in childhood to the same school, let them join in the same sports, read and spell in the same classes, until their different circumstances fix their business for life; but let the most eloquent orator that ever mounted a western stump, attempt to prejudice the minds of one part against the other, and so far from succeeding, the poorest of the whole would consider himself insulted, and from his own knowledge stand up in defence of his more fortunate schoolmate. The ties of friendship formed at school, outlive every other where relationship does not exist. Can any man meet the schoolmate of by-gone days, without feelings that almost hallow the greeting?"

If such are the influences created by common schools, who would not wish to see them established in every corner of the State? Who would not wish to see such feelings cherished in every youthful breast? If the rich would but consult the future interests of their children, and not their pride and vanity; if they would raise them up to be beloved and respected, and not to become a by-word and a reproach among all their neighbors, and to be despised and pointed at with the finger of scorn whenever they pass the streets; they would countenance and support the establishment of public schools adequate to the wants of the whole community. Nothing more is wanting to put our schools on high and prominent ground than the general co-operation of the public and a full supply of well qualified teachers. Time and the measures going into operation will ere long furnish these, and there can be little doubt that the good sense and reflection of the public will soon lead to that co-operation. But whatever may be the obstacles to universal education, and however great and many the difficulties to be encountered, they must be met and overcome. "The people must be educated or the government cannot stand. The right of suffrage is universal—the means of knowledge must be co-extensive. Where the necessities for education are the greatest, there the difficulties are the greatest, and the means the least. Education does not and cannot, by any means yet devised and in operation, reach the mass of the peeple, adequate to qualify them for the duties and responsibilities of freemen. Nay, there are immense numbers who never enter a school or receive an education at all. It has been estimated, and the fact been published in Europe, that there are at least thirteen hundred thousand free white children and youth south and west of New York, totally destitute of the means of elementary instruction. These facts, with the practical commentary afforded by the riots, recklessness of law and order, by the deliberate organization of infuriated mobs on the slighest grounds, and for the most inadequate causes, are full of meaning, and cannot be misunderstood. These symptoms of disorganization and defiance of law have been manifested in every part of the country, and they demonstrate, with appalling certainty, that popular ignorance and vice do gain ground upon all the means of popular education now in action. How long the institutions of the country, based upon the intelligence of the people, and intended for the enjoyment of intelligent freemen, can withstand and survive the underminings of ignorance and corruption, and the shocks of reckless vice and crime, is a problem which it will not take many generations to solve."* "You may dig canals, construct railroads and turnpikes, establish manufactories, cultivate fields, erect your splendid mansions, accumulate wealth until you become the pride of the earth, if you do not keep a good moral education of the whole population in advance of all your other improvements, you are but making a richer prize for some bold, crafty and successful tyrant, who must ultimately be hailed as a welcome deliverer from anarchy and confusion. Whatever was written aforetime was written for our instruction. Let me refer you to the history of other nations and other times. Did not France desire to be free? Did she not deserve to be free,

*Hon. James G. Carter, Speech. House Representatives, Massachusetts, 1837.

if a sacrifice of blood and treasure could merit freedom. She was not without learned men. * * * But the great mass of the community were not learned. Hence they were imposed upon by the few, and the people, after enacting all that patriotism, bravery, wealth and numbers could do, and breasting the opposition of combined Europe, ultimately threw themselves into the arms of a Corsician soldier!—to save themselves from the ravages of an outraged and ignorant mob. And it is only through fear of re-enacting the same scenes, that France has recently submitted to a tyranny as much worse than that of the dethroned monarch as we can well conceive."* It is devoutly to be hoped that the Michigan school system may be found fully adequate, in the means it is providing and accumulating to qualify each and every individual for the duties and responsibilittes of a freeman and a citizen.—[J. D. PIERCE, *Superintendent*, 1838.

The object of education is to raise up, and not to pull down; to improve the condition of man, to advance the interests of the whole people, while increasing the individual happiness and prosperity of every member in the commonwealth. If education results in the perfection of government, it also leads to the like perfection in science, in the arts and in every species of improvement. It is education that unfolds the hidden mysteries of creation, and introduces man to the secret springs by which he is destined to arrive at the highest degree of physical, intellectual and moral attainment. The improvements she is yet to make, and which she alone can make, in machinery, in mechanic arts, and in the implements of husbandry, will secure to every man, with four hour's labor, a competence for himself and his family. The great balance of time, expended as it should be, in moral and mental culture, would introduce us at once to the golden age of man. A less amount of labor than this can never be desired. Such an amount is essential to the beauty and perfection of his physical nature—to the development, the healthy and vigorous action of his bodily constitution and power.

The people of the older States, sensible of the urgent necessity of education, are awaking to redoubled efforts in its behalf. Wise men in those States, confident that this is the only way to preserve a preponderating influence in the general government of our common country, have been, and are promoting every means to advance the cause of general education, with the avowed purpose of raising up men of distinguished attainments and ability, to guide and direct in their councils. This was the purpose of Jefferson, when he founded the University of Virginia. He perceived that power was gradually passing the mountains, and that, at no distant period, it was destined to take up its abode in the valley of the Mississippi; and instead of bewailing its departure, set himself to devise ways and means to retain and exercise all the influence that high attainments in literature, science and the arts can give to any people. Governor Everett, in his late address at the commencement of Williams' college,

*Address of Hon. Samuel Lewis.

urges education upon the people of Massachusetts for the same reason. "I am strongly convinced," says he, "that it behooves our ancient commonwealth to look anxiously to this subject, if she wishes to maintain her honorable standing in the union of the States."

Would Michigan attain a high rank and an honorable distinction in this matchless confederacy of States,—would she keep pace with the rapid march of improvement and of mind,—would she exert her just share of influence in the grand councils of the nation—let her stretch every nerve, and ply every means to move foward the glorious work. Let perseverance be written upon the walls of her capitol, and let this be the watchword of her people, till every child in the State shall become thoroughly educated, and fitted to fulfil his duty faithfully, to his country and his God. The object is high, the inducements great, and the rewards above all price.—[J. D. PIERCE, *Superintendent*, 1839.

While the desirableness of education, in the best sense of the term, is admitted by every reflecting mind, its importance, under a free government like ours, no one can fully estimate. Our fathers held it in their highest regard, for they planted their school houses, with their churches, beside the war path of the Indian, while yet their first rude cabins but half sheltered them from the cold blasts of a New England winter. Since the May-flower landed the "Anglo Saxon exiles," that band of noble spirits which laid the foundation of a far spreading and powerful empire, no period is to be found in the history of our country, when education has not been more or less generally regarded as an object of the highest public concernment.

It is most assuredly an omen of lasting good to this infant community, and also a matter of congratulation, that so many are disposed not only to listen to, but to enter upon, the discussion of a subject so transcendently important in all its bearings upon the great interests of man, as the education of a whole people. It is certainly desirable to extend a good education to every child in the State, of whatever name or complexion—such an education as is suited to his wants, to his condition and circumstances in life. To do thus much should be the settled purpose of every citizen of this rising commonwealth, and the high aim of its legislation and government.

As the desire of improvement is universal, why not extend the blessings of education to every individual of all classes? This desire is not only universal, but every member of the human family is capable of an endless progression in improvement. Progress is the great principle of human existence. Progress in knowledge, in morality, in expansion of intellect, in arts and the subjugation of all nature to his own uses—progress in civilization, in refinement, and in the more full enjoyment of his noble rational existence, is the all engrossing desire of man. Not of any one man—but of the entire race. Why then confine the blessings of education to a privileged few? It can be desired by that few only for the purpose of converting the balance of our race into mere hewers of wood and drawers of water.

Man has not only the capacity and the power of continual advancement, but he has advanced, often in the midst of the most adverse circumstances, from the beginning of time. Not every individual of every age and tribe, not every generation of man—but man in his social nature and condition, as a sensitive and percipient being—the human race as a great and mighty family, have always been moving forward more or less rapidly in civilization and improvement. Besides, all men admire new forms of beauty—all are pleased with elegant, graceful and sublime objects—all desire to better their condition, to improve themselves and families, to enjoy more of life in its best sense—and all may improve and better their condition by wisely directed efforts. Why then resist this generous and ennobling impulse of human nature—why continue to chain down both body and soul in all the misery, the degradation, the meanness, the despair, the blackness and darkness of perpetual ignorance? Why resist the onward march of improvement to universal empire?

Children, as well as men, love improvement. They love to learn, go forward, see, hear, examine, compare, combine. The God of nature has formed them for it, and made them as susceptible of advancement in all that can adorn and beautify, as the earth is of cultivation; and this desire of improvement can no more be eradicated from the constitution af man than he can cease to be. So long as men desire the comforts of life—pure air, wholesome food, suitable clothing and convenient dwellings—they must constantly desire to better their condition. Why then do such men as Peel and Wellington, and the Archbishop of Canterbury, regard with an evil eye, and resist to utter desperation, all efforts and plans to instruct and elevate the great body of the people? Why do they so strenously oppose the establishment of schools throughout the empire, of which they are so prominent and powerful members? Is it because in these institutions men would learn to understand and appreciate their rights, powers, obligations and duties, and hence be no longer capable of being used as mere instruments to administer to the ambition, the pride, the pleasure and self-exaltation of the noble few? Or is it because they apprehend, in case the schools succeed, that they and their families may be reduced to what is to them the most terrible of all evils, the necessity of laboring to provide for their own subsistence? But education, which is the cause of man, must and will triumph over all its enemies.

To educate, is to draw out, unfold, develop, enlarge and strengthen, all the powers, faculties and susceptibilities of human nature. Education is hence the great business of human existence. It is the all important end to be pursued through life; while instruction is the presentation of facts, the communication of light and knowledge, and is one principal means of accomplishing that end. It is true much depends on the nature of the education, which is obtained through the manifold instrumentality that may be employed. "As the twig is bent, the tree's inclined." This declaration is full of meaning. How desirable then that such an education be given and received, as will fit for continued and increasing usefulness?—J. D. PIERCE, *Superintendent*, 1840.

That knowledge which a good education furnishes, is exceedingly valuable in all that pertains to human life—in the direction of household affairs—in the supply, management and economy of the kitchen—in the laying out and proper cultivation of the garden—in all the arrangements and business of the farm—in the gathering and preservation of all the products both of the farm and garden—in the building of houses, barns, mills, factories and other edifices, whether public or private—in digging a race or canal—in constructing a mill dam or railroad—in the manufactory of every variety of articles, whether for domestic or foreign use—in navigation and the multifarious operations of commerce—in all the business of government—in legislation—in the administration of justice—in all the professions—in the practice of law and medicine—in the pulpit and teaching.

An ignorant man, in the midst of an educated community, must ever find it impossible to sustain himself. All with whom he has to do, seem to be above him. Others appear to enjoy the fruit of his labor. And why is it so? Because he has not sufficient acquired knwoledge to direct wisely his own efforts. Being unable to compete with his neighbors, he becomes disheartened and gives himself up to crime. The inmates of State prisons are generally ignorant, uneducated men. Those, therefore, who suffer their children to grow up uninstructed, leave them without the means necessary to improve their condition, protect their rights, or even to preserve what they may have gained for them. The same is true of a State in the midst of nations generally uneducated. No people can prosper without intelligence and skill to direct State affairs. An ignorant community can never compete with a State guided by superior knowledge. What has enabled the government of Great Britain to lay under heavy contribution large portions of the globe? What has enabled the few of that island to tax many millions of people in other parts of the world? Superior knowledge. As education with them is confined to the privileged orders, they have contrived by various monopolies to appropriate to themselves a great share of the wealth and proceeds of the labor of their own country and people.

The history of the world in by-gone ages furnishes a most instructive lesson. It teaches us what must ever be the fate of an ignorant, uneducated people.

Our own history strikingly illustrates the value of knowledge, among the great mass of the people. It lies at the foundation of all the improvements and enterprise of the country. It was the origin of that glorious revolution which gave birth to a great, widely extended, and growing republic, and liberty to all her citizens. Our fathers knew their rights. The people were all educated. No child was suffered to grow up ignorant of his rights, powers, obligations, duties. When of age, and called to act in the township assemblies, those pure democracies, to which a late distinguished writer has traced the origin of all our republican institutions—he was qualified to act his part with honor to himself and usefully to his country. When we can fully appreciate our present condition, prosperous and happy, in comparison with that of the great body of the people in other portions of the globe, we shall better understand, and form an inconceivably higher estimate of the value of knowledge among the people.—J. D. Pierce, *Sup't*, 1840.

IMPROVEMENT OF THE SCHOOLS.

Vast sums are yearly squandered to no purpose. If the books selected consist of extracts and compilations, wholly unsuited to the capacity of children—if the house is cold or crowded, inconvenient and uncomfortable—and especially if given over to the management of an incompetent teacher, the school becomes a scene of anarchy and confusion, and all is waste—the young mind becomes disgusted with books and schools and teachers, and hates learning forever after. There is need also of improvement in the selection of school house sites; it is not, as many seem to imagine, a matter of indifference where the school house is located. It ought to be the most healthy and attractive spot within the circle of the district, just regard being had to convenience. The building should be spacious and warm, and well ventilated, with a yard suitably enclosed for playful exercise. The entire premises, with all thereunto belonging, the construction of the house and its internal arrangements, should be a picture of order, of neatness and comfort; and present to the youthful mind a pleasing and lovely aspect. It should be an enchanting spot, sheltered alike from the cold blasts of winter, and the summer's scorching sun; a place of love, of kindness and good will; and not a place of whips, consternation, despotism and terror. Let all be, in and out of school, as it should be, and the young mind is led daily to contemplate the usefulness and beauty of method, which cannot fail to produce a refined taste, with habits of order. But these topics in regard to the internal condition of schools, their government and order—the branches to be taught—the books to be used; the improvements which may be introduced in the methods of teaching—what defects are to be supplied—what evils to be remedied; the comparative advantages and disadvantages of different systems, especially of the monitorial—and various other matters pertaining to schools, will naturally and necessarily come up for consideration, when some general system for their external organization shall be perfected. The foundations must be laid, and the frame work completed, before the edifice can receive its finish in the internal apartments.—[J. D. Pierce, *Sup't*, 1837.

CHARACTER OF INSPECTORS.

Upon the wisdom, fidelity and zeal of this board, the success of the whole system will in a great measure depend. They will be called to decide on the qualifications of teachers; and consequently to fix the standard of education in their respective townships. If this standard is low, the schools must suffer an irretrievable loss. For the maxim of the Germans is strictly true: "As is the master so is the school." If his capacity is small, and his acquirements small, he will lull to sleep rather than wake up the energies of the youthful mind. Should he prove to be a man of passion, he will inspire fear, rather than a love of knowledge. It will therefore be within the power of the board of inspectors to aid greatly in raising the standard of education. And as this board must be supposed to represent the sentiment and feeling of the communities in which they respectively rside, it will be essentially important to impress upon the townships the necessity of maintaining an efficient board of school inspectors. Let their powers be ample, and let them be adequately sustained in the discharge of their duties, and the work will be done. And then the fruit will be, a well educated and vigorous people—a people trained in the school of knowledge and virtue—a people understanding their rights and capable of sustaining them.

Whatever form of external organization it may be thought best to adopt, it will be remembered that the system cannot be executed without agents. And as already intimated, on the number, activity and energy of these agents, will the success of the system depend. Much must necessarily be committed to them, and left to their management and care. It is worthy of remark, that they will be intrusted with executive and not legislative powers. These agents will be trustees of the people, deputed to fulfill certain important trusts. They will not be makers, but officers of the law; it will be their duty to do its bidding. To insure success, we must have simplicity, combined with activity and energy. Hence the number of the agents should be just enough to secure these desirable ends. If there are too many to do the work, it will not be done. In such a state of things, there will sometimes be neglect, and sometimes confusion, rather than decision, efficiency and action. It is therefore submitted, as worthy of deliberate consideration, whether it will not be best to reduce, from what they now are, at least one-half, the officers of the district and township organization. Let the agents be few, let their duties be clearly defined, and let them, as in the Prussian system, be paid for their services. Whatever may be thought of the Prussian government, so strong is the sense of justice in that people, that they have no idea of taking the time and labor of individuals, and applying them to the public benefit, without compensation. And it is conceived to be equally against the spirit and letter of our constitution, to require the services of any without paying them for what they do. The time of every man is his property, and cannot either justly or constitutionally be taken and given to the public without remuneration. Hence, when the good of the public calls any of its members to the discharge of important duties, let them be paid for their labor. In this view of the subject, it will not be advisable to employ more agents in the school system than will be sufficient to insure its success. To employ more than enough, would be to impose an unnecessary burden, whether paid or unpaid.—[J. D. PIERCE, *Superintendent*, 1837.

What has here been said regarding a judicious choice of men to form the district board, applies, with increased force, to the selection of persons to constitute the township board of school inspectors. Their situation involves great responsibility. Their duties, if not the most arduous, are always important, and sometimes delicate. They have ample scope for the exercise of their talents, discretion and firmness. They have abundant opportunity to manifest their desire to advance the public education, morals and interest. A competent education of the entire man, universally enjoyed, would prevent many of the physical evils to which man is liable; and nearly all the vices, with all their consequent miseries, that infest the world. It promotes the most desirable objects that pertain to man. It has a direct bearing upon his happiness and honor, in his present and future existence. Hence its immense magnitude is apparent. Its paramount claims upon the highest regards and energies of mankind, individually, and in every form of society, are strong and imperative.—[O. C. COMSTOCK, *Superintendent*, 1845.

COURSE OF STUDIES PROPER TO BE PURSUED IN THE SCHOOLS.

The relations of life are many and various; and out of these relations spring all the duties of life. There are duties which men owe to each other as rational and moral beings, duties which they owe to the State that sustains them, and duties which they owe to the government of the State that protects them. These duties grow out of the relations which they bear to each other, to the State, and to its government. Without proper instruction, how can they know, much less discharge these duties? Without such instruction in early life, how can it rationally be expected that they will be properly qualified, judiciously to exercise the elective franchise, the most important duty of freemen? Without it, how can they go forward from time to time, and understandingly exercise that portion of the sovereignty of the State, which resides in themselves? Without it, how can they properly judge in regard to the most important questions and measures of government, and so determine in all cases as to promote the general welfare? It results, therefore, that our young men of all conditions in life, should be taught the great principles of the constitution and laws of the State, and of the United States. It is of the first importance for them to have a correct knowledge of these things, because the sovereignty of the State resides in a majority of its citizens. Such young men as have no correct understanding of these great subjects, must be miserably fitted for the active duties of life. For the want of this, they may be led unwittingly to invade the rights of others, and thereby forfeit their own. If unexpectedly called to fill important trusts, and discharge responsible duties, they are necessarily subjected to great inconvenience, as well as extreme mortification, and find themselves obliged to commence the study of those things which they ought to have learned in childhood and youth. The young men of our country can scarcely fail of being called to judge of measures for the improvement of the district in which they reside, for the government of the township to which they belong, for the promotion of the larger interests of the county organization, for the growth and enlargement of the State, and the full development of its abundant resources, and for the protection, advancement and permanent prosperity, peace, happiness and glory of this great and united republic. But without education, what can they do? What services can they render? They must sink down into utter insignificance.

There are also other branches of knowledge of great importance, with which the youth of our country ought early to be made acquainted; and branches, too, which have an especial reference to their own future prospects and interests; but to a knowledge of which they can never expect to attian without correct instruction. Most certainly it would be of great utility to them to have a general acquaintance with the business transactions of the country; with its foreign and domestic commerce and relations; with its manufacturing and agricultural productions; with its internal improvements, population and power, as well as with its geography, history, literature and language. These things are interesting in themselves, and as useful as they are interesting. They should also have some correct understanding of the great business of civil magistracy, and be made acquainted with the names of the different officers of government under the constitution of the United States, and of the respective States; and also of their appropriate duties. Nor should the young men of our country be suffered to grow up in utter ignorance of the business and course of legislation; of the organization, proceedings, and peculiar functions of courts of justice, and the object and duties of courts of equity. Without some knowledge of the kind, they are not qualified to read either with pleasure or profit to themselves, even the common newspaper publications of the day. In addition to these things, the arts of husbandry, the history and use of domestic animals; the principles of mechanism and the mechanic arts; the various agents and powers of nature, which have been called into the service of man; mensuration, civil engineering, architecture and gardening, are each and all of them highly important and profitable branches of knowledge. It may be thought, however, that so wide a range of studies is unnecessary, if not injurious. But the truth is, the more the mind acquires, the more it is capable of acquiring. On the mole hill, in the valley, the vision of man is limited; if led from this position to some eminence on the surrounding hills, no difficulty is felt; and if transported to the chief summit of the loftiest mountain upon earth, no injurious consequences result; the eye is found to be equally well adapted to this large sphere of observation; and the depth of the emotion felt, and the pleasurable sensations excited, are proportionate to this enlargement of view. So it is with the mind. A desire of knowledge is one of its original, innate elements. It is one of the essential principles of the human mind. It belongs to the constitution of man, and forms a part of his existence. It is early developed in children; they uniformly love to learn; and the more they study, the more they wish to study; and the more they read, the more do they wish to read, provided the books put within their reach are what they should be, plain and easy to be understood, and filled with useful and interesting matter.

Every new acquisition gives additional strength to the mind; and this additional strength increases the power for acquiring further knowledge. Besides, nature is one, and the arts and sciences, like her children, of one family and kindred. An acquaintance with one facilitates an acquaintance with another, and the light of one is the surest guide to a knowledge of the others. As all the colors are necessary to make up the white and pure light of day, so all principles of knowledge are but parts of one great and glorious whole. It has often been a matter of wonder, how any man could, like Sir William Jones, acquire in one short life a facility in speaking and writing twenty-eight living languages; yet when we consider that all languages have a common root, whose members are grouped in classes, we come to admire not so much a giant intellect as a patience of investigation worthy of all renown. But however desirable it may be to lead the children and youth of our State far onward in the paths of literature and science, it is nevertheless true that a much less amount of knowledge will be found to be sufficient for the ordinary transactions of life.

The education of Washington the great, was confined in early life to the ordinary branches of an English education, at a period when knowledge and the means of acquiring it were not what they now are. This fact strikingly illustrates the truth of the remark of a great man, that, "give a child a sufficient mastery of the English language to enable him to spell, read and write it, and out of this amount of instruction, with a desire of improvement, he would work his way to the highest achievements of intellectual power." Hence, says Paulding, in his life of Washington, "while it serves to exalt the character and abilities of this famous man, to learn that though his means of acquiring knowledge were not superior, nay, not equal to those now within the reach of all for whom I write, yet did he, in after life, by the force of his genius and the exercise of a manly perseverance, supply all his deficiencies; so that when called upon to take charge of the destinies of his country, and bear a load as large as was ever laid upon the shoulders of man, he was found gloriously adequate to the task, and bore her triumphantly through a struggle which may be likened to the agonies of death, resulting in immortality. As with him, so with my youthful readers, most of whose opportunities of acquiring knowledge are greater than those of Washington, and who, though they will not reach his fame, may rationally aspire to an imitation of his perseverance, his integrity, and his patriotism. Opportunities for great actions occur but seldom; but every day and every hour presents occasion for the performance of our duties." Who would not teach his children to lisp the name of Washington, and to emulate his virtues? Who would not wish every child of the State to study his character, and read the history of his splendid achievements? But a consummation so much to be desired, can be attained only by furnishing every such child with a good education. With such an education the children of our State universally can and must be furnished.—[J. D. Pierce, *Sup't*, 1838.

As there probably is some difference of opinion on the subject, it may be proper to consider at some length what is implied in a good education—in such an education as the primary schools ought to furnish. It appears evident to the undersigned, that the public expectation is not sufficiently raised in regard to what they are capable of doing. They are obviously fitted to do more, and to enter upon a higher career of usefulness, than has ever yet been asked of them. Let justice be done our schools, and they will soon exceed in their achievements the highest expectation of friends. The following considerations are presented as the result of experience and much reflection.

A good education necessarily implies a knowledge of ourselves. Know thyself, was one of the first precepts of an ancient teacher; and it is emphatically a precept of the first importance. A knowledge of what we are is essential. The nature of man is complexed—two elements, matter and mind, are combined in his present existence. The body is the dwelling place of the living rational agent. How important to know the laws by which this complex being is governed, and how these two principles mutually affect each other.

Children should be early informed in regard to their bodily constitution. They ought to have a clear and correct knowledge imparted to them of what is necessary to its highest beauty, perfection, activity, vigor and health. Much of their usefulness and enjoyment of life, through coming years, depend on the early attainment of this essential knowledge. Did the fairer portion of our land know more of their bodily frame, of its different vital organs and their uses, is it conceivable that so many of them, in obedience to the dictates of an imported prostitute fashion, would willingly incur the guilt of self-murder? Did they know themselves, is it to be believed that any of them would continue to lay violent hands upon that beautiful frame which God has given them, when certain that death must ensue? It is highly important to us as a people, to have a more accurate and thorough knowledge of that wonderful formation, and curious product of divine wisdom—the body—the house in which we are destined while here to live, move, think, feel and act. This knowledge of our frame—of its organization and parts—of its wants and relations to surrounding objects, is essential to preserve and prolong life. The average of human life, in different countries, will be found to be in exact proportion to the prevalence of such knowledge. A man who knows what his physical constitution is, and requires, will not be likely to be either a glutton or a drunkard—but temperate in all things.

If a good education implies a knowledge of our bodily frame, how much more a knowledge of our rational nature. This nature is obviously three-fold—intellectual, moral and religious. The chief intellectual powers are perception, memory, reason, association of ideas, imagination and fancy; the moral powers are, ability to distinguish between right and wrong—to will, choose and refuse; while the affections, emotions and passions, form the heart, and constitute our religious being. It is in the highest degree important, and essential to our welfare as individuals, to have a correct knowledge of this intellectual, moral and religious nature. We ought as a people to know more of the powers and susceptibilities of the human mind—

of its workings—of its relations; what it can and what it cannot achieve—when and under what circumstance it can be most easily enlarged and improved. Such knowledge is essential to the instructor, and equally so to parents. Children should be early taught to turn their thoughts back upon themselves, for the purpose of observing the varied operations of their intellectual, moral and religious being.

It is highly important to know more of the relation between matter and mind, and how each is affected by this relation. If the brain is the chief instrument of mind in all its operations, then whatever may affect the brain must necessarily affect the mind. Both parents and teachers should fully understand and appreciate this law of our present existence. Without this knowledge, a child in feeble health may be permanently injured, if not sent to an early grave. Being unable to do much else, the child is kept close at study—the worst thing that could be done. The brain being unduly stimulated and excited, the whole system becomes deranged, and unless timely arrasted, dissolution must ensue. It is also to be further observed, that in children, muscular energy is often excessive—hence they need much exercise. Long continued confinement renders them uneasy, fretful, restless, miserable. Punishment in no form, neither chiding nor flogging, will cure this; it is human nature. In no case should they be kept, either in or out of school, more than one hour at close study, without giving them full liberty for that kind of exercise which they need. If allowed to run, skip, hop, jump, romp—as nature dictates—they will not be likely either to pull down benches, or wrench off doors from their hinges. If kept longer than one hour, the laws of our being are transgressed; both body and mind injured; and the whole man, for the time being, rendered unfit for further improvement. Disgust, hatred of schools, books, teachers, is the sure result. These things ought to be more generally known. Parents should know them; teachers also should know them; a good education implies a knowledge of them.

It implies, moreover, a knowledge of our country. To be ignorant of the country which gave us birth—sustained and protected us—is highly disgraceful. Every child should know the geography of his native land—its boundaries, grand outlines and features—the relative position of its different mountains and valleys, bays and harbors, lakes and rivers, and navigable waters. Destitute of this information, no person can read understandingly a common newspaper. He may read of transactions upon the great lakes and rivers of our country, but he knows not whether they occurred among the Esquimaux, Hindoos, Hottentots or among his own people. It is equally important to know its political divisions—the number and relative position of the States—their capitols, chief towns, ports of entry, and principal commercial cities. Ignorance of such things pertaining to our country, should not be suffered, where primary schools exist. Nor should it be allowed in regard to its geological formation. In the bosom of the earth, there is an abundance of treasure—resources without limits—materials of untold importance and value; such as coal, salt, iron, gypsum, copper, lead, marble, silver and gold, with other useful articles; some of which must be had, being essential to human existence and comfort. Some knowledge of geology would save, oftentimes an immense amount of labor and expense in searching for these hidden treasures, and aid greatly in the procurement of them when found. Such an education as ought to be given, would include a knowledge of the different soils, their composition, fertility, power and adaptedness to different productions—whether fitted for grass or grain—whether this or that crop will best succeed. This, to farmers, is of the first importance. Nor should they be ignorant of the various productions of their country. It ought to be a shame to any one not to know where the articles he uses, which he wears, which he puts upon his table, were produced; whether in his own or some other State; whether in his own country or foreign lands. With this, every person should have some knowledge of the commerce of his country; what articles are imported, where procured, how and by whom produced, what are exported, where and to whom sent; whether this commerce is carried on by our people, and in their own ships, or by men and in ships of other nations. This would include a knowledge of the principal manufactures as well as agriculture of the country—as manufactured and agricultural productions form the chief articles of its commerce.

The institutions and laws of our country should be known. A correct knowledge of them is certainly implied in a good education. Hence they ought to be studied in all the primary schools. Every citizen should be acquainted with the government under which he lives, in its legislative, judicial and executive departments; and have a full understanding of the federal and State constitutions, which secures to every man his rights and liberties, civil, political and religious. No man can safely be ignorant of these things; no man can do his duty while ignorant of them. The names and duties of public officers, the tenure of their respective offices—how appointed; whether by direct vote of the people, or by some agent authorized by law to make the appointment, are matters of high concernment to every member of the republic. The same is true of public works; they ought to be known; children should be informed in regard to them. They are matters of general interest. They belong to the people; being their property. A good education must also carry along with it a knowledge of the manifold improvements of the age. These have changed the aspect of affairs throughout the civilized world; many of them are stupendous both in magnitude and power; the results exceed all previous computation. Who would be ignorant of these things? These improvements have settled Michigan, and other of the new States. Without them, these plains, openings, prairies and forests would still be what they were before the red man gave place to the white. Their moral effects have been astonishingly great. Nations are now more intimate, with oceans rolling between, than families of the same State were a few years ago. All this is for good or for evil. Increased activity, energy, enterprise, much thinking, constant discussion, investigation of first principles, thorough examination of old systems; discarding of such as are not founded in truth; the exaltation of many to rights long denied them; these are the results, and the causes which produced them are pressing down with a weight and power almost resistless, upon the worn out, corrupt, fraudulent institutions of the old world. They may soon sink under the pressure, and none be found to help them, is a consummation devoutly to be wished. Again, it is asked, who would be ignorant of these things?

The history of our country is another branch of knowledge implied in a good education. Who would not have his children told the story of the pilgrims? Their wrongs, sufferings, fortitude, self-denial, love of liberty, wisdom and perseverance, laid the foundation for the rich inheritance which has come down to us Who would not have his children told the story of Washington and his brave associates? Their heroic deeds and achievements in the war of the revolution, gave liberty and independence to our country. Who would not have his children told the story of those civic fathers that framed its present constitution and government? Their deliberations and counsels firmly established and secured to us what was begun by the pilgrims, and consummated by Washington and his associates in arms. It must be a burning shame to be ignorant of the history of one's own country—of such a history as ours—so full of novelty combined with instruction—so rich in incident, usefulness and entertainment—teaching by actual experiments, never before made, lessons of wisdom.

In addition to this knowledge of the geography, commerce, institutions, improvements and history of our own country, every child should have some general information imparted to him in regard to foreign lands. Most certainly, since we as a people have much to do with other nations, we ought not to be ignorant of their position and circumstances. We cannot safely, if we would, be ignorant of their history, productions, commerce, institutions and laws. We have so many interests, in common with them, that this knowledge is requisite for the protection of those interests.

Something should also be known of the mineral, vegetable and animal kingdoms. It is obviously important to large portions of the community to be versed in the history of metals—to know their strength, uses and relative value. To farmers some knowledge of the laws of vegetation—the germination of seeds and growth of plants, is exceedingly desirable. They are specially interested to know what is favorable to vegetable life—what is the necessary natural food of different species of plants—and the effect of cultivation upon them. They are equally concerned to have a correct knowledge of the animal economy. They ought to know the history of the different species—their peculiar properties, uses, relative value, and how improved. No husbandman can safely be ignorant of these things.

The principles of architecture and mechanism must not be forgotten. The power and uses of different natural agents, as well as the mechanic arts, are essential elements in the knowledge of a people, who have millions invested in their manufacturing establishments, and who are constantly adding to those millions. All should know something of these things; and for mechanics to be ignorant of these matters, is unpardonable.

In a republic like ours, every man needs to be acquainted with numbers. A knowledge of the first elements and rules of computation is essential. The ordinary trades, transactions, and business of life require it.

To this should be added a knowledge of book-keeping. With a commercial credit going people, accounts must be kept; and every person should know how to keep them.

As language is the instrument of thought, and medium of communication, a good education must carry along with it a knowledge of the proper construction, use and power of language. No one should be ignorant of his native tongue. Every individual should know how to speak it properly—to spell, read and write it correctly.

Above all, a knowledge of our relations, domestic and public, and consequent obligations and duties to each other, to our country and to God, is exceedingly importaut and desirable. Of things of this nature, no human being should be suffered to grow up in ignorance; and no one need be ignorant of them. Our schools should cover the whole ground and furnish the required information.

Here it may be proper to anticipate an objection. It may be said, if a good education implies what has been claimed for it, then it is useless for the children of tradesmen, farmers, mechanics, and other laborers to think of obtaining it. This objection has sometimes been urged with confidence against the introduction of any branches into the primary schools, beyond the simplest rudiments. It is affirmed, that such children must be employed a large share of their time in manual labor, and consequently reading, writing, and the first elements of arithmetic, is all they can be expected to learn. Though this objection may have prevailed to a considerable extent, it is nevertheless founded altogether in mistake. The nature of man is such, no limit is to be prescribed to his attainments—he is capable of endless progression. The more he learns, the easier it is for him to learn. The more he knows, the more readily does he advance from one field of science to another. What is still more important to his advancement, the light of one is reflected upon all the others; and his advance from one to another is made with a constant accumulation of light.

With proper instruction, children may obtain a correct, though in some cases, limited knowledge of all the subjects mentioned, before they are twenty years of age. In any event, many will do more than this. But it may be asked, shall they be kept in school the year round till they are twenty? By no means. From four to six months in the year, under good teachers, is all sufficient. During the balance of their time, if properly directed, whether in the kitchen, dining room or parlor, at home or abroad, in the field, workshop, mill or counting room, they will be constantly increasing in knowledge. And it may be added, that the knowledge thus obtained is an essential part of a good education. Experience teaches us that it is not necessary for young persons to spend all their time at books to become learned. The history of the greatest and best men in our country—of those who have attained the proudest eminence in literature, science and arts, makes it certain that high attainments and usefulness are not confined to those who have nothing to do in early life but go to school. Few of this class have ever been distinguished for anything but idleness, extravagance and dissipation.

* * * * *

It is while at home, in the infancy of days, that children learn the names of a multitude of objects. Here they learn the names of the different rooms and apartments which they occupy, with their uses, the names and places of different utentils, implements, and carriages, employed in and about the fraternal residence, whether upon the farm, or in the work-shop—the names and uses of domestic animals; these with a little care, they must learn in a short time. They learn also the names of the numerous objects with which their home is surrounded, with their peculiar properties and uses. They early become acquainted with the names of different trees, herbs, grasses, grain and roots, with the name of every kind of fruit and berries, with that of every shrub, bush and flower within their reach, and the names of the different earths, rocks and pebbles. Besides, they learn to apply to different actions the appropriate words. To one the word run, to another skip, to another hop, to another strike, to another leap, to another drive, to another ride, to another fly. They learn also to apply the proper appellations to distinguish the quality of objects, as good, bad—hard, soft—sweet, sour.

Here we have the first elements of language, and the first and most essential principles of knowledge, acquired before the child is of sufficient age to be sent to school. He has acquired a knowledge of things, and their names. He has not learned mere words, the signs of ideas. The process is simply this: an object is presented, it is viewed, perhaps, as children are wont to do, examined closely, the name of it is repeated, he associates with the object the name of it; whenever afterwards the object is presented, he calls it by this name. The child has thus learned the sign of an idea, but before learning it, he had acquired a knowledge of the thing signified by that sign. This is the order of nature. "It is plain therefore that a knowledge of the sign, and thing signified, is acquired as near together as may be."

But as parents have not, generally speaking, the requisite time, if they always had suitable qualifications, to give their children all the instruction which they need, public schools are established. At these schools, clear and definite instruction is expected to be given. Here they should be taught to spell the words they have already learned, and while learning to spell them, be taught how to put them together so as to form correct sentences. This may be done by requiring them to describe the objects with which they are acquainted. Let the first lesson be a description of the house in which they live; the next, a description of the objects around them; the next, a description of the objects between their own dwelling and the school house. The advantage of this course, which ought to be pursued for some time, would be the early formation of a habit of close observation and accuracy of description. Reading, writing and numbers, would, as a matter of course, come in from day to day. Easy lessons in geography and history would soon follow; and from time to time, the elements of other branches of knowledge should be introduced. It is hence obvious, that the amount of valuable instruction to be given in the primary schools may be amazingly augmented. Let this method be pursued, and it will soon appear that much may be done beyond mere reading, writing and first rules of computation. These are not the ends to be aimed at in our schools; they are to be regarded as means of attaining that end, and that end is a good education. As already intimated, the proposed method of instruction would lead in early life to habits of close observation, and clearness and accuracy in relating facts and circumstances. The reason why children often seem confused in telling a story, is for the want of closely observing what they see and hear. If early called to describe objects, with which they are familiar, this habit will soon be formed, and with it habits of thinking and reflection.

Children, moreover, are fond of making experiments. This is an important principle in human nature, and is early developed. Such experiments as they are ever disposed to make, and such also as teachers might make for them by way of illustration, are essential means in promoting a good education. Some, however, appear inclined to repress this spirit in children; but nothing can be more injudicious. This disposition may need direction, but should never be repressed; it ought rather to be encouraged. Certain things can be learned only by experiment. This, therefore, is the only source of knowledge so far as things of this nature are concerned. This is true of gravity, weight, resistance of bodies, the effects of physical force, action of fire and water, and the results when different substances are brought into contact. A knowledge of these and other laws, by which the universe is governed, can be acquired in no other way than by actual experiments. The philosopher is allowed to make his experiments, so should the child; for he is emphatically the greater philosopher—he is the most ardent lover of learning. More experiments should be introduced into our schools. Much might be done in this way with little or no additional expense. Many facts in geography, in natural history, in chemistry, in natural philosophy, in astronomy, and in other branches, may be readily illustrated and by the simplest apparatus. With such an apparatus, every primary school may and should be furnished. The happiest effects would result from its use. This is no mere conjecture, but sober reality.—[J. D. Pierce, *Sup't*, 1840.

In excluding sectarianism from all schools supported by the public purse, the cardinal virtues must not be banished. Without virtue, no system of instruction can perfect its work. If the teacher is fit to be placed over a school, he will, by precept and his own exemplary conduct, teach all that the most rigid morality can ask. More than this would be trenching on forbidden ground; less, would be conclusive evidence of unfitness for his place. Let justice, for instance, be taught upon every occasion that presents itself in the school. Make the child understand that stealing, false dealing, lying, fraud, oppression, bribery, and all other forms of injustice, are wrong, and if indulged in, surely productive of unhappiness. Let him talk against avarice, and while recommending the pursuits of industry and honest gain, keep constantly in mind the maxim that "money is the root of all evil." Let him condemn slander, hypocrisy in social and religious intercourse, anger, blasphemy, evil communications, and other pernicious practices, and by conversation, interwoven with instruction, depict their consequences. Let him inculcate brotherly love, duties to parents and society, and the peace giving pleasures of benevolence, kindness, amiable manners and forgiveness of injuries. Let him talk about temperance and the terrible evils of intemperance. A teacher who feels right on these subjects, and whose daily example is made to prove it, will make himself familiar with such maxims as these: "Do as you would be done by;" "Abhor evil and cling to that which is good;" "Evil communications corrupt good manners;" "Honor thy father and mother;" "Love your enemies;" "Forgive injuries;" and a multitude of similar maxims that can be gleaned from the Scriptures, and other good writings. Above all, let distinct ideas of the greatness and all pervading goodness of God be given, and but little of moral instruction will be left untaught.—[F. Sawyer, Jr., *Sup't*, 1843.

Popular education should be practical. Book-keeping, though generally neglected in our primary schools, should constitute a branch of their studies. Acquiring a knowledge of this science, would improve the penmanship of the pupil—show him a practical application of the utility and precision of arithmetic; and impart to him some notions, at least, of the affairs of business. The idea that this science is only, or chiefly, useful to merchants, is erroneous. Thousands of other persons have occasion to employ it. Transactions of a business character are diversified and increasing. Under our republican institutions, very many become the incumbents of public offices. The correct management of these private and public affairs, requires a systematic and accurate use of figures; and, shows the strong and growing claims of this science to the attention of educators and scholars. Account books, and papers suitably kept, would enable an individual, engaged in the most ample and multifarious business, to know, every hour, were he so inclined, the exact state of his matters. This would teach him what branches in trade to curtail, or abandon—what to continue or extend. In short, every necessary variation to the success of his operations. An acquaintance with the science in question, might often prevent embarrassments, strife and litigation—aye, bankruptcy and carnage of character. A man possessed of a thorough and accurate knowledge of the science of book-keeping, by double-entry, and of industrious and moral habits, will find it highly available to him in any part of the civilized world.

It has been lamented, that so many of our people, in all the vocations of life, are deficient in the useful and elegant art of composition. This fact does not evince their destitution of native talents, or their ignorance of general knowledge. It does evince, however, the imperfection of the system of instruction, under which they were educated. Composition, with which every person should be somewhat acquainted, though cultivated in our higher seminaries, has been almost entirely neglected in our primary schools. This has probably resulted from various causes. Many may have conceived this acquisition not generally necessary, or even attainable. Some teachers may have bnen incompetent to instruct in this branch, even had they been desired to do so, by the parents and guardians of their scholars. But surely an accomplishment which every one ought, in some degree, to possess, should not be disregarded in those schools in which three-fourths of the community are to receive all that education which they will ever acquire, under the immediate tuition of instructors. Grammar may have been studied. At least, many of its elementary rules may have been committed to memory. The pupil may have been accustomed to parsing; and in the view of sciolists in the science, acquitted himself on his public examination, regarding it with high reputation. But should he stop here, very little beyond increasing the capacity of his memory, and cultivating to some extent a habit of attention, will have been achieved. Let such an individual, untaught and unpractised in composition, attempt to read a few sentences, without capitals or punctuation, and he will scarcely read it intelligibly to others, and of course, understandingly to himself. Whereas, one habituated to composition, will experience no embarrassment in such a trial. Composition teaches the best choice of words, and the most just collocation of them to express an idea. It teaches perspicuity, force and ornament. Redundancy and ellipsis, will alike be avoided. Accurate composition leads to accurate thinking. This evolves, invigorates and disciplines the original faculties of the mind. A strong and clear perception of a subject, enables one to write with propriety and efficiency. Composition shows the practical application of grammar. It fixes its rules and principles in the mind. It is not only highly beneficial, but a source of rational enjoyment to those who practice it. It prepares one to record much interesting matter for the benefit and gratification of others. Nearly all our youth are capable of becoming respectable writers. Some among them may be destined to eminent usefulness and distinction, as authors—they may write themselves up to immortality. These latent powers of intellect will forever remain dormant—be lost in obscurity—without suitable cultivation. All valuable science may be employed as a defence against injuries. A strong fortress is not apt to be attacked. So a man, notorious for the vigor and adroitness of his pen, is on this account, the less liable to be assailed by the poisoned arrows of detraction.

Composition should be early taught. At this period of life, mental impressions are easily made, more tenaciously held, and readily recalled, than those received in adult years. Scholars are sometimes permitted to write on themes too vast and sublime for their capacities. This is unwise; not succeeding, they thus become discouraged; they may resort to plaigarism, attempt to shine in borrowed lustre. This is worse than useless—it is rather inglorious. A man of reading and discernment can readily perceive, on a view of the compositions, and on hearing the oral replies of the pupils to questions, whether they are mere copyists, repeating only from memory the perfect language of the text books—the real import of which they have not maturely considered, and do not understand—or whether they are displaying the attributes and attainments of their own minds. We like to hear recitations and answers to questions in the pupil's own language, no matter how simple, that are manifestly the result of his own thoughts, research and digested knowledge of his subject. This course reflects credit and honor upon the scholar and teacher. The subjects of composition should be adapted to the age, capicity and genius of the learner. Here, as in almost every thing pertaining to the management of a school, there is ample scope for the exercise of common sense, and sound discretion. The practice of composition not only improves one's mind in the knowledge of grammar and logic, but also in an indefinite variety of subjects. A writer must of necessity read, observe and think, to multiply his topics of narration, description and discussion. The habit of attention and study thus formed, is of itself a most valuable acquisition. Select schools derive a part of their celebrity from their teaching composition, holding public examinations, and receiving the personal attentions of boards of visitors. We see no good reason why these things may not be extended to our primary schools.

Elocution, which stands in intimate union with composition, has been justly held in high estimation by all nations blest with learning and refinement. It must be confessed, however, that it has been generally overlooked, in the tuition imparted in our primary schools. The causes referred to, that were supposed to have prevented the cultivation of composition in them, may have operated in producing the fact just stated. In our country, where every citizen may be called upon in the career of his life, to address the primary assemblies of the people, or perhaps parliamentary bodies, it is highly desirable that the art of speaking should compose a part of our popular education. It should be borne in mind, in this connexion, that many whose professions will lead them to speak much in public, will receive all their original education in these elementary institutes. As so many of the sciences are affiliated, oratory cannot be studied and practised without materially benefitting the mind in the cognate branches of learning; besides, the organs of speech, the voice and gestures are all improved by a proper course of training in elocution. Debility of the vocal organs, feebleness of voice, and even aphony have been removed, and health and energy—aye, great power of accomplishment, restored to these organs, by the scientific, skillful and persevering efforts of the elocutionists. In our legislatures, few only of the members participate in the debates; indeed, in our courts, many learned counsellors and astute pleaders, deliver no oral arguments. A young man may have successfully gone through all the branches of learning, as they are sometimes taught, from the common school to graduation at the college; he may also have read law—been admitted in the higher courts, and, after all, be unable to utter five sentences extempore, to a court, a jury, or any other audience, without fearful diffidence, confusion and trembling. This inaptitude, for public speaking, in these cases, is rarely the result of necessity; but merely of omission in an education which, in other regards, may have embraced various and lofty attainments. Should the young man in question add to all the studies we have described, the lucubrations of twenty years, utterly neglecting extemporaneous speaking, it would not remove the difficulty mentioned. The only way to escape this miserable situation, is, with suitable preparation, to practice habitually, extemporaneous speaking. This course should be commenced in boyhood and youth, in the common schools. It may be extended afterwards, as opportunities and occasion offer. The longer a young man delays the course recommended, the more Herculean will appear the task it involves. Many of our extemporaneous speakers have had no instruction in practical eloquence. No intelligent and faithful friend has hinted to them their defects, and suggested improvements. Hence early faults, chiefly the consequence of embarrassment, have sometimes ripened into inveterate habits, adhering to the speaker with the tenacity of a natural deformity. Speeches on subjects, profoundly studied, delivered from a brief, or without one, as may be conceived most advisable, and debates upon these subjects by the scholars, under the eye and instruction of the teacher, would prevent these evils, and prove extremely beneficial. The time and more particular character of these exercises, with the age and other circumstances of those who may participate in them, are left to the teacher and his appropriate counsellors.

Music is ranked among the liberal sciences. Vocal music should be introduced into our common schools. Some may doubt, however, whether this would be practicable or advantageous. A capacity to learn it is almost universal. There is no doubt, the same diversity in the abilities of individuals to acquire a knowledge of music, that there is to acquire a knowledge of any other branch of learning. All have not equal talents and aptitude to improve in any department of education. The universality of the capacity of mankind to acquire a knowledge of the science, or, at all events, of the *practice* of music, is attested by the reports of numerous schools in Germany and other places touching this point. All the teachers with whom Prof. Stow conversed, in Germany, regarding this thing, replied, that "they had never seen a child who was capable of learning to read and write who could not be taught to sing well and draw neatly, and, that, too, without taking any time which would at all interfere with, indeed, which would not actually promote, his progress in other studies." The introduction proposed is no wild innovation. In reference to it, we are far behind many parts of Europe and the age.

Vocal music has been taught in the schools of Germany, ever since the time of Luther. Said this great reformer, "Music is a fair gift from God, and near allied to divinity; next to Theology, it is to music that I give the highest place, and the greatest honor." "Whoso hath skill in this art, the same is of a good kind, fitted for all things." Further, he added, "we must by all means maintain music in schools. A schoolmaster ought to have skill in music, otherwise I would not regard him." Music is now being taught, in primary schools, in many portions of our own country; and with the high commendation of those whose experience, observation and reading, have prepared them to judge understandingly on this subject. Col. Young, whose opinions on every thing connected with popular education deserve the most profound consideration, in one of his eloquent reports to the legislature of New York, says: "The introduction of music, as a branch of elementary instruction in our common schools, is one of the most valuable improvements which have resulted from the increased attention which is now bestowed upon the science of education."

Music should be taught to the young. In the earlier periods of life, the vocal organs are flexible, readily developed, and disciplined. Thus, their power to perform, and to sustain exercise, is increased. Singing improves the voice, augments its force, and extends its compass. It renders the voice capable of those inflections and modulations which are among the graces of that elequence which commands the attention, and charms the soul of an audience. Music excites sentiments of love, courage, or devotion, according to the qualities it possesses, and the peculiar susceptibilities of those who may come within the sphere of its influence. It inspires the imagination, refines the taste, and rouses the intellect to vigorous action. In many of those compositions which are set to music, one becomes acquainted with the finest displays of literature and genius, of exalted sentiment and poetic fancy. It is an agreeable relaxation from the severer studies. It conduces to cheerfulness and animation. The humanizing and kindly influence which it exerts on both teacher and scholars, inspires mutual respect and affection, thus rendering easy and successful the government and instruction of the school.

A person must have a bad heart, who is not benignly affected by tasteful music. A bard, distinguished for his analysis of the human heart and character, and for his exhibitions of the richness and power of the English language, has said:

"The man that hath no music in himself,
Nor is not moved with concord of sweet sounds,
Is fit for treason, stratagems and spoils;
The motions of his spirit are dull as night,
And his affections dark as Erebus:
Let no such man be trusted."

When Professor Stowe was in Berlin, he visited an establishment for the reformation of youthful offenders. Dr. Kopf, who had the care of it, took him to a room, in which were some twenty boys making clothes for the establishment, and singing at their work. On retiring, the doctor remarked: "I always keep these little rogues singing at their work; for while the children sing, the devil cannot come among them at all; he can only sit out doors there, and growl; but if they stop singing, in the devil comes."

Dr. Potter writes: "The Germans have a proverb, which has come down from Luther, that where music is not, the devil enters. As David took his harp, when he would cause the evil spirit to depart from Saul, so the Germans employ it to expel obduracy from the hearts of the depraved." Music, daily practised in a family, would impart pleasure and usefulness to the domestic circle. It might attach to a lovely home and its enjoyments, a promising and endeared son, who, without the attractions of music and its attendant delights, would, perhaps, have been dishonored and lost in the paths of folly, sin and death. That music constitutes a part of the public worship of God, a part of it too, in which all may engage, should operate strongly in favor of its composing a branch of elementary instruction.

A variety of studies, and the modern modes of teaching in schools, prevent monotony and listlessness. Practical elocution and music, are well adapted to relieve, and obviate these things.

Various reasons manifest the propriety of introducing agriculture, as connected with science, into our common schools, as a branch of popular education. Horticulture and agriculture, the philosophy of which is identical, were the earliest and chief earthly employment of mankind. They were *to subdue the earth, to dress and to keep* the garden, and *to till the ground.* It is moreover written, that *the profit of the earth is for all.*

When our race were perfect, a garden fraught with beauty, fragrance and food, in rich variety, was prepared by their benificent Creator, for their abode. This was the theatre of their delightful toil—their pure and sublime enjoyment. In the imaginative minds of poets, rural scenes and exercises are essential to the highest, purest earthly bliss. Although God has said to man, "In the sweat of thy face shalt thou eat bread," and has thus declared that his maintenance shall be the fruit of his industry, yet he is not by consequence, doomed to perpetual ignorance and degradation. This deplorable state is not the necessary result of any condemnation or law under which man is placed by his Heavenly Father.

In whatever aspect we view agriculture, we see it invested with immense importance. From it we derive most of the necessaries, comforts and delicacies of life. They can be obtained from no other source. Without it, our condition in many regards, would be assimilated to that of barbarians. It is radical to the existence and prosperity of the arts—of manufactures, and of commerce; and of almost everything that constitutes the highest character of nations. We have a vast national domain. It possesses great fertility and variety of soil, with genial climes. It is capable, under a culture faithful to the laws of nature as applicable to this subject, of producing the most rich and abundant harvests. Without a proper respect to these laws, however, a succession of crops will soon exhaust nearly all the native fertility of the earth. Most of our learned professions are crowded. Many of our young men seem to have fancied that wealth, ease and honorable distinction, are almost exclusively allied to the professions of medicine, law or politics; and hence, have embraced one of these as the paramount object of pursuit. Too many, perhaps, have also embarked in merchandize, for the benefit of themselves and the country. There are likewise, it is presumed, more mechanics of some kinds than can prosper in their calling. Add to these, numbers of other individuals who have no profession—are out of employment; know not what to do—are discontented—but who are capable of being useful, happy and respectable, if suitably engaged in business. Multitudes among these may have all along imagined that the business of farming is necessarily associated with ignorance, rusticity and servile labor. They do not appear to recollect that the class of farmers have furinshed hosts of champions of the rights of man—many authors of useful discoveries and inventions—aye, men who have extended in various directions the boundaries of science. The practice of farming is a most noble and useful art. It is highly conducive to the health and vigor of both body and mind. Like all other arts, it is founded upon science—the science of agriculture. Let the laws of this science be discovered, studied and understood—let an enlightened application of them be made in the prosecution of agriculture, and its theory and practice will be highly interesting—it will be elevated and popular. A vocation thus rendered pleasing, lucrative and honorable, cannot fail to command the attention of vast multitudes of our fellow citizens. Among these will be many from the various ranks to which allusion has been made. The idea that manual labor is incompatible with intellectual and moral improvement, and refinement of manners, is utterly inadmissible. It is nullified by the physiology and history of man. Labor is favorable to observation, study and reflection. The most laborious person may frequently find minutes, hours and days of leisure, in which he may indulge a fondnees for reading, study and mental cultivation. Whatever shall diffuse abroad a literary and scientific taste, is a desideratum. Solid learning promotes individual and social prosperity and happiness. It is material to the improvement and perpetuity of our political institutions.

Agricultural education in our common schools, from well adapted text books and otherwise, and by competent teachers, and introducing into our school, and other public libraries, books of a popular character, on agriculture connected with science, will, among other advantages, cultivate and diffuse that taste and learning which are so desirable. Agriculture is an ample subject. It has many auxiliary branches. The appropriate text books will no doubt be obtained or prepared. Adaptation in these, as in many other things, is all important. From the agricultural education acquired in our primary schools—extended by reading books on the subject, drawn from our public libraries, and from other sources, very many of our youth will elect farming as a livelihood. This, it must be confessed, would be a wise election—for surely it is a calling for which Heaven has many smiles. It is obvious that the text, and other books suitabe for our township libraries, should be plain—divested so far as practicable, of all technicalities—free from that obscurity usually consequent upon prolix and involved sentences. They should, at the same time, be written in a manner sufficiently pleasing, animated and ornate, to be interesting and attractive to the great mass of readers.

It is a matter of surprise and regret, that a great agricultural people, as are those of the United States, should have so long postponed that attention to this subject which its intrinsic and relative importance demands. But the prospect grows more animating. Farmers, philosophers and statesmen, are now, in great numbers, directing their earnest attention to this important interest. They have poured much light upon this department of useful knowledge, and won for it the public favor. It is respectfully submitted, whether it would not be wise and prudent, to provide by law, for the delivery of lectures, annually, in every school district, upon agriculture and its kindred sciences. The salutary influence these lectures would produce on the public mind, in reference to agriculture and rural economy, those cardinal interests of our country, would evidently increase the wealth, respectability and power of the State.

In the view of the preceding considerations, and many others that might be suggested, the undersigned is decidedly in favor of the introduction into our common schools, of agricultural education, and into our township libraries, books, of a popular character, on agriculture connected with science.—[O. C. Comstock, *Sup't*, 1845.

SCHOOL LIBRARIES.

It is deemed unnecessary to advert to the immense value and importance of common school libraries. The question of their utility has been settled by the decision of experience in other States, where liberal appropriations for the purpose have been granted. To accomplish the greatest degree of good, in our State, district libraries must be established; not only that the useful information contained in well selected books, may be generally conveyed, but that teachers may have the benefit of acquiring the most extended and important theoretical information. Means for educating young men to become teachers in our primary schools, have been devised; but by the acquirement of all that these means afford, they have only reached the threshold of the temple of knowledge, and are not fitted to work out the highest degree of good without the study of books, and the consequent information and instruction they afford. Too much value indeed can hardly be attached to the establishment of school libraries; and it is believed when once rightly established, they will be the means of effecting an equal amount of good, with the schools themselves.—[J. D. Pierce, *Sup't*, 1839.

TEXT BOOKS.

Suitable books and teachers constitute another important means of promoting a good education. Such books are highly valuable, but competent teachers are essential to the success of schools. A thoroughly trained and skillful teacher, with the most ordinary books, will do vastly more for his school than an incompetent teacher can, with the best books ever written. A good spelling book is important; so is a good reading book. Both should be adapted to the capacities of those for whom they are designed. The object of a spelling book is not the definition of words; but as the designation imports, it is intended chiefly to teach correct orthography; and it should be specially adapted to this purpose. A reading book is for improvement in the art of reading, and hence should contain some variety of composition. Every piece should contain something entertaining and useful, and be written in plain, simple and elegant language—in such language as children use—in language easy to be understood.

But it is to be remembered, that because a book comes with numerous commendations, it is not certain that it is adapted to the school room. Those concerned in the book trade find no difficulty in procuring them for any work, which they may wish to publish and have introduced. It is a money making business to exclude a book already in general use, and introduce into its place a new work. But to the public, it is a money expending operation; and is often done without any adequate compensation. A real improvement, *one of essential value*, should be introduced, cost what it may. But to exclude an old work, for a new book of little or no additional worth, is ministering to individual profit at the public expense. To lay aside the spelling book now in general use, for a new one, would cost our State in the outset an expenditure of from five to ten thousand dollars. It highly concerns the public to determine whether enough is to be gained to pay the price of the exchange. It is confidently believed that it would be far more profitable to the people to expend that amount in giving additional qualifications to teachers.

We have a multitude of writers of school books; but few indeed are the persons qualified to write for children; and it is because only here and there one can throw himself back to the days of childhood, and call to mind how children think, feel and reason. Hence the general want of adaptedness in school books to the capacities of children. In the midst of that multitude is to be found a Webster, a Gallaudet, a Pierpont, a Peter Parley, and the accomplished Mrs. Sigourney. Perhaps to this list should be added a few others. The works of these authors will live, because to high literary attainments and talents, they have superadded that particular adaptedness, without which a school book is of little value.

The spelling book in general use is constructed on a principle of the utmost importance, so far as uniformity of pronunciation throughout the country is concerned. In the work which is now sought to be substituted in place of it, and all others indeed, this principle is entirely abandoned. "But the change of the usual mode of instruction will be followed by a consequence not generally foreseen. Most of the present generation have been instructed in elementary books, in which the words are classified according to the sounds of the letters, the number of syllables, the accented syllables, and the terminations. The effect has been that children learn with great facility, as uniformity and sameness assist the memory; and by the frequent repetition of words with the same accent, our common people have acquired a habit of correct pronunciation which is so remarkable as to be a subject of observation with foreigners—and by the general use of one book, this pronunciation is almost uniform from one extremity of our nation to the other. This excellent classification, which it is believed was first made by Mr. Webster, and which has been introduced into all elementary books—is now to be abandoned." The book, which is sought most earnestly to be introduced—"has no classification; all sorts of words are jumbled together, with no key to the pronunciation, either of vowels or consonants. For such a defect, there is no equivalent; the child loses what he cannot afterwards gain; and if he learns a few definitions, he learns what may be more correctly learned at a later period." Let this principle of classification be retained, and the same desirable uniformity of pronunciation will continue to prevail throughout the length and breadth of our widely extended country. But let it be abandoned and the foundation is at once laid for as many brogues and dialects as exist on the island of Great Britain, where the inhabitants of one county often find it exceedingly difficult to understand those of its nearest neighbor. Besides many of the definitions of the books proposed to be introduced, are as inaccurate as can well be imagined, and some of them supremely ridiculous. Words entirely different in their origin and signification, are put down as "definers of each other;" thereby introducing perfect confusion into the language.—[J. D. PIERCE, *Sup't*, 1840.

UNIFORMITY OF BOOKS.

The presentment against schools by the inspectors, for non-uniformity of books, is unanimous. All execrate the evil and demand a remedy. The district returns also show that not less than thirty-three different reading books are used in the schools, while nearly every known author or compiler of a spelling book, grammar, arithmetic and geography is represented, not merely in the State, but in every school. Who, under such circumstances, has not "fresh tears" to shed over the misfortunes of teachers? It is not enough to reduce his monthly wages one-fifth, but two-fifths of the time bought must be consumed in unavailing efforts to economize both time and money, by classification! If qualified for his place, and ambitious to exhibit a school that shall be creditable to him, how must he proceed? Twenty scholars of equal proficiency in a particular branch may be picked out and called the first, second or third class; what then? Half a dozen different text books in that class, all treating perhaps upon a similar subject, have conducted the several members through processes, and to results widely, and it may be, irreconcilably variant. * * * *

Districts change their teachers annually. Owing to a variety of circumstances, and this very want of uniformity is one of them, teachers are driven from place to place like so many birds of passage; with this difference, however, that while the bird returns to its wonted latitude, the schoolmaster takes good care never to be caught in the same district a second time. And every succession of teachers brings with it a succession of new books. The necessary books of last year are upon the shelf or in the garret, the useless lumber of the present. The teacher, from the paucity of his wages, cannot afford to accommodate himself to the circumstances of his district, nor as a general thing, are the parents disposed to accommodate the teacher. So the wheel turns round, bearing with it expense, defective classification, waste of time and means, mutual heart-burnings, district quarrels, eviction of the teacher, disgust of officers, dissolution of the district, and general dissatisfaction with the best system in the world. This is not an overdrawn picture. It is precisely what results in many cases, from a neglect to secure uniformity of books.

What is the remedy? In some States the district officers control the matter; in others, the township committees; the law enforcing their recommendations. It is evident that without an interposition of law in some form, the evil can never cease. One difficulty attending district regulations is the want of inducement in book-sellers to furnish the limited supply on the most economical terms. A provision requiring the inspectors to recommend the best books, and forbidding the use of any others, will measurably remedy the evil. Book-sellers will then find it an object to keep a supply on hand, and competition will regulate the price. Or better still, if the law should exact uniformity throughout the State, and authorize two, three or more competent persons to designate the books, providing for changes at proper intervals to meet the spirit of improvement ever at work, the axe would be laid at the root of the evil. Nor would very frequent changes be necessary. It is not every new edition of an old work, nor every book heralding what are called the "latest improvements," that commends itself to adoption. Many reading books, for instance, in use twenty years ago, are none the less useful now. Nor would such a law necessarily require the State to turn wholesale book-dealer, and monopolize a trade for purposes of economy that properly belongs to individuals. From all such speculations the State should keep aloof. Individual competition, limited only by the kind of books, would ensure an abundant supply and the desirable economy. At all events, the evil universally complained of cannot be tolerated much longer. One or the other remedies suggested, or a third yet to be devised, is indispensable to the success of our system. —[F. Sawyer, Jr., *Sup't,* 1843.

The books used in our schools should be approved by men of talents, learning and moral worth, whose habits of teaching or public situation have led them to examine such works with critical attention. There should be but few books on the same subjects in our schools, and they should be uniform throughout the State. To acquire solid learning, it is not essential to read a multiplicity of books, but to study profoundly and to understand thoroughly a few standard authors in the various departments of erudition.

Although the approvals referred to are not imperative, have not the sanction of law, yet the districts and towns, exercising a sound discretion, will usually be swayed by these recommendations.

To suitable books should be added black boards, maps and globes, with such philosophical apparatus, as advancing knowledge has discovered, and the pecuniary means of the district may justify.—[O. C. COMSTOCK, *Sup't*, 1844.

EXAMINATION OF TEACHERS.

It is the legal duty of the inspectors to divide the town into districts, to apportion the public money, make out and transmit to the county clerk all the statistical information furnished by the several districts, and, most important of all, examine candidates for teaching "in regard to moral character, learning and ability." They have, then, high and responsible duties resting upon them. In the eyes of the law, they are the guardians of our common schools and ought therefore to be selected with great discrimination. Themselves the judges of what constitutes qualification for teaching, their own moral character should be stainless, their own learning adequate to the task imposed, their own ability undoubted. Otherwise, they cannot duly estimate such sterling qualities in those they examine. They must possess, too, great firmness of purpose—a moral courage that will shrink from the performance of no duty, whether in the exact line of their own predilections or not, which is demanded by the educational interests of the town. If a candidate for teaching come before them, they have no right to recognize him in any other capacity for the time than *as* a candidate, and the only questions they are bound to answer satisfactorily to themselves, are such as regard his moral character, learning and ability. If his habits are bad, he should be rejected at once; for the pure heart of youth should not be exposed to the contagion of evil communication or vicious example. Any known vice should be deemed a disqualification. If the candidate be intemperate, sooner keep children in ignorance for a while than subject them to so pestilential an influence. An attendant upon grog shops, or even a dram drinker at home, may do to train brutes, but never, never can he educate the human soul. Here, then, is a broad field for the discerning and severely scrutinizing mind of the inspector. Immorality, in any or all of its protean shapes, however specious may be its semblance of virtue, merits no quarter. It should be cut off at once from all hopes of success. With the *religious* views of the candidate, the inspector has no legal or other right to meddle. He may place high his standard of morals; practical virtue should be one test of fitness; but the teacher's *creed*, or the embodiment of his faith upon paper or within the deep recesses of his soul, is something with which only Divine wisdom can deal. The question is not, whether he is a Protestant or a Catholic, a Trinitarian or Unitarian, a Perfectionist, Latter Day Saint, Mormon or Transcendentalist; but whether he has such an unblemished moral character as will enable him to impart healthful principles to his scholars and be to them a living example of all that is beautiful and good.

As to the kind and degree of *learning* required by law, much is left to the examiner's sound discretion. Generally, the circumstances of the school over which the teacher is to be placed must govern.

College learning, certainly, is not contemplated; for that is hardly wanted in common schools. If sought by any, the University is expected to give it. Nor are the higher branches of academic learning essential, particularly in the present condition of our schools. An elementary school, where the rudiments of an English education only are taught, such as reading, spelling, writing and the outlines barely of geography, arithmetic and grammar, requires a female of practical common sense, with amiable and winning manners, a patient spirit, and a tolerable knowledge of the springs of human action. A female thus qualified, carrying with her into the school room the gentle influences of her sex, will do more to inculcate right morals and prepare the youthful intellect for the severer discipline of its after years, than the most accomplished and learned male teacher. In most of our common schools, the ages of our scholars require female teachers; and the reports show that the summer and some of the winter schools are kept by them. But the inspectors cannot scrutinize their qualifications too nicely. An unqualified female is less to be tolerated than an unqualified male teacher, because her influence, if wrongly directed, is by far the most dangerous.

But we have schools in which children of larger growth seek to perfect the education which in boyhood was only begun. And as the State increases in population, and the necessities of a pioneer existence give way to the intellectual wants which stated periods of leisure are sure to create, we shall find such schools rapidly springing up. Then comes the test of an inspectors fitness for duty. Then comes the time when the common school begins to assume that high and noble and respected station which is due to it. Then comes the necessity of employing teachers who can supply the mental and moral aliment demanded of them, and thus impel the school onward to the attainment of its purposes among the people.

The *ability* required, undoubtedly means the *power to teach.* The inspectors must be satisfied, not only that the candidate has a good moral character and sufficient learning, but that he is versed in the art of teaching. This is all important, and it is dwelt upon for a moment because some districts, in their reports, have suggested such an amendment of the law as would enumerate more specifically the qualifications of teachers. But it is believed that, if the term *ability* be defined as above, no amendment can be necessary. The annals of school keeping every where, show that the purest minds and profoundest scholars do not always, nor indeed often, understand the art of teaching. If Horace had given the world as rich a practical treatise on this most difficult of all arts, as he has on the art in which he himself excelled, many a rejected pedagogue of modern times would have blessed him.

In some foreign countries—Holland, Prussia and others—the *art of teaching* is taught like any other art; and such has been the conviction of its necessity in Massachusetts, that no less than three Normal schools, or schools for educating teachers, have been established. The two great objects of those schools, say the board of education in their annual report of 1839, are, first, to impart to the pupils a more correct and thorough knowledge of the various branches required to be taught in the schools; and second, to teach the principles of communicating instruction, both in theory and in practice, at a model school connected with the main institution.

If, then, the *ability to teach* constitutes a qualification, the *legal* duty of an inspector is not exhausted by one examination, especially if that examination be made before the teacher has opened his school. On such an examination, the power to teach, or faculty of communicating instruction, cannot be tested. It is only by following the candidate into the school; and there watching the gradual or sudden developments of his disposition, his modes of teaching, and the manner in which he disciplines his scholars and otherwise governs his school that the demand of the law can be met. We all know how easy it is to be deceived in these matters. A candidate may pass a good examination, and *theoretically* be pronounced qualified; yet in the school room exhibit anything but the traits of a school master. His plan of operations may be as eccentric as that which, to insure punctuality, compelled every tardy urchin to walk a mile with a fool's cap drawn over his head, and one of the punctual scholars to follow at some distance to see that the delinquent did not steal an occasional impunity by tearing off the cap and putting it in his pocket; which, to discipline the intellect, awarded a prize to that boy or girl, who at the end of the quarter and on examination day, should recite with the greatest rapidity, giving each word precisely as printed, all the rules in Adams' arithmetic, all those in Murray's grammar, and the Assembly's catechism from beninning to end; and which, by way of punishment for the minor faults of each hour, forced the luckless sinner to stand upon one foot, with the huge quarto bible at arm's length in one hand and a pitcher of water in the other, while a second law-breaker was stationed hard by, brandishing a rattan, that neither burthen might be dropped or the balance lost. It is not positively asserted that such a teacher can be found in Michigan, but simply this, that *precisely* that way of "teaching the young idea how to shoot," *might* not be inconsistent with a fautless examination *out* of the school. No inspector, then, should deem his *legal* duty ended with one examination. Having placed the candidate in school, he should keep his eye upon him; and if *practically* that candidate belies the certificate he has received, the law says such certificate may be annulled.—[F. SAWYER, JR., *Sup't*, 1842.

BLACKBOARD INSTRUCTION.

The communications received evince an almost universal neglect in our district school teachers to use the blackboard, as a means of instruction; and even in the few instances where it has been tried, but an occasional teacher appeared to comprehend its object or understand its use. Now, it is safe to say that no mechanical invention ever effected greater improvements in machinery, no discovery of new agents more signal revolutions in all the departments of science, than the blackboard has effected in schools; and certain it is, that no apparatus at all comparable with it for simplicity and cheapness, has to such a degree facilitated the means, and augmented the pleasures of primary instruction.—[F. SAWYER, Jr., *Sup't*, 1843.

THE NECESSITY OF GOOD TEACHERS.

Eligible teachers are all important. This fact is now more deeply and generally impressed on the public mind than formerly. A new science, founded on the nature of man, has been ascertained and taught. It is pedagogics, or the science of teaching. This is a distinct and most valuable science. On it the successful investigation of all other sciences depends. Its application is the art of teaching. It was once imagined that almost every man of a competent education could teach a school. But to this proposition there are many exceptions. It does not follow that because a man has received a liberal education, he is therefore a lawyer or physician. With all his attainments, he can be neither till he shall have faithfully studied one of these learned professions. And by a parity of reasoning, it is plain that an acquaintance with general literature and science does not, of necessity, prepare one for the arduous, but delightful business of educating the undying mind. Such a preparation is chiefly derived from the study of the science and art of teaching. Firmly persuaded of this truth, many of the governments of the old world, and some of our sister States have instituted normal schools, in which the science and art of teaching are elucidated and enforced. Model schools are formed and taught in these institutions. Here candidates for the office of teacher see many beneficial demonstrations in reference to classification, methods of teaching and government; and in short, whatever is valuable within the range of human knowledge, regarding this paramount interest. A teacher should be a man of learning and virtue. At all events, he should perfectly understand what he professes to teach. Among other attainments, he should know something of physical education. Sound health, a development of all the physical faculties, and an improvement of all the senses, are things too important to be overlooked in a system of popular education. He should be able and disposed to take a sort of paternal care of the health, morals and manners of his priceless charge.

To govern his school properly, it is essential that he govern himself, subjecting all his passions, desires and affections to the control of reason and conscience. Industry, kindness and patience should be prominent traits in his character. His moral qualities, bearing and deportment, should be approvable and worthy of imitation. He should have a fondness for books, learning and study, evincing a correct taste, and that he deems his education unfinished so long as his capacity to advance it remains. He will thus keep pace with the discoveries and improvements of the age, extend the sphere of his usefulness, partake of the most sublime enjoyment, and exhibit a laudable example to those upon whose reputation he will make a lasting impression. A teacher should be ardently devoted to his useful and honorable vocation. He should love children and youth. Their progressive acquirements, in all those branches of education which ennoble and adorn humanity, should afford his benevolent heart the highest delight. Teaching should be a profession, ranking with the professions of law and medicine. One should embrace it as a business for years, or for life. It is a calling of the most solemn responsibility. On the manner of its execution hang the most eventful consequences. The influence of early tuition may decide the character of an individual for time and eternity. It may be intimately connected with his happiness or misery during all the periods of his interminable existence.

It is apparent that a person uniting in his character the attributes, exercises and relations of an eligible teacher, is entitled to the highest consideration. He should be courteously greeted in the best circles of society. His employment should be permanent and lucrative. This would be greatly beneficial to all concerned. Teachers would be encouraged, respected and happy. Scholars would learn as much in two, as they now do in many schools, in six years. Besides, they would be rightly taught—taught to think—taught the power of application. All the original faculties of the mind would be developed in due proportion. A proper balance would be maintained. While the mind is acquiring in the wisest method, useful knowledge, it is disciplined to intense, enduring, triumphant thought, upon any subject submitted to its examination.

One word before leaving this topic regarding female teachers. The qualifications requisite to successful teaching and government are not exclusively confined to the male sex. All acquainted with the mind and manners of accomplished females, and with the character of children and youth, would class such females among the most eligible teachers. That such is the fact, appears from the concurrent testimony of numerous individuals, in several States, whose appointments had led them to make on the behalf of legislative bodies, critical examinations into the learning and government of many female schools. To these schools, composed of both sexes, were accorded the palm of excellence. It is devoutly to be wished that parents and teachers—all those whose official duties relate to schools, with all the friends of learning, may often meet on the subject of education. Let it be the theme of lectures, essays and debates. Let inquiries, observations and facts respecting its interests, everywhere meet the public eye on the pages of newspapers and periodicals. Truth invites discussion. It profits by examination. The more the subject of education, we repeat the idea, is agitated, the more its prosperity will be found strongly allied to the most valuable blessings of our beloved country, and of all mankind.—[O. C. Comstock, *Sup't*, 1844.

SMALL DISTRICTS.

A small district is unprofitable, and, so far as practicable, should be avoided. It will rarely possess numbers, wealth and efficiency enough to establish and sustain a good and prosperous school. In a large and successful school there is something inspiring to scholars and teachers; indeed, to all concerned. But a small school and its usual concomitants, exerts a contrary influence. A small district commonly employs a teacher who can be obtained for low wages; it has not alwas a due regard to his qualifications for his momentous employment. It will ordinarily keep a school in operation but a few months in a year. Such a district and its teacher are prone to change their relations to each other; and they often gratify this propensity; hence, the latter is engaged and dismissed in frequent succession. The injurious consequences resulting from these changes are numerous and apparent. A teacher who instructs a school but a short time only, cannot feel that lively interest in its welfare that he would, should he have it under his tuition during many terms. Besides, if the teacher deserves it, the scholars will, after a while, imbibe a respect for his character, which will progressively increase with the revolution of months and years. This respect is material to their improvement, and the teacher's happiness. When a teacher knows, from the general character of his district, that his labors in it will probably be short, he does not feel at home; he rather regards himself as a passenger, liable every hour to be called by the horn to prosecute his journey. He has not all those motives before his mind, to exhibit such a character, in all respects as a teacher, as should secure to him permanency, support and respectability in his calling. When a teacher is employed for the first time in a district, he often changes a part of the school books, the mode of teaching and the discipline. This is a source of embarrassment to the school, and expense to its patrons. There is usually a considerable interval between the time when one teacher leaves and another comes. This interrupts the habit of reading and study, and impairs that fondness for attending school which had been formed by the scholars. Their minds become dissipated; hence much time, pains and effort are requisite to bring them back to a state favorable to advancment in learning, to the enjoyment of the school. This mutability and the causes which induce it, are to be deprecated; they should be removed.

The advantages of having a school near one's house—advantages which sway the minds of many in voting to divide districts, or to organize small ones, cannot atone for the evils suggested. We had better oblige our children to enjoy the salutary exercise of walking one or two miles, to a reputable school, than to send them to one though at our door, which, for various reasons, is exceptionable.—[O. C. Comstock, *Sup't,* 1845.

CONSOLIDATION OF DISTRICTS.

The consolidation of districts, in our cities and rising villages, is highly desirable. A district thus augmented would be rendered capable of erecting and furnishing a building containing four rooms for graduated schools. The rule of graduation should have reference alone to degrees of scholarship. The lowest department should receive new beginners, and the highest those who intend to acquire the most liberal education these institutions could confer. Other departments should be occupied by the intermediate classes of pupils. These graduated schools would obviate the necessity of select seminaries. Education obtained in these, is always much more expensive than it would be, if imparted in the graduated schools; since these would be so organized and managed as to entitle them to a due proportion of the school fund. The necessity of select schools is founded in the imperfect character of the primary schools. Elevate these, and select schools will be superceded.—[O. C. Comstock, *Superintendent*, 1845.

PHYSICAL EXERCISE.

In childhood the excitability is highly accumulated. This is peculiarly the case when a child is deprived of sufficient exercise. In this state a sense of uneasiness pervades the entire system; the head especially feels disordered; the mind is confused; it does not perceive clearly; it cannot grasp a subject triumphantly; debility, irritation and peevishness are apt to ensue. Under these circumstances a child is temporarily disqualified for all agreeable and successful study. To demand it of him just at this period, is cruel. To expect that it could be profitable, is folly. Such a course would be at war with the laws of both body and mind. A scholar often treated in this way would regard the school house as a dreary prison, and his studies as a painful punishment. The necessary recesses and exercise in the open air, will obviate this melancholy train of things. Suitable play grounds attached to a school house are all important.

A child requires much exercise. This is indispensable to develop, strengthen and discipline the corporal faculties—to exhaust a part of the superabundant excitability—to restore and maintain an equable diffusion of blood and sensorial power—things which are essential to physical health, mental vigor, and delightful study. What I have said in reference to the physical system of children, applies in a great measure, to all animals. When they are young they are extremely sportive—a sort of perpetual motion. The animal universe demands air and action. Without these, all sentient beings lose their vitality.—[O. C. Comstock, *Sup't*, 1845.

THE TEACHER'S CALLING.

The teacher's calling should rank among the learned professions. The lawyer is required to devote a series of years to a regular course of classical study and professional reading before he can find employment in a case in which a few dollars only are pending. With this we find no fault. But it should not be forgotten that the teacher's calling is as much more important than the ordinary exercise of the legal profession, as the unperishable riches of mind are more valuable than the corruptible treasures of earth.

We seek out from among us men of sound discretion and good report to enact laws for the government of our State and nation. And with this, too, we find no fault. It is right and proper that we should do so. But it should be borne in mind that it is the teacher's high prerogative not only so to teach the rising generation that they shall rightly understand law, but to infix in their minds the principles of justice and equity, the attainment of which is the high aim of legislation. While our legislators enact laws for the government of the people, the well qualified and faithful schoolmaster prepares those under his charge to govern themselves. Without the teachers conservative influence, under the best legislation, the great mass of the people will be lawless; while the tendency of his labors is to qualify the rising generation who constitute our future freemen and our country's hope, to render an enlightened, a cheerful and a ready obedience to the high claims of civil law. The well qualified, faithful teacher, becomes the right arm of the Legislature. Once more: The physician is required to become thoroughly acquainted with the anatomy and physiology of the human body; in a word, to become acquainted with "the house I live in;" to understand the diseases to which we are subject, and their proper treatment, before he is allowed to extract a tooth, to open a vein, or administer the simplest medicine. Nor with this do we find fault, for we justly prize the body. It is the habitation of the immortal mind. When in health, it is the mind's servant, and ready to do its biddings; but darken its windows by disease and it becomes the mind's prison house. But while the physician, whom we honor and love, is required to make these attainments before he is permitted *even to repair* the house I live in, should not he who teaches the *master* of the house be entitled to a respectable rank in society? He should, in the unanimous opinion of every enlightened citizen who duly appreciates the importance of the teacher's profession.—[IRA MAYHEW, *Sup't,* 1846.

UNION SCHOOLS.

Section ninety-two of the revised school law provides, as we have seen, for the organization of such schools in this State. A considerble number of districts have already availed themselves of this provision, and several large and commodious Union school houses have been built, in which schools are in successful operation. Other similar houses are now in process of erection, and taxes have been voted in other cases, with reference to building another season.

In that school are combined all the advantages of the well conducted common school, the academy for young gentlemen, and the seminary for young ladies. Children may there commence with the alphabet, and pass from one grade to another, until, on leaving the school, they are prepared to enter any college or university in the United States.

Union schools should be established at the earliest practicable period, in every county of this State, and in all the principal villages, in which students may qualify themselves to enter the University. Union schools constitute the only reliable connecting link between our primary schools and the State University.

The following are among the advantages which well conducted Union schools possess:

1. *They are open to all.* In this respect, they are like our common schools. The course of instruction is also considerably extended, and ample provision is thus made for the thorough education of every child residing within the districts in which they are established.

2. *They may be better than our common and select schools now generally are.* In them, the principle of a division of labor is recognized. In this respect they resemble our colleges and universities, in which each professor has his distinct department. When a teacher instructs in a few branches only, he has an opportunity of attaining greater skill and aptness, than when he has occasion to direct his attention to eight or ten distinct recitations, in the short space of three hours. The course of instruction may also be more thorough than in our common or select schools; each pupil being required to sustain a satisfactory examination in every branch of study he pursues, before he is permitted to enter a higher class. This is very different from the course usually pursued in select and private schools. Children generally desire to advance rapidly. Parents, also, are commonly anxious to have them. Teachers understanding this, and hence, desirous of pleasing both children and parents,that they may continue their patronage, are frequently more solicitous to advance their scholars *rapidly* than *thoroughly*. This is a great error, and is productive of more mischief than most persons are aware of. We are the creatures of *habit*, and become accustomed to do things thoroughly or carelessly—well or ill. The evil consequences of bad habits who can estimate? The good, also, that results from the early formation of correct habits, so far from being confined to early childhood, only begins to discover itself at this period, and is not fully developed until late in life. "What is worth doing at all, is worth doing well," has become a proverb.

3. *Union schools are not only better, but they are cheaper than other schools.* Each teacher has large classes, and hence employs his time more profitably than he otherwise could. A good teacher can just as well instruct a class of fifteen or twenty, as only three or four. The scholars, also, will generally be more stimulated, and will hence apply themselves more closely to their studies, and with better results, with large classes than with small ones.

4. *Common schools and Union schools are democratic institutions*, while select schools are aristocratic in their character and tendency.

5. *Union schools are very good substitutes for Normal schools or teachers' seminaries.* I perhaps ought not to speak of them as *substitutes*. I may, however, safely say, that in the absence of Normal schools, well conducted Union schools cannot fail to accomplish much in the improvement of common school teachers. In them the course of instruction is extensive, thorough and practical; just what every teacher needs to qualify him for his work. In addition to this, the principal might organize a teacher's class, fall and spring, and give a course of instruction specially adapted to the wants of those who contemplate teaching. These instructions might be exemplified by frequent visits to the several departments of the union school, which should be so conducted as to constitute it a *model school*.

6. *The government is usually better in well regulated common schools, and especially in Union schools, than in select or private schools.* Select school teachers are apt to indulge their pupils to their serious injury, and they not unfrequently resort to questionable means to se-

cure their good will; for they know that if the child is displeased his parents usually are, and then the child may be withdrawn and sent to another school. Sometimes children are sent to half a dozen schools, from frivolous causes, in as many months. The public school teacher is less under the influence of this temptation, and is not so apt to be moved by the freaks of falsely indulgent parents, being generally sustained by his employers in the administration of wholesome discipline.

The manner in which children are governed, exerts a great influence upon their future weal or woe. If, when at home, they are imprudently indulged, and know not parental restraint, they will claim the same indulgence when sent to school. If they do not receive it, they are dissatisfied, and are perhaps sent to another and a more indulgent teacher. This makes the matter worse. They have been accustomed to disobey father and mother with impunity, and they are now encouraged to disobey their teacher. Soon they will be found throwing off all the restraints of society, and trampling under foot the laws of the land. Should they occasionally attend church, and listen to the reading of the Scriptures, and the counsels of the man of God, having been accustomed to disobey father and mother, the precepts of their teachers, and the laws of their country—in short, having established the HABIT *of disobedience*—they will disregard the authority of conscience, and heed not the monitions of Heaven. But if children are taught *obedience* at home and in the school, they will more readily yield to the claims of society, in compliance with the laws of the land. Having been accustomed to obedince—having formed the HABIT of obeying those whose right it is to govern them—they will be more apt to heed the voice of conscience, ponder the counsels of their spiritual teachers, and yield a ready and cheerful obedience to the sublime precepts of the Bible. What vast and far-reaching consequences, then, depend upon the early training of children? and what wisdom and discretion are required to teach and govern them aright?—[IRA MAYHEW, *Sup't*, 1848.

LOCATION AND VENTILATION OF SCHOOL HOUSES.

In this State six hundred and forty acres of land in every township are appropriated to the support of common schools. Suppose there are ten school districts in a township; this would allow sixty-four acres to every school district. It would seem that when the general government has appropriated *sixty-four acres* to create a fund for the support of schools, that each district might set apart *one acre* as a site for a school house. Once more: one school district usually contains not less than twenty-five hundred acres of land. Is it asking too much to set apart *one acre* as a site for a school house in which the *minds* of the children of the district shall be cultivated, when *twenty-four hundred and ninety-nine* acres are appropriated to clothing and feeding their *bodies?*

I would respectfully suggest, and even *urge* the propriety of locating the school house on a piece of firm ground of liberal dimensions, and of enclosing the same with a suitable fence. The enclosure should be set out with shade trees, unless provided with those of nature's own planting. Scholars would then enjoy their pastime in a pleasant and healthful yard, where they have a *right* to be protected alike from the scorching sun and the wintry blast. They need then no longer be hunted as *trespassers* upon their neighbors' premises, as they now too frequently are.

Although there is a great variety in the dimensions of school houses, yet there are few less than sixteen by eighteen feet on the ground, and fewer still larger than twenty-four by thirty feet. Exclusive of entry and closets, when they are furnished with these appendages, school houses are not usually larger than twenty by twenty-four feet on the ground, and seven feet in heighth. They are, indeed, more frequently smaller than larger. School houses of these dimensions have a capacity of three thousand three hundred and sixty cubic feet, and are usually occupied by at least forty-five scholars in the winter season. Not unfrequently sixty or seventy, and occasionally more than a hundred scholars occupy a room of this size.

A simple arithmetical computation will abundantly satisfy any person who is acquainted with the composition of the atmosphere, the influence of respiration upon its fitness to sustain animal life, and the quantity of air that enters the lungs at each inspiration, that a school room of the preceding dimensions does not contain a sufficient quantity of air to sustain the healthy respiration of even *forty-five* scholars, three hours, the usual length of each session; and frequently the school house is imperfectly ventilated between the sessions at noon, or indeed, for several days in succession. * * *

The prevailing practice with reference to their ventilation, is opening and closing the door, as the scholars enter and pass out of the school house, before school, during the recesses, and at noon. Ventilation, *as such*, I may safely say, has not hitherto been practiced in one school in fifty. It is true, the door has been occasionally set open a few minutes, and the windows have been raised, but the object has been, either to let the smoke pass out of the room, or to *cool* it when it has become *too warm*, NOT TO VENTILATE IT. Ventilation by opening a door or raising the windows, is imperfect and frequently injurious. A more effectual and safer method of ventilation is to lower the upper sash of the windows, or in very cold or stormy weather, to open a ventilator in the ceiling, and allow the vitiated air to escape into the attic. In this case, there should be a free communication between the attic and the outer air, by means of a lattice window, or otherwise. A ventilator may be constructed in connection with the chimney, by carrying up a partition in the middle. One half the chimney, in this case, may be used for a smoke flue, and the other half for a ventilator. But it may be asked why it is not just as well to raise the lower sash of the windows as to lower the upper ones. There are two good reasons why lowering the upper sash is the better method:

1. *Ventilation is more effectual.* In a room which is warmed and occupied in cold weather, the warmer and more vitiated portion of

the air rises to the upper part of the room, while the colder and purer air occupies the lower part. The reason for this may not be readily conceived, especially when we consider that carbonic acid, the vitiating product of respiration, is specifically heavier than common air. Three considerations will make the reason apparent: 1. Gases of different specific gravity mix uniformly, under favorable circumstances. 2. The carbonic acid which is exhaled from the lungs at about blood heat, is hence rarified, and specifically lighter than the air in the room, which inclines it to ascend. 3. The ingress of cold and heavier air from without, is chiefly through apertures near the base of the room. Raising the lower sash of the windows allows a portion of the purer air of the room to pass off, while the more vitiated air above is retained. Lowering the upper sash allows the impure air above to escape, while the purer air below remains unchanged.

2. Lowering the upper sash is the *safer method of ventilation.* It not only allows the impure air more readily to escape, but provides also for the more uniform diffusion of the pure air from without, which takes its place through the upper part of the room. The renovated air will gradually settle upon the heads of the scholars, giving them a purer air to breathe, while the comfort of the body and lower extremities will remain undisturbed. This is as it should be. Warm feet and cool heads contribute alike to physical comfort and clearness of mind. Raising the lower sash of the windows endangers the health of scholars, exposing those who sit near them, to colds, catarrhs, &c. Indeed, when it is very cold or stormy, it is unsafe to ventilate by lowering the upper sash of the windows. At such times, provision should be made for the escape of impure air at the upper part of the room, and for the introduction of pure air at the lower part.—[Ira Mayhew, *Sup't,* 1848.

CONSTRUCTION OF SCHOOL HOUSES.

There are few school houses the internal construction of which is in all respects alike; yet, by far the majority of them will rank in one of the three following classes:

1. The first class embraces those which are constructed with one or two tiers of desks along each side of the house, and across one end of it; the outer seat having the wall of the house for its back, and the front of each tier of desks constituting the back to the next inner seat. There is usually an alley on each side of the house and at the end of it, leaving the seats of sufficient length to accommodate from five to eight scholars. Those sitting next the alleys can pass to and from their seats without discommoding others. All the rest, (usually not less than three-fourths the entire number,) disturb from one to five or six scholars every time they pass to or from their seats; unless, (which is about as commonly practised, especially with the scholars most distant from the alleys,) they *climb over the desks* in front of them.

Occasionally the desks are shorter, accommodating three or four scholars; and, sometimes, they are intended to accommodate two scholars only, so that each of them, (excepting the outer ones at the end desks,) sits adjacent to an alley, and can pass to and from his seat without disturbing others. There is usually a desk, or table, for the teacher's use, (or at least a *place* for one,) at the end of the house not occupied by the cross seats.

2. The second class embraces those in which the desks extend across the house, with an alley through the middle of it lengthwise, and occasionally one around the outside of the room. All the desks of the second class front the teacher's desk or table.

3. The third class embraces those which are constructed with a row of desks along each side of the house, and across one end of it, the desks fronting the walls of the house, so that the backs of the scholars, while sitting at them, are turned towards the teacher. In this class of houses there are usually three long seats without backs, just within the desks. Sometimes the seats are joined at the corners so as to continue unbroken, twice the length of the house and once its width, a distance of forty-five of fifty feet. There is usually a second tier of seats, and sometimes desks within them, fronting the central part of the room.

There is one impropriety in the construction of a majority of school houses. The desks are generally constructed with close fronts extending to the floor, whereby a free circulation of air, and consequent equilibrium of temperature, are interrupted, which would take place were the seats and desks so arranged as to allow suitable channels of communication. The scholars behind the desks are necessarily troubled with cold feet, unless the room is kept too warm. Were this evil removed, the first class, with short desks, would constitute a very comfortable and convenient arrangement, except from the circumstance that the children are placed opposite each other, which is a serious evil, especially were both sexes are in the same room, as is the case in nearly all of our common schools.

Another objection to long desks, is the inconvenience to which the scholars are subjected in passing to and from their seats. This objection exists to a considerable extent in the second class of houses, especially where there is not an alley around the outside of the room. Were it not for this inconvenience, which might be obviated by introducing a greater number of alleys and shortening the desks, so as to accommodate but two scholars, each of whom would sit adjacent to an alley, and could pass to and from his seat without disturbing others—the *second* would, in my judgment, constitute the preferable plan. All the scholars should face the teacher, but none of them should face each other. This is particularly important where both sexes attend the same school.

And what shall I say of the third class? I can readily enumerate some of its inconveniences, but its real advantages are, in my opinion, few. The following are some of the inconveniences: 1. There is little or no uniformity usually, in the position of the scholars. Some of them face the walls, others the inner part of the room, and others sit astride the seat. 2. When the teacher desires the attention of the school, a portion of the scholars must either turn about, or sit with their backs towards him while he addresses them. 3. In changing their positions in foul weather the scholars are apt to muddy the seats, and the clothes of those who sit adjacent to them. 4. The change of position is frequently embarrassing to the girls. 5. Front lights are less pleasant, and more injurious to the eyes than the side lights or back ones, are. 6. Sitting on a plain seat without a back is uncomfortable, and often engenders diseases of the spine, especially in childhood and youth.

The principal supposed advantage of this construction is, I believe, that it affords the teacher a better opportunity for detecting the scholars when engaged in mischief. I do not see how any material advantage of this kind can exist, till the bodies of children become transparent.

But were the *supposed* advantage real, it seems to me to be tempting children to do wrong, to give the teacher an opportunity of displaying his skill in detecting them. When children cannot see their teacher, they frequently think he cannot see them, and conduct accordingly.

There are several inconveniences not yet specified, existing to a less or greater extent, in each of the three classes of houses I have described.

1. The height of the seats, although sometimes adjusted with great care, is frequently determined without any apparent regard to the size and comfort of the scholars who are to occupy them. I have visited many schools in which the majority of the scholars reverse the ordinary practice of *standing up* and *sitting down*. They literally *sit up* and *stand down*, their heads being higher while *sitting* than when *standing*.

2. The desks with their close fronts, are frequently several inches too high. I have visited many schools in which all that could be seen of a majority of the scholars occupying the back seats, was a *part of their heads*, and that too, when they sat erect upon their seats. The desks, moreover, are frequently inclined twenty-five or thirty degrees, so that a book laid upon them immediately slides off. An inclination of one inch to the foot will be found more convenient than greater obliquity. A space of three inches on the most distant portion of the desk should be left horizontal, for inkstands, pencils, pens, &c.

3. The floor is sometimes considerably inclined, for the purpose, I suppose, of giving the teacher a better opportunity of seeing the more distant scholars. The whole school is not only subjected to the inconvenience of walking up and down an inclined plane, but what is much worse, when scholars sit upon their seats and rest their feet upon the floor, when within reach, they are constantly sliding from under them.

School houses are not generally furnished with suitable conveniences for disposing of the loose wearing apparel of the scholars, their dinners, &c. There are sometimes a few nails or shelves in a common entry, through which all the scholars pass, upon which a portion of their clothes may be hung or laid, and where dinners may be deposited. But in such cases, the outside door is usually left open, the rain and snow beat in, and the scholars in haste to get their own clothes, frequently pull down as many more, which are trampled under foot. Moreover, the dinners are frozen, and not unfrequently they are devoured by dogs, and even by the hogs that run in the street. But the majority of school houses are not furnished with an entry; and where there is one, frequently not even a nail can be found in it, upon which a single article of clothing may be hung. Neither are there nails or shelves for this purpose within the school room. Scholars generally are obliged to throw their clothes across the desks, upon the seats, or into the windows.

School houses should be so constructed as to contribute to the health, comfort and convenience of both teacher and scholars. They should, then, be made of larger dimensions than they usually are. And especially should provision be made for their ventilation, which should be frequent and thorough. Every child, even the youngest in school, should be furnished with a seat and desk at which he may sit with ease and comfort. The school room should be so seated as to allow every child to pass to and from his seat without disturbing any other. This end can be accomplished with short desks to accommodate two scholars, as is represented in one of the plans for school houses in this report. It can, however, be better accomplished with long desks and pivot chairs, by allowing sufficient space in rear of the seats, for scholars to pass to and from them, without discommoding others.—[Ira Mayhew, *Sup't*, 1848.

We do not seek splendor for our school houses. Justice will be satisfied, and children will not complain, if we make them simple and cheap; for cheapness and simplicity are not incompatible with the most perfect convenience and comfort. Log houses we have and must have for years; but, because it is a log house, it must not be, of necessity, a prison or a barn. Nor is the veriest economy any bar to correctness or neatness of construction. Many a school-house, log, frame and brick, has cost double what was necessary to render it far more convenient and comfortable than it is. Whether it costs one, three or six hundred dollars, situated in city, village or corner of a town, every school house claims, as a matter of right, certain indispensable things to make it answer its purpose, and these comport with economy.

In the first place, its location should be healthy. This is a matter of judgment, not one of the pocket. And while, at the time, a healthy location costs no more than an unhealthy one, economy of health, in the long run, renders the first vastly the cheapest. That is a point on which there can be no dispute. One who has studied the subject long and thoughtfully, Mr. Mann, would build the school house "where some sheltering hill or wood mitigates the inclemency of winter; where a neighboring grove tempers the summer heat; remove it a little from the public highway, and from buildings where noisy and clattering trades are carried on; and above all, rescue it from sound or sight of all resorts for license and dissipation." In traversing the State during the last two summers, many such locations were observed. Michigan abounds with them.

The next things to be considered are the materials and construction of the school house. These depend somewhat upon the resources of the district; but in all districts, the money voted should be made to buy the greatest possible amount of convenience and comfort. If one hundred dollars, it should not be all expended in materials, leaving nothing for construction. The first question should be—What material is the best and cheapest, logs, hewn timber and boards, or brick? If, in the particular locality, logs are the best, decide upon logs; but do not select, cut and lay them without reference to quality, neatness, comfort and health. Logs, as nearly equal in diameter as possible should be selected. In placing them one upon the other, care, above all things, should be taken to expose the smallest possible number of crevices, so that the labor and expense of chinking be measurably saved. With proper attention, it is easier and much cheaper to make an air-tight log house than a frame one.

If hewn timber and boards be decided upon, let the best be selected. So of brick. Who, in selecting bricks for his dwelling house would prefer, as a matter of economy, miserable, soft, limestony ones to such as consist of good clay, and are well burned? The same hints will answer for school houses that cost more than the sum named. In all cases, let it be a maxim to make the most of the money raised.

As for construction, whatever the size contemplated, let proportion exist throughout—always bearing in mind that health requires at least a certain height between the floor and the ceiling, and a certain quantity of space for each scholar. With good health, a child may accomplish any amount of study and make it useful to him; without health, every mental acquisition is a curse. All writers agree as to the necessity and *humanity* of allowing every scholar a certain quantity of pure air; but they differ slightly in the precise amount. The general opinion, however, seems to be that the minimum cubic space for each child should be one hundred and fifty feet. Thus, if the area in which he sits be three feet square, the height of the room should be sixteen or seventeen feet. This is the smallest allowance compatible with good health.

Another important item is light. And here it may be said that, while in the old and populous villages of other States excess of light is the burden of complaint, a deficiency of that material is the prevailing evil of our interior towns, especially in log school houses. This fact was constantly forced upon my attention during the official tour of the past summer. Log houses, and many frame ones, stood out upon the public road with but a solitary inlet for the glorious light of day; and this, in very numerous instances, consisting of six seven by nine panes (they should be called pains,) of glass thrust into a single sash like the one eye of Polyphemus. It is often said of man, that he is the creature of circumstances; and if any one circumstance exercises over his mind a predominant influence, it is nature when presented to him in her brightest and most beautiful aspect. And what can spread cheerfulness over a school like sunlight streaming through two or three windows? Who blames a child for "playing truant," when the penalty for attending school is an almost utter deprivation of that which gives life to inanimate, and diffuses gladness through all animate nature? The severest punishment that can be inflicted upon a felon is incarceration in a dark cell. Solitary confinement is nothing, comparatively, if light be only vouchsafed. There is no reason in the world why log school houses should be stinted of their light. What are four or five dollars in comparison with cheerfulness, contentment, happiness?

Too much light, on the other hand, is as bad as too little; for it may injure the eyes beyond cure. And in school house where the desks are attached to the walls, children directly opposite every window are fearfully exposed to the consequences of this excess. The sun's rays should never fall directly upon the eye. If children must be compelled to face the window, the least that humanity can do for their safety is to elevate the window still somewhat above their heads. Curtains of a proper texture essentially modify the light and relieve the eyes.—[F. SAWYER, Jr., *Sup't*, 1843.

APPURTENANCES.

There are, perhaps, in the majority of school houses, a pail for water, cup, and broom, and a chair for the teacher. Some one or more of these are frequently wanting. I need hardly say every school house should be supplied with them all. In addition to these, every school house should be furnished with the following articles: 1. An evaporating dish for the stove, which should be supplied with clean pure water. 2. A thermometer, by which the temperature of the room may be regulated. 3. A clock, by which the time of beginning and closing school, and conducting all its exercises, may be governed. 4. A shovel and tongs. 5. An ash pail and ash house. For want of these, much filth is frequently suffered to accumulate in and about the school house, and not unfrequently the house itself takes fire and burns down. 6. A woodhouse, and well supplied with seasoned wood. 7. A well, with provisions not only for drinking, but for the cleanliness of pupils. 8. And last, though not least, in this connection, two privies, in the rear of the school house, separated by a high close fence, one for the boys and the other for the girls. For want of these indispensable appendages of civilization, the delicacy of children is frequently offended, and their morals corrupted.—[IRA MAYHEW, *Sup't*, 1848.

EDUCATION OF TEACHERS.

"As is the teacher, so will be the school," has become a proverb. In our efforts, then, to advance the interests of education, we should look carefully to the character of the teachers employed in our primary schools; for the schools will never advance beyond the attainment of their teachers. Teachers, then, should be models of excellence. They may possess a sufficient amount of learning to pass a creditable examination in the branches usually taught in common schools, and still be poorly qualified to take the charge of schools. Instructors of youth should be thorough scholars, it is true. In addition to this, they should be *apt to teach*. Moreover, their personal, intellectual, social and moral habits should, in all respects, be what their scholars may safely copy. To qualify teachers for the proper discharge of the duties of their profession, they need a specific training. An academical institution, or a college, whose graduates are not good school teachers, should no more be condemned *as a literary institution*. than one whose graduates are not good lawyers, physicians, or divines. The graduates of literary institutions should be *good scholars*. They are then qualified to enter advantageously upon a course of professional study. A mere graduate, or scholar, can hardly be supposed to be better qualified to teach school, than to practice medicine. I should place as high an estimate upon the judgment of a man who would employ such a person as a family physician, as upon the judgment of one who would employ him as the teacher of his children.

To qualify a person for the most efficient and successful discharge of the duties of an instructor of youth, he should himself receive his training, from the very first, in the best schools. Well conducted Union schools, hence become the very best preliminary training places for teachers. But these alone are not sufficient. A regular course of Normal instruction should subsequently be given. This is as important—I may say, as essential—to enable the *mere scholar* to become a *good teacher*, as are the exercises and developments of the *dissecting room* to constitute him a *good physician*. In addition to these, the latter needs hospital practice with an experienced physician. The former, likewise, needs practice in the model school, under the supervision of a Normal professor. But, neither all teachers, nor all physicians, can avail themselves of such advantages, desirable as they are. They should, however, seek the best opportunities that are afforded them, to become proficients.—IRA MAYHEW, *Sup't*, 1849.

The following regulations, extracted from the editions of laws prepared by the Superintendents of schools of the States of Massachusetts, New York and Rhode Island, are commended to the school officers of Michigan as embodying the true principles upon which candidates for teaching should be examined.

MORAL QUALIFICATIONS.

The committee must be satisfied of the good moral character of a teacher. * * * * No talents, however profound, no genius, however splendid, no attainments, however ample, can atone for any deficiency in moral character. In the beautiful language of the law, it is the "duty of the president, professors and tutors of the University at Cambridge, and of the several colleges, and of all preceptors and teachers of academies, and all other instructors of youth, to exert their best endeavors to impress on the minds of children and youth, committed to their care and instruction, the principles of piety, justice, and a sacred regard to truth, love to their country, humanity, and universal benevolence, sobriety, industry, and frugality, chastity, moderation and temperance, and those other virtues, which are the ornament of human society, and the basis upon which a republican constitution is founded; and it shall be the duty of such instructors to endeavor to lead their pupils as their ages and capacities will admit, into a clear understanding of the tendency of the above-mentioned virtues to preserve and perfect a republican constitution, and secure the blessings of liberty, as well as to promote their future happiness, and also to point out to them the evil tendency of the opposite vices."

The school committee may be satisfied respecting the moral character of the candidate, by actual knowledge, derived from long personal acquaintance; or, in the case of a stranger, they may have well authenticated testimonials of the fact. The committee should note, in their record-book, all letters or certificates of recommendation exhibited by any candidate, whom they shall approve, with the names of their authors; and, when practicable, the letters and certificates themselves should be put on the committee's files, so that their authors may be held to a rigid accountability for the truth of the credentials they have given. If, before the civil tribunals, a man is held to a strict pecuniary liability for accrediting an insolvent as a man in good mercantile standing, or for recommending a swindler as a man of integrity, how much more stringent ought the rule of a moral tribunal to be, when the dearest and most sacred interests of children are periled by means of false testimonials of good character, whether knowingly or heedlessly given!

LITERARY QUALIFICATIONS.

The committee must satisfy themselves, "by personal examination," of the "literary qualifications" of the candidates; that is, they must *personally* examine the candidates in all the branches they will be called upon to teach. * * Even for the lowest grade of schools known to the law, the teacher must be competent to give instruction in orthography, reading, writing, English grammar, geography and arithmetic. This is the minimum of literary qualification. It is lawful for districts to employ teachers who are competent to teach higher branches; or who are able to teach the required branches better, because they are masters of higher ones; who, for instance, can teach reading better, because familiar with the principles of elocution and rhetoric, and with the etymology of words, from whatsoever language they may be derived; who can teach writing better, because adepts in writing; who can teach English grammar better, because familiar, from the study of other languages, with the principles of universal grammar; who can teach geography better, because acquainted with astronomy, geology, statistics, and civil and natural history; and who can teach arithmetic better, because masters of the higher mathematics. So, too, a knowledge of Human Physiology may be required in a teacher, in order to secure the health of the children; because, on health depends their ability to go to school at all, and much also of their ability to study when in school.

CAPACITY TO GOVERN.

The committee must also make special inquiry as to the capacity of each candidate for the government of a school. * * * * * No ambiguous indications, on this point, will be given by the general air and manner of a candidate, the expression of the countenance, the tone of the voice, the firmness or fickleness legible in the eye, the self-esteem, or the servility proclaimed by the natural language.

When a candidate has taught school before, and has succeeded in maintaining good order, without the use of improper means, or without the use of proper means to an improper extent, this fact is strong evidence in favor of a capacity for government. Especially is it so, if the general circumstances and condition of the schools are substantially alike.

Visiting a school in which a candidate may be engaged, and actually witnessing the manner in which he conducts it, is also a valuable means of ascertaining the same fact.

But it is supposed that neither nor all of the above methods can supercede an actual questioning of the candidate as to his views of the principles on which a school should be conducted. It is of primary importance to know whether the fundamental idea of government, in his opinion, is the will of the teacher, or the applause of the neighborhood—which may be for one quality in one place and for another quality in another—or the good of the governed—whether on the one hand he would succumb to resistance and be driven away before rebellion, rather than to strike a blow; or, on the other, whether he would flout the docile, and be capricious towards the obedient, to prove whether there exists in them an unreasoning and unconditional submission to his claim of sovereignty.

If a candidate has no views respecting the great principles on which the government of a school should proceed, the committee cannot affirm that he has a capacity to govern. If such a person has any capacity, it must be in a latent state; but the committee must be satisfied, not of a possible or potential, but of an actual capacity; it must be in a developed state.

Probably few provisions, if any, in the statute book, have been more efficacious and serviceable in improving our schools, than the one which requires committees to examine teachers—as a few considerations will abundantly show.

There are annually employed in the Public Schools of Massachusetts, between five and six thousand different persons as teachers. I suppose it to be indisputable that no section of the Union, of equal population, supplies so large a proportion of young men for the professions, and for the various departments of educated labor, as New England; and among the New England States, Massachusetts, in this respect, is doubtless pre-eminent. The Public Schools of many towns, and the large number of highly respectable academies and private schools, carry forward a numerous body of young men and women to such a degree of literary attainment as enrolls them in the list of candidates for school keeping. Students in our colleges; ambitious young men, who are looking forward to some other employment, actually more lucrative, and, in public estimation, more honorable, and who must obtain a little money as a means of securing their ultimate object; many mechanics and farmers, possessed of more than ordinary intelligence and attainment, and who were renowned, when they went to school, for doing all the "hard sums" in the arithmetical text books; all these have been condidates for public school keeping. Added to this, the average rate of compensation given to teachers in Massachusetts has far exceeded that which has been given in any of the neighboring States. Hence, in the autumn of the year, hosts of adventurers flock hither from Maine, from New Hampshire, from Vermont, and from Connecticut, in quest of employment as teachers in our schools. Some of these are full, not only of enterprise, but of talent; but, under such circumstances, it would be strange indeed, if among the fine gold there should not be found something of dross. All these are competitors for our public schools. They often exhibit recommendations of a highly imaginative character—recommendations which prove the good will of their signers, far more than their good sense of their trustworthiness; for it is well known that the facility with which such recommendations can be obtained is the scandal of our people. What barrier, then, but the vigilance and intelligence of our school committees, shall prevent our schools from being invaded by practical immorality, by literary imposture, and by an inaptitude for all government except the government of fear and force? What but the fidelity of school committees shall prevent sound knowledge and high talent from being thrust aside by ignorance and pretension? The interests of all good teachers, emphatically the interests of the rising generation, demand, by every consideration that can appeal to patriotism, to philanthropy, or to the sense of religious obligation, that the legal duty of examining teachers should be performed without fear or favor, or exception. It has happened a thousand times, that prosperity or adversity has shone or frowned upon the schools of a town—like sunshine or frost upon the early flowers of spring, as it has been blest or cursed with a faithful or a neglectful school committee.

Yet it cannot be denied that for every public consideration demanding a thorough examination of teachers, there is a selfish one which resists it. Individuals in a district or a town, who, in their own minds, have appropriated to themselves the ensuing term of the schools, may, by management or collusion, secure the choice of a committee, who, either through inability or favoritism, will make the examination only a polite and facile ceremony of introduction into the school; or, what has not unfrequently happened, the expectants will secure the choice of a prudential committee, who will open to them the door of the school house without any examination at all. Sometimes it is not difficult for a person, through his relatives and friends, to create an apparent public opinion in a district, which shall seem to demand that the individual shall be selected to keep the school who has himself been the fraudulent author of the factitious opinion that points to him. All persons, too, who are intending to obtain a school, but who are fearful of the results of an examination, will, of course, be opposed to the principle of the law which requires an examination, and will therefore be ready to aid those who strive to evade it.—*Massachusetts Regulations.*

NEW YORK AND RHODE ISLAND REGULATIONS.

EXAMINING TEACHERS.

The examination of persons wishing to teach as principals or assistants, the granting of certificates of qualification, and the annulling of such certificates, are among the most important duties devolving on the school committee, and on their faithful performance the efficiency of the law mainly depends.

The inefficiency of the former school system in many of the towns was owing to the fact that the duties of examining teachers and visiting the schools were too generally neglected or ill performed.

In making such examinations, whether by the whole board, or by the sub-committee, they should inquire *first, as to moral character*. On this point, the committee should be entirely satisfied, before proceeding further. Some opinion can be formed from the general deportment and language of the applicant, but the safest course will be, with regard to those who are strangers to the committee, to insist on the written testimony of persons of the highest respectability in the towns and neighborhoods where they have resided; and especially to require the certificate of the school committee and parents where they have taught before, as to the character they have sustained, and the influence they have exerted in the school and in society.

While a committee should not endeavor to inquire into the peculiar religious or sectarian opinions of a teacher and should not entertain any preferences or prejudices founded on any such grounds, they ought, without hesitation, to reject every person who is in the habit of ridiculing, deriding or scoffing at religion.

And while the examination should in no case be extended to the *political* opinions of the candidate, yet it may with propriety extend "to their manner in expressing such belief, or maintaining it. If that manner is in itself boisterous and disorderly, intemperate and offensive, it may well be supposed to indicate ungoverned passions, or want of sound principles of conduct, which would render its possessor obnoxious to the inhabitants of the district, and unfit for the sacred duties of a teacher of youth, who would instruct by examples as well as by precept."—[*N. Y. Regulations.*

Second, as to literary attainments.—The lowest grade of attainments is specified in the school law. Every teacher must have been found qualified by examination, or by previous experience, which must have come to the personal knowledge of the committee, to teach the English language, arithmetic, penmanship, and the rudiments of geography and history. An examination as to the attainments of the teacher in these branches might be so conducted as to test his capacity, in those particulars, to teach any grade of schools. Some reference, therefore, must be had to the condition and wants of the district schools as they now are. But no person should be considered qualified to teach any school, who cannot speak and write the English language, if not elegantly, at least correctly. He should be a good reader, and be able to make the hearer understand and feel all that the author intended. He should be able to give the analysis as well as explain the meaning of the words of the sentence, and explain all dates, names and allusions. He should be a good speller, and to test this, as well as his knowledge of punctuation, the use of capitals, &c., he should be required to write out his answers to some of the questions of the committee. He should understand practically the first principles of English grammar, as illustrated in his own writing and conversation. He should be able to write a good hand, to make a pen, and teach others how to do both. He should show his knowledge of geography by applying his definitions of the elementary principles to the geography of his own town, State and county, and by questions on the map and globe. He should be able to answer promptly all questions relating to the leading events of the history of the United States and his own State. In arithmetic, he should be well versed in some treatise on mental arithmetic, and be able to work out before the committee, on the black board or slate, such questions as will test his ability to teach the text books on arithmetic prescribed for the class of schools he will be engaged in.

Third, his ability to instruct.—This ability includes aptness to teach, a power of simplifying difficult processes—a skill in imparting knowledge—of inducing pupils to try, and try in such a way that they will derive encouragement as they go along, which must be given by nature, but may be cultivated by observation and practice. An examination into the literary qualifications of a candidate as ordinarily conducted, and even when conducted by an experienced committee-man, or even by a teacher, will not always determine whether this ability is possessed, or possessed in a very eminent degree. Hence it is desirable for the committee to ascertain what success the candidate has had in other places, if he has taught before; and if this evidence cannot be had, whether he has received any instruction in the art of teaching; or has been educated under a successful teacher; or has visited good schools. In conducting the examination to ascertain this point, the candidate should be asked how he would teach the several studies. He should be asked how he would proceed in teaching the alphabet to a child who had never been instructed at all in it; as for example, whether he would give him words or single letters; or letters having a general resemblance; or in the order in which they are ordinarily printed; or by copying them on a slate or black-board, and then repeating their names after the teacher; or by picking them out of a collection of alphabet blocks, &c., &c. So in spelling. He should be asked how he would classify his scholars in this branch, and the methods of arranging and conducting a class exercise; how far he would adopt with the class the simultaneous method, and how far the practice of calling on each member in regular order; how far he would put out the word to the whole class, and after requiring all to spell it *mentally*, name a particular scholar to spell it *orally;* how far he would adopt the method of writing the word, and especially the difficult words, on a slate or blackboard; how far he would connect spelling with the reading lessons, &c.

It will be more satisfactory sometimes, perhaps. to have a class of small scholars present at the examination, and let the candidate go through a recitation with them, so that the committee can have a practical specimen of his tact in teaching each branch of study; in explaining and removing difficulties, &c.

The same method of examination should be carried into reading, and every other branch. It is more important to know that the teacher has sound views as to methods, than that he is qualified as to literary attainments.

Fourth, ability to govern. This is an important qualification, insisted upon by the law, and indispensable to the success of the schools. On this point the committee should call for the evidence of former experience, wherever the candidate has taught before, and when this cannot be had, the examination should elicit the plans of the teacher as to making children comfortable, keeping them all usefully employed, and interested in their studies, his best system of rewards and punishments, and examples of the kinds of punishment he would resort to in particular cases, and all other matters pertaining to the good order and government of a school. In this connection, the age, manners, bearing, knowledge of the world, love and knowledge of children, &c., of the applicant, will deserve attention.

In addition to these qualifications which the law requires, the address and personal manners and habits of the applicant should be inquired into, for these will determine in a great measure the manners and habits of the children whom he will be called upon to teach.

The most thorough and satisfactory mode of conducting the examination is by written questions and answers; it will be desirable, if the examination is conducted orally, to keep minutes of the questions and answers.

The school committee must remember that on the thoroughness and fidelity with which this duty is performed, depends in a great measure the success or failure of the school system. The whole machinery moves to bring good teachers into the schools, and to keep them as long, and under as favorable circumstances as possible.

If the teacher adds to his other qualifications, a knowledge of the art of singing, it will be an additional recommendation to him with those who desire to have a good school. Singing in school serves as a recreation and amusement, especially for the smaller scholars. It exercises and strengthens their voices and lungs, and by its influence on the disposition and morals, enables a teacher to govern his school with comparative ease.

The committee should exercise a sound discretion in the examination. If a person has been before examined by them, and the committee have often visited his school, and know him to be a good teacher, the law allows them to give him a certificate founded on this experience. But re-examinations can in no case do any injury, and by gradually increasing their rigor and adding to the requirements, much may be done towards raising the general standard of education. The committee should, for convenience of reference, keep a tabular list of the names of all persons examined by them, either on their common record book, or in a book kept for that purpose, with columns for the date, age, place of residence of the applicant, the result of the examination, and any other remarks that may appear worthy of remembrance.—*Rhode Island Reg.*

RATE BILL AND WARRANT.

The following decision has been published while the foregoing part of this document has been passing through the press, and is taken from MANNING'S MICHIGAN REPORTS, VOL. 1, Page 269:

WALL VS. EASTMAN: Where the moderator of a school district refused to sign a warrant to a rate bill for teacher's wages, and a judgment was afterwards recovered by the teacher against the district for the amount due him, which was paid by a tax on the district, a tax payer who was assessed, and paid his part of the tax, cannot sustain an action against the moderator to recover what he has paid.

CASE reserved from Jackson Circuit Court. Eastman sued Wall in a Justice's Court, in an action on the case, to recover eight dollars tax which he, as a resident of a school district, had been compelled to pay, by reason of Wall's refusal, as moderator of the district, to sign a warrant to the rate bill for teacher's wages. The substance of the declaration which was demurred to, is stated in the opinion of the Court. The Justice rendered judgment for Eastman. Wall appealed to the county court, which also gave judgment against him, when he carried the case to the circuit court by certiorari.

By the Court: Green, J.—The question reserved in this case is, whether the declaration contains a cause of action, in favor of the plaintiff below, against the defendant below. The declaration sets forth in substance, that in February, 1847, Wall, the defendant below, was director of a school district in Sandstone, Jackson county; that a teacher was hired, who taught the school in that district, and made out a rate bill for wages due him, and requested Wall to issue his warrant as director, for the collection thereof, which Wall refused to do; and that thereupon, the teacher sued the district, and recovered a judgment for the wages so due him—the amount of which judgment was levied upon the taxable property within the district, and collected—that the plaintiff below was a resident of the district, and owned taxable property therein, and that by reason of the premises he was compelled to pay a portion of said judgment, to wit: the sum of eight dollars thereof, which sum he claims to recover of the defendant below. To this declaration the defendant below demurred, and assigned several special cases of demurrer, all of which, however, embrace but one proposition in substance, namely, that the declaration does not contain a cause of action.

The counsel for the plaintiff below, referred to 5th John. R. 175, and 15 id. 250, and these are the only adjudged cases cited on either side. The question involved in the case in 5 John. R. referred to, was whether the imposition of a penalty for official misconduct, or neglect of duty, took away the right of action for damages. The law relating to primary schools and the duties and liabilities of school district officers in force when the cause of action in this case, if any arose, was the act of 1843, Session Laws 1843, page 88. By the 71st section of that act a penalty of ten dollars was imposed upon every person, who, having been elected to the office of moderator, director or assessor of a school district, and having entered upon the duties of his office, should neglect or refuse to perform any duty required of him by virtue of his office. Section 77 provides that in all cases not otherwise provided for in that act, in which a duty shall be enjoined upon any person, officer, or board of officers, such person, officer, or board, as the case may be, shall be liable to any party aggrieved, in the full amount of all damages sustained by the wilful neglect, or unfaithful performanee of such duty. This last provision introduces no new principle, but is in affirmance of the common law, and seems to have been incorporated into the statute by the Legislature, for the purpose of precluding any conclusion to the contrary, which might otherwise be supposed to arise from other provisions of the statute.

* * * * * *

By the second subdivision of section 21 of the act before referred to, it is made the duty of the director, by and with the advice and consent of the moderator or assessor, to contract with and hire qualified teachers *for the district:* which contract is required to be in writing, and to specify the wages per week or month, as agreed by the parties. To this contract the district, in its corporate capacity, is a necessary party, and in that capacity it is bound to perform it; and in case of a failure to do so, is liable in damages to the teacher for its non-performance. The district in its corporate capacity receives the moneys apportioned to it from the primary school fund, or derived from other sources for the payment of teachers; and if more is required for that purpose, it is to be collected from those sending children to the school, in proportion to the number of scholars, and the time they attend. For this purpose the teacher is to note the daily attendance of each scholar, and make return of the same to the director. The director is then to ascertain the amount due from each person sending children to school, and to make out a rate bill, and annex thereto a warrant for the collection thereof, to be signed by him and the moderator. This warrant is to be directed to the district assessor, who is required to collect all rate bills of the district made and delivered to him, in accordance with the seventh subdivision of section 21, of the act aforeraid, in obedience to the command of the warrants annexed to such rate bills, and to make a written return of the same to the director. When such moneys have been collected by the assessor, they are school moneys belonging to the district, and the assessor and his sureties are liable therefor, if not applied by him according to law, upon the bond which he is required to give to the district; and they are to be drawn by an order of the moderator upon the assessor, as moneys to be disbursed by the district, according to section 19 of the act aforesaid. If the moneys so required to be collected had been lost to the district by reason of the defalcation of the assessor, after they came into his hands, there can be no question but that the district, in its corporate capacity, might have recovered the amount in an action upon the assessor's bond; and it is equally clear that the members of the corporation could not in such a case, have sustained actions in their individual names, for their respestive portions of the loss. The converse of the last proposition would be a most palpable violation of that wise maxim, which declares that the law abhors a multiplicity of actions, and which forbids an individual to bring separate actions upon different items of the same account.

How does the case before us differ in principle from the one just supposed, of a loss sustained by the defalcation of the assessor? In that case, the loss would fall upon the district in the first instance, in its corporate capacity, and indirectly upon the owners of taxable property within the district. And so in this case. By reason of the refusal of the defendant below to issue his warrant for the collection of the rate bill, the district lost the amount which should have been collected from the individuals sending pupils to the district school for the payment of the teacher; and was obliged to collect by a tax upon the property within the district, the amount required—in consequence of which, the plaintiff below, being an inhabitant of the district, owning taxable property therein, was compelled to pay a tax of eight dollars, for the recovery of which, this suit was brought. If any right of action accrued, it was in favor of the corporation of which the plaintiff below was a member, and not to him individually. If the plaintiff below could sustain this action, every person who paid any portion of the judgment in favor of the teacher against the district, might also sustain a separate action for the amount paid by him; and upon the same principle, in case of the default of the county treasurer, every individual in the county who should be compelled to pay a tax to make good the fund lost, might also maintain a separate action against the treasurer for the amount paid by him. No such principle, it is believed, has ever been sanctioned or recognized by any judicial tribunal whose decisions have been reported in the books. The result to which the foregoing conclusions lead does not deprive the plaintiff below of a full and adequate remedy for the injury he complains of. If the defendant below has made himself liable by the omission of official duty, charged in the declaration in this case, a recovery against him by the district will not only make the plaintiff below good, but all the members of the district who suffered a like injury from the same cause. As the injury to the plaintiff below was indirect, and sustained by him in common with the other members of the corporation, as such, so must be his remedy.

PART III.

LAWS RELATING TO PUBLIC INSTRUCTION

AND

INCORPORATED INSTITUTIONS OF LEARNING

OF THE STATE OF MICHIGAN.

[No. 99.]

AN ACT prescribing the duties of the Superintendent of Public Instruction, and to repeal Chapter fifty-six of the Revised Statutes of eighteen hundred and forty-six, and an act to amend said Chapter fifty-six, approved March twenty-ninth, one thousand eight hundred and fifty.

Section 1. *The People of the State of Michigan enact,* That the Superintendent of Public Instruction shall have general supervision of public instruction, and it shall be his duty among other things to prepare annually and transmit a report to the Governor, to be transmitted by him to the Legislature at each biennial session thereof, containing:

1. A statement of the condition of the University, and its branches, of all incorporate literary institutions and of the primary schools;

2. Estimates and amounts of expenditures of the school money;

3. Plans for the improvement and management of all educational funds, and for the better organization of the educational system, if in his opinion the same be required;

4. The condition of the Normal school;

5. All such other matters relating to his office and the subject of education generally, as he shall deem expedient to communicate.

Sec. 2. He shall make all necessary abstracts of the reports of school inspectors, transmitted to him by the clerks, and embody so much of the same in his report as may be necessary.

Sec. 3. He shall prepare and cause to be printed with the laws relating to primary schools, all necessary forms, regulations and instruments for conducting all proceedings under said laws, and transmit the same, with such instructions relative to the organization and government of such schools and the course of studies to be pursued therein, as he may deem advisable, to the several officers entrusted with their care and management.

Sec. 4. School laws, forms, regulations and instructions shall be printed in pamphlet form, with a proper index, and shall have also annexed thereto a list of such books as the Superintendent shall think best adapted to the use of the primary schools, and a list of books suitable for township libraries, with such rules as he may think proper for the government of such libraries.

SEC. 5. He shall annually, on receiving notice from the Auditor General of the amounts thereof, apportion the income of the primary school fund among the several townships and cities of the State, in proportion to the number of scholars in each between the age of four and eighteen years, as the same shall appear by the reports of the several township inspectors of primary schools, made to him for the year last closed.

SEC. 6. He shall prepare annually a statement of the amount in the aggregate payable to each county in the State from the income of the primary school fund, and shall deliver the same to the Auditor General, who shall thereupon draw his warrant upon the State Treasurer in favor of each county for the amount payable to such county.

SEC. 7. He shall also send written notices to the clerks of the several counties of the amount in the aggregate to be disbursed in their respective counties, and the amount payable to the townships therein respectively; which notice shall be disposed of as directed by an act entitled an act to amend chapter fifty-eight of the revised statutes of one thousand eight hundred and forty-six, approved March twenty-eighth, one thousand eight hundred and fifty.

SEC. 8. Whenever the returns from any county, township or city, upon which a statement of the amount to be disbursed or paid to any such county, township or city, shall be so far defective as to render it impracticable to ascertain the share of public moneys which ought to be disbursed or paid to such county, township or city, he shall ascertain by the best evidence in his power the facts upon which the ratio of such apportionment shall depend, and shall make the apportionment accordingly.

SEC. 9. Whenever, by accident, mistake, or any other cause, the returns from any county, township or city, upon which a statement of the amount to be disbursed to any such county, township or city, shall not contain the whole number of scholars in such county, township or city, between the age of four and eighteen years, and entitled to draw money from said fund, by which any such county, township or city shall fail to have apportioned to it the amount to which it shall justly be entitled, the Superintendent, on receiving satisfactory proof thereof, shall apportion such deficiency to such county, township or city, in his next annual apportionment; and the conditions of this section shall extend to all cases which accrue in the year one thousand eight hundred and fifty.

SEC. 10. Upon all sums paid into the State treasury upon account of the principal of any of the educational funds, except where (other) provision is or shall be made by law, the Treasurer shall compute interest from the time of such payment, or from the time of the last computation of interest thereon, to the first Monday of April in each and every year, and shall give credit therefor to each and every school fund, as the case may be; and such interest shall be paid out of the general fund.

SEC. 11. The Superintendent shall, at the expiration of his term of office, deliver over on demand to his successor, all property, books, documents, maps, records, reports, and all other papers belonging to his office, or which may have been received by him for the use of his office.

SEC. 12. Chapter fifty-six of the revised statutes of one thousand eight hundred and forty-six, and an act to amend said chapter fifty-six, approved March twenty-ninth, one thousand eight hundred and fifty, are hereby repealed.

Approved April 4, 1851.

[No. 151.]

AN ACT to provide for the Government of the State University, and to repeal Chapter fifty-seven of the Revised Statutes of eighteen hundred and forty-six.

SECTION 1. *The People of the State of Michigan enact,* That the institution established in this State, and known as the University of Michigan, is continued under the name and style heretofore used.

SEC. 2. The University shall provide the inhabitants of this State with the means of acquiring a thorough knowledge of the various branches of literature, science and arts.

SEC. 3. The government of the University is vested in the Board of Regents.

SEC. 4. The Board of Regents shall constitute the body corporate, with the right as such of sueing and being sued, of making and using a common seal, and altering the same.

SEC. 5. The Regents shall have power to enact ordinances, by-laws and regulations for the government of the University; to elect a president, to fix, increase and reduce the regular number of professors and tutors, and to appoint the same, and to determine the amount of their salaries.

SEC. 6. They shall have power to remove the president, and any professor or tutor, when the interest of the University shall require it.

SEC 7. They shall have power to appoint a secretary, librarian, treasurer, steward, and such other officers as the interests of the institution may require, who shall hold their offices at the pleasure of the board, and receive such compensation as the board may prescribe.

SEC. 8. The University shall consist of at least three departments:

1. A department of literature, science and the arts.
2. A department of law.
3. A department of medicine.
4. Such other departments may be added as the Regents shall deem necessary and the state of the University fund shall allow.

SEC. 9. The Regents shall provide for the arrangement and selection of a course or courses of study in the University, for such students as may not desire to pursue the usual collegiate course, in the department of literature, science and the arts, embracing the ancient languages, and to provide for the admission of such students without previous examination as to their attainments in said languages, and for granting such certificates at the expiration of such course or term of such students, as may be appropriate to their respective attainments.

SEC. 10. The Regents shall make provision for keeping a set of meteorological tables at the University, after the forms adopted and furnished by the Smithsonian Institution, the record of which shall be transmitted with their report to the Superintendent of Public Instruction, who shall embody the same into his report.

SEC. 11. The immediate government of the several departments shall be entrusted to the president and the respective faculties; but the Regents shall have power to regulate the course of instruction and prescribe, under the advice of the professorships, the books and authorities to be used in the several departments; and also to confer such degrees and grant such diplomas as are usually conferred and granted by other similar institutions.

SEC. 12. The fee of admission to the regular University course in the department of literature, science and the arts, shall not exceed ten dollars, but such course or courses of instruction as may be arranged under the provisions of section nine of this act, shall be open without fee to the citizens of this State.

SEC. 13. The University shall be open to all persons resident of this State, without charge of tuition, under the regulations prescribed by the Regents; and to all other persons under such regulations and restrictions as the board may prescribe.

SEC. 14. The moneys received from such source shall be paid to the treasurer, and so much thereof as shall be necessary for the purpose, shall be expended by the Regents in keeping the University buildings in good condition and repair, and the balance shall be appropriated for the increase of the library.

SEC. 15. The board of Regents shall make an exhibit of the affairs of the University in each year, to the Superintendent of Public Instruction, setting forth the condition of the University and its branches; the amount of receipts and expenditures; the number of professors, tutors and other officers, and the compensation of each; the number of students in the several departments and in the different classes; the books of instruction used; an estimate of the expenses for the ensuing year; a full transcript of the journal of their proceedings for the year; together with such other information and suggestions as they may deem important, or the Superintendent of Public Instruction may require to embody in his report.

SEC. 16. From the increase arising from the interest of the University fund, the board of Regents may erect from time to time, such buildings as are necessary for the uses of the University, on the grounds set apart for the same; but no such buildings shall be erected until provision shall be made for the payment of the existing indebtedness of the University, nor until one branch of the University shall be established in each judicial circuit of the State.

SEC. 17. The board of Regents shall have power to expend so much of the interest arising from the university fund, as may be necessary for the improving and ornamenting the University grounds, for the purchase of philosophical, chemical, meteorological, and other apparatus, and to keep the same in good condition.

SEC. 18. As soon as the income of the University interest fund will admit, it shall be the duty of the board of Regents to organize and establish branches of the University, one at least in each judicial circuit or district of the State, and to establish all needful rules and regulations for the government of the same. They shall not give to any such branch the right of conferring degrees, nor appropriate a sum exceeding fifteen hundred dollars, in any one year, for the support of any such branch.

SEC. 19. The Regents may establish and organize a branch or branches, by the creation of a trusteeship for the local management of the same, or they may, in their discretion select for a branch, under the restrictions aforesaid, any chartered literary institution in the State.

SEC. 20. The meetings of the board may be called in such manner as the Regents shall prescribe; five of them shall constitute a quorum for the transaction of business, and a less number may adjourn from time to time.

SEC. 21. A board of visitors, to consist of three persons, shall be appointed biennially at the commencement of the collegiate year, by the Superintendent of Public Instruction. It shall be their duty to make a personal examination into the state and condition of the University, in all its departments and branches, once at least in each year, and report the result to the Superintendent, suggesting such improvements as they may deem important; which report shall be embodied into the report of the Superintendent.

SEC. 22. The Regents and Visitors to the University shall each receive pay for the actual and necessary expenses incurred by them in the performance of their duties, which shall be paid out of the University interest fund.

SEC. 23. All orders on the treasurer shall be signed by the secretary, and countersigned by the president.

SEC. 24. Chapter fifty-seven of the revised statutes is hereby repealed.

Approved April 8, 1851.

[No. 153.]

AN ACT relating to the State Library.

SECTION 1. *The People of the State of Michigan enact,* That the State library room shall be appropriated to the use of the Superintendent of Public Instruction, for his office.

SEC. 2. The State Librarian, in addition to the duties prescribed by law, shall keep a set of meteorological tables, after the forms adopted by the Smithsonian Institute, and under the direction of the Superintendent of Public Instruction; and the same shall be embraced with the annual report of the Superintendent, together with report of the Librarian.

SEC. 3. The Superintendent of Public Instruction shall cause the books, papers, maps, apparatus, &c., pertaining to his office, to be deposited in the State library; and it shall be his duty to collect such books, maps, apparatus, &c., as can be obtained without expense to the State, and deposit the same in the library.

SEC. 4. The librarian shall also act as assistant to and shall perform such duties as may from time to time be required by the Superintendent, free of expense to the State.

Approved April 8, 1851.

[No. 138.]

AN ACT to establish a State Normal School.

SECTION 1. *Be it enacted by the Senate and House of Representatives of the State of Michigan,* That a State Normal School be established, the exclusive purposes of which shall be the instruction of persons, both male and female, in the art of teaching, and in all the various branches that pertain to a good common school education; also, to give instructions in the mechanic arts, and in the arts of husbandry and agricultural chemistry, in the fundamental laws of the United States, and in what regards the rights and duties of citizens.

SEC. 2. The said normal school shall be under the direction of a board of education, and shall be governed and supported as hereinafter provided.

SEC 3. There shall be appointed by the Governor, by and with the advice and consent of the Senate, a board of education consisting of three persons, one of whom shall hold his office for three years, another for two years, and the other for one year. The Governor shall designate which person is to hold his office for one year, which for two years, and which for three years. At each session of the Legislature the vacancy occurring shall be filled as above directed. The Governor shall fill any vacancy that may occur when the Legislature is not in session. The Lieutenant Governor and the Superintendent of Public Instruction shall, by virtue of their offices, be members of said board, and the latter shall be their Secretary, and shall keep an exact and detailed account of their doings. He shall also communicate such reports to the Legislature as are required by this act.

SEC. 4. The board of education shall annually elect one of their number president, who shall be empowered to visit the various villages and places of importance in the State, and obtain donations and receive propositions for the establishment of said normal school.

SEC. 5. Said board of education shall appoint a principal and an assistant to take charge of said school. They shall also appoint such other teachers as may be required in said school, and fix the salary of each, and prescribe their several duties. They shall prescribe the various text books to be used in said institution, and shall make all the regulations and by-laws necessary for the good government and management of said school.

SEC. 6. Said board of education shall procure a site, and erect buildings thereon suitable for said institution, in or near some village in this State, where it can most conveniently be done, and where in their judgment it will most subserve the best interests of the State.

SEC. 7. They shall also establish a model school in connection with a normal school, and shall make all the regulations necessary to govern and support the same.

SEC. 8. As soon as said institution is prepared to receive pupils, the Superintendent of Public Instruction shall give notice of the fact to each county clerk in the State, and shall publish said notice in the State paper.

SEC. 9. The normal school board shall ordain such rules and regulations for the admission of pupils to said school as they shall deem necessary and proper. Every applicant for admission shall undergo an examination under the direction of the board, and if it shall appear that the applicant is not a person of good moral character, or will not make an apt and good teacher, such applicant shall be rejected.

SEC. 10. Any person may be admitted a pupil of said school who shall pass a satisfactory examination: *Provided*, That the applicant shall, before admission, sign a declaration of intention to follow the business of teaching primary schools in this State: *And provided further*, That pupils may be admitted without signing such declaration of intention, on such terms as the normal school board may prescribe; and that each county shall be entitled to send pupils in the ratio of the representatives to which it may be entitled, not to exceed three times the number of representatives.

SEC. 11. When the said school shall have commenced a term, it shall be visited by one of the appointed members of the board of education. Visits to said school shall be monthly; each appointed member making a visit once in three months. When a member makes a visit as aforesaid, he shall examine thoroughly into the affairs of the school, and report to the Governor and Superintendent of Public Instruction, his views with regard to its success and usefulness, and any other matters he may judge expedient.

SEC. 12. The said board of education shall annually make to the Legislature, a full and detailed report of their doings, and of all their expenditures, both in cash and land warrants, and the moneys received for tuition, and their opinion with regard to the prospects, progress and usefulness of said school.

SEC. 13. Those pupils who are admitted to the said school as provided by the ninth section of this act, shall not be charged for tuition or for the use of any apparatus, or for attendance on any lectures for one year. Lectures on chemistry, comparative anatomy, astronomy, the mechanic arts, agricultural chemistry, and on any other science, or any branch of literature that the board of education may direct, shall be delivered to those attending said school by the professors of the University, provided the regents shall give their consent thereto.

SEC. 14. As soon as any person has attended said institution twenty-two weeks, said person may be examined in the studies required by the board, and if it shall appear that said person has received the proper training, and possesses the learning and other qualifications necessary to teach a good common school, said person shall receive the proper certificate from the principal and board of education, certified by the Superintendent of Public Instruction.

SEC. 15. For the purpose of defraying the expenses of the erection and completion of the building proposed by the sixth section of this act, and for the purchase of the necessary apparatus and books for the said institution, and for various other incidental expenses of said school, there is hereby appropriated ten sections of the salt spring lands. The Auditor General shall, on the presentation of the certificate of the president of the board of education, countersigned by the Governor, draw his warrant on the Commissioner of the State Land Office, not bearing interest, and payable only in salt spring lands, to the holder of such certificate, for the amount therein specified, said lands to be those located as the normal school building lands.

SEC. 16. For the purpose of paying the principal of said normal school and his assistants, the board of education, immediately after their appointment, shall locate fifteen sections of the salt spring lands, and the same shall be denominated "the normal school endowment fund," and shall never be appropriated for any other purpose. They shall also locate the ten sections required by section fifteen, and the same shall be denominated the normal school building fund.

The said board of education shall give due notice to the Commissioner of the State Land Office, that they have located the lands required by this act, and shall file in his office a proper description of said lands.

SEC. 17. The normal school endowment fund shall be under the control of the board of education, and shall be disposed of according to the provisions of this act. The State Treasurer shall be treasurer of said board; and all orders or drafts for moneys or other funds shall be signed by the president of said board, and be countersigned by the Governor.

SEC. 18. The principal and other teachers employed, shall be paid for their services out of the normal school endowment fund, and from moneys received for tuition. The board of education shall be paid for their services, two dollars per day, with warrants drawn on the salt spring lands.

SEC. 19. This act shall take effect and be in force from and after its passage.

Approved March 28, 1849.

[No. 139.]

AN ACT to consolidate and amend the Laws relative to the establishment of a State Normal School.

SECTION 1. *Be it enacted by the Senate and House of Representatives of the State of Michigan,* That all acts done and contracts made by and with the board of education under and by virtue of "an act to establish a State Normal school," approved March twenty-eighth, eighteen hundred and forty-nine, and the act supplementary thereto, approved March thirty-first, eighteen hundred and forty-nine, be and they are hereby ratified and confirmed.

SEC. 2. That a State Normal school be established and continued at Ypsilanti, in the county of Washtenaw, upon the site selected by the said board of education, the exclusive purposes of which shall be the instruction of persons, both male and female, in the art of teaching, and in all the various branches that pertain to a good common school education. Also to give instruction in the mechanic arts, and in the arts of husbandry and agricultural chemistry; in the fundamental laws of the United States, and in what regards the rights and duties of citizens.

SEC. 3. The said Normal school shall be under the direction of a board of education, and shall be governed and supported as herein provided. Said board shall provide for the erection of suitable buildings on the site selected as soon as the title thereto is vested in them in fee, and the means in their hands for that purpose are sufficient, and they may appoint a suitable person to superintend the erection of said buildings.

SEC. 4. Said board of education shall hereafter consist of six members, three of whom shall be appointed by the Governor, by and with the advice and consent of both branches of the Legislature. The members of said board heretofore appointed shall hold their offices for the term for which they were designated. At the session of the Legislature for the year eighteen hundred and fifty, and annually thereafter, the vacancies occurring shall be filled as above directed by appointment, the term of which shall be three years. The Governor shall, by appointment, fill any vacancy that may occur when the Legislature is not in session; such appointment to expire at the close of the next session of the Legislature. The Lieutenant Governor, the State Treasurer, and the Superintendent of Public Instruction, shall, by virtue of their offices, be members of said board, and the latter shall be their secretary, and shall keep an exact and detailed account of their doings. He shall also communicate such reports to the Legislature as are required by this act. The State Treasurer shall, by virtue of his office, be treasurer of said board, and the members thereof shall annually elect one of their number president And no member of said board of education shall, during his continuance in office as a member, of said board, act as the agent of any publisher or publishers of school books or school library books, or be or become interested in the publication or sale of any such books as agent or otherwise. And the Governor of this State is hereby authorized and required, upon satisfactory evidence being produced to him that any member of said board is employed as such agent, or is interested in the manner aforesaid, to remove such member of said board from office, and to appoint another member in his place to fill such vacancy.

SEC. 5. Said board of education shall have power to appointment a principal and assistant to take charge of said school, and such other teachers and officers as may be required in said school, and fix the salary of each, and prescribe their several duties. They shall also have power to remove either the principal, assistant, or teachers, and to appoint others in their stead. They shall prescribe the various books to be used in said school, and shall make all the regulations and by-laws necessary for the good government and management of the same.

SEC. 6. Said board shall also establish an experimental school in connection with the Normal School, and shall make all the regulations necessary to govern and support the same, and may in their discretion admit pupils free of charge for tuition.

SEC. 7. Said board shall have the power, and it shall be their duty, from time to time, as the means at their disposal may warrant, to provide suitable grounds and buildings, implements of husbandry and mechanical tools, either by purchase or lease, for the purpose of more effectually and experimentally carrying out the provisions of the second section of this act, "to give instruction in the mechanic arts, and in the arts of husbandry any [and] agricultural chemistry."

SEC. 8. As soon as said Normal School is prepared to receive pupils, the Superintendent of Public Instruction shall give notice of the fact to each county clerk in the State, and shall publish said notice in a newspaper published in each senatorial district.

SEC. 9. The board of education shall ordain such rules and regulations for the admission of pupils to said school as they shall deem necessary and proper. Every applicant for admission shall undergo an examination in such manner as may be prescribed by the board; and if it shall appear that the applicant is not a person of good moral character, or will not make an apt and good teacher, such applicant shall be rejected. The board of education may, in their discretion, require any applicant for admission to said school—other than such as shall, prior to such admission, sign and file with said board a declaration of intention to follow the business of teaching primary schools in this State—to pay, or secure to be paid, such fees for tuition as to said board shall seem reasonable.

SEC. 10. Any person may be admitted a pupil of said school who shall pass a satisfactory examination: *Provided*, That the applicant shall, before admission, sign a declaration of intention to follow the business of teaching primary schools in this State: *And provided further*, That pupils may be admitted without signing such declaration of intention, on such terms as the Normal School board may prescribe; and that each county shall be entitled to send pupils in the ratio of the representatives in the State Legislature to which it may be entitled, not to exceed such number as the board may prescribe.

SEC. 11. After said school shall have commenced its first term, and at least once in each year thereafter, it shall be visited by three suitable persons, not members, to be appointed by the board of education, who shall examine thoroughly into the affairs of the school, and report to the Superintendent of Public Instruction their views with regard to its condition, success and usefulness, and any other matters they may judge expedient. Such visitors shall be appointed annually.

SEC. 12. It shall be the duty of the Superintendent of Public Instruction, once at least in each term, to visit said school; and he shall annually make to the Legislature a full and detailed report of the doings of the board of education, and of all their expenditures, and the moneys received for tuition, and the prospects, progress and usefulness of said school, including so much of the reports of said visitors as he may deem advisable.

SEC. 13. Lectures on chemistry, comparative anatomy, astronomy, the mechanic arts, agricultural chemistry, and on any other science, or any branch of literature that the board of education may direct, may be delivered to those attending said school, in such manner, and on such terms and conditions as the board of education may prescribe.

SEC. 14. As soon as any person has attended said institution twenty-two weeks, said person may be examined in the studies required by the board, in such manner as may be prescribed; and if it shall appear that said person possesses the learning and other qualifications necessary to teach a good common school, said person shall receive a certificate to that effect from the principal, to be approved by the Superintendent of Public Instruction.

SEC. 15. The board of education shall have the power and authority to demand and receive the sum or sums donated and subscribed by the citizens of Ypsilanti and its vicinity, in such manner as said board may prescribe, and apply the same to the erection and completion of the necessary buildings, the purchase of the necessary books, apparatus, furniture and fixtures, and for various other incidental expenses to be incurred by said board in pursuance of the provisions of this act; and if any surplus shall remain, to apply the same in defraying the expenses of conducting said school. And any deficit which may arise in the erection and completion of said buildings and purchases aforesaid, shall be paid out of the principal to be received on the sale of lands hereinafter mentioned, not to exceed the sum of ten thousand dollars. Such sum shall be paid from time to time on the warrant of the Auditor General, to be drawn in pursuance of the certificate of the superintendent of the building or secretary of the board, and countersigned by the president of the board of education; and no such certificate shall be issued until work shall be done, or services rendered, or buildings erected, or books, apparatus, fixtures or furniture purchased for the Normal School, under the direction of the board of education, entitling the applicant to such certificate, according to a contract or agreement with said board for that purpose, or for services and expenses of the board or some member thereof, in connection with the selection of the site, or the erection of the Normal School buildings, or the improvement of the grounds.

SEC. 16. The ten sections of salt spring lands, located by the board of education under the provisions of sections fifteen and sixteen of "an act to establish a State Normal School," approved March 28, 1849, together with the fifteen sections of said salt spring lands located under the provisions of section sixteen of said act, and all such lands as may be granted by Congress, or received or set apart (in any manner) in lieu of any portion of said land to which the title may prove insufficient, and all donations, in land or otherwise, to the State in trust or to the board of education for the support of a Normal School, shall constitute a fund, to be called the Normal School endowment fund, and shall be reserved from sale until the same shall be appraised. The minimum price of said lands shall be four dollars per acre; and it shall be the duty of the officer authorized to sell said lands, to cause the same to be appraised as soon as practicable, in the manner provided for the appraisal of other lands; none of said lands shall be sold for less than the minimum price fixed by law. It shall not be necessary to appraise any of said lands which have heretofore been appraised under existing provisions of law; and the proceeds of sales of any of said lands heretofore appraised and sold, shall constitute a part of the fund herein provided. After such appraisal, such land shall be and remain subject to sale at the State land office, as is now or shall be hereafter provided by law; and the principal shall be and remain a perpetual fund for the use of said institution, (except as herein provided.) The instalments of principal paid by the purchasers, shall be paid into the State treasury; and the interest thereon from the time of its receipt, or from the time of the preceding computation of interest, as the same may be, shall be computed by the Auditor General and State Treasurer, at the close of each fiscal year, at the rate of six per cent. per annum, and together with all interest paid by purchasers of any portion of said lands, shall be passed to the credit of the Normal School interest fund, to be drawn therefrom upon the warrant of the Auditor General, issued in pursuance of a certificate of the board of education, signed by their secretary and countersigned by their president, that the money is due and payable to the principal of the Normal School, or his assistants, or the teachers or officers employed, or to the members of the board, or the board of visitors, as herein authorized, or for necessary incidental expenses in the support or maintenance of said school or some of its departments.

Sec. 17. Said funds shall be under the direction and control of the board of education, subject to the provisions herein contained. The treasurer of said board shall pay out of the proper fnnd all orders or drafts for moneys to be expended under the provisions of this act. Such orders or drafts to be drawn by the Auditor General on certificates of the secretary, countersigned by the president of the board. No such certificates shall be given except upon accounts audited and allowed by the board at a regular meeting.

Sec. 18. The services and all necessary traveling and other expenses already or hereafter to be incurred by any member of the board of education, or the board of visitors, shall be paid on the proper certificate out of any funds belonging to said institution in the hands of the treasurer, until the erection and completion of the necessary buildings. The principal, assistants, teachers and other officers employed in said school, shall be paid out of the Normal school interest fund, and from receipts for tuition; and the services and expenses of the board of education, after the erection of the necessary buildings, and other expenses incident to said institution, shall be paid for out of the Normal school interest fund, in the same manner, as near as may be, as is required in regard to moneys drawn for the payment of the principal or other teachers. The members of the board of education and the visitors shall be entitled to two dollars per day for their actual services, and to their necessary traveling and other expenses.

Sec. 19. For the purpose of rendering more efficient their organization and to enable them the more fully to carry into effect the provisions herein contained, the members of the board of education now holding their offices under the provisions of "an act to establish a State Normal school," approved March 28th, 1849, and their successors in office, are hereby constituted a body politic and corporate, by the name of "the board of education," for the purposes herein contemplated, and subject to such modifications as may be made thereto, and in that name shall have perpetual succession, and shall be and they are hereby empowered to purchase, have, hold, possess and enjoy to themselves and their successors, lands, tenements, hereditaments, goods, chattels and effects of every kind, and the same to grant, alien, sell, invest and dispose of, to sue and be sued, plead, and be impleaded in all courts in this State, to have and to use a common seal, and the same to change, alter and renew at pleasure, and to make such by-laws and regulations as they may deem proper for the well ordering and government of said corporation and the transaction of its business: *Provided,* The same be not repugnant to the constitution or laws of this State or of the United States.

Sec. 20. Said corporation shall be subject to the provisions of chapter fifty-five of the revised statutes of 1846, so far as the same can apply, and are not inconsistent with the provisions of this act. They shall have power to transact all necessary business at any meeting, a quorum being present; and meetings may be called in such manner as their by-laws may provide; and a quorum shall consist of a majority of the members. The first meeting under this act may be held at such time and place as may be directed by the secretary, and no publication of notice thereof shall be necessary; and the attendance of a quorum shall render valid the proceedings of such meeting. All process against said corporation shall be served on the president or secretary thereof.

Sec. 21. Sections four, fifteen and sixteen of "an act to establish a State Normal school, approved March 28th, 1849, and all of the provisions of said act and the act supplementary thereto, which are inconsistent with the provisions of this act, are hereby repealed.

Sec. 22. This act shall take effect and be in force from and after its passage, and the Legislature may at any time alter, amend or repeal the same by a vote of two-thirds of the members present in each house.

Approved March 25, 1850.

[No. 180.]

AN ACT to amend an act to consolidate and amend the laws relative to the establishment of a State Normal School, approved March 25th, 1850.

SECTION 1. *Be it enacted by the Senate and House of Representatives of the State of Michigan*, That an act to consolidate and amend the laws relative to the establishment of a State Normal School, approved March twenty-fifth, eighteen hundred and fifty, be amended by striking out in section four of said act, the words "both branches of the Legislature," and by inserting in lieu thereof, the words "the Senate and House of Representatives in joint convention."

SEC. 2. This act shall take effect and be in force from and after its passage.

Approved March 29, 1850.

LAWS RELATING TO THE FREE SCHOOLS OF DETROIT.

[No. 70.]

AN ACT relative to Free Schools in the City of Detroit.

SECTION 1. *Be it enacted by the Senate and House of Representatives of the State of Michigan*, That the City of Detroit shall be considered as one school district, and hereafter all schools organized therein, in pursuance of this act, shall, under the direction and regulations of the board of education, be public and free to all children residing within the limits thereof, between the ages of five and seventeen years, inclusive.

SEC. 2. In lieu of the school inspectors now required to be elected in said city, there shall be twelve school inspectors, to be elected in the manner following: At the next annual charter election, there shall be elected in each ward of said city, two school inspectors, one of whom shall hold his office for two years, and the other for one year; and at every annual election thereafter, there shall be elected in each ward, one school inspector, who shall hold his office for two years. No school inspector shall be entitled to receive any compensation for his services.

SEC. 3. In case of a vacancy in the office of school inspector, the common council of the city of Detroit may fill the same, until the next annual election, when, if such vacancy happen in the first year of the term of said office, the electors of the proper ward may choose a suitable person to fill the remainder of such term: *Provided*, The city clerk shall give notice of such vacancy prior to such election, as may be required in other cases.

SEC. 4. Every person elected to the office of school inspector, who, without sufficient cause, shall neglect or refuse to serve, shall forfeit to the board of education, for the use of the library, the sum of ten dollars, to be recovered in an action of debt in some competent court: *Provided*, No person shall be compelled to serve two terms successively; and the said board shall make all necessary rules and regulations relative to its proceedings, and punish by fine, not exceeding five dollars for each offence of any member of the board who may, without sufficient cause, absent himself from any meeting thereof, to be collected as they may direct.

SEC. 5. The school inspectors, together with the mayor and recorder of said city, (who are declared to be ex-officio school inspectors,) shall be a body corporate, by the name and style of "The Board of Education of the City of Detroit;" and in that name, may be capable of suing and being sued, and of holding or selling and conveying real and personal property, as the interest of said common schools may require; and shall also succeed to, and be entitled to demand, all moneys and other rights belonging to, or in possession of, the board of school inspectors, or any member thereof, or of any school district board, or any member thereof, or any real and personal property or other rights of any such district in said city, and the clear proceeds of all such property which may come into the possession of said board, as last aforesaid, shall be accounted for and distributed among the several persons of whom the same may have been collected, in such manner as the said board may deem just and proper.

SEC 6. The board of education, (eight members whereof may form a quorum,) may meet from time to time at such place in said city as they may designate: the mayor shall be president of the board, and shall preside at all meetings thereof; but in case of his absence, or the absence of the recorder, a majority of the inspectors present at any meeting, may choose one of their number president *pro tempore*.

SEC 7. The clerk of said city shall be *ex-officio* clerk of said board, and shall perform such duties as the board of education may reasonably require. In case of the absence of said clerk, or for any other cause, the board may choose some suitable person to perform his duties, either as principal or deputy clerk.

SEC. 8. The recorder of said city shall be entitled to a seat at the meeting of said board, for the purpose of deliberation, and of acting on committees, but shall have no vote therein, except when the mayor shall be absent, in which case he shall act as president.

SEC. 9. The board of education shall have full power and authority, and it shall be their duty, to purchase such school houses, and apply for and receive from the county treasurer or other officer, all moneys appropriated for the primary schools and district library of said city, and designate a place where the library may be kept therein. The said board shall also have full power and authority to make by-laws and ordinances relative to taking the census of all children in said city between the ages of five and seventeen years; relative to making all necessary reports and transmitting the same to the proper officers, as designated by law, so that said city may be entitled to its proportion of the primary school fund; relative to visitation of schools; relative to the length of time schools shall be kept, which shall not be less than three months in each year; relative to the employment and examination of teachers, their powers and duties; relative to regulation of schools and the books to be used therein; relative to the appointment of necessary officers, and prescribe their powers and duties; relative to any thing whatever that may advance the interest of education, the good government and prosperity of common schools in said city, and the welfare of the public concerning the same.

SEC. 10. The mayor's court shall have jurisdiction of all suits wherein said board may be a party, and of all prosecutions for violation of said by-laws and ordinances.

SEC. 11. The said board shall annually, in the month of February, publish in some newspaper of the city, a statement of the number of schools in said city; the number of pupils instructed therein the year preceding; the several branches of education pursued by them, and the expenditures for all things authorized by this act, during the preceding year.

SEC. 12. The board of education shall establish a district library, and for the increase of the same, the common council are authorized annually to lay a tax on the real and personal property within said city, of a sum not exceeding two hundred dollars, which tax shall be levied and collected in the same manner as the moneys raised to defray the general expenses of said city.

SEC. 13. The common council of said city are hereby authorized, once in each year, to assess and levy a tax on all the real and personal property within said city, according to the city assessment roll of that year, which shall not exceed one dollar for every child in said city between the ages of five and seventeen years; the number of children to be ascertained by the last report on that subject, on file in the office of the clerk of the county of Wayne, or in the office of the clerk of said board of education, and certified by the president thereof, and the said tax shall be collected in the same manner as the moneys raised to defray the general expenses of said city; all such moneys shall be disbursed and expended by the authority of said board for the support and maintainance of said schools, and for no other purpose whatever.

SEC. 14. The treasurer of said city shall be the treasurer of said board, unless otherwise directed by said board; he shall keep all moneys belonging to said schools separate from the moneys belonging to the corporation of said city; and he shall not pay out or expend the school moneys, without the authority of the said board.

SEC. 15. The collector of said city, when he shall have paid any school moneys to said treasurer or other person, shall take a receipt therefor, and file the same with the clerk of said board; and it shall be the further duty of the collector, when he shall have made his final return concerning the collection of said tax, to make a report to said board, stating the whole amount of school tax, the amount collected, and the amount returned by him to the common council as unpaid or uncollected.

SEC. 16. The collector and treasurer shall, before they enter on their duties under this act, enter into such bonds to said board, and with such sureties as may be deemed necessary, conditioned for the faithful discharge of their duties respectively, under this act.

SEC. 17. All parts of acts, so far as they relate to the city of Detroit, inconsistent with this act, are hereby repealed; and it shall not be necessary to elect any school district officers in said city, as heretofore required by law.

SEC. 18. This act shall take effect from and after its passage.

Approved February 17, 1842.

[No. 20.]

AN ACT to amend an act entitled "an act relative to free schools in the city of Detroit."

SECTION 1. *Be it enacted by the Senate and House of Representatives of the State of Michigan,* That all taxes which have been, or may hereafter be assessed and levied by the common council of the city of Detroit, under and by virtue of the authority conferred on said common council by the thirteenth section of an act, entitled "an act relative to free schools in the city of Detroit," shall be set forth in the assessment roll of said city, in a separate column, apart, and distinguished from all other city taxes; and that the collector of said city, shall collect, and is hereby authorized and required to collect said taxes in money, and said collector shall not be required or permitted to receive in payment of said taxes, any liabilities or evidences of debt against said city.

SEC. 2. That all the fifth section of said act after the words "as the last aforesaid," in the thirteenth line of said section, be stricken out, and thefollowing be inserted in its place: "shall be expended and disbursed by and under the authority of said board of education, for the support of the said schools, after paying all just and legal demands existing against the several school districts heretofore existing in said city: *Provided,* That said board shall not be liable to pay an aggregate amount of indebtedness against any one district, greater than the amount received from the same by said board."

Approved February 13, 1843.

[No. 87.]

AN ACT to amend an act entitled "an act relative to Free Schools in the city of Detroit," approved February seventeenth, eighteen hundred and forty-two.

SECTION 1. *Be it enacted by the Senate and House of Representatives of the State of Michigan,* That the collectors of the city of Detroit, elected in the different wards of said city, shall act as collectors of the school tax assessed and levied in said city in their respective wards, under and by virtue of the provisions of the act to which this act is amendatory; and that each of said collectors previous to his entering upon his duties, shall, in addition to the bond now required by law, make and execute to the board of education of said city of Detroit, a bond with two good and sufficient sureties to be by them approved, in the penal sum directed by said board, conditioned for the faithful performance of his duties as such collector; and that in case of neglect or refusal of any one of said collectors to execute and obtain such bond according to the provisions of this section, he be subject to a penalty of one hundred dollars, to be collected in an action of debt, which may be brought in any court in this State at the suit and in the name of the said board of education of the city of Detroit.

SEC. 2. The board of education of the city of Detroit may elect one of their own number president of the board, who shall perform all the duties and be vested with all the powers conferred by the act to which this act is amendatory, upon the mayor and recorder of said city of Detroit, or either of them; and all the provisions of the act to which this act is amendatory, providing that the mayor or recorder of said city shall be president of said board, are hereby repealed. The term of office and time and mode of election of said president to be prescribed by said board.

SEC. 3. Six members of the board shall constitute a quorum for the transaction of business.

SEC. 4. This act shall take effect and be in force from and after its passage.

Approved April 28, 1846.

[No. 40.]

AN ACT to amend an act entitled "an act relative to free schools in the city of Detroit," approved February seventeenth, one thousand eight hundred and forty-two.

SECTION 1. *Be it enacted by the Senate and House of Representatives of the State of Michigan,* That in addition to the taxes mentioned in the act to which this act is amendatory, the common council of the city of Detroit is hereby authorized and empowered to levy and collect a tax not exceeding fifteen hundred dollars in any one year, to be expended in the purchase of lots in said city for the use of the public schools thereof, and in the erection and building a school house or school houses, with the necessary out buildings and fixtures, on any lot or lots which may be so purchased, or any other lots now owned by the board of education of said city, or which the said board may hereafter acquire: *Provided,* That said tax, when so levied and collected, shall be paid to the treasurer of said board of education, and be vested in said board, to and for the purpose hereinbefore stated, and no other, and also that the title to such lots purchased shall also be vested in said board for the purposes aforesaid.

SEC. 2. Said tax shall not be levied or collected, unless, at a meeting of the freemen of said city, called for such purpose as hereinafter provided, a majority of the freemen present shall assent to the same.

SEC. 3. It shall be the duty of the mayor, or recorder, in case of the absence of the mayor, or a vacancy in his office, to call such a meeting of the freemen of said city, for the purpose of giving their assent or dissent to such tax, when it shall be requested by petition signed by twenty-four freemen of said city; which call shall particularly express the object of such meeting, and shall be published in two of the daily newspapers, published in said city of Detroit, one week previous to such meeting: *Provided,* That the mayor may call such meeting upon the notice herein mentioned, without such petition at his own option.

SEC. 4. If the said mayor or recorder shall refuse to call such meeting upon the presentation to either of them of such petition, or shall neglect to do so for three days after the presentation of such petition, any two members of the common council of said city, may, on like petition, call such meeting upon a like notice and publication thereof, in the manner and for the time hereinbefore specified in the case of a call by the mayor or recorder. Such meeting may be adjourned from time [to time] by vote of a majority of those present.

Sec. 5. The said tax shall be levied and collected in the same manner as the tax provided for in the thirteenth section of the act to which this act is amendatory, and shall be consolidated therewith on the tax rolls; but it shall be the duty of the said board of education in each and every year when such tax is levied and collected, to separate the amount thereof from the gross amount of money received by said board for such year, and set it apart as a fund to be reserved for the purposes specified in the first section of this act.

Sec. 6. The board of education of the city of Detroit is hereby authorized from time to time, on such term or terms of payment as they may deem proper, to borrow a sum of money not exceeding in all the sum of five thousand dollars, for the purposes specified in the first section of this act, at a rate of interest not exceeding seven per cent. per annum, payable semi-annually, and to issue the bonds of said board in such form, and executed in such manner as said board may direct: *Provided,* That said board shall issue no bond for a less sum than fifty dollars: *And provided,* That no such sum of money shall be borrowed until authorized by a majority of all the voters present at a meeting to be called as provided in section three.

Sec. 7. The bonds issued under this act shall be a charge upon all the property of said board, which shall constitute a security for the payment thereof: *Provided,* That no legal proceedings shall be instituted to enforce such lien or to sell any property of said board for the payment of the principal money of any of said bonds until one year after such principal shall become due, according to the tenor and effect thereof.

Sec. 8. It shall be the duty of the board of education, whenever they shall borrow any money under the provisions of this act, annually to appropriate a sufficient sum out of any money which may come into their hands, to pay the interest upon the same; and also in addition thereto, an annual sum equal to five per cent. upon the amount so borrowed to be invested under the direction of said board in bonds of the city of Detroit, bearing interest at such prices as the same can be purchased, to accumulate as a sinking fund for the payment of the principal of the sum so borrowed; both of which appropriations shall take precedence of all others.

Approved March 12, 1847.

[No. 58.]

AN ACT to amend an act entitled an act relative to Free Schools in the city of Detroit.

Section 1. *Be it enacted by the Senate and House of Representatives of the State of Michigan,* That the thirteenth section of the act entitled an act relative to free schools in the city of Detroit, approved February seventeenth, in the year one thousand eight hundred and forty-two, be and the same is hereby amended by striking out the words "five" and "seventeen," in said section, and inserting in place thereof the words "four" and "eighteen;" so the first clause in said section shall read as follows: "The common council of said city are hereby authorized once in each year to assess and levy a tax on all the real and personal property within said city, according to the assessment roll of that year, which shall not exceed one dollar for every child in said city between the ages of four and eighteen years."

Sec. 2. Section six of an act entitled an act to amend an act entitled an act relative to Free Schools in the City of Detroit, approved February seventeenth, one thousand eight hundred and forty-two, is hereby amended by striking out all of said section six after the words "fifty dollars," in the ninth line of said section, so that said section shall read as follows:

"The board of education of the city of Detroit is hereby authorized, from time to time, on such term or terms of payment as they may deem proper, to borrow a sum of money not exceeding in all the sum of five thousand dollars, for the purposes specified in the first section of this act, at a rate of interest not exceeding seven per cent. per annum, payable semi-annually, and to issue the bonds of said board in such form, and executed in such manner, as said board may direct: *Provided*, That said board shall issue no bond for a less sum than fifty dollars."

SEC. 3. The removal of any member of the board of education of the city of Detroit, from the ward for which he is elected school inspector, after such election, shall not operate to vacate his office; but notwithstanding such removal, any inspector so removing shall continue to hold his said office, and to be a member of said board, and all provisions of any act or acts which make such removal a vacation of said office, are hereby repealed: *Provided*, The removal of such member shall not be from the city.

SEC. 4. This act shall take efect from and after its passage.

Approved March 5, 1850.

CITY OF ANN ARBOR.

SEC. 33. The common council of said city is hereby authorized and required to perform the same duties in and for said city as are by law imposed upon the township boards of the several townships of this State, in reference to schools, school taxes, county and State taxes, the support of the poor, and State, district and county elections; and the supervisor and assessor, justices of the peace, recorder, school inspectors, directors of the poor, and all other officers of said city who are required to perform the duties of township officers of this State, shall take the oath, give the bond, perform like duties, and receive the same pay and in the same manner, and be subject to the same liabilities, as is provided for the corresponding township officers, excepting as is otherwise provided in this act, or as may be provided by the ordinances of the common council.

SEC. 33. The common council shall have authority to assess, levy, and collect taxes on all the real and personal estate taxable in said city, which taxes shall be and remain a lien upon the property so assessed until the same shall be paid: *Provided*, That they shall not raise by general tax more than five hundred dollars in any one year, exclusive of school taxes and taxes for highway purposes, unless authorized thereto by a vote of the property tax payers of said city who are electors, when convened for that purpose pursuant to previous notice.

SEC. 34. Whenever the common council shall deem it necessary to raise a greater sum in any one year than five hundred dollars, exclusive of taxes for school and highway purposes, they shall give at least five days notice in writing, to be posted up in five public places in said city, which notice shall state the time and place of such meeting, and shall specify the objects and purposes for which the money proposed to be raised is to be expended; and when such meeting shall be assembled in pursuance of such notice, such electors, by a viva voce vote shall determine the amount of money which shall be raised for each object specified in the notice: *Provided*, That such tax shall not in any one year exceed one per cent. upon the valuation of the real and personal estate taxable within the limits of the city: *And provided also*, That not more than two such meetings shall be holden in any one year to determine the amount of tax to be raised; at all such meetings, the mayor, or in his absence, the recorder shall preside.

SEC. 35. The common council may appoint the aldermen to assist the supervisor in taking the assessment of property in the respective wards where the alderman resides; and all State, county and school taxes in said city, and all city taxes which shall be raised by general tax, shall be levied and collected, as near as may be, in the same manner as is provided by law for the assessment and collection of taxes by township officers; and all the proceedings for the return, sale, and redemption of real estate for non-payment of taxes shall be in conformity with the proceedings for the return, sale and redemption of real estate by township officers.

CITY OF MONROE.

SEC. 2. The inhabitants of said city shall be liable to the operation of any and all laws relating to township government, except so far as relates to the laying out and construction of streets and highways, and the labor to be performed thereon within the limits thereof.

CITY OF GRAND RAPIDS.

SEC. 49. The common council of said city is hereby authorized and required to perform the same duties respecting said city as are by law imposed upon the township boards of the several townships of this State in reference to schools, school taxes, county and State taxes, [and] all the other matters hereinafter mentioned.

INCORPORATED LITERARY INSTITUTIONS.

GENERAL LAW IN RELATION TO INCORPORATED ACADEMIES.

[No. 19.]

AN ACT requiring certain returns to be made from Incorporated Academies and other Literary Institutions.

SECTION 1. *Be it enacted by the Senate and House of Representatives of the State of Michigan,* That it shall be the duty of the president of the board of trustees of every organized academy or literary or collegiate institution, heretofore incorporated, or hereafter to be incorporated, to cause to be made out by the principal instructor or other proper officer, and forwarded by mail or otherwise, to the office of the Superintendent of Public Instruction, between the first and fifteenth days of December in each year, a report setting forth the amount and estimated value of real estate owned by the corporation, the amount of other funds and endowments, and the yearly income from all sources, the number of instructors, the number of students in the different classes, the studies pursued and the books used, the course of instruction, the terms of tuition, and such other matters as may be specially requested by said Superintendent, or as may be deemed proper by the president or principal of such academies or institutes, to enable the Superintendent of Public Instruction to lay before the Legislature a fair and full exhibit of the affairs and condition of said institutions.

Approved March 4, 1839.

AN ACT to incorporate Marshall Academy at White Pigeon.

SECTION 1. *Be it enacted by the Senate and House of Representatives of the State of Michigan,* That there shall be established at White Pigeon, in the county of St. Joseph, an academy for the purpose of educating youth, the style, name and title whereof shall be and are hereby declared to be as hereinafter mentioned and defined, that is to say, the said academy shall be under the direction, management and government of seven trustees, and Geo. Bowman, Nath'l Bacon, D. Clark, Neal McGaffey, P. W. Warner, M. Judson, and Henry Chapin, Jr., shall be and are hereby appointed the first trustees. That the first meeting of the trustees under this act shall be held on the first Monday of May next, and shall hold their office until their successors are chosen in the manner hereinafter provided.

Sec. 2. That the stock of funds of the corporation shall be considered as divided into four hundred shares, of fifty dollars each, such as are not taken up being vested in the proprietors and at the disposal of the trustees. The stockholders shall meet on the first Monday of May, eighteen hundred and thirty-seven, and annually thereafter on the first Monday of May, and shall elect by ballot seven trustees who shall hold their office one year and until their successors are chosen, and each share shall entitle its holder to one vote; the stockholders may increase the number of trustees to fifteen.

Sec. 3. That the shares shall be considered as personal property, and shall be transferrable; but no transfer shall be valid unless signed by the treasurer and secretary, who, before confirming the transfer of any share shall first secure to the corporation whatever may be due thereon.

Sec. 4. In case any holder of stock in this company shall refuse or neglect to pay to the treasurer any legal assessment, or any just demand for tuition, or any other object, the treasurer shall have power under the direction of the trustees, after giving ten days notice in writing in some public place in White Pigeon, to sell at auction the share or shares of such delinquent, and after satisfying the claims of the company and reasonable charges, shall, on application of the holder or his attorney, pay over any surplus which may remain from the proceeds of the stock sold under this provision.

Sec. 5. That it shall be the duty of the secretary to make out and deliver to any stockholder at his request, a certificate of the share or shares he or she may hold in the stock of this company, and this may be transferred, subject to the provisions of this act.

Sec. 6. The said trustees and their successors, shall forever hereafter be and they are hereby established and declared to be a body politic and corporate, with perpetual succession in deed and in law, to all intents and purposes whatsoever, by the name, style and title of "The Trustees of Marshall Academy;" by this name and title they and their successors shall be capable at law and in equity of suing and being sued, holding property necessary for the use of said academy, not exceeding twenty thousand dollars, real, personal and mixed, of buying and selling, and otherwise lawfully disposing of the same, and shall have power to make and use a common seal, and to alter the same at their pleasure; and further, any five of the said trustees shall be a quorum; in case said number is increased as aforesaid, any number nearest two-thirds of the whole number shall be a quorum to transact business.

Sec. 7. That it shall and may be lawful to and for the said trustees from time to time to apply such part of their funds and estate in such manner as they may think most conducive to the promotion of literature and the advancement of useful knowledge within the State: *Provided*, That when grants shall be made to them for certain use and purposes therein expressed and declared, the same shall not be applied either in whole or in part to any other uses without the consent of the grantor.

Sec. 8. The said corporation shall appoint by ballot a treasurer and secretary, to continue in office during the pleasure of the corporation, the treasurer shall keep fair and true accounts of all moneys by him received and paid out, and the secretary shall keep a fair journal of the meetings and proceedings of the corporation, in which the yeas and nays on all questions shall be entered, if required by two-thirds of the trustees present, and to all books and papers of the corporation every trustee shall always have access, and be permitted to take copies of them.

Sec. 9. The said trustees may establish an academy at such time and in such place in the township of White Pigeon, in said county, as may seem to them most expedient, and it shall be the duty of said trustees to appoint such preceptors, instructors and other officers for said academy as they shall think necessary, to fix their compensation and to remove them from office when such trustees shall think proper; and it shall be the duty of said trustees to visit and inspect said academy, to examine into the state and system of education and discipline therein, and to make such by-laws and ordinances not inconsistent with the laws of the United States or of this State, as they may judge most expedient for the government of said academy or for the accomplishment of the trust hereby reposed in such trustees.

SEC. 10. No religious test whatever shall be required from any stockholder, trustee, teacher or pupil; nor shall the tenets of any particular religious denomination be inculcated in said academy.

SEC. 11. This law or any part thereof may be repealed or modified by the Legislature: *Provided,* That such power of repeal never extend to divert to any other purposes than those expressed therein, if any shall be expressed, any grant of property to such corporation; but such property in the event of the dissolution of such corporation shall revert to the grantor or his heirs.

Approved March 28, 1836.

[No. 32.]

AN ACT to incorporate the Michigan Central College at Spring Arbor.

SECTION 1. *Be it enacted by the Senate and House of Representatives of the State of Michigan,* That Elijah Cook, Drusus Hodges, Jonathan L. Videto, Justus H. Cole, Joseph C. Bailey, Henry S. Limbocker, Lemuel W. Douglass, Lewis J. Thompson, and Enos W. Packard, and their successors in office, shall be and they are hereby constituted and declared a body corporate, by the name and title of the Michigan Central College at Spring Arbor, and shall be trustees of the said college, to have perpetual succession, capable by its name in law to sue and be sued, to plead and be impleaded, in any court within this State, and to receive, possess and retain and enjoy any lands, rents, tenements or hereditaments of what kind soever, and to alien the same, and also to purchase any lands or estates, real and personal, to receive any charity, donation or bequest, which may be made to them, the said trustees, for the use of the said college, and be capable to sell, lease or otherwise dispose of any lands, chattels, real or personal, of any kind whatever, that may come to them by purchase, gift, or bequest, or in any other way whatever, or to hold the same in perpetuity, or for a term of years: *Provided,* That the property, real or personal, of said corporation, shall not at any time exceed thirty thousand dollars on a just valuation.

SEC. 2. There shall at all times be nine trustees of said college. The term of office of three of said trustees shall expire on the first Wednesday of January, 1846, the term of office of three more of them on the first Wednesday of January, 1847, and three on the first Wednesday of January, 1848, as shall be determined by lot among themselves, within thirty days from and after the passage of this act; at the expiration of the regular term of office of any of the said trustees, or their successors in office, others shall be elected in their stead, and in case any of said trustees or their successors should refuse to act, resign, die, or remove out of the State, the remainder of the trustees or a majority of them shall have power to elect others in their stead; and that the said trustees or a majority of them shall have power and authority to make, alter or amend any by-laws for their own government, or regulation, that they may deem proper and necessary, which are not repugnant to the laws of this State or the United States, and have full power and authority to carry the same into effect.

SEC. 3. The trustees of the said college shall have a common seal, which they may alter or renew at pleasure, have power to appoint or remove their professors or teachers, and to make such rules and regulations therefor as they or a majority of them may think proper and expedient, and the said trustees shall have power to make such rules and regulations for the admission or dismission of students, as they may deem necessary.

SEC. 4. No person shall be excluded from any privelege, immunity or situation in said college on account of his religious opinions: *Provided*, That he demean himself in a sober, peaceable and orderly manner, and conform to the rules and regulations thereof.

SEC. 5. The said trustees shall keep an accurate account of all their proceedings in regard to the property granted as aforesaid, and of all moneys or valuables received or expended for the benefit of said college, which, whenever so required, they shall lay before the Legislature for their information.

SEC. 6. The trustees of said college shall be jointly and severally liable for all judgments obtained against the corporation: *Provided*, That no execution shall issue against the individual property of said trustees until the property of the corporation shall first have been exhausted.

SEC. 7. The Legislature shall have power at any time to alter, amend or repeal this act.

Approved March 19, 1845.

[No. 34.]

AN ACT to amend an act entitled "an act to incorporate the Michigan Central College at Spring Arbor."

SECTION 1. *Be it enacted by the Senate and House of Representatives of the State of Michigan*, That section two of said act be amended by inserting after the word "stead," in the ninth line, the words "by the stockholders of said college."

Also, add one new section, as follows:

SEC. 8. It shall be the duty of the Superintendent of Public Instruction to attend the examinations of said college once in each year, and to report at each annual session of the Legislature the condition and prospects of said college.

Approved March 25, 1846.

[No. 121.]

AN ACT to amend an act entitled "an act to incorporate the Michigan Central College at Spring Arbor."

SECTION 1. *Be it enacted by the Senate and House of Representatives of the State of Michigan*, That "an act to incorporate the Michigan Central College at Spring Arbor," approved March 19th, 1845, be and the same is hereby amended as follows: by adding to section three of said act the following words: "and to confer such degrees and grant such diplomas as are usually conferred and granted by other colleges: *Provided*, That the course of study pursued in said college shall be in all respects as comprehensive and thorough as that required or which shall hereafter be required in the University of Michigan."

SEC. 2. The said college shall always be subject to the visitation and examination of a board of visitors, three in number, to be annually appointed by the Superintendent of Public Instruction, and such visitors shall report to the said Superintendent as soon after an examination as practicable.

Sec. 3. There shall at all times after the next annual election be fifteen trustees of said college, the terms of office of five of whom shall expire on the first Wednesday of January in each and every year.

Sec. 4. The term of office of the additional number of trustees created by this act, shall expire, two of them one year, two of them two years, and two of them three years, from and after the next annual election, as shall be determined by lot, within thirty days from and after their election.

Sec. 5. The proviso to section one of said act is also hereby amended, so as to read as follows: *Provided*, That the property, real and personal, of said corporation, shall not at any time exceed one hundred thousand dollars.

Sec. 6. Said corporation shall not hold any real estate more than fifteen years after the same shall have been conveyed to them; excepting, always, such real estate as shall be necessary for the objects of said corporation.

Sec. 7. This act shall take effect immediately.

Approved March 20, 1850.

AN ACT to incorporate the Trustees of Spring Arbor Seminary.

Whereas, an annual conference of the Methodist Episcopal Church have resolved to patronize a literary institution within the Territory of Michigan, for the promotion of arts and sciences, and the general instruction of youth;

And whereas, proposals for the location of said institution in Spring Arbor, Jackson county, have been made and accepted; therefore,

Section 1. *Be it enacted by the Legislative Council of the Territory of Michigan*, That the said institution be established at Spring Arbor, on the site marked on Farmer's Map "Indian Village," to be known by the style, name and title, of Spring Arbor Seminary.

Sec. 2. That A. B. Gibson, Moses Benedict, Randall Hobart, W. Smith, B. H. Packard, Hiram Thompson, Nathan Comstock, Isaac Van Fossen, Milton Barney, Marcus Swift, Samuel W. Dexter, William R. Thompson, John Stockton, Elijah Woolsey, B. F. Burnet, Orin White, Wm. Cross, James P. Greves, Daniel Coleman, Justus Norris, and Samson Stoddard, are hereby appointed the first trustees of said seminary, with the power to fill all vacancies which may occur in their own body: *Provided*, That there be always retained in the board, (which shall be confined to the number of twenty-one,) two-thirds, at least, who are members of the Methodist Episcopal Church.

Sec. 3. That the said trustees, and their successors in office, shall forever hereafter be, and they are hereby declared to be a body politic and corporate, with perpetual succession,* in deed and in law, to all intents and purposes whatsoever, by the name and style of the Trustees of Spring Arbor Seminary; by which name and style they and their successors shall be capable at law and in equity, of suing and being sued, of holding and conveying property, real, personal and mixed: *Provided*, The said property shall be necessary for the purposes of the said institution, and shall at no time exceed in value the sum of fifty thousand dollars; they shall have power to make and use a common seal, and to alter the same at pleasure; and a majority of said trustees shall be a quorum.

Sec. 4. That said trustees shall have power to elect or appoint their own officers, to elect or appoint the faculty of said seminary, to fix the amount of their salaries, to regulate the price of tuition, to make such arrangements as may be necessary to connect with the institution the Manual Labor System, to pass by-laws, and direct and manage the affairs of the said corporation, in such manner as they may deem best calculated to promote the objects of this act.

Sec. 5. That the conference of the Methodist Episcopal Church, which shall now, or at any time hereafter, embrace the location of the said seminary within its limits, shall be authorized to appoint annually a board of visitors, who shall examine into the state thereof, and report its condition and their proceeding to the conference.

SEC. 6. The first meeting of the trustees shall be held at Spring Arbor, on the second Tuesday in May, one thousand eight hundred and thirty-five; and in case a sufficient number do not appear to do business, it shall be lawful for those who may be present, to adjourn from time to time, until a quorum shall appear; at which meeting their officers shall be chosen, and such further business done as may be considered necessary to carry into effect the purposes of this act.

Approved March 23, 1835.

[No. 48.]

AN ACT to amend an act entitled "An act to incorporate the trustees of the Spring Arbor Seminary," approved March 23, 1835.

SECTION 1. *Be it enacted by the Senate and House of Representatives of the State of Michigan,* That the trustees of said seminary shall be divided by lot, as may be provided by the by-laws of said trustees, into four classes, to be numbered first, second, third and fourth class; those falling into the first class shall go out of office in one year from the first day of May next; the second class shall go out of office in two years from the first day of May next; the third class shall go out of office in three years from the first day of May next; and the fourth class shall go out of office in four years from the first day of May next; and the vacancies shall be filled by the remaining trustees, at their first general meeting, after said vacancies shall occur.

SEC. 2. Said trustees are hereby authorized and empowered to sell and give a deed of any lands which they now own and are desirous of selling; and any deed by them made for the conveyance of any land by them sold, shall be good and valid in law, to convey the title of said land to the purchaser or purchasers, excepting twenty acres of land on which said seminary is now located.

Approved March 17, 1837.

[No. 53.]

AN ACT to amend an act entitled "An act to incorporate the trustees of Spring Arbor Seminary," passed March 23, 1835.

SECTION 1. *Be it enacted by the Senate and House of Representatives of the State of Michigan,* That the above recited act shall be so amended that there shall hereafter be only thirteen trustees instead of twenty-one.

SEC. 2. The location shall be changed from Spring Arbor to Albion, in the county of Calhoun.

SEC. 3. The name of said seminary shall hereafter be "the Wesleyan Seminary, at Albion."

SEC. 4. The following persons shall be the first trustees of said seminary, viz: Elijah Crane, Elijah H. Pilcher, Benjamin H. Packard, Almon Herrick, Alvan Billings, Thomas W. Pray, Marvin Hannahs, Jesse Crowell, Jesse Gardner, Wareham Warner, Peter Williamson, and Arza C. Robinson.

SEC. 5. The principal of said seminary shall hereafter be appointed by the conference of the Methodist Epispocal church, within whose bounds the seminary is or may be located.

SEC. 6. All lands heretofore conveyed to said seminary on condition of its being located at Spring Arbor, shall be reconveyed to the donors or their legal representatives; and all subscriptions made on like condition, shall be released at the option of the subscribers, and all funds paid on such subscriptions shall, if required, be repaid to the subscribers, by the trustees of the seminary, and compensation shall be made, if required, for all the materials delivered, or services rendered on account of the Spring Arbor seminary.

Sec. 7. The first meeting of trustees shall be held at Albion on the fourth Wednesday of April, 1839. The principal shall be ex-officio a trustee and the president of the board; and until a principal is employed, the trustees may appoint one of their number president. The trustees may hold real and personal property in trust for said seminary, not exceeding in value one hundred thousand dollars.

Sec. 8. This act shall take effect from after its passage.

Approved April 12, 1839.

[No. 11.]

AN ACT amendatory to the several acts incorporating the trustees of the Wesleyan Seminary at Albion.

Section 1. *Be it enacted by the Senate and House of Representatives of the State of Michigan*, That Loring Grant, Elijah Crane, Elijah H. Pilcher, Benjamin H. Packard, James S. Harrison, Almon Herrick, Thomas W. Pray, Marvin Hannahs, Jesse Crowel, Jesse Gardner, Wareham Warner, Peter Williamson and Arza C. Robinson shall be, and they are hereby constituted a body corporate by the name of the "Wesleyan Seminary at Albion," and shall be the trustees of said corporation, for the purpose of further establishing, maintaining and conducting the seminary of learning, for the education of youth generally, located at the village of Albion, in the county of Calhoun.

Sec. 2. There shall, at all times, be thirteen trustees of the said corporation, a majority of whom shall be members of the Methodist Episcopal church, and shall be divided into three classes, to be numbered one, two, three; the places of the first class, or number one, shall become vacant in one year from the first regular meeting of the board, after the passage of this act, (at which time the division shall be made by lot;) the places of the second class, or number two, shall become vacant in two years, and the third class, or number three, shall become vacant in three years from said meeting: *Provided, however*, That the said trustees shall continue to act until others are appointed in their places.

Sec. 3. The said trustees shall have power to fill all vacancies in their own board, to make by-laws for their own government, to elect or appoint the faculty of the institution, except the principal, who shall be appointed by the Michigan Annual Conference of the Methodist Episcopal Church; to prescribe the course of study, attend examinations and regulate the government and instruction of the students, and manage the affairs of said corporation, in such manner as they may deem best calculated to promote the object of this act.

Sec. 4. The said trustees shall be capable of suing and being sued, of receiving, holding and conveying property, real and personal: *Provided always*, That the annual income shall not exceed ten thousand dollars; they shall have power to make and use a common seal, and to alter the same at pleasure.

Sec. 5. No proceedings of the trustees of the Spring Arbor seminary, had or done according to the provisions of the act entitled "An act to incorporate the trustees of the Spring Arbor seminary," approved March 25, 1835, or any act amendatory thereof, or according to any other law, shall be rendered invalid by the passage of this act; nor shall any subscription, donation, bond, mortgage, or other security, executed to said trustees, be in any way invalidated by the passage of this act.

SEC. 6. All acts or parts of acts that relate to the Spring Arbor Seminary, or to the Wesleyan Seminary at Albion, which are inconsistent with, or contravene the provisions of this act, are hereby repealed; but the repeal shall in no wise affect any thing lawfully done under said act.

SEC. 7. This act shall be, and is hereby declared a public act; no nonuser of the privileges hereby granted to said corporation, shall create or produce any forfeiture of the same, and no misnomer of the said corporation, in any deed, will, testament, gift, grant, demise, or other instrument, contract, or conveyance, shall defeat or vitiate the same: *Provided*, The corporation be sufficiently described to ascertain the intention: *Provided further*, That no rights or privileges legally vested and existing at the time of the passage of this act, shall be impaired by the provisions of the same.

SEC. 8. This act shall take effect from and after its passage.

SEC. 9. The legislature may at any time alter, amend or repeal this act, by a vote of two-thirds of each house.

Approved March 6, 1841.

[No. 9.]

AN ACT to amend an act entitled an act "amendatory to the several acts incorporating the Trustees of the Wesleyan Seminary at Albion."

SECTION 1. *Be it enacted by the Senate and House of Representatives of the State of Michigan*, That the words "the said trustees shall have power to fill all vacancies in their own board," in the first and second lines of section three of an act entitled, an act amendatory to the several acts incorporating the trustees of the Wesleyan Seminary at Albion, approved March 6th, 1841, be stricken out, and that said section be amended to read as follows: "That the power to fill all vacancies accruing in the board of trustees of said Wesleyan Seminary at Albion, by removal, death, expiration of term of office, or otherwise, is hereby and hereafter vested in the Michigan Annual Conference of the Methodist Episcopal Church, who shall elect said trustees by ballot. All provisions in the act to which this is amendatory, to the contrary notwithstanding: *Provided*, The trustees who are now in office shall continue therein until the next meeting of the said annual conference, and that there shall then be an election of one class of trustees, and a like election at each session of said conference thereafter. Each trustee so elected shall receive a certificate from the secretary of said conference, which certificate shall be recorded in the county register's office of the county of Calhoun, and said trustees shall have power to make by-laws for their own government, to elect or appoint the faculty of the institution, except the principal, who shall be appointed by the Michigan annual Conference of the Methodist Episcopal Church, to prescribe the course of study, attend the examinations, and regulate the government and instructions of the students, and manage the affairs of said corporation in such manner as they may deem best calculated to promote the object of this act."

SEC. 2. This act shall take effect and be in force from and after its passage.

Approved February 17, 1845.

[No. 28.]

AN ACT to enlarge the powers of the Trustees of the Wesleyan Seminary at Albion.

SECTION 1. *Be it enacted by the Senate and House of Representatives of the State of Michigan,* That the trustees of the Wesleyan Seminary at Albion, be and they are hereby authorized and empowered to establish at Albion, as a branch of said Seminary, a Female College, with powers and privileges usually appertaining to such institutions, under the style and title of the Albion Female Collegiate Institute.

SEC. 2. That the principal of said seminary shall be president of said collegiate institute, and ex-officio a member of the board of trustees. The trustees shall have power to appoint such professors and teachers as may at any time be necessary for the instruction of the pupils therein, and shall have full power to make such rules and regulations, not inconsistent with the laws of this State, as they may deem expedient for the goverment and conduct of said collegiate institute, to prescribe such course of study and such mode of instruction therein as they may judge best; and, on the recommendation of the faculty, to confer on those pupils whom they shall judge worthy thereof, all such literary honors as are usually conferred by the best female colleges and seminaries of the highest rank: *Provided however,* That nothing contained in this act shall be so construed as to confer the power upon the trustees, officers or faculty of this collegiate institute to confer literary degrees upon males educated at this institution, and that the course of study shall be at least equal in extent to the graduating course published in the catalogue of the Wesleyan Seminary at Albion, for the years eighteen hundred and forty-eight and eighteen hundred and forty-nine.

SEC. 3. That the annual income of said institution may equal but not exceed the sum of twenty thousand dollars.

SEC. 4. That no certificate of free tuition in said seminary shall entitle the holder thereof to free tuition in the said collegiate institute, unless it be so expressed on the face of the instrument.

SEC. 5. That all acts or parts of acts relating to the Wesleyan Seminary at Albion, contravening the provisions of this act, be and the same are hereby repealed.

SEC. 6. A board of visitors, consisting of three persons, shall be appointed by the Superintendent of Public Instruction, whose duty it shall be once in each year to make a personal examination into the state of said Seminary and Female Collegiate Institute in all its departments, and to report the result to the Superintendent of Public Instruction, suggesting such improvements as they may deem important; which report he may in his discretion embody in his annual report.

SEC. 7. This corporation shall be subject to the provisions of chapter fifty-five of the revised statutes, so far as the same shall be consistent with the provisions of this act.

SEC. 8. This act shall take effect and be in force from and after its passage.

Approved February 18, 1850.

[No. 105.]

AN ACT to amend an act entitled "an act to incorporate the Michigan and Huron Institute."

SECTION 1. *Be it enacted by the Senate and House of Representatives of the State of Michigan,* That from and after the passage of this act, the Michigan and Huron Institute, located at Kalamazoo, shall be, and the same is hereby known by the name and style of the Kalamazoo Literary Institute.

SEC. 2. The trustees shall faithfully apply all funds by them collected, or hereafter collected, according to their best judgment, in erecting suitable buildings; in supporting suitable instructors, officers and agents; in procuring books, maps, charts, globes, philosophical, chemical and other instruments and apparatus, necessary to aid in the promotion of sound learning in said institution.

SEC. 3. The treasurer of said institute and all other agents, when required by the trustees, shall, before entering upon the duties of their office, give bonds for the security of said corporation in such penal sum as the board of trustees shall require.

SEC. 4. All process against said corporation shall be by summons; the service of the same shall be by leaving an attested copy of the same with the treasurer of the corporation, at least thirty days before the return day thereof.

Sec. 5. The said institute and departments shall be open to all Christian denominations, and the profession of any religious faith shall not be required of those who become students; all persons may, however, be expelled or suspended from the privileges of said institution, whose habits are idle or vicious, or whose moral character is bad.

SEC. 6. The trustees may receive by gift, grant or donation, for the use and benefit of said corporation, any land, money or materials; and the said corporation may hold estate, real, personal or mixed, not exceeding one hundred and fifty thousand dollars.

SEC. 7. It shall be at all times open to the inspection of any committee or other agent appointed by the Legislature; and it shall be the duty of the officers of said institute at all times to exhibit to any committee or agent appointed by the Legislature, a full and complete statement of the general or particular concerns of the institute.

SEC. 8. It shall be at all times competent for the Legislature to alter or amend this act, by a vote of two-thirds of each house.

SEC. 9. So much of the act to which this is an amendment as contravenes the provisions of this act, is hereby repealed.

Approved March 21, 1837.

[No. 1.]

AN ACT to enable the President of the board of Trustees of the Kalamazoo Literary Institute, to sell and convey real estate.

SECTION 1. *Be it enacted by the Senate and House of Representatives of the State of Michigan*, That the president of the board of trustees of the Kalamazoo literary institute be and he is hereby authorized and empowered to sell and convey by proper deeds and assurances, such parts or portions of the lands and real estate belonging to said institute, and for such considerations, and on such terms and conditions as the trustees of said institute or a majority of them, at any meeting regularly called, may direct to be sold and conveyed: *Provided*, such terms and conditions be not inconsistent with the provisions of an act entitled "An act to incorporate the Michigan and Huron institute," and the act to amend the same, approved March 21st, A. D. 1837.

SEC. 2. That before the said president shall sell and convey any such lands or real estate, he shall execute to the said trustees and their successors in office, a bond with such surety or sureties as shall be deemed sufficient by said trustees, or a majority of them, for the faithful application of the moneys or proceeds of such sale or sales, according to the provisions of an act entitled "an act to amend an act entitled 'an act to incorporate the Michigan and Huron institute,'" approved on the 21st day of March, A. D. 1837, and according to the by-laws or regulations of said institute.

SEC. 3. That all acts and parts of acts inconsistent with the provisions of this act, be and the same are hereby repealed.

Approved January 29, 1838.

[No. 78.]

AN ACT to incorporate the Tecumseh Academy.

SECTION 1. *Be it enacted by the Senate and House of Representatives of the State of Michigan,* That from and after the passage of this act, George W. Jermain, Stillman Blanchard, Henry L. Hewett, George Spafford, Seneca Hale, Daniel Pittman, Daniel G. Finch, Ezra F. Blood and Michael A. Patterson, of the county of Lenawee, and their successors, be and they are hereby constituted, ordained and declared to be a body corporate and politic in fact and in name, to be styled "the trustees of the Tecumseh Academy;" that by that name they and their successors shall and may have perpetual succession, and shall be persons in law capable of suing and being sued, pleading and being impleaded, answering and being answered, defending and being defended in all courts of record whatever, and in all manner of suits, actions, complaints, matters and causes whatever; and that they and their successors may have a common seal, and change and alter the same at their pleasure; and that they and their successors, by the name of the trustees of the Tecumseh Academy, shall be in law capable of acquiring and holding by purchase, gift, grant, devise, bequest or otherwise, and of selling, conveying or leasing any estate, real, personal, or mixed, for the use of said corporation; and that they and their successors shall have full powers to make and enter into contracts, to make such rules and by-laws as they may deem necessary for the good government and success of said institution: *Provided,* Such by-laws are not inconsistent with the constitution and laws of the United States, or of this State.

SEC. 2. Said trustees of Tecumseh Academy, shall have power to establish, at such time and at such place in the village of Tecumseh and county of Lenawee, as they may judge best, an institution for the instruction of youth, suited to the wants and demands of the surrounding country.

SEC. 3. That the said George W. Jermain, Stillman Blanchard, Henry L. Hewett, George Spafford, Seneca Hale, Daniel Pittman, Daniel G. Finch, Ezra F. Blood and Michael A. Patterson shall be the trustees of said academy, and have and exercise the power and franchise herein granted, until others be appointed in their place; they and their successors shall have power to fill all vacancies in their own body, which may happen by death, resignation or otherwise; they shall appoint a president of said academy, who shall, ex-officio, be president of the board of trustees, and have the power of giving the casting vote, in case of an equal division; a majority shall constitute a quorum for the transaction of business.

SEC. 4. The board of trustees shall faithfully apply all funds, in money or otherwise, by them collected, received or acquired, according to their best judgment, in erecting suitable buildings, supporting the necessary officers and instructors, in procuring books, maps, or other articles necessary to insure the success of said acadamy, or in lessening the expense of education at the same, or in improving the health of the students belonging thereto.

SEC. 5. All process against said corporation shall be by summons, and the service of the same shall be by leaving an attested copy thereof with the president of said academy, or in his absence, at his last usual place of abode, at least five days previous to the return day thereof.

SEC. 6. That at the first meeting of said trustees, they divide themselves into three classes of three members each; the term of office of the first class shall terminate at the end of the first year; the term of office of the second class shall terminate at the end of the second year; and the term of office of the third class shall terminate at the end of the third year, so that one-third of the number of trustees shall be chosen annually.

SEC. 7. This act shall be favorably construed to effect the purposes thereby intended, and the same is hereby declared to be a public act, and copies thereof, printed by authority of the State, shall be received as evidence thereof in all courts of this State.

SEC. 8. The legislature shall have the power at any time of amending or repealing this act, by a vote of two-thirds of both branches.

Approved April 2, 1838.

[No. 50.]

AN ACT to incorporate the Trustees of the Grand River Theological Seminary.

SECTION 1. *Be it enacted by the Senate and House of Representatives of the State of Michigan,* That from and after the passage of this act, Isaac Jennings, Thomas Blossem, John J. Shipherd, Josiah Yale, Erastus Ingersoll, Charles W. Gurney, Samuel Chadwick and E. P. Ingersoll, be and they are hereby constituted, ordained and declared to be a body corporate and politic, in fact and name, to be styled "The trustees of Grand River Theological Seminary;" that by that name, they and their successors shall and may have perpetual succession, and shall be persons in law capable of suing and being sued, of pleading and being impleaded, of answering and being answered, of defending and being defended, in all courts of record whatever, and in all manner of suits, actions, complaints, matters and causes whatever; and that they and their successors may have a common seal, and change and alter the same at their pleasure; and that they and their successors, by the name of "The trustees of the Grand River Theological Seminary," shall be in law capable of acquiring and holding, by purchase, gift, grant, devise, bequest or otherwise, and of selling, conveying or leasing any estate, real, personal or mixed, for the use of said corporation; and that they and their successors shall have full powers to make and enter into contracts; to make such rules and by-laws as they may deem necessary for the good government and success of said institution: *Provided,* That such by-laws are not inconsistent with the constitution and laws of the United States or of this State.

SEC. 2. Said trustees of Grand River Theological Seminary, shall have power to erect, in the village of Orion, in Eaton and Clinton counties, (the county line running through the village,) such buildings as they may judge the interests of the institution may at any time demand.

SEC. 3. That the several individuals named above as trustees, shall have power to increase their number to twelve; that they and their successors shall have power to fill all vacancies in their own body which may be occasioned by death, resignation or otherwise, to appoint a president of said Seminary, who shall, ex-officio, be president of the board of trustees, and have the power of giving the casting vote in case of an equal division; and three trustees, together with the president, shall constitute a quorum for the transaction of business.

SEC. 4. The board shall faithfully apply all funds in their possession in such a manner as, in their judgment, will most promote the interest of the institution.

SEC. 5. The president and several professors of the Seminary shall constitute the Faculty, who shall have power to govern the students and all the internal regulations of the institution.

SEC. 6. All professors shall be appointed by the board of trustees, with the concurrence of the Faculty.

Sec. 7. All process against said corporation shall be by summons, and the service of the same shall be by leaving an attested copy thereof with the president of said Seminary, or in his absence at his last usual place of abode, at least five days previous to the return day thereof.

Sec. 8. At the first meeting of said trustees, they shall divide themselves into three classes of four members each, exclusive of the president; the term of office of the first class shall terminate at the end of the first year, the term of office of the second class shall terminate at the end of the second year, and the term of office of the third class shall terminate at the end of the third year, so that one third part of the trustees shall be chosen annually.

Sec. 9. This act shall be favorably construed to effect the purposes thereby intended, and the same is hereby declared to be a public act, and copies thereof, printed by the authority of the State, shall be received as evidence thereof in all the courts of this State.

Sec. 10. The Legislature shall have power at any time to amend or repeal this act by a vote of two-thirds of both branches thereof.

Approved April 11, 1839.

[No. 41.]

AN ACT to incorporate the Grass Lake Academy and Teacher's Seminary.

Section 1. *Be it enacted by the Senate and House of Representatives of the State of Michigan,* That Alonzo Brewer, James Faulkner, Henry A. Francisco, Robert Davis, John M. Ellis, Joshua G. Knight, David Durand, Foster Tucker, James Courier, William H. Pease, Jona B. Taylor, Peter Brown, Job Rice, Miller Yeckley and Joshua Jones, of Grass Lake, Jackson county, and their successors, be and hereby are created a body politic and corporate, to be styled "The board of trustees of the Grass Lake Academy and Teacher's Seminary," and by that name to remain in perpetual succession, with full powers to sue and be sued; to acquire, hold and convey property, real and personal; to have and to use a common seal, to alter and renew the same at pleasure; to make and to alter from time to time such by-laws as they may deem necessary for the government of said institution, its officers and servants: *Provided,* Such by-laws are not inconsistent with the constitution of this State or of the United States.

Sec. 2. The said Academy shall be located in the township of Grass Lake, in the county of Jackson, and shall be erected on a plan sufficiently extensive to afford instruction in the liberal arts and sciences, and in the languages, as opportunity and ability may hereafter admit, or the trustees direct.

Sec. 3. The board of trustees shall from time to time appoint such officers and instructors, and also such servants of the institution as may be necessary, and shall have power to displace any or each of them for good and sufficient reasons. They may also have power to expel any of their own members for dishonorable and improper conduct, whenever two-thirds of the board at any regular meeting shall concur in such decision. The board may also prescribe the course of studies to be pursued in said institution or its departments. They shall also have power to fill all vacancies in said board that may happen by death or otherwise.

Sec. 4. The board of trustees shall consist of fifteen members, any seven of whom may constitute a quorum for doing business; and said board of trustees shall hold their first meeting at Grass Lake Centre, on the first Monday of May, one thousand eight hundred and thirty-nine, and afterwards on their own appointments; but in any emergency, the president of the board, with advice of two trustees, may call a special meeting of the board, or any five members may call such meeting, by giving notice to each member at least ten days before the time of said meeting.

SEC. 5. The board of trustees shall faithfully apply all funds collected or received by them, according to their best judgment, in erecting suitable buildings, supporting instructors, in procuring books and apparatus, and whatever may, in their judgment, be best fitted to promote the best success of the institution; but said corporation shall not, under any circumstances, be permitted to issue any note, bill or other negotiable paper or obligation for the payment of money: *Provided*, That in case any bequest or donation shall be made for a particular purpose, accordant to the design of this institution, and the corporation shall accept and receive the same, it shall be applied in conformity to the conditions or design expressed by the donor: *Provided further*, That the property to be held by the institution shall not, at any one time, exceed the sum of twenty thousand dollars.

SEC. 6. The treasurer of this institution shall always, and all other agents when required, before entering on the duties of their appointment, give bonds for the security of the corporation and the public, in such penal sums and with such securities as the board of trustees shall approve; and all process against the corporation shall be by summons, and the service of the same shall be by leaving an attested copy thereof with the treasurer of the institution.

SEC. 7. The institution hereby incorporated, shall always be subject to the examination or inspection of a board of visitors, or any officers appointed or authorized by the Legislature.

SEC. 8. The Legislature may at any time alter, amend or repeal this act, by a vote of two-thirds of each house.

Approved April 4, 1839.

[No. 60.]

AN ACT to incorporate Marshall College.

SECTION 1. *Be it enacted by the Senate and House of Representatives of the State of Michigan*, That John P. Cleveland, Sidney Ketchum and James P. Greves, of the county of Calhoun; John M. Ellis, William Page and Marcus Harrison, of the county of Jackson; Ira M. Wead, of the county of Washtenaw; Eurotus P. Hastings, Robert Stuart and Arthur L. Porter, of the county of Wayne; Austin E. Wing and Oliver Johnston, of the county of Monroe; George W. Jermain, of the county of Lenawee; Ashbel S. Wells, of the county of Oakland; Mitchell Hinsdell, of the county of Kalamazoo; Elisha P. Champlin, of the county of Hillsdale, and Phanuel W. Warriner, of the county of St. Joseph, and their successors, be and they are hereby created a body politic and corporate, to be styled "the board of trustees of Marshall College," and by that name shall remain in perpetual succession, with full powers to sue and be sued, plead and be impleaded; to acquire, hold and convey property, real and personal; to have and to use a common seal, to alter and renew the same at pleasure; to make and alter, from time to time, such by-laws as they may deem necessary for the government of said institution, its officers and servants; provided such by-laws are not inconsistent with the constitution and laws of the United States, or of this State.

SEC. 2. The said college shall be located in the township of Marshall, in the county of Calhoun; and shall be erected on a plan sufficiently extensive to afford instruction in the liberal arts and sciences; and the trustees may, as their abilities shall increase, and the interests of the community require, erect additional departments for the study of any or all of the liberal professions.

SEC. 3. The board shall, from time to time, appoint a president, vice president, secretary and treasurer, together with such other officers, instructors and servants of the institution, as may be necessary; and shall have power to displace any or either of them, for good and sufficient reasons; and also to fill vacancies which may happen by death, resignation or otherwise, in said board, or among said officers, instructors and servants; and also to prescribe and direct the course of study to be pursued in said institution and its departments.

SEC. 4. The president of the college shall be, ex-officio, a member of the board of trustees, and president of the same; and in his absence, the vice president shall preside in the meetings of the board; and in the absence of both president and vice-president, the board shall elect one of their own number to preside for the time being.

SEC. 5. The board of trustees shall consist of sixteen members, exclusive of the president, any nine of whom shall constitute a quorum to do business; said board of trustees shall hold their first meeting at the call of the members resident in the village of Marshall, within two months from the approval of this act, and afterwards they shall meet on their own appointments; but in cases of emergency, the president and secretary may call special meetings of the board, or any five members may call such meeting, by giving notice to each member, at least ten days before the time of such meeting.

SEC. 6. The board of trustees shall faithfully apply all funds collected or received by them, according to their best judgment, in erecting suitable buildings, supporting the necessary officers, instructors and servants, both in the collegiate and preparatory departments, and in procuring books, maps, charts, globes and other apparatus necessary to the success of the institution or for the purposes of lessening the expense of education or promoting the health of the students: *Provided, nevertheless,* That in case any donation or bequest shall be made for particular purposes accordant with the general designs of this institution, and the corporation shall accept and receive the same, every such donation or bequest shall be applied in conformity with the condition or design expressed by the donor.

SEC. 7. The treasurer of the college shall always, and all other agents when required, before entering on the duties assigned them, give bonds for the security of the corporation and of the public, in such penal sums, and with such sureties, as the board of trustees shall approve; and all process against the institution shall be by summons, and the service of the same shall be by leaving an attested copy thereof with the treasurer of the college, at least thirty days before the return thereof.

SEC. 8. The institution hereby incorporated shall always be subject to the examination or inspection of a board of visitors, or of any officer or officers appointed or authorized by the legislature; and after said institution shall have commenced operations, the Governor, by and with the advice and consent of the Senate, shall annually appoint three disinterested persons, not connected with the aforesaid or any other literary institution in the State, as a board of visitors, whose duty it shall be to visit said institution, at its annual collegiate commencement, or at such other time or times as they may deem expedient, or be directed thereto by the legislature, and report the result of their visit and examination into its condition and affairs, to the legislature at its next annual session. The necessary expenses of said board of visitors, in visiting and examining said institution, not exceeding to each visitor the sum of thirty dollars, shall be chargeable on and paid from the funds of said corporation.

SEC. 9. The trustees shall have power to confer the honors and degrees usually conferred by collegiate institutions upon those whom they may deem worthy, when it shall appear from the report of the board of visitors, on the report of a committee appointed by the legislature, that the institution is possessed of permanent funds, yielding an average yearly income of at least five thousand dollars, exclusive of any income arising from tuition fees, or other annual contingent contributions: *Provided, however,* That the primary degrees shall not be conferred on any students, who shall not have passed through a course of studies, similar or equivalent to, and at least as thorough as that prescribed by the regents of the University for candidates for the like degrees.

SEC. 10. This act shall not take effect until all the subscribers to a college contemplated to be established at or near the village of Marshall, by the name of Michigan College, who may so request the same, shall have had an opportunity of withdrawing their subscriptions, and a guarantee for twenty thousand dollars for said proposed college, given by Sidney Ketchum, John D. Pierce and A. L. Hays, of Marshall, shall have been released, and all moneys advanced on said subscriptions or guarantee refunded, if requested by the respective individuals advancing such moneys, or their legal representatives.

SEC. 11. The legislature may at any time alter, amend or repeal this act, by a vote of two-thirds of each house.

Approved April 16, 1839.

[No. 51.]

AN ACT to incorporate the Marshall Female Seminary.

SECTION 1. *Be it enacted by the Senate and House of Representatives of the State of Michigan*, That from and after the passage of this act, Sidney Ketchum, Oliver C. Comstock, Azrah C. Robinson, Jabez S. Fitch, James P. Greves, Thompson S. Hollister, Samuel Buel, Daniel Hudson, and James W. Gordon, of the county of Calhoun, and their successors, be and they are hereby constituted, ordained and declared a body corporate and politic, under the name and style of " The Marshall Female Seminary;" that by that name, they and their successors shall and may have perpetual succession, and shall be persons in law, capable of suing and being sued, pleading and being impleaded, answering and being answered, defending and being defended in all courts of record whatever, and in all manner of suits, actions, complaints, matters and causes whatever; and that they and their successors may have a common seal, and change and alter the same at their pleasure; and that they and their successors, by the name of the "Marshall Female Seminary," shall be in law capable of acquiring and holding by purchase, gift, grant, devise, bequest or otherwise, and of selling, conveying or leasing any estate, real, personal or mixed, for the use of said corporation; and that they and their successors shall have full power to make and enter into contracts; to make such rules and by-laws as they may deem necessary for the good goverment and success of said institution: *Provided*, Such by-laws are not inconsistent with the constitution and laws of the United States or of this State.

SEC. 2. Said corporation shall have power to establish at such time and at such place, in or near the village of Marshall, in the county of Calhoun, as may be judged best, an institution for the education of females, suited to the wants and demands of the surrounding country.

SEC. 3. That there shall be nine trustees of said Seminary: *Provided, nevertheless*, That no more than three of said trustees shall be taken from any one denomination of Christians, and that Sidney Ketchum, Oliver C. Comstock, Azrah C. Robinson, Jabez S. Fitch, James P. Greves, Thompson S. Hollister, Samuel Buel, Daniel Hudson and James W. Gordon, shall be such trustees, and have and exercise the power and franchise herein granted, until others be appointed in their place; and they and their successors shall have power to fill all vacancies in their own body, which may happen by death, resignation or otherwise; they shall appoint one of their number president of said Seminary, who shall be ex-officio president of the board of trustees, and have the power of giving the casting vote, in case of an equal division; a majority shall constitute a quorum for the transaction of business.

SEC. 4. The board of trustees shall faithfully apply all funds, in money or otherwise, by them collected, received or acquired, according to their best judgment, in erecting suitable buildings, supporting the necessary officers and teachers, in procuring books, maps, or other articles necessary to insure the success of said Seminary.

SEC. 5. All process against such corporation shall be by summons, and the service of the same shall be by leaving an attested copy thereof with the president of said Seminary, or in his absence, at his last usual place of abode, at least six days previous to the return day thereof.

SEC. 6. This act shall be favorably construed to effect the purposes thereby intended, and the same is hereby *declared a public act*, and copies thereof, printed by authority of the State, shall be received as evidence thereof in all courts of this State.

SEC. 7. The Legislature shall have the power, at any time, of amending or repealing this act, by a vote of two-thirds of both branches.

Approved April 11, 1839.

[No. 65.]

AN ACT to incorporate St. Philip's College.

SECTION 1. *Be it enacted by the Senate and House of Representatives of the State of Michigan,* That the Right Reverend Frederick Rese, Roman Catholic Bishop of Detroit, and his successors in said office of Bishop of Detroit, duly appointed by the See of Rome, be and are hereby ordained, created and constituted a body politic and corporate, in fact and in name, under and by the name of St. Philip's College, and by that name he and his successors shall have perpetual succession, and shall be capable of suing and being sued, pleading and being impleaded, answering and being answered unto, defending and being defended, in all suits, complaints, matters and causes whatsoever, either in law or equity; of having and using a common seal; of enacting all by-laws for the regulation of said college, and of the members thereof; of altering from time to time the same; of acquiring by gift, devise, purchase or otherwise, and of holding and conveying any real, personal or mixed estate whatsoever, necessary and proper for the object of this incorporation; of transacting all business, directing all the affairs, controlling and disposing of all the funds, estate and effects of said college, and of doing every other act, matter and thing necessary and proper for the well being and good government of the same, not inconsistent with the constitution and laws of the United States, or of this State.

SEC. 2. Said Bishop and his successors shall keep in existence and operation a collegiate institution, under the name of St. Philip's College, for the purpose and on a plan sufficient to afford instruction in the liberal arts and sciences; which institution may be increased so as to afford an opportunity for the study of the liberal professions. The college shall be located in the county of Wayne.

SEC. 3. The said Bishop and his successors shall, from time to time, appoint such officers, instructors and servants of the institution, as may be necessary or proper; and also to displace any or either of them; to fill all vacancies, and to prescribe and direct the course of study to be pursued in said college and its departments.

SEC. 4. The said Bishop and his successors may, in contemplation of absence, and whenever it may be necessary so to do, choose and appoint in writing, under the corporate seal, some proper person to fill his place, who, until said appointment be revoked by said Bishop or his successors, may do and perform every thing for the welfare, conduct and regulation of said college, which said Bishop and his successors might and could do by virtue of this act; and in the event of a vacancy occurring at any time in the said office of Roman Catholic Bishop of Detroit, by death or otherwise, upon such occurrence, and until the vacancy be filled according to the rites and ceremonies of said church, the person filling at that time the office of vicar general of the diocese of Detroit, shall represent said corporation, and do and perform, under said corporate name, every act and thing, and exercise every power and authority which said Bishop and his successors are hereby granted and vested with; but as soon as said vacancy shall be filled as aforesaid, and the person filling the same arrives in said diocese, then the powers and authority hereby vested in said vicar general shall cease.

SEC. 5. The institution hereby incorporated shall always be subject to the examination of a board of visitors, three in number, to be annually appointed by the governor, by and with the advice and consent of the Senate; and said visitors shall report to the Legislature, at its next annual session after their appointment and examination of said institution.

SEC. 6. The said Bishop and his successors shall have power to confer the honors and degrees usually conferred by collegiate institutions, upon such persons as may be deemed worthy, when it shall appear from the report of the board of visitors, or the report of the committee appointed by the Legislature: *Provided however,* That the primary degrees shall not be conferred on any students who shall not have passed through a course of studies equivalent to and as thorough as that prescribed by the Regents of the University for candidates for degrees.

SEC. 7. The Legislature may at any time alter, amend or repeal this act.

Approved April 16, 1839.

[No. 15.]

AN ACT to incorporate the Allegan Academy.

SECTION 1. *Be it enacted by the Senate and House of Representatives of the State of Michigan,* That Samuel Newberry, Elisha Ely, Silas F. Littlejohn, Chester Wetmore, Elihu G. Hackley, Abraham J. Deederick, Eber Sherwood, Joseph Fisk, Nathan Mason, Jr., Jacob B. Bailey, Amos P. Bush, and Flavius J. Littlejohn, all of the county of Allegan, and their successors, be and they are hereby created a body corporate and politic, to be styled "The Board of Trustees of the Allegan Academy," and by that name shall remain in perpetual succession, with full powers to acquire, hold and convey property, real and personal, not exceeding in value five thousand dollars; to have and use a common seal, and alter the same at pleasure; to sue and be sued, plead and be impleaded; to make, alter and modify from time to time, such by-laws, rules and regulations as they may deem necessary for the government of said institution, its officers and employees: *Provided,* Such by-laws, rules and regulations are not inconsistent with the constitution and laws of the United States and of this State.

SEC. 2. Said Academy shall be located in or near the village of Allegan, and shall be erected upon a plan sufficiently extensive and commodious for the purposes of an academic institution; and the said trustees, as the wants of the community require, may erect additional departments for instruction in the liberal arts and sciences.

SEC. 3. The board of trustees shall consist of twelve members, maintaining a perpetual succession by the annual election of four to supply the vacancy occasioned by the expiration of the term of a like number.

SEC. 4. The board of trustees shall annually elect from their number a president, secretary and treesurer, and shall, from time to time, appoint a principal and other necessary instructors and officers of the institution, and shall have power, for good and sufficient reasons, to remove any or either of them; and also to fill vacancies which may happen by death, resignation or otherwise, and also to prescribe and direct the general plan of instruction, the books to be used, and the tuition fee per term or quarter in said institution and its departments.

SEC. 5. Said board shall faithfully apply all funds by them collected, in money or otherwise, and all sums received or required in erecting suitable buildings, supporting the necessary officers and teachers, and in procuring books, maps or other articles necessary to ensure the success of said institution, or for the purpose of reducing the expense of instruction.

SEC. 6. A public examination of the students in the various branches of study by them pursued, shall be had at the close of each term, and a public exhibition shall be had once in each year, at such time and place as the board of trustees shall from time to time designate.

SEC. 7. The first annual meeting of said board of trustees shall be holden on the first Monday of September next, and special meetings of the same may be called at any time, on the application of two members to the secretary, who shall forthwith proceed to notify the board of the time and place of such meeting.

SEC. 8. That the said trustees shall be held indivdually liable for all debts contracted by said corporation.

SEC. 9. This act shall take effect and be in force from and after its passage.

Approved February 2, 1843.

[No. 76.]

AN ACT to incorporate the Grand Rapids Academy.

SECTION 1. *Be it enacted by the Seuate and House of Representatives of the State of Michigan,* That from and after the passage of this act, Daniel Ball, John Almy, James Ballard, Francis H. Cumming, Jonathan F. Chubb, Charles Shepard, Samuel F. Butler, Amos Rathbone and Truman H. Lyon, of the county of Kent, and their successors, be and they are hereby constituted and declared to be a body corporate and politic, in fact and in name, to be styled "the Trusteees of the Grand Rapids Academy;" that by that name they and their successors shall and may have perpetual succession, and shall be persons in law capable of suing and being sued, pleading and being impleaded, answering and being answered, defending and being defended, in all courts of record whatever, and in all manner of suits, actions or complaints whatever; and that they and their successors may have a common seal, and change and alter the same at their pleasure; and that they and their successors, by the name of the Trustees of the Grand Rapids Academy, shall be in law capable of acquiring and holding, by purchase, gift, grant, devise, bequest or otherwise, and of selling, conveying or leasing, any estate, real, personal or mixed, for the use of said corporation, for the purposes hereinafter mentioned, and no other; and that no sale of real estate shall be made without the vote of two-thirds of all the trustees, and that they and their successors shall have full power to make and enter into contracts, to make such rules and by-laws as they may deem necessary for the good government and success of said institution: *Provided,* Such by-laws are not inconsistent with the constitution and laws of the United States or of this State: *And provided further,* That the amount of the property held by such corporation shall not exceed the sum of thirty thousand dollars.

SEC. 2. Said trustees of Grand Rapids Academy shall have power to establish at such time, and at such place at or near the village of Grand Rapids, in the county of Kent, as they may judge best, an institution for the instruction of youth in the various branches of literature.

SEC. 3. That the said Daniel Ball, John Almy, James Ballard, Francis H. Cumming, Jonathan F. Chubb, Charles Shepard, Samuel F. Butler, Amos Rathbone and Truman H. Lyon, shall be trustees of said Academy, and have and exercise the power and franchise herein granted, until others be appointed in their places; they and their successors shall have power to fill all vacancies in their own body, which may happen by death or resignation. They shall appoint a president of said Academy, who shall, ex-officio, be president of the board of trustees, and have the power of giving the casting vote in case of an equal division; a majority shall constitute a quorum for the transaction of business, except otherwise determined by the rules and by-laws which may hereafter be adopted by the board.

SEC. 4. That at the first meeting of said trustees, they shall divide themselves into three classes of three members each; the term of office of the first class shall terminate at the end of the first year; the term of the office of the second class shall terminate at the end of the second year; and the term of the office of the third class shall terminate at the end of the third year; so that one-third of the number of trustees shall be chosen annually.

SEC. 5. The board of trustees shall apply all funds in money or otherwise, by them collected, received or acquired, according to their best judgment, in erecting and keeping in repair suitable buildings, supporting the necessary officers and instructors, in procuring books, maps, or other articles, necessary to insure the success of said institution, or in lessening the expense of education at the same, or improving the health of the students belonging thereto.

SEC. 6. Any three of the before mentioned trustees are hereby authorized to call and name the time and place for the first meeting of the board, and this act is hereby declared to be a public act, and copies thereof printed by authority of the State, shall be received as evidence thereof in all courts of this State.

SEC. 7. The Legislature shall have the power at any time of amending or repealing this act.

Approved March 11, 1844.

[No. 52.]

AN ACT to incorporate the Utica Female Seminary.

SECTION 1. *Be it enacted by the Senate and House of Representatives of the State of Michigan,* That Ephraim Calkin, Samuel Axford, William A. Burt, John Stockton, Jeremiah Curtis, Jacob Summers, Oliver Adams, Charles W. Chapel, David M. Price, Pliny Powers, George Gordon, Gurdon G. Deshon, together with such other persons as may become members of the incorporation, hereby created, shall be and they are hereby constituted and declared to be a body corporate and politic, by the name of the Utica Female Seminary, and in their corporate name may sue and be sued, may have a common seal, which they may renew at pleasure, and shall have, enjoy, and may exercise, all the powers, rights and privileges, which appertain to corporate bodies for the purposes mentioned in this act.

SEC. 2. The capital stock of the said corporation, shall not exceed the sum of five thousand dollars, and shall be divided into shares of ten dollars each.

SEC. 3. The corporation hereby created, shall be forever capable in law to purchase, take, receive, hold and enjoy, any estate, real and personal whatever, to an amount not exceeding five thousand dollars, and to lease, sell and convey, or otherwise dispose of the same.

SEC. 4. There shall be forever hereafter twelve trustees of the said corporation, who shall be members thereof, and who shall manage all the affairs thereof; and the first trustees shall be Ephraim Calkin, Samuel Axford, William A. Burt, John Stockton, Jeremiah Curtis, Jacob Summers, Oliver Adams, Charles W. Chapel, David M. Price, Pliny Powers, George Gordon, and Gurdon G. Deshon, who shall hold their offices until the first day of January, 1845, and until others are elected in their place.

SEC. 5. There shall be, on the first Monday in January, 1845, and on the first Monday in January, in every succeeding year, a general meeting of the members of said corporation, at some convenient place in the village of Utica, to be designated by the by-laws of said corporation; and a majority of the members who shall meet in person or by proxy, shall elect by ballot twelve of their members to be trustees of the said corporation for the year then next ensuing.

SEC. 6. The trustees of said corporation shall have power to choose from out of their number, a president, a treasurer, and a secretary, who shall immediately enter upon the duties of their offices, and hold the same from the time of their election until the first Monday of January of the ensuing year, and until others are chosen in their stead; and in case any of the trustees shall die, resign, refuse or neglect to act, then, and in every such case, the remaining trustees may, within thirty days thereafter, elect by ballot other members of said corporation in their stead, who shall hold their offices in the same manner as those first elected.

SEC. 7. Each member to be entitled to one vote for each share of which he shall be the holder. And the said trustees shall receive subscriptions for shares in said corporation, until the capital stock may be subscribed; the said shares shall be assignable and transferable, according to such rules as the board of trustees shall from time to time make and establish, and shall be considered personal property.

SEC. 8. In case it should at any time happen, that an election of the trustees should not be made on any day when, pursuant to this act, it ought to have been made, the said corporation shall not for that cause, or any non-user, be dissolved; but it shall and may be lawful, on any other day, to hold an election for trustees in such manner as shall be provided by the laws and ordinances of the said corporation.

SEC. 9. This act shall take effect and be in force from and after its passage.

Approved March 11, 1844.

[No. 76.]

AN ACT to incorporate the Ann Arbor Female Seminary.

SECTION 1. *Be it enacted by the Senate and House of Representatives of the State of Michigan,* That from and after the passage of this act, James Kingsley, Thomas Mosley, Fitch Hill, Edwin Lawrence, Luther Boyden, Thomas Wood and Samuel W. Dexter, of the county of Washtenaw, and their successors, be and they are hereby constituted, ordained and declared a body corporate and politic under the name and style of "the Ann Arbor Female Seminary;" that by that name they and their successors shall and may have perpetual succession, and shall be persons in law capable of suing and being sued, pleading and being impleaded, answering and being answered, defending and being defended in all courts of record whatever, and in all manner of suits, actions, complaints, matters and causes whatever, and that they and their successors may have a common seal, and change and alter the same at their pleasure, and that they and their successors, by the name of "the Ann Arbor Female Seminary," shall be in law capable of acquiring and holding by purchase, gift, grant, devise, bequest or otherwise, and of selling, conveying or leasing any estate, real, personal or mixed, for the use of said corporation, not exceeding ten thousand dollars, and that they and their successors shall have full power to make and enter into contracts, to make such rules and by-laws as they may deem necessary for the good government and prosperity of said institution: *Provided,* Such by-laws are not inconsistent with the constitution and laws of the United States or of this State.

SEC. 2. Said corporation shall have power to establish in or near the village of Ann Arbor in said county of Washtenaw, an institution for the education of females.

SEC. 3. Of the said seminary there shall be seven trustees, and the above named persons shall be such trustees, and shall have and exercise the power and franchise herein granted until others be appointed in their place; that they and their successors shall have power to fill all vacancies in their own body which may happen by death, resignation, or otherwise, to appoint a president, secretary and treasurer of their own body, and to prescribe such studies and regulations in said institution as to them shall seem best.

SEC. 4. Said trustees, or a majority of them, shall hold their first meeting in the said village of Ann Arbor, on the first Monday of May next; and the president and secretary of said board of trustees may at any time call a meeting of said board, by giving six days notice of the same to the said trustees, and that a majority of said trustees shall constitute a quorum for the transaction of business.

SEC. 5. Said trustees shall faithfully apply all funds in money, or otherwise, by them collected or acquired, according to their best judgment in the erection of suitable buildings, in the support of necessary officers and teachers, and in procuring a suitable library and other articles necessary to insure the success of said institution.

SEC. 6. All process against said corporation shall be by summons, and the service of the same shall be by leaving an attested copy with the president of said board of trustees, or in his absence, at his last place of abode, at least six days previous to the return day thereof.

SEC. 7. This act is hereby declared a public act, and copies thereof, printed by the authority of the State, shall be received as evidence thereof in all courts of this State.

SEC. 8. The legislature may amend or repeal this act at any time by a vote of two-thirds of each branch thereof.

SEC. 9. The trustees of said seminary shall be jointly and severally liable for all judgments obtained against the corporation: *Provided*, That no execution shall issue against the individual property of said trustees until the property of the corporation shall first have been exhausted: *And provided further*, That any trustee resigning, shall not thereby be released from any liability accrued during the period while he was such trustee until a responsible successor shall be appointed and enter upon the discharge of his duties.

SEC. 10. This act shall take effect and be in force from and after its passage.

Approved March 24, 1845.

[No. 75.]

AN ACT to incorporate the Ypsilanti Seminary.

SECTION 1. *Be it enacted by the Senate and House of Representatives of the State of Michigan*, That Lyman H. Moore and William Moore, of the county of Washtenaw, and their successors in office, be and they are hereby constituted and declared a body corporate and politic, in fact and in name, to be styled the proprietors of the Ypsilanti Seminary; by that name they and their successors in office shall and may have perpetual succession, and shall be persons in law capable of suing and being sued, pleading and being impleaded, answering and being answered unto, defending and being defended in all courts whatever.

SEC. 2. That they and their successors in office may have a common seal and change the same at their pleasure. That they and their successors in office, by the name of the proprietors of the Ypsilanti Seminary, shall be capable in law of acquiring and holding by purchase, gift, grant, devise, bequest or otherwise, and of selling, conveying or leasing any estate, real, personal or mixed, for the purposes hereinafter mentioned, and none other; and that they and their successors in office shall have full power to make and enter into contracts, to make such rules and by-laws as they may deem necessary for the good government and success of said seminary: *Provided*, Such by-laws are not inconsistent with the constitution and laws of the United States and of this State: *And provided further*, That the amount of property held by such corporation shall never exceed the sum of ten thousand dollars.

SEC. 3. Said proprietors shall have power to establish and continue in the township of Ypsilanti a seminary of learning, for the instruction of persons in the various branches of literature, or to continue the institution now established and known as the Ypsilanti Seminary.

SEC. 4. The individual as well as corporate property of said proprietors and their successors in office shall be liable for all debts against the said corporation, and may be proceeded against jointly or severally as in the case of debts against individuals.

SEC. 5. The legislature may at any time amend or repeal this act.

SEC. 6. This act shall take effect and be in force from and after its passage.

Approved March 24, 1845.

[No. 8.]

AN ACT to incorporate the Adrian Seminary.

SECTION 1. *Be it enacted by the Senate and House of Representatives of the State of Michigan,* That Parley J. Spalding, Alfred W. Budlong, William Wolcott, Theodore D. Billings, James J. Newell, Charles R. Watson, Daniel D. Sinclair, Harry Wood and Francis J. King, together with such other persons as may be associated with, and may become stockholders of the incorporation hereby created, shall be, and they are hereby constituted and declared a body corporate and politic, by the name and style of the "Adrian Seminary;" and in their corporate name may sue and be sued, defend and be defended in all courts of this State; may have a common seal which they may renew or change at pleasure, and shall have, enjoy and exercise all the powers, rights and privileges which appertain to corporate bodies, for the purposes expressed in this act.

SEC. 2. The capital stock of the said corporation shall not exceed the sum of ten thousand dollars, and shall be divided into shares of ten dollars each.

SEC. 3. The said corporation hereby created shall be capable in law of acquiring and holding by purchase, gift, grant, devise, bequest, or otherwise, and of selling and conveying or leasing any estate, real, personal or mixed, for the purposes mentioned in this act, and none other; and the trustees thereof and their successors in office, shall have full power to make and enter into contracts, to establish such rules and by-laws as they may deem necessary for the good government of the said seminary, and for the holding and disposing of its property and effects for the purposes mentioned in this act, not inconsistent with the constitution and laws of this State: *Provided,* That the amount of property held and owned by such corporation shall never exceed the sum of ten thousand dollars.

SEC. 4. There shall be nine trustees of the said corporation, who shall be stockholders thereof, and who shall manage and control all the affairs of the same, maintaining perpetual succession, three of whom shall be elected at the annual meeting in each year, to fill the vacancy of a like number, whose term of office shall expire upon the election of their successors; and the persons named in the first section of this act shall be the first trustees; and the said nine trustees shall, at their first meeting, proceed to cast lots for the terms of one, two and three years, by drawing numbers; and the three persons who shall draw the three highest numbers shall hold their office for the term of three years from and after the first day of January, A. D. one thousand eight hundred and forty-six; and the three persons who shall draw the next three highest numbers, shall hold their office for the term of two years from and after the first day of January, A. D., one thousand eight hundred and forty-six, and the remaining three persons shall hold their office for the term of one year from and after the first day of January, A. D. one thousand eight hundred and forty-six.

SEC. 5. There shall be a meeting of the stockholders of said corporation on the first Monday of January, A. D. one thousand eight hundred and forty-seven, and on the first Monday in January in every succeeding year, at some convenient place in the village of Adrian, to be designated by the by-laws of said corporation; and a majority of the stockholders who shall meet in person or by proxy, shall elect three of the stockholders to be trustees in the place of those whose term may expire, each person being entitled to one vote for each share he may hold in his own right, or by proxy.

SEC. 6. The said trustees shall have power to choose from their own number a president, treasurer and secretary, who shall hold their offices during the pleasure of the said trustees, and in case any of the trustees shall die, resign, refuse or neglect to act, the remaining trustees may, within thirty days after any such vacancy shall occur, elect by ballot other trustees, of stockholders of said corporation, to fill such vacancy.

SEC. 7. The said trustees are authorized to receive subscriptions for shares to the capital stock of said corporation, and such shares shall be assignable and transferable agreeably to such by-laws as the said trustees shall from time to time establish, and shall in law be considered personal property.

SEC. 8. The said trustees are hereby empowered and authorized to establish in the township of Adrian, in the county of Lenawee, an institution for the instruction of young persons in the various branches of literature, science and the arts, and shall faithfully apply the funds by them from time to time received, under the provisions of this act, in providing suitable buildings, employing professors and teachers, procuring books, maps, philosophical and other apparatus necessary to insure a successful prosecution of study in said institution.

SEC. 9. In the collection of debts against said corporation, if corporate property cannot be found sufficient to satisfy any execution issued against it, the trustees shall be liable as partners in trade, for any debt created by them whilst trustees in behalf of said corporation; and if such debts cannot be collected from the corporate property of said institution, or the property of the trustees as aforesaid, then each stockholder shall be individually liable therefor.

SEC. 10. The said trustees shall, at least ten days previous to each annual election of trustees as aforesaid, cause a list of the names of all the trustees and stockholders of said corporation, together with a statement of the amount of stock owned by each, duly authenticated by affidavit, to be filed in the office of the county clerk of the county of Lenawee; and the said list and statement shall be prima facie evidence that the individuals therein named are the trustees and stockholders of said corporation, and that the statement of the stock is the amount owned by each individual respectively.

SEC. 11. That said seminary shall be subject to the annual visitation of the Superintendent of Public Instruction, and the trustees of said seminary shall annually, on or before the twentieth day of October, in each year, make to said Superintendent a full report of the literary and pecuniary condition of said seminary.

SEC. 12. This act shall be under the control of any future Legislature, to alter, amend or repeal, as the public good may require.

Approved January 30, 1846.

[No. 70.]

AN ACT to amend an act entitled an act to incorporate the Adrian Seminary, approved January thirteenth, eighteen hundred and forty-six.

SECTION 1. *Be it enacted by the Senate and House of Representatives of the State of Michigan,* That the first section of the act entitled an act to incorporate the Adrian Seminary, approved January thirteenth, eighteen hundred and forty-six, be amended by striking out the names of Alfred W. Budlong, William Wolcott, Francis J. King and Harry Wood, and inserting the names of Abel Whitney, Daniel K. Underwood, John A. Rice and Langford G. Berry; and by striking out the words "Adrian Seminary," and inserting "Adrian Academy."

SEC. 2. The first meeting of said corporation shall be held at such time and place as may be designated, in accordance with the provisions of the third section of chapter fifty-five of the revised statutes of eighteen hundred and forty-six.

SEC. 3. This act shall take effect from and after its passage.

Approved March 16, 1847.

[No. 13.]

AN ACT to incorporate the Clinton Institute.

SECTION 1. *Be it enacted by the Senate and House of Representatives of the State of Michigan,* That from and after the passage of this act, Ebenezer Hall, Thomas M. Perry, Henry M. Dodge, Aaron G. Parke, Joseph Cole, Chester Spalding, Harlehigh Cartter, Pliny Power and Morton Shearer, of the county of Macomb, and their successors be and they are hereby constituted, ordained and declared a body corporate and politic under the name and style of "The Clinton Institute;" that by that name they and their successors shall and may have perpetual succession, and shall be persons in law capable of suing and being sued, pleading and being impleaded, answering and being answered, defending and being defended in all courts of record whatever, and in all manner of suits, actions, complaints, matters and causes whatever; and that they and their successors may have a common seal, and change and alter the same at their pleasure; and that they and their successors by the name of "The Clinton Institute," shall be in law capable of acquiring and holding by purchase, gift, or otherwise, and of selling, conveying or leasing any estate, real, personal or mixed, for the use of said corporation, not exceeding ten thousand dollars; and that they and their successors shall have full power to make and enter into contracts, to make such rules and by-laws as they may deem necessary for the good government and prosperity of said institution: *Provided,* Such by-laws are not inconsistent with the constitution and laws of the United States or of this State.

SEC. 2. Said corporation shall have power to establish at or near the village of Mount Clemens, in the county of Macomb, an institution for the instruction and education of young persons.

SEC. 3. There shall be nine trustees of the said corporation, who shall be stockholders thereof, and who shall manage and control all the affairs of the same, and the above named persons shall be the first trustees, and shall hold their offices until the first Monday in July, one thousand eight hundred and forty-six, and until others are elected in their places; and they or their successors shall have power to fill all vacancies in their own body, which may happen by death, resignation, or otherwise, to appoint a president, secretary and treasurer of their own body, and to prescribe such studies and regulations in said institution, as to them shall seem best.

SEC. 4. There shall be a meeting of the stockholders of said corporation on the first Monday in July, one thousand eight hundred and forty-six, and on the first Monday in July in every succeeding year, at some convenient place in the village of Mount Clemens, to be designated by the by-laws of said corporation; and a majority of the stockholders who shall meet in person or by proxy, shall elect nine of the stockholders to be trustees of said corporation for the year then next ensuing, and until others are elected in their places; each share of stock entitling the stockholder to one vote, either personally or by proxy.

SEC. 5. The capital stock of said company shall be ten thousand dollars, in shares of ten dollars each, and the trustees are hereby authorized to receive subscriptions thereto, at such times and places as they or a majority of them shall designate; said shares to be assignable and transferable agreeably to such by-laws as the trustees may from time to time establish, and shall in law be considered personal property.

SEC. 6. The trustees of said corporation shall be jointly and severally liable for all debts of the said corporation: *Provided,* That no execution shall issue against the individual property of said trustees until the property of the corporation shall first have been exhausted: *And provided further,* That any trustee resigning shall not thereby be released from any liability accrued during the period which he was in office, until a responsible successor shall be appointed and enter upon the discharge of his duties.

SEC. 7. The board of trustees shall cause to be transmitted to the Superintendent of Public Instruction, annually, on or before the tenth day of November, a full statement of the condition of the institute.

SEC. 8. This act may be amended or repealed at any time by a vote of two-thirds of any future Legislature.

Approved February 12, 1846.

[No. 128.]

AN ACT to incorporate the Owasso Literary Institute.

SECTION 1. *Be it enacted by the Senate and House of Representatives of the State of Michigan*, That Elias Comstock, Alfred L. Williams, Benjamin O. Williams, Amos Gould, Charles L. Goodhue, Anson B. Chipman and John B. Barnes, of the county of Shiawassee, and their successors in office, be, and they are hereby constituted and declared a body corporate and politic, in fact and in name, under the name and style of the "Owasso Literary Institute;" and by that name they and their successors in office shall and may have perpetual succession, and shall be persons in law capable of suing and being sued, pleading and being impleaded, answering and being answered unto, defending and being defended in all courts whatever.

SEC. 2. That the persons named in the preceding section, and their successors in office, may have a common seal, and change the same at their pleasure, and by the name of the Owasso Literary Institute, shall be capable in law of acquiring and holding by purchase, gift, grant, devise, bequest or otherwise, and of selling, conveying or leasing any estate, real, personal or mixed, for the purposes hereinafter mentioned, and no other; and they and their successors in office, shall have full power to make and enter into contracts, to make such rules and by-laws as may be necessary for the good government and success of said institute: *Provided*, Such by-laws are not inconsistent with the constitution and laws of the United States or of this State.

SEC. 3. The capital stock of the said corporation shall not exceed the sum of ten thousand dollars, and shall be divided into shares of ten dollars each.

SEC. 4. Said corporation shall have power to establish and continue in the township of Owasso, an institution of learning for the instruction of persons in the various branches of literature, and the arts and sciences.

SEC. 5. There shall be seven trustees of the said corporation, who shall be members thereof, and who shall manage all the affairs thereof; and the first trustees shall be Elias Comstock, Alfred L. Williams, Benjamin O. Williams, Amos Gould, Charles L. Goodhue, Anson B. Chipman and John B. Barnes, who shall hold their offices, and have and exercise the powers and franchises hereby granted, until the first Monday in January, eighteen hundred and forty-seven, and until others are elected in their places.

SEC. 6. There shall be, on the first Monday of January, eighteen hundred and forty-seven, and on the first Monday of January in every succeeding year, a general meeting of the stockholders of said corporation, at some convenient place in the village of Owasso, to be designated by the by-laws of said corporation; and a majority of the stockholders who shall meet in person or by proxy, shall elect by ballot seven of the stockholders to be trustees of said corporation for the year then next ensuing.

SEC. 7. The trustees of said corporation shall have power to choose of their own number, a president, treasurer, and a secretary, who shall immediately enter upon the duties of their offices, and hold the same from the time of their election until the first Monday of January of the ensuing year, and until others are chosen in their stead; and in case any of the trustees shall die, resign, refuse or neglect to act, then, and in any such case, the remaining trustees may, within thirty days thereafter, elect by ballot other stockholders of the said corporation in their stead, who shall hold their offices in the same manner as those first elected.

SEC. 8. Each stockholder shall be entitled to one vote for each share of which he shall be the holder; and the said trustees shall receive subscriptions for shares in said corporation, until the capital stock may be subscribed. The said shares shall be assignable and transferable according to such rules as the board of trustees shall from time to time make and establish, and shall be considered personal property.

SEC. 9. In case it should at any time happen that an election of trustees should not be made on any day when, pursuant to this act it ought to have been made, the said corporation shall not for that cause be dissolved; but it shall and may be lawful on any other day to hold an election for trustees in such manner as shall be provided by the by-laws and ordinances of said corporation.

SEC. 10. The said trustees shall faithfully apply all funds in money or otherwise, by them collected or acquired, according to their best judgment, in the erection of suitable buildings, in the support of necessary officers and teachers, and in procuring a suitable library and other articles necessary to insure the success of said institution.

SEC. 11. All process against said corporation shall be by summons, and the service of the same shall be by leaving an attested copy with the president of said board of trustees, or in his absence, at his last place of abode, at least six days previous to the return day thereof.

SEC. 12. The Legislature may alter, amend or repeal this act.

SEC. 13. The trustees of said institution shall be jointly and severally liable for all debts against the corporation: *Provided*, That no execution shall issue against the individual property of said trustees until the property of the corporation shall first have been exhausted.

SEC. 14. This act shall take effect and be in force from and after its passage.

Approved May 11, 1846.

[No. 82.]

AN ACT to incorporate the Vermontville Academical Association.

SECTION 1. *Be it enacted by the Senate and House of Representatives of the State of Michigan*, That from and after the passage of this act, W. W. Benedict, Oren Dickinson, S. S. Church, W. S. Fairfield, David Barber, W. J. Squier, M. S. Norton, D. H. Robinson, Levi Merrill, of the county of Eaton, and their successors be and they are hereby constituted, ord ined and declared a body corporate and politic, under the name and style of "The Vermontville Academical Association;" that by that name they and their successors shall and may have perpetual succession, and shall be persons in law capable of suing and being sued, pleading and being impleaded, answering and being answered, defending and being defended, in all courts of record whatever, and in all manner of suits, actions, complaints, matters and causes whatever; and that they and their successors may have a common seal, and change and alter the same at their pleasure; and that they and their successors, by the name of the "Vermontville Academical Association," shall be in law capable of acquiring and holding by purchase, gift, or otherwise, and of selling, conveying or leasing any estate, real, personal or mixed, for the use of said corporation, not exceeding ten thousand dollars, and that they and their successors shall have full power to make and enter into contracts, to make such ru'es and by-laws as they may deem necessary for the good government and prosperity of sa'd insti ution: *Provided*, Such by-laws are not inconsistent with the constitution and laws of the United States or of this State.

SEC. 2. Said corporation shall have power to establish at or near the village of Vermontville, in the county of Eaton, an institution for the instruction and education of young persons.

SEC. 3. There shall be nine trustees of said corporation, who shall be stockholders thereof, and who shall manage and control all the affairs of the same; and the above named persons shall be the first trustees, and shall hold their offices until the first Monday of July, eighteen hundred and forty-six, and until others are elected in their places; and they or their successors shall have power to fill all vacancies in their own body, which may happen by death, resignation or otherwise, to appoint a president, secretary and treasurer of their own body, and to prescribe such studies and regulations in said institution as to them shall seem best.

SEC. 4. There shall be a meeting of the stockholders of said corporation on the first Monday of July, eighteen hundred and forty-six, and on the first Monday in July in every succeeding year, at some convenient place in the village of Vermontville, to be designated by the by-laws of said corporation; and a majority of the stockholders, who shall meet in person or by proxy, shall select nine of the stockholders to be trustees of said corporation for the year then next ensuing, and until others are elected in their places, each share of stock entitling the stockholder to one vote, either personally or by proxy.

SEC. 5. The capital stock of said company shall be ten thousand dollars, in shares of ten dollars each. And the trustees are hereby authorized to receive subscriptions thereto at such times and places as they or a majority of them shall designate; said shares to be assignable and transferable, agreeably to such by-laws as the trustees may, from time to time establish, and shall, in law, be considered personal property.

SEC. 6. The trustees of said corporation shall be jointly and severally liable for all debts of the said corporation: *Providxd*, That no execution shall issue against the individual property of said trustees until the property of the corporation shall first have been exhausted: *And provided further*, That any trustee resigning shall not thereby be released from any liability accrued during the period while he was in office, until a responsible successor shall be appointed and enter upon the discharge of his duties.

SEC. 7. The board of trustees shall cause to be transmitted to the Superintendent of Public Instruction annually, on or before the tenth day of November, a full statement of the condition of the institute.

SEC. 8. This act may be amended or repealed at any time by a vote of two-thirds of any future Legislature.

Approved April 28, 1846.

[No. 39.]

AN ACT to incorporate the White Pigeon Academy.

SECTION 1. *Be it enacted by the Senate and House of Representatives of the State of Michigan*, That Levi Baxter, Edwin Kellogg, Elias S. Swan, John Redfern, Charles Kellogg and George W. Beisel, of the county of St. Joseph, and their successors in office, be and they are hereby constituted and declared a body corporate and politic, in fact and in name, under the name and style of the "White Pigeon Academy," and by that name they and their successors in office shall and may have perpetual succession, and shall be persons in law capable of suing and being sued, pleading and being impleaded, answering and being answered unto, defending and being defended in all courts whatever.

SEC. 2. The persons named in the preceding section, and their successors in office, may have a common seal, and change the same at their pleasure, and by the name of the White Pigeon Academy, shall be capable in law of acquiring and holding by purchase, gift, grant, devise, bequest or otherwise; and of selling, conveying or leasing any estate, real, personal or mixed, for the purposes hereinafter mentioned, and no other; and they and their successors in office, shall have full power to make and enter into contracts, to make such rules and by-laws as may be necessary for the good government and success of said academy: *Provided*, Such by-laws are not inconsistent with the constitution and laws of the United States and of this State.

Sec. 3. The capital stock of the said corporation shall not exceed the sum of ten thousand dollars, and shall be divided into shares of five dollars each.

Sec. 4. Said corporation shall have power to establish and continue in the township of White Pigeon, an institution of learning for the instruction of persons in the various branches of literature and the arts and sciences.

Sec. 5. There shall be six trustees of the said coporation, who shall be members thereof, and who shall manage all the affairs thereof; and the first trustees shall be Levi Baxter, Edwin Kellogg, John Redfern, Eilas S. Swan, Charles Kellogg and George W. Beisel, who shall hold their offices, and have and exercise the powers and franchises hereby granted, until the first Monday in January, eighteen hundreen and forty-eight, and until others are elected in their places.

Sec. 6. There shall be, on the first Monday of January, eighteen hundred and forty-eight, and on the first Monday of January in every succeeding year, a general meeting of the stockholders of said corporation at their academy building in the village of White Pigeon, or at any other place to be designated by the by-laws of said corporation; and a majority of the stockholders who shall meet in person or by proxy, shall elect by ballot six of the stockholders to be trustees of said corporation for the year then next ensuing.

Sec. 7. The trustees of said corporation shall have power to choose of their own number a president, treasurer and secretary, who shall immediately enter upon the duties of their offices, and hold the same from the time of their election until the first Monday of January of the ensuing year, and until others are chosen in their stead: and in case any of the trustees shall die, resign, refuse or neglect to act, then and in such case the remaining trustees may, within thirty days thereafter, elect by ballot other stockholders of the said corporation in their stead, who shall hold their offices in the same manner as those first elected.

Sec. 8. Each stockholder shall be entitled to one vote for each share of which he shall be the holder, and the said trustees shall receive subscriptions for shares in said corporation until the capital stock may be subscribed. The said shares shall be assignable and transferable according to such rules as the board of trustees shall from time to time make and establish, and shall be considered personal property.

Sec. 9. Each person residing in said county at the date of the passage of this act, who were subscribers and donors for erecting a building in said village in the year eighteen hundred and forty, for a branch of the university, shall be stockholders to the amount they have severally subscribed and paid for the benefit of said branch.

Sec. 10. That all the real and personal estate at any time heretofore donated to the regents of the University for the use of said branch by said subscribers, shall hereafter belong to and be owned by said corporation for the use of said institution.

Sec. 11. In case it shall at any time happen that an election of trustees should not be made on any day when pursuant to this act it ought to have been made, the said corporation shall not for that cause be dissolved; but it shall and may be lawful on any other day to hold an election for trustees, in such manner as shall be provided by the by-laws and ordinances of said corporation.

Sec. 12. The said trustees shall faithfully apply all funds in money or otherwise, by them collected or acquired, according to their best judgment, in the erection of suitable buildings, in the support of necessary officers and teachers, and procuring a suitable library and other articles necessary to insure the success of said institution.

SEC. 13. All process against said corporation shall be by summons, and the service of the same shall be by leaving an attested copy with the president of said board of trustees, or in his absence, at his last place of abode, at least six days previous to the return day thereof.

SEC. 14. The trustees of said corporation shall be jointly and severally liable for all debts against the corporation: *Provided,* That no execution shall issue against the individual property of said trustees until the property of the corporation shall have first been exhausted.

SEC. 15. The principal of the academy shall, on or before the first day of November of each year, report to the Superintendent of Public Instruction the number of pupils in said academy, the studies pursued, the books used, and the general condition of the institution.

SEC. 16. The legislature may at any time alter, amend or repeal this act.

SEC. 17. This act shall take effect and be in force from after its passage.

Approved March 12, 1847.

[No. 101.]

AN ACT to incorporate the Raisin Institute.

SECTION 1. *Be it enacted by the Senate and House of Representatives of the State of Michigan,* That Elijah Brownell, Eliphalet Jones, William E. Warner, Samuel A. Hubbard, Joseph L. Peters, Stephen Allen and Anson Backus, of the county of Lenawee, together with such other persons as may be associated with them for that purpose, shall be and they are hereby constituted a body politic and corporate, by the name and style of the "Raisin Institute," subject to the provisions relating to corporations, contained in chapter fifty-five of the revised statutes of eighteen hundred and forty-six, and such amendments thereof as may from time be made by the legislature.

SEC. 2. The trustees shall have power, and they are hereby authorized to establish in the township of Raisin, in the county of Lenawee, an institution for the instruction of young persons in ancient or modern languages or literature, and the arts and sciences, and shall faithfully apply all funds received by them for that purpose, by subscription, bequest or otherwise, in providing suitable buildings, employing professors and teachers, procuring books, maps, philosophical and other apparatus necessary or proper for the successful prosecution of study in said institution.

SEC. 3. The capital stock of said corporation shall not exceed the sum of ten thousand dollars, and shall be divided into shares of ten dollars each, which shall be considered personal property; and they may hold any property or estate, real, personal or mixed, for the purposes mentioned in this act, and none other, not exceeding in value the amount of capital stock herein authorized.

SEC. 4. In collection of debts against said corporation, if corporate property cannot be found sufficient to satisfy any execution issued against it, the trustees shall be liable as partners in trade for any debt created by them, whilst trustees in behalf of said corporation; and if such debts cannot be collected from the corporate property of said institution, or from the property of the trustees as aforesaid, then each stockholder shall be individually liable therefor.

SEC. 5. The institution shall be subject to visitation at any time by the Superintendent of Public Instruction; and the trustees shall annually, on or before the twentieth day of October, in each year, make to the Superintendent a full report of the literary and pecuniary condition of said institution.

SEC. 16. The legislature may at any time alter, amend or repeal this act.

Approved March 17, 1847.

[No. 121.]

AN ACT to incorporate the Howell Academy.

SECTION 1. *Be it enacted by the Senate and House of Representatives of the State of Michigan,* That Josiah Turner, F. C. Whipple, Elijah F. Burt, Alvan Isbell, Gardner Wheeler, Geo. W. Lee, Jonh Kenyon, Jr., Almon Whipple, and Edward E. Gregory, together with such other persons as may be associated with them, and may become stockholders of the incorporation hereby created, shall be and they are hereby constituted and declared a body corporate and politic, by the name and style of "Howell Academy," and in their corporate name may sue and be sued, defend and be defended, in all courts of this State; may have a common seal, which they may renew or change at pleasure; and shall have, enjoy and exercise all the powers, rights and privileges which appertain to corporate bodies for the purposes expressed in this act.

SEC 2. The capital stock of said corporation shall not exceed ten thousand dollars, and shall be divided into shares of five dollars each.

SEC. 3. The said corporation hereby created shall be capable in law of acquiring and holding by purchase, gift, grant, bequest or otherwise, and of selling and conveying, or leasing any estate, real, personal or mixed, for the purposes mentioned in this act, and none others; and the trustees thereof and their successors in office, shall have full power to make and enter into contracts, to establish rules and by-laws as they may deem necessary for the good government of the said academy, and for the holding and disposing of its property and effects for the purposes mentioned in this act, not inconsistent with the constitution and laws of this State.

SEC. 4. There shall be nine trustees of the said corporation, who shall be stockholders thereof, and who shall manage and control all the affairs of the same, maintaining perpetual succession; three of whom shall be elected at the annual meeting in each year, to fill the vacancy of a like number whose term of office shall expire upon the election of their successors; and the persons named in the first section of this act shall be the first trustees; and the said nine trustees shall, at their first meeting, proceed to cast lots for the terms of one, two and three years, by drawing numbers; and the three persons who shall draw the three highest numbers shall hold their office for the term of three years from and after the first day of January, one thousand eight hundred and forty-eight; and the three persons who shall draw the next three highest numbers shall hold their office for the term of two years from and after the first day of January, one thousand eight hundred and forty-eight; and the remaining three persons shall hold their office for the term of one year from and after the first day of January, one thousand eight hundred and forty-eight.

SEC. 5. There shall be a meeting of the stockholders of said corporation on the first Monday of January, one thousand eight hundred and forty-nine, and on the first Monday in January in each succeeding year, at some convenient place in the village of Howell, to be designated by the by-laws of said corporation; and a majority of the stockholders who shall meet in person or by proxy, shall elect three of the stockholders to be trustees, in place of those whose term may expire, each person being entitled to one vote for each share he may hold in his own right, or by proxy.

SEC. 6. The said trustees shall have power to choose from their own number, a president, treasurer and secretary, who shall hold their offices during the pleasure of the said trustees; and in case any of the trustees shall die, resign, refuse or neglect to act, the remaining trustees may, within thirty days after any such vacancy shall occur, elect by ballot other trustees of stockholders of said corporation to fill such vacancy.

SEC. 7. The said trustees are authorized to receive subscriptions for shares to the capital stock of said corporation, and such shares shall be assignable and transferable, agreeably to such by-laws as the said trustees shall from time to time establish, and shall in law be considered personal property.

SEC. 8. The said trustees are hereby empowered and authorized to establish in the township of Howell, in the county of Livingston, an institution for the instruction of young persons in the various branches of literature, science and the arts, and shall faithfully apply the funds by them from time to time received under the provisions of this act, in providing suitable buildings, employing professors and teachers, procuring books, maps, philosophical and other apparatus necessary to insure a successful prosecution of study in said institution.

SEC. 9. The said trustees shall, at least ten days previous to each annual election of trustees as aforesaid, cause a list of the names of all the trustees and stockholders of said corporation, together with a statement of the amount of stock owned by each, duly authenticated by affidavit, to be filed in the office of the county clerk of the county of Livingston; and the said list and statement shall be prima facia evidence that the individuals therein named are the trustees and stockholders of said corporation, and that the statement of the stock is the amount owned by each individual respectively.

SEC. 10. That said academy shall be subject to the annual visitation of the Superintendent of Public Instruction; and the trustees of said academy shall annually, on or before the twelfth day of October in each year, make to said Superintendent a full report of the literary and pecuniary condition of said academy.

SEC. 11. In case it shall at any time happen that an election of trustees shall not be made on any day, when pursuant to this act it ought to have been made, the said corporation shall not for that cause be dissolved, but it shall and may be lawful to assemble on any other day to hold an election for trustees, in such manner as shall be provided by the by-laws and ordinances of said corporation.

SEC. 12. Said company shall be subject to the provisions of chapter fifty-five of the revised statutes of eighteen hundred and forty-six, so far as the same may be applicable.

Approved March 27, 1848.

[No. 110.]

AN ACT to incorporate the Leoni Theological Institute.

SECTION 1. *Be it enacted by the Senate and House of Representatives of the State of Michigan,* That Samuel Bebans, A. W. Curtis, Rufus Thayer, John Diamond, William Holmes, William M. Sullivan, G. J. Barker, William D. Moore, Marcus Swift, Jason Steele, Jeptha Hewit, and S. P. Rice, of the State of Michigan, and their successors, be and they are hereby created a body corporate and politic, to be styled "The Board of Trustees of the Leoni Theological Institute, and by that name shall have perpetual succession, with full power to acquire, hold and convey property, real and personal, not exceeding thirty thousand dollars, and to have and use a common seal, to sue and be sued, plead and be impleaded, to make, alter and modify, from time to time, such by-laws and regulations as they may deem necessary for the government of said institute, its officers and employees: *Provided,* Such by-laws and regulations are not inconsistent with the constitution and laws of the United States or of this State.

SEC. 2. Said institute shall be located in the village of Leoni, county of Jackson; and the said trustees may proceed in the erection of buildings upon a plan sufficiently extensive for the purposes of a thorough theological education.

SEC. 3. At the first meeting of the trustees, after the passage of this act, they shall, by ballot, divide themselves into three classes of four members each; the term of office of the first class shall terminate at the session of the Michigan Annual Conference of the Wesleyan Methodist

Connection, in the summer or fall of eighteen hundred and forty-eight, and their places supplied by an election of said conference. The second shall go out of office at the next session of said Annual Conference, and their places supplied in like manner; and so of the third; so that each year one-third of said trustees shall be elected by said Annual Conference.

Sec. 4. The above named trustees, and their successors in office, may have power to fill vacancies which may occur in their own body, by death, removal or resignation. They may also appoint from their own members, a president, secretary and treasurer, whose duties shall be prescribed in the by-laws of said institute.

Sec. 5. Said board of trustees shall be in law capable of acquiring and holding, by purchase, gift, grant, devise or bequest, or otherwise, and of selling, conveying or leasing any estate, real, personal or mixed, for the use of said corporation, and for the interest of said institute, and no other, and shall be held liable for all debts as partners in trade, after the corporation property shall have been exhausted.

Sec. 6. The Legislature shall have the power at any time of amending or repealing this act; also to demand of the trustees of said institute a statement of the amount of property, real and personal, belonging to the same.

Approved March 25, 1848.

[No. 138.]

AN ACT to incorporate the Leoni Seminary.

Section 1. *Be it enacted by the Senate and House of Representatives of the State of Michigan,* That Wilder B. Mack, Jacob Sagendolph, Aaron Rowe, Abel Scott, Andrew Brown, 2d, William Jackson, Benajah Bayne, Ira W. Kellogg, Mason Branch, Samuel Lapham, Jared Warner and Isaiah Raymond, of the State of Michigan, together with such other persons as may be associated with them, and their successors for that purpose, shall be and they are hereby constituted a body politic and corporate, by the name and style of the "Leoni Seminary," subject to the provisions relating to corporations, contained in chapter fifty-five of the revised statutes of eighteen hundred and forty-six, and such amendments thereof as may from time to time be made by the Legislature.

Sec. 2. The trustees shall have power, and they are hereby authorized to establish in the village of Leoni, in the county of Jackson, an institution for the instruction of young persons in ancient or modern languages or literature, and the arts and sciences, and shall faithfully apply all funds received by them for that purpose, by subscription, bequest or otherwise, in providing suitable buildings, employing professors and teachers, procuring books, maps, philosophical and other apparatus, necessary or proper for the successful prosecution of study in said institution.

Sec. 3. Said board of trustees shall be in law capable of acquiring and holding, by purchase, gift, grant, devise or bequest, or otherwise, and of selling, conveying or leasing any estate, real, personal or mixed, in value not exceeding the sum of twenty-five thousand dollars, for the use of said corporation, and no other, and shall be held liable for all debts as partners in trade, after the corporate property shall have been exhausted.

Sec. 4. The institution shall be subject to visitation at any time by the Superintendent of Public Instruction; and the trustees shall annually, on or before the 20th day of October, in each year, make to the Superintendent a full report of the literary and pecuniary condition of said institution.

Sec. 5. This act shall take effect and be in force from and after its passage.

Approved March 29, 1848.

[No. 44.]

AN ACT to incorporate the Olivet Institute.

SECTION 1. *Be it enacted by the Senate and House of Representatives of the State of Michigan,* That James Douglass, Carlow Reed, Oramel Hosford, William Hosford, Enoch N. Bartlett, John G. Barnes, Chas. M. Bordwell and Wilson C. Esdell, of the county of Eaton, together with such other persons as may be associated with them and their successors, for that purpose, shall be and they are hereby constituted a body politic and corporate, by the name and style of the Olivet Institute, subject to the provisions relating to corporations, contained in chapter fifty-five of the revised statutes of eighteen hundred and forty-six, and such amendments thereof as may from time to time be made by the legislature.

SEC. 2. The trustees shall have power, and they are hereby authorized to establish in the township of Walton, in the county of Eaton, an institution for the instruction of young persons in ancient or modern languages or literature, and the arts and sciences; and shall faithfully apply all funds received by them for that purpose, by subscription, bequest or otherwise, in providing suitable buildings, employing professors and teachers, procuring books, maps, philosophical and other apparatus, necessary or proper for the successful prosecution of study in said institution.

SEC. 3. Said board of trustees shall be in law capable of acquiring and holding, by purchase, gift, grant, devise or bequest or otherwise, and of selling, conveying or leasing any estate, real, personal or mixed, in value not exceeding the sum of twenty-five thousand dollars, for the use of said corporation, and no other, and shall be held liable for all debts as partners in trade, after the corporate property shall have been exhausted.

SEC. 4. The institution shall be subject to visitation, at any time, by the Superintendent of Public Instruction, and the trustees shall annually, on or before the 20th day of October, in each year, make to the Superintendent a full report of the literary and pecuniary condition of said institution.

SEC. 5. This act shall take effect and be in force from and after its passage.

Approved February 22, 1848.

[No. 42.]

AN ACT to incorporate the Woodstock Manual Labor Institute.

SECTION 1. *Be it enacted by the Senate and House of Representatives of the State of Michigan,* That James G. Birney, William P. Russell, Prior Foster, Joseph Hewitt, William W. Jackson, and Joseph Foster, of the State of Michigan, together with such other persons as may be associated with them and their successors for that purpose, shall be, and they are hereby constituted a body politic and corporate, by the name and style of the Woodstock Manual Labor Institute, subject to the provisions relating to corporations, contained in chapter fifty-five of the Revised Statutes of eighteen hundred and forty-six, and such amendments thereof as may from time to time be made by the Legislature.

SEC. 2. The trustees shall have power, and they are hereby authorized to establish in the township of Woodstock, in the county of Lenawee, an institution for the instruction of persons of color, and others, in ancient or modern languages, or literature and the arts and sciences, and shall faithfully apply all funds received by them for that purpose, by subscription, bequest or otherwise, in providing suitable buildings, employing professors and teachers, procuring books, maps, philosophical and other apparatus necessary or proper for the successful prosecution of study in said institution.

SEC. 3. Said board of trustees shall be in law capable of acquiring and holding, by purchase, gift, grant, devise or bequest, or otherwise, and of selling, conveying, or leasing any estate, real, personal or mixed, in value not exceeding the sum of twenty-five thousand dollars, for the use of said corporation, and for the interest of said institute, and no other, and shall be held liable for all debts as partners in trade, after the corporate property shall have been exhausted.

SEC. 4. The institution shall be subject to visitation at any time, by the Superintendent of Public Instruction, and the trustees shall, annually, on or before the twentieth day of October, in each year, make to the Superintendent a full report of the literary and pecuniary condition of said institution.

SEC. 5. The Legislature may at any time alter, amend or repeal this act.

SEC. 6. This act shall take effect and be in force from and after its passage.

Approved February 19, 1848.

[No. 168.]

AN ACT to incoporate the Oakland Female Seminary.

SECTION 1. *Be it enacted by the Senate and House of Representatives of the State of Michigan,* That Alfred Williams, Origen D. Richardson, Horace C. Thurber, Willard M. McConnel, Benjamin B. Morris, Hester L. Stevens, Samuel M. Stelle, Jacob Hendrickson and Ezra H. Buddington, together with such other persons as may become members of the incorporation hereby created, shall be and they are hereby constituted and declared to be a body corporate and politic, by the name of the Oakland Female Seminary, and in their corporate name may sue and be sued, may have a common seal which they may renew at pleasure, and shall have, enjoy, and may exercise, all the powers, rights and privileges, which appertain to corporate bodies for the purposes mentioned in this act.

SEC. 2. The capital stock of said corporation shall not exceed the sum of ten thousand dollars, and shall be divided into shares of ten dollars each.

SEC. 3. The corporation hereby created shall be forever capable in law to purchase, take, receive, hold and enjoy any estate real and personal whatever, to an amount not exceeding five thousand dollars, and to lease, sell and convey, or otherwise dispose of the same.

SEC. 4. There shall be forever hereafter, eight trustees of the said corporation, who shall be members thereof, and who shall manage all the affairs thereof; and the first trustees shall be Alfred Williams, Origen D. Richardson, Horace C. Thurber, Willard M. McConnel, Benjamin B. Morris, Hester L. Stevens, Samuel M. Stelle, Jacob Hendrickson and Ezra H. Buddington; who shall hold their offices until the first day of January, eighteen hundred and fifty, and until others are elected in their places.

SEC. 5. There shall be on the first Monday of January, eighteen hundred and fifty, and on the first Monday of January in every succeeding year, a general meeting of the members of said corporation at some convenient place in the village of Pontiac, to be designated by the by-laws of said corporation; and a majority of the members who shall meet in person or by proxy, shall elect by ballot eight of their number to be trustees of the said corporation for the year then next ensuing.

SEC. 6. The trustees of said corporation shall have power to choose from out of their number a president, a treasurer, and a secretary, who shall immediately enter upon the duties of their office, and hold the same from the time of their election, until the first Monday of January of the ensuing year, and until others are chosen in their stead; and in case any of the trustees shall die. resign, refuse or neglect to act, then and in every such case, the remaining may, within thirty days thereafter, elect by ballot, other members of said corporation in their stead, who shall hold their offices in the same manner as those first elected.

Sec. 7. Each member to be entitled to one vote for each share of which he shall be the holder. And the said trustees shall receive subscriptions for shares in said corporation until the capital stock may be subscribed; the said shares shall be assignable and transferable according to such rules as the board of trustees shall from time to time make and establish, and shall be considered personal property.

Sec. 8. In case it should at any time happen that an election of the trustees should not be made on any day when, pursuant to this act, it ought to have been made, the said corporation shall not for that cause, or any non-user, be dissolved; but it shall and may be lawful on any other day, to hold an election for trustees in such manner as shall be provided by the laws and ordinances of said corporation.

Sec. 9. No male teacher shall at any time hereafter forever be employed in the seminary hereby incorporated. The trustees may, by their by-laws, make all necessary rules and regulations for calling special meetings, and for all other purposes, and five trustees shall constitute a quorum for the transaction of business.

Sec. 10. This act shall take effect and be in force from and after its passage, and shall be subject to the provisions of chapter fifty-five of the revised statutes of eighteen hundred and forty-six.

Approved March 30, 1849.

[No. 37.]

AN ACT to incorporate the Tecumseh Literary Institute.

Section 1. *Be it enacted by the Senate and House of Representatives of the State of Michigan,* That Sirrell C. Le Baron, Alonzo B. Palmer, Increase S. Hamilton, Salmon Crane, Stillman Blanchard, Perley Bills and Charles Spafford, and their successors in office, be and they are hereby constituted and declared a body corporate under the name and style of the "Tecumseh Literary Institute," subject to the provisions relating to corporations contained in chapter fifty-five of the revised statutes of 1846, and such amendments thereof as may from time to time be made by the legislature.

Sec. 2. The persons named in the preceding section, and their successors in office, shall have power, and they are hereby authorized to establish and continue in Tecumseh, in the county of Lenawee, an institution of learning for the instruction of persons in the various branches of literature and the arts and sciences; and to establish rules and by-laws for the government and management of the same: *Provided,* Such rules and by-laws are not inconsistent with the constitution and laws of the United States or of this State, and shall faithfully apply all funds or other property received by them for that purpose, by subscription, bequest or otherwise, in providing suitable buildings, employing professors and teachers, procuring books, maps, philosophical and other apparatus necessary or proper for the successful prosecution of study in such institution.

Sec. 3. Said board of trustees shall be in law capable of acquiring and holding by purchase, gift, grant, devise or bequest or otherwise, and of selling, conveying or leasing any estate, real, personal or mixed, in value not exceeding the sum of twenty-five thousand dollars, for the use of said corporation and no other; and shall further hold for the use of said corporation, any estate, real or personal, heretofore conveyed to the members of the said board for that purpose, and shall be held liable for all debts of said corporation, as partners in trade, after the corporate property shall have been exhausted.

Sec. 4. This act shall take effect and be in force from and after its passage.

Approved February 13, 1849.

[No. 149.]

AN ACT to incorporate the Clarkston Academical Institute.

SECTION 1. *Be it enacted by the Senate and House of Representatives of the State of Michigan,* That Nelson Abby, Horatio Foster, Jr., David A. Wright, Amos Orton, William C. Scranton, Arthur Davis, Marcus W. Riker, George P. Thurston, Albert G. Robinson, Joseph Gambell, David McKnight, Arza C. Crosby, Alexander Turbush, Nelson W. Clark, Thomas Johnson, Jacob Walter and Edward Bartlett, together with such other persons as may be associated with them as members of the Clarkston Academical Association, or under this act are hereby created, shall be and they are hereby constituted and declared to be a body corporate and politic by the name of the Clarkston Academical Institute, which shall be located in the village of Clarkston, in the county of Oakland; and in their corporate name may sue and be sued, and may have a common seal which they may alter or renew at pleasure, and shall enjoy and may exercise all the powers rights and privileges which may appertain to corporate bodies for the purpose mentioned in this act; and all obligations and liabilities created or existing to or with said association, are hereby transferred to said incorporation, and may be enforced by said incorporation as fully as by said association.

SEC. 2. The capital stock of said corporation shall not exceed the sum of six thousand dollars, and shall be divided into shares of ten dollars each: *Provided,* That the real estate which said corporation may hold shall only be such as shall be necessary for the object of said corporation.

SEC. 3. The corporation hereby created shall be forever capable in law to purchase, take, receive, hold and enjoy, any estate real and personal whatever, to an amount not exceeding six thousand dollars, and to lease, sell and convey, or otherwise dispose of the same for the benefit of the stockholders.

SEC. 4. There shall be forever hereafter seventeen trustees of said corporation, who shall be members thereof, and who shall manage all the affairs thereof; and the first trustees shall be Nelson W. Clark, president; Thomas Johnson, vice president; Edward Bartlett, secretary; Jacob Walter, treasurer; Nelson Abby, Horatio Foster, Jr., David A. Wright, Amos Orton, William C. Scranton, Arthur Davis, Marcus W. Riker, George P. Thurston, Albert G. Robinson, Joseph Gambell, David McKnight, Azra C. Crosby and Alexander Turbush, who shall hold their offices until the third Wednesday in August, 1850, and until others are elected in their places.

SEC. 5. There shall be, on the third Wednesday in August, 1850, and on the third Wednesday in August in every succeeding year, a general meeting of the members of said corporation at some convenient place in the village of Clarkston, to be designated by the laws of said corporation; and a majority of the members who shall meet in person or by proxy, shall elect by ballot, a president, vice president, treasurer and secretary, and seventeen trustees of the said corporation, who shall constitute a board for the management of its affairs, who shall immediately enter upon the duties of their offices, and who shall hold the same from the time of their election until the third Wednesday in August of the ensuing year, and until others are chosen in their stead; and in case any of the trustees shall resign, die, refuse or neglect to act, then and in every such case the remaining trustees may elect by ballot other members of said corporation in their stead, who shall hold their offices in the same manner as those first elected.

SEC. 6. Each member shall be entitled to one vote for each share of which he shall be holder; and the said trustees shall receive subscriptions for shares in said corporation until the capital stock may be subscribed; and said shares be assignable and transferable according to such rules as the board of trustees shall from time to time make and establish.

SEC. 7. In case it should at any time happen, than [that] an election of trustees should not be made on any day when pursuant to this act it ought to have been made, the said corporation shall not for that cause be dissolved, but it shall and may be lawful on any other day to hold an election for trustees in such manner as shall be provided by the laws and ordinances of said corporation.

SEC. 8. The trustees may by their by-laws make all necessary rules and regulations for calling special meetings, and changing the time of the annual meetings, and for the government and maintainance of said institute, and for no other purpose whatever; and a majority of the trustees shall constitute a quorum for the transaction of business.

SEC. 9. A board of visitors shall be appointed annually by the trustees, whose duty it shall be to attend all examinations, and from time to time make a personal examination into the state of the institute in all its departments, and report the result to the trustees, suggesting such improvements as they may deem important.

SEC. 10. It shall be the duty of the trustees to submit to the Superintendent of Public Instruction an annual report, exhibiting the number of pupils in the institute, and the condition thereof in all its departments, and he may submit the same to the Legislature in his annual report.

SEC. 11. This act shall take effect from and after its passage.

Approved March 25, 1850.

[No. 243.]

AN ACT to incorporate the Clinton Institute.

SECTION 1. *Be it enacted by the Senate and House of Representatives of the State of Michigan*, That from and after the passage of this act, Abner C. Smith, William Jenny, John Stephens, Horace H. Cady, John J. Traver and David Shook, of the county of Macomb, and their successors, be and they are hereby constituted, ordained and declared a body corporate and politic, under the name and style of "The Clinton Institute;" and by that name they and their successors shall and may have perpetual succession, and shall be persons in law capable of suing and being sued, pleading and being impleaded, answering and being answered, defending and being defended in all courts of record whatever, and all manner of suits, actions, complaints, matters and causes whatever; and that they and their successors may have a common seal, and change and alter the same at their pleasure; and that they and their successors, by the name of the "Clinton Institute," shall be in law capable of acquiring and holding, by purchase, gift or otherwise, and of selling, conveying or leasing, real, personal or mixed estate, for the use of said corporation, not exceeding ten thousand dollars; and that they and their successors shall have full power to make and enter into contracts, to make such rules and by-laws as they may deem necessary for the good government and prosperity of said institution: *Provided*, Such by-laws are not inconsistent with the constitution and laws of the United States or of this State.

SEC. 2. Said corporation shall have power to establish at or near the village of Mt. Clemens, in the county of Macomb, an institution for the instruction and education of young persons.

SEC. 3. There shall be six trustees of the said corporaton, who shall be stockholders thereof, and who shall manage and control all the affairs of the same; and the above named persons shall be the first trustees, and shall hold their offices until the first Monday in July, one thousand eight hundred and fifty, and until others are elected in their places; and they or their successors shall have power to fill all vacancies in their own body which may happen by death, resignation or otherwise; to appoint a president, secretary and treasurer, of their own body, and to prescribe such studies and regulations in said institution as to them may seem best.

Sec. 4. There shall be a meeting of the stockholders of said corporation on the first Monday in July, one thousand eight hundred and fifty, and on the first Monday in July in every succeeding year, at some convenient place in the village of Mt. Clemens, to be designated by the by-laws of said corporation; and a majority of the stockholders who shall meet in person or by proxy, shall at their first annual meeting, elect six trustees, who shall immediately be divided by lot into three classes; the first class to hold their offices one year, the second two years, and the third three years; so that thereafter there shall be two trustees elected annually; each trustee so elected to hold his office until his successor shall have been elected.

Sec. 5. The capital stock of said company shall be one thousand dollars, in shares of ten dollars each; and the trustees are hereby authorized to receive subscriptions thereto, at such times and places as they or a majority of them shall designate; said shares to be assignable and transferable agreeably to such by-laws as the trustees may from time to time establish, and shall in law be considered personal property.

Sec. 6. The trustees of said corporation shall be jointly and severally liable for all debts of the said corporation: *Provided,* That no execution shall issue against the individual property of said trustees, until the property of the corporation shall first have been exhausted: *And provided further,* That any trustee resigning, shall not thereby be released from any liability accrued during the period which he was in office, until a responsible successor shall be appointed, and enter upon the discharge of his duties.

Sec. 7. The board of trustees shall cause to be transmitted to the Superintendent of Public Instruction, annually, on or before the tenth day of November, a full statement of the condition of the institute.

Sec. 8. This act may be amended or repealed at any time, by a vote of two-thirds of any future Legislature.

Approved April 1, 1850.

[No. 29.]

AN ACT to incorporate the Young Ladies' Seminary of the City of Monroe.

Section 1. *Be it enacted by the Senate and House of Representatives of the State of Michigan,* That Charles Noble, Dan B. Miller, William H. Boyd, Robert McClelland, S. R. Arnold, George Landon, Wedworth W. Clark, David A. Noble, Thomas G. Cole, Norman R. Hascall, Ira Mayhew, Warner Wing, H. Morgan, H. H. Northrop, C. F. Lewis and Charles G. Johnson, together with such other persons as may become members of the incorporation hereby created, shall be and they are hereby constituted and declared to be a body corporate and politic, by the name of "The Young Ladies' Seminary of the City of Monroe;" and in their corporate name may sue and be sued; may have a common seal, which they may renew at pleasure; and shall have, enjoy, and may exercise all the powers, rights and privileges which appertain to corporate bodies for the purposes mentioned in this act.

Sec. 2. The capital stock of said corporation shall not exceed the sum of ten thousand dollars, and shall be divided into shares of ten dollars each.

Sec. 3. The corporation hereby created shall be capable in law to purchase, take, receive, hold and enjoy any estate, real and personal, whatever, to an amount not exceeding ten thousand dollars, and to lease, sell and convey, or otherwise dispose of the same.

Sec. 4. There shall be sixteen trustees of said corporation, who shall be members thereof, and who shall manage all the affairs thereof; and the first trustees shall be Charles Noble, Dan

B. Miller, William H. Boyd, Robert McClelland, S. R. Arnold, George Landon, Wedworth W. Clark, David A. Noble, Thomas G. Cole, Norman R. Hascall, Ira Mayhew, H. H. Northrop, C. F. Lewis, H. Morgan, Warner Wing and Charles G. Johnson, who shall hold their offices until the third Wednesday in August, eighteen hundred and fifty, and until others are elected in their places.

Sec. 5. There shall be, on the third Wednesday in August, eighteen hundred and fifty, and on the third Wednesday in August in every succeeding year, a general meeting of the members of said corporation, at some convenient place in the city of Monroe, to be designated by the by-laws of said corporation; and a majority of the members who shall meet in person or by proxy, shall elect by ballot, sixteen of their number to be trustees of the said corporation for the year then next ensuing.

Sec. 6. The trustees of said corporation shall have power to choose from out of their number, a president, a treasurer and secretary, who shall immediately enter upon the duties of their offices, and hold the same from the time of their election until the third Wednesday in August of the ensuing year, and until others are chosen in their stead; and in case any of the trustees shall resign, die, refuse or neglect to act, then, and in every such case, the remaining trustees may, within thirty days thereafter, elect by ballot, other members of said corporation in their stead, who shall hold their offices in the same manner as those first elected.

Sec. 7. Each member shall be entitled to one vote for each share of which he shall be the holder. And the said trustees shall receive subscriptions for shares in said corporation, until the capital stock may be subscribed; and said shares be assignable and transferable according to such rules as the board of trustees shall from time to time make and establish, and shall be considered personal property.

Sec. 8. In case it should at any time happen that an election of trustees should not be made on any day, when, pursuant to this act, it ought to have been made, the said corporation shall not for that cause be dissolved, but it shall and may be lawful on any other day to hold an election for trustees in such manner as shall be provided by the laws and ordinances of said corporation.

Sec. 9. The trustees may, by their by-laws, make all necessary rules and regulations for calling special meetings, and changing the time of the annual meetings, and for all other purposes necessary to carry on the true intent and meaning of this act, and not inconsistent with the laws of this State; and a majority of the trustees shall constitute a quorum for the transaction of business.

Sec. 10. A board of visitors, consisting of twelve ladies, shall be appointed annually by the trustees, whose duty it shall be to attend all examinations, and from time to time make a personal examination into the state of the seminary, in all its departments, and report the result to the trustees, suggesting such improvements as they may deem important.

Sec. 11. It shall be the duty of the trustees to submit to the Superintendent of Public Instruction, an annual report, exhibiting the number of pupils in the seminary, and the condition thereof in all its departments; and he may, in his discretion, submit the same to the Legislature in his annual report.

Sec. 12. The said corporation shall incur no debt whatever, except such as may be necessary for the current expenses of each current year: *Provided*, Nothing herein contained shall prohibit said corporation from executing a mortgage or other security for the balance now due for the purchase of property which has been already made for them.

Sec. 13. This act shall take effect and be in force from and after its passage. The Legislature may at any time alter, amend or repeal this act, by a vote of two-thirds of each House.

Approved February 18, 1850.

[No. 112.]

AN ACT to incorporate St. Mark's College at Grand Rapids.

SECTION 1. *Be it enacted by the Senate and House of Representatives of the State of Michigan,* That the Right Reverend Samuel A. McCoskry, Bishop of the Protestant Episcopal Church in the Diocese of Michigan, and his successors in said office, together with Francis H. Cuming, James M. Nelson, George Kendall and Alonzo Platt, of the county of Kent, Charles C. Taylor, of the county of Washtenaw; Charles Reighley, of the county of Genesee; Richard S. Adams, of the county of Lenawee; Algernon S. Hollister, of the county of Livingston; Richard S. Elder, of the county of Hillsdale; Charles C. Trowbridge and Henry P. Baldwin, of the county of Wayne; Daniel T. Grinnell and Ira Backus, of the county of Jackson; Charles E. Stuart, of the county of Kalamazoo; James L. Glen, of the county of Berrien; Hiram Adams and George C. Gibbs, of the county of Calhoun, and their successors, be and are hereby created, ordained and constituted a body politic and corporate, in fact and in name, by the title of St. Mark's College; and by that name they and their successors shall remain in perpetual succession, with full power to sue and be sued, plead and be impleaded; to acquire, hold and convey property, real and personal; to have and to use a common seal; to alter and renew the same at pleasure; to make and alter from time to time such by-laws as they may deem necessary for the government of said institution, its officers and servants; and of doing every other act, matter and thing necessary and proper for the well-being and government of the same, not inconsistent with the constitution and laws of the United States and this State: *Provided,* That nothing in this section shall be construed to authorize said corporation to hold at one time more than one hundred thousand dollars in property, real and personal.

SEC. 2. The said college or institution, as well as the preparatory school attached thereto, shall be located in the township of Grand Rapids, county of Kent, and shall be for the purpose of affording instruction in the liberal arts and sciences to such extent as their means may justify, and also for the study of all or any of the liberal professions; the preparatory department may embrace instruction for both male and female students.

SEC. 3. The board shall, at their first meeting, appoint a secretary and treasurer, together with such other officers and instructors as may be necessary, and shall have power to displace any or either of them; and also to fill vacancies which may happen by death, resignation, removal from the State, or otherwise, in said board, or among said officers, instructors and servants; and also to prescribe and direct the course of study to be pursued in said institution and its departments.

SEC. 4. The Bishop of said Church shall also be a member of said board and president thereof; when he is absent, or if there be a vacancy in said office of Bishop, the board shall elect one of their own number to preside for the time being. The secretary and treasurer shall be elected at each annual meeting of the board.

SEC. 5. The board of trustees shall consist of seventeen members, exclusive of the president, any eight of whom may constitute a quorum for the transaction of business; said board shall hold their first meeting at the call of the president of the same, within two months from the approval of this act, and afterwards they shall meet on their own appointment; special meetings may be called when necessary, by the president, or when required by any five members, each member of the board having been notified, in writing, of such meeting, at least seven days before the time of meeting.

SEC. 6. The treasurer of the college shall always, and all other agents when required, before entering on the duties assigned them, give bonds for the security of the corporation and the public, in such penal sums, and with such sureties, as said board shall approve; and all process against the institution shall be by summons, and the service of the same shall be by leaving an attested copy thereof with the treasurer of the college, at least thirty days before the return thereof.

Sec. 7. The institution hereby incorporated, as well as the preparatory school attached thereto, shall always be subject to the examination of a board of visitors, three in number, to be annually appointed by the Superintendent of Public Instruction, and such visitors shall report to said Superintendent as soon after an examination as practicable.

Sec. 8. The trustees shall have the power to confer the honors and degrees usually granted by collegiate inslitutions upon such persons as may be recommended by the professors of said institution to be worthy thereof: *Provided*, That the primary degrees shall not be conferred on any students, who shall not have passed through a course of studies equivalent to and as thorough as that prescribed by the Regents of the University of Michigan for candidates for degrees.

Sec. 9. Said corporation shall not hold any real estate more than fifteen years after the same shall have been conveyed to it: excepting, always, such real estate as shall be necessary for the objects of said corporation.

Sec. 10. The legislature may at any time alter, amend or repeal this act.

Approved March 20, 1850.

[No. 314.]

AN ACT to incorporate the St. Mary's Academy, at the village of Bertrand in Berrien county.

Section 1. *Be it enacted by the Senate and House of Representatives of the State of Michigan*, That Aglac De la Cheptais, Mathurine Salon, Theresa Dussaulx, Prosperine Chanson, and their associates and succesors in office, be and they are hereby constituted and declared a body corporate and politic by the name and style of the St. Mary's Academy; and by that name they shall have perpetual succession, with full power and authority to elect a president, professors, teachers and other officers and agents, as they may deem proper for the benefit of said academy; to form constitutions and by-laws for the good government of the institute; to contract and be contracted with; to acquire, hold, enjoy and transfer property, real or personal, in their corporate capacity; to make, have and use a common seal, and the same to alter at pleasure; to sue and be sued; to plead and be impleaded in any court of law or equity; to receive or accept of any grant, gift, donation, bequest or conveyance by any person, company or corporation, of any property, real or personal; and to hold and enjoy and dispose of the same as may be deemed by them the best for the interest of the institution; to make, ordain, establish and execute such rules and ordinances, not inconsistent with the constitution of the United States or this State, as they shall think proper for the welfare of said academy, and to do all other acts in pursuance thereof, necessary for the promotion of the arts and sciences and the prosperity of said academy: *Provided*, Said corporation shall not hold any real estate more than five years after they shall have become owners of the same, except such real estate as shall be necessary for the objects of the corporation: *And provided further*, That the amount of real and personal estate which said corporation may hold, shall not at any time exceed fifty thousand dollars: *Provided further*, That no deed or devise of lands made to said corporation by any person or persons during his or her last sickness shall be valid.

Sec. 2. This act is declared to be a public act, and the same shall be construed favorably for every beneficial purpose therein intended. The Legislature may at any time alter, amend or repeal this act. This act shall take effect and be in force from and after its passage.

Approved April 2, 1850.

LITERARY ASSOCIATIONS.

AN ACT to incorporate the members of the Detroit Young Men's Society.

SECTION 1. *Be it enacted by the Senate and House of Representatives of the State of Michigan*, That the members of the Detroit Young Men's Society, and all such persons as shall be associated with them for the purposes hereinafter mentioned, and their successors be and they are hereby ordained, constituted and appointed a body poltic and corporate, in fact and in name, under the name of the "Detroit Young Men's Society," for the purpose of moral and intellectual improvement, and by that name they and their successors may have perpetual succession, and shall be capable of suing and being sued, pleading and being impleaded, answering and being answered unto, defending and being defended in all suits, complaints, matters and causes whatsoever, either in law or equity; of having a common seal, of enacting all by-laws, for the regulation of the officers and members of said society, of acquiring by gift, devise, purchase or otherwise, and of holding and conveying any real, personal or mixed estate whatsoever, necessary and proper for the object of this incorporation: *Provided*, The same shall at no time exceed the sum of twenty-five thousand dollars.

SEC. 2. And for carrying into effect the purposes aforesaid, there shall be a president, vice-president, corresponding and recording secretaries, treasurer, auditor, and seven managers, who together shall constitute a board of directors, and shall, as such, keep a record of their proceedings, be empowered to establish and superintend a library, elect members, and for good cause expel the same, subject to an appeal to the society, fill all vacancies occurring between each annual meeting in their own body—transact all business—direct all the affairs, control and dispose of all funds, estate and effects of said society, and do every other act, matter and thing necessary and proper for the good government of the same, not inconsistent with the by-laws and this act of incorporation, seven of whom shall constitute a quorum for the transaction of business.

SEC. 3. There shall be an annual meeting of the society on the first Monday in July in each year, at which shall be held an election of officers and managers, who shall be elected by a majority of the members present, and shall hold their offices for one year, or until others be chosen in their places: *Provided*, That in case it shall at any time happen that an election of officers and managers shall not be made on the day aforesaid, the said corporation shall not be dissolved; but it shall and may be lawful to hold such election at any time thereafter, pursuant to public notice given in one or more papers printed in the city of Detroit.

SEC. 4. That the lands, tenements and hereditaments, which it shall be lawful for the said corporation to purchase, shall be only such as shall be required for its accommodation in relation to the convenient transaction of its business; and it shall be the duty of the board of directors whenever required by the Legislature to furnish a statement under oath or affirmation, the amount of capital actually paid in, the amount of their real estate, and other property, and containing a true and faithful exhibit of the entire state of said society.

SEC. 5. That of the said Detroit Young Men's Society, John L. Talbott shall be president, John Owen vice president, Franklin Sawyer Jr., corresponding secretary, Henry N. Walker recording secretary, Henry T. Stringham treasurer, Alexander H. Sibley, auditor, and Francis Raymond, Andrew T. McReynolds, Francis Dwight, Asher S. Kellogg, Marshal J. Bacon, Alexander W. Buel and Charles W. Penny, managers—who, together shall constitute the first board of directors of said society; and shall hold their said offices until the first Monday of July, A. D. 1836, or until others shall be chosen in their stead, according to the provisions of this act.

SEC. 6. This act may be altered, amended or repealed by any future Legislature, with the assent of at least two-thirds of the members of each house.

Approved March 26, 1836.

[No. 244.]

AN ACT to incorporate the Union Hall Association of the City of Monroe.

SECTION 1. *Be it enacted by the Senate and House of Representatives of the State of Michigan,* That W. P. Clarke, W. H. Boyd, Samuel Acker, D. B. Miller, P. S. Underhill, Isaac Lewis, B. F. Fifield, J. M. Sterling and Alexander Ragan, and all persons who now are or hereafter may become associated with them, are hereby constituted a body corporate, by the name of "The Union Hall Association of the City of Monroe;" and by that name shall have succession, and be capable of taking and holding by gift or grant, or of purchasing, holding and conveying by sale, lease or otherwise, any estate, real and personal, necessary for the purposes of said corporation: *Provided always,* That the said corporation shall not at any time hold or possess real and personal estate exceeding in value the sum of ten thousand dollars: *Provided also,* That the said sum shall be exclusively employed for the object stated in the second section of this act: *And also provided,* That the said association shall not at any time be empowered to sell or otherwise dispose of their real estate, or any portion thereof, without the consent of two-thirds of all the stockholders, at a meeting called for that purpose, first had and obtained.

SEC. 2. The object of this association shall be to purchase a site and to erect thereon a convenient edifice for the accommodation of all such orders and associations, and all such library and reading rooms, historical and scientific associations, and those for the promotion of arts, and such school, lecture and meeting rooms as to said association shall seem meet and proper: *Provided, however,* That if said edifice shall consist of three or more stories, it shall be lawful for the said association to lease the first and second stories thereof for mercantile or other business purposes: *Provided also,* That no part of said edifice shall at any time be let or used for the sale of ardent spirits, wine, beer, cider, or any other spirituous liquors whatsoever.

SEC. 3. The government of said association, and the management of its property and affairs, shall be vested in such officers, and according to such rules and regulations as the by-laws thereof shall from time to time ordain: *Provided,* That such by-laws shall not conflict with any law of this State, and the constitution of the United States and of this State.

SEC. 4. It shall and may be lawful for the Legislature at any time to demand a statement of the amount of property, real and personal, belonging to the said corporation, and of the debts due to and from said corporation, and the purposes for which disbursements shall have been made; and shall also have the right to authorize one or more persons to inspect such general accounts in the books of said corporation.

SEC. 5. The said corporation shall possess the general powers granted to corporations for the purposes mentioned in this act; and in the name of its corporate title may sue and be sued.

SEC. 6. The stockholders of said association shall be severally liable for all the debts of said association, to an amount equal to the amount of their stock.

SEC. 7. The Legislature may at any time alter or repeal this act.

SEC. 8. This act shall take effect immediately.

Approved April 1, 1850.

[No. 19.]

AN ACT to incorporate the Adrian Lyceum and Benevolent Association.

SECTION 1. *Be it enacted by the Senate and House of Representatives of the State of Michigan,* That Parley J. Spalding, Alfred W. Budlong, Elihue L. Clark, Frederick W. Macy, Jesse Treadwell, John Barber, Ahira G. Eastman, Fernando C. Beaman and Daniel D. Sinclair, and all persons who may hereafter become associated with them, are hereby, under the provisions of this act, created a body corporate by the name of the Adrian Lyceum and Benevolent Association, and by that name shall have succession, and be capable of taking and holding by gift or grant, or of purchasing, holding and conveying by sale, lease or otherwise, any estate, real and personal, necessary for the purpose of said corporation, not at any time exceeding in value the sum of twenty thousand dollars.

SEC. 2. The said association is hereby authorized to purchase a site, and to erect thereon a convenient edifice for the accommodation of a library, reading room and apartments for natural history, science and the arts, school, lecture and meeting rooms, and to provide for the education of orphan children.

SEC. 3. There shall be nine directors of the said corporation, who shall be stockholders thereof, and who shall manage and control all the affairs of the same, maintaining perpetual succession, three of whom shall be elected at the annual meeting in each year, to fill the vacancy of a like number whose term of office shall expire upon the election of their successors; and the persons named in the first section of this act shall be the first directors; and the said nine directors, at their first meeting, shall proceed to cast lots for the terms of one, two and three years, by drawing numbers; and the three persons who shall draw the three highest numbers shall hold their offices for the term of three years, from and after the first day of January, eighteen hundred and forty-six, and the three persons who shall draw the next three highest numbers shall hold their offices for the term of two years from and after the period last aforesaid; and the remaining three persons shall hold their offices for the term of one year from and after the said first day of January, in the year last aforesaid.

SEC. 4. There shall be a meeting of the stockholders of said corporation on the first Monday of January, one thousand eight hundred and forty-seven, and on the first Monday in January in any succeeding year, at some convenient place in the village of Adrian, to be designated by the by-laws of said corporation; and a majority of the stockholders, who shall meet in person or by proxy, shall elect three of the stockholders to be directors in the place of those whose terms may expire, each person being entitled to one vote for each share he may hold in his own right, or represent by proxy.

SEC. 5. The said directors are authorized and required, at their first meeting, to elect from their own number, a president, secretary and treasurer, who shall hold their offices for such terms, report to the board of directors, and be liable to removal under such rules and by-laws as said board shall from time to time adopt.

SEC. 6. The government of said association, and the management of its affairs and property, shall be vested in said board of directors, a majority of whom shall constitute a quorum for the transaction of all business relative to the same, and the directors are authorized to make such rules and by-laws as may from time to time be ordained and adopted by said association: *Provided,* That said rules and by-laws shall not conflict with the laws of this State, or of the constitution of the United States or of this State.

SEC. 7. The said corporation shall possess the general powers granted to corporations, for all the purposes mentioned in this act, and in the name of its corporate title may sue and be sued.

SEC. 8. In the collection of debts against said corporation, if corporate property cannot be found sufficient to satisfy any execution issued against it, the directors shall be jointly liable as partners in trade, for any debt created by them whilst directors of said corporation; and if such debts cannot be collected from the corporate property of said association, or the individual property of said directors, then the stockholders shall be individually liable therefor to the amount of stock by them severally owned.

SEC. 9. It shall and may be lawful for the legislature at any time to demand a statement from the officers of said association, of the amount of property, real and personal, belonging to, and of the debts due to and from said corporation, and the purpose for which disbursements shall have been made, and shall also have the right to authorize one or more persons, under resolution, to examine such general accounts, in the books of said association.

SEC. 10. The legislature may, at any time hereafter, amend, alter or repeal this act.

SEC. 11. This act shall take effect and be in force from and after its passage.

Approved February 19, 1846.

[No. 268.]

AN ACT to incorporate the Almont Young Men's Society.

SECTION 1. *Be it enacted by the Senate and House of Representatives of the State of Michigan,* That the members of the Almont Young Men's Society, and all such persons as shall be associated with them for the purposes hereinafter mentioned, and their successors, be and they are hereby ordained, constituted and appointed a body politic and corporate, in fact and in name, under the name of the Almont Young Men's Society, for the purpose of moral and intellectual improvement; and by that name they and their successors may have perpetual succession, and shall be capable of suing and being sued, pleading and being impleaded, answering and being answered unto, defending and being defended in all suits, complaints, matters and causes whatsoever, either in law or equity; of having a common seal; of enacting all by-laws for the regulation of the officers and members of said society; of acquiring by gift, devise, purchase or otherwise, and of holding and conveying any real, personal or mixed estate whatsoever, necessary and proper for the objects of this incorporation: *Provided,* The same shall at no time exceed five thousand dollars.

SEC. 2. And for carrying into effect the provisions aforesaid, there shall be a president, vice president, secretary, treasurer, auditor, librarian and seven managers, who, together, shall constitute a board of directors; and shall, as such, keep a record of their proceedings, be empowered to establish and superintend a library, elect members, and for good causes expel the same, subject to an appeal to the society, fill all vacancies occurring between each annual meeting in their own body, direct all the affairs, control and dispose of all funds, estates and effects of said society, and do every other act, matter and thing necessary and proper for the good government of the same, not inconsistent with the by-laws and this act of incorporation; seven of whom shall constitute a quorum for the taansaction of all business.

SEC. 3. There shall be an annual meeting of the society on the first Monday in July in each year; at which shall be held an election of officers and managers, who shall be elected by a majority of the members present; and they shall hold their offices for one year, or until others be chosen in their places: *Provided,* That in case it shall at any time happen that an election of officers and managers shall not be made on the day aforesaid, said corporation shall not be dissolved, but it shall and may be lawful to hold such election at any time thereafter: *Provided,* There be a public notice given three weeks prior to the time said election is to be held.

SEC. 4. That the lands, tenements, &c., which it shall be lawful for said corporation to purchase, shall be only such as shall be required for its accommodation in relation to the convenient transaction of its business; and all moneys belonging to said corporation, whether derived from dues, fees, gifts or otherwise, shall be expended for the purchase of such books as the society shall direct: *Provided*, Such money or a portion thereof shall not be required to defray the necessary expenses of said corporation.

SEC. 5. That of the said Almont Young Men's Society, Virgil Parmalee shall be president, N. H. Readman, vice president, Gavin E. Calkin, secretary, Hiram C. Welles, treasurer, George W. Culliver, librarian, and James Taggart, auditor; S. D. McKeen, O. P. Strowbridge, James S. Johnson, Henry Osborne, W. A. Hitchcock, Amaziah Roberts and John Parmalee, managers; who, together, shall constitute the first board of directors of said society, and shall hold their said offices until the first Monday in Juty, A. D. 1850, or until others be chosen in their stead, according to the provisions of this act.

SEC. 6. This act may be altered, amended or repealed by any future Legislature, with the assent of at least a majority of the members of each house. The directors of said society shall be jointly and severally liable for all debts contracted while they are in office, but no execution shall issue against the individual property of the trustees, until the property of the society shall have been first exhausted.

SEC. 7. This act shall take effect and be in force from and after its passage.

Approved April 2, 1850.

[No. 306.]

AN ACT to incorporate the Lawrence Literary Institute Association.

SECTION 1. *Be it enacted by the Senate and House of Representatives of the State of Michigan*, That from and after the passage of this act, John Andrews, John L. Marvin, Horatio N. Phelps, Tobias Miles, Henry W. Hurlbut, Jonathan N. Hinckley, Nelson S. Marshall, Humphrey P. Barnum and Philotus Hayden, of the county of Van Buren, and their successors, be and they are hereby constituted and ordained and declared a body corporate, under the name and style of "The Lawrence Literary Institute Association;" and by that name they and their successors shall have perpetual succession, and shall constitute a body corporate, in law capable of suing and being sued, pleading and being impleaded, answering and being answered, defending and being defended, in all courts of record whatever, and in all manner of suits, actions, complaints, matters and causes whatever; and they, as a body corporate, may have a common seal, and may change or alter the same at their pleasure; and the said body corporate, under the name, style and title of the Lawrence Literary Institute Association, shall be capable in law of acquiring and holding by purchase or gift, or otherwise, and of selling, conveying or leasing any estate, real, personal or mixed, for the use of said corporation, not exceeding in amount ten thousand dollars: *Provided*, Said corporation shall hold no real estate more than fifteen years, after the same shall have been conveyed to them, except such real estate as shall be necessary for the objects of said corporation. And the said body corporate shall have full power to make and to enter into contracts; to make such rules and by-laws as they may deem necessary for the good government and management of the affairs of said incorporation: *Provided*, Such by-laws contain no reqnirements, prohibitions or penalties inconsistent with the laws and constitution of the State of Michigan.

SEC. 2. The management and control of the affairs of said corporation shall be vested in a board of nine trustees, who shall elect from their number a president, secretary and treasurer. Said trustees shall be elected annually from among the stockholders, on the third Tuesday of June, by a majority of the stockholders present and voting; and the above named persons mentioned in this act of incorporation shall be the first trustees, who shall hold their offices until the third Tuesday in June, eighteen hundred and fifty-one, or until such time as others are elected in their stead; and said board may have power to fill all vacancies that may occur in their own body, either by death, removal or resignation.

SEC. 3. Said corporation shall have the power to establish in the village of Lawrence, in the county of Van Buren, an institution for the instruction of young persons in the ordinary and higher departments of learning.

SEC. 4. The capital stock of said corporation shall be limited to ten thousand dollars, in shares of ten dollars each; and the trustees are hereby authorized to receive subscriptions thereto, at such times and places as they or a majority of them shall designate. Said shares to be assignable and transferable agreeably to such by-laws as the trustees may enact, and shall in law be considered personal property.

SEC. 5. The board of trustees shall cause to be transmitted to the Superintendent of Public Instruction, annually, on or before the tenth day of November, a full statement of the condition of the institute.

SEC. 6. The trustees of said association shall be jointly and severally liable for all debts contracted while they were in office, but no execution shall issue against the individual property of all the trustees until the property of the association shall first have been exhausted.

SEC. 7. The Legislature may at any time alter, amend or repeal this act.

Approved April 2, 1850.

[No. 308.]

AN ACT to incorporate the Niles Union Hall Association.

SECTION 1. *Be it enacted by the Senate and House of Representatives of the State of Michigan,* That Robert Wilson, James Brown, Harvey Palmer, Benjamin F. Fish and Alfred L. Dennison, and all persons who now are, or may become associated with them, are hereby constituted a body corporate and politic, by the name and style of "The Niles Union Hall Association;" and by that name shall have succession, and be capable of taking and holding by gift or grant, or purchasing, holding and conveying by sale, lease or otherwise, any estate, real and personal, necessary for the purposes of said corporation: *Provided,* Said corporation shall only hold such real estate as shall be necessary for the objects of said corporation: *Provided also,* The amount of real and personal estate which said corporation may hold, shall not at any time exceed the sum of ten thousand dollars.

SEC. 2. The object of this association shall be to purchase a site and erect thereon a convenient edifice for the accommodation of public and private assemblies, and for lecture and reading rooms.

SEC. 3. The government of said association, and the management of its affairs and property, shall be vested in such officers, and according to such rules and regulations as the by-laws thereof shall from time to time ordain: *Provided,* That such by-laws shall not conflict with any laws of this State, and the constitution of the United States or of this State.

SEC. 4. The Legislature may at any time demand a statement of the amount of property, real and personal, belonging to said corporation, and of the debts due to and from said corporation, and the purposes for which disbursements shall have been made; and shall also have the right to authorize one or more persons to inspect such general accounts in the books of said corporation.

SEC. 5. The said corporation shall possess the general powers usually granted to corporations for the purposes mentioned in this act, and in the name of its corporate title may sue and be sued.

Sec. 6. The corporators mentioned in this act, shall be jointly and severally liable for the payment of any debts contracted by such corporation: *Provided,* The third subdivision of section four of an act to provide for the assessment and collection of taxes, approved March eighth, eighteen hundred and forty-three, shall not apply to this corporation.

Sec. 7. The Legislature may at any time amend or repeal this act.

Sec. 8. This act shall take effect immediately.

Approved April 2, 1850.

[No. 34.]

Preamble and Joint Resolutions relative to Mons. Vattemare's system of International Literary Exchanges.

Whereas, Mons. Alexander Vattemare, a citizen of France, has, with an unexampled zeal, devoted his time, his energies and his fortune, to the philanthropic effort of establishing an intellectual confederacy among the nations of the earth;

And whereas, His system of international literary exchanges is not only promotive of science and the improvement of literature and the arts, but is also conducive to the fraternization of governments and the diffusion of civilization through the globe;

And whereas, The project has been approved by the Chambers and Ministers of France, by the Congress of the United States, and the Legislatures of several of the States, and by the statesmen and literati of both nations; be it therefore

Resolved by the Senate and House of Representatives of the State of Michigan, That in grateful acknowledgment of his disinterested labors in the cause of humanity and civilization, and for the valuable works presented by him to the State, the thanks of the people of Michigan are respectfully tendered to Mons. Alexander Vattemare, by the Representatives of the people in Legislature convened;

Resolved, That His Excellency, the Governor, be and he is hereby authorized and requested to receive the parcel of books transmitted by Mons. Vattemare, through Lewis Cass, Jr., Esq., to the State of Michigan, and also the parcel consigned to E. Thayer & Co., forwarding merchants, in the city of New York, and to place the same in the State library.

Resolved, That His Excellency be, and he hereby is further authorized and requested to transmit to Mons. Vattemare, a copy of the revised statutes and session laws of the State of Michigan, together with the journals and documents of both Houses of the Legislature, and such maps of the several counties as are now completed.

Resolved, That the State Geologist be and he hereby is authorized and requested to examine and report to the next Legislature what duplicate specimens of the natural history of Michigan are in his department of the University.

Resolved, That our Senators in Congress be instructed, and our Representativds be requested to use their best efforts to obtain the appointment of Mons. Alexander Vattemare as an agent of the general government, to act in behalf of this State, with power to conduct literary exchanges between France and the United States.

Resolved, That His Excellency be and he is hereby requested to transmit a copy of these resolutions, and the report of the committee on education, to Mons. Vattemare, and to each of our Senators and Representative in Congress.

Approved March 12, 1844.

[No. 107.]

AN ACT to provide for the support of a system of International Exchange.

SECTION 1. *Be it enacted by the Senate and House of Representatives of the State of Michigan,* That the governor of this State be, and he is hereby authorized to appoint some suitable person residing in the city of Paris, in France, to be the agent of this State in transmitting to, and receiving from this State, all such works and objects as are intended as the subjects of international exchange.

SEC. 2. The sum of two hundred dollars, annually, is hereby appropriated to defray the expenses of the said agency in the city of Paris, in receiving from and transmitting to this State such works as may be made the subject of international exchange.

SEC. 3. When the Secretary of State shall have been officially informed that the agency provided for in the first section of this act has been duly established, he shall, upon his order, annually draw from the treasury and transmit to said agent the said sum of two hundred dollars, provided for in the second section of this act, and the said agent shall report annually to the Governor of this State, all his transactions relative to said agency.

SEC. 4. This act shall take effect and be in force from and after its passage.

Approved March 19, 1849.

EDUCATION OF THE DEAF AND DUMB, &c.

[No. 187.]

AN ACT to establish an Asylum for the Deaf and Dumb and the Blind and also an Asylum for the Insane of the State of Michigan.

SECTION 1. *Be it enacted by the Senate and House of Representatives of the State of Michigan,* That there shall be established in this State institutions under the title and style of the "Michigan Asylum for the Educating the Deaf and Dumb and the Blind," and "Michigan Asylum for the Insane," and that eight sections of the State salt spring lands be and is hereby appropriated for the erection of suitable buildings therefor.

SEC. 2. The government of said asylums shall be vested in a board of trustees to consist of five members, who shall be elected annually by the legislature of this State in joint convention: *Provided*, The Governor shall have the authority to appoint the first trustees under this act.

SEC. 2. The trustees authorized pursuant to the foregoing section, shall constitute a body corporate with the name and title of the "Trustees of the Michigan Asylums," with the right as such of suing and being sued, of making and using a common seal, and altering the same at pleasure.

SEC. 4. It shall be the duty of the above named trustees to meet at such time and place as the Governor shall appoint, and elect of their own body, a treasurer and clerk, who shall hold their offices one year and until their successors are chosen and qualified.

SEC. 5. Said trustees shall meet once in every three months, on their own adjournments, or oftener if they deem it advisable; have power to pass such by-laws and adopt such rules and regulations for the management and control of the institution as they may deem just and right.

Sec. 6. The trustees shall have power, and it shall be their duty to enact laws for the government of said asylums, and also to appoint a principal for each institution, whose respective salaries shall not exceed eight hundred dollars per annum, and who shall nominate for the action of the board of trustees all necessary subordinate officers, who may be dismissed by said respective principals for inefficiency or misconduct; but in case of every removal a detailed statement of the causes shall be reported to the board of trustees by the principal making the removal.

Sec. 7. The trustees shall be the judges of the ability of the candidate of this State for admission, to defray his or her expenses, and shall require the parent or guardians in all cases to pay the necessary expenses where they possess the ability, otherwise the same to be defrayed out of the asylum funds. They shall likewise admit into either institution candidates from any other State: *Provided*, The necessary expenses be defrayed by the parents or guardians of such persons.

Sec. 8. The board of trustees shall make out annually and report to the legislature, a detailed statement of the operations of said institution.

Sec. 9. The expenses necessarily incurred by such trustees in the discharge of their duties shall be reimbursed to them to be paid as the other expenses of the institution.

Sec. 10. Said board, when organized, is hereby authorized to receive proposals for donations of lands, money or other materials for the location and building of such asylums, and upon receiving a title of any lands, or the delivery of any money, materials, bonds or other security for such purpose, to and in behalf of the State for the benefit of such asylums.

Sec. 11. The board of trustees shall appoint one of their number as acting commissioner, whose duty it shall be to make immediate selection of the lands hereby appropriated, and file a notice of such selection with the Commissioner of the State Land Office, which lands shall thereupon be under the exclusive control of the board of trustees, who shall have power to order the sale of such portions, from time to time, under the supervision of the Commissioner of the State Land Office, as they may deem proper, and for the best interests of the State.

Sec. 12. The acting commissioner shall also have the superintendence of the erection of the necessary buildings, under the direction of the board of trustees, whose salary shall not exceed eight hundred dollars per annum, and which shall be in full for all his services, except the necsssary traveling fees.

Sec. 13. The proceeds of the lands and all other moneys shall be paid to the treasurer authorized by this act, who may be required to give bonds with sureties to be approved by the board, and filed with the Auditer General of the State; and all necessary expenses incurred in carrying out the provisions of this act shall be paid therefrom on a warrant drawn by the clerk and approved by the chairman or president of the board.

Sec. 14. This act shall take effect and be in force from and after its passage.

Approved April 3, 1848.

[No. 133.]

AN ACT to amend an act entitled "an act to establish an Asylum for the Deaf and Dumb and Blind, and also an Asylum for the Insane of the State of Michigan."

Section 1. *Be it enacted by the Senate and House of Representatives of the State of Michigan*, That section eleven of an act entitled "an act to establish an asylum for the deaf and dumb and blind, and also an asylum for the insane of the State of Michigan," be so amended as to read as follows: "It shall be the duty of the Commissioner of the State Land Office, to make immediate selections of the lands appropriated by this act, and keep on file, in his office, a list of the same; which lands shall thereupon be under the control of the board of trustees, who shall have power to order the sale of the same or portions of the same, from time to time, under the supervision of the Commissioner of the State Land Office, as they may deem proper and for the best interests of the State; and the proceeds of the same, when paid into the State Treasury, shall be passed to the credit of a fund called the 'asylum fund.'"

SEC. 2. That section twelve of said act be so amended as to read: "the board of trustees shall appoint one of their number as acting commissioner, whose duty it shall be to take charge of, direct and superintend the erection of the necessary buildings, under the direction of the board of trustees, whenever the proceeds of said lands, paid in the State treasury, shall be deemed sufficient by the governor and trustees for the erection of a suitable building for an asylum of the insane, shall be realized, or means derived for that purpose from other sources, by donation, bequest, or otherwise; and said board of trustees are hereby required to report annually to the governor of the State, on or before the first day of December, a full statement of their action in the premises, and a correct statement of the receipts and expenditures of the asylum fund, verified by the oath or affirmation of the commissioner of the board."

SEC. 3. That section one be so amended that the word "eight," in the fifth line, be stricken out, and the word "fifteen" be inserted.

SEC. 4. This act shall take effect and be in force from and after its passage.

Approved March 26, 1849.

[No. 282.]

AN ACT to amend an act entitled an act to establish an Asylum for the deaf and dumb and blind, and also an asylum for the insane of the State of Michigan, and the act amendatory thereto.

SECTION 1. *Be it enacted by the Senate and House of Representatives of the State of Michigan,* That ten additional sections of salt spring lands, or as much thereof as are unappropriated, not to exceed ten sections, be and the same are hereby appropriated for the erection of suitable buildings, and for the support and maintenance of the "Michigan Asylum for the educating of the Deaf and Dumb and the Blind," and "Michigan Asylum for the Insane."

SEC. 2. It shall be the duty of the president of the board of trustees of the Michigan Asylums, to make immediate selections of the additional salt spring lands appropriated by this act, and file a list of the same in the State Land Office; and the said lands shall thereupon be under the control of the board of trustees, and be disposed of in the manner provided in section one of act number one hundred and thirty-three of the session laws of 1849.

SEC. 3. The terms of office of the trustees of the Michigan Asylums, elected or to be elected in the year eighteen hundred and fifty, shall be as follows: two of them shall hold their office for one year, and three of them for two years; and it shall be their duty at the first meeting of the board after the passage of this act, to decide by lot, the terms of office of the members respectively, and file a list of the same in the office of the Secretary of State: *Provided,* That after the expiration of the terms of office of those holding but one year, their successors shall hold their offices for the term of two years.

SEC. 4. That the sum of five thousand dollars be and the same is hereby appropriated out of the general fund, and the same shall be passed to the credit of the asylum fund, on the books of the State Treasurer, to be used by the board of trustees of the Michigan asylums, from time to time, as it shall become necessary in the construction of asylums for the insane, the deaf and dumb, for the blind, and for other necessary expenses, and shall be drawn therefrom on warrants drawn by the clerk and approved by the president of the board: *Provided,*

That no more than one thousand dollars of the above sum shall be so drawn within one year from the passage of this act, nor a sum exceeding three thousand dollars the year following, or in any one year thereafter.

SEC. 5. The proceeds of all the lands selected for the benefit of the asylum fund shall be paid into the State Treasury, and five thousand dollars of the first proceeds shall be passed to the credit of the general fund to reimburse to the State the amount appropriated by this act.

SEC. 6. So much of any act or acts as controvene the provisions of this act are hereby repealed.

SEC. 7. This act shall take effect and be in force from and after its passage.

Approved April 2, 1850.

ACTS RELATING TO SCHOOL AND OTHER LANDS.

CHAPTER 59, REVISED STATUTES OF 1846.

OF THE STATE LAND OFFICE, AND THE OFFICERS CONNECTED THEREWITH.

SECTION 1. The State Land Office established in the village of Marshall in the county of Calhoun, shall be continued at the place aforesaid, until otherwise provided by law. [By act No. 217, Session Laws of 1849, the State Land Office is now established at Lansing.]

SEC. 2. The chief officer of the Land Office, shall be called the Commissioner of the Land Office, and shall be appointed by the governor, by and with the advice and consent of the Senate, and shall hold his office for the term of two years, and until his successor shall be appointed and qualified. [The revised Constitution makes the office of Commissioner elective by the people.]

SEC. 3. The Commissioner of the State Land Office shall receive a salary of one thousand dollars, payable quarter yearly. [Fixed at $800 by the revised Constitution.]

SEC. 4. Before entering upon the duties of his office, he shall take the oath prescribed by the twelfth article of the constitution of this State, and cause the same to be filed with the Secretary of State, and shall also execute to the people of this State, a bond in the penal sum of fifty thousand dollars, with two sufficient sureties, to be approved by the Auditor General and State Treasurer, and deposit the same with the Secretary of State.

SEC. 5. The condition of said bond shall be, that the said commissioner shall faithfully discharge the duties of his said office, and that he will honestly and truly account for and pay over all moneys and evidences of debt that may come into his hands by virtue of his office, or into the hands of his deputy or clerk, according to law.

SEC. 6. The said commissioner shall appoint a deputy, and may also appoint one clerk, if the business of his office shall require it, each of whom shall receive a salary not exceeding five hundred dollars, payable quarter yearly. [Amended.]

SEC. 7. Said deputy and clerks shall severally, before entering upon the duties of their office, take and subscribe the constitutional oath of office, and cause the same to be filed with the Secretary of State, and the commissioner may remove them or either of them at his pleasure; and the said commissioner and his sureties shall be responsible for their official acts.

SEC. 8. The commissioner shall keep a record of the sales of lands and of the moneys received by him on account either of principal or interest, the date of such sale or payment, the description of the lands sold, with the number of acres thereof, and the name of each purchaser, or person paying such moneys, to whom he shall give a receipt for such moneys, and shall credit the proper fund therewith.

SEC. 9. He shall, on or before the first Monday of each and every month, cause to be made out and transmitted to the State Treasurer, a statement showing the amount of money, or evidences of debt received by him, the name of the persons paying the same, the time of payment, the number of the certificate upon which such moneys were paid, the kind of funds received, and the proper fund to be credited therewith.

SEC. 10. He shall also, on the first Mondays of March, June, September and December in each year, and at any other time when required by the State Treasurer, deliver and pay over to said treasurer all moneys and evidences of debt received by him as aforesaid.

SEC. 11. The said commissioner shall have the general charge and supervision of all lands belonging to the State, or which may hereafter become its property, and also of all lands in which the State has an interest, or which are or may be held in trust by the State for any purpose mentioned in this title, and may superintend, lease, sell, and dispose of the same in such manner as shall be directed by law.

SEC. 12. He shall annually make a report to the legislature, of his official proceedings, showing the quantity of land sold or leased, and the amount received therefor; the amount of interest moneys received to the credit of the several funds, and all such other matters relating to his office as he may think proper to communicate.

[The following five sections have been amended by subsequent acts; but they are not important for the purposes of this document.]

SEC. 13. There shall also be appointed by the governor, an officer who shall be called the Recorder of the Land Office, who shall hold his office for the term of two years, and until his successor shall be appointed and qualified, and shall keep his office in the said land office *aforesaid*, and receive an annual salary of four hundred dollars a year, payable quarter yearly.

SEC. 14. The said recorder may appoint a deputy, but without additional expense to the State, for whose official acts he shall be responsible; both of whom shall severally, before entering upon the duties of their office, take and subscribe the constitutional oath of office, and cause the same to be filed with the Secretary of State.

SEC. 15. It shall be the duty of the recorder or his deputy, to countersign every certificate of purchase, receipt or other official instrument in writing, which may be issued or given by the said commissioner, and which purports to be evidence of moneys received by him; and unless such certificate, receipt or official instrument be so countersigned, it shall not be evidence of payment, nor valid in law.

SEC. 16. The said recorder, upon countersigning any certificate, receipt or other instrument as aforesaid, shall charge the commissioner with the amount received by him as therein mentioned, and credit the proper fund therewith, and shall also keep a record of the names of the persons paying the same, the number of the certificate upon which the amount shall be paid, and the time of payment.

SEC. 17. The recorder shall also, after comparing the accounts kept by him with those kept by the commissioner, on the first Monday of each and every month, transmit to the State Treasurer a statement of all the several certificates, receipts and other official instruments, which have been issued or given by the commissioner, and countersigned as aforesaid, together with the dates, numbers and amounts thereof, the names of the several persons paying such sums, and the several funds to which they respectively belong.

CHAPTER 60.

OF THE SUPERINTENDENCE AND DISPOSITION OF THE PUBLIC LANDS.

University and School Lands.

SECTION 1. The minimum price of the unsold and unimproved University lands, shall be twelve dollars per acre, and the minimum price of the unsold and unimproved school lands shall be four dollars per acre; but no such lands shall be otherwise sold until they shall once have been offered for sale at public auction, and no such lands shall be sold for less than the aforesaid prices respectively, nor shall any treasury notes or warrants be received for University lands hereafter forfeited to the State.

SEC. 2. The terms of payment on the sale of University and school lands, shall be twenty-five per centum of the purchase money to be paid at the time of the purchase, the balance of the principal at any time thereafter, at the option of the purchaser, with interest at the rate of seven per cent. per annum on the unpaid balance, payable on the first day of January, or within sixty days thereafter, in each and every year, at such place or places as shall be specified in the certificate of purchase. [Amended—page 39, laws of 1847.*]

SEC. 3. At the time of the sale of any such lands, the Commissioner shall make out and deliver to the purchaser or purchasers thereof a certificate, in which the said Commissioner shall, in the name of the people of this State, certify the description of land sold, the quantity thereof, and the price per acre, the consideration paid and to be paid therefor, and the time and terms of payment.

SEC. 4. The said certificate shall further set forth, that in case of the non-payment of the interest due by the first day of January, or within sixty days thereafter, in each and every year, by the purchaser or purchasers, or by any person claiming under him or them, then the said certificate shall, from the time of such failure, be utterly void and of no effect, and the said Commissioner may take possession thereof and re-sell the same as is hereinafter provided. [Amended—page 39, laws of 1847.]

SEC. 5. Any purchaser of University or school lands, his heirs or assigns, who shall have paid, on or before the first day of March, in the year one thousand eight hundred and forty-two, a sum equal to twenty per cent. of the purchase money on his certificate, together with the interest up to said day; and any person who shall have become such purchaser since the thirteenth day of April, in the year one thousand eight hundred and forty-one, his heirs or assigns, who shall have paid according to the terms of his certificate, shall be privileged to pay the balance of principal due on his purchase at any time hereafter at his option; but in all cases the interest on the unpaid balance of principal shall be paid on the first day of January, or within sixty days thereafter, in each and every year. [Amended—page 39, laws of 1847. See also act No. 52, laws of 1851, page 84.]

SEC. 6. In case of non-payment, either of principal or interest, when due, according to the provisions of the preceding section, or according to the terms of the certificate of sale, as the case may be, such certificate shall become void and of no effect from the time of such failure, and the Commissioner may take immediate possession thereof and re-sell the same.

SEC. 7. The Commissioner shall, whenever in his opinion the interest of the State will not be secured by the payment in this chapter required to be made at the time of the purchase, require of the purchaser such security for the payment of any moneys to become due and payable according to the terms of the certificate of purchase, as in his judgment will secure the respective funds against loss.

SEC. 8. The Governor of the State shall sign and cause to be issued patents for said lands as described in the certificates of sale, whenever the same shall be presented to him with the further certificate of the Commissioner endorsed thereon, that the whole amount of principal and interest specified therein has been paid according to law, and that the holder of the certificate of purchase is entitled to a patent for the lands described therein. [Amended—page 85, laws 1851.]

SEC. 9. The fee of each and every parcel of the said lands shall be and remain in the State until patents shall issue for the same respectively, upon full payment as aforesaid; and in case of a non-compliance by the purchaser, his heirs or assigns, with the terms of the certificate as aforesaid, or with the provisions of law applicable thereto, any and all persons being or

---

* The several acts amendatory of the statutes relative to the care and disposition of school and other educational lands, will be found in this document immediately following this chapter.

continuing in possession of any such lands after a failure to comply with the terms of the certificate as aforesaid, or with such provisions of law as aforesaid, without a written permission of the Commissioner of the Land Office, shall be deemed and held to detain such lands forcibly, and without right, and to be trespassers thereon.

Sec. 10. In all cases where security has been taken from the purchaser, pursuant to the provisions of the seventh section of this chapter, the commissioner shall have power to sue for and recover all such sums as may become due and payable, for which such security was given.

Sec. 11. All the improved portions of the university and school lands remaining unsold, shall be subject to sale at the respective prices at which they were severally offered at the last annual public sales, until the improvement on the same shall have been appraised as provided in this chapter.

Sec. 12. Whenever either the university or school fund will, in the opinion of the commissioner, be improved by laying off any section or tract of university or school lands, into small parcels, or village lots, the said commissioner may cause the same to be done, and may sell the same at the respective minimum prices established in this chapter; or if in his opinion any of such parcels or lots exceed in value such prices, he shall cause the same to be appraised by three disinterested freeholders of the county in which such parcels or lots are situated.

Sec. 13. Such freeholders shall be appointed by the commissioner, and after being first duly sworn so to do, shall appraise the several parcels or lots directed by said commissioner to be appraised by them, at their true value respectively, and shall make a return of such appraisement, duly certified by them, to the commissioner.

Sec. 14. All parcels or lots so appraised, shall be subject to sale in the same manner, and upon the same terms and conditions, and the certificates of purchase shall have the same effect as in the case of other university or school lands, according to the provisions of this chapter, at the prices at which the same were severally appraised, until a new appraisal shall be made, which the commissioner may, in his discretion, cause to be had in the manner aforesaid, and with the like effect; but no lots or parcels so appraised shall be sold for less than the minimum price of said lands established in this chapter.

Sec. 15. The said commissioner may also, in his discretion, reserve and withhold from sale, such portions of the university and school lands as in his opinion it may not be advantageous to sell and dispose of, and for so long a time as in his opinion will be most beneficial to the several funds affected thereby.

Sec. 16. All university and school lands which have been, or may be forfeited by the non-payment of either principal or interest, and which have not been offered at public auction after forfeiture, before the same shall be subject to private entry, shall be re-offered for sale at public auction, and the minimum price of all portions or tracts upon which improvements shall have been made, shall be such as shall be determined by the commissioner in the manner hereinafter in this chapter provided.

Sec. 17. The sale of such forfeited lands shall be held at such times and places as shall be designated in a notice containing a description of the lands so forfeited, which notice shall be published once in each week at least four weeks successively before the time of sale, in a newspaper printed in the county where the lands are situated, if there be one; if not, then in a newspaper printed in an adjoining county, if there be one; and if there be none printed in an adjoining county, then in such newspaper as the commissioner shall designate.

Sec. 18. Certificates of purchase issued pursuant to the provisions of law, shall entitle the purchaser to the possesion of the lands therein described, and shall be sufficient evidence of title to enable the purchaser, his heirs or assigns, to maintain actions of trespass for injuries done to the same, or ejectment, or any other proper action or proceeding to recover possession thereof, unless such certificate shall have become void by forfeiture; and all certificates of purchase in force, may be recorded in the same manner that deeds of conveyance are authorized to be recorded.

SEC. 19. Any purchaser of university or school lands, may pay to the State Treasurer the amount due on his certificate of purchase, whether principal or interest, and for the amount paid the Treasurer shall give his receipt, which shall be countersigned by the Auditor General; and a statement of all such payments shall be transmitted by said Treasurer to the Commissioner of the Land Office on or before the first Monday of each month.

SEC. 20. In all cases where the rights of a purchaser shall have become forfeited under the provisions of this chapter, by his failure to pay the amonnt due upon his certificate of purchase, if such purchaser, his heirs or assigns shall, before the time appointed for the sale of the lands described in such certificate, at public auction, pay to the Commissioner of the Land Office, the full amount then due and payable upon such certificate, and twenty-five cents on each dollar of such amount in addition thereto, such payment shall operate as a redemption of the rights of such purchaser, his heirs or assigns; and said certificate, from the time of such payment, shall be in full force and effect, as if no such forfeiture had occurred.

SEC. 21. On or before the first day of June in each year, the Commissioner of the Land Office shall prepare and transmit to the clerks of the several counties in which the same are situated, lists of all the forfeited lands in the several townships therein, and of all the unsold university, school, and State building lands which he may have cause to believe are improved, together with proper forms of returns and certificates of appraisement, to be forthwith distributed by such clerks respectively to the several supervisors of townships to whom the same may be directed.

SEC. 22. Every supervisor of a township, upon receiving the lists and forms as aforesaid, shall proceed to estimate and appraise the value of all the improvements upon the several tracts or parcels of land mentioned in such lists, and after making such appraisement according to the forms prescribed by said commissioner, he shall make returns thereof duly certified by him to the commissioner, on or before the first day of August in the same year: *Provided,* That the provisions of this section shall not apply to any settler mentioned in or contemplated by the "act to provide for the sale of certain lands to the settlers thereon, and for other purposes," approved March twenty-fifth, one thousand eight hundred and forty, and the several acts amendatory thereof, whose lands have been forfeited to this State, or who has not become a purchaser of the lands on which he resides, and on which his settlement is made; nor shall it apply to any person who has made, or who hereafter may make improvements on any of the university, school or State building lands, and who shall hereafter become a purchaser of the same; but such settler or other person shall be entitled to enter the same upon the terms herein established for the sale of unimproved university lands, irrespective of the value of said improvements, and he shall not be chargeable for the value of said improvements so made by or assigned to him.

SEC. 23. On the return of such appraisement, the amount of the appraised value of improvements on each tract or parcel shall be divided by the number of acres contained therein; and the result, together with the minimum price per acre of unimproved lands of the same description as established in this chapter, shall be the specific minimum price per acre of such tract or parcel, the improvements upon which shall have been so appraised, until the same shall be changed by a subsequent appraisal.

SEC. 24. The unimproved forfeited lands shall continue at the minimum price per acre of unsold and unimproved lands, as established in this chapter.

SEC. 25. The Commissioner of the Land Office may, from time to time lease, for terms not exceeding one year, and until the same are disposed of according to law, all such university and school lands, and other lands belonging to the State, as shall have improvements on them; and such leases shall contain proper covenants to guard against trespasses and waste.

SEC. 26. The university lands of this State, lying near Toledo, in the State of Ohio, shall be excepted from the provisions of this chapter. [Amended—session laws of 1847, page 39.]

SEC. 27. Whenever it shall appear to the commissioner necessary, in order to ascertain the true boundaries of any tract or portion of the lands mentioned in this chapter, or to enable him to describe and dispose of the same, in suitable and convenient lots, he may cause all such necessary surveys to be made; and the expenses thereof shall be paid out of the proper fund, in the same manner as the other incidental expenses of the land office.

State Salt Spring Lands.

[These lands are now "Normal School." See act 139, session laws of 1850, page 123; see also, act 130, session laws of 1850, page 180.]

SEC. 30. The minimum price of the lands selected for this State as salt spring lands, and which shall not have been improved, shall be four dollars per acre; and the minimum price of the improved salt spring lands shall be such as may be determined by the commissioner in the manner provided in this chapter for determining the minimum price of improved university and school lands, but none of said lands shall be sold for less than four dollars per acre.

SEC. 31. The terms and conditions, and manner of sales of said lands, and of payment, both of principal and interest therefor, shall be the same in all respects as are prescribed in this chapter for the sale of university and school lands and payment therefor, and the Commissioner of the Land Office shall issue certificates of purchase upon the sale thereof, in the same form, and with the like effect, as upon the sale of university or school lands.

SEC. 32. None of the said salt spring lands shall be subject to private entry until they shall have been first advertised and offered for sale at public auction in the manner prescribed in this chapter for advertising and selling forfeited university and school lands.

SEC. 33. Such of the said lands as have been improved by the State, by boring thereon for salt springs, and such other of said lands as in the opinion of the Governor, State Geologist and commissioner, should not be sold, shall be withheld from sale until otherwise provided by law.

SEC. 34. Whenever, in the opinion of the commissioner, the interests of the State will be promoted by laying off any section or tract of said lands into small parcels or village lots, he shall cause the same to be done, and such lots or parcels to be appraised in the manner provided in this chapter, for appraising university and school lands laid off into small parcels or village lots, and such appraisal shall be the minimum price at which such lots or parcels shall be respectively sold.

SEC. 35. All sums received on account of the sale of said salt spring lands, shall be paid into the treasury of the State, to the credit of the general fund.

Miscellaneous Provisions.

SEC. 49. The Commissioner of the Land Office shall have the custody of all books and papers relating to any of the public lands mentioned in this chapter, except such as properly belong to the records or files of other offices.

SEC. 50. The State Geologist shall furnish the Land Office with a map of each of the several counties of this State, as soon as the same are completed.

SEC. 51. The said commissioner shall, on or before the third Monday in March in each year, transmit to the treasurer of each county in which any lands mentioned in this chapter may have been sold during the year then next preceding, a description of each parcel of the lands so sold in such county, and the names of the purchasers, distinguishing university and school lands from others.

SEC. 52. Whenever the Commissioner shall lay off any tract of land into small parcels or village lots as provided in this chapter, he shall cause a correct map of the same to be entered of record in the county where said lands may be situated; and all parcels or lots heretofore laid out, shall in like manner be entered of record.

SEC. 53. The several county treasurers receiving such descriptions shall, on or before the first Monday of April, deliver to the supervisor of each township in which any of such lands are situated, a description of such lands t herein, with the names of the purchasers of the same.

SEC. 54. The registers of deeds of the several counties are authorized to record all patents issued by the Governor pursuant to the provisions of this chapter, and the record thereof shall have the same effect as the record of other conveyances executed according to the laws of this State.

SEC. 55. The necessary incidental expenses of the Land Office shall be paid out of the several funds, respectively, in relation to which they were incurred, and upon the presentation of satisfactory vouchers therefor to the board of State Auditors, shall be allowed by them at their annual settlement with the Commissioner.

SEC. 56. In case of any sale made by mistake, or not in accordance with law, or obtained by fraud, the same shall be void; and no certificate of purchase issued thereon shall be of any effect, but the holder of any such certificate shall be required to surrender the same to the Commissioner, who shall thereupon refund the amount paid in the like funds received by him on such certificate.

SEC. 57. The legal assignees of all bona fide purchasers of any of the lands mentioned in this chapter, shall be subject to, and govenred by, the provisions of law applicable to the respective purchasers of whom they are the assignees, and they shall have the same rights in all respects, as original purchasers of the same class of lands.

SEC. 58. All sales of lands by the Commissioner, shall be made according to the subdivisions thereof by the United States surveys, unless the same shall have been laid off into smaller lots as provided in this chapter, or unless, in the opinion of the Commissioner, any of said lands can be more advantageously disposed of according to other divisions to be ascertained and distinctly described by him.

SEC. 59. When an original certificate of purchase shall have been issued by the Commissioner for a quarter section or more of said lands, according to the legal subdivisions thereof, he may in his discretion, upon the surrender of such certificate, and the payment of one dollar for each new certificate requested, issue a new certificate for each smaller legal subdivision included in such original purchase, not being less than one-fourth of a quarter section; if in his opinion no injury will result therefrom.

SEC. 60. All damages recovered for any trespass or other injury upon or to any of the lands mentioned in this chapter, shall be paid over to the Commissioner of the Land Office, or into the State treasury, for the benefit of the fund to which the same may properly belong.

SEC. 61. Every person who shall commit any wilful trespass upon any of the lands owned, or held in trust or otherwise by this State, either by cutting down or destroying any timber or wood, standing or growing thereon, or by carrying away any timber or wood therefrom, or who shall injure or remove any buildings, fences, improvements, or other property belonging or appertaining to said lands, or shall aid, direct or countenance any such trespass or other injury, shall be deemed guilty of a misdemeanor, and on conviction thereof shall be punished by imprisonment in the county jail not more than one year, or by a fine not exceeding five hundred dollars, or both such fine and imprisonment, in the discretion of the court.

SEC. 62. It shall be the duty of every court having jurisdiction of the same, specially to charge the grand jury at each term of such court, to inquire into all offences against the provisions of this chapter, and present any person who may be guilty of any such offence within their county.

SEC. 63. Any person who shall commit any trespass upon any of the lands owned, or held in trust or otherwise by this State, shall be held liable in treble damages, in an action of trespass to be brought in the name of the people of this State, if such trespass shall be adjudged to have been wilful: and single damages only shall be recovered in such action, if such trespass shall be adjudged to have been casual and involuntary.

SEC. 64. In case any person shall hold or continue in possession of any of the lands mentioned in this chapter, without express authority in writing from the Commissioner of the Land Office, or contrary to the conditions or covenants of any lease or written agreement, he shall be liable to an action of forcible entry and detainer, or any other proper action or actions for the recovery of possession of such lands, and damages for the detention of the same.

SEC. 65. The prosecuting attorneys of the several counties shall promptly report to the Commissioner, all trespasses committed upon any of said lands, which may come to their knowledge, and shall, when directed by the Commissioner, prosecute all actions for any trespass or injury thereto, or for the recovery of possession thereof, or otherwise.

SEC. 66. It shall be the duty of each of said prosecuting attorneys, whenever requested by the commissioner, to advise with and give their opinion upon all questions of law which may be submitted to them by the said commissioner, relating to the duties of his office, without unnecessary delay, and without charge to the commissioner or to the State.

SEC. 67. The seal now in use in said land office shall continue to be the seal of said office, and in case the same should be lost or destroyed, another seal, with a similar device, shall be procured for said office by the commissioner thereof.

SEC. 68. All treasury notes or warrants bearing interest, drawn by authority of law, on the treasurer of this State, shall be received in payment of principal for any of the university lands which have been heretofore sold, or which may hereafter be sold, and which have not once been sold and forfeited, in the same manner as they are by law receivable for any lands owned by this State, subject to the limitations hereinafter contained.

SEC. 69. The whole amount of such notes and warrants which may be received under the provisions of the preceding section, shall not exceed the residue of the sum of one hundred thousand dollars which shall remain after deducting the full amount of all sums which shall have been credited to the Regents of the University, or to the university fund, on the principal of the "Michigan University State Stock," in pursuance of "an act authorizing the receipt of obligations of this State in payment of university lands," approved February twenty-eighth, one thousand eight hundred and forty-four, and of "an act for the relief of the University of Michigan," approved March eleventh, one thousand eight hundred and forty-four, and one hundred and fifty-six thousand dollars in addition thereto.

SEC. 70. The State Treasurer shall, on the first days of January, April, July and October, in each year, make out a statement of the notes or warrants received in payment of principal for university lands, pursuant to the provisions of the sixty-eighth section of this chapter during the preceding quarter, with an interest account upon the same, and shall thereupon credit the university fund with the amount of such notes or warrants and interest.

SEC. 71. From the date of each and every such credit, the university fund shall be relieved from the payment of interest on an amount of the said "Michigan University State Stock," equal to the amount of such credit; and when the amount of said "Michigan University State Stock" shall have been received into the State treasury, the State Treasurer shall continue to make quarterly statements of the amount of treasury notes or warrants received, and credit the same to the university fund, and interest shall thereupon accrue, and shall annually be paid by she State to the treasurer of the board of Regents, for the use of the University.

SEC. 72. The seal of the land office affixed to any certificate of purchase, receipt or other instrument issued by the Commissioner of the Land Office, according to the provisions of this chapter, shall be prima facia evidence of the due execution of such certificate.

[No. 30.]

AN ACT to amend Chapter sixty of the Revised Statutes of eighteen hundred and forty-six, relative to the Public Lands, and the superintendence and disposition thereof.

SECTION 1. *Be it enacted by the Senate and House of Representatives of the State of Michigan,* That sections number two, four and five, of chapter number sixty of an act entitled an act for revising and consolidating the general statutes of the State of Michigan, be each severally amended by striking out the word "January," and substituting in lieu thereof, the word "March;" so that the time specified in each of said sections for the payment of interest, shall be on the first day of March, or within sixty days thereafter in each and every year.

SEC. 2. Strike out the twenty-sixth section of chapter sixty of said act, and insert as follows: "It shall be the duty of the commissioner to inquire into the situation and condition of the university lands lying near Toledo, in the State of Ohio, and if in his opinion it would be advantageous to the fund to sell said lands, or be proper to offer them for sale, he is hereby authorized so to do. And in case it is deemed proper to offer the said lands for sale, and the commissioner is of opinion that their value exceeds the minimam price of twelve dollars per acre, he may procure an appraisal of the same by three disinterested persons under oath; and the said lands shall be offered at such appraisal, upon such terms and conditions of payment and forfeiture as the commissioner may deem most advantageous to the fund: *Provided,* That notice of the offering of said lands at public sale, shall be published in the newspapers at Toledo, and in the State paper at Detroit; and that none of said lands shall be sold at a less price than twelve dollars per acre."

SEC. 3. This act shall take effect and be in force on and after the first day of March next.

Approved March 1, 1847.

[No. 82.]

AN ACT to amend chapter sixty, title twelve of the Revised Statutes.

SECTION 1. *The People of the State of Michigan enact,* That section five of chapter sixty, title twelve of the revised statutes, be amended by adding to said section the words following, to wit: "and any purchaser of the right, title and interest of an original purchaser, his heirs or assigns, at an execution or mortgage sale, shall be deemed an assignee of the person whose right, title and interest was sold by virtue of such execution or mortgage;" so that said section as amended shall read as follows, to wit:

"SEC. 5. Any purchaser of university or school lands, his heirs or assigns, who shall have paid on or before the first day of March, one thousand eight hundred and forty-two, a sum equal to twenty per cent of the purchase money on his certificate, together with the interest up to said day; and any person who shall have become such purchaser since the thirteenth day of April, in the year one thousand eight hundred and forty-one, his heirs or assigns, who shall have become such purchaser since the thirteenth day of April, in the year one thousand eight hundred and forty-one, his heirs or assigns, who shall have paid according to the terms of his certificate, shall be privileged to pay the balance of principal due on his purchase at any time thereafter at his option; but in all cases the interest on the unpaid balance of principal shall be paid on or before the first day of January or within sixty days thereafter, in each and every year; and any purchaser of the right, title and interest of the original purchaser, his heirs or assigns, at an execution or mortgage sale, shall be deemed an assignee of the person whose right, title and interest was sold by virtue of such execution or mortgage."

SEC. 2. Section eight of said chapter is hereby amended by adding thereto the words following: "and the Governor shall in like manner sign and cause to be issued patents of said land to any purchaser of the right, title and interest of the original purchaser, his heirs or assigns, at an execution or mortgage sale, upon the presentment to him of the certificate of the commissioner, that the whole amount of principal and intekest due thereon has been paid according to law, and that such purchaser at execution or mortgage sale is entitled to a patent for the lands described in such certificate;" so that the same as amended shall read as follows, to wit:

"SEC. 8. The Governor of the State shall sign and cause to be issued patents for said lands as described in the certificates of sale, whenever the same shall be presented to him, with the further certificate of the commissioner endorsed thereon, that the whole amount of principal and interest specified therein has been paid according to law, and that the holder of the certificate of purchase is entitled to a patent of the lands described therein; and the Governor shall in like manner sign and cause to be issued patents of said lands to any purchaser of the right, title and interest of the original purchaser, his heirs or assigns, at an execution or mortgage sale, upon the presentment to him of the certificate of the commissioner that the whole amount of principal and interest due thereon has been paid according to law, and that such purchaser at execution or mortgage sale is entitled to a patent for the lands described in such certificate."

Approved April 4, 1851.

[No. 49.]

AN ACT requiring the Commissioner of the State Land Office to make an Annual Report to the Regents of the University of Michigan.

SECTION 1. *Be it enacted by the Senate and House of Representatives of the State of Michigan,* That the Commissioner of the Land Office shall make out and transmit to the Secretary of the Board of Regents of the University, by the first day of July next, an accurate statement of each and every parcel of University land that shall have been sold up to that date, and the price for which it was sold. Also, of all forfeitures and re-sales, with an amount of the loss or gain attending such forfeitures and re-sales, and also an amount or list of each parcel of University land unsold.

SEC. 2. Said Commissioner shall annually thereafter, report to the Board of Regents, all sales and forfeitures of University lands, with an amount of the receipts and expenditures attending the same.

SEC. 3. Said Commissioner shall also report annually, the expenses lawfully charged to and deducted from the University interest fund, together with the nett income.

SEC. 4. Said Commissioner shall with each of his reports, furnish an accurate statement of all moneys loaned from said fund, to whom loaned and when payable, with the interest annually paid thereon, and the annual interest due and unpaid. Also, the amount of internal improvement warrants paid for University lands, with the annual interest paid thereon by the State.

SEC. 5. The Regents of the University shall severally be entitled to receive from the Secretary of State, in the same manner as other public officers, a copy of the annual laws of the State.

SEC. 6. This act shall be in force from and after its passage.

Approved March 3, 1849.

[No. 217.]

AN ACT to provide for the removal of the State Land Office to the seat of Government.

SECTION 1. *Be it enacted by the Senate and House of Representatives of the State of Michigan,* That the State Land Office now established and being at Marshall, in the county of Calhoun, shall be removed to and be established in the village of Lansing, in the county of Ingham, and for that purpose the Commissioner shall, as soon after the tenth day of May next as the business of the said office will permit, and not later than the fourteenth day of said month of May, close his said office at Marshall, and shall immediately thereafter remove all the books, maps, papers, furniture, fixtures and other things belonging to said office, to said village of Lansing, and arrange the same for business at some convenient place, to be designated by the Auditor General.

SEC. 2. Upon closing the said Land Office at Marshall, as provided in the preceding section, the office of the Recorder of the Land Office shall be and is hereby abolished.

SEC. 3. The duties of the Commissioner of the Land Office shall remain and continue as provided by existing laws, until the first day of February next, except as herein otherwise provided.

SEC. 4. All moneys received at the said Land Office shall, after the removal thereof as provided in section one of this act, be paid to the State Treasurer, who shall give a receipt for the same, and which said receipt shall be countersigned by the Auditor General as in other cases.

SEC. 5. From and after the said first day of February next, the office of Commissioner of the Land Office shall be, and hereby is declared to be abolished, and the duties required of said Commissioner by existing law shall devolve upon and be performed by the Auditor General.

SEC. 6. All accounts for incidental expenses of said office, accounts for traveling expenses and postage of Superintendent of Public Instruction, accounts for surveys of village lots or other lands, improvements in Lansing, and all other accounts and charges heretofore allowed and paid by the said commissioner, from moneys in his hands, shall hereafter be audited by the board of State Auditors, on the certificate of the commissioner, and when audited and allowed shall be paid from the State treasury on the warrant of the Auditor General, drawn on the proper fund.

SEC. 7. Any purchaser of salt spring, university or primary school lands, his agent or attorney, may pay to the county treasurer of the county in which such lands lie, the amount due on his certificate from time to time, either for principal or interest, and for the amount so paid, the said treasurer shall give to such person his receipt, specifying the amount so paid, and whether for principal or interest or both, and the amount of each, and which said receipt shall be countersigned by the county clerk; and when so given and countersigned, shall have the same force and effect as if it had been given by the Commissioner of the State Land Office or State Treasurer: *Provided,* The several county treasurers authorized to receive money under the provisions of this act, are required to execute and give to the State a bond with good and sufficient sureties, in an amount to be fixed by the Commissioner of the State Land Office or by the Auditor General, the sureties to be approved by the prosecuting attorney and register of deeds of their respective counties, conditional that the said moneys shall be paid over to the State Treasurer, as provided in this act.

SEC. 8. The said county treasurer shall issue duplicate receipts for all moneys received under the provisions of the preceding section, one of which shall be left with the county clerk of such county.

SEC. 9. The duplicates of such receipts shall be filed with the county clerk, who shall also make an entry of the amount for which such receipt was given, and whether the same was for principal or interest, with the name of the person paying the same, in a book to be provided by him for that purpose, at the expense of the county, and shall, on the first Monday of each month, forward all receipts on file in his office, to the Commissioner of the Land Office or Auditor General, in such manner as he may direct.

SEC. 10. It shall be the duty of the Commissioner of the State Land Office, on or before the first day of July next, and of the Auditor General, on or before the first day of July in each year thereafter, to transmit to the county treasurers of the several counties where payments may be made under the provisions of this act, a statement of all salt spring, university or primary school lands within such counties upon which any interest or principal is due, or to become due, the amount of principal due on each description, the amount of interest annually due or to become due thereon, with such directions and instructions as may be necessnry to enable said county treasurers fully to carry out the provisions of this act; and the said Commissioner of the State Land Office or the Auditor General shall also transmit to the several county treasurers with the statemeuts mentioned in this section, a bond to be executed by them, in the penal sum of at least twice the amount which may be received by the said county treasurer; upon the election of any county treasurer in any county where payments may be made under the provisions of this act, they and each of them shall at the time of their executing their ordinary bond of office, and before entering upon the duties of their office, also execute the bond provided for in this act, and forward the same to the Auditor General, as herein provided.

SEC. 11. The said county treasurers shall, on the receipt of the statements and bonds, execute in the manner provided in this act, the bonds, and forward the same to be filed in the Auditor General's office, and for any failure to pay over to the State Treasurer any or all money received under the provisions of this act, by any county treasurer, the county in which such failure may occur shall be liable for all losses that may occur from such failure, and the State Treasurer shall charge the same to such county.

SEC. 12. The moneys received by said county treasurers under the provisions of this act, shall be held subject at all times to the order of the State Treasurer; and all such moneys so received shall be paid over to the State Treasurer on or before the first day of May in each year.

SEC. 13. This act shall take effect from and after its passage.

Approved March 31, 1849.

[No. 317.]

AN ACT to provide for the collection and payment of taxes assessed upon sold and part-paid-for university and primary school lands.

SECTION 1. *Be it enacted by the Senate and House of Representatives of the State of Michigan,* That the supervisor of every township in which there shall be assessed the interest of any purchaser of university or primary school lands, as personal property, shall, on or before the first day of November in the year when the same was so assessed, transmit to the treasurer of his county a list of all such lands, containing a full description thereof, together with the name of the persons to whom respectively the same was so assessed.

SEC. 2. That the several county treasurers shall, at the same time and in the same manner they are now required to return to the office of the Auditor General lands delinquent for taxes in their respective counties, return to the State Land Office a statement of all university and primary school lands upon which, from returns made to them by the township treasurers, it appears the taxes assessed have not been paid and cannot be collected.

SEC. 3. The Commissioner of the State Land Office shall provide suitable books and enter in the same the description of every parcel of land so returned to his office, and the taxes assessed on the same.

SEC. 4. The purchaser or purchasers of any parcel of the land so returned, or the person or persons claiming to have any interest in the same as the assignee or legal representative in any other capacity of such purchaser, shall, under pain of forfeiting his or their interest in such lands and in the certificate of sale thereof, within the time in which the annual interest is required to be paid on the purchase money of such lands, pay to the State Treasurer the amount of taxes assessed upon any description of the lands so returned, with interest thereon from the first day of February following the assessment of the same, at the rate of fifteen per cent. a year, and in addition thereto on each description the sum of twenty-five cents to defray the expense of the collection of such taxes.

SEC. 5. Every parcel of land returned under the provisions of this act, upon which the taxes and the interest and charges aforesaid shall remain unpaid at the expiration of the time within which payment thereof is required to be made by the next preceding section, shall be deemed to have been forfeited to the State by the purchaser thereof, his assignee or other legal representative; and the lands so forfeited shall be subject to sale in the same manner that other forfeited and unsold university and primary school lands are.

SEC. 6. The said Commissioner shall, on or before the first day of May and November in each year, make out and furnish to the Auditor General a statement containing a description of the lands upon which the taxes have been paid, and the amount of taxes, interest and charges paid on such lands.

SEC. 7. The Auditor General shall credit to the proper counties the taxes so paid, with the rate of interest allowed on other delinquent taxes, and place the balance of moneys arising from such interest and charges to the credit of the general fund.

SEC. 8. This act shall take effect and be in force from and after its passage.

Approved April 2, 1850.

[No. 214.]

AN ACT to amend an act to provide for the removal of the State Land Office to the seat of government, and to revive certain laws relative to the same.

SECTION 1. *Be it enacted by the Senate and House of Representatives of the State of Michigan*, That section five of an act to provide for the removal of the State Land Office to the seat of government, approved March 31, 1849, be and the same is hereby repealed; and the office denominated "The Land Office of the State of Michigan," in the act entitled "an act to organize a Land Office and to regulate the sale of public lands," approved March 6, 1843, be and the same is hereby re-established, the chief officer of which shall be called the Commissioner of the Land Office, as provided for in said last mentioned act.

SEC. 2. All the laws relative to the State Land Office which were in force at the time when the act to which this is amendatory took effect, not contravening the provisions of this act, or the act to which this is amendatory, are hereby revived, and shall be, after the passage of this act, in full force.

SEC. 3. Section seven of the said first mentioned act is hereby amended by striking out all after the word "approved," in the fifteenth line, to and including the word "deeds," in the sixteenth line, and inserting instead thereof the words "by the judges of the county court."

SEC. 4. This act shall take effect from and after its passage.

Approved April 1, 1850.

APPENDIX.

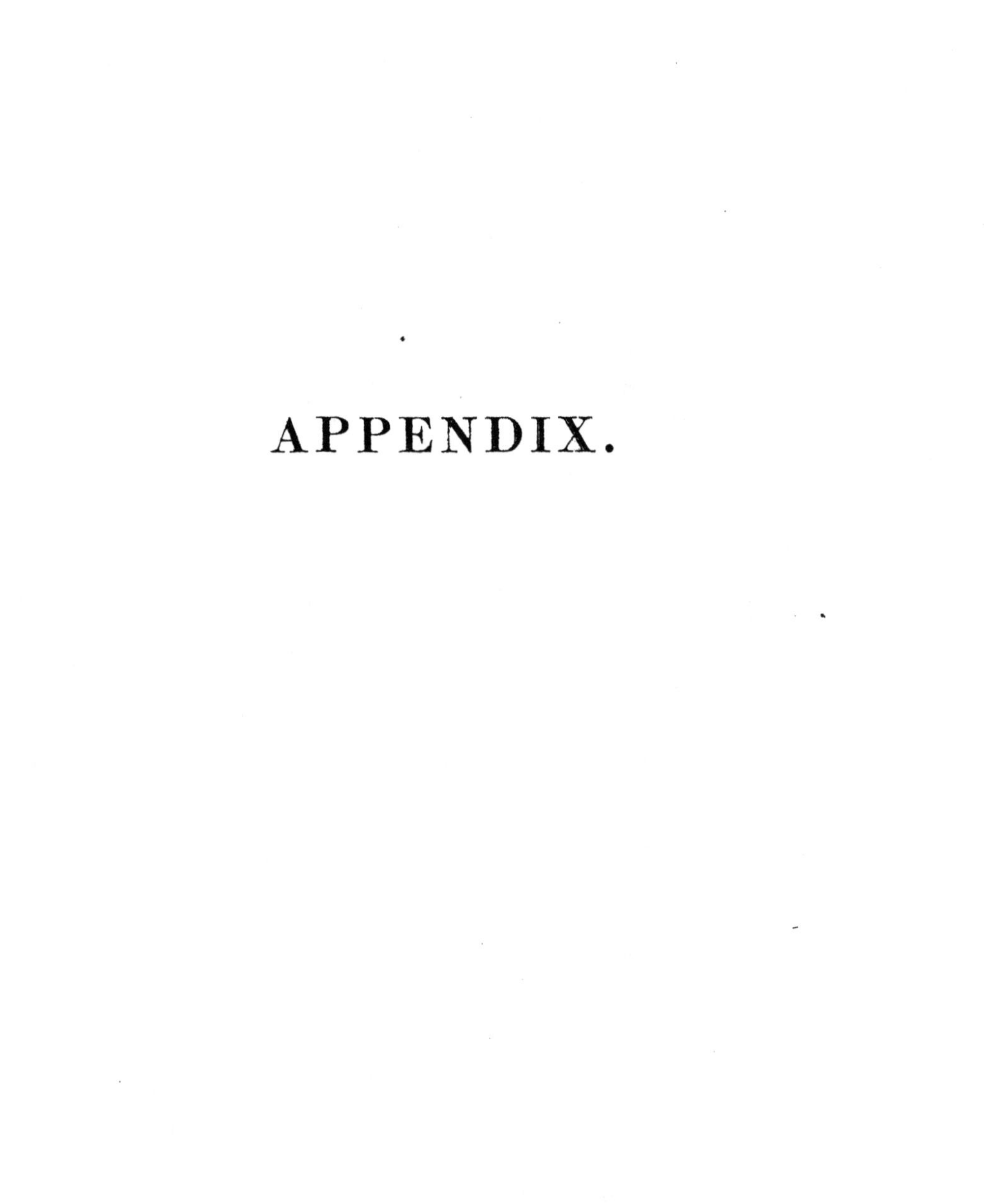

UNIV.
OF
MICH.

COMMUNICATIONS

EMBRACING ACCOUNTS OF UNION SCHOOLS, &c.

WESLEYAN SEMINARY, ALBION.

To the Superintendent of Public Instruction:

SIR:—In the year 1833, Dr. B. H. Packard, then of Ann Arbor, Rev. H. Colclazer and Rev. E. H. Pilcher, having consulted together, resolved to seek to establish a seminary of learning under the patronage of the Annual Conference of the M. E. Church, which embraced this country.

In conformity with this design, an invitation was given to persons in different localities, to make propositions of what they would do for the purpose of securing its establishment among them. In the summer of 1834, several such propositions were made and submitted to the Ohio Conference, which, at that time, had jurisdiction here. At this session of that body, a committee was appointed, with full powers to accept of the best proposition and to secure from the Legislative Council a charter. That committee fulfilled its duties—accepted the proposition from Spring Arbor, in Jackson county, and in March, 1835, the charter of the "Spring Arbor Seminary" was passed and approved. Soon after this the board of trustees was organized, and various efforts were made to secure the erection of buildings and the establishment of the school, without success. The friends of the enterprise and the original projectors became much discouraged, and feared that the scheme would have to be abandoned for the present, on account of the difficulties thrown in the way by some who were the professed friends of the object. But in the summer and fall of 1838, the proprietors of the village of Albion, and other residents, made an offer of liberal assistance to the trustees, provided the location could be changed to that place. This offer was accepted, and their consent for the necessary change in the charter was sent into the Legislature. The charter was amended as desired, and the board of trustees was reorganized in the village of Albion, on the 29th of April, 1839. Nothing of any importance was done towards the erection of buildings, until the spring of 1840, when an agent was appointed to solicit donations and subscriptions, and to take preparatory steps for building. At this time a system of scholarships was adopted, which succeded well for a time, but ultimately became a source of embarrassment. That system was, to give a certificate of free tuition for four years for every hundred dollars subscribed, but not available to the holder until the whole amount was paid.

The reason of the embarrassment growing out of this system, was, that the available subscription was mostly used up in the erection of buildings, and nothing was left to support the faculty.

The corner stone of the centre building in the plan, was laid in August, 1841, and it was ready to be occupied in November, 1842, when the school was opened with a large number of pupils. The first public examination and exhibition took place in March, 1843.

On the 6th day of June, 1849, a new plan of scholarships was adopted and put into operation, with a view to raise a permanent endowment fund, which has succeeded very well. By an amendment of the charter, at the session of the Legislature in 1850, the "Female Collegiate Institute" was engrafted on the Seminary. The first class in this department graduated in August, 1851.

From this Seminary have already gone out a large number of young men, who have entered the various active avocations of life; and also of young ladies, to fill up their sphere of active duties, as teachers and matrons. These all hold a very pleasing recollection of the days passed in this institution.

We should probably be safe in saying, that for the nine years and a half that this institution has been in operation, not far from two thousand five hundred youth of our State have received a considerable portion of their mental culture within its walls. It is now enjoying a tide of prosperity almost unparalleled in the history of literary institutions.

Yours truly,

E. H. PILCHER.

OLIVET INSTITUTE.

To the Superintendent of Public Instruction:

The Olivet Institute is situated in Olivet, Eaton County, Michigan. The Institution was commenced in the spring of 1844, by a colony of Christian men who came here with their families for this express purpose.

The main design in its establishment was to furnish a thorough Christian education to that class of youth whose circumstances were too limited to admit of their pursuing a thorough course of study elsewhere.

The first year of their labor was one of severe trial. Being entirely unacquainted with the peculiarities of the climate, and business pressing hard, the colonists, although admonished by friends, labored beyond measure, until their strength was gone, and they were completely prostrated. Then followed months of suffering and distress, notwithstanding the efforts of surrounding friends to furnish relief. During this period of great debility and consequent discouragement, the founder of the Institution, the Rev. J. J. Shipherd, was removed by death.

For a time it seemed that the enterprise must be given up. Several who were ardent in the outset, and full of hope for the future, when the day of trial came, were disheartened, and returned to their former homes. These accumulated discouragements necessarily had an influence on those who remained. But as the people recovered their health and strength, they renewed their determination to go on with the work. The school was opened in the autumn of the same year, in a private room. This proving exceedingly inconvenient, it was immediately determined to erect a small edifice that might serve the double purpose of chapel and recitation rooms.

Owing to the great feebleness of the community, the work progressed but slowly, and the winter came on before it was possible to enclose the house. The snow was falling fast, and the chilling winds were fiercely blowing as the shingles were nailed to the roof. Notwithstanding all this, the enclosure was effected, the floors laid, the partition put up, and the second or upper story nearly lathed. The people were now looking forward with fond anticipations to the time when the work should be completed. But in an unsuspecting moment a spark from a stove which it was found necessary to use, it being now mid-winter, communicated the flames to the light materials around, and in a few moments, the labor of wearisome days, and nights too, was a mass of smouldering ruins.

Disheartened and dejected, the little band met to devise plans for the future. The question with a part was seriously considered whether they should not relinquish the enterprise; whether it was not, after all, entirely impracticable for so few to undertake so great a work.

Having seriously and prayerfully considered the matter, they concluded that what they had already done they could do again, and resolved immediately to rebuild upon the same site. The first building was erected with the assistance of the district, and they were to occupy the lower room, for school purposes. It was to be rebuilt upon the same plan. This was completed before the opening of the next fall term of the school.

An attempt was now made to obtain a charter for the Institution, which entirely failed, for two reasons. One was, that the State at that time determined to reserve to the State University the exclusive power to confer degrees, and would not grant that privilege to any other institution. The other was the opposition felt by some of the leading men in the Legislature, to the manual labor features of the Institute. This failure, together with the cold indifference manifested by those who ought to have been deeply interested in such an enterprise, tended to discourage those who had at so great an expense of not only money, but health and comfort, been laboring for the good of many youth of the State. Yet they still determined to toil on, so long as there was any reasonable prospect of final success.

The constant increase of students demanded additional accommodations, and it was thought advisable to erect an edifice three stories in height, finished with rooms in the upper stories for the accommodation of students, and the lower story furnishing recitation rooms, &c. To effect this required the united efforts of all, together with the aid that could be obtained from abroad.

The expense of the edifice has been about three thousand dollars. Two years were spent in its erection. The cost is small, it is true, and the time occupied long, but when viewed in connection with the fact that there were so few to do the work, and they possessed of but small means, the work accomplished seems a large one. This finished, the community had hoped for one year's respite. In this they were disappointed, for fire from a burning dwelling was conveyed to the chapel and in a few moments that was again in ashes.

Another chapel is now in the process of erection, much larger than the other, which it is hoped will be completed this fall.

The school has been steadily increasing in numbers and interest from its commencement. The number of students in attendance the past year was about one hundred and fifty.

The present year has opened with most favorable prospects. Not less than one hundred students will be present during this term. Many who are anxious to avail themselves of the advantage for mental culture here offered, are prevented from want of accommodations.

For several years past, about fifty of the students have been employed some part of the year as teachers in common schools, yet the demand for instructors has been by no means supplied.

The chief aim of the trustees heretofore has been to prepare teachers thoroughly for their work, and to fit young men for college or prepare them for an advanced standing, if they chose. In their efforts thus far they have not been entirely unsuccessful. A charter was obtained a year or two since granting all privileges save that of conferring degrees. Under this charter the present board of trustees was formed.

The board now purpose enlarging the operations of the institution as there shall seem to be a demand. The formation of various departments is proposed, each of which shall have a course of instruction complete in itself. Not that the studies of one department shall be entirely distinctive. All in the various departments may for a time pursue the same branches, but in the course of their progress one class shall pursue thoroughly certain branches which may fit them for a particular occupation in life, while another class shall pursue as thoroughly other branches, such as may fit them for a different sphere.

For instance, let there be a farmers' department. Those entering that, would be required to master the branches belonging to such department, such as chemistry, botany, geology, mineralogy, and all the branches requisite for a scientific farmer. Then the merchant's department, in which shall be taught those branches to fit one for mercantile life; the mechanics' department, and others which may be demanded.

The time of entering fully upon this plan will depend very much on the funds of the institute. With the limited means now at command, but little could be realized. But with a moderate fund a course of instruction might be given which would be of great value to those who are soon to become the business men in the State.

The report for the year will be similar to the one forwarded last year. The whole number of students in attendance during the

Spring term	40
Fall "	103
Winter "	88

A large number of the students pursued the higher branches of science, and several were engaged in a course of preparation for college. Four instructors have been employed during the entire year, and a fifth during the fall and winter terms.

The academical year of the Institute commences on the second Wednesday in April, and is divided into three terms. The Spring term begins on the second Wednesday of April, and continues till the last Wednesday in June. The Fall term begins on the last Wednesday of September and continues fourteen weeks. The Winter term commences at the close of the Fall term and continues till the second Wednesday in April, at which time the public examinations and commencement exercises occur. There is one vacation, from the last Wednesday in June till the last Wednesday in September.

EXPENSES.

Tuition in any department, except those hereafter specified, is for:

Gentlemen, per annum	$12 00
Ladies, " "	9 00

EXTRA CHARGES.

Book-keeping, per quarter	1 00
Music on Piano, "	8 00
Painting in Oil, "	7 00
do in Water Colors, per qr	3 00
Drawing, "	1 00
Penmanship, "	1 00
Incidental expenses per annum	1 25
Room Rent	5 00
Library fee, per term	12

Boarding in families is from $1 to $1,25 per week, exclusive of fuel and lights. Most of the students defray a considerable portion of this expense by manual labor.

LIBRARY, READING ROOM AND APPARATUS.

The library numbers more than one thousand volumes. The reading room is supplied with various valuable publications from various States. The apparatus consists of an air pump, electrical machine, galvanic battery, and chemical apparatus sufficient for most experiments in this study. This apparatus was purchased of N. B. & D. Chamberlain, of Boston.

There is also belonging to the Institute a superior Piano, manufactured by Mr. Chickering, the celebrated Piano manufacturer of Boston.

SOCIETIES.

There are three societies in connection with the Institute, which hold regular meetings during term time—the Society of Inquiry, the Philoalethian, and the Young Ladies' Literary Society.

New classes are formed at the beginning of each term, and also at the middle of the Fall and Winter terms.

Most of the books included in the course of study, are kept on hand by the Teachers, and supplied to the students on low terms.

CARLO REED,
Chairman of the Board of Trustees.
E. N. BARTLETT,
Secretary of Board of Trustees.

Olivet, Oct. 6, 1851.

ST. MARK'S COLLEGE.

HON. F. W. SHEARMAN:

DEAR SIR—The following report relative to the history and condition of St. Mark's College and Schools, I would respectfully present:

For several years before the present charter was obtained, the subject of an institution for academical, collegiate, and theological learning had been brought up annually at the convention of the Episcopal Church in this Diocese. During the session of the legislature for the year 1850, a charter was procured under the title of St. Mark's College, to be located in the village (now the city) of Grand Rapids. The first meeting of the trustees of St. Mark's, was held in Detroit, on the 18th day of May, 1850, at which time the charter was accepted. At the same time the Rev. Mr. Cuming was authorized to put the preparatory department for females into operation. This he did by securing the services of two young ladies of established reputation, as teachers. The first term of the female department commenced in the spring of 1850, and numbered fifty pupils.

At the meeting of the trustees, in September, 1850, the Rev. Charles C. Taylor was elected President, and at the same time an arrangement was made to have the male department go into operation, under the care and instruction of Mr. D. D. Van Antwerp.

The catalogue which was published in November, 1850, at the close of the second quarter of the female, and the first of the male department, records the names of 116 pupils. The schools have probably averaged about 100. The present term has already numbered from 120 to 130. It is the design of the trustees to make the institution fully competent, and of sufficient merit to meet the entire educational wants of the community.

The courses of study in St. Mark's, will, as far as possible, be so arranged that with the approbation of the Faculty, the guardians of the pupils may select the course which shall best qualify the students for usefulness and eminence, whatever occupation or profession may be chosen. Students are received for any portion of time, and permitted to pursue the studies of such classes as shall be considered most appropriate to their attainments and designs, and on leaving can receive a certificate of their matriculation, standing and acquirements. Whenever any one shall have pursued a course of study fully equivalent (however it may differ) to the course of study in the University of Michigan, and shall have sustained in it a satisfactory examination, he shall be entitled to the degree of Bachelor of Arts; and when a student can sustain a similar examination in the course of study required in either of the professions, he can receive a diploma accordingly.

The institution is already furnished with six professors and teachers, five of whom have been constantly engaged in instruction. The trustees think themselves fortunate in having secured the services of able teachers, who have had much experience in the instruction of youth. The success of the enterprise has surpassed the expectations of its friends. By the most economical management the income has nearly met the expenditures. A committee of the trustees during the present week have succeeded in purchasing a lot, which, of all others, they have long regarded as the most desirable, for the site of the preparatory departments;

and they are now taking measures to secure upon it before another autumn, the erection of buildings, not unlike the plan forwarded to you with this report.

With much respect, your obedient servant,

CHARLES C. TAYLOR.

Grand Rapids, Feb. 6th, 1852.

YOUNG LADIES' SEMINARY, MARSHALL.

In compliance with a request made by the Superintendent of Public Instruction, this brief report of the Young Ladies Seminary is now given.

This institution was opened in March, 1850, under the superintendence of Miss S. Burgess, and has now been in operation nearly two years, A building was erected by the citizens, capable of accommodating forty pupils, with the intention of enlarging it when necessary. This is carpeted, and tastefully furnished. A more attractive school room is no where to be found. Its location is retired, and one of the best in the village.

The ultimate design is, to furnish a school of the highest grade, for the education of young ladies. It was entered upon as an experiment. The number of pupils has varied; yet such are the present prospects, that the friends and founders of the institution are sanguine that their hopes will be realized.

Arrangements will be made hereafter for the accommodation of pupils from abroad, and it is designed as soon as practicable to have a boarding house connected with the school, where they may be under the immediate supervision of their teachers.

The course of instruction pursued embraces the elementary and higher English branches, (including Algebra and Geometry,) French, Latin and Drawing. As soon as circumstances render it expedient a musical department will be added. Exercises in composition are required weekly, from which no one is excused, except by a request from their parents or guardians. The scholastic year consists of two terms, or four quarters of eleven weeks each. The Fall term commences the second week in October. The Spring term about the 20th of March.

In consequence of the frequent changes in the school, and the limited time for which many pupils are entered, it is deemed advisable that a public examination should be held at the close of each quarter.

Especial care is taken that the instruction given should be as thorough as possible under the existing counteracting circumstances; and every effort is used to induce habits of attention, of thinking, reasoning, and punctuality. Pupils are not allowed to pass over their studies superficially. The principle is adopted, that the quantity learned is not of so much importance as the manner in which it is learned, and the character of the discipline given to the mind—that it is not so necessary to impart knowledge as to create a desire for it—to bring out ideas, and teach the pupil how to learn every thing.

The practical duties of life are ever kept in view. To lead young ladies to feel their high responsibility in the cultivation of their intelleetual faculties—to fully understand their relations to God, to their fellow creatures, and their duties to society at large, and fit them for scenes of future usefulness, is most prominent in the instruction given.

S. BURGESS.

Marshall, Jan. 31, 1852.

FAYETTE UNION SCHOOL—JONESVILLE.

To the Superintendent of Public Instruction:

At a public school meeting, held May 28th, 1844, the expediency and feasibility of establishing and sustaining a union school, of a character to meet the entire wants of our community in that regard, were fully discussed. It was finally resolved by a large majority to be both

Fayette Union School.

feasible and expedient, and that no time should be lost in making the necessary preparations. A suitable house must be erected. A committee was appointed to prepare plans, and submit estimates. At a subsequent meeting this committee submitted several plans: one of which was adopted; and a brick house, 32 by 60 feet, two stories high, was erected, at a cost of $2,100, a plan of which is hereto attached.

The house was completed January 1st, 1848, and the school opened uner the auspices of A. S. Welch, A. M., as principal, with two competent assistants. The year was divided into two terms, of twenty-two weeks each, the first term commencing the 1st of September, with a short vacation of two weeks at its close, and a vacation of six weeks at the close of the summer term. The amount paid teachers the first year, was $900. The number of scholars in attendance, was two hundred and twenty-two; the whole number of persons in the district betwen the ages of four and eighteen, being only two hundred and twenty.

At the close of the first year the experiment of employing experienced and highly educated teachers, though at an expense far exceeding the amount the people had been accustomed to regard as a liberal compensation to teachers of district schools, had proved so eminently successful, that the district with great unanimity, determined to continue the school under the same auspices, with an increased salary to the principal, and an additional number of assistant teachers. Mr. Welch continued in charge of the school until the summer of 1849, when he was compelled by the state of his health, to relinquish it; and Rev. C. S. Kingsley, A. M., was employed to succeed him. The sum of $600 was paid to teachers for the first term of 1849, and yet cost of tuition was only from $1 to $1,50 to each scholar, for the term. Mr. Kingsley continued in charge of the school until the fall of 1850, with from two to four assistant teachers, at a cost to the district of between $1,000 and $1,100 per year. The cost to each scholar during this time ranged from $1,50 to $3 per term.

In the fall of 1850, the Rev. S. C. Hickok, A. M., was employed to take charge of the school, at a salary of $600 per year, with authority to employ such assistants as he might require, at an expense not exceeding $600, in addition to his own salary. Mr. Hickok was shortly afterward taken sick, and after an ilness of some weeks, died. It was then too late for the district board to secure the services of such a teacher as was desired, and they were compelled to employ for a short time, a person capable of teaching only the common branches of an English education. The principal received $35 per month, and was furnished with two competent assistants; but owing to the fact that only the common branches were taught, the school was not so fully attended, and the cost of tuition per scholar was much greater than when teachers had been paid at the rate of $1,200 per year.

The division of the year into two terms, being found inconvenient, a change was made in the spring of 1851, and the year divided into three terms, two of sixteen weeks each, and one of twelve weeks. Mr. Welch having fully recovered his health, was again induced to take charge of the school, at a salary of $700 per year. During the summer term he had three assistant teachers, who were paid at the rate ef $600 per year, and yet the cost of tuition per scholar was only $1,20 for the term.

The fall term has just commenced, and the number in attendance is so large that four assistant teachers have already been employed, and it is probable that some classes will still be placed under the tuition of advanced scholars, who are pursuing a course of study with especial reference to the profession of teaching. Though so large an amount is paid for teachers, it is confidently believed by the school board that the cost per scholar will be less than for any previous year.

It has been the aim of the board and the district, to afford facilities for education in this *district school*, equal to those afforded by the best academies and grammar schools of the country. Especial attention has been paid to those preparing themselves for teachers. Classes in Latin, Greek, Spanish, Chemistry, Algebra, Geometry, &c., have been advanced considerably beyond what is usually required for admission into even an advanced class in college; and yet there has been no want of attention to the minor and rudimental branches. Indeed, it has been found that much greater thoroughness has been secured in elementary studies than is usually attained in schools where these studies are alone pursued, and the general effect has been to secure an unusual degree of thought, attention and mental development.

The experience of this school has shown that as a matter of economy alone, it is *poor policy* to employ *cheap* teachers—that when the district has paid the highest wages, and secured experienced and highly educated teachers, the cost of tuition per saholar has been least.

It has shown, too, the practicability and the policy of affording facilities for the study of the classics, and the higher branches of English, in our district schools. A large proportion of the youth of our country have access to no other schools; and though their parents or guardians could not be induced to send them to academies or colleges, they are ever ready to afford them facilities for the attainment of *all the knowledge* to be obtained in the *district school.* Let these be made what they should, and what they may, without any greatly increased expense, and we shall have no need of academies and grammar schools.

W. J. BAXTER.

UNION SCHOOL AT BATTLE CREEK.

To the Superintendent of Public Instruction:

The district board of the Union School at Battle Creek, would respectfully report, that the first term of the Union School, since the completion of the school buildings, closed December 24th. Four hundred and thirty-six scholars were in attendance during the term. Twenty-seven non-resident scholars have been admitted into the school.

Instruction was given during the term in the highest branches of mathematics, French and Latin, and weekly exercises in composition and declamation. The school is separated into three departments, two teachers in each under the superintendence of the principal. Teacher's wages per term, $511 00. The year is divided into three terms of fifteen weeks each. There are six hundred and one children in the district, between the ages of four and eighteen.

The Union School House is constructed of brick, three stories in heighth, forty by sixty, containing three large rooms and three convenient rooms for recitation. The house is situated on a beautiful eminence, with two acres of land attached to it, which will be filled with forest and ornamental trees the coming spring. The first school district in this place was organized in June, 1834, with a sparse population, embracing twelve sections, known as school district No. 3, township of Milton. A tax of $60 was raised, for which a school house was erected, which answered the demands of the district until 1837. During the years 1837 and 1838, $500 were raised to prepare a more commodious building. In 1840 a library was attached to the school, and a resolution adopted to support the school through the academic year. In the year 1844, the friends of universal education started the project of a Union School, and were encountered by strong opponents who were unceasing in their efforts to defeat the raising of a sufficient tax to execute their plans, and were successful for a time. The board of inspectors in the year 1845, not favoring the principles of Union Schools, attempted to divide the district into several, but were checked by the active exertions of those who believed such an act would prove injurious to the cause of popular education. Public meetings were called, and the question discussed for some months with a beneficial result.

In 1847, the inspectors of Emmet, Battle Creek and Bedford formed a Union school district, composed of fractional parts of said townships, including a territory equal to five and five-eighths sections. At the annual meetiug of 1848, a resolution passed to raise $2,000 to purchase a site and build a house suitable for the Union school. The tax was duly assessed and mostly collected; a site had been secured and arrangements were being made for the erection of an edifice suitable for the district; but by the ingenuity of the enemies of the investment of a capital for the benefit of the rising generation, an injunction was placed upon the treasurer and the amount which had been collected was refunded; the district was obliged to relinquish their claims on an enviable site and await a proper time for another effort, suffering much from an unnecessary expense and delay. In 1849 they succeeded in passing a resolution to raise another tax, and were successful in collecting it. A site was procured and the building commenced. In 1850, men were selected to fill the offices of the district with perseverence sufficient to overcome all obstacles which were presented in their way, and the speedy completion of the building was the result; and we are happy to report the present prospects of the school encouraging. The building and site has been obtained at an expense of $5,500. The board feel determined to do all in their power to make this school worthy the patronage so liberally bestowed. The district is in much need of apparatus and a district library, and we believe if the Union schools could have their share of the township libraries and of the library fund, much more benefit might be derived than is now obtained.

S. WRIGHT,
Secretary of the Board.

Battle Creek, Jan. 3, 1852.

YPSILANTI UNION SCHOOL.

YPSILANTI, April 30, 1852.

HON. FRANCIS W. SHEARMAN, *Superintendent of Public Instruction:*

DEAR SIR—The directors of Ypsilanti Union School respectfully transmit, subject to your disposal, the following brief report of the rise, progress and present condition of this instuittion.

This school was organized in October, 1849, under a special aet of legislation authorizing the directors to adopt any system which would not conflict with the general school law.

It was a bold and in many respects an unprecedented experiment, undertaken by one district alone, and involving an amount of pecuniary responsibility which nothing but zeal in the cause of education could have induced its projectors to assume, and which nothing but great faith in the feasibility of their enterprise could have justified them in assuming.

In October 1851, two years from the time the school was organized, a second district united with the first, and since then it has been sustained by the united efforts of the two districts—still leaving two others in our village which have not seen fit to unite with us. While under the control of a single district it was known as a model school, but soon after the union of the two, there then being no school in this part of the country which afforded advantages superior to those of the common district school, it was deemed advisabie to extend the course of instruction, not only that our own children might receive a finished as well as a thorough and practical education at home, and under the parents' immediate protection, but also as an inducement for pupils from abroad to become connected with the institution. In this respect it is believed we have gone beyond most institutions in this and other States.

In a large majority of the Union Schools in the State of New York, the course of instruction is limited to that of the common district school, while but few give advantages of a classic or even an extended English course. Owing to this deficiency, they are in many instances compelled to support as separate schools, both an Academic and a Union School. We have aimed to unite both of these in one; and how far we have succeeded, the present condition of the school will show. From its character, the privileges it afforded and the large and comprehensive course of study then adopted, it insensibly, and by a kind of common consent, became known as Union Seminary, which name it has since borne, without, it is believed, giving offence to other seminaries, or bringing discredit upon the name.

If it is the first institution of the kind which has assumed this well merited distinction, it is to be hoped it will not be the last, for surely such schools taking the rank and doing the labor of seminaries, in our populous and enterprising villages, are the hope of the State, not only as seats of academical learning, but as preparatory schools for our University; and there can be no good reason why they should not take *title* and position in keeping with their real rank and importance.

The buildings belonging to the district are valued at $8,000; the annual expense of school $2,300; the average attendance of pupils, 250; the average amount raised by tax for payment of teachers' salaries, 200; and the expenses per scholar to the inhabitants of the district, for common school privileges, $5.

This average per district scholar, though no higher than in many common district schools, we are in hopes soon to reduce at least one half.

The following course of studies have been adopted, and is now pursued by the classes in the school. Some will have completed the course at the expiration of the present term:

COURSE OF STUDIES—PREPARATORY.

Orthography, Reading, Penmanship, Modern Geography, Grammar, Arithmetic written and mental, Geography of the Heavens, History of the United States and Analysis.

FIRST YEAR.

First—Higher Arithmetic, Advanced Grammar, Ancient Geography.

Second—Algebra begun, Higher Arithmetic, Advanced Grammar.

Third—Book Keeping, Algebra finished, Syntax and Prosody.

Fourth—Bourdon begun, Physiology, Botany.

Composition during the year—Parker's Aid.

SECOND YEAR.

First—Bourdon finished, Botany, Geometry.

Second—Geometry finished, History, Rhetoric.

Third—Trigonometry, History, Rhetoric.

Fourth—Calculus, History, Logic.

Composition during the year—Parker's Aid.

THIRD YEAR.

First—Surveying, Geology and Mineralogy, Mental Philosophy.

Second—Chemistry, Mental Philosophy, Natural Philosophy.

Third—Natural Philosophy, Mental Philosophy, Agricultural Chemistry.

Fourth—Astronomy, Moral Scienee, Elements of Criticism.

Composition during the year.

There are two Primary departments for youeg pupils, and a Preparatory, which students are required to pass through before entering upon the other course.

TERMS OF TUITION PER QUARTER FOR FOREIGN PUPILS.

Primary Department,	$2 00
Common English branches,	2 50
Common English, with one high English,	3 00
Common, with one or two high English,	4 00
Languages,	4 50
Music, with use of Piano extra,	9 00
Painting and Drawing, Extra,	2 00

It is worthy of remark that the course of study is as thorough and extensive as in any other institution in the State, and that the rates of tuition are lower than in most.

In addition to the English course, just attention is paid in preparing young men for college, and much time and labor devoted to instruction in the modern languages. During the past year there have been large classes in French, German, Music, Painting and Drawing.

A philosophical, chemical and mathematical apparatus of considerable value, belongs to the Seminary, and the town library, containing over one thousand volumes, is kept in the building. The Encyclopedia Americana, and several other valuable books for reference have been recently added, and are accessible to the members of the school. There are now in the University at Ann Arbor, a number of students from this school, several of whom entered one year in advance.

The number of foreign pupils connected with the school has increased very much since it was first opened; and during the past year, as our catalogue will show, a large number have been in attendance from different parts of this State, and some few from other States. Our building, which will accommodate from sixty to seventy with rooms for study, has usually been full, and during the fall and winter quarter, several applications for admission have been refused, for want of additional room accommodations in the building. This large number of foreign pupils who have been united with the school, and without any special effort or solicitation on our part, plainly shows that our course of instruction, the method of teaching pursued by our teachers, and the management of the school, are appreciated, and that a school based upon the Union System may compete with the best institutions of our land.

Our school year is divided into two terms of twenty-two weeks each, and each term into two quarters of eleven weeks.

At the close of each term there is an examination, at which time the classes are publicly examined in the branches they have pursued, and at the close of the third quarter there is a public examination and exhibition.

There are two literary societies connected with the school, which have regular monthly public exercises, and before one of which, during the past winter, public lectures on different subjects pertaining to popular education have been delivered.

It has been an object in this sketch to state as briefly as possible, the most important features of our school, that the public generally may know what we have accomplished in so short a space as two and a half years, and what may be accomplished in almost every village in our State in the same laudable enterprise. What public spirit has done in Ypsilanti it will do elsewhere; and if others see anything commendable in our example we trust it will be speedily followed in other places, and the advantages of a liberal and through English and classical education be placed within the reach of numbers by whom it cannot now be obtained.

From the success which has crowned our efforts, and the high position which our school has attained in so short a period, we cannot bring this report to a close without urging the friends of education in other places to hazard at least an experiment in the union system; neither do we hesitate to express an opinion that although much our colleges and universities may do in the cause of education, the *great work* of educatnig the rapidly increasing population of this commonwealth must be performed in and through the influence of union schools or seminaries. Upon these the safety and perpetuity of our national superstructure will mostly depend.

C. JOSLIN, *Sec. District Board.*

LANSING UNION SCHOOL.

LANSING, May, 1852.

To the Hon. FRANCIS W. SHEARMAN, *Superintendent of Public Instruction, &c.:*

DEAR SIR—Having the cause of popular education at heart, and regarding as I do with deep interest the efforts which are being made from time to time, not only in our own State but also in many others, to bring within the reach of every youth the means of acquiring a thoroughly *practical* if not liberal education, thereby placing each individual member of the rising generation on the same great democratic platform of equality and intelligence, which is the basis of our republican institutions, giving to them greater permanency and inciting to a healthy advancement in the cause of human progress, do I most gladly comply with your very reasonable request in transmitting you a brief history of the origin, rise and present prospects of the "LANSING UNION SCHOOL," located in the northern, or as it is termed, the "lower town" portion of this village. School District No. 2, in the township of Lansing, Michigan, was first organized in 1847, comprising at that time five sections of land, (the greater portion, however, covered with dense forest,) including the north one-third part of this village; a school house of ordinary capacity was erected, in which a school has been kept up on an average of six months each year. But owing to the rapid influx of population, the school building soon proved inadequate to the wants of the district, and, as a legitimate result, petty *select* schools sprung into existence, drawing from the *people's* school its most effectual aid and care, and finally its influence and character in community.

This state of things could not long remain unnoticed and without correction, while healthier influences were exerted all about us. The beneficial workings of the *Union School system*, as put into operation at Marshall, Battle Creek, Jonesville, and other places, had attracted the attention of many of the most active and influential citizens of the district, and not unfrequently was it made the topic of conversation; its applicability to the existing wants of the district was discussed, and its happy effects on community made known. The examination of the merits and feasibility of the plan strengthened the conviction that in every respect it was well calculated to afford to the community at once, an economical and yet thorough system, and means of education, yielding them every advantage to be derived from the best conducted High Schools and Academies, without their attendant evils and expense, fully commensurate with their wants, open alike to all, and within the reach of all.

Such being the light in which the Union School system of education was regarded here, that at the Annual School meeting on the 30th September, 1850, the practicability and expediency of erecting a suitable building and sustaining a "Union School," was fully and ably discussed, and resolutions to purchase a site, to raise the necessary funds, and to enter at once in right good earnest into the work of erecting a large and commodious building, with a suitable bell and school apparatus, were almost unanimously agreed to. A committee was appointed to prepare plans, and estimates of costs, &c., and to report the same at an adjourned meeting in January, then following.

The committee deserve great credit for their earnest endeavors to make the building what it should be, and yet avoid unnecessary expense and outlay of funds, as appears from the plans and estimates submitted at the January meeting, as also have the building committee exhibited much good sense and faithfulness in the carrying of those plans into execution, as the building itself will most clearly evidence. The work has advanced so nearly to completion that the district board have decided to open the school for the reception of pupils about the 7th of June next. The effort is indeed as praiseworthy as the building is beautiful. Erected at an expense (including site, etc.,) of about $5,000, on a most delightful elevation, retired from the business portion of the village, commanding a distinct view of almost the entire village, it is being fitted up with especial reference to health, comfort and convenience, and is sufficiently large to accommodate from 250 to 300 pupils. The building is constructed of brick, two stories high and basement beneath, standing thirty-six by sixty feet on the ground.

The basement will contain the fuel and (in case the original design is carried out) also the apparatus for warming the various rooms by means of heated air conveyed to them in pipes. The first story, twelve feet high, is separated by a hall in the centre into two rooms of equal size. The second story is mainly occupied by one general school room, which will serve also for an assembly room. The north end of this story is divided into two small rooms, one to contain the literary and school apparatus, the other will be devoted to the wishes of the principal either as a private apartment or recitation room. The windows are large and high, and will admit of every requisite ventilation, clearly indicating that physical education has not been lost sight of by those having its erection in charge. Another feature, too often regarded of little moment, is the arrangement and division of the play grounds; these are entered by separate doors from the rear of the hall, and each surrounded by a high, close board fence, and furnished with suitable out-buildings.

The Board have secured the services of Mr. John S. Dixon, as principal, whose acknowledged ability and ripe scholarship, together with his long experience and success in conducting schools of this character, have gained for him an enviable reputation. They will also employ such number of competent assistant teachers as the wants of the school may indicate. It is earnestly hoped and expected that the institution may in no degree disappoint the expectations of those who have so nobly cared for our village youth, who, as past experience shows, must receive an education somewhere, either at some well conducted school, or amid the haunts of vice and folly.

The course of educatiou will comprise a primary, middle, and classical department, and the Board express the determination that no effort on their part shall be wanting to secure competent teachers, and suitable apparatus to make the school one of the very best in the State; so that the various branches from the primary lessons of childhood, up to the higher and more abstruse branches of a classical education, can be pursued in it, with profit and success.

In conclusion, permit me to add that the establishment of such a school in this section of the State is peculiarly gratifying to all who feel a lively interest in the progress of the educational cause. May this system of schools, of which we have good reason to be proud, raise its standard still higher, until there is afforded to the youth of every community throughout the entire State—and all have a moral right to exercise their minds in contemplating all that is grand and beautiful in the vast creation of thought—that intellectual culture and social improvement which will enable them to act well their part in the great drama of life; that as they look abroad on the rich splendors of God's material universe, and investigate more truly the laws which govern matter and mind, they may be only the better prepared to disseminate and make known the rich rewards of a TRUE EDUCATION over the State—the nation and the wide world.

Very respectfully and truly yours,

S. S. CORYELL.

DETROIT LADIES' ACADEMY.

This institution, organized but a few months since, has met with the most liberal encouragement, and it is confidently hoped that the anticipations of those who have manifested so friendly an interest in its success may be realized in its future usefulness and prosperity.

It is the determination of those engaged in the enterprise, to make the Academy, in all respects, a school of the highest order. That they may, by rendering its establishment permanent, the more effectually secure this object, the large and commodious mansion of Dr. Russel, on Fort street, has been purchased, and will be fitted up expressly for this purpose. A competent board of instructors, carefully selected with reference to their experience and ability to teach, will be employed, and the most thorough instruction in all the useful and ornamental branches of education, will be furnished, while, at the same time, the morals, deportment and social habits of the pnpils will receive unwearied attention. All Sectarian views will be studiously avoided in the influenee exerted by the Teachers over those committed to their care. The young Ladies who are members with the family, will be expected to attend such places of Religious Worship as their friends may specify.

In the Government of the School no more rules are enjoined than are indispensably necessary, but with these a strict and uniform compliance will be required. A faithful record will be kept, showing the punctuality, conduct and standing of each pupil in every class, which will be transmitted to her parents or guardian at the close of every term.

The Academic Year is divided into three Terms of fourteen weeks each.

The First Term commences on the second Monday in September; the second on the first Monday in January; and the third on the fourth Monday in April—giving two weeks vacation at the close of the Spring and Fall terms.

There will be an examination of the Academic Department at the close of each term, and a public examination of the whole School at the close of the Scholastic Year, during the last week of July; at which time Diplomas will be granted to all who have completed the entire course of study, and sustained a satisfactory examination in each department.

DEPARTMENTS AND COURSE OF STUDY—PRIMARY DEPARTMENT.

Eclectic Primer, Eclectic Spelling Book, Eclectic Readers, 1st and 2d, Mitchell's Small Geography, Arithmetic, Thompson's First Lessons, Exercises on Slates and Blackboards.

PREPARATORY.

Town's Fourth Reader, Eclectic Speller, Mental Arithmetic—Colburn, Young Analyzer, McElligot, Geography—Mitchell, Grammar—Smith, History United States—Wilson, Arithmetic—Thompson's 2d Book, Botany for Beginners, Parker's Exercises in Compositions.

ACADEMIC COURSE—FIRST YEAR.

Manual of Orthography to Definition—McElligott, Grammar—Brown, Higher Arithmetic—Thompson, Ancient Geography—Mitchell's, Mental Algebra—Tower, Natural Philosophy—Parker, General History—Willard.

Parker's Exercises, Reading and Writing.

SECOND YEAR.

Algebra—Davie's 1st Lessons, Physiology—Lambert's 3d Book, Chemistry—Johnson, Botany—Wood, Book-Keeping—Mayhew, Domestic Economy—Beecher, Natural Theology—Paley, Astronomy—Mitchell's Burritt, Mental Philosophy—Upham, Logic—Hedges.

Parker's Aids to Composition.

THIRD YEAR.

Geometry—Davies' Legendre, Geology—Ruschenberger, Algebra—Davies' Bourdon, Paradise Lost—Milton, Rhetoric—Newman, Moral Science—Wayland, Evidences of Christianity, Paley, General Review.

Particular attention given to Reading, Orthography, Pronunciation, Composition and Penmanship, throughout the entire course.

EXPENSES

Tuition in Primary Department, per term of fourteen weeks,	$4 00
" Preparatory " " "	6 00
" Academic Course—1st year's studies,	8 00
" " " —2d and 3d year's studies,	10 00
" Languages, (Extra,) each,	5 00
" Music—Piano or Guitar,	12 00
" Drawing or Painting in Water Colors,	6 00
Use of Piano for Practice,	3 00
Board, together with Fuel, Lights, Washing, Furnished Rooms, and Tuition in Preparatory Department, per year,	150 00
" " with Academic Course—1st year,	156 00
" " " " —2d and 3d years, each,	162 00

Payment each term in advance. No deduction made for students who enter at any time after the commencement of the term, nor for absence after they have entered, unless on account of protracted illness.

MISS S. HUNT.

GREGORY'S COMMERCIAL COLLEGE.

DETROIT, October 6, 1851.

To FRANCIS W. SHEARMAN,

Superintendent of Public Instruction of the State of Michigan:

DEAR SIR—Your letter with a copy of your annual report, came to hand to-day. Agreeable with your request, I send the following report, also one of my circulars.

In May, 1850, with the encouragement of a number of the first business men of this city, I organized a school to be known by the name and style of Gregory's Commercial College, myself acting as principal of said institution, with E. C. Walker, Esq., as lecturer on Commercial Law. The object of which is to secure to young men (who never have had the expe, rience of the diversified functions of the counting-room,) a thorough and practical commercial education. The course of study proposed embraces penmanship, book-keeping by double-entry, commercial calculations, and commercial law. The system of teaching in said institution discards the use of text-books, and relies upon oral and black-board instruction. Pupils are instructed individually and not in classes, so that they may enter at any time and proceed in ratio of their capacity and assiduity. The school, though small at first, has from month to month gradually increased until we have found it necessary to procure assistant teachers. The first year ending June 1st, 1851, the number of students that entered the college was 63. It usually takes young men of ordinary capacity three months to complete the course of instruction as arranged for this class of institutions.

The Commercial College serves as a connecting link between the academic institution and the counting-house of the merchant. The literary and scientific institution contributes to the discipline and general information of the mind, breadth and comprehensiveness of view, and the enlargement of the understanding. While the discipline of the Commercial College contributes directly and largely to these ends, it also enables the possessor of these attainments to apply them to the practical details of business, in one of the most important pursuits of life. Occupying this vantage ground, the beginner in a mercantile career is not appalled or embarrassed by the difficulties which inevitably beset the man who is destitute of a commercial education. A man may have natural sagacity, but without this discipline, or the information which is more speedily obtained by this discipline than is usually obtained by years of experience, he can hardly expect success in business, or an eminent standing in his profession.

In conelusion, the undersigned feels confident, from his experience both in the practice and theory of the subjects of instruction, and with the aid of such assistants as may be required, that he will be enabled to advance those who avail themselves of the advantage offered to the rank of thorough and accomplished accountants.

Respectfully yours,

URIAH GREGORY.

METEOROLOGY.

Under article XI. of the revised constitution, relating to Education, it is made the duty of the legislature to encourage the promotion of intellectual, scientific, and agricultural improvement. It would seem to be the province of the department of Public Instruction to recognize as a legitimate field of reflection, the efforts which have been made by the national government to reduce to a system the important science of meteorology. The legislature of Michigan has already made an appropriation for the requisite instruments, and provided by law for the keeping of the proper tables, under the forms adopted by the Smithsonian Institution, at Washington. It is also made the duty of the Regents to provide for keeping meteorological records, which are to be hereafter published with the report of the Superintendent of Public Instruction.

ANN ARBOR, 27th April, 1852.

HON. FRANCIS W. SHEARMAN, *Superintendent of Public Instruction:*

DEAR SIR—I accede with pleasure to your request for a copy of the table communicated by me to the Smithsonian Institute, exhibiting in inches and decimals of an inch, the monthly fall of RAIN in this city, for the three years named.

The instrument which I use is DeWitt's nine inch Conical Rain Gage, the principle and construction of which you may find described in Silliman's Journal of Science, Vol. XXII., page 321. Tables like the following, sometimes include with the rain, an account also of the water of melted snow. It should be observed that this does not.

	1849.	1850.	1851.
January	,63.	,66.	,99.
February	,14.	,80.	2,48.
March	1,69.	2,47.	1,02.
April	2,13.	,95.	3,90.
May	3,59.	,30.	5,85.
June	3,46.	3,44.	2,41.
July	3,27.	2,15.	5,04.
August	3,10.	6,52.	4,18.
September	3,90.	1,86.	2,08.
October	3,38.	1,09.	2,94.
November	1,66.	1,73.	2,48.
December	,37.	,93.	2,27.
Total	27,33.	22,90.	35,64.

From this table it would appear that the variation in the annual amount of rain which falls here is large. The quantity which fell the last year exceeded that of 1850 by nearly thirteen inches. *Is the rise and fall of the waters in our great lakes due to the varying quantity of rain which falls in different years, in the region which they occupy?*

The annual average in this place, for the three years above named, is 28,62 inches. The annual average in Boston is stated to be 39 inches; in the States of New York and Ohio, 36; in Rome, 39; in England, 32; in Paris, 22; in St. Petersburgh, 16; in Calcutta, 81; in Vera Cruz, 278; and in San Luis, S. A., 280.

The peculiar situation of our State in relation to the great lakes, in addition to those reasons which are common to us with other States, urges to the establishment of a well appointed system of meteorological observations. It cannot be doubted that the faithful prosecution of such a system for a few years, would result not only in a valuable contribution to science, but in the developement of facts and principles of much importance to the agricultural interests of our State.

I am happy to know that the subject has strongly attracted your attention, and can but hope that you may be completely successful in the accomplishment of your utmost desires in regard to it.

Very respectfully yours,

L. SMITH HOBART.

RULES

FOR THE GOVERNMENT OF TOWNSHIP LIBRARIES, &c.

NOTE. By section 144, the township board have power to suspend the operations of section 115 of the school law, which provides for the distribution of the books once in three months, and to restore the same. See sections 115 and 144. The following rules are taken from the pamphlet edition of the school laws of 1848:

DUTIES OF LIBRARIAN.

1. The township librarian shall keep a catalogue of all the books belonging to the township library, in a blank book to be provided for that purpose, and he shall be accountable to the township for their safe keeping. In said book he shall enter in a legible hand, the *title* and *number* of each book belonging to the library, with such additions as may from time to time be made thereto.

2. He shall label each book belonging to the township library, before it is drawn therefrom, thus.

"——— *Township Library.* *No.* ——.
"This book is returnable to the director the last Saturday of every month. The drawer is responsible for all damages done to it while in his possession."

The preceding label should, if practicable, be *neatly printed,* and snugly pasted on the inner side of the cover. The name of the township to which the library belongs should be inserted in the first blank. The number of the several volumes should be filled with a pen, commencing with No. 1.

3. Section 51 provides that "the director shall draw from the township library, the proportion of books to which the district may be entitled, and return the same to the township library at the expiration of every three months." The times for drawing books from the township library, and returning the same, shall be the first Saturday of January, April, July and October, between the hours of 12 o'clock M. and 3 o'clock P. M.

According to section 115, the books of the township library are to be distributed by the township librarian among the several districts of the township, in proportion to the number of children in each between the ages of four and eighteen years, as the same shall appear by the last report of the director thereof. But all maps, charts, engravings and lexicons, belonging to the library, shall remain therein, and at all proper times be open to inspection by the citizens of the township. [See section 144.]

4. The librarian shall, in a book to be provided for that purpose, charge every director with the books he may draw from the township library, by their *numbers;* and in like manner credit the same when they shall be returned.

5. He shall make a written report to the school inspectors, between the 25th and 31st days of March in each year, setting forth the number of books in the library, and their condition. The report shall also state what books have been added to the library during the year; what books have been lost, if any; what injured; and what amount of fines have been imposed and collected; together with such other particulars as the inspectors shall direct; which report shall be placed on file with papers of their office.

DRAWING BOOKS.

1. No person, except directors of school districts, shall be permitted to draw books from the township library; nor shall *they* be entitled to draw at any other times than specified above.

Nevertheless the librarian may allow directors who have not drawn books for any quarter, to receive them at other times.

2. None but inhabitants of school districts shall be entitled to draw books from the directors; and no director shall loan a book to any person who is not a resident of his district.

3. No person shall be permitted to draw more than one book at a time, unless there are books enough in the library to accommodate all persons that are entitled to draw therefrom. And in no case shall any person be permitted to draw, at one time, more than one book for himself, and one for each member of his family that is able to read.

4. The library shall be open for drawing and returning books, every Saturday, (except those days when the director returns books to the township library, and draws anew,) from 12 o'clock M. until 2 o'clock P. M., unless the director, with the consent of the district board, shall change the time, in which case he shall give due notice thereof. The director may, at his discretion, allow persons entitled to receive books, to draw them at other times, as may suit the convenience of the parties. But all books, whenever drawn, shall be returned to the director the last Saturday of every month.

5. Different persons wishing any book or books, shall be entitled to draw the same according to the priority of their applications.

FINES AND DAMAGES.

1. For every volume retained beyond the time established by these rules, a fine of five cents shall be imposed for the first day, and a fine of ten cents per week thereafter, until the book shall be returned.

2. For turning down leaves, tearing, greasing, or in any way mutilating or injuring books beyond their natural wear, the director is authorized to impose a fine of not less than five cents, nor more than twenty, for each and every offence. No person, against whom fines stand unpaid, shall be entitled to draw books. But any person dissatisfied with fines imposed by a director, shall be entitled to appeal to the township librarian, whose decision shall be final.

3. Any person losing a book belonging to the township library, shall pay therefor not less than the first cost of the same, and not more than twice that amount, to be determined by the director; or, if lost by a director, to be determined by the librarian; and if lost by a librarian, to be determined by the board of school inspectors.

4. All fines received by directors shall be paid to the township librarian, who shall pay the same into the township treasury for the benefit of the township library.

RULES FOR THE GOVERNMENT OF THE MEDICAL COLLEGE IN THE UNIVERSITY OF MICHIGAN, ADOPTED BY THE BOARD OF REGENTS OF THE UNIVERSITY, JULY, 1850.

CATALOGUE OF MEDICAL FACULTY.

Abram Sager, M. D.,—Professor of Obstetrics and Diseases of Women and Children.

S. H. Douglass, M. D.,—Professor of Medical Jurisprudence and Pharmaceutical Chemistry.

Samuel Denton, M. D.,—Professor of Theory and Practice of Physic snd Pathology.

Moses Gunn, M. D.,—Professor of Anatomy and Lecturer on Surgery, &c.

J. Adams Allen, M. D.,—Professor of Materia Medica and Physiology.

OF THE FACULTY AND THEIR DUTIES.

1st. This department of the University shall be styled the "Department of Medicine and Surgery in the University of Michigan."

2d. The Professors now or hereafter to be appointed, shall constitute the Faculty of this Department, who shall be styled the "Faculty of Medicine and Surgery."

3d. The immediate government of this department shall be vested in the Faculty, whose duty it shall be to instruct the students in the several branches of learning taught in this department of the University.

4th. One of the Professors appointed annually by the Faculty, as President thereof, shall preside at stated meetings of the Faculty, and be empowered to call special meetings whenever in his judgment necessary, or upon application of any two Professors.

5th. At all meetings of the Faculty a majority shall constitute a quorum. In the absence of the President, a President *pro tem.* shall be appointed by the Faculty, who shall discharge the duties of the President. The presiding officer shall be always entitled to a vote.

6th. The Faculty shall annually appoint one of their number Secretary, who shall keep a record of all their proceedings and submit the same to the Regents at the annual meeting, for inspection.

7th. The President of the Faculty shall keep a book in which shall be registered the time of entrance, name, and age of each student, with his place of residence.

8th. The Faculty shall present at the annual meetings of the Regents, a report on such matters touching the interests of the department, as in their view call for the action of the Board.

OF ADMISSION.

1st. Every candidate for admission shall present satisfactory evidence of good moral character, shall exhibit evidence of a good English education, the knowledge of Natural Philosophy, the Elementary Mathematical Sciences, and such an acquaintance with the Latin and Greek languages as will enable him to appreciate the technical language of medicine, and read and write prescriptions.

Provided, these literary requirements shall not be insisted upon for the two first years, until the student becomes a candidate for the degree of M. D.

TERMS OF STUDY—SYSTEM OF INSTRUCTION, &C.

1st. The course of study in this department shall commence the first Wednesday in October, and continue until the first Wednesday in April.

2d. There shall be four Lectures daily, (Saturdays excepted.)

3d. Each Professor shall daily examine the class upon the subject of the lecture of the previous day.

4th. All text books used shall be selected by the Faculty, subject to the revision of the Board of Regents.

5th. Candidates for graduation shall announce themselves as such at the close of their first course, or the commencement of their second, and shall be examined upon the subjects of Anatomy, Physiology, Materia Medica, and chemistry.

6th. Candidates for graduation shall be required to write a thesis upon some Medical or Surgical subject, once in two weeks, which thesis shall be read and defended before the class, on such Saturdays as may be appointed by the Faculty.

OF INITIATION FEES.

1st. Every student on entering shall pay the sum of ten dollars, as an initiaton fee, which money is to be appropriated to the increase of the Library, Museum, and other means of illustration.

2d. Clergymen, members of the legal profession, and graduates of other respectable medical institutions, may be permitted to attend the course of instruction, as honorary members of the Medical Department.

DEGREES.

1st. All degrees shall be conferred by the Board of Regents, upon the recommendation of the Medical Faculty.

2d. In order that a student may be recommended for the degree of Doctor of Medicine, he shall exhibit evidence of having pursued the study of Medicine and Surgery for three years, with some respectable practitioner of Medicine; must have attended two courses of lectures, the last in the Medical Department of the University of Michigan; must have submitted to the Faculty an original thesis on some Medical subject, and have passed an examination, held at the close of the second course, satisfactory to the Faculty.

3d. An allowance of one year from the term of study may be made in favor of graduates of the departments of Science and Arts, and of other respectable literary colleges, and respectable practitioners, of four years' standing, may be admited to the degree of M. D., by attendance upon one course of lectures, on passing the requisite examination.

Adopted at the annual meeting of the Board, July, 1850.

E. N. WILCOX, *Secretary.*

As an incentive to effort on the part of the student, a regulation to conform to the following has been authorized by the Board of Regents.

The Medical Faculty transmitted the following communication which was read, and the Faculty authorized to make the regulation recommended:

The Medical Faculty beg leave to add to their report as presented, the following recommendation, viz: to provide for the publication of one or more such thesis as may be selected by the Faculty, at each annual commencement of this Department.

Adopted July, 1851.

TEXT BOOKS.

The law does not make the recommendation of the Superintendent imperative upon school officers to adopt the books. Nor is it believed that good policy would require it to be so, for evil might ensue, by its arbitrary force upon those who are indeed good judges and good teachers, but who might be of opinion that they could be more successful in adopting and teaching from books other than those recommended. Without the cordial co-operation of school officers, teachers and parents, neither the law nor the recommendation would result in any practical good. It cannot be expected, however much it might be desired, that all can agree upon the merits of the same book or books, any more than all can agree upon one system of belief in matters of faith, or upon the merits of an agricultural implement. The ***best book***, like the best farming utensil, eventually gains its way into use, recommendation or no recommendation. The examination and recommendation of a person whom the legislature deems to be competent, it was supposed, would not be without its benefits, in facilitating information and presenting useful books to the view of teachers and others, thus making way for their gradual introduction into schools, not in a forced, imperative manner, but by eliciting the examination and investigation of all interested. Nor can this be viewed in any other light than the requirement of a good policy, which ensures improvement and progression. For, if it be urged that each successive officer is to recommend the same series, without reference to his own judgment, or that the same officer is to perpetuate his own recommendations, *there is an end to all further advancement.* Our scholars and our schools, in the next quarter of a century, would be found far back in the path of retrogression and behind the light of the age.

It does not follow, that in consequence of the recommendation of a list or series of books, different from those which may have been recommended, that the books which are in our schools are to be thrown promiscuously out of the doors of our school houses—that parents are forced to the necessity and expense of furnishing new books—that teachers are to close their lessons from before the eyes of their pupils; all this would be confusion, and far from the object intended by the law. The useful results anticipated, will be found in throwing out before the public, before teachers and school officers, a list of books from time to time, which have been examined and compared with those in use, and which, like all other lists they have had before them, it may be hoped, might afford some facility to them in their own good work of investigation; leaving such books, after announcing the result of such examination by this office, where the law itself leaves them—subject to adoption or rejection, to change or otherwise, as the best judgment of school officers and teachers, and their knowledge of the local wants of the schools or districts, shall afterwards dictate.—*Superintendent's Report*, 1850.

* * * * * *

There certainly can be no serious objection to the recommendation of works which, in the judgment of this department, seems best adapted to the purposes and uses of teachers; leaving such works to find their way into our schools upon their actual merits, and both teachers and scholars free to avail themselves of such authorities as in their opinion might most effectually aid their investigations. It is not contemplated, either in the law or by this department, to make such recommendations imperative. The great object of this requirement would seem to be that a list of suitable books, properly and carefully examined, should be thrown before teachers and school officers, in the hope of facilitating their own examinations, and by some *unity of action*, that something useful may be accomplished towards a desirable uniformity. No reason has yet occurred to this office, to modify or change the ground assumed npon this subject, in its last communication to the Legislature.

The organization of schools and academies, the establishment of Universities, liberal endowments and apppropriations for teachers, are but first steps. They are all preparatory to that system of training and development which is called education. This system does not consist in the acquisition of mere facts, learned without order, and remembered without arrangement, but in that orderly training which develops in their right direction, the whole physical, intellectual and moral nature. Education, therefore, demands system and order. There must be correspondence and unity in all its parts.

In a perfect system, each branch has its appropriate ideas, properly classified and arranged. For this, much study and much experience in teaching are indispensable. The mechanic or farmer learns his business only by labor and toil, continued through many years. Systems of instruction for the young, that are to furnish food for the mind and give character to our schools, can only be contstructed by varied knowledge, aided by long experience. They can be formed only from ripe knowledge, made practical by much experience in teaching, and become well known only by the fruits they bear. Under such impreasions, the attention of this office was directed at an early season to the subject of text books. Our schools were filled with multifarious systems, having no connection with each other, and consequently carrying forward no common system of education. In mathematics, where uniformity of system is most necessary, and most easily attainable, various systems, differing from each other in their organic structure, were often to be found in the same school, and frequently in the same class. Systematical instruction in the exact sciences, based upon uniform and settled principles, could not thus be given. Under this state of things, it seemed to be necessary to make selections and recommendations which would secure at least a uniformity in the same school, and if possible, in the same district. In accomplishing this, it was to be expected that differences of judgment and opinion would arise, not only among practical educators and teachers, but among various authors and publishers, whose interests were more or less affected. It is perhaps due to the interests of our schools that the reason for some of the principal selections made and recommended by this office, should be given.

The works of Professor Davies, on the subject of mathematics, and which were much in use in our schools, were greatly preferred, because of their scientific arrangement, the clearness and precision of their rules, and their eminently practical character. The author of these works had long been at the head of the mathematical department in the military school at West Point, had prepared a course of mathematical text books long since adopted and used in that institution, and in whole or in part, in most of the collegiate institutions of the country. A second series was also prepared, on the same general plan, for academies, and a third, embracing an arithmetical course, for schools. Our University had adopted, and now use the higher course. To have the same system in the schools, the preparatory institutions and the University, appeared to be of the first importance. The principles of exact science are the same in arithmetic, in algebra, and in the higher branches of mathematics, and should be taught and explained in the same manner, so that a pupil who has thoroughly learned his arithmetic, will have acquired those habits of thought which prepare him for the study of the advanced course. The course of Professor Davies is the only complete one now before the public, in which all the subjects forming a full course of mathematical instruction are taught according to one general method. This course has been rendered of still greater value as a system of education, by a recent publication entitled the "Logic and Utility of mathematics." This work gives a full analysis of mathematics as a subject of knowledge, explains the mental processes which the study develops, the nature of the reasoning employed, and the best method of imparting instruction. It is a work which should be in the hands of every practical teacher, and its superior merit entitles it to a place in every district library of the State.

In the selection of text books for history, the same considerations governed. The series of Mrs. Willard embraces a school history of the United States, a larger history for advanced classes, and a general history, ancient and modern, all constructed upon the same general plan. This series, more than any other, seems to connect chronology, geography and the physical development and growth of our country, with the rise and fall of nations and the progress of civilization. They are marked by a wide range of thought, a pure and ardent spirit, a warm patriotism, and a methodical arrangement particularly adapted to instruction.

For the work on natural philosophy, we are indebted to the system of public instruction established in the schools of Boston. Mr. Parker, whose philosophical works are recommended, has been long known as the head of the public schools of that city. His works have passed the ordeal of adoption and use, not only in that city, but in other places equally distinguished for good schools and general intelligence. Their peculiarity consists particularly in clearness of style, correct arrangement and copiousness of matter.

Grammar, it has been known from long experience, has been taught mechanically. To break up this false system, the author of the work recommended for use in our schools, has adopted a method which subjects every step to careful analysis, obliges the pupil to chalk out on the black board the results of every lesson, and compare every principle with those which have preceded. Thus was substituted a series of *connected principles*, for a set of arbitrary rules, making Grammar a science, enlightening and expanding the mind, instead of a dubious art, loading and clogging the memory.

No reason need be assigned for recommending a return to the elementary works of Dr. Webster. Although perhaps subject to objection, others in some respects are no more perfect. Besides, his dictionary is the standard of our language, and has become a national treasure, as well as the monument of his industry and genius. To discard his elementary works from schools, while we adopt the higher as the basis of our literature, would seem to be unwise. Connection and uniformity in systems of instruction, will alone raise the mind to clear and connected trains of thought, while different and conflicting systems, like opposite winds and opposing currents, only produce agitation and froth.

Having thus explained the general principles which have governed this department in the recommendation of text books, it is a cause of much satisfaction that distinguished and able educators of our own State have so efficiently aided in giving the right tone to an already enlightened public sentiment on this subject.

LIST OF TEXT BOOKS.

Webster's Elementary Speller.
Swan's Spelling Book, for advanced classes.
McGuffey's 1st, 2d and 3d Readers.
Parker's Rhetorical Reader, and series of Readers.
Instructive Reader.
McElligott's Young Analyzer.
do Analytical Manual.
Davies' First Lessons in Arithmetic.
do School Arithmetic.
do University Arithmetic.
do Elementary Algebra.
do Elementary Geometry.
do Drawing and Mensuration.
do Bourdon's Algebra.
do Legendre's Geometry.
do Elements of Surveying.
do Analytical Geometry.
do Diff. and Integral Calculus.
do Descriptive Geometry.
do Shades and Shadows.
Willard's School History.
do History of the United States.
do Universal History, perspective.
do American Chirographer, a chart to aid in the study of Willard's U. S.
do English Chronographer.
do Temple of Time—a chronological chart of Universal History.
do Historical Guide for Schools.
The first Book of History, by Peter Parley.
Robbins' Outlines of History.
Mitchell's series of Geographies and Atlases—Ancient and Modern.
Clark's New English Grammar.
Parker's Progressive exercises in English composition.
Parker's Aid to English Composition.
Northend's Little Speaker.
do School Dialogues.
do Am. Speaker.
Dr. Watt's Improvement of the Mind.
Parker's First Lessons in Philosophy.
do Natural Philosophy.
Smith's Illustrated Astronomy, for Districts and Schools.
McIntyre's Astronomy and Treatise on the Globes.
Olmstead's large Philosophy, for advanced classes.
Olmstead's Astronomy, for advanced classes.
Reid & Bain's Chemistry and Electricity.
Page's Geology.
Hamilton's Physiology.
Clark's elements of Drawing.
Wood's Botany.
Liebeig's Chemistry, in its application to Agriculture and Physiology.
Sherwood & Britton's School Song and Hymn Book.
Kingsley's Juvenile Choir—for teaching vocal music.
Fulton & Eastman's Chirographic charts.
do Key to "
do Writing Books.
do Copy Books.
do Penmanship.
do Book-Keeping.
do Blank Account Books for Merchants.
do Blank Account Books for Farmers and Mechanics.

LIBRARY BOOKS.

DICTIONARIES, BOOKS OF REFERENCE, &C.

	Vols.
Penny Cyclopedia;	27
Encyclopedia Americana,	14
Webster's dictionary,	1
Worcester's dictionary,	1
Crabb's Synonymes,	1
Liddell & Scott's Greek Lexicon; or Pickering's,	1
Leverett's Latin Lexicon,	1
Anthon's Greek and Roman antiquities,	1
Fisk's Manual of classical literature,	1

Anthon's classical dictionary, ... 1
Brande's Encyclopedia of science, art and literature, ... 1
McCulloch's Universal Gazetteer, ... 2
Murray's Encyclopedia of Geography, ... 3
McCulloch's Commercial Dictionary, ... 2
Cyclopedia of Biography, ... 1
Chambers' Cyclopedia of English Literature, ... 2
Chambers' Information for the People, ... 2
Baldwin's Pronouncing Gazeteer, ... 1
Encyclopedia of Agriculture, ... 1
Ure's Dictionary of Arts and Science, ... 2
Webster's Encyclopedia of Domestic Economy, ... 1
Morse's North American Atlas 1
Universal Atlas, ... 1
Butler's Ancient Geography, ... 1
Potter's Hand-Book for Readers, ... 1
Pycroft's Course of Reading, ... 1

RELIGION, NATURAL AND REVEALED.

Kitto's Cyclopedia of Biblical Literature, ... 1
The obligations of the world to the Bible, by Dr. Spring, ... 1
Horne's introduction to the study of the Bible, ... 1
Butler's analogy of natural and revealed Religion, ... 1
Paley's natural theology, with Lord Brougham's notes, ... 2
Wiseman on the connection of science and religion, ... 1
Paley's evidences of Christianity, ... 1
Turner's sacred history of the world philosophically considered, ... 3
Bibilical legends of the Mussalman, ... 1
Milman's history of the Jews, ... 1
Milman's history of Christianity, ... 1
Ranke's history of the Popes, ... 1
History of Missions, ... 1
History of the different religious denominations in the U. States by members of the respective denominations, ... 1
Imitation of the life of Christ, ... 1

LAW AND GOVERNMENT.

The Constitution—published by order of U. S. Senate, ... 1
Wheaton on the law of Nations, ... 1
Gardner on the moral law of nations and American policy, ... 1
Blackstone's commentaries on the common law of England, ... 4
Hallam's constitutional history of England, ... 3
Constitutions of the several States, ... 1
Story on the constitution of the United States, ... 1
The Federalist, by Madison, Jay and Hamilton, ... 1
Kent's commentaries on the constitution and American law, ... 4
Messages (annual and special) of the several Presidents of the United States to Congress . . . 2
Marshall's decisions of cases of constitutional law 1
Class book on the constitution of the United States, by Hart, ... 1
Democracy in America, by De Tocqueville, ... 2
Democracy in France, by Dumas, ... 1
The people in France, by Michelet, ... 1
The legal rights of Woman, by Mansfield, ... 1
The citizen of a republic, ... 1
Cushing manual of Parliamentary practice, ... 1
Statutes of Michigan, ... 1

EDUCATION.

Schools and School systems.

Connecticutt common school journal, 1838—'42, ... 4
Connecticutt common school manual, 1846—'7, ... 1
Massachusetts common school journal, 1839—'47, ... 8
New York district school journal, 1844—'45, ... 1
Journal of the Rhode-Island institute of instruction, ... 1
Pennsylvania common school journal, 1844, ... 1
Common school system of New York. *S. S. Randall*, ... 1
School laws and returns of school committees of Massachusetts.
Reports relating to the public schools of Providence, ... 1
Barnard's report on the public schools of Rhode Island, ... 1
Annals of education for 1836—'37, ... 1
Education of mothers. *L. Aime Martin*, ... 1
Theory and practice of teaching. *D. P. Page*, ... 1
The school and school master, ... 1
History of Sunday schools. *Lewis G. Pray*, ... 1
Exercises on the black board. *John Goldsbury*, ... 1
The teacher's institute. *Wm. B. Fowle*, ... 1
The teacher's manual. *Thomas H. Palmer*, ... 1
Lectures on education. *Horace Mann*, ... 1

The teacher taught. *Emerson Davis*, ... 1
The district school as it was. *W. Burton*, ... 1
Slate and black board exercises. *W. A. Alcott*, ... 1
Mental cultivation and excitement. *A. Brigham*, ... 1
Confessions of a schoolmaster. *W. A. Alcott*, ... 1
Common schools and teacher's seminaries. *C. E. Stowe*, ... 1
History of education. *H. I. Smith*, ... 1

Domestic Education and Economy.

Humphrey's domestic education, ... 1
Beecher's domestic economy, ... 1
" " receipt book, ... 1
The mother's book, by Mrs. Child, ... 1
Phelps' fireside friend, ... 1
Combe on infancy, ... 1
Thompson's management of the sick room, ... 1
Shaw's medical remembrancer, ... 1
Hand book of needle work, ... 1
Leslie's lady's receipt book, ... 1
Frugal housewife, by Mrs. Child, ... 1
Webster's Encyclopædia of domestic economy, ... 1

Physical Education and Physiology.

Education of the senses, ... 1
Air and its uses. 1
Griscom's animal mechanism and physiology, ... 1
Combe's principles of physiology, ... 1
" constitution of man, ... 1
Johnson's economy of health, ... 1
Alcott's house I live in, ... 1
Warren on the preservation of health, ... 1

Self Education, &c.

Pycroft's course of reading, ... 1
Cobbett's advice to young men, ... 1
Beecher's lectures to young men, ... 1
Sprague's letters to a daughter, ... 1
" " young men, ... 1
Hawes' lectures to young men, ... 1
Nott's counsels to the young, ... 1
Sedgwick's morals of manners, ... 1
The young lady's friend, ... 1
Jewsbury's letters to the young, ... 1
The young maiden, by Muzzy, ... 1
The young lady's home, ... 1
Self-culture for young men, by Dr. Channing, ... 1
Self-training for young women, by Miss Sedgwick, ... 1

AGRICULTURE.

Fruit and fruit trees of America, ... 1
Agricultural chemistry, ... 1
New American Gardener, ... 1
Farmer's dictionary, ... 1
The farmer's companion, ... 1
The complete farmer, ... 1
Catechism of agricultural chemistry, ... 1
American farmer's encyclopedia, ... 1
Youatt on the horse, ... 1
do do pig, ... 1
Cultivation of the grape vine, ... 1
American flower garden directory 1
The American florist, ... 1
The American gardner, ... 2
The farmers' instructor, ... 1
American husbandry, ... 1
Agriculture and gardening, ... 1
The American poultry book, ... 1
The honey bee, ... 1
The cultivator, ... 1
The farmer's library, ... 1
Journal of agriculture, ... 1
The American polterer's companion, ... 1
Ladies' companion to the flower garden, ... 1

COMMERCE.

History of British commerce; by Clark.
Book of commerce.
McCulloch's commercial dictionary.

MANUFACTURES AND TRADES.

Beekman's history of inventions, ... 2
Panorama of trades and professions, by Hazen, ... 1
The useful arts, by Bigelow, ... 2
British manufactures, ... 6
American factories and their operatives, ... 1
Lowell as it was and it is, ... 1
Days at the factories, ... 1
Pastoral life and manufactures of the ancients, ... 1
Manufacture of porcelain, ... 1
Enterprize, industry and art of man, ... 1
Familiar illustrations of mechanics, ... 1
The book of the feet, ... 1
A tour in the manufacturing districts of England, ... 1
History of cotton manufactures in the United States, ... 1

ARCHITECTURE AND LANDSCAPE GARDENING.

Hand-Book of architecture, ... 1
Glossary of architecture, by Mrs. Tuthill, ... 1
Hints to young architects, by Wightwich, ... 1
Builder's guide, by Hill, ... 1
American house carpenter, by Hatfield, ... 1
Downing's cottage residences, ... 2
Hints on landscape gardening and rural architecture, ... 1
Browne's trees of America, ... 1
Emerson's trees and shrubs of Massachusetts, ... 1

FINE ARTS.

Reynolds' (Joshua,) discourses on the fine arts, ... 1
Lassing's history of the fine arts, ... 1
Lanzi's history of painting, ... 3
Hand-Book of painting, ... 1
Cunningham's lives of painters and sculptors, ... 2

MORAL AND MENTAL SCIENCE.

Boyd's eclectic and moral philosophy, ... 1
Wayland's elements of moral science, ... 1
Abercrombie on the moral feelings, ... 2
Henry's history of intellectual philosophy, ... 1
Abercrombie on the intellectual powers, ... 1
Whewell's elements of morality, ... 1
Dymond's essays on morality, ... 1
Coleridge's aids to reflection, ... 1

LOGIC, RHETORIC, COMPOSITION AND ELOCUTION.

Whately's elements of logic, ... 1
Mills' system of logic, ... 1
Whately's elements of rhetoric, ... 1
Kame's elements of criticism, ... 1
Parker's aids to composition, ... 1
Macery's principles of eloquence, ... 1
Russell's vocal culture, ... 1
Comstock's system of elocution, ... 1
Coldwell's manual of Elocution, ... 1
Mandeville's system of reading, ... 1
Lovell's young speaker 1
Russell's juvenile speaker, ... 1

POLITICAL ECONOMY.

Wayland's elements of political economy, ... 1
Smith's wealth of nations, ... 1
Sedgwick's public and private economy, ... 2
Claims of labor, ... 1
Capital and labor, ... 1

SCIENCES.

Objects, advantages and pleasures of science, by Brougham, ... 1
Somerville on the physical sciences, ... 1

Astronomy.

Herschell's astronomy, ... 1
Olmsted's rudiments of astronomy and natural philosophy, ... 1
" letters on " 1
" elements of " 1

Dick's Sidereal Heavens,....................1
" scenery of the Heavens,....................1
" practical astronomy,....................1
Somerville's mechanism of the Heavens,....................1
Nichol's architecture of the Heavens,....................1

Natural Philosophy.

Outlines of natural philosophy,....................1
Olmsted's school philosophy,....................1
" rudiments of,....................1
Renwick's,....................1
Chamber's,....................1
Euler's letters on,....................1

Natural History.

Smellie's philosophy of natural history,....................1
Good's book of Nature,....................1
Goldsmith's animated Nature,....................5
Duncan's sacred philosophy of the seasons,....................4
Howitt's book of the seasons,....................1
Godman's American natural history,....................2
Uncle Philip's conversations on natural history,....................1
History of insects,....................1
" birds,....................1
" quadrupeds,....................1
" the elephant,....................1
White's natural history of Selborne,....................1
Parley's anecdotes of the animal kingdom,....................1
Naturalist's library, by Sir W. Jardine,....................21
Mudies' guide to the study of Nature,....................6

Chemistry.

Silliman's chemistry,....................1
Draper's " 1
Renwick's, " 1
Liebig's agricultural chemistry,....................1

Mineralogy and Geology.

Lee's geology and mineralogy,....................1
Dana's geology,....................1
Lyall's,....................2
Page's geology.

Botany, and Vegetable Physiology.

Gray's botanical text book,....................1
Elements of vegetable physiology,....................1

Science, applied to the Arts.

Lardner's lectures on science and art,....................1
Parnell's chemistry applied to the arts,....................1
Arnott's elements of physic,....................1
Practical treatise on dyeing and calico printing,....................1
Engineer's and mechanic's companion,....................1
Farmer's land measurer,....................1
Practical treatise on road making,....................1
Renwick's practical mechanic,....................1
Working man's companion,....................1
Allen's mechanics,....................1

HISTORY.

General Works.

Pycroft's course of reading,....................1
Cyclopedia of history,....................1
Munsell's every day of chronology,....................2
Taylor's manual of ancient and modern history,....................1
Great events, by great historians,....................1
Muller's universal history,....................6
Tytler's do 4
White's, Robbin's, Worcester's, Willard's do.

Ancient.

The Scriptures of the old testament,....................1
Josephus' history of the Jews,....................2

Rollin's ancient history, ... 8
Ancient history, by various authors, ... 4
Connexion of sacred and profane history, by Davidson, ... 2
Russell's history of Palestine, ... 1
Ruins of ancient cities, ... 2
Glidden's ancient Egypt, ... 1

Greece.

Outline of Grecian history, by Christian knowledge society, ... 1
Pinnock's Goldsmith's Greece, ... 1
Heroditus and Thucydides, ... 5
Heeren's ancient Greece, ... 1
Thirlwall's history of Greece, ... 5
Demosthenes' Orations, ... 1

Rome.

Outline of Roman history, by Christian Knowledge Society, ... 1
Pinnock's Goldsmith's Rome, ... 1
Schmidt's Rome, ... 1
Furguson's Roman Republic, ... 1
Michelet's " " 1
Arnold's " " 1
Livy, Cæsar, and Salust, (translated,) 2
Cicero's orations and life, by Middleton, ... 8
Keightley's Roman Empire, ... 2
Guizott's Gibbon's decline and fall, ... 4

Asia and Africa.

History of China, by Davis, ... 2
" Btitish India, by Barrow, ... 1
" Nubia and Abysinia, by Russell, ... 1
" Arabia, by Crichton, ... 1
" Mahomet, ... 1
" Barbary States, by Russell, ... 1
" Mesopotamia and Syria, by Frazer, ... 1
" Japan, ... 1
" Palestine, by Russell, ... 1
" Moors, ... 1
" Polynesia, by Russell, ... 1

Europe.

Guizot's history of civilization in Europe, ... 4
Arnold's Lectures on modern history, ... 1
Michelet's elements of modern history, ... 1
Smythe's lectures on modern history, ... 2
Froissart's chronicles, ... 1
Hallam's middle ages, ... 2
Digby's ages of faith, ... 1
James' history of chivalry and the crusaders, ... 1
" " Charlemagne, ... 1

Italy and Switzerland.

Sismondi's Italian Republics, ... 1
Machiavelli's Florentine histories, ... 2
Smedley's Venetian history, ... 2
Spaulding's Italy, ... 1
Roscoe's de Medici and Leo X., ... 5
History of Switzerland, ... 1

Germany and North of Europe.

Kohlrausch's history of Germany, ... 1
Coke's history of Austria, ... 1
Schiller's thirty years' war, ... 1
" Revolt of the Netherlands, ... 1
Fletcher's history of Poland, ... 1
Wheaton's Denmark, Sweden and Norway, ... 1
Grattan's Netherlands, ... 1
History of Iceland, Greenland, &c., ... 1
Bell's Russian Empire, ... 2

Barrow's Peter the Great, ... 1
Voltaire's do do 1

France, Spain and Portugal.

Pictorial history of France, ... 1
Crowe's history of France, ... 3
Michelet's do do 2
The French revolution, by Theirs, ... 4
do do Carlyle, ... 1
do do Allison, ... 4
do do do abridged, ... 1
The Consulate and Empire, by Theirs, ... 2
Life of Napoleon, by Scott, ... 2
do do Hazlitt, ... 2
Camp and Court of Napoleon, ... 2
Napoleon and his Marshals, by Headly, ... 2
Napoleon's expedition into Russia, ... 1
History of Spain and Portugal, ... 5
Robertson's Charles V., ... 1
Prescott's Ferdinand and Isabella, ... 3
Napier's Peninsular war, ... 4

British Empire.

Compendium of English history, by Christian knowledge society, ... 1
do do do Keightley, ... 2
do do do Goldsmith, by Pinnock, ... 1
Turner's history of the Anglo Saxons, ... 2
Hume and Smollett's England, ... 8
Knight's Pictorial England, ... 4
Guizot's English revolution, ... 2
Carlyle's letters and speeches of Cromwell, ... 2
History of Scotland, by Scott, ... 2
do Ireland, by Moore, ... 2
do British Colonies, by Martin, ... 10
Vol. 1 Canada. 2 & 3. West Indies. 4. Gibralter and Malta. 5. Nova Scotia. 6. Good Hope. 7. Ceylon and Northern Africa. 8 & 9. East India Co. 10. South Wales, &c.

America.

General history of America, outlines of,
do do Willard, ... 1
do do Robertson, ... 1
Conquest of Mexico, by Prescott, ... 3
do Peru, by do 2
British America, by Murray, ... 3
History of United States, by Hale, ... 1
do do Willard, ... 1
do do Bancroft, ... 3
do do Graham, ... 2
Pictorial history of the United Stetes, by Frost, ... 2
do do do Goodrich, ... 2
Cooper's naval history, ... 1
Frost's book of the Navy, ... 1
do do Army, ... 1

American Indians.

Drake's book of the Indians, ... 1
Thatcher's Indian biography, ... 2
do traits of Indian character, ... 2
Poetry and history of Wyoming, ... 1
Frost's book of the Indians, ... 1
Stone's border wars, ... 2
Catlin's Indians of North America, ... 2

Particular States.

Chronicles of Plymouth, by Young, ... 1
do Massachusetts, do 1
Barber's historical collections of New England, Massachusetts, Connecticut, New York, New Jersey, Pennsylvania, Virginia, Ohio—1 volume each, ... 8
History of Virginia, Connecticut, New Hampshire, New York, Massachusetts, Michigan, and Wisconsin, ... 8

BIOGRAPHY.

Plutarch's lives, ... 4
Lives of ancient philosophers, ... 1
Zenophon's Cyropædia, ... 1
Famous men of ancient times, ... 1

Life of Alexander, 1
do Julius Cæsar, 1
do Belizarius, 1
do Mahomet. 1

VOYAGES AND TRAVELS.

Circumnavigation of the Globe, by Magellan and others. 1
Voyages around the Globe, by Cook, 1
Parry's Voyages for a Northwest Passage, 2
Discoveries in the Polar Seas and Regions, 1
Voyages of Discovery in the Arctic Regions, from 1818 to 1846, 1
Progress of Discovery in North America, 1
Lives and Voyages of Drake, Cavendish and Dampier, 5
Seaward's Shipwreck and Discoveries in the Caribbean Sea, 1
Mutiny of the Ship Bounty, and discovery of Pitcairn's Island, 1
Narratives of Shipwrecks, 1
Expedition to Siberia and the Polar Sea, 1
Dana's Two Years before the Mast, 1
United States Exploring Expedition, 1
Journal of a Naturalist in a voyage around the World, 3
Keppel's expedition to Borneo, 1
Travels in China and the East, by Marco Polo, 1
" to Mount Ararat, by Parrot, 1
Military operations in Afghanistan, 1
Travels in Africa, by Bruce, 2
" " Mungo Park, 1
" " the Landers, 2
" " Dedham and Clappenter, 1
" Southern Africa, by Moffat, 1
" Egypt, Nubia, Arabia proper, Palestine, by Stephens, 2
" " by Pres. Olin, 2
" " by Dr. Durbin, 2
" Algiers, 1
Eothen, by Kinglake, 1
Crescent and the Cross, by Warburton, 2
Travels in Greece, Turkey, &c., by Stephens, 2
Greece of the Greeks, by Peddicari, 1
Travels in Italy, by Headly, 1
" Switzerland, by Headly, 1
" on the Continent of Europe, by Dr. Fisk, 1
" " " " Dr. Durbin, 2
German Watering Places, by Dr. Granville, 1
" " Bubbles, &c., by Head, 1
Notes of a traveler in Germany, by Laing, 1
Rural and domestic life in Germany, by Howitt, 1
Belgium and the Rhine, by Mrs. Trollope, 1
Travels in the North of Europe, by Dr. Baird, 2
" Russia, by Rohl, 1
" Sweden, &c., by Laing, 2
" Austria, by Trumbull, 2
" Spain, by Barrow, 2
" " Ford, 2
" England, Ireland and Scotland, Pukler, Muskau, 1
" " " " by Kohl, 1
" " " by Z. Allen, 2
A tour in the manufacturing districts of England, 1
Scotland and the Scots, by Sinclair, 2
Shetland and the Shetlanders, by Sinclair, 1
Travels in New England, by Dr. Dwight, 4
Society in America, by Miss Martineau, 2
Winter Studies and Summer Rambles in Canada, 2
The Emigrant, by Sir Francis Head, 1
Lewis & Clark's Travels, 2
Fremont's Exploring Expedition beyond the Rocky Mountains, 1
Gregg's Commerce of the Prairies, 2
Travels in California, 1
Rambles in Yucatan, 1
Stephen's Yucatan and Central America, 4
Humbolt's travels and researches in Central America, 1
Argentine Republic, 1
Kidder's Brazil, Howitt's visits to remarkable places, 2
America and American people, 1
Miller's Rural Sketches, 1
Paraguay, 1
Parker's Tour to the Rocky Mountains, 1
Prairie Land, 1
Distinguished men of modern times, 4
Georgian era, or modern British biography, 2

Modern British Plutarch, ... 1
Belknap's American biography, ... 3
Spark's American biography, [first series,] 10
" " [second series,] 13
Dwight's signers of the declaration of Independence, ... 1
Thatcher's Indian biography, ... 2

Artists and Literary and Scientific Men.

Martyrs of Science, by Brewster, ... 1
Distinguished Painters, by Cunningham, ... 5
Authors of England, or a new spirit of the age, ... 2
Men of letters and science in the reign of George III., ... 1
Life of Dr. Samuel Johnson, by Boswell, ... 2
" Sir Walter Scott, by Lockhart, ... 5
" Sir Isaac Newton, by Brewster 1
" Dr. Arnold, ... 1
" John Foster, ... 1
" Addison, ... 1
" Cowper, ... 2
" Leibnitz, ... 1
" Mozart, ... 1

American.

Life of Columbus, by Irving, ... 1
Lives of Pizarro and Cortes, ... 1
Life of Americanus Vespucio, ... 1
" Capt. John Smith, by Simms, ... 1
" William Penn, ... 1
" Washington, by Bancroft, ... 2
" " by Sparks, ... 2
Lives of Washington and his Generals, by Headley, ... 2
Life of Jefferson, by Tucker, ... 2
" De Witt Clinton, by Renwick, ... 1
Lives of Jay and Hamilton, ... 1
" American naval officers, ... 1
Life of John Paul Jones, ... 2
" Putnam, ... 1

English.

Life of George Canning, ... 1
Statesmen of Commonwealth of England, ... 1
Orators of the age, ... 1
Southey's life of Nelson, ... 1

Female.

Biography of Pious Women, by Burder, ... 1
" Good Wives, by Mrs. Child, ... 1
" English Church Women, ... 1
Lives of Female Sovereigns, by Mrs. Jameson, ... 1
Lives of the Queens of England, by Agnes Strickland, ... 1
Lives of Famous Women, by Parley, ... 1
Memoirs of Mrs. Hemans, ... 9
" Hannah Moore, ... 1
" Charlotte Elizabeth, ... 2
" Jane Taylor, ... 1
" Empress Josephine, ... 1
" S. L. H. Smith, ... 1
" Isabella Graham, ... 1
" Mrs. Fry, ... 1
" Mrs. Van Lenope, ... 1
" Mrs. Duncan, ... 1
" Madame D'Arblay, ... 2

Mechanics and Self-Taught Men.

Life of Smeaton, and history of Light-Houses, ... 1
Biography of Eli Wheaton, ... 1
Memoirs of Samuel Slater, ... 1
Memoirs of a working man, ... 1
Biography of self-taught men, ... 2
Pursuit of Knowledge under difficulties, ... 2

Legal aud Medical.

Eminent British Lawyers, ... 1
Lives of the Lord Chancellors of England, ... 3
Life of Sir Matthew Hale, ... 1
Memoirs of Chief Justice Marshall, ... 1
Memoirs of Judge Storey, ... 1
Thatcher's medical biography, ... 1
Williams' " " 1

POETRY.

Treatise respecting Poetry.

Lowth on Hebrew poetry, ... 1
Herder's spirit of Hebrew Poetry, ... 2
Coleridge on the study of the Greek and Roman poets, ... 1
Hunt's Italian poets, ... 2
Montgomery's lectures on poetry, ... 2
Hazlett's lectures on English poetry, ... 2

Latin and Greek Poets.

Homer's Iliad and Odessy—translated by Pope, ... 3
Virgil's Eclogues, and Ænead—translated by Dryden, ... 2
Peters' specimen of the poetry of the ancients, ... 1

Italian, Spanish, German, &c.

Longfellow's specimens of the poetry of Europe, ... 1
Tasso—translated by Hunt, ... 1
Dante—translated by Carey, ... 1
Schiller—translated by Bulwer, ... 1

British.

Walsh's British poets, ... 50
Aiken's British poets, ... 1
Frost's continuation of Aikin, ... 1
Griswold's poetry of England of the XIXth century, ... 1
Halleck's selections from British poets, ... 2
Lamb's specimens of the dramatic poets, ... 2
Sharkspear's works, ... 6
Milton's poetical works, ... 2
Heman's poetical works, ... 2
Pope, Young, Thomson, Cowper, Montgomery, Goldsmith, Gray, Campbell, Wordsworth, Coleridge, E. Scott, Rogers, Kirk White, Elliott, ... 14
Byron—selections from, ... 1
Burns—selections from, ... 1
Motherwell's poems, ... 1

American Poets.

Bryant's selections from American poets, ... 1
Griswold's American poetry, ... 1
Bryant's poems, ... 1
Longfellow's " 1
Whittier's " 1
Hillhouse's " 1
Sigourney's " 2
Gould's " 1

Miscellaneous and Juvenile.

Poetry for home and school, ... 1
Keble's Christian year, ... 1
Keble's Child's Christian year, ... 1
Lays for the Sabbath, ... 1
Hart's class book of English poetry, ... 1
Cleveland's compendium of English poetry, ... 1
Taylor's poems for infant minds, ... 1
Beauties of Shakspeare, ... 1
Poetry of the passions, affections, flowers, sentiments, ... 1

STATEMENT OF EXPENDITURES AND RECEIPTS OF UNIVERSITY, FROM ITS ORGANIZATION (1837,) TO DECEMBER 31st, 1851, COMPILED FROM REPORT OF REGENTS.

In the aggregate there has been expended as follows, viz:

For Branches, ...	$35,935 00
" Janitor, ...	539 72
" Printing, ...	823 50
" Secretary, ...	2,252 40
" Treasurer, ...	637 51
" Librarian, ...	700 01

" Minerals,		5,898 38
" Library,		7,449 26
" Regents' Expenses,		1,317 73
" Professors' Houses,		30,933 27
" Main buildings,		20,101 25
" "		12,755 25
" Medical buildings,		8,300 00
" Wells,		786 05
" Grounds,		1,845 87
" Trees and plants,		234 00
" Fixtures,		2,474 00
" Insurance,		1,516 00
" Professors' salaries,		31,060 25
Total,		$185,460 20

NOTE.—In the above cost of the main University building first erected, under the superintendence of Harper Lum, is included the cost of woodhouse, and privies for Professor's dwellings, and five water cisterns; also, salary ($1,478 07) paid said Lum; also his traveling and extra incidental expenses, so that the actual cost of this main building alone, may be estimated at about $10,000. The appropriation for the main building last erected, under the superintendence of J. Kearsley, was $13,000, of which $244,75 was expended for fixtures, leaving the actual cost of this edifice, $12,755 25.

In addition to the above sum of		$185,460 20
Is to be added expenditures for plans, interest on bonds, &c,		81,617 25
Making total disbursements,		$267,077 45

RECEIPTS.

1837. From old board of trustees of University,		$5,454 71
Loan from Bank of Michigan, on State bonds,	100,000 00	
Premium on Loan,	6,000 00	
Interest on Premium,	38 50	
Per contract with Bank of Michigan on interest account,	10,555 67	
Total proceeds of Loan,		$116,594 17
From State Treasurer, from 1838, to July 1, 1850,		145,028 57
		$267,077 45
Disbursements brought down,		$267,077 45

Agreeably to a communication of the Commissioner of the State Land Office, dated March 1, 1851, it appears that up to that period there has been sold, as follows:

Of university lands, acres, 21,366.31

Unsold university lands, " 23,055.00

Total acres located, 44,421.31

Amount due from purchasers, ... $137,168 18.

Interest on the above annually, at 7 per cent,	$9,601 77
Interest from counties on $24,500 02,	1,715 00
" " State on $12,789 87,	895 29
	$12,716 06
Interest due from A. Mann,	504 00
	$12,716 06

As it is believed the interest due from the State is exclusive of the $6,000 and charges, payable in New York annually, the resources of the university interest fund for educational purposes may be safely estimated as above, with such gradual increase as may accrue from additional sales of land. By a report of the Commissioner of the State Land Office, dated July 11, 1850, it appears that 623.93 acres of land and 76 lots in Niles, were sold during the year ending June 1, 1850, for $10,682 47, the interest on which will accrue on the 1st of June, 1851, amounting to $747 77, which will make the university interest fund for the year ending June 30, 1851, $13,468 83, or after deducting interest due from Mr. Mann, (504,) the present annual interest may therefore be estimated at $12,959 83.

The above statement includes the fiscal transactions of the Board of Regents up to July 15, 1851. By a supplemental statement, it appears that up to December 31, inclusive, when the term of the old Board expired, there had been expended as follows:

For printing,	$298 88	
secretary,	274 00	
treasurer	177 83	
library,	247 50	
Regents' expenses,	335 88	
medical building,	950 00	
fixtures,	676 15	
insurance,	374 00	
professors' salaries,	16,516 56	
Total supplemental statement,		$19,850 77
" statement dated July 15, 1851,		267,077 45
Aggregate disbursements,		$286,928 22

According to the statement of the Board of Regents and Treasurer of the University, there were outstanding unpaid warrants, December 31, (inclusive,) 1851, the sum of æ11,822 70.

December 31, 1851.

COMPARATIVE STATEMENT OF THE SALES OF PRIMARY SCHOOL LANDS.

[FROM THE REPORT OF THE COMMISSIONER OF THE STATE LAND OFFICE FOR 1851.]

YEARS.	Acres.	Net amount of sales.
Total amount of sales up to April 1, 1843, inclusive,	52,392.81	[illegible]3 9,261 39
Part year ending November 30, 1843,	6,159.94	32,1[illegible]1 00
1 do do do 1844,	7,[illegible]5[illegible].66	3[illegible],860 60
1 do do do 1845,	5,009.93	6,974 17
1 do do do 1846,	6,879.63	[illegible]5,169 70
1 do do do 1847,	18,9[illegible]0.32	[illegible]5,817 15
1 do do do 1848,	15,0[illegible]6.84	68,763 88
1 do do do 1849,	8,9[illegible]6.66	[illegible]8,509 74
1 do do do 1850,	10,9[illegible]8.79	47,111 23
1 do do do 1851,	19,[illegible]9.95	83,4[illegible]9 [illegible]9
	149,029.56	$816,0[illegible]1 88
Less for forfeiture of land sold J. M. Barber, charged back in 1851, should have been charged in 1847,	6[illegible]0.00	4,315 52
Net sales of primary school lands,	148,289.56	$811,76[illegible] 36
Total amount of primary school fund,		$811,766 36

COMPARATIVE STATEMENT OF THE SALES OF UNIVERSITY LANDS.

YEARS.	Acres.	Net amount of sales.
Total amount of sales up to April 1, 1843, inclusive,	10,254.31	$123,[illegible]09 90
From April 1, 1843, to November 30, 1843,	809.59	8,0[illegible]0 70
1 year ending November 30, 1844,	4,155.57	41,154 05
1 do do do 1845,	1,881.53	23,296 19
1 do do do 1846,	1,323.21	16,0[illegible]0 52
1 do do do 1847,	1,017.46	11,839 77
1 do do do 1848,	662.74	8,075 46
1 do do do 1849,	3[illegible]2.48	5,800 09
1 do do do 1850,	7[illegible]1.22	12,896 52
1 do do do 1851,	1,289.59	15,266 29
Net sales of university land,	22,497.70	$268,639 49
Total amount of university fund,		$268,639 49

ABSTRACT OF SCHOOL INSPECTOR'S

ALLEGAN

TOWNSHIPS.	Whole districts.	Fractional districts.	Whole No. from which reports have been received.	No. of children in each township between the ages of 4 and 18 in which school has been taught by a qualified teacher.	No. of children that have attended during the year under 4 years of age.	No. that have attended during the year over 18 years of age.	Whole No. that have attended school during the year.	Whole amount of wages paid to teachers in the township.	Am't of money received from township treasurer, apportioned by township clerk.	Whole amount of money raised by the districts.	Purpos's
											To build school house.
Alle gan, ...	4	3	7	294	10	9	263	$579 00	$155 82	$693 75	$201 89
Dorr, ...	1	..	1	20	...	2	20	22 75	16 00	122 75	100 00
Fillmore, ...	4	..	4	196	1	112	....	118 00	53 70	175 57	75 00
Gunplain, ...	..	..	...	238	...	8	198	209 91	90 06	53 00	......
Ganges, ...	6	..	5	80	...	10	74	175 75	56 04	162 32	......
Leighton, ...	..	..	...	45	...	...	28	21 00	7 83	100 47	50 00
Manlius, ...	1	1	2	36	...	...	37	94 50	13 60	40 00	......
Martin, ...	4	1	4	126	1	3	88	168 48	48 12	69 30	......
Monterey, . . .	6	..	3	105	3	2	88	162 29	106 02	88 00	15 00
Newark, ...	1	1	1	28	...	...	28	63 00	32 00	....	......
Otsego, ...	8	..	6	283	...	...	246	357 25	142 42	327 13	173 00
Pineplains, . . .	1	1	2	18	4	...	18	65 25	2 78	117 54	100 00
Trowbridge, . .	4	2	6	148	2	2	158	152 50	22 37	321 74	230 00
Watson, ...	3	1	4	131	3	8	123	166 79	43 86	203 47	75 00
Wayland, ...	..	3	3	103	4	6	78	144 04	24 36	232 84	......
Total, ...	43	13	48	1851	28	162	1,447	$2,500 51	$814 98	$2,707 88	$1019 89

BARRY

TOWNSHIPS.	Whole districts.	Fractional districts.	Whole No. from which reports have been received.	No. of children in each township between the ages of 4 and 18 in which school has been taught by a qualified teacher.	No. of children that have attended during the year under 4 years of age.	No. that have attended during the year over 18 years of age.	Whole No. that have attended school during the year.	Whole amount of wages paid to teachers in the township.	Am't of money received from township treasurer, apportioned by township clerk.	Whole amount of money raised by the districts.	To build school house.
Assyria, ...	5	2	5	120	...	6	97	$163 50	$31 96	$228 00	$200 00
Baltimore, . . .	2	2	12	......	...	...	....	....	....	....	......
Barry, ...	3	4	4	98	...	9	144	176 50	28 42	54 52	......
Castleton, . . .	3	2	5	148	...	2	131	144 50	38 31	66 00	......
Carlton, ...	2	2	4	116	2	...	10	152 97	27 52	115 00	......
Hastings, ...	3	..	3	229	1	...	121	178 17	86 01	....	......
Hope, ...	..	..	...	41	...	7	51	51 00	18 32	32 76	......
Irving, ...	1	..	1	68	...	6	69	....	20 06	57 00	......
Johnstown, . . .	7	..	6	151	2	15	154	....	79 00	200 65	......
Maple Grove, . .	3	3	3	31	....	6	38	73 50	9 18	51 00	......
Orangeville, . . .	4	1	4	154	3	10	117	144 25	49 63	145 50	68 50
Prarieville, . . .	7	..	5	199	12	10	16	59 74	63 81	121 00	......
Rutland, ...	5	1	3	76	....	1	5	101 25	25 09	243 87	198 00
Thornapple, . .	4	..	4	137	4	....	9	181 84	37 27	581 88	200 00
Woodland, . . .	3	4	3	105	...	....	9	91 25	34 00	37 00	......
YankeeSprings	5	..	4	100	2	....	6	96 38	44 05	26 00	......
Total, ...	57	21	66	1,773	26	72	1,48	$1,614 85	$592 63	$1,960 16	$666 50

RETURNS BY TOWNSHIPS, FOR 1851.

COUNTY.

Repairs of school house. (for which it was raised, and amount raised for each particular purpose)	Support of school including pay of teachers.	To pay past indebtedness.	Any other purpose.	Amount raised by rate bill.	No. of vols. in the township library.	Amount of mill tax assessed by the supervisor and collected for support of school and township library. [Sec. 107.]	Amount of tax voted at the annual district meeting in addition to other taxes for the support of schools. [Sec. 140.]	Amount of fines, penalties and forfeitures of recognizance received of county treasurer for the purchase of books and township library.
$91 50	$639 51	$102 18	$112 50	$262 41	110	$99 00	$00 00	
....	22 75	....	....	6 75	144	27 65	....	
....	73 12	22 45	5 00	....	101	....	73 12	
45 00	....	8 00	....	168 63	....	....	....	
75 00	211 03	8 20	5 00	165 27	226	....	....	
97	65 00	4 50	63	14 83	....	....	....	
....	40 00	....	....	65 00	94	22 26	40	
43 64	72 14	....	....	81 00	190	25 00	....	
....	....	35 00	....	78 77	74	159 75	....	
....	....	....	....	47 95	137	....	....	
54 00	123 00	4 00	5 13	155 43	223	60 79	....	
....	17 54	....	....	65 25	75	....	....	
....	112 25	1 99	....	36 00	190	....	321 74	
5 00	92 05	1 00	....	92 66	....	22 38	42 65	
14 25	169 13	12 96	36 50	94 26	148	25 00	....	
$329 36	$1,637 52	$200 28	$164 76	$1,334 21	1,712	$441 83	$437 91	

COUNTY.

Repairs of school house.	Support of school including pay of teachers.	To pay past indebtedness.	Any other purpose.	Amount raised by rate bill.	No. of vols. in the township library.	Amount of mill tax assessed by the supervisor and collected for support of school and township library. [Sec. 107.]	Amount of tax voted at the annual district meeting in addition to other taxes for the support of schools. [Sec. 140.]	Amount of fines, penalties and forfeitures of recognizance received of county treasurer for the purchase of books and township library.
$0 00	$163 50	$18 47	$0 00	$114 40	245	$26 18	$28 00	
....	....	....	....	....	58	....	....	
300 00	154 75	....	....	105 51	120	33 84	80 00	
8 00	58 01	....	....	79 85	193	24 50	....	
45 00	32 50	....	....	28 01	130	....	....	
....	....	....	....	92 15	585	80 00	....	
5 00	....	....	....	....	....	....	....	
7 00	....	....	....	20 00	146	....	....	
56 00	....	....	....	89 63	156	25 00	....	
5 00	31 50	14 50	....	52 38	109	....	....	
10 50	66 50	1 00	....	53 64	200	23 17	66 50	
77 00	....	....	....	93 81	200	....	....	
....	77 25	....	2 00	17 18	136	....	40 50	
4 00	72 44	19 69	....	40 73	385	....	....	
6 00	71 42	....	....	36 73	300	25 00	....	
....	71 88	....	....	36 53	351	21 81	....	
$623 50	$799 75	$53 66	$2 00	$860 55	3,314	$259 50	$215 00	

BERRIEN

TOWNSHIPS.	Whole districts.	Fractional districts.	Whole No. from which reports have been received.	No. of children in each township between the ages of 4 and 18 in which school has been taught by a qualified teacher.	No. of children that have attended during the year under 4 years of age.	No. that have attended during the year over 18 years of age.	Whole No. that have attended school during the year.	Whole amount of wages paid to teachers in the township.	Amount of money received from township treasurer, apportioned by township clerk.	Whole amount of money raised by the districts.	Purpos's
											To build school house.
Bainbridge,...	6	1		222	23	21	250	$336 66	$65 98	$117 11	$55 00
Bertrand,.....	7	3	8	405	20	35	358	466 08	196 13	498 59	180 00
Benton, ...	4	4		132	3		113	31 81	28 41	31 81	180 00
Berrien,......	6	3	7	311	4	24	286	377 44	110 02	146 41	
Buchanan,....	5	2	4	292	5	7	266	252 25	140 36	103 00	30 00
Galien, ...	3		2	135	10		71		33 29		
Hager, ...	3	2		58	1		44		19 59	7 00	
Lake, ...	3	1	4	82	4	7	93	129 00	64 55	156 45	75 00
New Buffalo,..	3		2	210	100	4	144	232 38	83 94	174 00	
Niles, ...	10	6	13	1,297	3	35	758	1940 21	646 81	1465 66	
Oronoko,.....	5		5	289	1	13	277	498 61	103 47	559 10	
Pipestone, ...	8	1	6	147		4	130	228 00	45 44	263 00	209 00
Royalton,.....	5		2	63			46		26 76	171 25	
St. Joseph,....	1	1	1	116	10	6	132	50 00	30 00		
Watervliet, ...	1	1	2	75	3		61	43 25	32 98	132 45	101 45
Wesaw, ...	3		3	107		7	81	121 62	24 13	148 50	
Total,......	73	25	59	3,941	187	163	3,110	$4,707 31	$1,641 86	$3,974 33	$830 45

BRANCH

TOWNSHIPS.	Whole districts.	Fractional districts.	Whole No. from which reports have been received.	No. of children in each township between the ages of 4 and 18 in which school has been taught by a qualified teacher.	No. of children that have attended during the year under 4 years of age.	No. that have attended during the year over 18 years of age.	Whole No. that have attended school during the year.	Whole amount of wages paid to teachers in the township.	Amount of money received from township treasurer, apportioned by township clerk.	Whole amount of money raised by the districts.	To build school house.
Algansee	7	3	5	141	6	6	141	$133 96	$63 27	$98 50	$80 00
Batavia, ...	6	4	6	306	9	18	269	336 75	202 95	284 38	150 00
Bethel........	3	5	4	224	2	16	151	193 74	156 31	102 00	
Butler, ...	5		5	202		2	165		149 61	127 70	
Bronson, ...	5	3	7	310	5	21	224	255 26	208 05	179 43	
California,....	3	3	6	244	1	8	212	275 87	88 15	187 72	
Coldwater	13	3	11	710	12	82	687	1,222 73	276 91	1,218 68	780 00
Gerard	7	2	9	348	1	22	117	485 37	236 97	169 79	23 00
Gilead, ...	3	4	4	218	5	6	163	146 70	107 66	17 87	180 00
Kinderhook,..	4		3	119	2	8	112	163 05	70 70	149 59	135 00
Mattison,.....	4	3	4	145		15	131	146 37	114 88	121 65	
Noble	4	1	5	236	1	11	228	231 00	139 42	92 62	
Ovid,.........	6	2	8	282	7	7	259	314 92	106 57	238 36	75 00
Quincy.......	6	4		487	4	31	505	539 52	298 22	616 06	470 00
Sherwood,....	6	1	7	267	5	14	241	326 61	148 31		
Union........	8	2	9	452	5	15	391	694 50	269 12	295 64	69 00
Total,......	90	40	93	4,691	65	282	3,996	$5,466 35	$2,637 10	$3,899 99	$1962 00

COUNTY.

for which it was raised, and amount raised for each particular purpose.								
Repairs of school house.	Support of school, including pay of teachers.	To pay past indebtedness.	Any other purpose.	Amount raised by rate bill.	No. of vol's in the township library.	Amount of mill tax assessed by the Supervisor and collected for support of school and township library. [Sec. 107.]	Amount of tax voted at the annual district meeting in addition to other taxes, for the support of schools. [Sec. 140.]	Amount of fines, penalties and forfeitures of recognizance received of county treasurer for the purchase of books and township library.
$27 11			$25 11	$270 6[illegible]	237	$[illegible]9 6[illegible]		
13 60	$272 20	145 40	12 00	234 39	45[illegible]	60 57		
					[illegible]6		6 [illegible]0	
3 00	132 41	11 00		314 08		62 10	11 00	6 37
	74 00			165 37		6 56		
					91			
7 00				48 87	121	14 [illegible]8		
3 00	129 00			6[illegible] 45	2[illegible]5	[illegible]1 75	15 00	
12 00	163 00				4[illegible]6	85 73	174 00	
135 48	2,030 70	135 00		528 76	5[illegible]0	2[illegible]7 32	767 00	
5 00	206 50	350 60		166 91	[illegible]65	25 [illegible]0	2[illegible]6 50	
15 25	228 00	109 00	10 00	145 9[illegible]	2[illegible]0	4[illegible] 2[illegible]	40 [illegible]0	
					198			
	50 00			20 00	148	2[illegible] 00		
	70 81			16 [illegible]5	174	5 53	40 00	
13 00	116 13	59 05	11 50	6 00	[illegible]50	3[illegible] [illegible]	[illegible]6 00	
$234 44	$3,472 75	810 05	$58 61	$2 080 68	3,811	$6[illegible]3 97	$1 295 50	$6 37

COUNTY.

Repairs of school house.	Support of school, including pay of teachers.	To pay past indebtedness.	Any other purpose.	Amount raised by rate bill.	No. of vol's in the township library.	Amount of mill tax assessed by the Supervisor and collected for support of school and township library. [Sec. 107.]	Amount of tax voted at the annual district meeting in addition to other taxes, for the support of schools. [Sec. 140.]	Amount of fines, penalties and forfeitures of recognizance received of county treasurer for the purchase of books and township library.
	$88 46		18 50	$109 10	[illegible]23	$31 00		
6 50	341 75			13[illegible] 80				
	202 53	32 56		18 9[illegible]	2[illegible]0	2[illegible] 85	159 97	
68 00				65 46	[illegible]26		25 [illegible]0	
	80 37	99 [illegible]6		64 [illegible]2	[illegible]68	62 00		
	379 00			187 [illegible]2	2[illegible]1	21 [illegible]0		
142 50	806 64	26 00	20 22	6[illegible] 48	[illegible]11	11[illegible] 15		
67 29	61 [illegible]1		18 50	16 59	2[illegible]0	[illegible]0 0		
2 19	[illegible]6 70	111 9[illegible]	6 00	49 75	[illegible]68		15 75	
14 50	163 [illegible]5	11 00		1[illegible]0 64	[illegible]	[illegible]4 [illegible]0		
3 25	91 00	7 00		66 40	[illegible]97	28 50		
	92 62			92 62	[illegible]0	[illegible]7 50	12 00	
3 00	315 51		5 00	4 5[illegible]	[illegible]9	5[illegible] 68		
60 85	31 76	21 87	31 50	[illegible]4 21	[illegible]5			
				146 [illegible]2	[illegible]9	64 18		
34 15	149 00	3 54		2[illegible] 12	[illegible]9		[illegible]94 50	
$402 23	$2,899 40	$313 02	$99 72	$2,368 74	[illegible]909	[illegible]0 [illegible]6	[illegible]60[illegible] 2	

CALHOUN

TOWNSHIPS.	Whole districts.	Fractional districts.	Whole No. from which reports have been received.	No. of children in each township between the ages of 4 and 18 in which school has been taught by a qualified teacher.	No. of children that have attended during the year under 4 years of age.	No. that have attended during the year over 18 years of age.	Whole No. that have attended school during the year.	Whole amount of wages paid to teachers in the township.	Am't of money received from township treasurer, apportioned by township clerk.	Whole amount of money raised by the districts.	Purpos's
											To build school house.
Athens, ...	4	1	5	191	2	15	149	$261 11	$88 55	$38 00	$0 00
Albion, ...	9		6	452		8	281	193 52		318 81	
Battle Creek, . .	5	3	8	916	9	28	746	123 05	478 39	1,720 00	1,500 00
Bedford, ...	6	6	8	265		12	245		116 53	494 15	441 00
Burlin gton, . . .	6		5	254		15	198	296 00	98 70	74 53	
Clarence, ...	5	3	6	197	5	6	162	209 32	81 10	192 98	88 00
Clarendon, . . .	4	4	5	277	1	24	307	353 60	124 73	16 00	
Convis, ...	8	4	5	191		5	177	229 50	66 89	156 00	68 50
Emmett, ...	5	3	8	270	16	3	191	352 31	109 69	172 27	
Eckford, ...			7	243	3	12	237	351 25	108 95	12 75	
Fredonia, ...	6	4	9	282	2	2	221	460 14	159 46	440 63	100 00
Homer, ...	5	6	8	304	2	12	280	444 65	162 93	205 00	
Lee, ...	5	3	4	161	2	7	133	153 49	48 20	209 20	105 00
Leroy, ...	5	2	7	293	9	13	311	445 69	132 96	128 37	
Marshall, ...		3		938	31	10	189	1,453 00	566 33	4,918 40	3,928 35
Marengo, ...	8	3	11	365	3	13	340	458 33	227 14	306 04	14 75
Newton, ...	2	6	5	182		6	163	209 22	94 09	7 94	
Pennfield, ...	3	3		233	4	12	251	308 50	98 99	626 22	225 00
Sheridan, ...	2	2		130	1	9	217		105 35	211 32	979 00
Tekonsha, ...	5	1	6	259	2	19	251	354 87	114 38	353 90	310 00
Total, ...	93	57	113	6,403	92	231	5,049	$7,757 55	$2,983 36	$10,601 91	$7759 60

CASS

TOWNSHIPS.	Whole districts.	Fractional districts.	Whole No. from which reports have been received.	No. of children between 4 and 18 taught by a qualified teacher.	No. under 4 years of age.	No. over 18 years of age.	Whole No. that have attended school during the year.	Whole amount of wages paid to teachers.	Am't of money received from township treasurer.	Whole amount of money raised by the districts.	To build school house.
Calvin, ...	6	1	6	236	2	17	208	$276 05	$87 80	$415 38	$100 00
Howard, ...	11		5	186	4	13	147		71 25	30 00	
Jefferson, ...	8		8	352		31	324	460 00	124 73	314 70	
Marcellus, ...	4		4	103	1	1	82	107 67	73 07	41 00	
Mason, ...	5	2	5	187	1	8	169	182 50	46 75	219 11	
Milton, ...	4	2	6	289	4	11	238	335 73	124 47	37 60	180 00
Newberg, ...	3	2	5	140	3	3	106	110 45	42 50	20 00	
Ontwa, ...	5	2		272	3	4	184	447 00	105 92	435 21	
Pokagon, ...	5	2	7	830	2	36	391	650 30	193 72	262 81	314 69
Penn, ...	6	1	6	283	5	14	285	434 75	147 77	175 96	250 00
Porter, ...	9	3	9	466	6	38	453	607 46	180 17	396 56	
Silver Creek, . .	5		5	202	3	5	166	198 36	55 42	254 00	
Lagrange, . . .	7	2	8	449	6	10	439	667 60	206 84	188 02	175 00
Volinia, ...	6		6	219		9	202	237 00	81 76	9 00	
Wayne, ...	8	1	5	234	1	12	191	262 00	100 06	108 00	100 00
Total, ...	92	18	85	4,448	41	212	3,585	$4,976 87	$1,642 23	$2,907 35	$1119 69

CHIPPEWA

TOWNSHIPS.	Whole districts.	Fractional districts.	Whole No. from which reports have been received.	No. of children between 4 and 18 taught by a qualified teacher.	No. under 4 years of age.	No. over 18 years of age.	Whole No. that have attended school during the year.	Whole amount of wages paid to teachers.	Am't of money received from township treasurer.	Whole amount of money raised by the districts.	To build school house.
St. Marie, ...	1	1		349			75	$150 00	$80 58		

COUNTY.

for which it was raised, and amount raised for each particular purpose.								
Repairs of school house.	Support of school, including pay of teachers.	To pay past indebtedness.	Any other purpose.	Amount raised by rate bill.	No. of vols. in the township library.	Amount of mill tax assessed by the supervisor and collected for support of school and township library. [Sec. 107.]	Amount of tax voted at the annual district meeting in addition to other taxes for the support of schools. [Sec. 140.]	Amount of fines, penalties and forfeitures of recognizance received of county treasurer for the purchase of books and township library.
$5 00	$33 00	$0 00	$0 00	$112 18	310	$43 46	$0 00	$0 00
	137 97				433			
60 00			160 00	744 66	600	116 97		8 77
11 00	127 75			101 74	276	77 78		
				177 34				3 09
	209 32		6 00	128 46	239	3 83		
3 00		6 00	1 50	257 82	387	52 00		
13 00				102 12	313	50 00		1 85
				221 62	350	115 68		
7 95	115 75			205 72	420	70 00	6 75	
14 23	398 54	2 19	10 00	148 39	280	110 27		2 38
58 25	94 00	40 00	12 75	246 00	448	93 06	56 00	3 47
4 00	234 50	4 00		29 51	162			
4 20	247 56	12 30	3 75	192 36	266	25 00		3 01
35 60	967 64		215 00	347 74	735	288 67	967 14	9 43
50 46	135 96	19 14	4 38	168 47	380	135 57		
7 94	217 16			77 67	159	46 44		
10 00	101 22	260 00		132 18	308	70 37		2 14
					285	52 43		
	335 50	15 00	32 90	259 42	350	50 00		
$284 63	$3,355 87	$358 63	$446 28	$3,656 43	6,701	$1,401 53	$1,029 89	$34 14

COUNTY.

Repairs of school house.	Support of school, including pay of teachers.	To pay past indebtedness.	Any other purpose.	Amount raised by rate bill.	No. of vols. in the township library.	Amount of mill tax	Amount of tax voted	Amount of fines, penalties and forfeitures
$23 28	$112 88	$8 28	$10 00	$157 94	397	$0 00	$0 00	$0 00
16 25				115 16	400			16 00
10 02	469 68		15 00	247 86		55 00	40 00	3 90
25 50	16 40	15 50			308	11 68	47 00	5 00
13 10	50 68		3 86	115 26	279			
	144 40			192 39				
10 00				67 95				
27 88		92 64		356 79				
5 00		7 81		513 97	123	59 64		8 83
30 00	330 75	3 92	5 00	152 02	425			5 00
22 06	411 09			388 32			35 30	
50	52 00	8 50		81 68	340		70 00	3 99
45 00	249 88		9 00	318 31	400			
				52 93	300	50 00		
6 00			2 00	166 95	331	46 28		5 81
$234 59	$1,837 76	$136 65	$44 86	$2,927 53	3,303	$222 60	$192 30	$48 53

COUNTY.

Repairs of school house.	Support of school, including pay of teachers.	To pay past indebtedness.	Any other purpose.	Amount raised by rate bill.	No. of vols. in the township library.	Amount of mill tax	Amount of tax voted	Amount of fines, penalties and forfeitures
				$16 74	66	$68 00	$54 00	

CLINTON

TOWNSHIPS.	Whole districts.	Fractional districts.	Whole No. from which reports have been received.	No. of children in each township between the ages of 4 and 18 in which school has been taught by a qualified teacher.	No. of children that have attended during the year under 4 years of age.	No. that have attended during the year over 18 years of age.	Whole No. that have attended school during the year.	Whole amount of wages paid to teachers in the townships.	Am't of money received from township treasurer, apportioned by t'wnship clerk.	Whole amount of money raised by the districts.	Purpos's — To build school house.
Bath,........	4		3	35		2	33		$11 50	$106 00	
Bengal,......	3	2		45	1	3	59	$59 75	10 54	120 50	$120 00
Bingham,.....	3	1	2	64	2	3	60	74 05	18 05	70 00	65 00
De Witt,.....	4	1	4	251		12	231	354 50	121 94	275 65	
Duplain,......	4	1	4	179	2	5	148	141 50	72 46	1 50	
Eagle,........	6		6	219	3	12	214	231 75	43 29	142 25	
Essex,........	8		3	73			58	54 75	22 48	15 00	15 00
Greenbush,...	5		3	115	2	7	102		33 99	54 00	54 00
Lebanon,.....	4		2	51	2	2	51		14 96	61 00	
Olive,........	4		3	81	4	5	87		21 38	180 30	
Ovid,.........	2	2	4	101		3	66	85 25			
Riley,........	1	1	2	90	1	6	91	105 50	25 16	20 00	
Victor,......	3	1	3	108	2	3	118	167 34	29 92	137 42	
Watertown,..	4	1	4	126	2	10	143	200 76	36 72	140 50	75 00
Westphalia,...	2		2	238	3	2	127		82 96	85 00	
Total,.......	57	10	45	1,776	24	75	1,591	$1,475 15	$545 35	$1,415 12	$329 00

EATON

TOWNSHIPS.	Whole districts.	Fractional districts.	Whole No. from which reports have been received.	No. of children in each township between the ages of 4 and 18 in which school has been taught by a qualified teacher.	No. of children that have attended during the year under 4 years of age.	No. that have attended during the year over 18 years of age.	Whole No. that have attended school during the year.	Whole amount of wages paid to teachers in the townships.	Am't of money received from township treasurer, apportioned by t'wnship clerk.	Whole amount of money raised by the districts.	Purpos's — To build school house.
Brookfield,...	4		4	102		1	88	$111 43	$28 90	$122 39	$75 00
Bellevue,......	5	2	4	204		5	173		66 86	39 17	
Benton,......	5	2	4	113	1		90	122 00	31 96	251 50	200 00
Chester,......	4	5	5	186	5	3	150	198 13	54 06	456 43	380 00
Carmel,......	5	2	7	271	5	3	208	247 66	92 04	112 50	
Delta,........	5		5	87			86			117 00	
Eaton,........	5	4	9	164	1	7	152	223 75	68 69	320 00	200 00
Eaton Rapids,.	11	2	13	563	7	23	495	536 59	181 09	186 29	75 00
Kalamo,......	7		6	194	4	13	192		53 38	115 25	
Oneida,.......	4	4	8	259	2	13	231	270 68	57 14	273 50	195 00
Roxand,.....	3	2	5	129	2	5	120	193 92	43 17	128 75	
Sunfield,......	1	1	1	21			12	19 50	5 12	14 38	
Vermontville,.	3	1	4	130	1	4	144	180 00	58 14	130 50	10 00
Windsor......	4		4	98	2	4	121	192 75	34 55	255 71	72 00
Walton,......	6	1	7	210	3	2	166	217 75	90 87	133 63	
Total,......	72	26	86	2,731	33	83	2,428	$2,514 16	$865 97	$2,657 00	$1207 00

COUNTY.

for which it was raised, and amount raised for each particular purpose.								
Repairs of school house.	Support of school including pay of teachers	To pay past indebtedness.	Any other purpose.	Amount raised by rate bill.	No. of vols. in the township library.	Amount of mill taxed assessed by the supervisor and collected for support of school and township library. [Sec. 107.]	Amount of tax voted at the annual district meeting in addition to other taxes for the support of schools. [Sec. 140.]	Amount of fines, penalties and forfeitures of recognizance received of county treasurer for the purchase of books and township library.
$72 00					240			
25 00	$8 00			$32 50	450		$26 50	
5 00				56 00	219	$41 00	7 00	
40 00	114 00	$104 65		99 52	240	71 80		
1 50				69 04	210	45 03		
	142 25				500	47 00	142 25	
					200	39 81		
					215	22 35		
				44 00	250	27 15		
172 80				58 87		31 52		
				85 25		26 75		
20 00				81 00	252	22 00		
137 42				60 42	309		77 00	
	55 50				231			
					200	26 38		
$473 72	$319 75	$104 00		$586 60	3,516	$400 79	$252 75	

COUNTY.

Repairs of school house.	Support of school including pay of teachers	To pay past indebtedness.	Any other purpose.	Amount raised by rate bill.	No. of vols. in the township library.	Amount of mill taxed assessed by the supervisor and collected for support of school and township library. [Sec. 107.]	Amount of tax voted at the annual district meeting in addition to other taxes for the support of schools. [Sec. 140.]	Amount of fines, penalties and forfeitures of recognizance received of county treasurer for the purchase of books and township library.
$15 89	$46 00		$5 00	$46 66	226	$24 05	$26 50	
13 00				193 56	371	48 40		
	51 50			33 34	242	25 00		
	40 00	$9 93	26 50	106 71	300	25 00	40 00	
	221 16	24 25	9 69	101 33	335	43 62	111 50	
25 00				13 50	199	25 00		
2 00	29 50			76 06	227	51 15		
2 50	129 00	41 52		75 54				
				155 47	231	27 78		
7 00	30 00		41 50		182	34 33	47 00	
22 00	74 81	5 00	4 75	47 88	150			
				14 38	226	14 81		
	71 00	49 50		39 39	308	11 58		
4 25	192 75	4 56	15 00	91 90	220	28 69	68 00	
5 00	167 75		14 00	54 66	153	35 68	77 50	
$96 64	$1,053 47	$134 76	$116 44	$1,050 38	3,370	$395 09	$370 50	

GENESEE

TOWNSHIPS.	Whole districts.	Fractional districts.	Whole No. from which reports have been received.	No. of children in each township between the ages of 4 and 18, in which school has been taught by a qualified teacher.	No. of children that have attended during the year under 4 years of age.	No. that have attended during the year over 18 years of age.	Whole No. that have attended school during the year.	Whole amount of wages paid to teachers in the township.	Amount of money received from township treasurer, apportioned by township clerk.	Whole amount of money raised by the district.	Purpos's: To build school house.
Argentine....	4	1	5	210	8	6	165	$214 46	$73 73	$160 00	$160 00
Atlas........	10		9	488	1	46	352	39 00	217 15	259 18	
Clayton,.....	3	5	5	187		7	172	255 87	79 25	11 00	
Davison......	7	3	7	141	1	1	117	162 64	35 26	278 00	160 00
Forrest......	3		3	69			52	82 50	24 82	81 50	
Flint........	14	6	16	1140	11	44	953	1100 00	406 14	632 35	550 00
Fenton.......	4	2	6	431	6	8	313	393 63	138 88	409 62	175 00
Flushing.....	7	1	8	295	5	13	268	398 00	112 61	389 05	14 00
Genesee......	7	3	9	399		34	364	473 87	135 49	184 89	
Grand Blanc..	6	2	8	375	12	33	373	378 75	168 92	625 07	310 00
Gaines.......	2	3	5	90	3	13	115	184 96	74 30	256 50	400 00
Montrose.....	1		1	20		1	14	51 00	8 61		
Mundy........	6		6	327	7	14	263		94 26	210 00	
Richfield....	4	2	5	193	10	1	159	160 75	53 96	67 01	
Thetford.....	4	2	6	175	3	9	158	186 50	70 89	139 48	80 00
Vienna.......	1	1		67							
Total.......	83	31	99	4,607	67	230	3,838	4,081 93	$1,694 29	$3,703 65	1,849 00

HILLSDALE

TOWNSHIPS.	Whole districts.	Fractional districts.	Whole No. from which reports have been received.	No. of children in each township between the ages of 4 and 18, in which school has been taught by a qualified teacher.	No. of children that have attended during the year under 4 years of age.	No. that have attended during the year over 18 years of age.	Whole No. that have attended school during the year.	Whole amount of wages paid to teachers in the township.	Amount of money received from township treasurer, apportioned by township clerk.	Whole amount of money raised by the district.	Purpos's: To build school house.
Adams........	8	2	10	432	8	25	394	$636 51	$172 53	$227 76	
Allen,.......	9	3	8	348	4	20	348	519 01	137 38	394 92	$150 00
Amboy........	5	1	3	95	6	6	110	92 50	25 86	145 45	75 00
Cambria......	7	3	6	213	4	7	212	293 38	69 23	61 00	
Camden.......	5	2	5	209			156	165 27	76 16	44 50	
Fayette......	5	6	10	902	18	43	716	1579 25	214 61	1047 81	37 00
Jefferson,...	7	1	7	279	9	5	270	335 82	121 79	249 93	
Litchfield...	5	5	9	543	1	17	555	718 50	224 90	161 00	
Moscow.......	5	3	8	3\\4	8	24	346	549 91	178 14	141 50	
Pittsford....	8	2	8	392	4	20	389	532 01	148 72	518 29	50 00
Ransom.......	6	1	5	214	3	8	217	223 90	63 53	226 40	
Reading......	7	2	9	367	2	20	352	317 78	106 42	168 98	250 00
Somerset.....	4	4	6	294	3	34	298	427 59	107 54		482 50
Scipio.......	7	5	8	261	3	7	146	254 55	117 17	168 73	
Wheatfield,..	9	4	11	520	5	39	532	613 75	284 42	691 83	430 00
Wright.......	6	1	7	260	11	17	257	318 62	111 08	328 20	169 00
Woodbridge..	7		5	155		2	108	129 73	38 76	622 59	498 63
Total.......	110	45	125	5,848	89	294	5,406	7,708 08	$2,193 24	$5,198 80	2,142 13

COUNTY.

for which it was raised, and amount raised for each particular purpose.								
Repairs of school house.	Support of school including pay of teachers.	To pay past indebtedness.	Any other purpose.	Amount raised by rate bill.	No. of vol's in the township library.	Amount of mill tax assessed by the Supervisor, and collected for support of school and township library. [Sec. 107.]	Amount of tax voted at the annual district meeting in addition to other taxes, for the support of schools. [Sec. 140.]	Amount of fines, penalties, and forfeitures of recognizance received of county treasurer for the purchase of books and township library.
	$213 96			$66 00	176	$34 28		
107 88				23 38	264	34 00		
5 00		$6 00		166 62	260			
5 00	381 77	58 00	$16 00	91 38	250	25 37	$36 00	
17 50	64 00				106			
229 73	151 62					208 44		
48 64	263 58		7 00	198 81	203	44 00		
13 00	414 00			107 87	450			
	95 54	5 75	8 00		315			
90 84	328 31	99 19	30 09	175 21	208	59 10	52 00	
5 00	205 46			137 76	105		40 00	
				42 39	94		20 00	
195 00						30 09		
38 85	126 75	5 17		40 79	200	33 08	63 00	
85 50	199 93	20 75	10 00	88 91	144	24 52		
771 94	$2,444 92	194 86	$74 09	$1,139 12	2,775	$492 79	$211 00	

COUNTY.

Repairs of school house.	Support of school including pay of teachers.	To pay past indebtedness.	Any other purpose.	Amount raised by rate bill.	No. of vol's in the township library.	Amount of mill tax assessed by the Supervisor, and collected for support of school and township library. [Sec. 107.]	Amount of tax voted at the annual district meeting in addition to other taxes, for the support of schools. [Sec. 140.]	Amount of fines, penalties, and forfeitures of recognizance received of county treasurer for the purchase of books and township library.
$50 00	$152 06	$11 90	$14 12	$252 61	350	$68 43	$152 74	
9 50	392 38	3 00	19 50	203 06	350	123 76	394 92	
3 00	59 00	8 45		9 45	171	33 60		
5 00	54 50	1 50		113 44	234	37 52		
	34 50	10 00		15 00				
55 00	1021 25	321 00	351 00	1,271 34				
92 20	121 66	28 27	6 00	86 57	250			
44 00	118 60	8 50	14 50	358 93	486	64 72		
31 05	239 96	12 56	1 50	197 34				
21 00	388 29		4 00	322 37	278	47 00		
2 50	223 90	7 89		164 88	173			
20 50	51 37	27 00	9 50	284 93				
16 58	460 71			278 69		44 83	47 42	
17 50	257 91			235 53	206	40 98	3 50	
13 00	212 71	14 66	21 46	211 35	376	95 00		
28 00	125 50		5 70	105 38	320	27 12	119 00	
	102 13	24 87		13 45	170	51 53		
408 83	$4,016 43	$479 60	$447 28	$4,124 32	3,364	$634 49	$717 58	

INGHAM

TOWNSHIPS.	Whole districts.	Fractional districts.	Whole No. from which reports have been received.	No. of children in each township between the ages of 4 and 18 in which school has been taught by a qualified teacher.	No. of children that have attended during the year under 4 years of age.	No. that have attended during the year over 18 years of age.	Whole No. that have attended school during the year.	Whole am't of wages paid to teachers in the township.	Amount of money received from township treasurer, apportioned by township clerk.	Whole amount of money raised by the districts.	Purpos's
											To build school house.
Alaiedon, ...	4	2	5	167	3	10	166	$199 96	$51 34	$68 45	
Aurelius, ...	4	4	6	263	4	14	245	313 00	95 94	505 64	$282 90
Bunker Hill, ..	5	1	6	178	4	14	183	220 25	46 91	116 73	
Delhi, ...	3	1	4	170	5	8	157	211 17	62 97	61 25	
Ingham, ...	4	2	6	336	1	18	296	327 51	91 79	326 31	355 50
Lansing, ...	4	1	4	413	2	4	307	599 44	234 71	502 00	45 00
Le Roy, ...	3	1	4	145	4	10	125	123 50	35 70	135 29	
Leslie, ...	7	4	8	290	4	5	262	384 17	112 59	185 64	
Locke, ...	4	4	4	82	2	1	74	82 25	18 14	432 00	350 00
Meredian, ...	5	1	6	159	4	6	132	204 11	75 61	283 50	115 00
Onondaga, ...	6	6	6	222	7	6	227	257 99	87 26	454 78	350 00
Phelpstown, ..	5		5	170	2	12	168	274 75	52 09	323 08	250 00
Stockbridge ..	7	1	6	281	3	44	222	284 87	86 67	317 82	329 00
Vevay, ...	5	1	6	324	13	19	351	446 75	111 52	638 33	511 00
Wheatfield, ...	1	1	2	55	1	1	46	33 64	21 76	42 65	
White Oak, ...	6	1	6	181	2	3	135	145 19	38 50	240 94	120 00
Total, ...	73	31	84	3,436	61	175	3,096	$4,108 55	$1,223 50	$4,634 41	$2708 40

IONIA

TOWNSHIPS.	Whole districts.	Fractional districts.	Whole No. from which reports have been received.	No. of children in each township between the ages of 4 and 18 in which school has been taught by a qualified teacher.	No. of children that have attended during the year under 4 years of age.	No. that have attended during the year over 18 years of age.	Whole No. that have attended school during the year.	Whole am't of wages paid to teachers in the township.	Amount of money received from township treasurer, apportioned by township clerk.	Whole amount of money raised by the districts.	To build school house.
Berlin, ...	2	3	2	62			54	$102 25	$26 84	$62 00	$1 00
Boston, ...	3	2	4	159	3	13	179	303 75	56 32	149 00	
Campbell, ...	1		1	29			20	15 00	5 78		
Danby, ...	3	2	1	40		1	36		23 80	43 00	
Easton, ...	5	1	6	213	5	15	228	245 49	66 46	334 14	233 00
Ionia, ...	4	5	6	354	2	4	295	16 50	137 07	218 03	140 50
Kane, ...	5	2	6	268	5	24	264	398 75	89 30	84 34	
Lyons, ...	5	3		331	3	14	256	550 28	185 28	366 58	175 00
North Plains..	2	2	3	129		4	117	170 50	58 49	113 50	
Odessa, ...	1		1	45		3	34	40 25	11 22	7 26	
Orange, ...	4	8	6	170	5	6	154	222 85	55 26	155 00	75 00
Orleans, ...	3	1	4	148	3	10	151	175 50	40 14	157 50	65 00
Otisco, ...	6	2	5	301	30	36	198	361 00	128 59	84 89	
Portland, ...	5	5	10	375	3	15	314	560 52	108 12	320 73	67 00
Roland.	5	2	7	196	6	8	227	267 76	73 96	387 27	231 70
Sebewa, ...	2	1	2	64	2		66	66 33	15 63	51 70	
Total, ...	56	39	64	2,884	67	153	2,593	3,496 73	$1,082 26	$2,534 90	$988 20

COUNTY.

for which it was raised, and amount raised for each particular purpose.								
Repairs of school house.	Support of school including pay of teachers.	To pay past indebtedness.	Any other purpose.	Amount raised by rate bill.	No. of vols. in the township library.	Amount of mill tax assessed by the supervisor and collected for support of school and township library. [Sec. 107.]	Am't of tax voted at the annual district meeting in addition to other taxes for the support of schools. [Sec. 140.]	Amount of fines, penalties and forfeitures of recognizance received of county treasurer for the purchase of books and township library.
$33 45	$35 00			$113 64	176		$34 00	
3 00	203 00	$33 40	$14 00	24 30	191	$32 88	110 00	
	93 60			93 23	152	32 28		
				88 38	208		121 50	
4 20	129 64	83 30		145 21	171	42 24		
29 00	179 00	79 73		174 97		146 00	350 00	
20 29	88 25			12 00	245	25 00		
25 50	409 67			73 26	230	84 56	116 25	
	89 00						82 00	
10 00	129 88	22 00	46 00	67 83	247			
5 25	149 48	1 25	11 00	114 85		45 34	52 28	
2 62	29 00		50	81 76	305	34 70		
26 00	420 62			156 19	198	44 57	65 50	
11 50	113 00		2 50	259 49	245	48 65		
	42 65			16 51	256	58 92	26 00	
		117 94		111 21	221	32 41		
$170 81	$2,111 39	$337 62	$74 00	$1,532 83	2,845	$627 55	$957 53	

COUNTY.

Repairs of school house.	Support of school including pay of teachers.	To pay past indebtedness.	Any other purpose.	Amount raised by rate bill.	No. of vols. in the township library.	Amount of mill tax assessed by the supervisor and collected for support of school and township library. [Sec. 107.]	Am't of tax voted at the annual district meeting in addition to other taxes for the support of schools. [Sec. 140.]	Amount of fines, penalties and forfeitures of recognizance received of county treasurer for the purchase of books and township library.
$5 00	$97 28				193	$37 50	$29 00	
65 00	84 00			$159 41	150	35 86		
				9 22	27	13 31		
4 00	59 25			6 25	111	25 00	39 00	
20 04	184 29		$12 38	134 77	250			
3 30		$37 50	22 08	229 10				
12 39	461 19			257 40				
17 78	279 22	15 11	11 94	241 35	281	11 27		
30 00	33 50		50 00	87 03	240	32 40	33 50	
3 00	21 72		4 26	14 46	58	10 00	22 50	
2 00	77 00		1 00	33 65	197	28 90		
15 00	193 00			31 05	109			
50 89	44 00			253 10	244	50 98		
25 52	250 54		15 00	364 65	177	50 00		
2 50	202 51			109 29	120	35 00		
				8 70				
$256 42	$1,987 50	$52 61	$116 58	$1,939 48	2,157	$330 22	$124 00	

JACKSON

TOWNSHIPS.	Whole districts.	Fractional districts.	Whole No. from which reports have been received.	No. of children in each township between the ages of 4 and 18 in which school has been taught by a qualified teacher.	No. of children that have attended during the year under 4 years of age.	No. that have attended during the year over 18 years of age.	Whole No. that have attended school during the year.	Whole am't of wages paid to teachers in the township.	Am't of money received from township treasurer, apportioned by township clerk.	Whole amount of money raised by the districts.	Purpos's
											To build school house.
Columbia, . . .	8	7	10	416	7	30	448	$565 25	$216 15	$225 10	$0 00
Concord, ...	5	4	7	334	4	17	285	436 25	201 04	331 93	150 50
Grass Lake,. . .	11	1	12	509	3	27	368	682 75	228 66	272 03	210 00
Hanover, ...	7	3	6	296	6	18	299	399 14	141 39	696 49	414 75
Henrietta, . . .	5	2	7	309		24	303	420 00	105 64	301 00	
Jackson,. . . .	13	4	15	1376	9	39	1,087	2,557 75	836 03	1,704 85	112 00
Leoni,.	5	3		526	14	23	313	382 50	125 80	174 18	
Liberty, ...	6	5	7	283	5	31	278	329 00	112 03	785 18	670 00
Napoleon, . . .	8	3	11	490	3	22	365	674 80	250 09	735 42	250 00
Parma, ...	5	3	8	458	5	16	468	576 64	183 06	606 57	505 00
Pulaski, ...	4	3	7	279	2	20	305	372 19	122 94	394 63	144 00
Rives, ...	5	3	5	176	4	5	175	220 64	82 24	299 00	150 00
Sandstone,. . .	5	7	8	315	8	2	266	478 90	132 57	256 91	150 00
Spring Arbor,	6	1	6	297	1	24	256	387 50	136 95	499 14	305 00
Springport,. . .	5	2	7	280	8	15	198	371 12	94 72	6 00	
Tompkins, . . .	5	4	6	192	2	9	172	235 00	97 83	157 60	100 00
Waterloo, . . .	5	5	10	502	4	33	442	517 89	244 97	410 34	305 00
Total, ...	108	60	132	7,036	85	355	6,028	$9606 82	$3,312 11	$7,856 37	$3466 25

KALAMAZOO

TOWNSHIPS.	Whole districts.	Fractional districts.	Whole No. from which reports have been received.	No. of children in each township between the ages of 4 and 18 in which school has been taught by a qualified teacher.	No. of children that have attended during the year under 4 years of age.	No. that have attended during the year over 18 years of age.	Whole No. that have attended school during the year.	Whole am't of wages paid to teachers in the township.	Am't of money received from township treasurer, apportioned by township clerk.	Whole amount of money raised by the districts.	To build school house.
Alamo,.	3	2	4	101		7	104	$137 16	$48 28	$447 50	$333 00
Brady, ...	4	2	6	219	8	8	213	300 66	68 76	74 00	
Cooper, ...	6	1	7	302	9	19	300	415 50	98 83	333 55	10 00
Charleston, . . .	7	3	7	306	2	9	265	427 75	146 20	273 61	
Climax, ...	6	1	6	270	4	11	203	279 95	102 72	191 25	165 00
Comstock,. . .	8	1	9	477	6	36	361	584 88	153 00	530 58	75 00
Kalamazoo,. . .	15	3	12	1,041	12	27	712	1,091 25	209 39	609 57	180 00
Oshtemo,. . . .	8	1	6	238	1	5	293	398 60	74 82	127 52	
Pavilion,. . . .	4	4	5	161	1	10	154	229 73	53 04	103 00	
Portage, ...	5	2	7	256	16	23	146	394 50	76 44	450 00	200 00
Prarie Ronde,.	5	1	6	273	3	18	239	366 99	150 89	11 96	
Richland,. . . .	7		7	296		1	115	96 17	38 00		
Ross,.	3	5	6	240	17	9	249	323 78	138 33	365 74	90 00
Schoolcraft,. . .	8	2	7	373	4	18	223	474 50	83 71	413 75	200 00
Texas, ...	3	3	2	83		3	87	122 00	42 87	81 63	
Wakeshma,. . .	3	1	2	35	3	2	28	47 75		169 40	150 00
Total, ...	95	32	99	4,671	86	206	3,692	$5691 17	$1,485 28	$4,183 06	$1403 00

COUNTY.

for which it was raised, and amount raised for each particular purpose.								
Repairs of school house.	Support of school, including pay of teachers.	To pay past indebtedness.	Any other purpose.	Amount raised by rate bill.	No. of vols. in the township library.	Amount of mill tax assessed by the supervisor and collected for support of school and township library. [Sec. 107.]	Amount of tax voted at the annual district meeting in addition to other taxes for the support of schools. [Sec. 140.]	Amount of fines, penalties and forfeitures of recognizance received of county treasurer for the purchase of books and township library.
$73 18	$0 00	$0 50	$15 50	$134 00	245	$89 12	$0 00	$0 00
85 91	65 00			259 69	298	77 63		
9 70	119 35	2 93		194 01				
5 12	234 96			203 21	398	62 14	81 75	37 00
12 00	356 98			216 83	300			
116 40	1,146 42	431 15	295 25	924 81	264	25 00		
32 00					430			
	159 68	20 00		131 00	155	53 24		
40 03	389 09	56 30		389 09	390	84 54		
31 51	514 04	19 57		329 19	336	94 57	32 00	
5 77	247 86	150 49		152 25	318	35 71		
	149 00			87 00	221	26 63		
3 49	209 42		11 00	142 87	159	41 90		
25 00	252 32	7 00		252 32	335	47 71		
6 00				257 90	145	50 79		
24 76	146 92			101 86	172	47 85		
32 00	447 89	33 34		240 95	168		40 00	
$502 75	$4,438 93	$721 28	$321 75	$4,016 98	4,334	$736 83	$153 75	$37 00

COUNTY.

Repairs of school house.	Support of school, including pay of teachers.	To pay past indebtedness.	Any other purpose.	Amount raised by rate bill.	No. of vols. in the township library.	Amount of mill tax assessed by the supervisor and collected for support of school and township library. [Sec. 107.]	Amount of tax voted at the annual district meeting in addition to other taxes for the support of schools. [Sec. 140.]	Amount of fines, penalties and forfeitures of recognizance received of county treasurer for the purchase of books and township library.
$5 00	$68 00	$105 00	$22 50	$155 05	191	$0 00	$0 00	
2 00	300 66		9 00	157 32	109			
70 00	372 68	29 13	41 75	194 37	300			
26 06	326 06	3 00	18 00	197 24	400			
10 00	100 25			158 81	192	42 00		
42 17	434 70	40 00	20 00	314 42	180	31 50	75 67	
69 00	311 77	20 45	18 50	482 20	150			
5 00	78 27	25	10 00	142 88	280		17 00	
				176 69	167		103 00	
40 00					200			
3 00	262 01			248 47	265	10 00	4 00	
	15 00	6 35	8 62	182 91				
20 00	205 59	21 60	9 00	89 22	214	60 64	42 00	
98 00	85 75	20 00	10 00		150			
2 50				81 63	200			
	19 40			22 40				
$392 73	$2,580 14	$245 78	$167 37	$2,603 61	2,998	$144 14	$241 67	

KENT

TOWNSHIPS.	Whole districts.	Fractional districts.	Whole No. from which reports have been received.	No. of children in each township between the ages of 4 and 18 in which school has been taught by a qualified teacher.	No. of children that have attended during the year under 4 years of age.	No. that have attended during the year over 18 years of age.	Whole No. that have attended school during the year.	Whole amount of wages paid to teachers in the township.	Amount of money received from township treasurer, apportioned by township clerk.	Whole amount of money raised by the districts.	Purpos's
											To build school house.
Alpine, ...	4	5	6	215	2	2	72	$183 82	$15 44	$100 00	
Ada	6	3	6	179		9	187	289 11	65 06	207 62	$95 62
Algoma, ...	2	3	1	53		8	55	73 00	9 31	25 00	
Byron	4		3	113	1	1	101	107 98	41 08	139 90	65 00
Bowne, ...	4		4	95		8	55		13 26	140 00	
Courtland, . . .	5		4	159	3	3	136	150 73	25 84	218 75	160 00
Cascade, ...	4	2	6	225	3	8	202	262 25	55 42	327 50	173 50
Caledonia	2		2	39	2	1	34	76 83	24 10	99 50	
Cannon, ...	6	2	8	353	5	13	297	437 50	128 65	246 80	
Grattan, ...	6		4	160	1	8	148		54 06	193 00	
Gaines, ...	6		6	133		7	140	200 62	75 07	457 00	375 00
G'd Rapids t'n.	6	4	7	226	2		125	193 38	76 56	739 50	430 00
do city,	1	2	3	1122	2	27	608	596 95	284 58	1,533 12	200 00
Lowell, ...	3	2		130	6	3	81	120 00	36 00	136 50	
Oakfield	3	3	3	129	6	10	151	197 00	41 78	78 84	
Plainfield, ...	3	1	3	177	3	3	83	102 00	34 36		
Paris	6	2	6	140		6	147	182 76	54 58	370 00	295 00
Sparta	6		4	82		1	79		26 27		
Vergennes . . .	6	2	8	403	7	15	360	547 00	114 50	468 95	
Walker	6	6	6	250		6	218	331 52	94 91	256 49	180 00
Wyoming, . . .	4			175	2	2	85	208 00	82 44	36 00	
Total, ...	93	37	90	4,558	45	141	3,374	$4,265 45	$1,353 27	$5,774 47	1,974 12

LAPEER

TOWNSHIPS.	Whole districts.	Fractional districts.	Whole No. from which reports have been received.	No. of children in each township between the ages of 4 and 18 in which school has been taught by a qualified teacher.	No. of children that have attended during the year under 4 years of age.	No. that have attended during the year over 18 years of age.	Whole No. that have attended school during the year.	Whole amount of wages paid to teachers in the township.	Amount of money received from township treasurer, apportioned by township clerk.	Whole amount of money raised by the districts.	To build school house.
Almont, ...	2	7	7	478	8	18	413	$280 50	$161 75	$350 00	$350 00
Attica	5	5	4	118	1	3	109	105 02	14 29	86 00	75 00
Dryden	12	3	11	478	11	24	477	487 62	167 37	582 92	336 00
Elba, ...	5		5	112		3	65	154 22	26 18	120 00	80 00
Hadley, ...	10		6	303	8	21	315		119 18	269 00	
Imlay, ...	3	3	1	21	1		21	35 75	10 11	163 00	130 00
Lapeer, ...	9	9	10	512	5	17	447	531 07	212 11	15 30	
Marathon, . . .	3		2	57	4	1	190	59 81	12 58	305 81	200 00
Metamora, . . .	4	3	6	285		8	263	429 00	109 60	149 50	60 00
Oregon	2	3	2	56			57	111 00	38 74	89 50	
Total, ...	55	33	*54	2,420	38	95	2,357	$2,193 99	$931 91	$2,131 03	1,231 00

COUNTY.

for which it was raised, and amount raised for each particular purpose.				Amount raised by rate bill.	No. of vol's in the township library.	Amount of mill tax assessed by the Supervisor, and collected for support of school and township library. [Sec. 107.]	Amount of tax voted at the annual district meeting in addition to other taxes, for the support of schools. [Sec. 140.]	Amount of fines, penalties and forfeitures of recognizance received of county treasurer, for the purchase of books and township library.
Repairs of school house.	Support of school, including pay of teachers.	To pay past indebtedness.	Any other purpose.					
				$68 56	170			
$1 00	$86 50	$97 62		132 90	186		$86 50	
	122 50			40 37	90	$25 63	25 00	
5 75	66 90	1 75	50 00	66 90	159	29 71	18 00	
105 00					131			
8 78	95 00		8 00	79 83		27 73	22 00	
52 75	264 75			109 40	212	27 47	82 50	
10 00	60 00	58 00		15 90	100	21 71	27 00	
48 08	194 00	4 00	75	116 81	160	38 79	194 00	
166 00								
9 00	203 02		9 00	105 40	172	31 50		
85 00			77 05	123 45	115	56 80		
23 97	978 11	275 28	150 00	741 28	180		1104 00	
	237 00			43 50	143		35 00	
5 00	58 00	4 84	11 00	64 99		25 00	57 00	
2 50				63 06	165	33 29		
16 75	178 50			77 07	189			
97 50					150			
34 12	432 83		2 00	356 69	200	34 59		
49 00	17 00		9 49	79 33	296	50 49		
	55 90		7 00	6 72	105			
$720 17	$3,049 11	$441 49	$324 29	$2,292 16	2,923	$402 71	$1661 00	

COUNTY.

1 18	$4 60	$5 44		$91 56				
	116 02			54 52	260	25 00	11 00	
10 12	159 05	74 10	$3 75	110 79				
3 00	37 00			94 60	230	29 85	21 00	
160 00					385	78 93		
	18 00	5 00	10 00	3 66	106			
3 10		7 00	5 10	326 72		107 51		
10 00	59 81			45 78				
10 00	53 50	15 00	5 00	260 76	296	50 [illegible]		
2 00		3 00		12 12	164	20 [illegible]		
$199 40	$447 98	$109 54	$23 85	$1,000 51	1,441	$311 36	$32 00	

LENAWEE

TOWNSHIPS.	Whole districts.	Fractional districts.	Whole No. from which reports have been received.	No. of children in each township between the ages of 4 and 18, in which school has been taught by a qualified teacher.	No. of children that have attended during the year under 4 years of age.	No. that have attended during the year over 18 years of age.	Whole No. that have attended school during the year.	Whole amount of wages paid to teachers in the township.	Amount of money received from township treasurer, apportioned by township clerk.	Whole amount of money raised by the district.	Purpos's: To build school house.
Adrian, ...	9	6	15	1670	23	27	1096	$2628 54	$5?2 95	$3,422 10	$2337 00
Blissfield, ...	6	2	6	390	4	17	357	227 55	158 92	246 80	
Cambridge, ..	6	2		305	4	13	191	315 50	162 42	153 38	
Dover, ...		2	10	483	10	34	518	683 25	216 73	311 62	180 00
Franklin ...	7	3	10	522	3	23	440	573 90	223 57	338 02	294 00
Fairfield, ...	11	3	11	547	9	20	529	630 71	279 12	314 07	177 07
Hudson, ...	8	7	10	485	7	12	457	666 03	181 72	45 50	
Medina, ...	13		12	666	13	28	654		230 93	1013 83	507 00
Madison, ...	6	5	8	397	2	25	311	517 63	189 44	164 13	
Macon, ...	6	1		425	7	17	310		126 48	75 90	75 00
Ogden, ...	6	2	7	317	4	23	257	299 04	116 06	116 00	180 00
Palmyra, ...	8	2	9	387	2	25	345	474 42	169 03	386 57	264 00
Ridgeway, ...	2	4	4	260		20	213	336 87	111 98	56 00	
Rollin, ...	7	5	6	324	1	24	259	37 00	325 77	328 97	130 00
Rome, ...	8	3	11	553	2	23	470	590 46	296 16	368 99	275 00
Riga, ...	2	2	4	78			72	128 66	23 54	79 00	
Raisin, ...	5	7	11	501	10	32	409	208 00	262 05	141 25	100 60
Seneca, ...	7	1	8	430	2	10	345	304 46	162 29	278 51	180 00
Tecumseh, ..	10	2	11	921	8	41	752	1664 66	542 70	809 27	520 00
Woodstock ..	7	3	9	389	8	28	373	461 25	147 44	120 42	
Total, ...	134	62	162	10,050	119	442	8359	10747 93	4,519 30	8,769 51	5219 67

LIVINGSTON

TOWNSHIPS.	Whole districts.	Fractional districts.	Whole No. from which reports have been received.	No. of children in each township between the ages of 4 and 18, in which school has been taught by a qualified teacher.	No. of children that have attended during the year under 4 years of age.	No. that have attended during the year over 18 years of age.	Whole No. that have attended school during the year.	Whole amount of wages paid to teachers in the township.	Amount of money received from township treasurer, apportioned by township clerk.	Whole amount of money raised by the district.	Purpos's: To build school house.
Brighton, ...	8	3	8	337	7	10	259	$379 80	$107 44	$78 03	
Conway, ...	3	2	5	181		4	153	202 62	58 54	397 07	$316 57
Deerfield, ...	11	1	8	331	1	23	287	391 25	123 51	59 97	20 00
Green Oak, ..	5	2	6	295		25	347	338 00	144 67	95 54	
Genoa, ...	5	4	8	344	5	16	297	390 51	124 91	115 79	1 14
Hartland, ...	7	1	8	335	6	38	287	376 82	130 98	301 89	
Hamburg, ...	6	1	7	289	3	7	260	339 26	115 90	257 33	197 50
Howell, ...	5	3	8	474	6	13	433	918 05	163 20	950 48	433 00
Handy, ...	6		5	167		6	147	156 25	49 33	444 00	498 00
Iosco, ...	5	2	5	201	7	4	186	154 36	76 64	109 94	
Marion, ...	6	4	10	368		17	384	499 01	113 33	532 00	257 00
Oceola, ...	7	2	8	318	4	15	317	274 13	133 79	25 00	
Putnam, ...	6	3	9	431	2	15	442	492 00	156 63	22 64	149 00
Tyrone......	7		7	295		8	260	296 24	112 82	251 00	240 00
Tuscola, ...	4	5	6	196	6	8	191	272 35	63 23	336 91	180 00
Unadilla, ...	8	4	8	356	9	23	333	335 52	99 96	365 68	365 68
Total, ...	99	37	116	4918	56	232	4583	5816 17	1774 88	4343 27	2657 89

COUNTY.

for which it was raised, and amount raised for each particular purpose.								
Repairs of school house.	Support of school including pay of teachers.	To pay past indebtedness.	Any other purpose.	Amount raised by rate bill.	No. of vols. in the township library.	Amount of mill tax assessed by the supervisor and collected for support of school and township library. [Sec. 107.]	Amount of tax voted at the annual district meeting in addition to other taxes for the support of schools. [Sec. 140.]	Amount of fines, penalties and forfeitures of recognizance received of county treasurer for the purchase of books and township library.
$100 50	$396 38	$10 23	1 20	265 23				
22 64	317 75	59 29		466 36				
23 50	28 21	3 50	8 00	101 23	87	$68 00		$2 60
27 64	247 56		75	385 68	600	79 00		4 53
5 08			10 00	186 99	815			
31 00	39 00		12 00	327 42	406			4 17
34 38			8 00	477 08	349			4 04
17 00	70 19			426 99				
51 01	270 09	13 00		330 73	356	175 80		3 35
9 00	140 69	16 13	7 78	97 57	329			
24 75	474 92	3 25	1 16	272 17	320	65 00		2 46
45 00	11 00			209 07	420		$56 00	2 00
5 50	269 86	6 98	9 28	66 20	387	180 50		2 83
55 85	571 05	8 00		279 27	428	81 00		4 45
	71 00			40 56	430	25 00	78 00	17
46 00	130 00			117 25	386	134 00		6 00
32 00	54 00	1 25	11 25	188 54	424			3 35
72 50	153 61	46 68		321 00				
26 00	133 42	12 00		185 34	344	58 00		3 26
629 33	3,378 73	180 31	69 42	4,744 70	6081	866 30	134 00	43 21

COUNTY.

Repairs of school house.	Support of school including pay of teachers.	To pay past indebtedness.	Any other purpose.	Amount raised by rate bill.	No. of vols. in the township library.	Amount of mill tax assessed by the supervisor and collected for support of school and township library. [Sec. 107.]	Amount of tax voted at the annual district meeting in addition to other taxes for the support of schools. [Sec. 140.]	Amount of fines, penalties and forfeitures of recognizance received of county treasurer for the purchase of books and township library.
$50 00		8 03	20 00	178 59				
	$80 50			76 67	290	29 99	80 50	
34 25	64 50	23 47		57 51	296			
23 51	83 51			21 00	187	50 00	25 00	
11 00	118 20			199 16	314	34 62	44 50	
9 18	292 39	10 32		259 94	301	50 00		
5 00			29 83	200 55		25 00	25 00	
62 00	228 00	93 06	20 00	413 63	285	52 07		
25 00	84 94			79 74	267	41 46		2 08
3 00	131 00	101 00	40 00	238 77	340	45 00	131 00	
12 00	10 00	3 00		167 53	140			
47 00					200		22 64	
9 00		2 00		198 58	168	40 00		
	131 91		25 00	77 71	300	32 25		2 00
90 94	1224 95	240 88	134 83	2169 38	3088	400 39	328 64	4 08

MACOMB

TOWNSHIPS.	Whole districts.	Fractional districts.	Whole No. from which reports have been received.	No. of children in each township between the ages of 4 and 18 in which school has been taught by a qualified teacher.	No. of children that have attended during the year under 4 years of age.	No. that have attended during the year over 18 years of age.	Whole No. that have attended school during the year.	Whole amount of wages paid to teachers in the township.	Amount of money received from township treasurer, apportioned by township clerk.	Whole amount of money raised by the districts.	Purpos's To build school house.
Armada....	3	7	3	504	7	26	438	$631 00	$203 66	$14 00	
Bruce......	8	2	9	716	3	34	489	736 44	317 10	27 71	
Chesterfield...	5	2	5	297		5	223	234 11	114 80	174 92	60 00
Clinton.....	7	3	10	977	3	15	553	1112 00	289 61	344 00	400 00
Erin,.......	6	2	3	217	6		86	127 68	77 91	53 44	
Harrison,....	2		2	199			77	99 00	18 35	10 00	
Lenox......	7	3	8	295	4	11	258	404 90	103 89	241 00	125 00
Macomb....	4	5	8	445	3	13	303	389 75	143 96	72 72	
Ray........	9	5	11	476	4	21	440	438 89	203 02	242 40	138 25
Richmond...	7	2	8	418		15	371	539 53	171 17	28 30	
Shelby,.....	7	1	8	594	10	33	496	559 66	228 55	508 35	
Sterling,.....	3	2	5	284	5	5	259	374 50	97 57	243 00	195 00
Washington,..	6	6	8	444	3	29	413	570 13	223 62	346 55	300 00
Warren,....	5	1	6	287	2	3	124	169 00	94 98	201 01	175 00
Total, ...	79	41	94	6,063	50	210	4,630	$6,386 59	$2,288 19	$2,507 50	1,393 25

MONROE

TOWNSHIPS.	Whole districts.	Fractional districts.	Whole No. from which reports have been received.	No. of children between 4 and 18	Under 4	Over 18	Whole No. attended	Wages paid to teachers	From township treasurer	Raised by the districts	To build school house.
Ash........	5	6	8	467	3	10	391	$536 49	$202 73	$289 00	
Bedford....	6		6	328	5	20	244	343 63	125 60	134 87	
Dundee,....	10	2	12	513	29	38	564	661 40	155 59	306 25	
Erie,.......	5		4	407	3	9	181	233 00	192 97	71 81	
Exeter,.....	5		4	218	1	1	97	117 00	78 97	52 21	
Frenchtown,..	14	4	8	470	1	7	306	368 25	150 84	324 00	75 00
Ida........	3	2	4	164	1	2	94	199 00	61 25	74 00	
La Salle,....	8	2	8	439	1	18	312	332 75	145 18	128 00	75 00
London,....	4	3	6	263	6	17		403 00	105 92	273 42	76 81
Milan,......	5	4	7	296	5	9	261	215 14	107 03	232 73	184 00
Monroe city,..	5		5	1045	11	7	350	821 00	572 13	213 00	
do towns'p,	3		3	279			113	132 25	135 06	166 00	150 00
Raisinville...	5	5	8	470		9	280	490 50	179 24	399 73	75 00
Summerfield..	5		4	165	2	10	160	169 60	59 96		
Whiteford...	6	2	7	296	1	12	284	404 32	114 42	119 00	
Total,....	89	30	94	5,850	69	169	3,637	$5,427 33	$2,387 89	$2781 02	$635 81

COUNTY.

for which it was raised, and amount raised for each particular purpose.								
Repairs of school house.	Support of school including pay of teachers	To pay past indebtedness.	Any other purpose.	Amount raised by rate bill.	No. of vols. in the township library.	Amount of mill taxed assessed by the supervisor and collected for support of school and township library. [Sec. 107.]	Amount of tax voted at the annual district meeting in addition to other taxes for the support of schools. [Sec. 140.]	Amount of fines, penalties and forfeitures of recognizance received of county treasurer for the purchase of books and township library.
16 12	$321 90			$387 10				
4 42			23 29	427 10	216	88 00		
30 00	232 75		2 00	119 57	141	28 00		
40 38				689 64	395	113 97	144 00	
20 00		10 00		61 96	95	39 86		
2 00			8 00	88 65	212	23 35		
				146 90	387	52 76	116 00	
5 30	344 75			118 66	103			
12 65	126 08	17 35		154 01	240	64 52		
25 00		2 50	80	367 56	263	19 74		
32 00	564 23			532 50				
				196 35	240		10 00	
46 69		7 26	2 08	349 70	164	114 97		
20 00		5 00	1 00	104 05	890	33 00		
$254 56	$1,559 81	$42 11	$37 17	$3,743 15	2,646	$578 17	$270 00	
COUNTY.								
$16 75	$230 50	3 50	12 00	$59 34	275	59 59		
8 12	332 50		8 43	80 44	133	47 39	168 62	
46 88	218 00	29 00	6 00	207 90				
10 25	124 75			52 00	325			
					250	28 00		
27 00	327 25	20 50	5 50	41 13	228	72 67		
14 50	49 00		5 00	33 93	280			
3 00	34 50		6 00	129 25	382			
•	147 00			147 00	320	29 74		
7 94	50 02	3 81		70 90	290			
4 00	880 00	19 00	12 00	292 09	160	224 94	212 00	
13 00	150 25			3 00	117	58 39		
24 07	328 58	6 43		310 82	200	46 74		
29 00	150 60				275			
15 26	94 00	4 74	5 00	46 18	310	42 19	94 00	
$219 77	$3,167 95	$86 98	$59 93	$1,473 98	3,545	$609 65	$474 62	

MONTCALM

TOWNSHIPS.	Whole districts.	Frational districts.	Whole No. from which reports have been received.	No. of children in each township between the ages of 4 and 18 in which school has been taught by a qualified tracher.	No. of children that have attended during the year under 4 years of age.	No. that have attended during the year over 18 years of age.	Whole No. that have attended school during the year.	Whole amount of wages paid to teachers in the townships.	Am't of money received from township treasurer, apportioned by t'wnship clerk.	Whole amount of money raised by the districts.	Purpos's — To build school house.
Eureka, ...	6		4	128		6	129	$59 66	$35 36	$155 97	$126 00
Bushnell, ...	1			38			24	60 00	12 92		
Fairplain, ...	3			66	3	2	64		10 88	26 34	
Total, ...	10		4	232	3	8	217	119 66	59 16	182 31	126 00

MICHILIMACKINAC

TOWNSHIPS.	Whole districts.	Frational districts.	Whole No. from which reports have been received.	No. of children between 4 and 18 taught by a qualified tracher.	No. under 4 years of age.	No. over 18 years of age.	Whole No. that have attended school during the year.	Whole amount of wages paid to teachers.	Am't of money received from township treasurer.	Whole amount of money raised by the districts.	To build school house.
Holmes, ...	2		2	282		4	143	438 00	44 00	341 00	
Inverness, ...	1		1	38			26				
Peaine, ...	5			287	15	17	189				655 00
Total, ...	8		3	607	15	21	358	438 00	44 00	341 00	655 00

OAKLAND

TOWNSHIPS.	Whole districts.	Frational districts.	Whole No. from which reports have been received.	No. of children between 4 and 18 taught by a qualified tracher.	No. under 4 years of age.	No. over 18 years of age.	Whole No. that have attended school during the year.	Whole amount of wages paid to teachers.	Am't of money received from township treasurer.	Whole amount of money raised by the districts.	To build school house.
Addison, ...	5	1	6	287	2	20	297	315 60	122 89	240 00	200 00
Avon, ...	9	3	12	603	2	25	582	784 84	295 28	203 96	
Bloomfield, ...	6	9	10	624	5	29	581	725 38	180 96	40 75	
Brandon, ...	6	4	8	323	3	19	329	440 06	107 68	339 13	
Commerce, ...	6	9	10	459	2	18	459	524 20	223 44	637 39	287 00
Farmington, ..	6	5	10	648	5	51	648	730 88	411 84	348 98	
Groveland, ...	5	7	5	339	1	7	273	256 20	109 24	26 25	
Highland, ...	5	2	6	298	3	14	214	408 85	137 70	128 86	
Holly, ...	7	2	8	268	5	5	222	318 25	109 35	109 00	
Independence,	8		7	384	3	14	331	446 83	177 84	233 50	400 00
Lyon, ...	6	4	6	350	5	21	260	379 00	160 12	10 00	
Milford, ...	10	1	11	614	5	30	492	676 66	261 88	582 45	
Novi, ...	7	4	11	586	6	25	410	631 56	310 86	648 25	172 70
Oakland, ...	5	2	7	392	5	35	312	518 06	196 34	127 71	64 00
Orion, ...	6	3	7	452	11	8	276	404 25	158 28	30 00	
Oxford, ...	2	6	6	456	14	35	315	316 43	139 23	409 42	270 00
Pontiac, ...	8	4	11	1025	7	39	864	1545 19	486 84	2845 04	2440 38
Rose, ...	7	2	7	323	3	70	181	288 20	113 79	769 50	
Royal Oak, ...	4	3		420	4	8	257	34 98	180 83	183 68	100 00
Southfield, ...	5	4	9	606	16	24	486	694 00	274 23	64 58	
Springfield, ...	3	2	8	388	7	7	153	434 63	129 92	468 73	
Troy, ...	8	9	9	444	3	30	451	77 07	248 50	213 85	
Whiteford, ...	7	4	10	411	23	12	393	595 21	188 60	436 40	129 00
White Lake, ..	6	5	8	358	4	9	275	363 50	135 46	53 00	
W. Bloomfield,	6	5	7	372	3	11	283	525 88	195 17	407 65	
Total, ...	153	100	199	11,430	147	566	9344	12435 71	5,056 27	9,558 08	4,063 08

COUNTY.

for which it was raised, and amount raised for each particular purpose.								
Repairs of school house.	Support of school, including pay of teachers.	To pay past indebtedness.	Any other purpose.	Amount raised by rate bill.	No. of vols. in the township library.	Amount of mill tax assessed by the supervisor and collected for support of school and township library. [Sec. 107.]	Amount of tax voted at the annual district meeting in addition to other taxes for the support of schools. [Sec. 140.]	Amount of fines, penalties and forfeitures of recognizance received of county treasurer for the purchase of books and township library.
	53 27			25 84	75			
	53 27			25 84	75			

COUNTY.

Repairs of school house.	Support of school, including pay of teachers.	To pay past indebtedness.	Any other purpose.	Amount raised by rate bill.	No. of vols. in the township library.	Amount of mill tax.	Amount of tax voted.	Amount of fines, penalties, etc.
7 50	407 50	38 00	17 00	24 50	1	112 56	394 00	
				80 00			19 00	
46 50			110 00	98 00			100 00	
54 00	407 50	38 00	127 00	202 50	1	112 56	513 00	

COUNTY.

Repairs of school house.	Support of school, including pay of teachers.	To pay past indebtedness.	Any other purpose.	Amount raised by rate bill.	No. of vols. in the township library.	Amount of mill tax.	Amount of tax voted.	Amount of fines, penalties, etc.
40 00				192 75	200	27 44		
9 00	297 38	15 22		497 76	325	25 00		7 09
18 90		13 08		465 43	152	115 00	8 27	5 62
39 75	466 22			369 13	336	48 03		3 49
115 00	287 09	16 43		367 81	431	91 06		5 45
71 37	16 00			336 40	466	148 00		
3 00	23 25			110 82	320	48 17		1 46
5 65		115 86		241 12	331	25 00		4 50
30 00	79 00			135 58	302		62 00	3 69
40 15	61 00			332 09	195	83 34	33 50	4 35
10 00				218 88	297	60 40		4 00
33 50	553 90	12 50	3 50	477 85	400	74 23		
103 95	696 31	20 21		624 31	217	118 85		7 50
21 21	299 00			373 87	280	62 06		
11 58	173 66	22 42		208 91		41 26		
90 00	300 89			225 75	224	57 85		2 51
34 54		171 53	328 59	1099 93				
8 00	99 31				260		54 50	
12 00	167 50			234 54	311	25 00		
6 04	51 54		7 00	469 77	541	96 80		
23 00	505 17			215 23	189	58 52	50 50	
62 56	349 10	47 34		517 73	393	110 10		6 72
54 00	323 58	129 00	9 00	296 13	320	76 65		
12 00	362 00	1 00		190 15	262	55 77	41 00	1 72
51 10	538 74			330 92	298	81 66		4 58
906 30	5,650 64	564 59	347 09	8,532 86	7,050	1,530 19	249 77	62 73

OTTAWA

TOWNSHIPS.	Whole districts.	Fractional districts.	Whole No. from which reports have been received.	No. of children in each township between the ages of 4 and 18 in which school has been taught by a qualified teacher.	No. of children that have attended during the year under 4 years of age.	No. that have attended during the year over 18 years of age.	Whole No. that have attended school during the year.	Whole amount of wages paid to teachers in the township.	Am't of money received from township treasurer, apportioned by township clerk.	Whole amount of money raised by the districts.	Purpos's — To build school house.
Allendale, . . .	1	1	1	15	1	1	22	48 00		108 00	40 00
Chester, ...	1	3	4	153	2	4	123	159 13	31 38	172 25	51 00
Crockery, . . .	1		1	41			26	47 28	10 00	10 00	
Georgetown, . .	4		3	51	2		53		60 50	49 76	
Holland, ...	1	1	1	150			80	80 00	111 70	100 00	
Ottawa, ...	1		1	116	3	5	140	260 00	296 00	253 00	
Polkton, ...	1	3	4	66	1	2	60			76 00	
Ravenna, ...	3		3	24		1	29	46 00	24 00	159 25	132 25
Tallmadge, . . .	3		3	152	20	2	128	138 50	46 52	106 61	
Wright, ...	4	3	5	139	4	3	136	207 75	38 76	81 50	
Zealand, ...	1	1	2	203			91	99 00	63 92	42 00	
Total, ...	21	12	28	1112	33	18	888	1085 66	682 78	1158 37	223 25

SAGINAW

TOWNSHIPS.	Whole districts.	Fractional districts.	Whole No. from which reports have been received.	No. of children in each township between the ages of 4 and 18 in which school has been taught by a qualified teacher.	No. of children that have attended during the year under 4 years of age.	No. that have attended during the year over 18 years of age.	Whole No. that have attended school during the year.	Whole amount of wages paid to teachers in the township.	Am't of money received from township treasurer, apportioned by township clerk.	Whole amount of money raised by the districts.	Purpos's — To build school house.
Bridgeport, . . .	2	1		61			43	35 50	14 00	21 50	
Hampton, . . .	2	1		97	5	2	40	120 00		120 00	
Northampton,	1	1		44			32	65 00	19 04		
Saginaw, ...	3	3	1	282		1	64	298 00	231 31	256 00	
Taymouth, . . .	1	1		67	1		21	19 00		20 00	
Tittabawassee,	5	5		161	6	1	146	196 75	51 70	62 00	
Total, ...	14	12	1	712	12	4	346	834 25	316 05	479 50	

COUNTY.

Repairs of school house.	Support of school, including pay of teachers.	To pay past indebtedness.	Any other purpose.	Amount raised by rate bill.	No. of vol's in the township library.	Amount of mill tax assessed by the Supervisor and collected for support of school and township library. [Sec. 107.]	Amount of tax voted at the annual district meeting in addition to other taxes, for the support of schools. [Sec. 140.]	Amount of fines, penalties and for feitures of recognizance received of county treasurer for the purchase of books and township library.
for which it was raised, and amount raised for each particular purpose.								
	48 00		20 00	33 00	90		15 00	
10 00	140 00		4 25	36 01	74	36 10	107 00	
3 00	50 28				84			
30 00		50 00	20 00		50		150 00	
125 00	128 00				303	97 00	128 00	
50 00				60 00	87	28 76	33 00	
	27 00			22 00		18 10	27 00	
28 11	47 00			49 00				
	79 50	2 00		94 67	185			
	42 00			42 00			412 75	
246 11	561 78	52 00	44 25	336 68	873	179 96	872 75	

COUNTY.

Repairs of school house.	Support of school, including pay of teachers.	To pay past indebtedness.	Any other purpose.	Amount raised by rate bill.	No. of vol's in the township library.	Amount of mill tax assessed by the Supervisor and collected for support of school and township library. [Sec. 107.]	Amount of tax voted at the annual district meeting in addition to other taxes, for the support of schools. [Sec. 140.]	Amount of fines, penalties and for feitures of recognizance received of county treasurer for the purchase of books and township library.
10 00	35 50		6 20	21 50	64	48 87	10 00	
3 00			4 00	124 00	92			
	15 00			23 32	80	30 00		
52 00	18 80			126 45	114	137 30		
	15 85	4 50	10 00	15 85				
					118			
65 00	134 35	4 50	20 20	311 12	468	216 17	10 00	

SANILAC

TOWNSHIPS.	Whole districts.	Fractional districts.	Whole No. from which reports have been received.	No. of children in each township between the ages of 4 and 18 in which school has been taught by a qualified teacher.	No. of children that have attended during the year under 4 years of age.	No. that have attended during the year over 18 years of age.	Whole No. that have attended school during the year.	Whole amount of wages paid to teachers in the township.	Am't of money received from township treasurer, apportioned by township clerk.	Whole amount of money raised by the districts.	Purpos's: To build school house.
Lexington . . .	6	2	6	371	7	5	302	$176 75	176 82	225 00	
Sanilac	3		3	70		2	44	57 00	13 26	171 84	100 00
Wright.	4		2	139		6	106		68 55	22 50	
Total, ...	13	1	11	580	7	13	452	$233 75	258 63	419 34	100 00

SHIAWASSEE

TOWNSHIPS.	Whole districts.	Fractional districts.	Whole No. from which reports have been received.	No. of children in each township between the ages of 4 and 18 in which school has been taught by a qualified teacher.	No. of children that have attended during the year under 4 years of age.	No. that have attended during the year over 18 years of age.	Whole No. that have attended school during the year.	Whole amount of wages paid to teachers in the township.	Am't of money received from township treasurer, apportioned by township clerk.	Whole amount of money raised by the districts.	Purpos's: To build school house.
Antrim, ...	1	3	4	130		2	126	133 25	32 10	203 50	150 00
Bennington. . .	5	4	6	210	2	10	199	225 95	57 37	104 50	12 00
Burns.	7	1	6	221	9	18	234	382 33	100 67	194 67	
Caledonia, . . .	5	1	5	220	5	10	232	270 25	54 40	474 00	40 00
Hazleton, ...	1			9							
New Haven, . .	1	1	2	44	3	6	56	81 83	15 64	85 00	10 00
Owasso.	3	2	5	154	2	6	139	233 50	52 02	351 00	180 00
Perry, ...	1	3	4	109	2	13	132	116 16	44 86	56 61	
Rush.	1		1							82 75	60 00
Sciota	3		3	60		2	78	108 41	16 66	102 00	150 00
Shiawassee, . . .	4	3	7	362	1	16	264	423 31	105 36	538 00	500 00
Venice, ...	4		4	97	3	4	82	127 74	21 36	249 00	170 00
Vernon.	7	1	8	303	7	16	264	284 53	93 74	43 25	
Woodhull, . . .	4		3	73		3	70	49 00			
Total, ...	47	19	58	1,992	34	106	1,876	2436 26	594 18	2,484 28	1272 00

COUNTY.

for which it was raised, and amount raised for each particular purpose.								
Repairs of school house.	Support of school, including pay of teachers.	To pay past indebtedness.	Any other purpose.	Amount raised by rate bill.	No. of vols. in the township library.	Amount of mill tax assessed by the supervisor and collected for support of school and township library. [Sec. 107.]	Amount of tax voted at the annual district meeting in addition to other taxes for the support of schools. [Sec. 140.]	Amount of fines, penalties and forfeitures of recognizance received of county treasurer for the purchase of books and township library.
	$161 40				200	$54 80	$75 00	
$28 00	57 00			$43 74	115	16 40	41 00	
10 00				38 89	138	47 00		
$38 00	$218 40			$82 63	453	$118 20	$116 00	

COUNTY.

Repairs of school house.	Support of school, including pay of teachers.	To pay past indebtedness.	Any other purpose.	Amount raised by rate bill.	No. of vols. in the township library.	Amount of mill tax assessed by the supervisor and collected for support of school and township library. [Sec. 107.]	Amount of tax voted at the annual district meeting in addition to other taxes for the support of schools. [Sec. 140.]	Amount of fines, penalties and forfeitures of recognizance received of county treasurer for the purchase of books and township library.
$50 00	$10 48			$94 04	132	$52 00		
25 00	67 50			118 78				
	171 00	$9 67	$14 00	151 12	210	47 13	$23 67	
2 50	306 00	120 00	3 25	222 38	256	25 00		
25 00	81 83	4 00		30 94	33		48 00	
	143 00	8 00	20 00	88 57	294	40 70		
	66 11			90 40	180	25 00	147 01	
	14 00	8 75				11 25	14 00	
5 00	34 00		13 00	104 80	130	17 58		
16 00	22 00			307 15	212	43 11		
31 00	28 00		11 00	86 08	200			
14 19	29 00			171 04	283	35 19		
				49 00	100			
$168 09	$972 98	$150 42	$61 25	$1,514 30	2,030	$296 96	$232 68	

ST. CLAIR

TOWNSHIPS.	Whole districts.	Frational districts.	Whole No. from which reports have been received.	No. of children in each township between the ages of 4 and 18 in which school has been taught by a qualified tracher.	No. of children that have attended during the year under 4 years of age.	No. that have attended during the year over 18 years of age.	Whole No. that have attended school during the year.	Whole amount of wages paid to teachers in the townships.	Am't of money received from township treasurer, apportioned by t'wnship clerk.	Whole amount of money raised by the districts.	Purpos's — To build school house.
Berlin, ...	4	2	6	258	3	12	224	$265 08	$100 42	$47 39	
Brockway, . . .	4		3	117		1	72	60 58	65 74	170 00	$150 00
Burchville, . . .	4		4	241			184	162 52	88 48	128 11	
Casco, ...	1	2	1	51		2	25	39 50	21 19		
China, ...	8		8	405	15	15	310	468 50	168 06	171 00	
Clay, ...	5		5	338	22	15	207	288 08	120 56	123 40	
Columbus, . . .	5	2	4	182		2	123	57 72	75 21		6 00
Cottrelville, . .	4		3	323	3	2	209	281 27	159 51	74 06	
Clyde, ...	6		6	305	2		208		94 53	122 41	
Ira, ...	3		3	300			125	254 00	172 24	388 94	125 00
Port Huron, . .	7		6	756	8	8	657	973 25	329 65	696 95	
Riley, ...	4		3	130	1		131	99 25	38 76	302 50	300 00
St. Clair, ...	6		6	597	6	33	413	645 00	246 54	792 52	300 00
Wales, ...	3		2	97	6	2	98	86 16	21 97	133 25	80 00
Total, ...	64	6	60	4,100	66	92	2,986	3,680 91	$1,702 86	$3,150 53	$961 00

ST. JOSEPH

TOWNSHIPS.	Whole districts.	Frational districts.	Whole No. from which reports have been received.	No. of children between 4 and 18.	Under 4 years of age.	Over 18 years of age.	Whole No. attended.	Wages paid to teachers.	Am't from township treasurer.	Raised by the districts.	To build school house.
Burr Oak, . . .	6	5	6	279	17	20	274	$309 00	$104 43	$223 94	$180 00
Colon, ...	3	2	5	289	3	12	284	295 00	108 77	110 00	
Constantine, . .	7	3	6	454	3	13	387	614 93	183 00	369 19	
Fabius, ...	5	3	4	170		6	152	173 87	60 43	91 00	
Florence, ...	2	5	6	292	2	23	220	372 00	127 39	356 18	
Flowerfield, . . .	2	3	3	184	1	7	152				
Fawn River, . .	5	2	4	179	3		132	147 75	46 20	12 00	185 00
Leonidas, ...	7		7	307	6	13	229	350 98	97 70	407 15	335 00
Lockport, . . .		2	3	337	6	18	303	424 52	170 86	704 00	660 00
Mottville, ...			4	225		1	110		68 52	79 34	
Mendon, ...	5	1	6	297	5	21	272	374 03	132 76	124 50	
Nottawa, ...	6	5	6	388		3	353	784 87	238 42	381 30	88 25
Park, ...	5	3	8	353	3	20	343	505 50	33 69	91 71	
Sherman, ...	4	4	8	101	1	4	96	156 48	20 21		
Sturgis, ...	4	1	5	376	17	36	371	581 50	156 59	511 89	
White Pigeon,	2	2		309	3	9	218	390 00	217 27	129 00	180 00
Total, ...	63	41	81	4,540	70	206	3,896	$5,480 43	$1,766 24	$3,591 20	1,628 25

TUSCOLA

TOWNSHIPS.	Whole districts.	Frational districts.	Whole No. from which reports have been received.	No. of children between 4 and 18.	Under 4 years of age.	Over 18 years of age.	Whole No. attended.	Wages paid to teachers.	Am't from township treasurer.	Raised by the districts.	To build school house.
Tuscola, ...	1			92			60				
Verona, ...		1		31			32				
Total, ...	1	1		123			92				

COUNTY.

for which it was raised, and amount raised for each particular purpose.								
Repairs of school house.	Support of school including pay of teachers.	To pay past indebtedness.	Any other purpose.	Amount raised by rate bill.	No. of vols. in the township library.	Amount of mill tax assessed by the supervisor and collected for support of school and township library. [Sec. 107.]	Am't of tax voted at the annual district meeting in addition to other taxes for the support of schools. [Sec. 140.]	Amount of fines, penalties and forfeitures of recognizance received of county treasurer for the purchase of books and township library.
$3 50	$43 00		$0 89	$20 00	236	$23 24	$43 00	
20 00					117	53 00		
22 00	164 52			21 00	275			
	39 50			19 20	117			
23 50	483 66	2 75	19	152 41	203	59 20	158 00	
33 00	90 00			17 24	220	39 91		
19 50				27 18	170	35 00		
6 76	233 75	1 19		115 94	198			
10 00	206 94				280	54 57		
	154 95		4 00	16 00	40	74 24		
98 00	350 48	180 60	54 32	201 50	204	138 94		
	101 75	2 50			188			
7 00	335 52	95 00	55 00	182 93	230	344 41		11 27
4 13	44 50	2 00	4 75		285		41 50	1 90
$247 39	$2,248 57	$284 04	119 15	$773 40	2,763	$822 51	$242 50	$13 17

COUNTY.

Repairs of school house.	Support of school including pay of teachers.	To pay past indebtedness.	Any other purpose.	Amount raised by rate bill.	No. of vols. in the township library.	Amount of mill tax.	Am't of tax voted.	Amount of fines, penalties, etc.
26 00		$10 00	3 00	$239 53	234	$48 92		8 67
27 00	61 50		13 00		133	33 00		
60 00					465	43 58		
71 00	189 63		5 00	99 85	236	44 89	15 00	4 90
169 65	391 65			134 52		66 65	141 95	15 14
					285	85 00		
12 00	158 00	7 66		59 60	189			
3 00	213 50	14 85		180 63	226	50 62		10 90
9 75	35 00			241 41	279	180 00	660 00	6 00
15 00								
10 00	373 45		8 50	195 73	219			11 02
3 00	238 20		77 26	356 82	270	77 28		14 46
3 00	62 71			309 24	384	33 99	62 71	12 63
				136 92	144			
13 50	471 39	23 00		440 89		73 99		
22 00	412 70			55 00	250	72 00	69 51	13 54
444 90	2,607 73	$55 51	$106 76	$2,450 14	3,314	$809 92	$949 17	$97 26

COUNTY.

VAN BUREN

TOWNSHIPS.	Whole districts.	Fractional districts.	Whole No. from which reports have been received.	No. of children in each township between the ages of 4 and 18 in which school has been taught by a qualified teacher.	No. of children that have attended during the year under 4 years of age.	No. that have attended during the year over 18 years of age.	Whole No. that have attended school during the year.	Whole am't of wages paid to teachers in the township.	Am't of money received from township treasurer, apportioned by township clerk.	Whole amount of money raised by the districts.	Purpos's — To build school house.
Arlington,....	2	1	3	50	2		31		$30 81	$200 75	$150 00
Antwerp.....	7		7	228	6		35	$416 12	113 38	88 65	
Almena,.....	3	4	3	95	3		62	84 00	30 38	160 50	150 00
Bloomingdale.		4	1	42	1	1	45	52 50	7 00		
Columbia,...		3	2	68	1		55	63 00	35 47	62 15	
Decatur.....	4		3	118		4	110	121 50	11 22	.332 00	245 00
Hartford,....	2	3	5	165	4	13	165	170 35	25 51	163 72	100 00
Hamilton....	5		4	150		9	140	168 56	40 12	321 00	200 00
Keeler,.....	5	1	4	159	1	9	136	158 50	34 00	243 00	200 00
Lafayette....	5	2	6	389	36	5	328	603 91	165 01	239 67	114 47
Lawrence,...	4	2	6	172	4	7	168	268 50	76 37	82 50	
Porter......	6	1	6	177		10	179	171 65	53 30	24 77	
Pine Grove,...	1	1	2	40	40	1	40	35 00	80 00	80 00	50 00
South Haven,.	3	2	3	59	1		50	96 00	36 60	96 25	
Waverly....	1	5	3	115	4	17	110	171 50	37 46	74 00	
Total,....	48	29	58	2,027	103	76	1654	2,581 09	$776 66	$2168 69	1,209 47

WASHTENAW

TOWNSHIPS.	Whole districts.	Fractional districts.	Whole No. from which reports have been received.	No. of children between 4 and 18 taught by a qualified teacher.	No. under 4 years of age.	No. over 18 years of age.	Whole No. that have attended school during the year.	Whole am't of wages paid to teachers.	Am't of money received from township treasurer.	Whole amount of money raised by the districts.	To build school house.
Ann Arb'r city		2	2	1027	18	8	742	$1308 12	$589 10	$974 20	
do t'ns'p.	8	6	8	463	3	29	420	637 50	242 86	336 79	$175 00
Augusta,.....			6	310		9	281	358 00	144 93	117 94	4 00
Bridgewater..	10		10	794	20	58	798	822 50	342 54	1190 65	724 51
Dexter,.....	6	2	7	345	24	6	323	436 56	151 97	254 89	
Freedom,....	7	2	9	494			293	309 06	164 90	188 82	40 00
Lyndon,....	3	7	6	301	8	15	239	275 59	77 52	94 21	
Lodi,.......	5	8	7	380	4	8	353	324 25	179 79	149 90	
Lima.......	7	1	7	249	8	14	221	425 65	135 63	317 05	
Manchester...	7	3	9	479	7	29	407	661 76	282 24	111 72	
Northfield,....	6	1	7	462	2	11	373	370 03	194 14	71 18	125 00
Pittsfield,.....	4	3	7	400	4	28	339	582 25	220 81	377 23	
Saline,......	6		10	668	9	33	472	801 60	829 55	240 00	215 00
Salem,......	5	5	6	420	2	12	378	462 00	268 19	148 42	
Scio.......	6	6	12	631	3	18	410	905 00	445 41	382 65	
Sharon,.....	8		8	302	3	13	258	438 04	161 82	95 00	70 00
Superior,....	6	3	9	427	1	36	366	585 25	246 75	88 92	
Sylvan,.....	4	3	7	384	4	14	275	500 24	163 33	432 91	80 00
Webster.....	5	2	7	326	5	20	337	455 78		323 68	265 00
York.......	4	9	6	431	8	20	395	532 50	220 60	696 90	565 00
Ypsilanti,....	11	2	13	1133	8	47	983	2146 25	674 63	1488 10	864 00
Total....	118	65	163	10,426	141	428	8693	13137 84	$5,236 71	$8,081 16	3,127 51

COUNTY.

for which it was raised, and amount raised for each particular purpose.								
Repairs of school house.	Support of school, including pay of teachers.	To pay past indebtedness.	Any other purpose.	Amount raised by rate bill.	No. of vols. in the township library.	Amount of mill tax assessed by the supervisor and collected for support of school and township library. [Sec. 107.]	Amount of tax voted at the annual district meeting in addition to other taxes for the support of schools. [Sec. 140.]	Amount of fines, penalties and forfeitures of recognizance received of county treasurer for the purchase of books and township library.
$15 00	$83 38		$ 50	$21 13	235	$27 06	$32 25	
18 00	426 30		10 00	232 58	294	43 26		
	10 50			44 39	182	29 44		
					221	20 07	21 00	
	62 15			62 15	142	41 43	9 50	
	87 00			34 50	187	29 37	87 00	
	105 72	30 72	2 34	101 62		27 43	33 00	
15 00	120 03	28 78		71 18	323			
10 00	192 75			125 51	337	3 48		
6 00	71 10	16 00	52 10	372 61	200	70 85	71 10	
24 50	241 75			133 44	175			
		16 30		124 66	207			
29 00			1 00		71	105 34		
	26 25	31		28 15	244	12 55	23 90	
1 14	171 50		31 86	91 00	210	24 55	41 00	
$118 64	$1,598 43	$92 11	$97 80	$1,442 92	3,028	$438 83	$318 75	

COUNTY.

Repairs of school house.	Support of school, including pay of teachers.	To pay past indebtedness.	Any other purpose.	Amount raised by rate bill.	No. of vols. in the township library.	Amount of mill tax assessed by the supervisor and collected for support of school and township library. [Sec. 107.]	Amount of tax voted at the annual district meeting in addition to other taxes for the support of schools. [Sec. 140.]	Amount of fines, penalties and forfeitures of recognizance received of county treasurer for the purchase of books and township library.
	$1,464 71	$252 50	$102 61		157	$25 00		
$31 70	563 51	12 22	5 34	$157 92	155			
24 94	67 00	1 00		187 62				
	411 88				330			
	254 89			254 89	310	152 00		
11 49	64 31	6 50		82 52	289	82 71		
5 00	192 70			117 91	240	50 84	24 10	
				149 90	158	93 79		3 44
8 40	424 45			308 55	225	31 00		
55 00		19 72	36 62	232 66	428	102 72		
7 00	265 68	1 00		209 96	230		29 00	
23 52	300 22	4 00	24 39	355 72	430	108 98		
17 00			8 00	384 87	409	385 71		
17 20	161 56			207 31	349	108 55		
31 68	680 26	7 50	23 92	130 23	300	120 46	46 00	
6 00		14 00	5 00	189 27	231	61 52		
54 20	334 26	19 76	15 05	315 22			70 00	
16 00	336 91			336 91				
11 42		26 00	20 30	293 51				
43 04	162 44		20 00	144 42	364	87 60		
218 16	549 99	198 79	77 92	912 93	755			
$581 75	$6,234 77	$562 99	$339 16	$4,972 32	5,370	$1,410 88	$169 00	$3 44

WAYNE

TOWNSHIPS.	Whole districts.	Fractional districts.	Whole No. from which reports have been received.	No. of children in each township between the ages of 4 and 18, in which school has been taught by a qualified teacher.	No. of children that have attended during the year under 4 years of age.	No. that have attended during the year over 18 years of age.	Whole No. that have attended school during the year.	Whole amount of wages paid to teachers in the township.	Amount of money received from township treasurer, apportioned by township clerk.	Whole amount of money raised by the district.	Purpos's
											To build school house.
Brownstown,	8		8	404	34	12	305	482 96	$147 88	$155 70	
Canton, ...	5	4	9	612	3	17	585	683 75	237 04	222 00	$180 00
Detroit City,.				7253			4250	6255 25		8665 00	1500 00
Dearborn, ...	8	2	8	549	8		339	38 61	197 94	39 25	46 61
Ecorse, ...	3		3	256	1		163	158 32	99 75	6 00	
Greenfield, ...	8	2	8	588	17	12	334	490 37	149 77	180 79	
Gross Point,.	5	1	6	475	20	4	257	433 00	206 59	249 50	
Huron, ...	1	3	4	182		15	189	265 99	56 96	143 00	
Hamtramck,.	7	2	5	498	2		220	429 00	351 55	658 50	400 00
Livonia, ...	8	1		495	3	28	456		225 01	397 98	180 00
Monguagon, .	3		3	337	12	16	152	168 50	162 50	559 00	559 00
Nankin, ...	7		9	630	4	27	424		211 33	629 17	
Plymouth, ...	10	5	15	904	6	67	938	1570 44	494 83	955 85	
Redford, ...	10	1	10	645	7	27	440	645 30	306 26	27 00	
Springwells, .	3	1	4	366			173	291 62	181 11	550 00	554 50
Sumpter, ...	2		2	106	2	2	102		37 11	120 00	
Taylor, ...	2	3	5	418	2	10	119	69 25	29 16	62 50	
Romulus, ...	4	6	1	237	1	7	183		75 88	132 44	
Van Buren, ..	7		8	432	5	20	371	329 69	183 07	283 24	
Total, ...	101	31	108	15,087	127	264	10000	12,312 05	3,353 74	14,036 92	3,420 11

COUNTY.

for which it was raised, and amount raised for each particular purpose.								
Repairs of school house.	Support of school including pay of teachers.	To pay past indebtedness.	Any other purpose.	Amount raised by rate bill.	No. of vols. in the township library.	Amount of mill tax assessed by the supervisor and collected for support of school and township library. [Sec. 107.]	Amount of tax voted at the annual district meeting in addition to other taxes for the support of schools. [Sec. 140.]	Amount of fines, penalties and forfeitures of recognizance received of county treasurer for the purchase of books and township library.
$23 00	$49 50	$5 00	$2 50	$164 96	369	$63 44		
9 47		27 84	4 69	445 02	226			$14 72
288 76	8,003 67	1347 21	29 50					184 06
	39 40	22 00		20 00	262			
6 00				19 50	270			5 76
33 00	24 19	10 60		151 68		63 63		16 31
51 00	328 00	7 00			262	25 00	$50 50	14 35
25 00	118 00			75 58	207	31 00		
43 00	215 50				326		298 50	12 96
52 50	482 14	8 81	7 00	322 28				
				152 29	192	62 00		24 34
453 80					350	47 94		14 00
59 10	303 18	524 71	23 32	894 68	374	180 82	303 18	26 97
22 00				335 56	355	100 00		
				42 85		71 00		
5 00					263	30 83		2 72
12 00	50 50			19 45	217	49 78		
4 56					161	25 00		
109 87	647 45	106 25		134 73				
1198 06	$10,261 53	2059 42	$67 01	$2,788 58	3,834	$750 44	$652 18	$316 19

RECAPITULATION OF SCHOOL INSPEC-

COUNTIES.	Whole districts.	Fractional districts.	Whole No. from which reports have been received.	No. of children in each Co. between the ages of 4 & 18 in which sch'l has been taught by a qualified teacher.	No. of children that have attended during the year under 4 years of age.	No. that have attended during the year over 18 years of age.	Whole No. that have attended school during the year.	Whole amount of wages paid to teachers in the township.	Amount of money received from township treasurer, apportioned by township clerk.	Whole amount of money raised by the districts.	Purpos's
											To build school house.
Allegan, ...	43	13	48	1851	28	162	1417	2500 51	$814 98	$2707 88	$1019 89
Barry, ...	57	21	66	1773	26	72	1489	1614 85	592 63	1960 16	666 50
Berrien, ...	73	25	59	3941	187	163	3110	4707 31	1641 86	3974 33	830 45
Branch, ...	90	40	93	4691	65	282	3996	5466 35	2637 10	3899 99	1962 00
Calhoun, ...	93	57	113	6403	92	231	5049	7757 55	2983 36	10601 91	7759 60
Cass, ...	92	18	85	4448	41	212	3585	4976 87	1642 23	2907 35	1119 60
Chippewa, . . .	1		1	349			75	150 00	80 58		
Clinton, ...	57	10	45	1776	24	75	1591	1475 15	545 35	1415 12	329 00
Eaton, ...	72	26	86	2731	33	83	2428	2514 16	865 97	2657 00	1207 00
Genesee, . . .	83	31	99	4607	67	230	3838	4081 93	1694 29	3703 65	1849 00
Hillsdale, . . .	110	45	125	5848	89	294	5406	7708 08	2193 24	5198 80	2142 13
Ingham, . . .	73	31	84	3436	61	175	3096	4108 55	1223 50	4634 41	2708 40
Ionia, ...	56	39	64	2884	67	153	2593	3496 73	1082 26	2534 90	988 20
Jackson, ...	108	60	132	7036	85	355	6028	9606 82	3312 11	7856 37	3466 25
Kalamazoo, . .	95	32	99	4671	86	206	3692	5691 17	1485 28	4183 06	1403 00
Kent, ...	93	37	90	4558	45	141	3374	4265 45	1353 27	5774 47	1974 12
Lapeer, ...	55	33	54	2420	38	95	2357	2193 99	931 91	2131 03	1231 00
Lenawee, . . .	134	62	162	10050	119	442	8359	10747 93	4519 30	8769 51	5219 67
Livingston, . .	99	37	116	4918	56	232	4533	5816 17	1774 88	4343 27	2657 89
Macomb, . . .	79	41	94	6063	50	210	4630	6386 59	2288 19	2507 50	1393 25
Monroe, ...	89	30	94	5850	69	169	3637	5427 33	2387 89	2784 02	635 81
Montcalm, . . .	10		4	232	3	8	217	119 66	59 16	182 31	126 00
Mackinac, . . .	8		3	607	15	21	358	438 00	44 00	341 00	655 00
Oakland, . . .	153	100	199	11430	147	566	9344	12435 71	5056 27	9558 08	4063 08
Ottawa, ...	21	12	28	1112	33	18	888	1085 66	682 78	1158 37	223 25
Saginaw, ...	14	1	12	712	12	4	346	834 25	316 05	479 50	
Sanilac, ...	13	1	11	590	7	13	452	233 75	258 63	419 34	100 00
Shiawassee, .	47	19	58	1992	34	106	1876	2436 26	594 18	2484 28	1272 00
St. Clair, ...	64	6	60	4100	66	92	2986	3680 91	1702 86	3150 53	961 00
St. Joseph. . .	63	41	81	4540	70	206	3896	5480 43	1766 24	3591 20	1628 25
Tuscola, ...	1	1		123			92				
Van Buren, . .	48	29	58	2027	103	76	1654	2581 09	776 66	2168 96	1209 47
Washtenaw, .	118	65	163	10426	141	428	8693	13137 84	5236 71	8081 16	3127 51
Wayne, ...	101	31	108	15087	127	264	16000	12312 05	3353 74	14036 92	3420 11
Total, ...	2313	994	2594	143272	2086	5784	115,165	155,469 30	55,897 44	130,196 38	57,348 52

TORS' RETURNS BY COUNTIES, FOR 1851.

for which it was raised, and amount raised for each particular purpose.								
Repairs of school house.	Support of school including pay of teachers	To pay past indebtedness.	Any other purpose.	Amount raised by rate bill.	No. of vols. in the township library.	Amount of mill taxed assessed by the supervisor and collected for support of school and township library. [Sec. 107.]	Amount of tax voted at the annual district meeting in addition to other taxes for the support of schools. [Sec. 140.]	Amount of fines, penalties and forfeitures of recognizance received of county treasurer for the purchase of books and township library.
$329 36	$1637 52	$200 28	$164 76	$1334 21	1712	$441 83	$437 91	
523 50	799 75	53 66	2 00	860 55	3314	259 50	215 00	
234 44	3472 75	810 05	58 61	2080 68	3811	633 97	1295 50	$6 37
402 23	2899 40	313 02	99 72	2368 74	3909	500 06	607 22	
284 63	3345 87	358 63	446 28	3656 43	6701	1401 53	1029 89	34 14
234 59	1837 76	136 65	44 86	2927 53	3303	222 60	192 30	48 53
				16 74	66	68 00	54 00	
473 72	319 75	104 00		586 60	3516	400 79	252 75	
96 64	1053 47	134 76	116 44	1050 38	3370	395 09	370 50	
771 94	2444 92	194 86	74 69	1139 12	2775	492 79	211 00	
408 83	4016 43	479 60	447 28	4124 32	3364	634 49	717 58	
170 81	2111 39	337 62	74 00	1532 83	2845	627 55	957 53	
256 42	1987 50	52 61	116 58	1939 48	2157	330 22	124 00	
502 75	4438 93	721 28	321 75	4016 98	4334	736 83	153 75	37 00
392 73	2580 14	245 78	167 37	2603 61	2998	144 14	241 67	
720 17	3049 11	441 49	324 29	2292 16	2923	402 71	1661 00	
199 40	447 98	109 54	23 85	1000 51	1441	311 36	32 00	
629 33	3378 73	180 31	69 42	4744 70	6081	866 30	134 99	43 21
90 94	1224 95	240 88	134 83	2169 38	3088	400 39	328 64	4 08
254 56	1559 81	42 11	37 17	3743 15	2646	578 17	270 00	
219 77	3167 95	86 98	59 93	1473 98	3545	609 65	474 62	
	53 27			25 84	75			
54 00	407 50	38 00	127 00	202 50	1	112 56	519 00	
906 30	5650 64	564 59	347 09	8532 86	7050	1530 19	249 77	62 73
246 11	561 78	52 00	44 25	336 68	873	179 96	872 75	
65 00	134 35	4 50	20 20	311 12	468	216 17	10 00	
38 00	218 40			82 63	453	118 20	116 00	
168 69	972 98	150 42	61 25	1514 30	2030	296 96	232 68	
247 39	2248 57	284 04	119 15	773 40	2763	822 51	242 50	13 17
444 90	2607 73	55 51	106 76	2450 14	3314	809 92	949 17	97 26
118 64	1598 43	92 11	97 80	1442 92	3028	434 83	318 75	
518 75	6234 77	562 99	339 16	4972 32	5370	1410 88	169 99	3 44
1198 06	10261 53	2059 42	67 01	2788 58	3834	750 44	652 18	316 19
11,265 60	76,734 06	9,108 34	411,290	69,085 37	97,158	17,140 59	14,086 66	666 12

STATEMENT OF INCREASE OF NUMBER OF CHILDREN RESIDING IN THE DISTRICTS, AND OF THE INCOME OF THE PRIMARY SCHOOL FUND FOR THE LAST TWO YEARS.

COUNTIES.	1850.			1851.		
	Am't per scholar	No. of schol'rs.	Amount apportioned.	Am't per scholar.	No. of scholars.	Amount apportioned.
Allegan......	34 cts.	1500	$510 00	40 cts.	1851	$740 40
Barry......	"	1526	518 84	"	1773	709 20
Berrien,......	"	4047	1375 98	"	3941	1576 40
Branch,......	"	4345	2611 20	"	4654	1861 60
Calhoun,.....	"	6490	2206 60	"	6403	2561 20
Cass,........	"	3806	1294 04	"	4448	1779 20
Chippewa,....	"	237	80 58	"	349	139 60
Clinton,......	"	1596	542 64	"	1776	710 40
Eaton........	"	2403	817 02	"	2731	1092 40
Genesee......	"	4191	1424 94	"	4471	1788 40
Hillsdale,.....	"	5250	1778 52	"	5848	2427 60
Ingham,......	"	3048	1036 32	"	3436	1374 40
Ionia........	"	2565	906 10	"	2884	1153 60
Jackson,......	"	6319	2214 46	"	7036	2814 40
Kalamazoo,....	"	4141	1407 94	"	4671	1868 40
Kent,........	"	4055	1378 70	"	4558	1823 20
Lapeer,.......	"	2445	831 30	"	2420	968 00
Lenawee,.....	"	9596	3262 64	"	10050	4020 00
Livingston,....	"	4711	1601 74	"	4918	1967 20
Mackinac.....	"	385	130 90	"	607	242 80
Macomb......	"	5165	1756 10	"	6063	3425 20
Monroe,......	"	5512	1874 08	"	5850	2340 00
Montcalm,....	"	174	59 16	"	232	92 80
Oakland......	"	11230	3818 20	"	11430	4572 00
Ottawa.......	"	1031	354 54	"	1111	444 40
Saginaw......	"	679	230 86	"	712	284 80
Shiawassee,....	"	1690	574 60	"	1992	796 80
St. Clair.......	"	3476	1181 84	"	4100	1640 00
St. Joseph....	"	4107	1429 38	"	4540	1816 00
Sanilac.......	"	539	183 26	"	580	232 00
Tuscola......	"	...	.....	"	123	49 20
Van Buren....	"	1644	558 96	"	2199	879 00
Washtenaw,...	"	10115	3439 10	"	10426	4170 40
Wayne.......	"	14592	4961 28	"	15087	6034 80
Total,......	....	132,610	$46,351 82	....	143,270	$57,308 00

INDEX.

A.

B.

C.

D.

N.

O.

P.

R.

S.

T.

U.

V.

W.

Y.

www.ingramcontent.com/pod-product-compliance
Lightning Source LLC
LaVergne TN
LVHW021051110826
845150LV00001B/47

* 9 7 8 1 4 2 5 5 6 7 5 0 7 *